Exploring Education Studies

Visit the *Exploring Education Studies* Companion Website at www.routledge.com/9781408218778 to find valuable **student** learning material including:

- Weblinks to relevant video material online, to facilitate your own research
- Suggested further reading for independent study
- Annotated links to useful websites referred to in the book
- An online glossary to explain key terms

Exploring
Education Studies

Edited by Vivienne Walkup

Routledge
Taylor & Francis Group

LONDON AND NEW YORK

First published 2011 by Pearson Education Limited

Published 2013 by Routledge
2 Park Square, Milton Park, Abingdon, Oxon OX14 4RN
711 Third Avenue, New York, NY 10017, USA

Routledge is an imprint of the Taylor & Francis Group, an informa business

Copyright © 2011, Taylor & Francis.

ISBN 13: 978-1-4082-1877-8 (pbk)

British Library Cataloguing-in-Publication Data
A catalogue record for this book is available from the British Library

Library of Congress Cataloging-in-Publication Data
Walkup, Vivienne.
    Exploring education studies / Vivienne Walkup.
        p. cm.
    Includes bibliographical references and index.
    ISBN 978-1-4082-1877-8 (pbk. : alk. paper)   1. Education—Great Britain.
2. Education—Great Britain—History.   I. Title.
    LA632.W27 2011
    370.941—dc22

                                                        2011001750

Typeset in 9.5/12.5 pt Stone Serif by 73

Brief contents

Contents

3 Alternative schooling   **55**

Annie Flower and Vanessa Cottle

PART 2
THE PSYCHOLOGY OF EDUCATION   **99**

4 The psychology of learning and education   **101**

Vivienne Walkup

5 Understanding and managing the behaviour of learners   **132**

Ann Kenny

6 Communication and change: transactional analysis and cognitive behavioural theory   **166**

Vivienne Walkup

9 The inclusion debate and special educational needs (SEN)   265

Jenny Thompson

Part 4
NEW PERSPECTIVES IN EDUCATION   301

10 Literacy learning in a postmodern world   303

Laura-Lee Duval

11 Engaging with innovative practice 347

Laura-Lee Duval

12 International education 383

John Dolan

Supporting resources

Visit www.routledge.com/9781408218778 to find valuable online resources

Companion Website for students

- Weblinks to relevant video material online, to facilitate your own research
- Suggested further reading for independent study
- Annotated links to useful websites referred to in the book
- An online glossary to explain key terms

For instructors

- Instructor's Manual, containing suggested answers and teaching notes for all questions and cases in the book
- PowerPoint slides of all table and diagrams from the book
- Links to articles and resources on the web

Also: The Companion Website provides the following features:

- Search tool to help locate specific items of content
- E-mail results and profile tools to send results of quizzes to instructors
- Online help and support to assist with website usage and troubleshooting

List of acronyms

ACL	Adult and Community Learning
ADHD	Attention Deficit Hyperactivity Disorder
APA	The American Psychiatric Association
APEL	Accreditation of Prior Experience and Learning
ASD	Autistic Spectrum Disorder
ATL	Association of Teachers and Lecturers (UK)
BECTA	The British Education Communications and Technology Agency
BfL	Behaviour for Learning
BTEC	Business and Technology Education Council (UK)
CBT	cognitive behavioural theory
CEOP	The Child Exploitation and Online Protection Centre
CLC	Community Learning Centre
CMS	Charter Movement School
CORA	Community, Opportunity, Responsibility, Accountability
CP	child protection
CPD	continuing professional development
CSJ	The Centre for Social Justice (UK)
CTC	Child Tax Credit (UK)
CTC	City Technology College (UK)
DCSF	The Department for Children, Schools and Families (UK 2007–2010)
DfES	The Department for Education and Skills (UK, 2001–2007)
EAL	English as an additional language
EAZ	Education Action Zone
EBD	education and behavioural difficulties
EFA	Education for All
EI	emotional intelligence
EiC	Excellence in Cities
ESOL	English for speakers of other languages
EU	European Union
FE	further education
FEC	further education college
GCSE	General Certificate of Secondary Education
HE	higher education
IAG	information, advice and guidance
ICT	information and communication technology
ILP	individual learning plan
IQ	intelligence quotient
ISTE	The International Society for Technology in Education

JISC	The Joint Information Systems Committee (UK)
KS1	Key Stage 1
LEA	Local Education Authority (UK)
LMS	local management of schools
LO	learning organisation
LTA	learning teaching and assessment
LTM	long-term memory
LTS	Learning and Teaching Scotland (UK)
MDG	Millennium Development Goals (UN)
MRI	magnetic-resonance imaging
NAACE	The National Association of Advisors for Computers in Education (UK)
NAGTY	The National Academy for Gifted and Talented Youth (UK)
NCES	The National Council for Educational Standards (UK)
NEET	'Not in Education, Employment or Training'
NHS	The National Health Service (UK)
NIACE	The National Institute of Adult Continuing Education (UK)
NLP	National Literacy Project (UK)
NLS	National Literacy Strategy (UK)
NLT	National Literacy Trust (UK)
NSPCC	The National Society for the Prevention of Cruelty to Children (UK)
NUS	The National Union of Students (UK)
NVQ	National Vocational Qualification
OECD	The Organisation for Economic Cooperation and Development
Ofqual	The Office of Qualifications and Examinations Regulation (UK)
Ofsted	The Office for Standards in Education (UK)
PE	physical education
PGCE	Postgraduate Certificate in Education (UK)
PSA	pupil support adviser
PSHE	personal, social, health and economic education
PTA	Parent–Teacher Association
QCDA	Qualifications and Curriculum Development Agency (UK)
SAT	Standard Assessment Test
SEAL	social and emotional aspects of learning
SEN	special educational needs
SENCO	special educational needs coordinator
SENDA	The Special Educational Needs and Disability Act 2001 (UK)
SEN RPs	special educational needs regional partnerships
SMART	specific, measurable, appropriate, recorded, time-framed
SWOT	strengths, weaknesses, opportunities, threats
TA	teaching assistant
TA	transactional analysis
TDA	The Training and Development Agency for Schools (UK)
TEACCH	Treatment and Education of Autistic and related Communication handicapped Children
TEEM	Teachers Evaluating Educational Multimedia
TLRP	The Teaching and Learning Research Programme
UKCCIS	The UK Council for Child Internet Safety

UN	United Nations
UNESCO	United Nations Educational, Scientific and Cultural Organization
UNICEF	The United Nations Children's Fund (formerly the United Nations International Children's Emergency Fund)
VAK	visual, auditory, kinesthetic
VLE	virtual learning environment
VSO	Voluntary Service Overseas
WDE	World Data on Education
WEA	Workers' Educational Association
WFTC	Working Families Tax Credit (UK)
ZPD	zone of proximal development

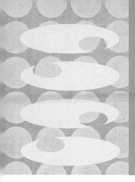

About the authors

Vanessa Cottle is a senior lecturer at the University of Derby with interests which span the field of education. After a long career in further education, she developed her specialism in NVQs and Professional Development, both reflected in her Masters dissertation of 1989. In 2007 she began to deliver Professional Development training freelance, worked for a short time within prison education, and began undergraduate lecturing in Education Studies at the University of Derby. Currently she lectures on a range of topics, including Lifelong Learning and Alternative Schooling.

John Dolan though now semi-retired, has developed and taught university courses in Education Studies for over thirty years, both in the UK and overseas. He is an external examiner at a number of national and international universities. John has also been the co-ordinator of two European transnational projects funded by the EU's Socrates programme. His interests in the history of education and concerns for educational equity and social justice stem from his days as a teacher in both primary and secondary schools in England, prior to his working in the higher education sector.

Laura-Lee Duval is a full-time lecturer on the Education Studies and PGCE HE programmes at the University of Derby. Specialising in the pedagogical potential of postmodern literacies at undergraduate level, her Doctoral work develops this theme in the adult (andrological) context of HE with a particular emphasis on the role of technology-enhanced learning to facilitate and support widening participation.

Annie Flower is a senior lecturer at the University of Derby on the Education Studies programme. Her background is in teaching English and Education Studies, and she has experience of lecturing both in further education and in higher education.

Ann Kenny is Programme Leader for the BA (Hons) Education Studies and a senior lecturer at the University of Derby. She has also worked for the Open University. Her long career in education includes teaching psychology in sixth-form centres, as well as working in schools and colleges of further education. She has recently completed a European project, working with Hogeschool Edith Stein and other European partners to explore new ways of training European teachers. Currently she is involved in research exploring the transition to university from A level to undergraduate study.

Deborah Outhwaite was formerly Head of Politics and Sociology in a sixth-form school in Bedford, having taught A levels for 12 years. She is author of a set of AS Politics Workbooks (Philip Allan, 2002), and has contributed regularly to both *Politics Review* and *Talking Politics*. She is now a lecturer at the University of Derby where she is studying for a Doctorate in educational inequality, and teaching on the Sociology Strand in Education Studies.

Fiona Shelton is a senior lecturer in Education Studies at the University of Derby. She previously worked as a Primary Adviser with the Primary Curriculum Review team at the Qualifications and Curriculum Development Agency. Fiona first qualified as a primary school teacher and taught for many years across the primary age range, before moving into Initial Teacher Education where she was the BEd Programme Leader at the University of Derby. She is the co-author of *Effective Behaviour Management in the Primary School* (OUP, 2008) and *101 Essential Lists on Managing Behaviour in the Early Years* (Continuum, 2006).

Rosemary Shepherd is a child care specialist and lecturer at the University of Derby. Currently in her final year of an MA in Education in Special Educational Needs, she has taught across a wide range of Education Studies modules including Education Policy, Educational Psychology and Language and Literacy Development.

Jenny Thompson is a specialist in Special Educational Needs, and a senior lecturer on the BA Honours Education Studies programme at the University of Derby. She is the Disability Coordinator for the Faculty of Education, Health and Sciences at the University. Jenny has in excess of ten years' teaching experience in special education schools, further education colleges and latterly in higher education. Jenny's current Doctoral research focuses on 'The issues of dyslexia in higher education'. Jenny is the author of *The Essential Guide to Special Educational Needs* (Pearson, 2010).

Vivienne Walkup is the Assistant Head of Education Studies at the University of Derby and has responsibility for both the BA Education Studies and Early Childhood Studies. She has a background in psychology and many years of teaching experience ranging from secondary to higher education. She has particular interests in human interactions and their importance within the learning situation. Vivienne has co-authored *Psychology in Education* (Pearson, 2008) and is currently working on a second edition. She has also contributed chapters to *Advanced Early Years Care and Education* (Heinemann, 2005 and 2008). Her research interests include self-esteem in access students and mothers returning to higher education and she is currently beginning work on research into homophobic bullying in secondary schools.

Case study 1.1

A personal history of education

The following short piece is taken from the website of Richard Cannon. Cannon began his website and blog after he chose to retire from his management job in the rail industry some eight years ago, and it has a wide readership. It was written as a piece of personal recollection rather than as 'serious' writing about education in the past. Even so, the writer's experience seems representative of that of many people of his generation. Most young people in Britain in the 1950s, 1960s and 1970s attended secondary modern schools; for good or ill, very few 'passed to go to the grammar'. Though there were marked regional and local variations, only between 10 per cent and 35 per cent of pupils ever attended grammar schools, and the rest attended secondary moderns (Szreter, 2004).

The 1950s saw me going to three schools. It should have been only two, but a move of house intervened (something I always blame failing the 11+ plus on!!).

Case studies opening and closing each chapter illustrate the complex realities of modern educational practice, showing you how the same issues can take very different forms.

History of education

CBT

- *Behavioural approaches* originated in the work of J.B. Watson in the first half of the twentieth century (Watson, 1913). Watson wanted to create an objective, scientific theory of human psychology which challenged the 'introspective' view current at this time. He and others, such as Pavlov (1927) and Skinner (1953), believed that only observable actions mattered because only they could be recorded and measured. Thus experiments (many of them on animals) formed much of the research supporting this approach. This was understandable at a time when science emerged as a dominant model within western culture.
- *Cognitive approaches* take the opposite view in some ways, believing that it is thought and internal processes that drive behaviour, and that it is therefore impor-

History of education summaries are informative and easy to read, filling in the essential background for all the major topics covered in the book.

Within the learning situation

Rhianna is a Year 11 (15/16-year-old) pupil who will be taking GCSEs at the end of the year. She is currently underperforming in terms of coursework (predicted overall B but work at E standard) for a number of subjects and this will affect the outcome of her exam results. During a discussion with her year tutor Rhianna revealed that she was leaving her work to the last minute and so rushing it. This resulted in poor-quality work which was brief and littered with errors. A contract was drawn up which clearly laid out the responsibilities of both Rhianna and her year tutor.

Rhianna

- Agreed that she would work productively on each of the three pieces of coursework for two hours per week and bring her work to her year tutor on a weekly

Within the learning situation puts a spotlight on practical examples of theory in practice, in a variety of educational settings.

Controversies

Has Eric Berne oversimplified?

Let us look here at two of the debates about TA so that we can consider these as we read the rest of the chapter.

Berne has been criticised by some writers who argue that he has reduced Freud's work to a simplistic model which does not accurately represent psychodynamic theory.

Agree: Shertzer and Stone (1980) suggested that TA is 'little more than a warmed-over simplified psychoanalytical theory' (p. 210).

Disagree: Berne deliberately shifted the focus of psychodynamics and used simple language in order to provide an accessible theoretical model. He focused on internal processes to the analysis of interpersonal interactions in order to address change rather

Controversies are topical discussion boxes tackling thorny issues, and showing two (or more) sides of the debate.

Stop and reflect questions within each chapter encourage you to compare what you've read with your own experiences of education.

> think, and to decide one's own destiny) draw upon **cognitive behavioural approaches** to understanding human behaviour because they focus on the way that individuals process and respond to information. These are explored more fully later in this chapter.
>
> ❓ Stop and reflect
>
> • Look again at the philosophy of TA. Do you find any of these principles surprising? If so, in what ways?
> • Do any of them challenge your own way of thinking about yourself and/or others?
>
> The key principles upon which TA is built are also fundamental to education itself, as within education assumptions are made about including and providing opportunities for all (people are OK), engaging learners in thinking (everyone can

Connect and explore pushes you further by providing links to the latest research and policy.

> ↖ Connect and explore
>
> Berne's ideas of the importance of human stimulation for healthy growth were based on the work of Renee Spitz (1945, 1946) which found that over a third of infants in an institution for abandoned babies did not survive despite adequate standards of cleanliness, food and medical care. This was compared with children reared by mothers in prison where conditions were much poorer in these respects but all the children survived. The critical difference was in the level of physical contact as those in the foundling institution (orphanage) were often in incubators whereas in the poorer prison they were held by the mothers. This suggested that people need physical contact (strokes) to survive.
>
> More current research (Ackerman, 1990; Walsh, 1991; Field, 1995, 1998; and Jinon, 1996) involving premature infants has also indicated the need for tactile stimulation in order for both physical and psychological development to proceed normally (Patterson and Hidore, 1997). This has been taken on board by maternity units in

Activity panels provide tasks and challenges for practical learning opportunities, which you can complete individually or as part of a group.

> *Activity*
>
> ### Defining contemporary education issues
>
> Look down the list of contemporary education issues on the left. What do you think each one means?
>
> Then, for each issue, look at the list on the right for potential reasons for importance. Did your understanding of the issue match the reason given here?
>
> | Issue | Potential reasons for importance? |
> | --- | --- |
> | Looked-after children | Poverty and child protection (CP) issues |
> | Refugee/asylum children | Use of immigration detention centres |
> | Traveller children | Poverty and human rights issues |

Key terms highlighted in the text are defined in a comprehensive Glossary at the end of the book.

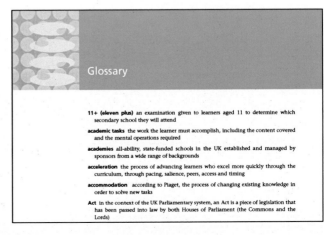

> ### Glossary
>
> **11+ (eleven plus)** an examination given to learners aged 11 to determine which secondary school they will attend
>
> **academic tasks** the work the learner must accomplish, including the content covered and the mental operations required
>
> **academies** all-ability, state-funded schools in the UK established and managed by sponsors from a wide range of backgrounds
>
> **acceleration** the process of advancing learners who excel more quickly through the curriculum, through pacing, salience, peers, access and timing
>
> **accommodation** according to Piaget, the process of changing existing knowledge in order to solve new tasks
>
> **Act** in the context of the UK Parliamentary system, an Act is a piece of legislation that has been passed into law by both Houses of Parliament (the Commons and the Lords)

Acknowledgements

The publishers would like to thank all those who provided feedback and suggestions for this book. Their insight and advice has been much appreciated.

Jane Andrews (*University of the West of England*)

Liz Barrett (*Sheffield Hallam University*)

Jane Bates (*Manchester Metropolitan University*)

David Blundell (*London Metropolitan University*)

Derek Bunyard (*University of Winchester*)

Gareth Dart (*University of Worcester*)

Sandra Leaton Gray (*University of East Anglia*)

Brenda Morgan-Klein (*University of Stirling*)

Stavros Moutsios (*Danish School of Education*)

Chris Neanon (*University of Portsmouth*)

John Rees (*Sheffield Hallam University*)

Nicola Spawls (*University of Middlesex*)

Roger Standaert (*University of Ghent*)

Publisher's Acknowledgements

We are grateful to the following for permission to reproduce copyright material:

Figures

Figures 6.1 and 6.2 from http://www.ta-tutor.com/ztatutor.html; Figure 6.5 adapted from 'Fairy tales and script drama analysis', *Transactional Analysis Bulletin*, 7(26), pp. 39–43 (Karpman, S. 1968); Figure 7.2 from www.millionplus.ac.uk/file_download/10/MOBILITY_190309.pdf; Figures 10.1 and 10.2 from McLean, N. (2007) 'Multimodal Literacies' presented at the Naace annual strategic conference, available from http://events.becta.org.uk/content_files/corporate/resources/events/2007/feb/niel_mclean_naace.ppt.

Tables

Table 7.1 after *Welfare-to-Work and the New Deal*, Centre for Economic Performance (Layard, R. 2001); Table 10.1 adapted from http://www.tlrp.org/dspace/retrieve/3692/IvanicRB50final.pdf; Tables 10.2 and 10.3 adapted from Clarke, D. (2009) 'Bloom's taxonomy of learning domains, the three types of learning', available from: http://www.nwlink.com/~Donclark/hrd/bloom.html; Table 11.1 adapted from *Game Cultures: Computer Games as New Media* Open University Press (Dovey, J. and Kennedy, H. W. 2006) p. 3, McGraw-Hill Education; Table 12.1 adapted from http://www.internetworldstats.com/stats.htm.

Text

Case Study 1.1 from http://www.downthelane.net/growing-up-50s-60s/going-to-school-1950s.php; Case Study 8.2 adapted from http://www.traintogain .gov.uk/casestudies/casestudiesitems/East_of_England/The+Ipswich+Hospital+ NHS+Trust.htm?listingPosition=1&AppendChannelPath=%2fEast_of_England& SECTORDROPDOWN=PublicSector&SIZEDROPDOWN=*, with permission of The Skills Funding Agency; Case Study 9.1 from 'Sharp rise in number of special needs pupils', *The Daily Telegraph*, 22/07/2010 (Prince, R.), copyright © Telegraph Media Group Limited; Case Study 12.3 the author is unable to provide source information, but the case study may come from the following website: http://www .col.org/SiteCollectionDocuments/L3Farmers_NetworksforLifelongLearning.pdf.

Photographs

The publisher would like to thank the following for their kind permission to reproduce their photographs:

(Key: b-bottom; c-centre; l-left; r-right; t-top)

13 Getty Images: Monty Fresco / Topical Press Agency; 18 Reproduced by permission of Durham County Record Office (l); Getty Images: Hulton Archives (r); 36 Alamy Images: Juice Images (r); Corbis: Hulton-deutch Collection (l); Rex Features: (c); 70 Pearson Education Ltd./Photodisc/Photolink; 74 Montessori St Nicholas & Montessori Centre International: www.montessori.org.uk; 75 Pearson Education Ltd/Jules Selmes; 77 Montessori St Nicholas & Montessori Centre International: www.montessori.org.uk; 137 Pearson Education Ltd/Jules Selmes; 156 Pearson Education Ltd/Sophie Bluy; 174 Getty Images: Echo; 184 Getty Images: DK images; 208 Getty Images: Hulton Archive; 217 Getty Images: Hulton Archive; 253 Getty Images: Thinkstock; 285 www.educationphotos.co.uk/walmsley, Copyright © John Walmsley 2011 All rights reserved (t); Alamy Images: Blend Images (c); Pearson Education Ltd/Photodisc/Geoff Manasse (b); 338 Pearson Education Ltd/Rob Judges; 408 Getty Images: Joseph Van Os.

All other images © Pearson Education

Every effort has been made to trace the copyright holders and we apologise in advance for any unintentional omissions. We would be pleased to insert the appropriate acknowledgement in any subsequent edition of this publication.

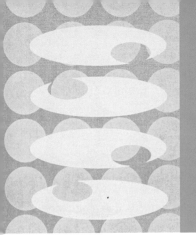

Introduction

Students thinking of studying education at university often ask, 'What is education studies exactly? Is it about training to teach? If not, what is it about?' They may receive the reply that education studies involves the academic study of education and issues related to it, which overlaps with, but goes beyond, educational practice. The key thing, and what many students often fail to realise, is the realisation that education is itself a complex concept worthy of academic study in its own right. The study of education encompasses a range of disciplines, including but not limited to psychology, sociology, history and philosophy. As a discipline, education studies also seeks to encourage serious debate about important educational issues.

About this book

This book is arranged in four parts, reflecting the multidisciplinary nature of education studies, and spotlighting the areas which the authors see as exciting and important. Our aim is to encourage critical engagement with education, and to equip readers with a basis from which to evaluate key issues. The authors are drawn from the education studies team at the University of Derby who have expertise in these particular areas and who have developed their programme with this in mind.

Part 1 provides a foundation for the study of education by considering the historical and philosophical underpinnings, and leading to thoughts about the future of education in Chapter 1, 'A history of education'. We introduce the background to mainstream education in the UK in Chapter 2, 'Teaching, learning and the National Curriculum', which looks at the origins, debates and recent reform of the National Curriculum. In Chapter 3, 'Alternative schooling', alternative curricula, rooted in differing philosophical views, are discussed, and the perspective broadened to include European and American educational contexts.

Part 2 of the book looks at ways in which psychology provides insights into education, beginning with a wide-ranging view in Chapter 4, 'The psychology of learning and education'. This chapter covers theoretical approaches to learning and development, intelligence and motivation before moving to some more specific applications. In Chapter 5, 'Understanding and managing the behaviour of learners', issues, research and approaches relating to behaviour in schools are examined.

Chapter 6, *'Communication and change: transactional analysis and cognitive behavioural theory'*, applies two psychological models within the educational context in order to facilitate learning.

In Part 3 we examine contemporary policies and developments within education. Chapter 7, *'Contemporary policies and issues'*, highlights key policies and links education with the idea of social justice in order to examine the social purpose and political importance of education. *'Lifelong learning'* is the subject of Chapter 8, an exploration of notions of 'lifelong learning', and ways in which government drivers have impacted upon practice. Chapter 9, *'The inclusion debate and special educational needs'*, discusses the challenges presented to educationalists within the wider context of an inclusive education system.

Part 4 considers new perspectives in education. In Chapters 10 and 11, *'Literacy learning in a postmodern world'* and *'Engaging with innovative practice'*, the focus is on literacy and ways in which notions of postmodernism and technological innovations are impacting on traditional views. The final chapter, *'International education'*, explores current debates about comparative and international education with regard to issues of education provision and the impact of globalisation.

Supporting your studies

Within the chapters you will find a range of regular features to support your learning.

- **Case studies** Each chapter opens with an establishing case study, designed to get you thinking more deeply about the subject of that chapter. A second case study at the end of the chapter is designed to let you apply what you have learned from your reading. Both cases aim to illustrate the key issues and problems addressed in the chapter.

- **History of education** Chapter 1 is dedicated to the history of education, but this important theme runs throughout the book. To that end, most subsequent chapters include a 'History of education' box, giving a brief account of where the topic originated and how it fits into the broader historical context of education.

- **Within the learning situation** These are brief examples of how a particular theory applies in practice. 'The learning situation' is a deliberately broad definition – encompassing not just the classroom, but the full range of educational settings.

- **Controversies** With this feature, the authors select a particular area of debate in their subject area and present some of the arguments for and against a contested topic.

- **Stop and reflect** These 'pauses for thought' are found regularly throughout all chapters and pose some questions to provide thinking space about the section you have just read.

- **Activities** These varied and practical suggestions for activities to support learning can be used in seminars, classes or, in many cases, individual study.

- **Connect and explore** These annotated links to further reading opportunities, many supported by weblinks (which you'll also find on the book's companion website), will add depth and breadth to your understanding.

- **Summary** An aid for revision or just to help you find a topic in the book more easily, every chapter features a summary recapping the main sections.

Companion website

In addition to these features in the book, you will also find a companion website for *Exploring Education Studies* online at www.routledge.com/9781408218778. Featuring weblinks to videos and further reading, as well as a range of resources for lecturers, make the *Exploring Education Studies* companion website your first port of call as you begin to explore the world of education for yourself.

We hope that you enjoy reading the book and that you find it both useful and accessible as a source of information and challenging as a stimulus for thought, further reading and debate.

Part 1

THE HISTORY AND PHILOSOPHIES OF EDUCATION

1

A history of education

John Dolan

Contents

Introduction

Ian Whitwham, a London comprehensive school teacher with nearly 20 years of experience, writes a very popular Sec.Ed. website blog (perhaps you are already familiar with it). In a recent posting he mused on the ways in which his own diverse and very modern students – typical of the great majority of students in schools – were obliged into conformity by school rules and procedures. 'These days,' he wrote, '[it's] all about modules and targets and uniforms . . . If we continue to treat them like this, we will lose them' (Whitwham, 2009).

Whitwham's wistfulness may well find resonance with many current practitioners and students alike. Yet there is nothing odd about this: his views give part expression

7

to one side of a debate about the purposes of schooling that has recurred throughout the 140 (or so) year history of state-provided education in this country. Some, like Whitwham, argue that education is about supporting children and young people to develop their knowledge, values and themselves in ways which are particular to them. For others, though, schooling is concerned to equip youngsters with the knowledge, skills and attitudes long respected by dominant society as relevant and useful for a purposeful adulthood.

When the 1870 Education Act established a national system of elementary schooling in the UK, their mere requirement to attend schools led children, some young people and their parents to protest in the streets, particularly in the industrialised towns of the north and in agricultural areas: in both, children as earners (whether full time or seasonal) were important in the family economy. How did schooling get from being a resented requirement on the individual to a closely managed opportunity from which those who are in any way unconventional might find themselves excluded?

This chapter is all about trying to map some of the landmarks of the debate about, and the reality of, schooling over the past 150 years or so. This provides us with a chance not only to understand our past education history and thereby to 'extend our imaginations' (Fielding, 2005), but also to think about what 'education' might be in the modern world of globalisation and of rapid and transforming information technologies. It is timely to do so for two reasons.

First, debates about the purposes of education (and schooling) are essentially ideological expressions. An **ideology** is best understood as a set of ideas and values about the world held by a group, influencing their behaviour and conversation or debate with others. These systems of understandings are usually seen as '"the way things really are" by the groups holding them, and they become the taken-for-granted ways of making sense of the world.' (Meighan et al., 2007). Whitwham's view of the purposes of education is expression of an ideology of **liberalism**, dating back at least as far as the eighteenth century; the alternative view is essentially an ideology of **conservatism**, sometimes termed **neo-liberalism** in the late twentieth century (Apple, 2004).

Second, the modern world demonstrates intense and increasing economic competition between nations and a belief that education is key to provision of marginal national advantage and yet, as internationally respected comparative educationalist Edmund King suggests, 'all . . . established systems [of schooling] . . . were developed for a world that no longer exists' (2000).

This chapter aims to:

- Develop your knowledge about selected developments in the history of education in Britain over the past 150 years or so.

- Provide closer examination of the ideological debate over schooling through a focus on to the provision of the history curriculum in English and Welsh schools.

- Discuss the enduring contribution to education thought and debate by selected international educationalists.

Case study 1.1
A personal history of education

The following short piece is taken from the website of Richard Cannon. Cannon began his website and blog after he chose to retire from his management job in the rail industry some eight years ago, and it has a wide readership. It was written as a piece of personal recollection rather than as 'serious' writing about education in the past. Even so, the writer's experience seems representative of that of many people of his generation. Most young people in Britain in the 1950s, 1960s and 1970s attended secondary modern schools; for good or ill, very few 'passed to go to the grammar'. Though there were marked regional and local variations, only between 10 per cent and 35 per cent of pupils ever attended grammar schools, and the rest attended secondary moderns (Szreter, 2004).

The 1950s saw me going to three schools. It should have been only two, but a move of house intervened (something I always blame failing the 11+ plus on!!).

Back then there was no Comprehensive system, just the 11+ and into either Secondary or Grammar education. Most of them were male/female segregated and it could be argued over this being a good policy or not!

I started at Chevening Primary in 1953 nestled away on the Chipstead to Chevening Road and not far from Chevening Halt, the railway station on the Dunton Green to Westerham Line, later shut by the infamous Mr Beeching and now the M25!

Probably the biggest difference between now and then was actually getting there and coming home. Not many parents would drive their young ones to School (mainly because not many people had cars). You were left more to your own devices and my sister Julia and myself would make the two mile walk over ground no Parent would ever allow now. It entailed going across fields, crossing two Stream's where no one would hear you if you fell in and along a fairly quiet Road.

Come the 11+ and I didn't get through, so it was off to Wildernesse Secondary for Boys, somewhere I enjoyed very much for many reasons pertaining to that period in time.

But, between these times, I did do a little work! The day would always start with Assembly, which would comprise of a Hymn, a Bible Reading, a Talk from the Headmaster, Prayers and another Hymn. Usually someone would faint at some point and often lead to a chain reaction. You'd hear thumps and bumps all round the Hall, quite amusing to most of us who didn't have that problem!

You took the basic subjects; Maths, English, PE, Geography, Music and History. To these there was some choice between Biology, Science, Physics etc. plus a 'skilled' class in either Woodwork or Metalwork.

I got branded the Class Creep as we progressed through the years. I'd always been a neat writer and loved maps. By chance, the Headmaster taught us Geography and would always use my Book work as the example of how it should be done.

To avoid the Cane on my [sic] from the Headmaster and spoiling my credibility after being caught throwing a Rubber Bung at the Stand-in Biology Teacher, I gave my name as Paul Eaton to him. He got six of the best and 48 years on he still doesn't know it was me!

I did get the cane once though. This followed a tremendous in-swinging snow ball landing right on the back of Mr Wright's (the Gardening Teachers) head. This comes back to me every time I put the Runner Bean poles up in Spring!

They were good schooling days though. After Assembly, we'd sit down in our Class and have to spell twelve words. If one single person got one wrong, we'd have that word again the next day. Any sign of 'cheating' was severely dealt with by a Chinese Grip on your elbow – and boy, did that hurt!

You would never wear your shirt outside your trousers, always wear your tie. You'd know your Anthem off by heart, drink your free one third of a pint bottle of milk at morning break and ALWAYS keep our handwriting upright!

Source: http://www.downthelane.net/growing-up-50s-60s/going-to-school-1950s.php

Of course, Cannon's is a personal rather than an academic account. However, we would argue that the work of educational historians (such as Szreter) suggests that we can place some reliance on it.

Questions for discussion

1 *What is your reaction to Richard's account of his schooling?*

2 *Does his experience mirror your own, or are there significant differences?*

3 *Overall, does his seem an education experience that you would have welcomed for yourself, or do you find it unappealing?*

A partial overview of education in Britain, 1870 to the present day

The word 'partial' is used here to reflect both of its meanings: partial can mean part of something larger, it is not complete. Equally, it can mean that one has a liking for something, that it accords with one's own taste or preferences. We use the term in both of these senses. History is a complex and intricate field of study. To expect comprehensive coverage of any historical topic (and especially to expect it in a short coverage of the topic) is unrealistic. However, a short overview, such as that that we offer here, has the virtue of helping to set a particular historical event, personality or experience into a wider frame of information and so aids understanding.

In addition, we would say that developments we have selected correspond with shifts in education policy that provide further illumination about the ideological debate surrounding education and schooling. Even so, what we provide here is our 'partial' overview of the history of education in Britain: it is not the only possible interpretation of the basic facts. (You could, of course, appraise what we say by going back to the original information and read the interpretations of that provided by others. If you are interested to do so, the bibliography may help you do that.)

We are going to concentrate on four main landmark events:

- The Elementary Education Act 1870 (aka the Forster Act), which established the first national system of elementary education (5- to 14-year-olds).
- The Education Act 1944 (aka the Butler Act), which systematised a selective structure of secondary education, with pupils attending either **grammar** or **secondary modern schools** post age 11 depending on their results in the competitive **11+** transfer examination.
- The Plowden Report 1967, which returned the focus sharply back from post-11 secondary education and to elementary provision, and on to infant and junior years (ages 5–11) in particular.

- The Education Act 1988, making the final achievement of the neo-conservative education project that really began with the Black Papers in the 1970s. In Britain, this project stemmed from a belief that schools and colleges in particular were generally failing to provide their students with a relevant and robust standard of education. This was married to a belief that the market, rather than central government, should increasingly be the driver of education reform and efficiency. For the then Prime Minister, Margaret Thatcher, and others, emphasis was placed on a need to re-establish the primacy of traditional subjects and knowledge (Jack Lam, 2001).

The Elementary Education Act 1870 (the Forster Act)

The history of education in the United Kingdom over the past 150 years cannot be fully understood without some acknowledgement of the dominance of the notion of 'liberalism' in British thought and social policy since the eighteenth century. Simply expressed, the idea of liberalism prioritises the individual rather than society as a whole. It also argues that the individual's own self-motivation underpins all action, including efforts at learning (Carr and Hartnett, 1996).

The Reform Act of 1832 began the process of political democracy in this country by extending the right to vote well beyond traditional boundaries; a process which continued until the achievement of universal suffrage in 1928 when the right to vote was extended to include women, of course. Rapid changes in economic prosperity and industrial technologies led to major social changes during the late eighteenth and the nineteenth centuries. Britain was largely transformed from a previously agricultural economy and society to a dynamic and dominant world leader in mining and manufacturing industries, and with its swelling population increasingly living in major towns and cities. These changes led some to argue that a democratic society had a duty to educate all of its members. The force of argument from influential voices in the period, such as the philosopher John Stuart Mill and the educationalist Matthew Arnold, eventually culminated in the Forster Elementary Education Act.

This Act established for the first time a national and compulsory system of elementary education for all children under the age of 12, paid for largely by local taxation (the so-called 'board schools', named after the local school boards which administered them, and further consolidated by the 1902 Education Act). This **state-funded system** incorporated, rather than replaced, the previous largely voluntary provision of elementary schooling provided by religious bodies (such as the Church of England's National Society, created in 1811). It needed to do so because there were powerful voices arguing that education was too important to be left to politicians alone, and that the religious organisations should continue to have a strong voice in shaping and regulating the character and scope of the education provided in the new schools.

Though with an elementary academic curriculum that would be considered modest in scope and provision by the standards of Britain in the twenty-first century, the Forster Act was an important piece of social legislation. This curriculum laid emphasis on manual skills training, appropriate for eventual employment in factories, mines, shipyards and the like for boys; and on skills for work either in domestic service or retailing, or in the home, for girls. Even so, it offered children and young people, regardless of family location or background, some genuine opportunities for social mobility – the chance to get paid employment and to seek to better it through their own continuing efforts – based on educational achievement and this contributed to the spread of social as well as intellectual knowledge. Through the experience of years being spent together in schooling, the previously disparate social groupings that made up the populations of earlier towns and cities came to share a body of curriculum knowledge transferred in the schools, and also a set of values and beliefs that increasingly tied people together as citizens and electors.

Given the compulsory and largely egalitarian nature of the Forster Act's provisions, it is perhaps unsurprising that it met with some initial resistance. This came from conservative opponents, who saw universal education as unnecessary and potentially costly, and also from some parents (and not a few of their children) who resented its requirement that children attend school rather than their being available to take up employment (whether full time or seasonal). However, the impact or size of neither set of opponents should be overstated.

Gardner (1984), for example, argues persuasively against the view that working-class parents who opposed the introduction of compulsory elementary education were dominant. He makes careful study of the so-called 'private' schools supported by working men and women throughout the nineteenth century. These schools were established by one or two individual teachers (some male, but most female) who then offered basic education for relatively small numbers of local children, each paying a few pence per week in fees. Despite the modest scale of these private schools, Gardner ends his study by concluding that most parents supported education provision for their children.

It is worth acknowledging here that, in our view, such historical attitudes in our own country perhaps find parallels with contemporary attitudes among parents of children in developing economies. These parents make enormous financial and other sacrifices to send their children to school when given the opportunity of state provision to do so (Commonwealth Secretariat, 1993). That this opportunity is still not universal is evidenced by the fact that such provision forms one of the United Nation's Millennium Development Goals, for achievement by 2015.

Britain was not the only country introducing such education reform in this period. Indeed, many continental countries, notably Germany and France, were well advanced in this project by the time of the Forster Act. These countries were increasingly characterised by urban populations, accompanied by demands for democratic structures of political representation and accountability. In such circumstances, education provision was viewed as a means of sustaining national identity, and achieving greater social cohesion. Though centrally determined by national government, education provision was invariably allowed to be administered by local authorities. Local variations in the character and quality of schooling therefore often resulted.

Though these administrative arrangements have endured even until the present day (at least in England), from the later twentieth century onwards there have been sustained and global efforts to minimise such qualitative variations (Hill, 2009).

Connect and explore ↖

Go to the Institute for Education Policy Studies website at **http://www.ieps.org.uk/index.php** to read a range of interesting papers by Dave Hill, who is referenced above.

The Education Act 1944 (the Butler Act)

The 1944 Butler Education Act instituted a demarcation between 'elementary' (primary) schooling in Great Britain and secondary schools, devised to meet the needs of young people. Butler set the school-leaving age at 15, and introduced free secondary schools. Pupils were selectively judged by process of examination at age 11+ (effectively an IQ test) that determined whether they were either 'vocationally' suited (and who therefore attended secondary modern schools, teaching a technical skills curriculum) or more 'academic' in their aptitudes (and who attended grammar schools, teaching an essentially academic curriculum). Richard Cannon, featured in Case study 1.1, might be seen as an early 'beneficiary' of the Butler Act.

The Butler Act has been termed 'the single most important piece of legislation during the War' (Rhodes-James, 1986). It certainly has had an enduring effect on shaping education in Britain (and its former colonial territories). Indeed, nostalgia for the age of selective education ushered in by the Butler Act in the reconstruction period following the end of the Second World War in Britain still resonates in contemporary debates about education. The Provost of Eton College, Sir Eric Anderson, wrote in 2007, for example, that 'Where selection remains in the state

Figure 1.1 R.A. Butler, who steered the 1944 Education Act through Parliament
Source: Getty Images: Monty Fresco/Topical Press Agency.

system . . . results show that selection works better [than comprehensive schooling]'
(Anderson, 2007).

↖ *Connect and explore*

To read the full article, go to 'Poorer pupils benefit most from selective education' at
http://www.telegraph.co.uk/comment/personal-view/3635845/Poorer-pupils-benefit-
most-from-selective-education.html

Even so, many have argued that the passing of this Act represented expression
of an ideological, liberal and egalitarian ideal which was determined that the
post-war years should achieve markedly greater economic prosperity and **social
mobility** and cohesion than had been achieved so far in the century (Carr and
Hartnett, 1996). And, indeed, up to 1944 as many as 80 per cent of young people
remained in elementary schools until the age of 14, when they left education
and entered into whatever employment they could find. At the same time, the
passing of the Act marks a moment of significant policy emphasis through which
central government (rather than local boards) began to actively direct the structure, quality and purposes of schooling, albeit a power shift based on concerns
for wider social and economic opportunities for increasing numbers of young
people (Batteson, 1999).

This Act looked forward to the task of economic and social reconstruction of
British society following the disruptions and destructions of the Second World
War years. It was concerned to foster a sense of renewed and redirected national
effort, as well as to provide a different set of education opportunities for young
people. It was also concerned to achieve an affordable and efficient system of
national schooling, mainly under the direction of central government, unlike the
patchy and expensive system of secondary education that characterised the century up to 1939. In other words, the Butler Act was an expression of conservative
ideology, albeit one which made concessions to neo-liberal concerns for individual needs and potentials.

In the rising economic prosperity and changing social circumstances of the late
1950s and 1960s, such a rigid view of young people's potential as that enshrined
in selection at age 11 came to be increasingly questioned by both educationalists
and politicians. Gradually this led to the renewal of ideas about how children and
young people might best learn, building on the tradition of eighteenth-century
liberalism found in the work of Jean Jacques Rousseau and the early twentieth-
century contribution of the American educationalist John Dewey. At secondary
level, the rise of non-selective comprehensive schools marked a change of direction from the established grammar versus secondary modern divide, under the
direction of mainly socialist politicians such as Anthony Crosland. In primary
schools, it led to an emphasis on a revised conceptualisation of the very notion of
'a child'. (Though apparently 'new', many of these ideas about education and
schooling had a long history of their own, as we shall see in the final section of
this chapter.)

The Plowden Report 1967

The Plowden Report emphasised the need to see children as individuals: 'Individual differences between children of the same age are so great that any class, however homogeneous it seems, must always be treated as a body of children needing individual and different attention.' This found its practical expression in an insistence that the curriculum should be based on the child's intrinsic interest in learning and should lead a child to learn for her or himself. It introduced into primary schools and classrooms a variety and freedom that some educationalists, teachers and policy-makers saw as liberating and enriching, and others saw as chaotic and excessive (Gillard, 2004).

Professor Colin Richards (1999), for example, recognises the limitations and excesses of some of those who espoused the Plowden Report's championing of a form of schooling which was responsive to the needs and potential of the individual child. Nonetheless, he goes on to make a compelling argument for the pivotal promise that the Report offered in terms of a new way of structuring primary education and new processes of creative **pedagogy**.

However, episodes such as the notorious 'William Tyndale affair' in 1974, in which a media frenzy translated an episode of school mismanagement into an attack on the principles of the Plowden Report, gradually had effect. Senior staff at the school promoted enquiry-based methods of teaching and learning, which were resisted by some classroom teachers. Both sides in the dispute claimed support from parents of children at the school for their views. In the end, following widespread media controversy and national debate, the school staff was replaced and the school's curriculum reforms were abandoned. Nonetheless, the controversy over these ideas seared the landscape of educational discussion for many years to follow (Davis, 2002).

When the then (Labour) Prime Minister, James Callaghan, made his Ruskin College speech in 1976, few doubted that his call for increasing central political control over education policy and provision marked a break with the tradition of schooling begun by the Forster Act of more than a century before. Callaghan's speech gave renewed furore to debate about education – its purposes, forms and standards – which, as we have seen so far in this chapter, continues into the present time.

The Education Act, 1988 to the present

The period since Callaghan's speech has been dominated, not just in Britain, but globally, by discussions centred on the 'human capital theory' of education, which espouses the view that education is critical to economic and social advancement (Simon, 1985). This has been accompanied by debate over whether learning should be didactically directed by the control of the curriculum and the teacher or the result of individual activity and curiosity on the part of the classroom student. The rhetoric of policy stressed a focus on the individual learner and a concern to develop each child or young person into a rounded, self-confident adult. However, the press of repetitive **inspection** on schools, publication of **'league tables'** and assessments of young people's learning achievements means that didacticism often takes precedence over more creative, exploratory forms of learning (Power and Whitty, 1999).

Margaret Thatcher was elected Prime Minister for the first time in 1979. The years
of the Thatcher governments in the 1980s witnessed the dominance of these ideas
and corresponding education policies, culminating in the Education Acts of 1988
(which firmly set in place the **National Curriculum** at both primary and secondary
phases) and 1992 (which required all schools to undergo inspection by Ofsted
every four years).

The significance of the National Curriculum in this context was that it ignored
all differences between individual students (regardless of whether of sex, class,
ethnicity or faith) and instead insisted on constructing a supposedly shared and
authentic 'national' body of accepted knowledge and standards. In practical
terms, this led to an emphasis on developing a common (or 'core') curriculum
and increasing regard for the measured achievement of expected educational outcomes of students. The National Council for Educational Standards (NCES) gave
voice to these twin priorities. Eventually, the NCES was effectively replaced by the
Office for Standards in Education (Ofsted).

Though controversy remains, the introduction and implementation of the
National Curriculum and its associated school reforms and accountability
changes are claimed by government to have led to an overall improvement in the
education achievements of children and young people, as indicated in Figure 1.2.

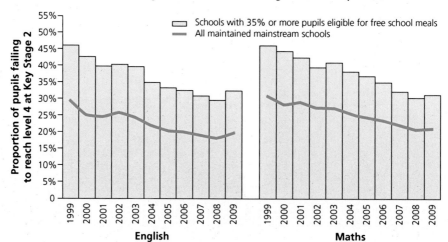

**Substantial progress has been made in the literacy and numeracy of 11-year-olds
including those in schools with high levels of deprivation**

Figure 1.2 **The proportion of pupils failing to reach level 4 at Key Stage 2 in English and
Maths**

Source: DCSF Performance Tables, England; updated December 2009.

Thus, after over a hundred years of state-provided universal education initially intended to cope with the upheavals of social, political and economic life, the urge for central government control of education had become dominant. In the next section we look at this in more detail through a case study of the history curriculum in schools in England.

As you read the next section, it will be useful to keep in mind this question: Were these changes in education policy and provision inevitable? Afterwards, in the final section, we look at some alternatives that were – and might still remain – possible.

Activity

● Look again at the four landmark events. Do these suggest to you an inevitable course of progress in education policy and provision? Do you think any of them are contradictory, either wholly or in part, of other main events discussed?

● What has been your own experience of Ofsted school inspection?

● If you are a parent or carer of a child presently in school, did you consult the Ofsted inspection report before deciding to send your child to this school? If you did, did you find the report useful? If so, in what ways?

● If you have recently left school, how well do you think it prepared you for the 'next steps' you've taken in your life since then?

The ideological debate over the history curriculum in England

As with any other study of history, the history of education demands that educational policies, ideas and provision are located in the specific circumstances and context that gave rise to them (Green and Cormack, 2008). All cognition – intellectual understanding – results not only from genetic events over millennia, but also from cultural events over thousands of years, and personal events taking place as they develop in their lifetime from childhood to adulthood (Tomasello, 1999). The implications for how we view education in the light of such perspectives are potentially profound and wide-ranging.

Up to now in this chapter, we have argued that 'education' is best understood 'as scientific, as sympathetic to the child, and as concerned with citizenship' (Baker, 2001). In this final section, we will examine the extent to which present-day debate about, and provision of, 'education' in England (and possibly in the United Kingdom as a whole) exhibits continuities or changes in relation to those of past times. We are going to do that by focusing specifically on the teaching of history (as a subject); very few other curriculum subjects arouse as much interest and debate among politicians and educationalists as has history (Jones, 2000).

Perhaps unsurprisingly, in June 2010, in one of the first acts of the newly formed Coalition government (Conservatives and Liberal Democrats) the new education secretary, Michael Gove, publicly appealed to pro-empire TV historian Niall Ferguson to help rewrite the history curriculum for English schools (Seamus Milne, 2010). Ferguson, it might be noted, has unashamedly championed British colonialism and declared that 'empire is more necessary in the 21st century than ever before'.

Let's first set this discourse into a wider context.

The present-day state (public) education systems in Europe and the USA were largely established in the late nineteenth and early twentieth centuries. This was a period of rapid and massive changes, affecting each of these countries. Populations were growing fast (largely as a result of both internal and international migrations) and increasingly living in urban areas – themselves sites of social changes. Old political systems were either under strain or being swept away, and there was an increasing emphasis on democratic forms of political representation and accountability. Indeed, it can be argued that mass education was both necessitated by and a necessary precursor of democracy (David, 1988). The period also saw transformations in industrial processes and the expansion of the transport system. Both of these developments demanded a workforce that was better taught and more flexibly skilled than perhaps had been the case in these countries previously. Taken together, in most of these countries schooling was viewed as a main way of producing both social cohesion and economic development through emphasising national identity and shared knowledge and values. Additionally, it can also be argued that these countries increasingly exported their cultural values – and advanced their own economic and military interests – through the imposition of imperial control of colonial regions and territories (Levinson et al., 2002).

In England, as in many other countries, the notion of a single national identity was the dominant discourse from the nineteenth-century debates about the purposes of schooling (Bracey, 2006). Attention increasingly focused on the teaching of history as one of the principal ways by which children and young people might be best inculcated with such 'identity'. Debate and clashes of interpretation over national identity, over the role which knowledge of the past plays in cementing a sense of **nationalism**, over the concept of national identity forming an essential part of the national culture to be transmitted to future generations, and over relationships within the United Kingdom in a multinational and **multicultural** society have been common and recurring (Cannadine, 2010).

Figure 1.3 **Two contrasting images of nineteenth-century education. On the left, a typical nineteenth-century school photograph showing a primary class in England. On the right, the Girls' School at Belgaum in Karnataka, India, taken by an unknown photographer c. 1870**
Source: (left) Durham County Record Office; (right) Getty Images: Hulton Archives.

In effect, the school history curriculum has become an area of concern both for those eager to see the stimulation of pride in national identity and those fearful of the rise of aggressive jingoism (intolerant and extreme patriotism) (Wood and Payne, 1999). In the 1980s, for example, the widely respected historian Geoffrey Elton, in many of his lectures, argued for a grand narrative approach to the past based on studies of British kings and queens, rather than multicultural or Third World history (GR Elton, 1991). At this time, too, David Cannadine (whose broadcasted views we have already cited) called for 'a new version of our national past which can regain its place in our general national culture' and lamented the growth of both global and micro studies of the past (Cannadine, 1987).

From the 1980s, when the Conservative government led by Margaret Thatcher was in power, politicians, policy-makers, employer organisations, the media and numerous other bodies have argued that the centralised authority of a National Curriculum for schools (at least those in England and Wales) was essential for the nation to assure its global competitiveness, based on 'world-class' educational standards. Specifically, students and teachers were to be held accountable to standards of achievement measured by national assessments, while the ultimate goal was that the public would be able to judge the success of a particular educational system by scrutinising the results of a centrally orchestrated testing mechanism (Foster, 1998). Let us look at some of the debate on history and the National Curriculum before reading on. The following 'Controversies' box shows both sides of the debate over the question of whether history works well in the National Curriculum.

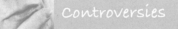

Controversies

'History works well in the National Curriculum'

Agree: The history National Curriculum was introduced in 1991 and was revised in 1995 and again in 2000. Though its introduction and revisions proved to be contentious among both historians and teachers, it seems that history teaching is one of the most successful areas of provision at secondary school level, with the Office for Standards in Education (Ofsted, 2005) claiming in successive subject reports that 'in 80 per cent of lessons seen . . . the teaching has been judged good or better, meaning that history is one of the best taught subjects'. And certainly, official examination results at the end of Key Stage 4 (GCSE) appear to back up this view.

Table 1.1 **History O level/GCSE**

	Annual entry	Passes grades A–C as % of history entries	% of all subject entries	Passes grades A and A* as % of history
1960	128,638	8.0	57.2	N/A
1970	162,514	7.3	57.5	N/A
1980	179,155	6.0	58.6	12.3
1990	195,680	5.7	52.0	11.5
2000	190,279	4.0	61.3	22.8
2007	205,200	4.4	67.2	29.3

Source: DES, *Statistics of Education*, DfES/DCSF website.

Disagree: Such evidence does not persuade everyone. Writing on the *Daily Mail* website, for instance, and also in 2007, Laura Clark suggests that 70 per cent of secondary students drop history before entering KS4 and that 'lessons had been reduced to a random collection of topics' (Clark, 2007).

What do you think? Which side of the argument do you favour?

Wherever the merits lie in this debate, what is more certain is that some teachers have consistently expressed concerns around the problem of educating students in the vital processes of historical thinking while at the same time covering an enormous amount of chronological content matter.

In truth, there is not now a great deal of curriculum time devoted to history in English schools. At primary level, history takes as little as 4 per cent of curriculum time, often concentrated in one- or two-week blocks in both years 3 and 4 of the primary school (Y5 and Y6). The official curriculum for the primary phase (Key Stage 2) suggests that every student should follow 6 Units – 1 a local history study, 3 chosen from a range of British history topics, and 1 of each of a European and a global history topic. At secondary level, comment has been made about the fact that 'Britain is out of step with virtually all other European countries in not making history compulsory up to the age of 16' (in some countries it is 18). The Qualifications and Curriculum Agency (QCA) recommends that secondary students at Key Stage 3 should follow some of the 22 developed Units outlined to teachers. At Key Stage 4 (GCSE) that those electing to study History should follow a minimum of 4 of the 32 Units outlined for the Key Stage. However, the QCA points out that: 'The scheme is not statutory; . . . [the teacher of history] . . . can use as much or as little as you wish. You could use the whole scheme or individual units' (QCA, 2010). Perhaps unsurprisingly, in 2006, for example, nearly half of the total of secondary schools in England entered no candidates for GCSE history (Mathews, 2009).

Indeed, criticism of the national standards for history has derived from unease felt by many educationalists who have examined the history standards and have gone on to identify serious flaws within them. Such critics, mainly from the political left, have argued, for example, that as standards typically exalt the 'official knowledge' of the dominant culture, they appear as yet another vehicle 'to silence, disable, and marginalize certain groups in society through the process of schooling' (Foster, 1998). Others, mainly from the political right, argue that history should be taught as a collection of universally accepted 'truths' to be absorbed by young people. In simplistic terms, school history ought to be a means to instil in the young a sense of unity and patriotism and a veneration of the nation's glorious heritage. Echoing Niall Ferguson's views that we reported earlier, even Gordon Brown, the New Labour Prime Minister defeated by the Conservative/Liberal Democrat Coalition in 2010, insisted that the 'days of Britain having to apologise for its colonial history are over'.

Where do these debates and schooling trends in respect of history teaching and learning leave the study of education and our opening claim that present-day policy and provision exhibit continuities with – as well as divergencies from – the past?

If education is really to be sympathetic to the child and to be concerned with citizenship (Baker, 2001) then the mere fact that children and young people reflect the multicultural and plural society characteristic of modern Britain raises important questions. Just whose 'history' is to be taught, given that many current school students have family heritages originating from previously colonised communities and cultures? What place is there in 'his-story' for examining and appraising the contribution of women in the nation's historical development? Is there really only one, national story to be told, or are there many, depending on variations of regionality, economic circumstances and social opportunities?

Answers to these questions are more problematic. Accordingly, we would suggest that 'history' is necessarily interpretative, complex and nuanced. The study of history depends upon the progressive development of skills (of chronology, knowledge and understanding, interpretations, enquiry, organisation and communication). From this viewpoint, therefore, school history ought to develop in the student an intelligent discernment and critical application of historical evidence, on historical research and on narrative construction. When learning progresses in this way, it is likely that young people will exhibit and value the diversity-related dispositions of understanding, tolerance and respect (Stevens and Charles, 2005). Indeed, from such understandings it might be that individual students can decide for themselves on the potential for social action and social transformation in the present (Hawkey, 2007).

This may not easily be achievable in the current state of education in this country. Though not the only study to do so, Ann Beers' recent and careful review of research from Britain and from Europe more widely (2003) points out that many young people are either confused or ignorant (or both) of their actual national history, even after years of secondary schooling. She concludes from her review of research that 'national history' (insular and inward-looking) predominates and influences the basic school history curriculum in all 12 of the European countries investigated, including England. She goes on to argue that many young people rely on a version of history closer to 'heritage history', rather than real historical knowledge. 'Heritage history', in this sense, is not so much an investigation of the reality of the past as a celebration of the mythic and nostalgic 'national story'. It may well be that this is to be expected in periods of rapid change, economic constraint and widespread social and cultural diversity. In such times, retreat to an imagined past can appear to offer certainty and comfort.

⑦ Stop and reflect

- *Do you think that 'heritage history' ideas and images are as pervasive among young people as we have suggested in this topic?*
- *How might a classroom teacher best set about the task of supporting students to understand the differences between 'heritage' and actual history?*

We go further and argue that the history of education shows that the official school curriculum, whether for history or for any other subject, is influenced throughout by the values which the educational system seeks to instil in its students. There is nothing neutral about the endeavour. Going back to Whitwham's musings which opened this chapter, therefore, we can now see that the all-pervasive 'rules and procedures . . . modules and targets and uniforms' that he sees as constraining the individuality and personal development of his school students are part of a tradition of conservative and neo-liberal education in the service of nation-building that has tended to dominate state provision since the late nineteenth century.

The contribution to education thought and debate by selected international educationalists

As our brief survey of the history of education in Britain suggests, education always takes place in an intricate context of political, social and economic variables (or factors), and often has ideological foundations which are themselves the result of the interpretation of this context by policy-makers. It is important to look at the underlying theories informing education ideologies. We are going to concentrate in this section on the educationalists who first developed them, often termed 'progressive'. Potts (2007) surveys the development of 'progressive education' and has concluded that it is one of the most ambiguous terms in education. Even so, no chapter dealing with the history of education can ignore those whose contributions to 'progressive education' have provided, and continue to offer, alternatives to dominant structures of schooling as defined by the state (any state).

Let us look first at the education ideas of a remarkable woman, born in the nineteenth century but whose main contributions to educational thought and provision were in the twentieth century and resonate right up to the present day. You may well have noticed the increasing number of mainly privately owned and operated 'Montessori' primary schools in cities and towns in Britain (www.montessori.org.uk/msa), and now totalling some 700 schools (a minority of which are 'maintained', i.e. government-funded, within the state system).

Maria Montessori

Maria Montessori, born in the Italian village of Chiaravelle in 1870, first trained to be a doctor (in fact, she was the first woman graduate of Rome University) but has had lasting impact as an innovator of classroom practices. Her ideas increasingly influence primary education provision in many countries worldwide. Working first with children from economically disadvantaged families, Montessori claims that children learn best when educated holistically. Her ideas stress the importance of allowing children to learn through activity, by doing. Children, she reasoned, need to develop positive self-images if they are to develop motivation for further learning. Self-image – the way in which an individual physically and socially judges or values her or his self – contributes directly to one's own self-concept and esteem; all are qualities necessary for continued learning.

Montessori developed a range of classroom resources to foster independent learning, in a structured and developmental setting, encompassing mental, physical and social aspects. The teacher's skills rely on timely interventions, observation of when the child is ready to move on in her or his own learning, in summary, 'a prepared environment in which the child, set free from undue adult intervention, can live its life according to the laws of its development' (Potts, 2007).

Montessori's philosophy is essentially optimistic (some might say idealistic) with regard to the development of the child. She held the belief that a child will naturally develop refined behaviours and rounded knowledge if given freedom from adult oppression, and from imposed learning of academic 'subjects' to do so. Her theory sees the child as passing through three development phases (3–6 years of age, 6–12, and ages 12–18). It is the first two stages which tend to be represented among existing Montessori provision in Britain, although elsewhere in Europe successful secondary Montessori schools do exist. Though the practice of learning and teaching has some variation between individual Montessori schools, there is general agreement on the main features of such education. These can be contrasted with the dominant model of learning in traditional school settings, as summarised in Table 1.2.

Table 1.2 **Comparison of Montessori and traditional schools**

Montessori	Traditional
Children of varying ages taught together	Children grouped for teaching according by age
Child at the centre of the learning process with teacher remaining in background	Teacher is the director of the child's learning
Child selects her own learning from her own interests and curiosity	The curriculum is determined by the teacher or the school and applied to all children
Child determines for herself how long to stay on task or on topic	Teacher directs how long the child should remain on task
Child sets her own pace of learning	The teacher usually structures the pace of the group's learning
Children are supported in learning concepts from self-teaching materials	The teacher seeks to guide the child to selected concepts and ideas
Learning materials are multi-sensory, encouraging varied explorations	Few sensory learning aids for motor and / or concrete learning
Collaboration and peer-supported learning positively encouraged	Learning tends to be individualized with collaboration limited
Learning environment structured to enable internalization of learning by the child, and self-discipline	Teacher tends to reinforce learning environment so that child's attention remains on the teacher
Child is able to work anywhere where she feels most comfortable for learning and movement is encouraged	Child often assigned a learning place by the teacher
Child is encouraged to take responsibility for, and ownership of the learning space	Little emphasis placed on care of the learning space nor on instruction on how best to do this
Learning opportunities include focus on both self-care and social responsibility	Teacher remains solely responsible for care of the learning space and well-being of children
Parents and carers actively promoted as partners in the child's learning (all have chosen to send their child to the school)	Parents and carers mainly seen as reinforcers of the school's learning priorities

Carl Rogers

The American psychologist and educationalist Carl Rogers (1902–1987) also stressed the need for freedom for the individual child or young person. He was concerned to help youngsters develop free from psychological strain or externally imposed requirements. He believed too that such 'freedom to learn' (the title of one of his main books, in fact) could be created within existing school structures. Rogers placed stress on the importance of human relationships for learning to be achieved, rather than emphasising the individual child, as did Montessori. For Rogers, the ideal teacher is the one who could create a classroom situation characterised by 'realness, prizing and empathy' and that 'learning how to learn' is more important than knowledge (Rogers, 1967). Thus, in this view the teacher becomes a 'facilitator' of 'experiential learning', avoiding direct or didactic (teacher-led) approaches, concerned to support rather than to control the learner and her or his efforts. Sharing and talking are, for Rogers, central to the achievement of real learning. However, Rogers also has high expectations of a teacher (or facilitator) of young people's learning:

Key concepts underlying Rogers' education theory

- **Realness in the facilitator of learning** – the most basic of the essential attitudes necessary for learning to take place is realness or genuineness in the teacher (facilitator of the student's learning).
- **Prizing, acceptance, trust** – successful facilitators of learning value the learner, respecting her feelings, her opinions and her person.
- **Empathic understanding** – once a student is able to trust her or his facilitator (teacher) then she or he is able to self-initiate experiential learning. Empathic understanding, when the teacher has the ability to understand the student's reactions from the inside, and a sensitive awareness of the way the process of education and learning seems *to the student* are fundamental to this process.

Paulo Freire

The Brazilian educator Paulo Freire (1921–1997) took up this notion of 'conversation' as a key component of effective learning. Though his own work can make for challenging reading, Freire's view of learning rejected any suggestion of 'banking knowledge', and so he rejected much of the stress on didactic and transactional teaching and learning found in many classrooms. For Freire, learning is concerned to develop both the individual and the community of which the individual is part (whether school, family or broader society). Such learning depends on action and activity, and requires a teacher to identify 'teachable moments' when the learner can be encouraged and supported to develop knowledge and skills based on ethical values, personal and social improvement, and community action. In his most famous work, *Pedagogy of the Oppressed*, Freire writes: 'Human existence cannot be silent, nor can it be nourished by falsewords, but only by true words . . . To exist humanly, is to name the world, to change it . . . Humans are not built in silence, but in word, in work, in action-reflection.'

All three of the educators we have looked at in this section place stress on education serving a purpose other than a purely economic function, whether of the individual or of society ('the nation'). All three have views of learning and schooling which begin with the needs and potentials of the individual, rather than with the achievement of an ideological project. Whether any of their ideas could sustain an entire system of education may be open to debate and question; even in those European countries where they presently can be most evidenced, none can be judged to be the dominant predication of schooling. However, elements of the ideas of all of them can be seen in present-day provision, in Britain and elsewhere, and offer a counterbalance to the view that education is a globalised and market-driven enterprise. There is even a faint echo of them, perhaps, in Ian Whitwham's observation (which we met in the introduction to this chapter) on the way in which his students are constrained by present-day schooling concerns and values. Individually and together they offer glimpses of how schooling might be reshaped in ways which, by starting with the learner, take account of and find place for difference and diversity. Their views do not sit easily alongside a priority for, say, the reinstatement of the esteem for Britain's imperial past, such as is called for by Niall Ferguson (cited above).

It seems to us that such a concern is one that will be of increasing importance for the future of education and learning in a fast changing, technologically driven age in which previously dominant cultural traditions and forms of information sharing and creation may no longer endure (ACU, 2008).

Stop and reflect

- *Can you see traces of the ideas of any of these three educationalists in present-day schools?*
- *Do you think that your own experience of education would have been better or worse if ideas similar to these had played a part in your own schooling?*
- *Do the ideas of any of these educationalists have a place, do you think, in the future development of schooling in this country? What about elsewhere in the world?*

Conclusion

Perhaps in our wireless connected communications age, it isn't so difficult to imagine what Illich's 'learning networks' (a 'new learning society') might look like on the ground (see Case study 1.2 on page 27). After all, computers and 3G devices already allow peer matching, peer knowledge exchange and – crucially – peer collaboration and creation. The operation of a peer-matching network would be simple. The user would identify himself by name and address and describe the activity for which he seeks a peer (or skilled or knowledgeable mentor). A computer would send him back the names and addresses of all those who have inserted the same description. It is amazing that such a simple utility has never been used on a broad scale for publicly valued activity of all types.

In its most rudimentary form, communication between client (learner) and computer could be done by return mail. In big cities, desktop or handheld terminals could provide instantaneous responses. The only way to retrieve a name and address from the computer would be to list an activity for which a peer is sought. People using the system would become known only to their potential peers, safeguarding privacy for both and security for the client learner. In the nations of the economically developing world, such centres are probably going to be community (social) amenities, shared and used by many, rather than the more individual and personal access to technology that we are used to in this country and elsewhere in economically developed countries.

A complement to the computer could be a network of bulletin boards and classified newspaper ads, listing the activities for which the computer could not produce a match. No names would have to be given. Interested readers would then introduce their names into the system. School buildings would become neighbourhood learning centres.

One way to provide for their most efficient and varied use would be to give over the space to people from the immediate neighbourhood. Each could state what he would do in the classroom and when – and a bulletin board would bring the available programmes to the attention of the inquirers. Access to 'class' would be free – or even purchased with educational vouchers, for those wedded to a marketplace view of education provision. The same approach could be taken towards **higher education**. Students could be furnished with educational vouchers which entitle them for ten hours yearly to private consultation with the academic of their choice, in combination with institution's library, the peer-matching network, and vocational or academic 'apprenticeships'. Something similar exists in the internship programmes now offered by many universities and their partner organisations for their own undergraduates in the UK.

Whilst traditional teachers would no longer be required, there would be need for new 'professional educators'.

Parents, in all likelihood, will need support in guiding their children on routes to responsible educational independence. Learners need experienced leadership when they encounter difficulties and setbacks. These two needs are quite distinct: the first is a need for pedagogy, the second for intellectual leadership in all other fields of knowledge. The first calls for knowledge of human learning and of educational resources, the second for wisdom based on experience in any kind of exploration. Both kinds of experience are indispensable for effective educational endeavour, and amounting together to what Illich termed 'conviviality'. Schools package these functions into one role ('the teacher') – and tend to view any independent exercise of either as at best suspect, and often as 'out of order'. It is a point of view that I suspect is very familiar to Ian Whitwham (quoted at the start of this chapter).

The wise student will periodically seek professional advice: assistance to set a new goal, insight into difficulties encountered, choice between possible methods. Is this what you did? In my experience, most persons would admit that the important services their teachers have rendered them are such advice or counsel, given at a chance meeting or in a tutorial.

This chapter has demonstrated that the study of the history of education is more than simply a rehearsal of dates and events. Instead, the discipline deals with debates and decisions which have important consequences on the lives of children and young people, as much today as in the past. Of course, acknowledgement has to be made of key developments and prominent figures within the history of education. However, such regard should not obscure the contemporary relevance of this aspect of education study.

Case study 1.2
Deschooling society

The following is a short series of extracts from Ivan Illich's celebrated (and admirably short) book, *Deschooling Society*. Like Montessori, Rogers and Freire, Illich offers us an alternative view of education and schooling, a remarkably prescient view considering it was written now nearly 40 years ago:

> I believe that a desirable future depends on our deliberately choosing a life of action over a life of consumption, on our engendering a lifestyle which will enable us to be spontaneous, independent, yet related to each other, rather than maintaining a lifestyle which only allows to make and unmake, produce and consume – a style of life which is merely a way station on the road to the depletion and pollution of the environment. The future depends more upon our choice of institutions which support a life of action than on our developing new ideologies and technologies. [In education, we can do this by creating]:
>
>> **Reference services** to educational objects – which facilitate access to things or processes used for formal learning. Some of these things can be reserved for this purpose, stored in libraries, rental agencies, laboratories and showrooms like museums and theatres; others can be in daily use in factories, airports or on farms, but made available to students as apprentices or on off-hours.
>>
>> **Skill exchanges** – which permit persons to list their skills, the conditions under which they are willing to serve as models for others who want to learn these skills, and the addresses at which they can be reached.
>>
>> **Peer-matching** – a communications network which permits persons to describe the learning activity in which they wish to engage, in the hope of finding a partner for the inquiry.
>>
>> **Reference services to educators-at-large** – who can be listed in a directory giving the addresses and self-descriptions of professionals, paraprofessionals and freelances, along with conditions of access to their services. Such educators . . . could be chosen by polling or consulting their former clients. (Illich, 1973:81)
>
> A radical alternative to a schooled society requires not only new formal mechanisms for the formal acquisition of skills and their educational use. A deschooled society implies a new approach to incidental or informal education. . . . . [W]e must find more ways to learn and teach: the educational qualities of all institutions must increase again. (Illich, 1973)

Questions for discussion

1 *Are you able to apply Illich's ideas as outlined above to your own experience of learning both in school and elsewhere? If so, in what ways?*

2 *What factors do you think presently limit the scope for Illich's ideas to be more widely adopted? Would it be better if these factors were overcome, or do you welcome their being present?*

Summary

A partial overview of education in Britain, 1870 to the present day

The first section of this chapter identified selective developments in the history of state (public) education provision in this country over the past 150 years or so. What is noticeable is that throughout this period, though there have been some important changes in the regulatory structures of education provision, there has been little debate about the nature of character of the education to be provided. What has endured until the present day is a model of learning essentially dependent on predetermined curricula being taught to all members of a class together and through the medium of teacher direction and instruction (a didactic rather than an exploratory form of education).

The ideological debate over the history curriculum in England

The second section looked at this more closely through the single lens of the enduring debate about the teaching of history. What is clear is that the essential model of the character and purposes of schooling is essentially that developed at the time of the Industrial Revolution. Technological innovations in classrooms remain subservient to the enduring didacticism and values of classroom life.

The contribution to education thought and debate by selected international educationalists

Our final section in this chapter outlined the innovatory ideas of selected educationalists – Maria Montessori, Carl Rogers and Paulo Freire. Though none of these has had significant impact on the education system in this country, all offer alternative suggestions to how learning and teaching might best be undertaken. It may well be that some of these possible developments, such as those presented in the work of Ivan Illich (Case study 1.2), are likely to have impact in the future, as technology becomes increasingly available and facilitates shifts in how learning is accessed and developed. Regardless of their impact to date, these educationalists provide models of how the undesirable split between 'the experience gained in more direct associations and what is acquired in the classroom' might best be avoided (Hecht, 2002).

References

Anderson, E. (2007) Poorer pupils benefit most from selective education. Available at www.telegraph.co.uk.

Apple, M. (2004) *Ideology and the Curriculum*, 3rd edn, New York: RoutledgeFalmer.

Association of Commonwealth Universities (ACU) (2008) *Dazzling Technologies: Seismic Shifts in Higher Education in a Fast-changing and Unequal World*. Conference Proceedings 28–30 November 2008. Available at http://hyderabad2008.acu.ac.uk/conference_papers (accessed November 2009).

Baker, B. (2001) *In perpetual motion: Theories of power, educational history and the child*, New York: Peter Lang.

Batteson, C.H. (1999) The 1944 Education Act Reconsidered, *Educational Review*, 51(1), pp. 5–15.

Bernstein, B. (1996) *Pedagogy, Symbolic Control and Identity: Theory, research critique*, London: Taylor Francis.

Bracey, P. (2006) Teaching for Diversity? Exploring an Irish Dimension in the School History Curriculum since c. 1970, *History of Education*, 35(6), pp. 619–35.

Brandon, G. and Hayward, J. (2010) New Academies, New Opportunities: An Assessment of Conservative Party Education Policy, Cambridge: Jubilee Centre.

Broadfoot, P. (2000) Comparative Education for the 21st Century: retrospect and prospect, *Comparative Education*, 36(3), pp. 357–71.

Cannadine, D. (2010) *A Point of View: Reflections on the teaching of history in schools*, BBC, Radio 4, 25 June.

Cannadine, D. (1987) British History: Past, Present and Future, *Past and Present*, 116, pp. 160–91.

Carr, W. and Hartnett, A. (1996) *Education and the Struggle for Democracy: The politics of educational ideas*, Buckingham: Open University Press.

Clark E. (2007) Consigned to history – 70 per cent drop key subject before GCSE, *Daily Mail*, 19 July.

Cowen, R. (1996) Last Past the Post: comparative education, modernity and perhaps postmodernity, *Comparative Education* 32(2), pp. 151–170.

Commonwealth Secretariat (1993) *Better Schools: Resource Materials for School Heads in Africa*, Module 1, London: Commonwealth Secretariat Education Programme.

Craft, A. (2010) *Creativity and Education Futures*, Stoke-on-Trent, UK: Trentham Books.

Daily Telegraph (2010) *Conservative Party's policies and manifesto for the general election 2010: key issues, the latest news and policy overview*. Available from http://www.telegraph.co.uk/news/election-2010.

Darling-Hammond, L. (2000) Futures of Teaching in American Education, *Journal of Educational Change*, 1(4), pp. 353–73.

Davis, J. (2002) The Inner London Education Authority and the William Tyndale Junior School Affair, 1974–76, *Oxford Review of Education*, 28(2/3), pp. 275–98.

DfES (2001) *Schools: achieving success*, Cm 5230, London, September.

Dreyfus, H.L. (2008) *On the Internet (Thinking in Action)*, London: Routledge.

Elton, G.R. (1991) *Return to essentials: Some reflections on the present state of historical study: The Cook Lectures delievered at the University of Michigan*, Cambridge: Cambridge University Press.

Fielding, M. (2005) Putting Hands Around the Flame: reclaiming the radical tradition in state education, *Forum: for promoting 3–19 comprehensive education*, 47 (2–3), pp. 61–70.

Foster, S.J. (1998) Politics, parallels and perennial curriculum questions: the battle over school history in England and the United States, *Curriculum Journal*, 9(2), pp. 153–64.

Freire, P. (1995) *Pedagogy of Hope. Reliving 'Pedagogy of the Oppressed'*, New York: Continuum Books.

Fryer, P. (1988) *Black People in the British Empire*, London: Pluto Press.

Gardner, P. (1984) *The Lost Elementary Schools of Victorian England*, Beckenham: Croom Helm.

Gillard, D. (2004) 'The Plowden Report', the encyclopaedia of informal education. Available at www.infed.org/schooling/plowden_report.htm.

Green, B. and Cormack, P. (2008) 'Curriculum history, 'English' and the New Education: Or, installing the empire of English? *Pedagogy, Culture & Society*, 16(3), pp. 253–67.

Grosvenor, I. (1999) There's no place like home, in McCulloch, G. (ed.) *The Routledge Falmer Reader in History of Education*, 2005. Abingdon, Oxon: Routledge.

Hawkey, K. (2007) Theorizing Content: Tools from cultural history, *Journal of Curriculum Studies*, 39(1), pp. 63–76.

Hecht, Y. (2002) *Democratic Education: A story with a beginning*, Jerusalem: Keter Publishing.

Hill, D. (ed.) (2009) *Contesting Neoliberal Education: Public Resistance and Collective Advance*, London and New York: Routledge.

Hofman, A. (2007) The politics of national education: Values and aims of Israeli history curricula, 1956–1995, *Journal of Curriculum Studies*, 39(4), pp. 441–70.

Holt, M. (1999) Recovering the Comprehensive Ideal, *Teacher Development*, 3(3), pp. 329–40

Illich, I. (1973) *Deschooling Society*, Harmondsworth: Penguin.

Jack Lam, A.L. (2001) Economic Rationalism and Education Reform in Developed Countries, *Journal of Education Administration*, 39(4).

Jones, G.E. (2000) The debate over the National Curriculum for history in England and Wales, 1989–90: The role of the press, *The Curriculum Journal*, 11(3) pp. 299–322.

Kamens, D.H. (1988) Education and Democracy: A comparative institutional analysis, *Sociology of Education*, 61(2), pp. 114–127.

King, E. (2000) *Comparative Education*, p. 267.

Knight, J. (2003) Updating the Definition of Internationalization, *International Higher Education*, 33 (Fall).

Levinson, D.L., Cookson, P.W. Jnr and Sadovnik, A.R. (eds) (2002) *Education and Sociology: An encyclopedia*, London: RoutledgeFalmer.

Lo, J.T-Y. (2004) The junior secondary history curricula in Hong Kong and Shanghai: A comparative study, *Comparative Education*, 40(3) pp. 343–61.

Louisy, P. (2001) Globalisation and Comparative Education: A Caribbean perspective, *Comparative Education,* 37(4), pp. 425–38.

Low-Beer, A. (2003) *School History, National History and the Issue of National Identity.* Available at http://www.heirnet.org/IJHLTR/journal5/Low-Beer.pdf.

Massachusetts Institute of Technology (MIT) available at http://sap.mit.edu/resources/portfolio/laptop/ (accessed December 2009).

Mathews, D. (2009) *The Strange Death of History Teaching: Fully explained in seven easy-to-follow lessons.* Available from http://www.cardiff.ac.uk/carbs/faculty/matthewsdr/history4.pdf.

Meighan, R. et al. (2007) *A Sociology of Educating,* London: Continuum.

Milne, S. (2010) *This attempt to rehabilitate empire is a recipe for conflict: Prepare for an outbreak of culture wars if Michael Gove's appeal to colonial apologists to rewrite school history is taken up.* Available from http://www.guardian.co.uk/commentisfree/2010/jun/10/british-empire-michael-gove-history-teaching.

Mitra, S. (2007) *How Kids Teach Themselves.* TED video recording. Available at http://www.ted.com/talks/sugata_mitra_shows_how_kids_teach_themselves.html (accessed December 2009).

Montessori St. Nicholas Charity (n.d.). Available at www.montessori.org.uk/msa (accessed December 2009).

Office for Standards in Education (Ofsted) Ofsted subject conference report: History 4–19: the relevance of history, London, 7/8 July 2005.

Phillips, R., Goalen, P., McCully, A. and Wood, S. (1999) Four Histories, One Nation? History teaching, nationhood and a British identity, *Compare: A Journal of Comparative and International Education,* 29(2), pp. 153–69.

Potts, A. (2007) New Education, Progressive Education and the Counter Culture, *Journal of Educational Administration and History,* 39(2), pp. 145–59.

Power, S. and Whitty, G. (1999) New Labour's Education Policy: First, Second or Third Way? *Journal of Education Policy,* 14(5), pp. 535–46.

QCA (2010) *Standards Site*: History at Key Stage 3.

Reimer, I. (1971) *School is Dead,* Harmondsworth: Penguin.

Rhodes-James, R. (1986) *Anthony Eden,* London: Weidenfeld & Nicolson.

Richards, C. (1999) *Primary Education at a Hinge of History?* London: Falmer Press.

Rogers, C. (1969) *Freedom to Learn,* Colombus, OH: Merrill.

Simon, B. (1985) Can education change society? In McCulloch, G. (ed.) *The Routledge Falmer Reader in History of Education, 2005,* Abingdon, Oxon: Routledge.

Stevens, R. and Charles, J. (2005) Preparing Teachers to Teach Tolerance, *Multicultural Perspectives,* 7(1), pp. 17–25.

Southgate, B. (2000) *Why bother with history?* Essex: Pearson Education Ltd.

Szreter, S. (2004) *Lecture,* University of Cambridge, Lent Term.

Tomasello, M. (1999) *The Cultural Origins of Human Cognition,* Cambridge, MA: Harvard University Press.

Whitwham, I. (2009) *At the Chalkface: Great Moments in Education,* London: Hopscotch Educational Publishers.

Wood, S. and Payne, F. (1999) The Scottish school history curriculum and issues of national identity, *Curriculum Journal,* 10(1), pp. 107–21.

2

Teaching, learning and the National Curriculum

Jenny Thompson, Rosemary Shepherd and Fiona Shelton

Contents

Introduction

If you were asked to make a list of words to describe the National Curriculum, what words would you choose? Prescriptive, old fashioned, compartmentalised, boring or irrelevant? Research by the Qualifications and Curriculum Development Agency (QCDA, previously QCA) has found that these are the words many head teachers and teachers have used to describe the current National Curriculum at public consultation events and conferences. More positively, some have also used the words entitlement, balance, and breadth. Clearly, the National Curriculum is an issue which, more than 20 years after its introduction, still has the power to divide opinion.

The National Curriculum was introduced in 1988 following many years of what may be considered an unstructured approach to teaching in the UK, in contrast to the increased incidence of planning and preparation in curriculum development which exists as a result of the implementation of the National Curriculum. This chapter looks at the impact of the National Curriculum on the teaching profession in the UK.

This chapter aims to:

- Discuss the impact of the National Curriculum.
- Consider the changing role of the teacher.
- Assess the impact of the National Curriculum on the teaching profession and the learner.

Case study 2.1
A teacher's experience of the National Curriculum

Mrs Brown has been a primary school teacher since qualifying in 1979. She really enjoyed the comparative freedom which was current when she began teaching and devoted considerable time to developing topics for her ten-year-old pupils which related to their own interests and environment. A particularly successful project (which had lasted a whole term) on 'Brewing in Burton-upon-Trent' (the town where the school was located and where monks had begun brewing centuries before) had resulted in some excellent work from the children, which incorporated creative writing, local history, maths, drama and science. Parents were involved, and many were delighted that their own local knowledge and work in the brewing industry were included in their children's learning, and that they were learning about 'real' things which were relevant to them. They had been invited to come into the school to see the children's work, and links had been made with the local brewing museum. However, following the introduction of the National Curriculum, Mrs Brown has found that she struggles to cope with the constraints of SATs, tests, Ofsted and the literacy and numeracy hours. She feels unable to divert from the curriculum for fear that her pupils will achieve worse results than another local school, which will have a negative impact upon the school's position in the league tables. The Head teacher makes sure that his staff are drilled in the importance of this, so although she is helping her class to achieve the required national standards, Mrs Brown feels that she is failing them in terms of offering lively, interesting and 'real-world' work.

Questions for discussion

1 *Is it better for a teacher to use their own judgement to choose topics for students to study, or do you think teachers should follow a curriculum?*

2 *If you were a newly qualified teacher, would you see the National Curriculum as supporting or constraining you?*

The problems encountered by Mrs Brown may illustrate one of the central issues about the National Curriculum: that it stifles the ability of teachers to decide upon what should be taught, and presents lessons which are 'too formal, too early' (Bartley, 2008). Bear these perspectives in mind as you read the rest of the chapter.

The National Curriculum – for better, for worse?

As a student of education studies in the twenty-first century, it is likely that you already know quite a lot about the National Curriculum. You may be a 'product' of the National Curriculum yourself, or you might have worked in a UK school where the National Curriculum was in evidence all around you. It is not the purpose of this chapter, therefore, to revisit the history of how and why the National Curriculum was introduced in 1988 – instead, we will take a more critical approach, and ask whether the impacts of the National Curriculum have been positive or negative.

The National Curriculum was divided into four key stages:

Key Stage 1: ages 5–7 years (Years 1–2)   Primary
Key Stage 2: ages 7–11 (Years 3–5)
Key Stage 3: ages 11–14 (Years 7–9)   Secondary
Key Stage 4: ages 14–16 (Years 10–11)

The National Curriculum is a legal requirement for all pupils in state education. It makes certain subjects mandatory for students depending on their age/level – so, for example, statutory subjects for pupils at key stages 1 and 2 include art and design, design and technology, English, geography, history, information and communication technology, mathematics, music, physical education, science and religious studies (QCA, 2009).

The National Curriculum was implemented in order to enable every individual child to develop his/her aims in life, specifically in relation to what the individual is good at, interested in and what career path they wish to take in life. In practice, as the curriculum is structured around a very limited number of subjects, this is not possible. The National Curriculum has been heavily criticised by educationalists since it was introduced. Some argue that, if an individual is academic, the path this individual will follow will lead from GCSEs, through A levels to Higher Education. However, these individuals may not receive the opportunity to experience other forms of learning, including vocational, hands-on experience. In contrast, for individuals who are not deemed 'academic' or find examinations difficult, the curriculum seems meaningless, and as a result they are at a disadvantage. Testing at the ages of 7 and 11 is considered inappropriate, as this may label the child from an early age, especially since some children may already find the academic route to education very difficult. This gets worse when the individual's ability is apparently questioned by tests and examinations. The degree of labelling is further reinforced if the child is ranked according to his/her ability by being streamed in specific subjects (such as literacy and numeracy), as currently occurs in the majority of mainstream primary schools. This may result in a child being limited by adhering to a test-based curriculum, regardless of their academic ability. The following 'Controversies' box looks at these, and other, criticisms in more detail.

Controversies

'The National Curriculum does not work'

Agree: Although the National Curriculum has been one of the most influential educational milestones, it has been criticised heavily by many educationalists (Bash and Coulby, 1989; Lawton and Chitty, 1988; Pring, 1989).

- By introducing tests to the curriculum, the educational experience available to the learner is distorted, as tests may demotivate the individual, especially if they are low achievers. Tests dominate the entire timetable and may label a child who is less academic.

- Although many teachers are not against testing in principle, many believe that if teachers were allowed to carry out continuous assessments through coursework, using tests only when they judged it appropriate, pupils would be far more motivated to learn and achieve.

- Art, drama, music and ICT are given less time than subjects such as mathematics, English and science on the timetable and, as such, children are not given enough time to be creative, when creativity is very important as a means to develop a child in terms of his/her ability to adapt to different situations and become open to different ideas.

- Teachers are unable to use their own sense of creativity due to the rigid structure of the National Curriculum (as there is a huge amount of content to be covered by the curriculum which leaves little time for informal learning).

Disagree: The National Curriculum has achieved what it set out to do in raising educational standards across all sectors of society.

- It is easy to be critical but it is facts and figures which count. The Government published figures in 2009 which showed that there was an overall improvement in the performance of pupils on tests of literacy and numeracy (DCSF Performance Tables).

What do you think? Which side of the argument do you favour?

It is important to remember that, when the National Curriculum was introduced in 1988, it was a guidance document which teachers and educators could follow in order to ensure that individual pupils received a 'broad and balanced' curriculum. However, teachers and educators see this document as a means to ensuring that the same subjects, with the same level of detail, are taught in every school in the UK. Therefore, in practice the curriculum is actually built around a set of subjects rather than a set of aims and outcomes. This places limitations on the individual in respect of their options and does not allow a greater breadth of experience for the individual.

In principle, if the government were to reform the National Curriculum and implement practical learning throughout the whole curriculum, the number of barriers to learning faced by individual children might be reduced. This calls to question whether the government should have the central role in deciding educational aims.

? Stop and reflect

Tyler (1949, cited in Kelly, 2004) advocates that the curriculum should be viewed as four elements including: objectives, content, methods and evaluation. Consider this suggestion, and answer the following questions:

- *What do you feel is the most important purpose of the National Curriculum?*
- *How can teachers/practitioners provide educational experiences that are likely to attain these purposes?*
- *Do you feel that curriculum content should be central to the planning of sessions or that the individual pupil should be central to the planning, matched with the curriculum content?*

We have seen that the National Curriculum has met with significant criticism since its introduction. Let us now consider the impact of the National Curriculum on teaching and learning.

The changing role of the teacher

The role of the teacher has changed radically from the role of educator to a multifaceted role involving education, social and psychological care, and the occasional parenting of the child (also known as *in loco parentis*, meaning 'in place of the parent'), whereby the teacher has a legal right to act in the best interests of a child while at school in terms of instructing, advising and correcting behaviour. Societal change has brought about a number of extra responsibilities for the teacher, including a range of skills often gained in a 'hands-on' setting beyond the bounds of **initial teacher training (ITT)**. Skills such as **mentoring** and **coaching**; **counselling**; working alongside agencies to manage disruptive, emotional and behavioural concerns; managing learners with both physical and mental disabilities; and the variety of cultural and social preferences among learners – all of these invoke the need for both resilience and tenacity in the teacher, as well as a broad knowledge of inclusion and equality policy relevant to the needs of diverse learners. There is also the need for the teacher to be able to demonstrate flexibility, and to adapt to constant change in role and subject knowledge, often at an alarming rate, as the sheer volume of consultations and new regulations from central government impose themselves upon classrooms with demands for almost immediate implementation.

Activity

Consider Figure 2.1 outlining some of the roles of a teacher.

- Are there any further roles you can identify?
- Which roles do you think are most important to:
  - The teacher?
  - The child/young person?
  - The government/LEA?
  - The parent?

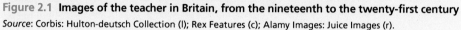

1800s   1970s   2010

Figure 2.1 Images of the teacher in Britain, from the nineteenth to the twenty-first century
Source: Corbis: Hulton-deutsch Collection (l); Rex Features (c); Alamy Images: Juice Images (r).

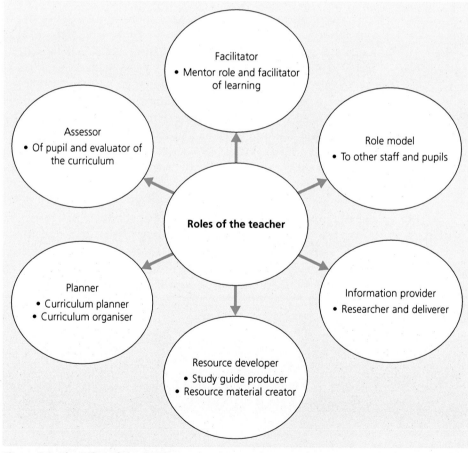

Figure 2.2 The roles of the teacher
Source: Adapted from Harden and Crosby (2000:2).

In contrast to current teaching roles, an insight into the role of the teacher during the late nineteenth century shows that the teacher was an educationist – essentially a conservative agent, or traditionalist, in that they largely transmitted traditional knowledge such as the 3Rs (Reading, wRiting and aRithmetic) (Hoyle, 1969). The level of knowledge delivered was relevant to the needs and levels of the industrial masses in society at that time (Gardner, 1998) where the teacher was seen as a wise, learned and often religious person, esteemed because they embodied certain values. Examples of this type of teaching can be seen in the character of the schoolmistress, Miss Temple, in Charlotte Brontë's *Jane Eyre*, who sought to correct errors and use praise 'liberally', and furthermore in Miss Scatcherd in the same novel, who was not quite as liberal with her praise but sought to deal with pupils who were careless and unorganised (Brontë, 1847, 1994:58). Although these teachers are taken from the imagination of a middle-class author who was considering her own middle-class schooling, they give some insight into the notion of the type of socialisation that was considered to be most significant in the role of the teacher, and the importance of teaching acceptable standards, along with the fundamental skills of literacy, numeracy and general knowledge (Hoyle, 1969). However, socialisation was not the only area for improvement at this time: for example, Dickens' *Hard Times* (1854, 1994) also reveals the perceived importance of learning facts in schools, and 'nothing but facts' (p. 1), which was done through what is called a **rote system**. This involved children learning facts off by heart. Dickens suggests in the same chapter that pupils were being prepared to have 'imperial gallons of facts poured into them until they were full to the brim' (p. 2). This is a system which the older generation of our time who attended schools up until the mid 1940s still bear testimony to in terms of the huge amount of knowledge they left school with. Clearly, although Dickens was to a significant extent satirising and making fun of this kind of approach, it was not without its supporters.

As society became more industrialised in the twentieth century, the teacher's role began to change, and while still considered to be a reasonably conservative agent (especially with young children), the teacher now had to adapt to the new technologies rising in society. These included the use of electronic devices in communication, such as calculators, and the onset of the computer and media communication age during the late 1970s. During the mid 1960s computers were introduced into some schools in the USA and used in administrative practices; however, it was not until 1981 that the first educational programs were developed by IBM for personal computers (Murdock, 2007). Each technology induced the need for a more open-ended independent form of education, requiring broader thinking in skills such as English, **information and communication technology (ICT)** and mathematics in order to encourage individuals to work confidently, effectively and independently (QCDA, 2009), qualities which are needed in society, particularly during the secondary years (Hoyle, 1969). However, as we shall see, the rise of the British National Curriculum in 1988 had a devastating effect on many teachers (such as Mrs Brown in Case study 1.1), and brought about even more changes in the teaching profession. The National Curriculum was to affect both professional status and classroom practice, and created the need for the additional staffing within the classroom to assist the teachers in their endeavour to reach every pupil. To understand the extent of the changes wrought, we review the post-war, pre-National Curriculum period, sometimes called 'the golden age of teaching'.

The golden age of teaching

Whitty (2002) shows that, before the rise of the National Curriculum, teachers had enjoyed relative freedom within their role, in terms of the planning, design and delivery of the curriculum. The years between 1944 and the mid 1970s could be, and indeed are still, considered by many educators to be the 'golden age' of teaching. During these years, teachers were considered to have experienced a reasonably free rein and control of the curriculum. By teaching to learner needs, using local, tried and tested teaching techniques, and supposedly offering an all-round curriculum, teachers enjoyed a considerable degree of privacy and autonomy in terms or teaching style and curriculum content (Hoyle, 1969); and 'parents . . . were expected to trust professionals and accept that teachers knew what was best for their children' (Whitty, 2002:66).

The **syllabus** or curriculum was rarely set out in any detail, as it was recognised that teaching could not 'consist of a blueprint' (Gillard, 2007): this gives further credence to the arguments surrounding the notion of a lottery curriculum, with further increasing measures of government control during the 1970s and 1980s, and teachers considering schooling and education as 'their concern' (Acker, 1990, cited in Helby and McCullock, 1997). Much of this freedom in the planning and design of the curriculum had come about because the **Local Education Authorities (LEAs)**, which were originally assigned the role of planning and design, 'had major problems with the management of buildings and staffing', and so had duly passed the task of curriculum planning to the teachers in schools (Lawton, 1989:35). However, Lawton also reminds us that schoolteachers had not always experienced this so-called freedom of planning and design within the curriculum, as prior to the 1944 Education Act there were considerable governmental controls and regulations in place.

Consider the following account, from a teacher who worked in a primary school during the 1970s:

> Before the National Curriculum I always had a good idea what I was going to teach because we had discussed ideas in staff meetings, but if a child brought in something interesting to share then I could just tell the head teacher that I was going to cover my originally planned lesson the next week and we would then explore the flowers, the object or book or whatever it was through discussion, perhaps write stories, copy, draw, or create something similar through cutting and pasting, or we would go out for a nature walk to find some more . . . We could be spontaneous to teaching moments . . .
>
> Mrs Ward, Retired school teacher reporting on experiences in primary school during the 1970s

Activity

Compare this account (and that of Mrs Brown in Case study 2.1) with your own experiences of primary schooling and consider the following:

- What are the distinct differences in today's teaching approach?
- What might be the advantages of spontaneity in the classroom?
- What do you think may be the concerns with having a 'free for all' curriculum?

Most primary schools followed a locally planned curriculum that provided an adequate learning experience to prepare children for secondary school which in turn would prepare them for future employment upon leaving school (see Chapter 1 for more on the tripartite system in secondary schools).

However, during the 1970s there were concerns from parents, school inspectors and local businesses that the progressive style of teaching, brought about originally in the USA by John Dewey and his colleagues in the early 1900s and re-established during the 1960s, was not proving to be as effective as the more traditional rote learning of facts (Lowe, 2007); and that this type of schooling was causing a decline in the educational standards and skills for work in young people (Jones, 2003). Progressive schooling asserted that 'children were unique individuals', that 'learning was the product of the active relationship between individuals and their environment', and that 'learning was best organised through collaboration between students, and between students and their teachers' (Cunningham, 1988:20, in Jones, 2003:54). Curtis (2008) informs that the approach is a more child-centred approach to teaching and a less formal setting, where children are seated facing each other at tables rather than the traditional rows of desks.

? Stop and reflect

- *Is progressive schooling still found in schools today?*
- *Which type of schooling did you experience?*

The discord about teaching styles and decline in academic standards in pupils brought about a major survey into the attitudes of industry and business, carried out by the National Youth Employment Council (NYEC) in 1974, which suggested that employers were managing the

> marked deterioration in the behaviour of young workers who were now 'more questioning', 'less likely to respect authority' and 'more likely to resent guidance about their general appearance'.
>
> NYEC, 1974:74, cited in Chitty, 2004:34

Ultimately, the government was bombarded with complaints from business and industry in terms of the ever-increasing cohorts of pupils entering the workplace with limited communication and social skills and often inadequate subject knowledge or experience in the tasks required for work, which brought about the historical Ruskin College speech from Prime Minister James Callaghan in 1976.

Callaghan's speech on skills for work

In his speech at Ruskin College in 1976, Prime Minster James Callaghan outlined his concerns in terms of the 'complaints from industry that new recruits from the schools sometimes [did] not have the basic tools to do the job . . .' Callaghan also voiced the notion that the goal of education from nursery through to adulthood was to 'equip children to the best of their ability for a lively constructive place in society and also to fit them to do a job of work' (Callaghan, 1976). It would appear that this was neither evident nor working effectively from the point of view of industry. The blame for the deficit in skills and 'most of the problems found in schools' fell on the teaching profession (Chitty, 2004:36), with the prevailing argument being that it was the teaching styles that were being used, and the varied curriculum being taught within schools, that were no longer effective (for more on Callaghan's Ruskin College speech, see Chapter 1).

It was at this time also that plans were steadily being advanced towards a more centralised and core curriculum, one that would enable the raising of standards in education, and strengthen the role of parents, teachers and professional bodies in order to ensure that young people were better equipped to make the transition from school to the workplace (Gillard, 2007).

➤ Connect and explore

http://education.guardian.co.uk/thegreatdebate/story/0,9860,574645,00.html
This website offers access to the full report 'Towards a National Debate' addressed by James Callaghan in his Ruskin College speech. This is useful when trying to understand the skills debate and the political effects of the education system on society.

The impact of the National Curriculum on the teaching profession

Wragg (1989), a professor of education and renowned trainer of teachers, informs us that the teaching profession in general was not opposed to the prospect of a National Curriculum: however, the majority of teachers did feel that the changes imposed on their role, from planner and designer to that of deliverer, did impact upon their work and autonomy as a professional. This meant that teachers had on the whole a largely negative response to the prospect of a National Curriculum.

Initially the teaching profession (particularly in primary schools) was concerned at what the National Curriculum would contain, and shared concerns in terms of their subject knowledge, and doubted whether they would be knowledgeable enough to teach such demanding content. Teachers were aware that the curriculum would be subject based, but had only been given limited information on how much time would need to be spent studying these individual subjects (Gillard, 1988). Anxiety over how they would manage the new assessments (**Standard Assessment Tests**, or **SATs**) and the increased administration connected to this all served to increase stress across all levels of the profession.

Deskilling and disempowering teachers

After such a long tradition of teacher autonomy, many teachers experienced what was termed as 'deskilling and disempowerment' (Helsby and McCullock, 1997:2), particularly in the early years of the National Curriculum. The National Curriculum was seen as dictating to teachers what content should be taught, how it should be taught and, furthermore, how it should be assessed (Coffrey, 2001), all of which were areas of expertise previously undertaken by the teachers at the individual school level. In many teachers' views, their professional skills in curriculum design had been passed on to government officials, thus deskilling teachers and leaving trained professionals with limited scope in terms of their new role as 'deliverers', which Sofer (1988, cited in Gillard, 1988) suggested now summed up the role of the teacher in the age of the National Curriculum.

Many teachers found this change in role demeaning to their professionalism, believing they were now expected to follow a new curriculum that had been designed without consulting them. Teachers who had previously taken control of the curriculum were now in the position of following a strict framework, which Gillard (1988:2) suggested felt like 'a straightjacket'.

Ambiguity in the curriculum?

The National Curriculum, although a framework, was considered by many teachers to be ambiguous and confusing. For example, where on the one hand the guidelines would indicate freedom and flexibility when planning curriculum content, on the other hand the guidelines would suggest that the curriculum content and assessment should be 'tightly defined', requiring teachers to plan subject content minute by minute (Gillard, 1988). Research from Webb and Vulliamy (2006) has shown that tightly defined schedules within the classroom have resulted in less time to respond to the children's interests during the school day. An example from Webb and Vulliamy's research suggests that attempts by learners to share experiences in class often could not be accommodated if they did not quite fit the discussion of the day:

> You have got news on Monday morning? Great, tell us Thursday afternoon because we have got five minutes then.
>
> SENCO, November 2004, cited in Webb and Vulliamy, 2006:149

We see an example here of teachers losing valuable communication time with learners who, after feeling enthused to show and tell, might well be disappointed by this response. Moreover, teachers felt too constrained by the curriculum guidelines to make time to listen.

? Stop and reflect

- *Are there questions about the use of anecdotal evidence such as the above statement from Webb and Vulliamy's research?*
- *How does such evidence compare with the quantifiable data from DCSF Performance Tables?*

The quality of interaction between pupils and teachers was also considered to be problematic as the national strategies for literacy and numeracy were introduced from 1998 onwards. Although, unlike the National Curriculum, the literacy and numeracy strategies were not statutory, they informed teachers on exactly how to teach literacy and numeracy in primary schools. Cassidy (2008) considers that teachers were no longer thinking on their feet or adapting lessons to individual needs. The school day was now controlled by the government, which provided guidance booklets suggesting schemes of work to support the system. Interestingly however, once these schemes were implemented, the government appeared to swiftly withdraw them, causing many teachers to experience confusion and despair – having made one set of changes to their planning, they were now expected to undertake more change. Gillard (2007) suggests that this was due to the government's constantly reviewing and revising the curriculum because of pressures from researchers and pressure groups that were unhappy with the curriculum.

On a more positive note, Helsby and McCullock (1997) show that some teachers looked for and found ways of adapting a more proactive role in accommodating the National Curriculum, and sought to impose their own insights on requirements. This was not easy to do, and required teachers to have a degree of confidence which in time grew as the National Curriculum became more established. However, for some, the confidence had been crushed, and took time to be re-established. Research by Cox and Sanders (1994:34) into the effects of the National Curriculum on teachers informs us that teachers in the early 1990s were:

> moving slowly along the path. Change [could not] be enforced – it [had] to happen gently. [It was a] gradual process to build up to the National Curriculum.

Sadly, the rise of the National Curriculum caused some teachers to leave the profession, mainly due to sheer overload, others because the job they had been trained to do was no longer there. However, many teachers were able to adapt to the changes and structures of the National Curriculum, and demonstrated resounding resilience in managing a curriculum that initially overwhelmed them. In the twenty-first century we can see that many trainee teachers were educated during the National Curriculum and so have become products of a curriculum which to them is 'the norm', and which would suggest that the tensions present among teachers during the late 1980s are now less likely to be present.

Standard Assessment Tests

Perhaps one of the most difficult pills of all for teachers to swallow was the introduction of the Standard Assessment Tests (SATs). The SATs were introduced to test the subject knowledge of children at the end of each Key Stage, as follows:

KS1   age 7
KS2   age 11
KS3   age 14
KS4   age 16

Initially, teachers administered the SATs and reported back to the government and parents on the progress of pupils based on the teachers' assessment and results taken from SATs (Acker, 1997). However, the SATs were seen by the teachers as just another test, which did not provide them with any more information on a pupil's progress than they already had from their own local tests. Some teachers considered the extra workload unnecessary and boycotted the 1993 SATs: however, the government, much to the dismay of the teaching profession, insisted that the SATs should remain intact and continue to be administered by teachers, but be marked externally. This was a blow to the teachers, who now felt they were not trusted to mark the tests that they still had to administer. Most teachers agree with the importance of regular testing in class for checking student understanding but, as the United Kingdom is considered to be among the highest tested countries in the world (Hall, 2008), and with the evidence of numerous reports on the increasing stress levels in young people who are constantly being tested, it is understandable that the teaching profession today is still seeking the abolition of SATs in favour of a more effective school-level assessment (Marley, 2008).

? Stop and reflect

Think about a time when you were taking exams or tests.
- *How well prepared were you for these tests, and what do you feel are the benefits of being tested, if any?*
- *Did your results reflect your actual knowledge?*

It should be noted that the teaching profession was not against the prospect of a National Curriculum and its testing schemes – the profession had agreed that the National Curriculum provided a helpful planning framework – but it was concerned about the overload of information, the exorbitant amounts of administration and record-keeping around the SATs, and the notion of being seen as deliverers rather than creators and designers of the curriculum, all of which added to the amount of pressure being placed upon them (Cox, 1996).

Slimming down the National Curriculum

Sir Ron Dearing (a cross bencher in the House of Lords) (1993, cited in MacLeod-Brudenell, 2004) suggested a slimming down in some subjects, and was followed in 1999 by the revised National Curriculum – entitled Curriculum 2000 – which was launched online to provide clearer guidance and place more emphasis on inclusion. A short period of optimism on the part of the teaching profession ended with still more clarity issues in terms of the foundation subjects and the structure of the exam timetables and still an over-prescription on objectives. A further concern was voiced by Weiner (1993, cited in Coffey, 2001) in terms of the gender bias found in the new history curriculum which 'did little to present re-visioned historical accounts of women' but rather seemed to present a 'malestream of white history' (p. 46) (see Chapter 1 for more on the history curriculum). Furthermore, the launch of the national strategies in literacy and numeracy, which were both assigned full hours in the classroom on a daily basis, seemed to be bringing about yet more work for teachers in what was supposed to be a slimmed-down curriculum.

The impact of the National Curriculum on the learner

The National Curriculum emphasises learning, and theorists with a psychological stance have long been involved in providing an understanding for teachers on the various ways that children are considered to learn. This includes their development of 'cognitive, social, emotional and physical skills as well as knowledge and understanding' (Hallet and MacLeod-Brudenell, 2004:248). In the early days of planning a core curriculum, the Plowden Report of 1967 had examined the ways that primary schools were running and how they catered for the developing child moving on into secondary school. One theorist mentioned in the report was Jean Piaget (1896–1980), a Swiss biologist whose stage theory of the cognitive development in young children seemed to make relative sense. Piaget suggested that children 'more or less naturally move through a series of stages of learning development in which they are able to handle progressively more complex concepts in progressively more complex ways' (Moore, 2000:9).

Table 2.1 demonstrates how Piaget's stage theory relates to the stages suggested for the National Curriculum and assessment.

Within the learning situation

Piaget's theory may be applied in practice, as teachers in the classroom are able to focus on the idea that children do not achieve a fixed level by a certain age: this allows for individual development. Goodall (1996, cited in Neumark, 1996) agrees with this idea, and suggests that this provides teachers with greater understanding of the experiences of the early stages of childhood cognition. According to Piaget (Woods, 1998) a child cannot learn or be taught functions at higher levels unless they have passed through the lower stages of development first, and should be in a state of 'readiness' before moving on to further stages. The role of the teacher is to identify the stage a child has reached and assess their learning readiness (Wood, 1998). Moreover, the teacher may need to evaluate Piaget's theory and its application to the National Curriculum in terms of 'discovery learning', where tasks are set to encourage children to explore the world for themselves. Compare this with the theories of Lev Vygotsky (1896–1934) and Bruner (1915–) who suggested that learning can be assisted at any stage through an approach referred to as **'scaffolding'**, wherein the child is supported in their learning by a teacher or more competent peer until a concept is understood and the child can continue unaided (Bruner, 1963, cited in Bentham, 2002).

As the National Curriculum developed, the government sought to provide opportunities for discovery learning, as suggested by Piaget (1978), and further to provide opportunities to support learning, as suggested by Vygotsky (1962). For more information on Piaget and Vygotsky, see Chapter 4.

Techniques like scaffolding and the acceleration of learning, using Vygotsky's **zone of proximal development (ZPD)**, which measures the distance between the child's actual development and their potential development (Vygotsky, 1962), are

Table 2.1 **Piaget's stages of cognitive development**

Piaget's stages of cognitive development	Characterised by	UK National Curriculum stages and Standard Assessment Tests
Sensori-motor (birth–2 years)	Babies learning through their senses	N/A
	They are egocentric and see the world from their own point of view	
	They achieve object permanence and realise that things continue to exist even when they can no longer see the object	
Pre-operational (2–7 years)	Learns to use language and to represent objects by images and words	**Foundation and Key Stage 1** Baseline Assessment Tests
	Thinking is still egocentric: has difficulty taking the viewpoint of others	Standard Assessment Tests – age 7
	Classifies objects by a single feature: e.g. groups together all the red blocks regardless of shape or all the square blocks regardless of colour	Achieve NC levels 1–3 in Key Stage 1 and attain level 2 at the end of the Key Stage
Concrete operational (7–11 years)	Can see things from another's point of view (decentre); can think logically about objects and events	**Key Stage 2** Standard Assessment Tests – age 11
	Achieves conservation of number (age 6), mass (age 7), and weight (age 9)	Achieve NC levels 2–5 in Key Stage 2 and attain level 4 at the end of the Key Stage
	Classifies objects according to several features and can order them in series along a single dimension such as size	
Formal operational (11 years and up)	Can think logically and test hypotheses systematically	**Key Stage 3** Standard Assessment Tests – age 14 (abolished in 2009)
	Becomes concerned with the hypothetical, the future, and ideological problems	Achieve NC levels 3–7 in Key Stage 3 and attain level 5/6 at the end of the Key Stage
		Key Stage 4 GCSE age 16
		A levels age 18

Source: Adapted from Tassoni et al. (1999) and http://www.learningandteaching.info/learning/piaget.htm.

discussed in Chapter 4. Both theories are considered as constructivist theories, meaning that learning is achieved by constructing knowledge by building upon prior knowledge, and developing through increasingly challenging tasks (Hallet and MacLeod-Brudenell, 2004). This can be seen in the Early Years Foundation

Stage where teachers plan activities that encourage children to build on experiences learnt in the home environment, through the play corner or the book corner. Using role play opportunities to explore different environments, such as going to the doctor's surgery or the hairdresser's, can encourage discovery learning through exploration (including verbal and tactile activity), and also provide opportunities for practitioners to support learning through questions, discussion and demonstration.

Activity

View the following video from teachers.tv: 'Professional Skills – Independent Learners: A whole school approach' (http://www.teachers.tv/video/5429).

- Having watched this video, what do you think are the benefits of discovery learning?
- How could scaffolding be incorporated in this case?

The new primary curriculum

In January 2008, the Secretary of State for Education, Ed Balls, asked Sir Jim Rose to undertake a review of the primary National Curriculum. He asked that Rose pay particular attention to standards in literacy and numeracy, flexibility, transition between phases of education, reducing prescription, personal, social and emotional capability and personalising learning (remit letter to Sir Jim Rose, January 2008), aspects of curriculum that have been contentious for many years. Following visits by Rose to many primary schools, discussions with teachers, head teachers, pupils and parents and researching the success of national curricula in other countries, the primary curriculum was reorganised (QCDA, 2010). The National Curriculum in England has always been subject-based: as a result of the review, an alternative 'areas of learning' curriculum was proposed, where the programmes of learning are set out in six broad areas which incorporate subjects. The intentions behind this move were to allow for better links to be made between subjects, and to give schools greater flexibility and freedom, enabling them to tailor learning to meet the needs of learners in their locality. Children's learning in school would therefore be given context in the real world.

How significant was the proposed change? Despite the perception that has developed following its initial introduction, in reality the National Curriculum had only ever prescribed subject content to teachers, and suggested a minimum weekly lesson time for each subject. It did not prescribe pedagogy, nor did it prescribe how much time should be dedicated to the teaching of each subject, or any particular curriculum design. However, while there is much that is good in the current National Curriculum, for primary schools in particular it remains overcrowded. *The Cambridge Primary Review* (2010), which was published after several years of extensive investigation into all aspects of primary education in England, found that children had insufficient time to engage adequately with every subject required by law. Teachers had become overstretched with the plethora of initiatives, QCA schemes of work, the Primary Strategy and other policies. Many schools (mistakenly) believed that all these were statutory initiatives, whereas some were in fact guidance. Some schools felt under so much pressure that they opted to follow the QCA schemes of work. In doing so, they felt there would be more security in terms of planning, subject knowledge and Ofsted compliance. There was also a feeling that, by using these schemes, curriculum content was being covered. On the other hand, there was a backlash feeling of being straitjacketed, of a loss of creativity and, as we saw earlier in this chapter, many teachers felt they were becoming deliverers of the curriculum rather than the designers of it.

Many schools across the country have exciting, rich curricula that inspire not only pupils but also teachers. These schools have designed curricula that are relevant to their context, their learners and their locality. They have been courageous in their curriculum design, and have relished the opportunity to develop compelling learning experiences with learners at the heart: 'The most successful schools based their reforms on considerable background research into theories of learning and different ways of approaching the curriculum' (Ofsted, 2008:5). Of course, schools will continue to face the pressure of Ofsted inspections, standards and SATs, but there is an argument that, if the process (in this case, the curriculum) is good, then the product (the educational outcomes) will be all the more likely to be good too.

One criticism of the original National Curriculum was that it was not derived from a set of aims – it was not until 2000 that the aims of the curriculum were overtly stated (Rose, 2009). Aims have been seen to be extrinsic (meaning they are imposed from outside) to the curriculum for many years: according to Kelly (2009), this has been a major downfall of curriculum change. When aims become intrinsic they become part of the process of education, the long-term aspiration for learning rather than the short-term objectives. 'Aims and processes cannot be separated; the aims are reflected in the processes and the processes are embedded in the aims' (Kelly, 2009:96). The new curriculum endeavours to 'establish guiding principles for the holistic education of a child with a unifying set of values and aims' (Rose, 2009:31) for the whole of education, from early years to primary and secondary, to offer greater continuity and coherence for children as they move through the different phases of their education. The primary curriculum review has sought to enable children to develop as human beings rather than bodies of knowledge, allowing them freedom of thought, critical awareness and autonomy.

There have been continuing and wide-ranging discussions about the curriculum and how it has been revised and reformed including the review of the primary curriculum in 2000, the Rose Review of the primary curriculum published in 2009 and the Cambridge Review (2010) (which explored all aspects of primary provision such as Special Educational Needs, pedagogy and curriculum, unlike the Rose review which looked solely at the curriculum). In these past 10 years we have seen significant change; for example, the use of technology in schools has moved on apace, so that students at primary and secondary schools use **virtual learning environments (VLEs)** where they can upload and download work. With the advent of Web 2.0, children have become participants, easily developing and utilising technology-based skills to become creators and contributors in the learning journey, sharing with both peers and teachers. For example, they produce podcasts, create, edit and share photographs and video materials and have their own school radios where they write the programmes and have learned how to use the technology so they can broadcast their programmes on air during school time. (See Chapters 10 and 11 for further discussion of the changing role of technology in educational settings.) Should the curriculum reflect the evolving world of technology? Is the curriculum concerned with more than learning subject knowledge? In a time of change, what does the future hold for the primary National Curriculum?

The new primary curriculum is built on a set of aims which link with the *Every Child Matters* outcomes and are the same as the aims of the secondary curriculum:

- **Successful learners** who enjoy learning, make progress and achieve
- **Confident individuals** who are able to live safe, healthy and fulfilling lives
- **Responsible citizens** who make a positive contribution to society.

(QCDA, 2010:12)

Underpinning the curriculum areas are 'essentials for learning and life' which are defined as the literacy, numeracy, ICT capability and personal learning, thinking and social skills necessary to achieve the aims of the curriculum. The 'essentials for learning and life' are implicit in the areas of learning and it is this focus on fundamental skills, dispositions and reflection that the government aspires to enable children to develop a lifelong love of learning (QCDA, 2010).

The areas of learning are:

- Understanding the arts
- Understanding English, communication and languages
- Historical, geographical and social understanding
- Mathematical understanding
- Understanding physical development, health and well-being
- Scientific and technological understanding.

If you look at other countries that have adopted areas of learning curriculum – Northern Ireland or New Zealand for example – you will notice that, although there are subject disciplines within each area, there are separate skills and knowledge for each subject within that area. One might argue that this does not constitute an areas of learning model; rather, it remains a subject-based model.

↖ Connect and explore

Go online and compare the curricula of Northern Ireland and New Zealand with the new primary curriculum. Look at the knowledge, understanding and skills of the Northern Ireland curriculum, the 'achievement objectives by learning area' in the New Zealand curriculum and the 'essential knowledge' and 'key skills' in the English National Curriculum. How are they different? How are they similar? What common elements do they share?

Northern Ireland: **http://www.nicurriculum.org.uk/docs/key_stages_1_and_2/ northern_ireland_curriculum_primary.pdf**

New Zealand: **http://nzcurriculum.tki.org.nz/Curriculum-documents/The-New-Zealand-Curriculum**

England: **http://curriculum.qcda.gov.uk/new-primary-curriculum/index.aspx**

The new primary curriculum considers what an area of learning represents and what is important to know and to be able to do as a result of the interaction and engagement within that area of learning. For example, in 'Understanding the arts', there are common sets of 'essential knowledge' and 'key skills' for the whole area of learning, regardless of whether you are learning about art and design, dance, drama or music:

Essential knowledge

Children should build secure knowledge of the following:

(a) how creative ideas can be developed in response to different stimuli and imaginative thinking;

(b) how different art forms communicate and evoke moods, thoughts and ideas;

(c) that designing, creating and performing require discipline, control, technique and practice;

(d) how and why people from different times and cultures have used the arts to express ideas and communicate meaning;

(e) that accepted forms and conventions can give structure and purpose to artistic works but can be adapted and changed.

Key skills

These are the skills that children need to learn to make progress:

(a) explore, investigate and experiment from a range of stimuli and starting points, roles, techniques, approaches, materials and media;

(b) create, design, devise, compose and choreograph their individual and collective work;

(c) improvise, rehearse and refine in order to improve their capability and the quality of their artworks;

(d) present, display and perform for a range of audiences, to develop and communicate their ideas and evoke responses;

(e) use arts-specific vocabulary to respond to, evaluate, explain, analyse, question and critique their own and other people's artistic works.

(National Curriculum website, 2010)

In order to make effective progress in school, children need to be able to identify the purposes of learning, to reflect on the processes of learning and to identify obstacles or problems and to plan ways to improve their learning. The 'essential knowledge' provides a base for what children need to know and understand in a specific area of learning; these are the foundations for deeper understanding in the later stages of education. The 'key skills' include the important skills and processes children need to develop to prepare them for future learning. Take a moment to look at the key skills: can you identify four strands – investigate, create and develop, communicate and evaluate? These are evident in each area of learning, in the key skills section, and are relevant to the essentials for learning and life. These strands provide a common framework across and within each area of learning.

The current context

Following discussions with the opposition parties, on 6 April 2010 the Labour Government tabled amendments to the Children, Schools and Families Bill to enable some parts of the Bill to be passed into law before Parliament was dissolved as a General Election was imminent. Some key provisions were taken out because no agreement could be reached between the government and opposition parties. These provisions included the reform of the primary curriculum. The statutory status of the new primary curriculum remained to be finalised after the election had taken place on 6 May 2010. It was widely expected that, if the Labour Party were voted back into office, the new primary curriculum would be implemented as planned in September 2011. Alternatively, the Conservatives had promised to reform the curriculum with an emphasis on traditional subjects, while the Liberal Democrats were planning to replace the National Curriculum with a 20-page Minimum Curriculum Entitlement document. The hung Parliament outcome of the 2010 election, and the subsequent formation of a coalition government by the Conservatives and the Liberal Democrats, meant that at the time of writing there was still much uncertainty over the new primary curriculum, but it is clear that the curriculum debate will remain ongoing, and a key political issue.

Conclusion

Changes to the National Curriculum will be ongoing. A new secondary curriculum was introduced in 2007 with new opportunities in terms of vocational qualifications and the notion of child-centred learning and creativity making a welcome return to the curriculum, with decisions regarding the outcomes of the primary curriculum review to be decided. Many teachers are starting to feel that they are regaining some of the autonomy and flexibility found prior to the National Curriculum. In the words of one teacher:

> I feel so tired, but invigorated at same time . . . it's hard to motivate yourself when it's the end of a long year . . . and you think you are doing something extra while others are starting to wind down . . . in reality no one winds down . . . this has left me feeling more positive about myself, my relationships and more confident in my ability to plan creatively in the future . . . it's worth being tired.
>
> Patterson and Kidd (2008)

Furthermore, through the research of Webb and Vulliamy (2006), we are beginning to see how the National Curriculum has provided more organisation and clarity to the education of children and young people, and how this has enabled professionals to improve both teaching and learning standards. This is evident in the following statement, from a teacher who had experienced many of the difficulties at the onset of the National Curriculum, but who now demonstrates the benefits of the National Curriculum for both teaching and learning:

> Going back a few years I didn't know what I was teaching, the kids didn't know what they were learning and at the end of the lesson we didn't know whether we'd learnt it and nobody bothered to find out whether we'd learnt it. Now I know what I'm teaching,

they know what they're learning and at the end of the lesson I'm going to know whether they've learnt it and what's more important they're going to know whether they've learnt it – and that's what's improved teaching.

Year 3 teacher, in Webb and Vulliamy (2006:152)

Although the National Curriculum was introduced after many years of an unstructured 'golden age' of teaching in the UK, and despite being the subject of many ongoing debates, there is evidence to suggest that it is succeeding. Nevertheless, the curriculum continues to undergo radical changes, and there is no doubt that the curriculum will be subject to many more changes in the future, depending on societal and political influences. It is essential that educators are aware of the need for constant change to the curriculum, and indeed to their role, in order to promote an inclusive educational environment which meets the needs of the individual learner. This may be a challenging consideration for potential teachers, as well as those teachers who are currently working hard to implement each strategy as it arrives in the classroom. However, the National Curriculum has changed the face of education, hopefully for the better, and provided a framework on which to build a greater element of equality for those who teach it and for those who receive it in the classroom.

Case study 2.2
A new teacher's experience of the National Curriculum

Amanpreet is 28 and has been teaching in a primary school for 6 years. She has experience of teaching each of the year groups from year 3 to year 6 with a specialism in English and feels settled in her teaching role as she prepares her current year 6 class for the up-and-coming Standard Assessment Tests. Amanpreet has attended a variety of staff development sessions over her time in the school and has recently achieved a Masters in Education in Teaching and Learning. She has a good working knowledge of the National Curriculum objectives at all stages. There was a change in the primary literacy strategy in her early years of teaching (2006) which she welcomed and thought that she had adapted to very well. During this time, Amanpreet got married and now has a 3-year-old toddler, who attends a local nursery. Being off on maternity leave did unsettle her a little, but Amanpreet soon caught up with the new policies that had been implemented into the classroom. However, she has now been informed by a fellow teaching friend that the primary curriculum has been under review and that the changes in the curriculum are likely to mean redesigning the curriculum and the ways she has been teaching the subjects she has become so well accustomed to. Some of the longer-serving teachers in the school have been talking in the staff room about the difficulties they experienced when the National Curriculum was brought into schools. Amanpreet is starting to feel some pressure and has come to you for advice.

Questions for discussion

1 *Considering your reading from this chapter, how would you allay Amanpreet's concerns?*

2 *What pitfalls could she avoid?*

3 *What might be the benefits of planning and delivering a revised curriculum to her continuing professional development?*

4 *How could Amanpreet use the following website introducing the new primary curriculum to help her prepare effectively for the changes afoot? http://curriculum. qcda.gov.uk/new-primary-curriculum/index.aspx*

Summary

The National Curriculum – for better, for worse?

Although the aim of the National Curriculum was to enable every individual to develop his or her aims in life, specifically in relation to what the individual is good at, interested in and what career path they wish to take, in reality the National Curriculum did not provide these opportunities, as it was structured around a limited number of subjects. This failed to take into account any vocational options, thereby resulting in any individual who was not 'academic' being disadvantaged in the education system.

The changing role of the teacher

The role of the teacher has changed radically over the last two centuries. Teachers have experienced a variety of government controls, leading them from the controls of the early 1900s to relative freedom in planning and design after the 1944 Education Act, often referred to as the 'golden age of teaching'. The 1988 Education Act and onset of the National Curriculum brought about a return to tightly controlled government policies, which aimed to raise achievement and ensure equality of opportunity for all learners.

The impact of the National Curriculum on the teaching profession

The impact of the National Curriculum brought about a host of attitudes among teachers that included feelings of being deskilled and disempowered in terms of their teaching role, moving from that of curriculum planner and designer to being just a deliverer. Feelings of confusion, due to ambiguities in the curriculum, and government distrust in terms of the delivery of target-driven assessments, caused more unrest among teachers, as did the onset of the national literacy and numeracy strategies after the slimming down of the National Curriculum, causing many teachers to leave the teaching profession.

The impact of the National Curriculum on the learner

The National Curriculum adopted and included useful theories from psychology in order to ensure that learners received an appropriate education, that addressed learning needs adequately, and with understanding of how children learn cognitively. Theory from Piaget acknowledged the importance of discovery learning and useful stages of development that could offer appropriate ages and stages for assessment. Theory from Vygotsky and Bruner advocated the use of scaffolding. Vygotsky recognised that children learn at different rates and may not conform to expected levels; however, with a more experienced adult or peer supporting them they could reach a stage earlier than expected.

References

Acker, S. (1997) Becoming a teacher educator: Voice of women academics in Canadian faculties of education, *Teacher and Teacher Education*, 13(1).

Alexander, R. (2010) *Children, their World, their Education*, London: Routledge.

Ball, S. (2003) *Class Strategies and the Education Market: The Middle Classes and Social Advantages*, London: RoutledgeFalmer.

Bartlett, S. and Burton, D. (2007) *Introduction to Education Studies*, London: Sage.

Bash, L. and Coulby, D. (1989) The Education Reform Act: Competition and Control, London: Cassell.

Bentham, S. (2002) *Psychology and Education*, Hove, Sussex: Routledge.

Brontë, C. (1847, 1994) *Jane Eyre*, London: Penguin Group.

Cassidy, S. (2008) Failed Political Interference is Damaging Children's Education, www.Independent.co.uk, 29 Feb. 2008.

Chitty, C. (2004) *Education Policy in Britain*, Basingstoke: Palgrave MacMillan.

Coffey, A. (2001) *Education and Social Change*, Buckingham: OUP.

Curtis, P. (2008) Children being failed by progressive teaching, http://www.guardian.co.uk/education/2008/may/09/schools.uk, accessed March 2010.

DCSF (2009) Performance tables, England. Available from http://www.dcsf.gov.uk/performancetables/, viewed July 2010.

DfES (2009) *The Early Years Foundation Stage*. Available from http://www.standards.dfes.gov.uk/eyfs/site/requirements/learning/goals.htm, viewed April 2009.

DfES (2006) *Primary National Strategy: Primary framework for literacy and mathematics*, DfES.

Dickens, C. (1994; first published in 1854) *Hard Times*, London: Longman.

Fowler, W.S. (1990) *Implementing the National Curriculum: The Policy and Practice of the Education Reform* Act, London: Kogan Page.

Gardner, P. (1998) Classroom Teachers and Educational Change, 1876–1996, *Journal of Education for Teaching: International Research and Pedagogy*, 24(1), April, pp. 33–49.

Gillard, D. (1988) The National Curriculum and the role of the primary teacher in curriculum development, http://www.dg.dial.pipex.com/articles/educ07.shtml, May 2009.

Gillard, D. (2004) 'The Plowden Report', *The encyclopaedia of informal education*, www.infed.org/schooling/plowden_report.htm, May 2009.

Gillard, D. (2007) Education in England: A brief history, http://www.dg.dial.pipex.com/history/index.shtml.

Hall, K. (2008) England young 'among those most tested'. Available from http://news.bbc.co.uk/2/hi/uk_news/education/7232897.stm.

Halpin, D. and Lewis, A. (1996) The impact of the National Curriculum on twelve special schools in England, *European Journal of Special Needs Education*, 11(1), Routledge.

Helby, G. and McCulloch, G. (1997) *Teachers and the National Curriculum*, London: Cassell.

Hoyle, E. (1969) *The Role of the Teacher*, London: Routledge and Kegan Paul.

Jones, K. (2003) *Education in Britain: 1944 to the Present*, Cambridge: Polity Press/Blackwell Publishing Ltd.

Kelly, A.V. (1986) *Knowledge and Curriculum Planning*, London: Paul Chapman Publishing.

Kelly, A.V. (2009) *The Curriculum: Theory and Practice*, London: Sage Publications.

Lawton, D. (1989) *Education, Culture and the National Curriculum*, London: Hodder & Stoughton.

Lawton, D. and Chitty, L. (eds) (1988) *The National Curriculum* (Bedford Way Papers, 33), London: University of London.

Lowe, R. (2007) *The death of progressive education: How teachers lost control of the classroom*, Abingdon: Routledge.

National Literacy Trust (2010) Literacy Policy in Scotland. Available from http://www:literacytrust.org.uk/policy/scotland.html, viewed January 2010.

Marley, D. (2008) Ofsted slams teaching to the test, http://www.tes.co.uk/article.aspx?storycode=6000653.

Moon, B., Shelton Mayes, A. and Hutchinson, S. (2002) *Teaching, Learning and the Curriculum in Secondary Schools*, Oxon: RoutledgeFalmer.

Moore, A. (2000) *Teaching and Learning: Pedagogy, Curriculum and Culture*, London: RoutledgeFalmer.

Murdock (2007) History, the History of Computers, and the History of Computers in Education. Available from http://www.csulb.edu/~murdock/histofcs.html, viewed January 2010.

Neumark, V. (1996) Thinking about thinking, *TES Magazine*, 13 September 1996, http://www.tes.co.uk/article.aspx?storycode=41567, viewed June 2009.

Ofsted (2004) *Special educational needs and disability: Towards inclusive schools,* London: Ofsted.

Ofsted (2008) *Curriculum Innovation in Schools*, London: Ofsted.

OPSI (1988) *Education Reform Act 1988*. Available from http://www.opsi.gov.uk/acts/acts1988/ukpga_19880040_en_2#pt1-ch1-pb1-l1g1.

Patterson, R. and Kidd, D. (2008) From compliance with the curriculum to creativity in the classroom, http://www.teachingexpertise.com/articles/from-compliance-with-the-curriculum-to-creativity-in-the-classroom-3243, viewed October 2008.

Piaget, J. (1978) *The Development of Thought: Equilibration of Cognitive Structures*, Oxford: Basil Blackwell.

Plowden Report (1967) *Children and their Primary Schools*, http://www.dg.dial.pipex.com/documents/plowden.shtml, viewed June 2009.

Pring, R. (1989) *The New Curriculum*, London: Cassell.

Qualifications and Curriculum Development Agency (2010) *Introducing the new primary curriculum*, QCDA.

Qualifications and Curriculum Development Agency (2010) National Curriculum, http://curriculum.qcda.gov.uk/new-primary-curriculum/areas-of-learning/understanding-the-arts/programme-of-learning/index.aspx?tab=2, accessed April 2010.

Qualifications and Curriculum Development Agency (2010), National Curriculum http://curriculum.qcda.gov.uk/key-stages-3-and-4/aims/index.aspx, accessed January 2010.

Qualifications and Curriculum Development Agency (2010) National Curriculum: About the Primary Curriculum, http://curriculum.qcda.gov.uk/key-stages-1-and-2/Values-aims-and-purposes/about-the-primary-curriculum/index.aspx, accessed February 2010.

Qualifications and Curriculum Development Agency (2010) Functional Skills, http://www.qcda.gov.uk/6062.aspx, accessed January 2010.

Rose, J. (2009) *Independent Review of the Primary Curriculum: Final Report*, Nottingham: DCSF Publications.

Shearn, P. and Waymen, A. (2004) A Review of National Curriculum (5–16 yrs) Guidance of England, Scotland and Wales. Report Number HSL/2005/25. Available from http://www.hse.gov.uk/research/hsl_pdf/2005/hsl0525.pdf, viewed January 2010.

Tassoni, P., Bulman, K., Beith, K., Burnham, L. and Eldridge, H. (1999) *Early Years Care and Education*, Oxford: Heinemann.

Teachernet (2009) Social and Emotional Aspect of Learning (SEAL), http://www.teachernet.gov.uk/teachingandlearning/socialandpastoral/seal_learning/, viewed April 2009.

Vygotsky, L.S. (1962) *Thought and Language* (E. Hanfmann and G. Vaktor, Trans.), Cambridge, MA: MIT Press.

Webb, R. and Vulliamy (2006) The Impact of New Labour's Education Policy on Teachers and Teaching at Key Stage 2, *Forum*, 48(2), http://www.wwwords.co.uk/pdf/freetoview.asp?j=forum&vol=48&issue=2&year=2006&article=5_Webb_FORUM_48_2_web, viewed October 2008.

Whitty, G. (2002) *Making Sense of Education Policy*, London: Paul Chapman Publishing.

Wood, E. (2004) A new paradigm war? The impact of national curriculum policies on early childhood teachers' thinking and classroom practice, *Teaching and Teacher Education*, 20(4), May 2004, pp. 361–74.

Wragg, E. (1989) Primary teachers and the national curriculum, *Research papers in Education*, 5(3), pp. 17–45.

3

Alternative schooling

Annie Flower and Vanessa Cottle

Contents

Introduction

This chapter provides you with a general introduction to approaches to education and school curricula by considering examples of schools from Europe and the USA which have a role in providing alternative curricula to the English National Curriculum and educational policy. We hope that, as you read, you will begin to ask questions about the purpose and nature of education and perhaps arrive at some answers. It is evident that education has been debated over many centuries and has developed according to the context of time and place. As you make links between historical approaches to education and current thinking, you can compare and contrast these ideas as well as develop your own about what the best sort of school would be for today's children. Think about the current context that schools need to respond to in order to provide the best education. It may well be that you come to more than one answer about what approach a school should take. Certainly you may find that your peers come to different conclusions about what is ideal – for this reason the issue of choice for parents and children is considered.

The chapter looks at the influence that educational thinkers and philosophers have had on shaping how education is delivered within schools; the lessons that can be learned from their ideas and the ways in which these ideas can be applied to improve our current school curricula. Specifically, the philosophies of educationalists Steiner and Montessori will be discussed, along with a consideration of the **alternative schools** that bear their names and reflect their philosophies today. We have also included a short overview of Reggio Emilia schools which have brought together a range of educational ideas that over the years have synthesised to create what many believe to be a unique approach to teaching pre-school children. As a comparison, Charter Movement Schools from the USA will also be considered. Charter Schools adopt an alternative approach to funding and management as well as teaching and learning and therefore provide a useful contrast. **Home schooling** is considered through the case studies at the beginning and end of this chapter, which provide insight into a potentially good example of this type of education. We also note, however, that there are other cases of home schooling which sadly do not result in the same kind of success, an extreme example being that of Kyra Ishaq who was brutally abused and eventually died in 2009. Kyra had been hidden from the authorities under the 'protection' of home schooling.

From reading this chapter we hope you will also be stimulated to do your own investigation of alternative schools near you.

This chapter aims to:

- Evaluate the factors contributing to a good, effective education.
- Gain knowledge of a historical perspective on education.
- Identify a number of key philosophers and thinkers, specifically Jean-Jacques Rousseau, Johann Wolfgang von Goethe, and John Dewey.
- Evaluate aspects of choice regarding education.
- Investigate characteristics of a number of popular alternative schools, specifically Montessori schools, Steiner Waldorf schools and Charter Schools.

Case study 3.1
Which school to choose?

Mr and Mrs Wilcox are keen for their son Charlie to receive a well-balanced education that will ensure that he will have an advantage when it comes to applying for jobs in an increasingly competitive market. They believe that it is important for Charlie to be well-schooled in traditional subject areas as well as in practical and key transferable skills. The Wilcoxes are both professionals and are willing to pay for Charlie's education.

Mr Wilcox was educated at a Steiner Waldorf school, which he believes provided him with a more balanced education that allowed him to develop a wide range of skills and as a result he has become an extremely successful businessman. Mrs Wilcox received a traditional state education and is now a talented teacher working part time since Charlie was born. Charlie is a gifted footballer and he wants to go to the same school as his friends James and Jenny, who live opposite.

The Local Education Authority has allocated Charlie a place at a local school, which has an excellent reputation for sports. However, because he lives over the road from James and Jenny, he is in a different catchment area and has, therefore, not been offered a place at the same school as them. (The term catchment area refers to the geographical area from which a school's pupils are drawn.) Mr Wilcox believes that Charlie will benefit most by attending an alternative school, whereas Mrs Wilcox is keen for Charlie to benefit from a traditional education. They are unable to agree on the best course of action to take and have asked you for guidance.

Questions for discussion

1 *What does it mean to be educated through a 'non-traditional route'?*

2 *In what ways might an alternative school be different?*

3 *What benefits and limitations are there for Charlie if his parents decide to pay for his schooling?*

4 *Is it fair that Charlie is denied a place at a school of his choice? Justify your answer.*

5 *What guidance would you offer Mr and Mrs Wilcox?*

Alternative to what?

In order to be able to consider alternative schooling, you need to know exactly what you want an alternative for. In Chapter 2 of this book, and probably through your own experience of learning and study, you will have become familiar with the English National Curriculum, and the debates surrounding it as it continues to develop. It is important that you have some understanding of this in order to evaluate alternatives. It is also necessary to consider why it is worthwhile even thinking about an alternative. Many parents do opt out of the state system of education in the UK (which is dominated by the National Curriculum) to seek alternative forms of schooling for their children – why do they feel compelled to do so? Change is always difficult: psychologically people will tend to resist change and usually don't like it. So you need to step back a little and think about the role, or purpose, of school. Once you have thought about this you can then begin to reflect on and make some judgements about the best way to achieve this purpose and decide whether the current school system is fit for purpose, or whether an alternative would be better. There are three important questions here:

1 Are alternative schools about offering better quality, for example in terms of higher student attainment or enhanced student experience? Or:

2 Are alternative schools about providing parents and children with freedom of choice and selection, enabling them to opt for a particular school that offers an approach or philosophy they believe to be appropriate? Or:

3 Are alternative schools about both of the above?

The answers to these questions are likely to be subjective, and based on what you believe the purpose of education to be.

By considering these ideas you are beginning to provide yourself with a picture of what makes a 'good' school. Popular opinion would generally agree that education is something that takes place within a school and is facilitated by the curriculum implemented within that school. Education and learning, however, are also about the social, cultural and economic contexts you live within – for example, social class, ethnicity, nationality or religion – and other external influences you have to respond to, which could include gaining the requisite skills and qualifications demanded by local employers. An individual may be motivated by a number of factors when pursuing an education such as learning for learning's sake, to develop self-confidence, to achieve qualifications, to understand the values and norms of the society in which they live, or simply for fun. You may have to take account of these as you read this chapter and try to conclude which alternative schooling approach, if any, would be the one you would choose to meet your needs. What aspects of alternative approaches would you like to integrate within the UK state school system? You may be surprised by some of the more novel alternatives, but it is worth giving them some serious consideration.

Setting the scene for schooling – where did it all begin?

It is worth having a historical perspective of how education developed so that you can reflect on the different ideas proposed by key educationalists and philosophers. Having a picture of education's historical routes should help you begin to grasp some of the ideas behind why schools have developed in the way they have. For centuries, those interested in education have reflected on the best ways to educate and on the purpose of education. Their philosophies and ideas can still be recognised in curriculum design today and yet governments, employers, teachers, parents and children continue to strive to get it right – could you select from their ideals to decide on the perfect school?

History of education

From ancient times to the nineteenth century

Education and learning is not a new phenomenon. In ancient civilisations in Egypt, China and India, subjects as diverse as writing, science, architecture, poetry, music and physical exercise were considered worthy of study. As today, a key purpose of education was to prepare potential leaders for their roles in the government. Today, it is often the English public school system that delivers the knowledge and skills required for those wishing to seek government office. Religion, too, has always influenced and played a significant part in English education: as early as the ninth century King Alfred the Great established educational institutions and supported religious education.

Until the 1800s, with the onset of the Industrial Revolution, formal education was almost exclusively for the upper social classes. But late in the eighteenth century, when the Church remained key in facilitating education, Sunday Schools appeared in England for poor and working children. The issue of providing all pupils, regardless of family income, equality of educational opportunity has today still not been resolved.

In the nineteenth century education began to attract interest and influence from the state as well as the Church when England and Wales set up state primary schools and public financial aid was given to church schools in the 1830s. The Industrial Revolution generated skills gaps in the job market and the need for employees who could read and write, skills that had not previously been required on the land. Again, there are strong parallels with today's skills gaps, not just hi-tech skills, but also literacy and numeracy skills. However, nineteenth-century Sunday Schools, which taught people to read the Bible, discouraged writing or arithmetic for fear of the lower classes rising above their station (Gillard, 2007). The nineteenth century, then, saw education for the masses developing, but very much organised on a class basis with higher education only available to the upper classes. During the twentieth century 'progressive education' or the system of teaching children according to their needs and potential within a culture of freedom was championed.

Connect and explore

Kirkpatrick, Jerry (2008) *Montessori, Dewey and Capitalism*, Claremont: TLJ Books. Read the excellent chapter on the historical origins of education to find out more.

Derek Gillard's website provides a really useful review of the history of education with links to key government policy that has shaped what we have today. He also has links to a range of articles that will be of interest: **http://www.educationengland.org.uk**.

Find out more about today's skills gap by reading the *Leitch Review of Skills 2006* – you can find this at: **http://www.hm-treasury.gov.uk/leitch_review_index.htm**.

The twentieth century: education as we know it

Today education is synonymous with school and to some extent, therefore, we pass the responsibility for teaching our children (our future adults) about our values and culture to their teachers. Teachers have to be qualified to specific standards which are formulated by government agencies. You can see, therefore, that government can indirectly, as well as directly through policy, influence the values and culture of our society.

Compulsory education is now very well established within the UK and much comment and thought is given to it by government, which is why a brief summary of recent developments that led to the current National Curriculum and approach to schooling in England should now be considered. Such developments may include changes in the economy and social attitudes, together with legislative responses to these changes.

Between 1900 and 1920 there was reaction to the highly disciplined approach to teaching that prevailed in the nineteenth century – there was the rise of socialism which drew attention to the plight of the underprivileged in society. This contributed to a desire for more freedom in education, an ideal which could well have been informed by educational thinkers such as Pestalozzi (1746–1827), Dewey (1859–1952), Montessori (1870–1952) and Steiner (1861–1925) who were all influenced by Rousseau (1712–1778) and Goethe (1749–1832) and their approaches to schooling. In particular, both Montessori and Steiner developed their own systems of education and schools which are available to children in most localities of England and other areas of the world today. Due to their alternative approaches and decisions to opt out of state governance within England, such schools are usually not supported by funding from the state – however, this may change, as in February 2010 plans for the first Montessori state school were being discussed.

During the 1960s the 'hippie' movement, which originated in the United States, reflected the question about whether the role of schools was to produce obedient civilians or critically thinking, free people. Hippies became prominent and noted for their rejection of established cultural norms. For example, they maintained a very relaxed work ethic and a dress code that seemed to be based on denim jeans, skimpy T-shirts and flowers in their hair, as opposed to the traditional tailored suits. They strongly disagreed with the seemingly never ending Vietnam War (into which the USA had become deeply entrenched at a cost of very many lives) and the power they felt government had over individuals. They favoured personal freedom above all else. These ideals very much reflected those of A.S. Neill's Summerhill School, which was started in the 1920s and based on a completely democratic approach to education and learning. Neill's philosophy was based on wanting children to live their own lives according to their own intrinsic motivation. He believed that, if a child wants to laze about, then that is what is important for them at a particular moment in their development and that only a child knows what is best for him/herself. Summerhill has been much criticised for the freedom it gives its pupils – if they don't want to attend lessons they simply don't have to. The school claims to provide a happy environment where well-balanced men and women develop. Certainly during the 1960s there was a tendency towards the humanist approach to schooling which the hippie movement stood for. For example, **comprehensive schools** were introduced to provide greater equality of opportunity, and these ideals of equality of opportunity grew as women's rights took hold and legislation on Race Relations came into effect in 1976. At a practical level in schools there was debate around the curriculum which reflected this move towards freeing up ideas. An example of this was around what was considered unnecessary penalties in examinations for incorrect use of English grammar; it was considered that overemphasising grammar would curb a child's writing creativity and flow of ideas.

Connect and explore

Summerhill School was founded in 1921 by A.S. Neill in Germany. Eventually the school moved to England and is currently sited in Suffolk. Use this website to find out more about Summerhill School: **http://www.summerhillschool.co.uk.**

As we saw in Chapter 2, however, James Callaghan's Ruskin College speech in 1976 led to more concern about the need for schools to be 'accountable' with regard to the amount of public money being spent on education. Moves requiring schools to demonstrate, or measure, whether or not they were achieving their purpose were set in motion. And, after many years of teachers feeling autonomous with regard to curriculum content and design, the Education Reform Act of 1988 gave rise to a prescribed National Curriculum. The requirements of this National Curriculum halted the rights of schools to determine their own curriculum (see Chapter 2 for more on this). There has been much debate and negative criticism about the National Curriculum, with teachers often feeling that their professionalism is devalued and that teaching to pass tests, rather than for enjoyment of learning, restricts the 'education' of children. Some stakeholders in education, for example political parties, employers and parents themselves, maintain that standards have fallen in spite of much government intervention.

As the new millennium unfolds, a new interest in a 'free' and child-centred approach to schooling is coming about. One particular response to this interest is discussed in the Badman Report (2009) which comments on the increasing interest in home schooling which provides parents with the opportunity to keep their children away from school and educate them within the home on a full- or part-time basis. Badman notes that, while it is known there are 20,000 children on the home schooling register in England, the number could be as high as 80,000. This discrepancy could be due to a number of reasons: for example, parents may just not register that their children are home schooled, particularly if the home schooling period is a temporary measure; there may also, in a very small minority of cases, be more sinister reasons for not registering, reflected by the Kyra Ishaq case in 2010 of a girl who was tragically abused by her parents. With the exponential developments in technology a virtual world can be brought into most homes almost instantly at the click of a mouse. The Digital Economy Bill 2009 confirmed the government's commitment to universal broadband, making it still easier for parents to access the resources required to take on the role of educator. Technology increasing the possibilities to genuinely appeal to all learning preferences and to provide a truly child-centred education is at the fingertips of many parents should they feel so inclined to home educate. For example, interactive courses, video and online communities could make learning effective for children who have not engaged in the mainstream classroom. The underlying philosophy or 'wisdom' which underpins education is relevant here to allow critical understanding of these views.

Philosophic views on education

Jean-Jacques Rousseau (1712–1778)

Jean-Jacques Rousseau was born in 1712 and has often been attributed as being the founder of 'modern education' (the term 'modern education' refers to 'experimental learning') (Oelkers, 2002). He was the author of one of the seminal works on developmental psychology, entitled *Émile, or On Education*, which was published in 1762 (O'Hagan, 2001). As long ago as 1762, Rousseau was advocating the idea that children should interact with their surroundings and actively engage in the process of learning. He was also keen to promote the concept of what we now refer to as the autonomous learner (O'Hagan, 2001). Rousseau regarded education as 'a process of natural growth' (Dewey and Dewey, 1985, cited in Oelkers, 2002: 685) and this notion has influenced many theorists in education, including Jean Piaget (1896–1980) (see Chapter 4 'The psychology of learning' for more information on Piaget), who acknowledged Rousseau as 'the first advocate of the child . . . the first "modernist" in education' (Oelkers, 2002:680).

The notion that human beings are good by nature is central to Rousseau's philosophy of education. In *Émile*, he implied that society was corrupt and that, by removing a child from society and manipulating the learning environment, the teacher would be able to ensure that the pupil was exposed to learning situations that were commensurate to his developmental stage (O'Hagan, 2001). Rousseau's philosophy is not so much about developing techniques that enable children to absorb information and concepts, but rather it is about ensuring that pupils develop a healthy sense of self-worth and morality, as these characterisitics will allow individuals to relate to others in a natural way (Delaney, 2006), thereby creating a better society. So, for Rousseau, the educational process should prepare individuals to not only take their place in society, but also to help create a better society.

Rousseau believed that men and women had complementary and fundamentally different roles to play in society and should, therefore, be educated accordingly – that is to say, they should receive separate, discrete educations. In recent years there has been a significant amount of discussion and debate regarding gender differences in education (Woolfolk, Hughes and Walkup, 2008:205–15) and, while Rousseau's ideas may, nowadays, appear somewhat extreme, nonetheless the notion of delivering a separate education to boys and girls is still practised today in some schools.

When Rousseau began writing *Émile*, he acknowledged that many writers had already citicised the 'current methods of education' (Rousseau, 2007:7). While he agreed that those methods were inadequate, Rousseau argued that it was no good criticising established methods of education without suggesting alternatives. Rousseau's contention was that there were few people knowledgeable enough to undertake the tutoring of others. He stated that the most authoritative writers on education concerned themselves with 'what a man ought to know, without asking what a child is capable of learning' (Rousseau, 2007:7). Rousseau believed that it was important to study children and childhood and to try to educate them accordingly. Rousseau maintained that:

> Our wisdom is slavish prejudice, our customs consist in control, constraint, compulsion. Civilised man is born and dies a slave. The infant is bound up in swaddling clothes, the corpse is nailed down in his coffin. All his life long man is imprisoned by our institutions.
>
> Rousseau, 2007:16

He claimed that from the moment a child is born he is physically confined and mentally restricted, forced to live by the values and beliefs imposed on him by society and various institutions. Education did not make a man free, instead it constrained him and forced him to conform.

In *Émile*, Rousseau charted the development of a fictitious child called Émile. He removed Émile from society and brought him up in the country. He made a conscious effort to shape and control the environment in which Émile lived and created situations based on imaginary, experimental scenarios. Despite the fact that this composition was based on a fictional situation, Rousseau's work had a significant impact on both parents and educationalists and has influenced many 'educational thinkers' including Maria Montessori and Jean Piaget (O'Hagan, 2001).

Rousseau argued that children go through different, distinct stages of development and that the learning process needs to be tailored accordingly by using different approaches to education. He stressed that it is of paramount importance for the teacher to know his pupil well before he begins to instruct him, and he implied that children should be allowed to be children and should learn for themselves rather than being told information. He maintained that, by reading books, children do not learn knowledge, they merely acquire words (Rousseau, 2007); the role of the teacher would, therefore, be that of a facilitator (recall from Chapter 2 the concerns about deskilling teachers) who stimulates the desire to learn and ensures that children have the requisite opportunities to learn through experimentation.

Émile consists of five books, each of which deals with a distinct developmental stage as follows:

- Book I: infancy (ages 0–2) – physical care and training
- Book II: childhood (ages 2–12) – development of physical qualities, specifically the senses
- Book III: age of reason (pre-adolescence, ages 12–15) – education of the intellect
- Book IV: age of passion (puberty and adolescence, ages 15–20) – education of the passions
- Book V: beginning of adulthood (age 20 on) – being reintegrated with society, finding a suitable partner. (Rousseau, 2007)

O'Hagan (2001) states that Rousseau 'added a three-stage schema of ethical development' (p. 57) which suggested that in infancy and childhood a child should be ruled by *necessity*; between childhood and puberty he should be ruled by *utility* and after the onset of sexuality he should be ruled by *morality*.

Johann Wolfgang von Goethe (1749–1832)

Johann Wolfgang Von Goethe was born in 1749 in Frankfurt am Main and his life spanned a period of intense change in social order, which was taking place at that time in both Britain and Europe; this change was largely brought about by the Agricultural and Industrial Revolutions and educational and administrative reforms (Williams, 1998). Goethe spent many years pursuing the study of science. He believed that the study of science is a dynamic pursuit and that, in order to gain insight into scientific processes and phenomena, you need to actively engage the complete range of human qualities including the less tangible attributes such as creativity, the use of senses and the ability to use your imagination, all of which he asserted were intrinsic components in the development of knowledge.

Goethe was a keen advocate of 'spiritual science', which looks at the spiritual development of human beings in conjunction with scientific developments and also considers the spiritual development of the Universe as a whole. Spirituality is a difficult concept to grasp, but put simply we would suggest that it covers intangible, sometimes intuitive beliefs – those concepts which are difficult to prove or disprove; nonetheless they may allow us to form a deeper understanding of the whole picture and provide us with the faith/motivation to carry out further scientific investigation.

Connect and explore

Explore the following link: **http://nationalstrategies.standards.dcsf.gov.uk/node/ 84045** and click on the 'Creative Development' link. Having studied this section, do you recognise any similarities between Goethe's thinking and the 'new and innovative' approach towards the Early Years Foundation Stage advocated by today's government initiatives? See Chapter 7 for more information on 'Contemporary policies and issues'.

Goethe believed that in nature 'the whole is reflected in each of its parts' (Edmunds, 2004); this suggests that the way in which an organism (or even a child) develops or matures during each stage is directly linked to the end product (the emergent adult). According to Goethe, by looking at the life cycle and taking into account how organisms are interrelated and dependent on one another, we will be able to understand how the world sustains itself. He reasoned that in nature each developmental stage (growth stage) is inextricably linked to the other stages. It therefore follows that a child's education should involve the development of all aspects of that child, because each facet of that child has a reciprocal effect on the resultant adult. Education should enhance and extend the mental, spiritual and physical dimensions, allowing a child to grow into a 'complete' individual.

Goethe's 'alternative' view of science and his philosophy of development had a profound impact on Rudolf Steiner who edited Goethe's scientific manuscripts (Steiner, 1886) and whose own philosophy of education will be addressed in due course. As you read further through this chapter you will be able to identify Goethe's influence upon 'alternative schooling'.

John Dewey (1859–1952)

John Dewey was born in 1859 in Burlington, Vermont, USA. Dewey was a philosopher and educational reformist, who believed that schooling was of paramount importance for intellectual development and ultimately social progress and reform. He is regarded as one of the major figures of American education, philosophy and politics, who not only wanted to understand the social world, but also wanted to change it (Apple and Teitelbaum, 2001). Dewey (1915) asserted that education should not be concerned with the individual, but should have broader, more social considerations. When Dewey first expounded this view, it was considered to be a novel approach to the concept of education. Nowadays, in the UK we often hear politicians espousing this view.

In line with other innovators, Dewey supported the view that education was not just about intelligence, but should also be linked to manual skills and physical and moral development (Leiding, 2008). At the time that Dewey was alive, manual skills were not considered to be a type of intelligence. The term intelligence was often synonymous with academic ability. Nowadays, thanks to people like Howard Gardner, who developed the theory of multiple intelligences, we recognise that 'intellect' is only one form of intelligence. Dewey was a vociferous supporter of what is now referred to as experiential learning. He criticised Rousseau and regarded Rousseau's approach to education as 'individualistic' – something that took place between a teacher and a pupil (Dewey, 1916). Dewey posited the idea that the main aim of education is to 'encourage the individual to participate in society' (Carnie, 2003:100).

Dewey regarded education as a social process, by which he meant that it is a shared or group process. As young children we often draw on the experience of others in addition to our own experiences in order to develop our understanding. Many of our beliefs and values are socially and culturally constructed. Dewey claimed that education should take a broader view that should include both knowledge and experience (experiential learning) and consider societal needs and values. He firmly believed that education should take place in communal situations and he reproached Rousseau for removing 'Émile' from society. He suggested that Rousseau relied solely on Nature as the educator of the child: in fact, Rousseau placed considerable emphasis on the role of the teacher in constructing a suitable environment for learning (Rousseau, 2007).

Dewey questioned the value of a subject-based approach to learning, favouring social activities such as cooking, sewing and manual training (Dewey, 1897). He reasoned that education should be informed by the experiences of the children and consequently children should be involved in decisions about their learning. He regarded the school as a community with a responsibility to extend the moral values of a child's home life and suggested that the teacher's role was not to impose particular ideas on a child, but to link the child's interests to educational experiences that would provide continuous mental growth (Apple and Teitelbaum, 2001).

Stop and reflect

Dewey believed that externally imposed educational aims, which are forced on a teacher, merely serve to inhibit the teacher and subsequently the child (Dewey, 1916). Consider this view in the light of the National Curriculum favoured by the UK's state system of education. During its inception, many teachers initially complained about the restrictive nature of the National Curriculum. Why do you think this might be?

The purpose of education

You have now read some of the key philosophical thinkers' views about how and why we should educate our children. Before we discuss some of the alternative approaches to schooling currently available, you need to be clear about the purpose of education in your own minds.

Activity

Compare and contrast the views of Rousseau, Goethe and Dewey with regard to the following questions:

- Who is education for?
- What is education for?
- What should be learned?
- How should learning be achieved?
- Who should provide education?

The case study of Charlie and his family and the subsequent activity will have highlighted some of the issues concerning the purpose of education and clarified your personal view. However, the function of education is a complex and contentious issue and this chapter aims to provide a more informed understanding by considering some of the alternative approaches to schooling that are currently available. Let's begin by considering the role of education today.

Many people agree that education has essentially two main roles:

- to enable children to cope with life in the adult world; and
- to provide society with people who are equipped with the necessary skills, knowledge and understanding to enable nations to remain economically competitive in an increasingly technological world.

The first of these roles centres on the individual, while the second benefits society as a collective. While there may be some agreement as to the purpose of education, what many people do not agree on is how best to achieve these aims. In recent years, following the implementation of *Every Child Matters: Change for Children,* published in 2004, there has been much government rhetoric about adopting a holistic approach to education and meeting the needs of the 'individual' in order to provide a 'meaningful learning experience'. However, Carnie (2003) suggests that because the National Curriculum segregates learning into different subject areas, the capability of mainstream schools to present integrated, holistic approaches to education is substantially reduced. This is essentially because the National Curriculum is split into statutory requirements, relating to subject areas such as English and mathematics, which teachers must cover, and non-statutory requirements, which teachers are able to address if they have time, including PSHE (personal, social, health and economic education).

Rathunde (2009) suggests that an education which concentrates on the cognitive aspect of learning, i.e. relating to thought processes, tends to demotivate students and may have a significant impact on the quality of their learning experience, often leading to a 'disembodied education' (p. 190) which, as the term implies, involves little active participation and engagement. He also posits the idea that the most extreme examples of 'disembodied education' prevalent in mainstream schools expect young people to spend a significant amount of time listening to teachers, sitting quietly and doing homework. While Rathunde (2009) acknowledges that some schools are attempting to reform education by adopting a **multi-sensory approach** to learning, this practice (particulary in secondary schools) is not widespread. A multi-sensory approach to learning requires children to use more than one of the senses, for example learning the shape of letters in the alphabet not only by looking at the shape of the letter, but also by drawing the shape of the letter in a tray of sand or physically mimicking the shape of a letter with their bodies.

We will now consider some of the alternative approaches to education currently available in various parts of the world.

Putting theory into practice

The Steiner philosophy of education

Following the devastation of the First World War, people longed for something new. Germany had suffered national defeat and many people despaired about the social inequalities of the time; in these conditions, Rudolf Steiner promoted his ideas for a new social order (Ashley, 2009). Central to Steiner's philosophy was the notion of freedom. Steiner believed that, in order to achieve 'freedom', education should be designed to meet the changing needs of children as they develop physically, mentally and emotionally. He studied 'anthroposophy' (spiritual science) – 'the belief that a human is a three-fold being of body, soul and spirit' (Wilkinson, 1993, cited in Cox and Rowlands, 2000:486). This was an important development in the concept of education because it considered all aspects of an individual and was very much in line with today's thinking regarding a holistic approach to education. Up until this point, learner needs were often given little or no consideration. What children were taught was essentially determined by the tutor, much the same as it had been in Rousseau's day.

Steiner established his first school in 1919 in Stuttgart, for children of the Waldorf-Astoria cigarette factory. The school was initially set up in order to provide children of workmen and employees, irrespective of their socio-economic status, '[with] the same teaching and education as that enjoyed by children of families with means . . .' (Avison, 1998:21). Steiner was acutely aware of the need for social change and acknowledged that:

> Parents who entrust their children to this school are bound to expect that the children shall be educated and prepared for the practical work of life . . . This makes it necessary, in founding the school, to begin from educational principles that have their roots in the requirements of modern life. Children must be educated and instructed in such a way that their lives fulfil demands everyone can support, no matter from which of the inherited social classes one might come. What is demanded of people by the actualities of modern life must find its reflection in the organization of this school. What is to be the ruling spirit in this life must be aroused in the children by education and instruction.
>
> Steiner, 1919

Steiner, a keen advocate of social reform, wanted to develop a system of education that would allow a child to develop as a balanced, healthy individual who was capable of making 'a meaningful and socially responsible contribution to society' (Clouder and Rawson, 2003). You may be surprised to learn how many of Steiner's principles are reflected in much of today's thinking regarding the purpose of education.

Steiner/Waldorf schools

The Steiner/Waldorf approach to education is based on:

> The desire to establish a harmony between the spiritual and the worldly – between intellectually-spiritual and the physically-corporeal – in the teaching of children and young people.
>
> Nobel, 1996:221

By bringing together the 'spiritual' and the 'worldly', Steiner believed that a balance would be achieved between intellectual, emotional and physical qualities, thereby developing a deeper understanding and empathy of both mankind and the world around us. In Steiner's view, the role of the teacher is to nurture a child's natural curiosity, imagination and creativity, to act as a role model and to facilitate learning, by providing the requisite conditions for a child to develop as a well-balanced and well-rounded human being.

For Steiner, development, not teaching or learning, forms the basis of education (Oelkers, 2001). Steiner suggested that development from childhood to adulthood comprises three distinct stages, each lasting approximately seven years:

- Stage 1: 0 to age 7 – this focuses on the development of will
- Stage 2: 7 to 14 years – this focuses on the development of feeling
- Stage 3: 14 to around 21 years – this focuses on the development of thinking skills.

The guiding principle of Steiner/Waldorf schools is rhythm – the rhythm of the day, the week, the seasons and the year. Activities are not restricted to the classroom, and the outdoors is regarded as an extension of the learning environment. Children explore the natural habitat of their surroundings and learn about the delicate balance of nature and the changing seasons through discovery and active learning.

Steiner/Waldorf schools adopt an essentially Goethean-based approach to science, which, as demonstrated in a large-scale study by Jelink and Sun (2003, cited by Ashley, 2009), produces students with superior skills in scientific reasoning in comparison with their counterparts who attend state schools (Ashley, 2009). Woods et al. (2005) suggest that pupils in Steiner schools are encouraged 'to observe and come to their own conclusions rather than proving someone else's theory' (p. 38), which may account for Jelink and Sun's findings. Does knowing this have any impact on your original views as to whether Mr and Mrs Wilcox should choose an alternative school for Charlie?

There are currently over 950 Steiner schools worldwide (Steiner Waldorf Schools Fellowship, 2008). Steiner education is practised in approximately 60 countries and in many of those countries it exists alongside state-run schools and receives government funding (Avison, 1998); this allows parents to choose which system of education they wish their children to attend, and is in line with Steiner's original ethos of offering accessible education to all children irrespective of their socio-economic background. This is not the case in the UK where (at the time of writing), with the exception of the new Steiner Academy in Hereford and two schools in Ireland, Steiner/Waldorf schools, unlike most of their counterparts in Europe, receive no state support (Steiner Waldorf Schools Fellowship, 2008).

Activity

Explore the Steiner Waldorf Schools Fellowship website to find out more about Rudolf Steiner and Steiner schools. Available from: http://www.steinerwaldorf.org/whatis-steinereducation.html.
See also 'An Introduction to Waldorf Education', available from http://wn.rsarchive.org/Articles/IntWal_index.html.

- Consider the ways in which your own experience of school differs from the Steiner/Waldorf system.
- If you experienced the Steiner/Waldorf system, how did this differ from traditional mainstream schooling?
- Based on what you know so far, what might be the benefits/disadvantages of attending a Steiner school?

Within the learning situation

We referred earlier to Steiner's 'notion of freedom'; this philosophy extends not only to the students, but also to the teachers and the content of the curriculum taught within Steiner schools. Steiner-influenced classrooms tend to be full of natural objects, such as wooden toys and puzzles, designed to stimulate imagination and a desire to learn (Cox and Rawson, 2000). Art, sculpture, music and drama all permeate much of the learning that takes place on a daily basis (Carnie, 2003); this encourages active participation and engagement with the learning process. The first two hours of the day are usually devoted to a 'main lesson' which is based on a specific theme and each theme is taught for approximately 4–6 weeks. Students develop numerous practical skills including woodwork, cookery and farming. Teaching methods throughout the

▶

curriculum aim to first consider the whole and then to understand the diverse parts in the context of the whole (Clouder and Rawson, 2003; Ashley, 2009), a view which echoes Goethe's philosophy.

Activity

Source: Pearson Education Ltd./Photodisc/ Photolink.

Look at the image above. In small groups of 3 or 4, and bearing in mind what you have learnt so far through reading this chapter and researching the Steiner Waldorf website, consider the ways in which this image might be incorporated into the learning experience in a Steiner school? Try to be creative!

In Steiner schools, the image of the butterfly could be used in a variety of ways to enhance the learning experience, for example:

- It might be used to encourage younger children to trace the outline of the butterfly's folded wings to form the basic shape of the letter 'B' by using a sandbox, drawing materials or through physical movement (look at the image of the butterfly and trace the outline of its wings with your finger).
- It could be used to inspire children to look for butterflies during a non-classroom-based activity perhaps as an extension to a nature and life science lesson on the theme of stages of development and life cycles.
- It might be used as a focus for an art lesson or used as pictorial representation on a poem in an English literature lesson.

Connect and explore

There are numerous possibilities of ways in which the butterfly image could be incorporated into lessons. Further examples of other resources can be found on the following websites: **http://www.straightlineandcurve.co.uk/class_1_main_lessons. htm; http://www.waldorflibrary.org/pg/newResources/newResources.asp.**

Steiner schools are non-selective, multicultural, co-educational and offer a comprehensive curriculum. They are all independent, self-administered and with no internal structures of managerial hierarchy (Clouder and Rawson, 2003). Each Steiner school is an **autonomous institution**, which means that it runs itself and it is not required to follow a prescribed curriculum. However, as a result of their common commitment to the principles and philosophy of Steiner education, there is a great deal of consistency among the schools in terms of the curriculum they offer (Woods et al., 2005).

The curriculum is based on a **spiral curriculum** (themes are revisited again and studied in more depth as the child develops). Steiner schools place the development of the individual at the centre of their teaching. The children are taught in age groups – classes are not segregated according to ability. Children learn from and through each other and the mixed ability classes allow students to appreciate other people's strengths and support them in their weaknesses. You may be able to make some links here with Vygotsky's ideas about the social aspect of learning and his concept of 'scaffolding' (see Chapter 4 for further information).

Key points about Steiner schooling

1 The curriculum advocates an integrated approach to learning, so children develop a range of academic and practical skills alongside one another. For example, while they are learning how to bake cakes, they will also learn about weights and measures and will also be encouraged to sell their products to parents and friends as a business enterprise, thereby learning about marketing opportunities and profit and loss margins.

2 The emphasis is on imagination and the ability to visualise. At the start of their education, children create their own textbooks and are encouraged to draw using their imagination, rather than using images and information from printed textbooks or the internet.

3 'The fundamental lesson children have to learn is that *they need the world and that the world needs them*' (Clouder and Rawson, 2003:89). Children need to learn respect for each other, for the environment and the world around them and to live in harmony.

4 Formal teaching of the 'three Rs' (reading, writing and arithmetic) does not begin until the seventh year; the belief is that these capabilities will develop more effectively if children are initially allowed time and opportunities to develop physically, socially and emotionally in secure, harmonious environments (Steiner Waldorf Schools Fellowship, 2008).

5 Prior to the age of 7, children learn primarily through imitation, modelling and play. For example, numeracy skills may be developed through teacher-initiated activities such as songs, clapping or puppet shows or role play, e.g. shop keeping.

6 Practical skills form an integral part of the curriculum – from an early age children are taught to cook, knit, make clothes and do woodwork. They are encouraged to grow produce or bake bread and cakes to celebrate various festivals. They also learn gardening and farming skills.

7 Art, sculpture, music and drama all permeate much of the learning that takes place on a daily basis (Carnie, 2003). These activities provide students with various opportunities for self-expression and for the improvement of coordination and motor skills.

8 Usually the first two hours of the children's day is based on a particular theme and a period of about four weeks is spent on each theme. In this way children are able to gain more in-depth knowledge of the various components/aspects and see how they link/relate not only to each other, but also to the world as a whole.

9 In addition to the more traditional subjects, children at Steiner schools study 'eurythmy' (an art of movement developed by Steiner) which is meant to help children develop harmoniously with mind, body and soul (Woods et al., 2005).

The following extract is taken from the 'Learning and Development' section of the National Strategies website for the Early Years Foundation Stage (EYFS):

> Children's creativity must be extended by the provision of support for their curiosity, exploration and play. They must be provided with opportunities to explore and share their thoughts, creativity, ideas and feelings, for example, through a variety of art, music, movement, dance, imaginative and role-play activities, mathematics, and design and technology.
>
> Department for Children, Schools and Families, 2009

Can you see that many of the requirements that are currently being heralded as innovative and 'new' reflect much of Steiner's philosophy of education? Look back at the 'Key points about Steiner education' and note any similarities.

Children need to be encouraged to develop higher level thinking skills, such as analysis and evaluation, if they are to develop their knowledge and understanding. Splitter (2009) suggests that learning should be meaningful, a term which he qualifies by stating that learning must not only be relevant, but also make sense. Steiner schools aim to enable children to make sense of the world around them and to develop to their full potential.

? Stop and reflect

- *Think back to your own experience of learning in school. How does your experience of learning differ from that of your parents or grandparents?*
- *Consider how children as individuals can 'make sense' of the world around them if they are constrained by limitations of environment and curriculum? In a classroom situation with a ratio of 1 teacher to 25 children, how can each individual's needs be met?*

Maria Montessori's philosophy of education

You have already been introduced to Maria Montessori in Chapter 1. In the context of alternative schooling, Montessori is a key figure, who, having trained as a physician, subsequently worked in psychiatric clinics with children who were regarded as being mentally deficient; it was there that she developed an interest in education (Lilliard, 2008). In 1901, Montessori aroused international attention when the mentally deficient children with whom she had been working passed state educational tests designed for 'normal' children (Lilliard, 2008).

In 1907 Montessori set up her first school, known as 'Casa dei Bambini' (Children's House) in San Lorenzo, a deprived area in Rome (Carnie, 2003). The underlying principle of the Montessori philosophy of education is that the child is regarded as 'a motivated doer, rather than an empty vessel' (Lilliard, 2008:28); the notion of active learning is one that you may recognise from Rousseau's philosophy of education. It was while Montessori was observing a three-year-old child who seemed to be totally immersed in what she was doing and apparently completely oblivious to the noise and distractions that were going on around her (almost as if she was isolated from her surroundings) that Montessori began to realise that being 'a motivated doer' was inherently linked to the ability to concentrate. Montessori believed that concentration was central to education and the acquisition of knowledge and that concentration was triggered by **intrinsic motivation** (Rathunde, 2009). She believed that children are naturally motivated to learn and that they should be allowed to develop at their own pace without adult intervention (Carnie, 2003).

Concentration has been described as the 'key that opens up to the child the latent treasures within him' (Standing, 1984:174, cited in Rathunde, 2009), suggesting that a child's abilities lie dormant within him/her, waiting to be awoken. Montessori believed that, when children are given the freedom to learn and explore in a safe environment and are provided with the requisite 'materials', then they will progress from 'concrete knowledge to the understanding of abstract concepts' (Carnie, 2003:72). She designed the 'requisite materials' herself; these resources were developed specifically to promote the learning of diverse concepts, and they were introduced in a specified order. Montessori advocated the idea that children would be able to develop according to their own interests and abilities without being corrected by an adult when they made a mistake. She further asserted that children would be naturally motivated to repeatedly re-attempt an activity until they had mastered it. The satisfaction gained by achieving the task would negate the need for extrinsic (external) rewards and motivate the child to repeat the activity (Rathunde, 2009).

Montessori schools

The Montessori approach emphasises that all children are individuals and is based on eight principles of education:

1 that movement and cognition are closely entwined, and movement can enhance thinking and learning;

2 that learning and well-being are improved when people have a sense of control over their lives;

3 that people learn better when they are interested in what they are learning;

4 that tying extrinsic rewards to an activity, like money for reading or high grades for tests, negatively impacts motivation to engage in that activity when the reward is withdrawn;

5 that collaborative arrangements can be very conducive to learning;

6 that learning situated in meaningful contexts is often deeper and richer than learning in abstract contexts;

7 that particular forms of adult interaction are associated with more optimal child outcomes; and

8 that order in the environment is beneficial to children.

(Lilliard, 2008:29)

Observation plays a key role in the Montessori approach to education. Montessori observed that the mind and body are closely linked: she said that in young children thinking and moving constitute the same process, and she put forward the idea that thinking is expressed by the hands before it can be expressed through words (Lilliard, 2008). If you observe a young child trying to complete a jigsaw puzzle, you will probably find that the child can correctly position a piece of the puzzle before she/he is able to articulate the reason she/he placed that particular piece in the specific location. She/he will have learnt through trial and error following a period of intense concentration. Through observing a similar process, Montessori developed an educational system that focused on the manipulation of objects and recent research seems to concur with her findings by implying that movement enhances the learning process (Lilliard, 2008). Everything in the Montessori classroom is designed to support the child's natural development. Examples of children learning through the manipulation of objects can be seen in the images below.

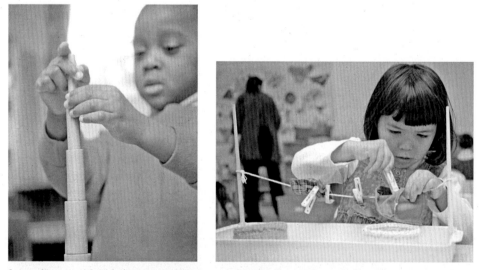

Source: Montessori St Nicholas & Montessori Centre International: www.montessori.org.uk

Connect and explore

Explore the Montessori Foundation website – **http://www.montessori.org/** – to find out more about Maria Montessori and Montessori schools.

Within the learning situation

An ordered environment (often referred to as the '**prepared environment**') is an important concept in Montessori schools and refers to both the conceptual and physical design of a classroom (Lilliard, 2008). This has significant implications for the Montessori teacher. Teachers are expected to adapt and design the learning environment to meet 'the needs, interests, abilities, and development of the children in the class' (Seldin, 2007). In order to facilitate the learning process, teachers provide opportunities that allow the individual to achieve his/her potential by bringing activities, materials and objects to the child's attention. Teaching 'materials', which were originally designed by Maria Montessori herself, are specially designed to be self-teaching and self-correcting; this means that teachers need to organise teaching materials in such a way that the children 'naturally' progress from one activity to another.

Children in Montessori schools have much greater freedom of choice than children attending mainstream schools. They decide what to work on, how long they want to work on it and with whom they want to work. Teachers are expected to inspire children by promoting sufficient curiosity to instigate a desire to explore and pursue active learning. They should be supportive, but not interfere, and should provide clear guidelines. Montessori teachers need to observe children closely and introduce new materials at an optimal time for the individual child, i.e. when the child is ready to progress (Lilliard, 2008). Because the children are allowed to select their own activities and materials, they are more focused and engage with the task in hand for longer periods of time (Isaacs, 2007), which allows teachers to observe the children for more extended periods.

Figure 3.1 **An example of a child engaging with self-selected materials**
Source: Pearson Education Ltd./Jules Selmes.

Montessori also believed that individuals learn better when they are encouraged to be independent and are given freedom of choice and freedom of movement. Consequently, she developed child-friendly chairs and tables, manufactured to an optimum size for the children, in order to provide a safe environment for the children to move around in and ensured that resources were situated at appropriate levels for the children (Kirkpatrick, 2008). If children are allowed to choose which activities they undertake and the teaching 'materials' are not only accessible, but designed to stimulate interest and engage the children, then children are more likely to be absorbed in learning (Lilliard, 2008); they are also apt to develop the ability to concentrate for longer periods, resulting in a more fulfilling, productive and meaningful learning experience.

Providing sufficient, appropriate 'materials' would prove to be expensive in a state school that is essentially dependent on the Local Education Authority for funding. As a result, children would neither be able to choose what activity they did nor would they be able to choose when they did it. Montessori schools charge **fees**, which precludes many children from poorer families from attending them. In Case study 1.1, Charlie's parents are affluent and can afford to pay the requisite fees, but this option is not available to many families.

In many mainstream schools, the physical environment would make it difficult to implement the Montessori method of teaching due to the lack of floor space available for the open-plan design of the Montessori classroom. Many of our older, traditional primary school classrooms do not appear to lend themselves readily to a design that necessitates a physically and conceptually organised layout – a design that is consistent with the Montessori classroom (Lilliard, 2008) where children are free to choose where they sit throughout the day.

Montessori schoolchildren are encouraged to be independent from an early age. They are expected to tidy up after themselves, not only in order to maintain an ordered environment and promote independence, but also to demonstrate respect for others by ensuring that 'materials' are ready for another child to use when they choose to do so (Lilliard, 2008); these expectations help to promote an ethos of calm and order.

Key points about Montessori education

1 Freedom of choice and movement are actively promoted; this point is closely linked to the next item and is in line with Montessori's belief (particularly

Figure 3.2 A Montessori classroom: a place for everything and everything in its place. Order, space and light are important aspects that are taken into consideration
Source: Montessori St Nicholas & Montessori Centre International: www.montessori.org.uk

with regard to young children) that thought and movement constitute the same process.

2 Learning is achieved through movement.

3 Classes usually consist of multi-aged groups spanning three-year age levels. In this way older children are able to model appropriate behaviour to the younger ones.

4 Learning from peers is actively encouraged; in order for this to operate effectively class sizes tend to be large, generally with between 30 and 35 children to one teacher (Lilliard, 2008).

5 Teachers need to observe the children closely in order to optimise their learning; this is crucial in order for teachers to be able to facilitate the appropriate opportunities and resources for learning to take place.

6 The teacher acts as a facilitator of learning and ensures that the environment is child-friendly and stimulating (Kirkpatrick, 2008).

7 Students learn through hands-on experience, investigation and research, all of which encourage active learning and increase motivation.

8 The curriculum is based on a spiral, integrated curriculum, which promotes mutual respect, similar to the Steiner philosophy of education; themes are revisited and studied in more depth as the child develops.

9 Teaching children to be kind and peaceful is an intrinsic part of the teacher's role.

10 Children are self-directed learners who learn in different ways and progress at their own rates (Seldin, 2000); this notion results in a child-centred approach to education.

? Stop and reflect

Before you move on to the next section of this chapter, consider ways in which Montessori's key notions on education differ from or reflect your own experience of learning.

- *If you attended a Montessori school, did you experience/can you identify any difficulties that might be experienced when transferring from a Montessori school into mainstream education or an alternative learning situation?*
- *If you did not attend a Montessori school, how different from your experience does the description in this chapter sound?*

Reggio Emilia schools

Reggio Emilia schools for pre-school children are an interesting example of how context shapes a philosophy, and how a philosophy from one particular region can influence school curricula throughout the world. It is also an example of how educational philosophies and ideas from other thinkers and educationalists can be used, shaped and applied within a new context. The Reggio Emilia philosophy, or approach, originated in the northern Italian city of Reggio Emilia (you might have heard of Parmigiano Reggiano parmesan cheese, for which the region is also famous). At the end of the Second World War, when Italy was economically devastated, a village on the outskirts of Reggio Emilia had the opportunity to sell a German tank, among other abandoned armaments. The proceeds of this enterprise were to be invested into one of two uses. The men of the village wanted to invest in a theatre, but the women wanted to build a school. They wanted an education for their children which would be 'loving and guaranteed', and a school that would 'free the children from an age old subjection by the official schools' (Barazzoni, 1985:18). The women had their way – perhaps significantly, this was at a time when Italian women had just received the right to vote – and with the proceeds of the armaments salvage and by reusing bricks, window frames and other materials from bombed buildings, the community literally built their school brick by brick. The Reggio Emilia pre-school and toddler centres (3 months to 6 years) were initiated.

There are many features embedded in the Reggio Emilia approach that set it apart, but which can be taken and applied into any other context. Arguably the whole could never be completely transported, as it is so fixed within the community, culture, history and psyche of the city itself. The main features or principles of Reggio Emilia are:

- Reggio Emilia exponents explain children's learning as a process of research which comes almost instinctively to that child – a parallel in adult education is what Geoff Petty (2009) refers to as 'making meaning'. This is achieved by providing a carefully planned environment in which children are stimulated but not rushed; an environment which facilitates a focus and a process, and in which the adult takes advantage of what Vygotsky calls the 'zone of proximal development' (ZPD) (Doherty and Hughes, 2009). The adult steps in only when the child cannot progress unaided.

- Children are allowed and encouraged to take a leading role in their own learning by constructing meanings from their experiences. Children are highly valued for themselves and it is acknowledged that they have rights. The term 'special needs' is not used, rather 'special rights', which reinforces the idea of empowering and valuing the voice of the child.

- A principle called 'one hundred languages' explains how, through their interactions (with each other, those who support their learning and their learning materials), children make meaning and build their own knowledge. The 'one hundred languages' are apparent in every way children speak, move, write, draw (and, for those too young to manipulate writing material with control, make marks), manipulate materials, think, interact and perceive.

- Adults working with children work closely and interact with each other. There are teachers who work on a daily basis with the children alongside people known as *Atelieristas*. These are artists who are employed to work with children on a daily basis as they work on their projects. In every school the cook, and his/her auxiliaries (assistants) are also fundamental to the children's learning opportunities, as they help with food preparation and serving of food. Other schools in Italy do not have their own kitchens, but bring in food from a central location. Parents contribute their time and skills as they work closely with the teaching team by, for example, preparing a vegetable patch and sewing vegetables to be grown and used in the school kitchen. Helping to develop an understanding of the learning processes are the *Pedagogistas* (Rinaldi, 2006). A *Pedagogista* has a degree in pedagogy or psychology and will work with a small number of schools. The combined participation of all these people generates values of shared aims, responsibility and cohesion.

- Art is fundamental to the Reggio approach, as children learn to develop their skills of communication in a creative way, increasing their understanding of the world around them. Children are allowed to develop their learning in a natural rather than linear pattern defined by someone else through a set curriculum.

- Reflection on, and particularly *in*, practice encourages 'listening' to how each individual child learns. The process of each child's learning journey is meticulously documented, and this so-called 'trace' of the child is available to the parents, for the child and for the teachers. The teachers use the documentation as part of their research, making new meanings of learning and deciding the direction of projects being undertaken.

- This concept of listening is taken in its broadest sense to include non-verbal communication, and not overwhelming a child by pushing them into particular areas or styles of learning.

The particular features of the environment in which children learn that add to the uniqueness of Reggio Emilia schools include 'atelier spaces' within the schools. These are rooms or areas where children focus on and engage with particular projects for a day, a week or longer. Although children are encouraged to be autonomous, they are helped to face and cope with (rather than avoid) obstacles, by skilful use of questioning and encouragement. Many projects are underpinned by artistic ideals, reinforcing the link between Reggio Emilia and art. Examples of the use of atelier spaces, which are small workshop rooms (a luxury in most English early years settings), include working with light boxes which project scenes from

Figure 3.3 **This image of a bicycle is representative of maybe two dozen which have been designed by Reggio Emilia pre-school children and blown up as murals to decorate the city underpass where the community can share in the beauty and pleasure of the children's work. On close inspection of the bicycles it can be seen that they have been created using recycled materials such as buttons, pieces of fabric and wire lengths. Recycling and care for the environment is another underpinning value that Reggio Emilia schools uphold**

Source: Vanessa Cottle.

an overhead projector. Such scenes are projected on to a white wall, which becomes a beach, countryside or even a moonscape, an image which is further reinforced with appropriate sounds and sometimes smells. Within these environments, children play, allowing their imaginations to run free and create their own meanings and questions. As they play, they are encouraged to develop their own ideas about how to progress, and in this way contribute fully to the planning of the direction of their learning.

So how did context shape this educational phenomenon? While the building of the first school (known as the April 25 School) was under way, a young teacher from Reggio Emilia, Loris Magaluzzi, visited the enterprise. Magaluzzi was inspired by the aspirations of the villagers, and became very involved as the number of schools grew. Magaluzzi recognised that the community and parent involvement with the school staff provided important underpinning values for the children's learning. He saw that school staff included everyone connected with the development of the school, including the cooks who, to this day, are considered core to the teaching team as they embed the Italian culture of the importance of food. The Reggio Emilia approach may have come about almost accidentally – a result of a particular time and place that could not be replicated – but it has developed and been sustained because a young teacher became fascinated by the event.

Magaluzzi's involvement was the driving force of the movement, which continues to develop today through the Friends of Reggio Children Association and the Loris Magaluzzi International Centre. It was Magaluzzi who conceptualised the 'one hundred languages' theory described above. His dedication to the education of young children inspired him to travel Europe to meet with educational thinkers in order to research ideas that could develop the schools' organic approach to teaching and learning, absorbing others' best practice. He was particularly influenced by Montessori, but also took ideas from Vygotsky. Later, Magaluzzi built a strong relationship with the American psychologist Jerome Bruner, who was given Honorary Citizenship of Reggio Emilia in 1998. Bruner has had a great influence on approaches to teaching and learning including, among many other ideas, his notion of scaffolding, which describes how teachers lead a child's learning in a step-by-step manner (Doherty and Hughes, 2009), which is consistent with Vygotsky's theories of cognitive development and ZPD. Magaluzzi and Howard Gardner became close friends and seem to have influenced each other's thinking: Magaluzzi's one hundred languages of children bears a striking resemblance to Gardner's influential theories of multiple intelligences (which will be discussed in Part 2 of this book).

At the Reggio Emilia Study Visit held in April 2010, over 350 delegates gathered with a view towards taking the Reggio philosophy back to all corners of the globe, and to implement the approach within early years education in countries as distant as New Zealand, Australia, Canada, USA, Belgium, Ireland, England, Wales, China, India, Singapore, Australia and Thailand. In Wales, the new Foundation Phase curriculum (aimed at 3-to 7-year-olds), which will be fully implemented by the 2011–2012 academic year, is already heavily influenced by the Reggio approach. Although it is clear that, as with all philosophies, Reggio Emilia approaches derive from a particular time and place, it is also clear that aspects can be taken and used to enhance other teaching and learning approaches. Perhaps the most powerful part of the Reggio approach is its commitment to embedded research and learning about learning, not only among teachers, *atelieristas*, *pedagogistas* and cooks, but by the children themselves.

Charter Movement Schools

A Charter Movement School (CMS) is an acknowledged alternative to traditional systems of education in the United States of America. The Charter, or performance agreement, sets out how the school will be run, its philosophies, aims and precise targets for student achievement. The Charter is designed by parents and professionals, but has to be approved and granted by local state legislation. These schools have come about in the USA as a response to problems experienced in high-poverty communities which are characterised by minority populations of students who tend to be underprivileged and disadvantaged – these include Hispanic, African-American, Native American, those with disabilities and who speak English as a second language, often known as EAL (English as an additional language) in the UK. The problems experienced by these groups of students result in significant achievement gaps between them and their white and Asian American peers who have the cultural and financial capital to cope with the education system they experience.

WestEd is an American non-profit research, development and service agency that works with education and other communities to promote excellence, achieve equity and improve learning for young people. WestEd have compiled a number of reports about the Charter Movement for the US Department of Education Office of Innovation and Improvement. Their 2007 report focused on how Charter Movement Schools contributed to closing the achievement gap mentioned above and explains how Charter Movement Schools work to overcome major barriers to attending school that many students experience. For some students the normally simple task of travelling to school can create barriers as they travel through areas where it is not uncommon to be threatened by potentially dangerous gang fights. This type of barrier along with a range of others with which you may be more familiar, for example those caused by poor language skills, lack of family support when parents have to hold down more than one job, different cultural perspectives (particularly the African-American youth sub-culture that perceives school as 'uncool') and previous disengagement with learning, are exacerbated when combined with the practical challenges that schools in inner cities face. These practical challenges include the need to divert financial and staff resources to policing bad behaviour, countering low expectations of prospective employers, parents, teachers and students and the resulting inability to attract high-quality teachers.

Having applied for and been granted a Charter, such schools receive some funding from their regional state (most states in the USA have Charter Schools), but are free from some state laws and district policies which apply to other schools. They have the freedom to create a curriculum which meets the specific needs of the community so long as the requirements of the agreed Charter are met. Thus, the school is allowed to run independently of the existing 'public' school system. (Note that in the USA the term 'public' is used to describe the state-funded system, unlike in the UK where 'public' refers to independently run, fee-paying schools.) In practice, therefore, Charter Schools, unlike their public counterparts, experience greater autonomy and control over, for example, the management of school budgets; employing teachers, and firing those who do not meet the standards required by the school management; approaches to teaching; class and school size and length of school day and year (WestEd, 2007). In short, they have more flexibility in their approach than other schools funded by the state in which they operate. Interestingly this autonomy can lead to criticism for many Charter Movement Schools which do not cater fully for children with learning difficulties, allowed as a result of the specific Charter agreement. However, there are examples of how Charters can work in favour of children with learning difficulties. One school is Gateway High, which is one of about 500 Charter Movement Schools in the state of California. Gateway High was founded by seven parents who all wanted their children to achieve a college education in spite of their learning difficulties (WestEd, 2007).

Because the amount of funding received will vary and some American states provide Charter Movement Schools with less financial support than traditional schools within that state's jurisdiction, Charter Movement Schools are allowed to supplement their budgets by generating income through parent and other sponsor donations. In order to achieve the terms of their Charter within the constraints of their budgets these schools have to be innovative on all levels of organisational management and curriculum development. In spite of these 'freedoms' and drivers to innovate, Charter Movement Schools are strictly accountable, to their sponsors and the State with whom the Charter has been agreed, for how they use their funding and how well the students achieve; as Rhim and Mclaughlin (2001:374) put it, this accountability '. . . will foster the creation of innovative, effective and efficient schools'. One way that Charter Movement Schools can save money is to cut back on teachers' salaries either by paying a lower salary than could be earned in the public system or by being prepared to employ unqualified teachers. This is, of course, controversial and at first could seem detrimental to the quality of education provided. However, it is a strategy that is used by many schools that operate independently of a central government control; for example, Steiner schools consider a teacher who shares the Steiner values as equally, if not more, important than being qualified to national teaching standards and Montessori schools have their own Montessori teacher training programme.

Reflect for a moment on what you have just read. You will notice a difference here in what constitutes an alternative school. Up to now, the alternatives have been derived from philosophies concerned with the manner in which children should be treated as well as how and what they should learn. The examples of Steiner and Montessori discussed earlier in this chapter provide alternatives to the English National Curriculum. However, it could be argued that the constraints of their philosophies, that is the very attributes making each a unique alternative, could be the very factor which restricts their capacity to be flexible in providing for the diverse range of needs inevitably apparent within every group of learners and in providing for cultural differences and developments. In the case of Charter Movement Schools, the emphasis shifts so that which is the 'alternative' characteristic is concerned with a range of aspects. On one level the alternative is regarding philosophies of how the school is managed, both at state level and within the school itself, as directed by the Charter agreed with the state legislature. On another level Charter Movement Schools are at liberty to design their own curriculum based on whatever philosophy they believe best for their children; they could, for example, take the best from the ideas of Steiner, and/or any other educational thinker, and recreate these ideas within a twenty-first-century American context. Certainly, the particular emphasis on accountability drives these schools to use innovative approaches to school structures and curriculum to ensure that the achievement targets agreed with the regional state legislation, which grant the Charters, are met, which in turn should ensure that children are equipped with the skills and knowledge required by a modern and global community.

Some of the innovative approaches to curriculum adopted by Charter Movement Schools include:

- Changing the length of the school day – usually making them longer – and often including Saturdays. These ideas can be very beneficial for parents who need to work for financial reasons and who may have concerns about their children being unsupervised out of normal school hours – you may see some parallels to the extended school system in England.
- Linking with local employers to arrange appropriate work placements.
- Linking with local universities to encourage students to experience higher education learning before leaving school.

- Having a 'stage not age' approach to class groups, which means that where a child does not achieve the standard required at a particular stage they repeat the stage, and conversely children can progress earlier than their peers if ready to do so. In practice this requires teaching for mastery – that is, children must learn and understand the basics before moving on.

- Offering different dress codes where some schools have uniforms, which works towards eliminating competition for designer labels, and some do not, often to avoid antagonising local gangs by inadvertently wearing colours of opposing gangs.

- Providing additional staffing to allow for smaller classes or to place two teachers with one group.

- Requiring parents to sign contracts to make them partners in family-style school cultures and this can include a requirement of an agreed amount of time committed to school duties throughout a school year. See also Chapter 6 which further discusses contracts in the context of education.

The first Charter Movement School legislation was passed in Minnesota in 1991 and was developed according to three basic values: opportunity, choice and responsibility for results, which encompass what has already been discussed in this section. By 2004 there were 2,996 Charter Movement Schools operating in the USA across 40 states with about 750,000 students taking part (WestEd, 2007). By 2010, according to EdReform (2009), there would be approximately 5,000 schools serving over 1.5 million students with approximately another 90 planned. The WestEd (2007) report suggested that the popularity of these schools could be the result of their 'ability to innovate to meet students' needs'. The report also states that:

> In some instances, charter movement schools have put reforms into place before traditional public schools in their states have been able to do so.
>
> WestEd (2007:3)

It is clear that individual Charter Movement Schools operate differently according to the needs of the local community. For example, their focus might be to provide educational access to students from low-income or minority backgrounds; they may well have a subject specialism such as art or science. There are Charter Movement Schools catering for all age ranges, from nursery age upwards. They are usually small schools with as few as one hundred students and are unlikely to have many more than a thousand students (within the USA context this is still a low number). As well as being innovative in the ways mentioned earlier, Charter Movement Schools are required to share certain characteristics in order to gain their Charter status.

- They aim to close the achievement gap between minority groups and others.
- They are mission driven (as recorded in the Charter document) – which means they have specific goals to work to which are shared by school staff and parents.
- They create a positive school culture through a 'safe learning environment'.

- They have tests aiming for in-depth understanding – this implies that tests must be valid and students must prove themselves.

- Families are seen as partners. One school, Oglethorpe, encourages all parents to sign a contract agreeing to serve the school for a given number of hours a year – included in the list of activities which contribute to the hours are: attending field trips; leading a club and preparing food for special events (Oglethorpe Charter Movement School (2009) available from http://www.oglethorpecharter.org).

- Charter Movement Schools hold themselves accountable for results – if the school does not achieve its stated aims, which include achievements, it can lose its contract to operate. It must also manage the budget precisely so that the mission is achieved. By 2010, while there had been increasing numbers of Charters being granted, a few Charter Movement Schools had lost their Charter though this was mostly as a result of financial rather than academic difficulties.

Within the learning situation

Below are three examples of practice from Charter Movement Schools (WestEd, 2006).

North Star Academy

Most Charter Movement Schools are founded in response to disengaged students who are not achieving the grades required to access a college education. Typically, such students are labelled as non-achievers and along with this will come feelings of low self-esteem and lack of belief in themselves. To help address these negative attitudes North Star Academy school students have this call-and-response during their community meetings:

Who are you? A Star! I shine brightly for others.

Why are you here? To get an education!

Why else? To be the great person I am meant to be!

And what will you have to do? Work! Hard!

And what will you need? Self-discipline!

And what else will you need? Respect for me, my peers, my teachers and all people!

Where are you headed? To college!

And when you succeed what will you do? Give back to others!

Although at first this might seem a rather strange approach, this very much reflects the USA culture of generating in a child a sense of allegiance and loyalty to their school. This in turn develops a sense of belonging and cohesiveness which can combat the very real feeling of loneliness felt by many children who do not belong to a gang. It is also about celebrating success and building esteem in particularly disengaged children. There are parallels to the school song which many of you might be aware of; certainly up until the time of secondary modern education all English schools had their own song to be sung every morning at assembly. Even today, Steiner schools have their morning song to help the children settle into their day. There is another parallel to this American approach to reaching disengaged learners. Recently there is a growing trend in English schools to cash in on 'street' culture and use rap singing to engage children in literacy learning, particularly creative writing and as a modern day rote learning technique.

Minnesota New Country School

At MNCS, students who have not adapted to traditional school curricula are allowed to develop their own projects to develop skills and knowledge; for example, 'one student researched chemicals in fast food and then developed a nutrition class for his peers' (WestEd, 2006:9).

Toledo School for the Arts

While most Charter Movement Schools are committed to ensuring that their students get to college and higher education, even if this means evening tutorials until 7 p.m. and extra classes on Saturdays, TSA's goal is lifelong learners and provision is made for students to experience work as artists in the community.

Connect and explore

Access the US Government Department of Education at **www.ed.gov** and search for the document 'Successful Charter Movement Schools' for further reading and take a look at **www.edreform.com/accountability** for an easy-to-view state-by-state update on how well Charter Movement Schools are doing – just click on the state of your choice.

Activity

Discuss (if possible in groups) the extent to which you believe it is the role of a school to celebrate success and build a child's self-esteem. Justify your answers. Assuming that it is a school's role to celebrate success and build a child's self-esteem, what kind of activities could achieve these goals? Try **www.teachers.tv/videos** to search for some examples of how rap and other innovative ideas give inspiration.

Charter Movement Schools provide parents and professionals, who identify a need and who can raise the additional funds required, opportunities to provide innovative structures and curricula aimed at closing the achievement gap experienced by disengaged and disadvantaged students. This is achieved by principles of strict accountability to the legislators combined with freedom to implement whatever strategies are required to achieve the stated goals. Those who support Charter Movement Schools claim that freedom to make curriculum and pedagogical decisions at a local level leads to excellent provision and student achievement; while those who oppose Charter Movement Schools claim that, on the contrary, freedom from central control can be detrimental to the quality of education. Whatever the detractors may say, the perceived success is such that in March 2010 Barack Obama, the US President, presented his blueprint for education to the American congress which calls for the expansion of the Charter Movement School system (Stanage, 2010). It can be said that Charter Movement Schools are about educational reform, where pupils attend the school of their own and/or their parents' choice. Although many Americans see this 'pick and choose' approach as being anti-democratic, unlike English alternatives which are fee-paying, funding follows the American pupils from the state provision to the preferred Charter Movement School.

? Stop and reflect

Think back on all your learning experiences; include those that might be referred to as formal within a school environment and those that might be referred to as informal and experienced as part of everyday life.

- *Which ones have had the most positive and most negative effect on you?*
- *Based on these experiences, what would your own Charter School curriculum be like?*

Activity

Draw up a table to identify the strengths and weaknesses of Charter Movement Schools. You could stretch yourself further and compare and contrast Charter Movement Schools with Montessori or Steiner/Waldorf schools (or any other alternative you can think of).

The debate about choice

There are some basic concepts to consider when the term 'choice' is used. In the first place, you have to have alternatives to provide choice – specifically, alternatives to a mainstream curriculum funded and directed by the state. If parents or learners opt for one of the alternative forms of schooling, as we saw in the earlier section 'Alternative to what?' this implies that the alternative offers something better than the state system. If alternative forms of schooling are not chosen, they are likely to lose funding and will cease to exist. To remain competitive, alternative schools need to offer something which enhances their appeal and makes them more attractive than the 'free' state system. League tables, which are used by government to rank schools according to how well their children achieve in SATs, GCSEs and A levels, often promote competition. For example, if one of two local schools is higher in the league tables than the other, this could attract not only more parents to choose it, but possibly more qualified staff to work there. The other school could be left with low numbers and be less attractive to aspirational staff looking for employment: this in turn would increase the success of the first school and worsen the failure of the other. Ultimately, if the second school was unable to develop strategies to improve then it could be classed as 'failing' and Ofsted would put the school into 'special measures'. Special measures could result in the school management being replaced and the school reopened in a new structure. This is perhaps an extreme example of competition; it is where, for example in the case of schools, not only does the organisation (school) have to continually improve its own performance, but it must be mindful of other schools' performance and qualities. It must perform better than them in the league tables and/or provide a unique selling point which will meet the needs of prospective customers. Here you might begin to recognise the language of marketing and, in the context of parental choice, begin to view the parent as consumer or customer, school as provider and education as a product. The theory is that the parent, as a consumer, has the power of choice. Choice, in a competitive market, will drive up the quality of the product – education will become better. The school which provides education will have to respond to the demands of the parent (customer) and, therefore, have to meet their needs. It follows that, as parents are the agents of their children, within a market analogy, if the parents' needs are met then the child's needs are also likely to be met. In short, by having choice, parents have the power to make change. Carnie (2003) discusses how, in the USA, choice is used to make change in response to a 'groundswell of desire' from parents and teachers for alternative approaches to education to better meet the academic, physical and emotional needs of children.

? Stop and reflect

What experiences have you and your friends had which demonstrate how choice, or the lack of it, has impacted on how you feel about your learning and your school/college/ university?

How do parents decide which school to choose – on what do they base their choices? Darlene Leiding is a principal at Oh Day Aki (Heart of the Earth Charter School) in Minnesota. She works with inner-city American Indian students and believes that:

> . . . if we are to understand our students and determine what kinds of schools will be most helpful to them, we must first consider how a changing world is shaping today's young people and their future.
>
> Leiding, 2008:169

She considers that '. . . work, learning, citizenship and motivation for learning' are the kind of skills that should be developed within a child's education. She supports the kinds of strategies that go to establishing child-centred classrooms 'where actual learning takes place'.

She also states that 'Children do not learn from adults who do not love them.' So, she seems to be claiming that parents' choice of school should be based on not just what, but *how* children will learn. However, Collins and Snell (2000) list more practical considerations that will influence a parent's choice. These include reputation of school, examination results, ease of access and sports facilities.

In addition to parents' choice there is also the issue of children's choice – children are, after all, the end users (they receive the education). You will almost certainly have experienced some choice within your own education; for example, you will have had some degree of choice with regard to your subject options at GCSE level, and then in later years chosen your AS/A levels and degree subject.

But choice is also a matter of importance for children long before they think about their GCSE exams. In line with Leiding's thinking there is another perspective of choice that parents might think about when investigating school ethos. This choice is based specifically on a school's approach to curriculum delivery, which could relate to the ideals of thinkers and philosophers already mentioned, or could be connected to the theories developed by psychologists such as Piaget. One psychologist who upholds the importance of choice as a significant stage in child development is Erik Erikson. The second stage of his theory of psychosocial development, known as the eight ages of man, is described as 'autonomy versus shame and doubt'. Within this stage, as stated by Mooney (2000:47), 'in order to develop a strong sense of independence, toddlers need to have reasonable opportunity for choice and control'. According to this theory, without this element of choice built into the curriculum, children will not be able to develop to their full potential.

Controversies

'Parents and children should be able to choose the schooling they receive'

Agree: In a democratic country it is the right of every individual to aspire to the type of school that will offer an education to meet their individual needs and personal values and ethics. Parents and children have an intimate insight into their own needs so choice is the only way in which personalised learning can be achieved. It is only in this way that children will be able to grow and learn in a fulfilling way. From a broader perspective choice promotes competition and competition drives up quality.

Parents and children are able to choose the schooling they receive in the following ways:

1 Every school provides information, normally through both electronic and printed media, which explains its mission statement, values and curriculum. Inspection reports from Ofsted and the School Inspection Service, which inspects independent schools, are made available. Blair (2005) claims that the information provided by league tables and inspections provides parents with the information that allows them to make their choices.

2 The Department for Children, Schools and Families (2002) lists 11 categories of school which include special schools, religious schools and independent schools from which to choose. There are 8 different types of specialist school ranging from arts through engineering to languages and, increasingly, diplomas are available. These options provide for subjects which meet the needs of diverse learning styles, interests and vocational or academic aspirations.

3 In practice parents have a right to express a preference for a place in any maintained, city technology or academy school; in some local authorities more than one preference can be identified; this provides the opportunity to 'choose' a school other than the one a child would automatically be selected to attend according to their postal code.

▶

4 In addition to the range of mainstream schools listed above, across the UK there are hundreds of independent alternative schools such as the ones discussed in this chapter which are not required to offer the National Curriculum. Although parents who can afford to do so are happy to pay school fees, many of these schools do attract an amount of state funding and some, including the most exclusive boarding schools Harrow and Eton, offer annual scholarships.

Disagree: Completely free choice is impractical and unlikely to be achievable. Many would consider free choice to be divisive as ultimately it reinforces social divide when those who cannot afford to pay school fees or travel to better schools are excluded from a better education. Free choice would not serve the country as a whole to best effect. In order to meet the social and economic needs of the country, schooling has to provide an education that equips children with the skills and qualities they need to be employable in jobs that will help the economy grow and be competitive in a global economy. The only way to achieve this is for the curriculum to be devised and guided centrally, informed by government policy.

Parents and children are not able to choose the schooling they receive because:

1 Unless the school is the one to which a child would automatically be allocated, information has to be asked for. Having to take the initiative to make this kind of 'official' request can cause barriers for those parents who may not have the cultural or educational capital to find their way around an unfamiliar system or even may not be aware that alternatives are available. There can be a lack of consistency between school policies which leads to confusion and lack of information. When you don't have information, you don't have choice.

2 Preference is not the same as choice. For example, parents are able to state a preference for a specific school; however, the child's potential ability, or inability, in a specialism is not taken into account. This can lead to a child being allocated to a specialist school where they have to study and take exams in subjects they would prefer not to study. School admission policies do not guarantee a place at a preferred school, even if the applicant lives in the catchment area of the preferred school.

3 'While parents can express a choice of school, there are not yet enough good schools in urban areas; such restrictions are greatest for poor and middle-class families who cannot afford to opt for private education or to live next to a good school, if they are dissatisfied with what the state offers' (Blair, 2005, Foreword).

4 Some schools remain overtly selective; for example, grammar schools which will select the academically most able applicants through the 11+ and city Technology Schools which select across the ability range. Mainstream schools select in a more covert way: simply by using the local catchment area policy ensures that children with specific addresses are first to be offered a place. Children from outside the area are excluded from their preferred school unless there are places available; such availability would be unlikely at a popular school with good Ofsted reports and which is placed high in the league tables.

5 Some parents may genuinely want their child to attend a school not in their natural catchment area for reasons other than the qualities of the school. For example, it may be located close to where the parent works, or close to a family member who will be responsible for collecting the child from school.

What do you think? Which side of the argument do you favour?

To find out about school choice in the state sector, go to:
**http://www.direct.gov.uk/en/Parents/Schoolslearninganddevelopment/
ChoosingASchool/DG_4016312**

A more in-depth study, which considers choice with reference to Charter Schools, is provided by **Plank and Sykes** (1999).

And for a more in-depth critique of marketisation of the state system, read Chapter 2 of **Ward and Eden** (2009).

Conclusion

The question of how to achieve learning in the way most appropriate to meet the needs of a diverse range of learners has been debated by educational thinkers for centuries. The lessons learned have been developed into successful and beneficial alternative curricula for those who have had the opportunity to access and opt into them. The examples referred to in this chapter, Steiner/Waldorf and Montessori schools, emphasise how freedom within the learning situation facilitates the learner to develop skills, knowledge and understanding at a rate appropriate to their own cognitive and psychomotor development. This in turn allows learners to enjoy and embrace learning without fear and to develop an intrinsic motivation towards embarking on new challenges. It is argued that children exposed to these philosophies are more able when it comes to making meaning in a critical way; being creative and innovative; developing self-esteem and confidence – they become learners who are unafraid of taking risks and of failure. We have also considered how the Charter Movement Schools' model can provide a different type of alternative, for example where communities have broken down, and like-minded people can come together to create a school curriculum that suits their particular needs and a particular time, often drawing on the philosophies of thinkers such as those considered in this chapter.

Of course this chapter can only provide a taste of the many alternative schools that are available. In the UK, 'alternative' usually means fee-paying, independent schools. There are, however, a range of alternatives for practical purposes, for example schools for children with severe learning difficulties; faith schools for children whose families feel that this aspect of their lives is significant; or 'schools' which provide education for children and young people while they are in hospital or who cannot access mainstream school due to their medical conditions. All of these are alternative in a specific way, but all offer the English National Curriculum and are state funded.

However, while alternative schools provide a choice for parents and children – and choice can provide a lever to drive up quality – choice is not always fully accessible to parents and children. Restrictions with regard to choice are as diverse as the students themselves and include many obvious barriers. For example, the location of a school of choice may simply prove too time consuming and/or expensive to travel to and from; the selection criteria may be exclusive; the cost of school fees may be prohibitive; and there may be hidden financial costs such as school uniform or extra-curricular activities such as trips abroad.

Across the world in most big cities there are also International Schools, which meet the needs of parents who are transient as a result of the jobs they hold. International Schools tend to be English-speaking, and usually offer the International Baccalaureate curriculum. This provides continuity for children who may be living in Hong Kong one year, England the next and then find themselves at school in Bangkok. While these children have continuity of study, many would argue that continuity of friendship and culture would meet their social and emotional needs better. Though, of course, in this digital age it is very much easier to maintain long-distance friendships than before the advent of Facebook, Skype and MSN.

These are just a few examples for you to think about; the one thing that they are likely to have in common is that they provide education based on philosophy that can be linked back to one of the great educationalists mentioned in this chapter.

Case study 3.2
The Wilcoxes make their choice

Mr and Mrs Wilcox have finally agreed on the alternative education option that would suit Charlie best: Mrs Wilcox will give up her part-time job and dedicate most of her time to home schooling Charlie.

This is the plan for Charlie

The study is redecorated to Charlie's choice with plenty of football posters, comfortable seating for study and for relaxing when watching TV or listening to music. There is a range of textbooks, novels and magazines such as *National Geographic*. A new PC is installed with wireless access to the internet and standard software for word processing, spreadsheet, database and basic art work. In addition, Google Earth is installed initially as a novel piece of software, but this becomes so fascinating that Charlie's interest in geography quickly stimulates him to independently study the subject.

Mrs Wilcox has contacted the local home schooling group and she will take Charlie on trips with other home schooled children. They will visit the theatre, museum and other similar venues followed by discussion over a pizza. As parents take turns to organise these trips Mrs Wilcox hopes to do some supply work on these occasions to help her keep up to date in her subject area of science.

Charlie has asked for a small patch of garden where he wants to teach himself to grow his own flowers and vegetables for the family and Mr Wilcox has offered to be on hand when he needs help. Mrs Wilcox is delighted with this and realises that cooking and related sciences will form a natural part of the curriculum.

One evening a week and at the weekend Charlie is booked into the local football club for training, and there is an option for an extra session if Charlie wants this. He is given 'time off' during the day so he is not over-tired when training. But he thinks that this time will be given over to visits to the park where he can practise his bike riding and skateboarding. Mrs Wilcox thinks there may be opportunities here to chat about environmental issues and horticulture if Charlie shows interest.

At all times Mrs Wilcox will be on hand to encourage and tap into the 'subjects' behind the activities Charlie undertakes, particularly when he shows an interest. She has built in some opportunities for formal study of maths and English, usually in the afternoon which is Charlie's optimum time for study, being a naturally late riser. The aim is that Charlie will eventually attend the local further education college to take GCSEs in maths, English and ICT; the last of these will be largely self-taught but Mr Wilcox is well qualified in this area. Now that Charlie and his mum will not be constrained by school terms they intend to increase their visits to France in order to develop their language skills and this self-taught approach will be supplemented by occasional private tuition.

Throughout this home schooling experience Mrs Wilcox expects Charlie to be setting his own targets for achievement and she will be there to support and encourage him. Should he wish to access higher education rather than go directly into a football career the Wilcoxes are confident that he will be able to enrol on an Access to HE course.

Questions for discussion

1 *Think about what you have learned in this chapter and reflect on your own school experiences to identify the strengths, weaknesses, opportunities and threats of home schooling.*

2 *Whose educational philosophy are the Wilcoxes emulating? Explain.*

Summary

Setting the scene for schooling – where did it all begin?

Education and learning have been valued since earliest times. The nature and purpose of study has changed according to the particular era and the economic, social (particularly religious attitudes) and political pressures at any given time. Early important thinkers include Confucius, Socrates, Aristotle and Plato. Lessons about learning from the seventeenth century include an emphasis on using experiential learning, including a variety of content and treating children as individuals. The English education system of didactic teaching stems from the Church of England's Sunday School system and in the nineteenth century government began to take more interest in educating the masses when state primary schools were funded. Today, compulsory education is very well established with a National Curriculum prescribed by government which expects children and young people to achieve national targets in subjects which are taught to government guidelines. The purpose of this type of schooling is to develop a nation of individuals who have the skills and qualities to be employed within an economy which needs to compete successfully in a global market.

Philosophic views on education

Rousseau argued that children go through different, distinct stages of development and that the learning process needs to be tailored accordingly by using different approaches to education. He stressed that it is of paramount importance for the teacher to know his pupil well before he begins to instruct him and he posited the idea that children should be allowed to be children and should learn for themselves rather than being told information.

Goethe believed that creativity, the use of the senses and the ability to use your imagination were intrinsic components in the development of knowledge.

Dewey supported the view that education was not just about intelligence. He argued that education should be linked to manual skills and physical and moral development. He also advocated the idea that children should be involved in decisions about their learning and he regarded the school as a community with a responsibility to extend the moral values of a child's home life. According to Dewey, the teacher's role was not to impose particular ideas on a child, but to link the child's interests to educational experiences. Several of these notions appear to be reflected by current ideologies relating to education.

Philosophy into practice – relevance in today's schools

Most people agree that education has essentially two main roles: to enable children to cope with life in the adult world as they work, engage in leisure and develop within their family and community (Winch and Gingell, 2006); and to provide society with people who are equipped with the necessary skills, knowledge and understanding to enable us to remain economically competitive in an increasingly technological world. Indeed it could be argued that education appears to be a cyclic process and that very little has changed regarding the concept of education over the past two hundred and fifty years.

Steiner/Waldorf schools and Montessori schools

Both the Steiner/Waldorf and Montessori methods of schooling stress the importance of discovery learning, active participation and engagement with the learning process. The role of the teacher is to nurture a child's natural curiosity and to act as a facilitator of education, while adopting a child-centred approach to learning. Teachers aim to provide resources which promote and support the child's natural development and foster autonomy in a safe and caring environment. Movement is regarded as an integral part of the learning process and learning from peers is actively encouraged. Many of these principles are regarded as good practice and they tend to promote a love of learning, freedom of choice and an ethos of inclusion, all of which are currently being advocated by the government through various frameworks such as *Every Child Matters*, the proposed new primary curriculum and the Early Years Foundation Stage.

Reggio Emilia schools

Reggio Emilia schools for pre-school children are an interesting example of how context shapes a philosophy, and how a philosophy from one particular region can influence school curricula throughout the world. It is also an example of how educational philosophies and ideas from other thinkers and educationalists can be used, shaped and applied within a new context. Loris Magaluzzi's determination to bring together the best educational research is demonstrated by his work with contemporary educational theorists such as Jerome Bruner and Howard Gardner. His impact on the city of Reggio Emilia is reflected in the Loris Magaluzzi International Centre for Educational Research.

Charter Movement Schools

Charter Movement Schools are the USA's response to problems in high-poverty communities with minority students in a bid to decrease the achievement gaps experienced between these students and their peers who do not experience these difficulties. These schools are designed and run by the parents and interested professionals who have identified a need and are able to apply for a Charter, which will detail how the school will be run, for example the curriculum and management structure. The parents and professionals have to be able to supplement the state funding received by Charter Schools and then use their funding to implement the requirements of the Charter. Strict principles of accountability to the legislators combined with freedom to implement whatever strategies are required to achieve their stated goals drive these schools to use innovative approaches to curriculum and structures.

The debate about choice

In spite of much debate about and investment in education, too many children are still disengaged from school, do not achieve targets set and remain unemployed for too long. Often schools do not meet the needs of individual children. Parents want alternatives for their children which better meet learners' individual needs and will equip them for a successful future. Indeed, choice for parents is seen by government as a key driver for quality in schools. However, while in principle parents and children do have opportunity to express their preference about which school their child will attend, there are many barriers to receiving this preference. Not least of these barriers is lack of state funding for those schools that do not offer the prescribed National Curriculum.

References

Apple, M.W. (2001). John Dewey, in Palmer, J.A. (ed.) *Fifty Major Thinkers on Education*, pp. 177–82, Milton Park and New York: Routledge.

Ashley, M. (2009) Education for Freedom: The Goal of Steiner/Waldorf Schools, in Woods, P.A. and Woods, G.J. (eds) *Alternative Education for the 21st Century*, pp. 209–25, New York: Palgrave Macmillan.

Avison, K. (1998) Waldorf Education: A Schooling for the Future, in *Balance in Education: Rudolf Steiner's contribution to mainstream and special education*, pp. 20–33, Launceston: Lanthorn Press.

Badman, G. (2009) *Report to the Secretary of State on Review of Elective Home Education in England*, TSO.

Barazzoni, R. (1985) *Brick by Brick, the History of the XXV Aprile People's Nursery School of Villa Cella*, Reggio Emilia: Reggio Children.

Bates, J. and Lewis, S. (2009) *The Study of Education: An Introduction*, London: Continuum.

Blair, T. (2005) Foreword by the Prime Minister, *Higher Standards, Better Schools for All: More choice for parents and pupils,* DfES HM Government. Available from http://www.dcsf.gov.uk, search parent choice.

Carnie, F. (2003) *Alternative Approaches to Education,* Abingdon: RoutledgeFalmer.

Centre for Education Reform (2009) *National Charter School and Enrolment Statistics 2009,* available at http://www.edreform.com/Issues/Charter_Connection/index.cfm, viewed April 2010.

Clouder, C. and Rawson, M. (2003) *Waldorf Education* (2nd edn), Edinburgh: Floris Books.

Collins, A. and Snell, M.C. (2000) Parental Preferences and Choice of School, *Applied Economics,* 32, pp. 803–813, University of Portsmouth, Hants, UK.

Cox, M.V. and Rowlands, A. (2000) The effect of three different educational approaches on children's drawing ability: Steiner, Montessori and traditional, *British Journal of Educational Psychology,* 70(4), pp. 485–503, available from http://ejournals.ebsco.com/direct.asp?ArticleID=5CK3GG3DUVEAU9AL9DFY, viewed August 2009.

DCSF (2002) *Secondary School Performance Tables 2002,* available from http://www.dcsf.gov.uk/performancetables/schools_02/glossary.shtml.

Delaney, J.J. (2006) *Jean-Jacques Rousseau,* available from http://www.iep.utm.edu/r/rousseau.htm#SH5b, viewed August 2009.

Department for Children, Schools and Families (2009) *Early Years Foundation Stage (EYFS) Principles: Learning and Development,* available from http://nationalstrategies.standards.dcsf.gov.uk/node/84045, viewed August 2009.

Department for Education, Schools and Families (2004) *Every Child Matters: Change for Children,* available from http://www.dcsf.gov.uk/everychildmatters/about/background/background/, viewed April 2010.

Dewey, J. (1915) *The School and Society: And the Child and the Curriculum,* 2nd edn, BN Publishing, www.bnpublishing.com.

Dewey, J. (1916) *Democracy and Education,* New York: Macmillan.

Doherty, J. and Hughes, M. (2009) *Child Development, Theory and Practice 0–11,* Harlow: Pearson Education Limited.

Edmunds, F. (2004) *An Introduction to Steiner Education,* 2nd edn, Sophia Books.

Gillard, D. (2007) *The History of Education in England,* available at: http://www.educationengland.org.uk/history/chapter02.html, viewed November 2010.

Isaacs, B. (2007) *Bringing the Montessori Approach to Your Early Years Practice,* Abingdon: David Fulton Publishers.

Kirkpatrick, J. (2008) *Montessori, Dewey, and Capitalism Educational Theory for a Free Market in education,* Claremont, California: TLJ Books.

Leiding, D. (2008) *The Hows and Whys of Alternative Education,* Maryland: Rowman & Littlefield Education.

Lilliard, A.S. (2008) *Montessori: The Science Behind the Genius,* updated edition, New York: Oxford University Press.

Mooney, C.G. (2000) *An Introduction to Dewey, Montessori, Erikson, Piaget and Vygotsky,* St Paul: Redleaf Press.

Nobel, A. (1996) *Educating Through Art: The Steiner Approach,* Edinburgh: Floris Books.

Oelkers, J. (2002) Rousseau and the image of 'modern education', *Journal of Curriculum Studies,* 34(6), pp. 679–98.

Oelkers, J. (2001) Rudlof Steiner, in Palmer, J.A. (ed.) *Fifty Major Thinkers on Education,* pp. 187–91, Milton Park and New York: Routledge.

Oglethorpe Charter Movement School (2009), available from http://www.oglethorpecharter.org.

O'Hagan, T. (2001) Jean-Jacques Rousseau, in Palmer, J.A. (ed.), *Fifty Major Thinkers on Education,* pp. 55–60, Milton Park: Routledge.

Petty, G. (2009) *Teaching Today, A Practical Guide,* 4th edn, Cheltenham: Nelson Thornes.

Plank, D.N. and Sykes, G. (1999) How Choice Changes the Education System: A Michigan Case Study, *International Review of Education,* 45(5/6), pp. 385–416.

Potts, A. (2007) New Education, Progressive Education and the Counter Culture, *Journal of Educational Administration and History,* 39(2), pp. 145–59.

Rathunde, K. (2009) Montessori and Embodied Education, in Woods P.A. and Woods G.J. (eds) *Alternative Education for the 21st Century: Philosophies, Approaches, Visions,* pp. 189–208, New York: Palgrave Macmillan.

Rinaldi, C. (2006) *In Dialogue with Reggio Emilia Listening, Researching and Learning,* Abingdon: Routledge.

Rhim, L.M. and Mclaughlin, M.J. (2001) Special Education in American Charter Movement Schools: state level policy, practices and tensions (1), *Cambridge Journal of Education,* 31(3), pp. 373–83.

Rousseau, J. (2007) *Émile or On Education* (B. Foxley trans.), Nu Vision Publications, www.nuvisionpublications.com/.

Seldin, T. (2007) *Finding an Authentic Montessori School,* available from The Montessori Foundation: http://www.montessori.org/story.php?id=265, viewed September 2009.

Seldin, T. (2000) *Montessori 101: Some basic information that every Montessori parent should know*, available from The Montessori Foundation: http://www.montessori.org/sitefiles/Montessori_101_nonprintable.pdf, viewed September 2009.

Splitter, L.J. (2009) *Authenticity and Constructivism in Education*, available from http://ejournals.ebsco.com/direct.asp?ArticleID=40D980A799AD3F14987E, viewed August 2009.

Stanage, N. (2010) Obama Knows Teachers Must Try Harder, in Guardian.co.uk, Tuesday 16 March 2010, available from http://www.guardian.co.uk/commentisfree/cifamerica/2010/mar/16/obama-teaching-unions-failing-schools-education, viewed April 2010.

Steiner, R. (1979) *The Theory of Knowledge Implicit in Goethe's World Conception*, 7th edn (W. Lindemann, trans.), available from http://wn.rsarchive.org/Books/GA002/English/AP1985/GA002_index.html, viewed August 2009.

Steiner, R. (1919) *An Introduction to Waldorf Education* (E. Bowen-Wedgewood, trans.), available from http://wn.rsarchive.org/Education/IntWal_index.html, viewed August 2009.

Steiner Waldorf Schools Fellowship (2008) *The Steiner Waldorf Schools Fellowship*, available from http://www.steinerwaldorf.org/, viewed August 2009.

Ward, S. and Eden, C. (2009) *Key Issues in Education Policy*, London: Sage.

WestEd for US Dept of Education Office of Innovation and Improvement (2006) *Charter High Schools, Closing the Achievement Gap*, US Department of Education.

WestEd for US Dept of Education Office of Innovation and Improvement (2007) *K-8 Charter Movement Schools, Closing the Achievement Gap*, US Department of Education.

Williams, J.R. (1998) *The Life of Goethe: A Critical Biography*, Oxford: Blackwell Publishers.

Winch, C. & Gingell, J. (2006), *Philosophy and Educational Policy*, London: Routledge.

Woods, P., Ashley, M. and Woods, G. (2005) *Steiner Schools in England*, available from http://www.dfes.gov.uk/research/data/uploadfiles/RR645.pdf, viewed January 2009.

http://www.telegraph.co.uk/education/primaryeducation/7126485/First-Montessori-state-school-planned-in-UK.html.

Part 2

THE PSYCHOLOGY
OF EDUCATION

4

The psychology of learning and education

Vivienne Walkup

Contents

Introduction

Learning is undeniably a fundamental aspect of education. The relationship between learning and education may seem obvious, but let us be clear about what learning actually is – and what it is not. In its broadest sense, learning takes place when experience results in a relatively permanent change in someone's knowledge or behaviour. This can be deliberate or by chance, may be helpful or unhelpful, correct or incorrect and conscious or unconscious (Hill, 2002) and can occur in any situation whether within or outside education. The key distinction is that the change in knowledge or behaviour happens because of the person's *experience* or *engagement with their environment*. Learning is gained; it is not simply change over time. This distinguishes it from biological or developmental change such as cutting teeth or one's hair turning grey. This chapter looks at ways in which psychology can inform our understanding of learning, and will look at some theoretical accounts of learning and consider their relevance within educational contexts.

However, before we move on to these accounts, let us consider some of the bigger underlying questions about learning, such as why people learn and why we put ourselves through the process of education. There are a number of different explanations about learning including the view that it is a survival mechanism which allows humans to adapt to and survive within different changing environments. At a micro level this involves the genetic structure of the brain and ways in which brain cells and connections flourish or die depending upon the ways in which they are needed within specific environmental conditions. Looking at learning and the whole person, Piaget's work initially with simple organisms (molluscs) which were able to adapt to different conditions caused him to ponder about human development. His subsequent studies which looked at the ways in which children's thinking changed as they matured is rooted in this view but also acknowledges the importance of experience as an integral part of that development. Behaviourists explain learning as a response to stimuli and so place the emphasis much more squarely on the environment. They argue that actions which are rewarded are more likely to be repeated (learned) so that the individual develops a repertoire of learned behaviours. Humanists, such as Maslow (1968, 1970) and Rogers (1969), take a different view, suggesting that learning is something people do in order to satisfy their needs for self-fulfilment or **self-actualisation**. Many current explanations assume a combination of factors but current focus is upon ways in which humans process information (**information-processing approaches**).

These differing views, however, are about learning rather than education, which itself is a continued subject of debate (see Part 3 of this book, 'Contemporary policies and debates in education'). Education is mandatory within developed countries and is usually seen as a way of transmitting worthwhile knowledge and acceptable standards in order to preserve that society and ensure its continued well-being. While this is fraught with contested issues about power and political manipulation, education is seen by most as important and necessary. It might be, however, that a person spends many years undertaking **compulsory education** but learns little from it for a range of reasons so, although education is dependent upon learning, the two do not necessarily go together.

This chapter aims to:

- Provide an outline of behavioural learning theories and their relevance within education.
- Explore the contribution of cognitive approaches to learning within the learning situation.
- Discuss the role of the brain in learning.

- Consider notions of IQ (intelligence quotient) and EQ (emotional intelligence) and their relevance within education.
- Examine learning preferences.
- Reflect upon motivation within the learning situation.
- Make links between psychology and learning within education studies.

Case study 4.1
Recipes for success

A group of students were asked to find ways to bring together different ethnic and social groups within their school and local area. The teacher suggested that they work in groups of four or five and then begin by 'brainstorming' various ideas, selecting their preferred ones and then putting these forward for the whole group to consider. The teacher then carried out a voting system to find the top three which were then taken up by the students. One of the suggestions which they agreed to take forward was to bring in favourite recipes from the three cultures represented in the neighbourhood (members of which were present in the group). The recipes were then scrutinised, translated and tested by the students and amendments made where necessary to ensure the quality of the recipes. The teacher suggested that the group divided up the work between them to reflect their own interests and strengths so that, for example, those who had artistic skills took on the illustrations and photographs and those with strong literacy skills checked for sense and correct spelling and grammar. After a good deal of editing and organising material, the book was sent to and approved by a local publisher and resulted in the successful publication of a recipe book (in three languages) which included favourite recipes from these three cultures. Although teaching staff acted as facilitators in terms of offering advice and suggestions when required, particularly about selection and presentation of materials and providing names and details of contacts, the whole initiative was student-driven, and they became fully engaged and motivated in the course of solving the problems involved.

Questions for discussion

1 *Does the role of the teachers in this case study match your understanding (or the stereotype) of what being a teacher involves? How is it different, if at all?*

2 *In what ways do you think this project 'educated' the students involved?*

Behavioural views of learning

Behavioural learning theories assume that the outcome of learning is a change in behaviour, and stress the effects of external events upon individuals. For example, if we have learned how to spell a word correctly then our future spelling of that word (our future *behaviour*) will change to take account of this.

The role of **conditioning** is seen as critical within behavioural approaches, which are based upon the work of key theorists such as Ivan Pavlov (1927) and B.F. Skinner (1953). **Classical conditioning** (so called to differentiate it from later types of conditioning) involves learning by association and helps to explain involuntary responses to various situations. Pavlov observed that dogs became conditioned to salivate when they heard the sound of someone bringing their food. At first the dogs salivated at the food (a natural, **unconditioned response**), then later at the sight of the feeder, and eventually at the sound of the feeder's approach (**conditioned responses**). His subsequent experiments found that sounding a buzzer at the same time as presenting food eventually resulted in salivation when only the buzzer sounded and no food was present. Thus a transferral of response was involved, from the food itself (the **unconditioned stimulus**) to the buzzer (the **conditioned stimulus**), so that although salivation started out as a reflex, unconditioned response it became a conditioned one. Thus the dogs had been conditioned to automatically respond to a stimulus. Further experiments suggest that humans may also be classically conditioned (Menzies, 1937) and more recent work indicates that personal concepts, such as self-esteem, can also be increased by classical conditioning (Baccus, Baldwin and Packer, 2004).

Within the learning situation

Classical conditioning helps to explain responses such as fear or anxiety which may interfere with effective learning. So, for example, learners who experience symptoms of fear and anxiety when presented with mathematical tasks may have been conditioned to do so by previous failure at maths which may have been humiliating and stressful. Procedures based on classical conditioning can be used to encourage more positive responses by pairing pleasant events with learning tasks; for example, making mathematical tasks fun by having learners decide how to divide refreshments equally and then allowing these to be eaten. This approach is commonly used at primary level, but a small project is currently under way with adult learners returning to further education who suffer from maths anxiety. They have been taught some relaxation and visualisation exercises which the tutor encourages them to carry out at the beginning of a session or whenever they feel anxiety or panic symptoms. As it is impossible to be relaxed and stressed at the same time, it is hoped that the learners' negative feelings which are conditioned responses to maths will be replaced by positive feelings as they are able to engage with the learning in a more relaxed way.

However, although classical conditioning helps to explain some involuntary responses to situations, most behaviours associated with learning involve voluntary rather than automatic responses. B.F. Skinner developed the concept of **operant conditioning** to account for ways in which people consciously learn new behaviours within their environment. Operant conditioning focuses on ways in which behaviour is strengthened or weakened by the events that go before it or the consequences which follow it. So, for example, operant conditioning would suggest that a learner who is rewarded for working hard (consequences) is more likely to work hard in the future. The reward plays an important role as a psychological **reinforcer**, a term which is used within operant conditioning to describe any consequence which strengthens the behaviour it follows.

Within the learning situation

Operant conditioning provides insights into learner behaviours. For example, a young person might receive **positive reinforcement** (a wished-for consequence) from his peers (in the form of laughter) for being rude to the teacher. This might cause the teacher to stop the lesson in order to deal with this student. In this case the behaviour may be doubly reinforced. In the first place it is reinforced by the student's classmates, who are giving him attention by laughing. Second, it is reinforced by the teacher, who is inadvertently reinforcing the behaviour since one of the student's wished-for consequences was to avoid working. The concepts of **negative reinforcement** and **punishment** also fit within this framework, and are often used together by teachers to deter undesired behaviour. Negative reinforcement strengthens appropriate behaviour by *removing* an unpleasant stimulus when the desired behaviour occurs. An example of this is a learner who has been kept behind after class to complete her work and who works hard and stays focused on the task so that she can go home. Thus she is removing the unpleasant stimulus (staying in the classroom) by her behaviour (working hard and staying on task). Punishment differs from negative reinforcement in that it involves *suppressing or decreasing behaviour* rather than strengthening it. An unwanted behaviour that is followed by a punishment (an unpleasant stimulus) is less likely to be repeated in similar situations in the future. So, for example, the removal of privileges such as exclusion from a school trip following inappropriate behaviour would constitute one form of punishment. So, in many ways, negative reinforcement and punishment are two sides of the same coin: but whereas punishment is given *following* the undesired behaviour and thus does nothing to encourage desired behaviour, negative reinforcement actually seeks to *motivate* the learner to act positively in order to remove the unpleasant stimulus.

In the context of schools, many **behaviour management** approaches (which increasingly include school-wide or 'whole-school' strategies in the UK) are based on positive and negative reinforcement, punishment and other behavioural principles of learning. These include concepts such as schedules of reinforcement (how often positive reinforcement should be given to make it most effective) and the role of antecedents (the events preceding behaviours such as a teacher standing quietly in front of a class or clapping his hands in order to indicate that it is time to listen) in behaviour change. A rising number of texts provide practitioners with guidelines for managing behaviour (Rogers, 2000, 2002, 2004, 2006; Cowley, 2003a, 2003b, 2006), and these are widely used both within primary and secondary school contexts.

However, useful as the behavioural view of learning is, it has often been criticised, both for viewing the learner as a passive recipient of external stimuli in the learning process, rather than an active learner, and for its emphasis on behaviour and observable responses which fails to take proper account of internal processes. Chief among these internal processes, for many theorists, is cognition.

Cognitive views of learning

Cognitive theorists view learners as being at the centre of their own learning rather than responding to the rewards and punishments around them. Learners are seen as actively constructing meaning from the events they experience and so are in control of their own learning. The views of the psychologists Piaget and Vygotsky, and the information processing approach, are considered here.

Piaget's theory of cognitive development

Piaget's theory became a dominant psychological approach within education in the 1960s. It suggests that children and young people develop their cognitive abilities in stages (Piaget, 1954, 1963). These stages involve qualitative changes in thinking, each of which builds upon the preceding stage. Thus development proceeds through a combination of **maturation** (changes in biological maturity) and **adaptation** (ways in which people adapt to the environment) which involves **assimilation** (the way that existing knowledge is used to solve problems) and **accommodation** (the process of changing existing knowledge in order to solve new tasks).

Piaget saw individuals as striving to maintain balance as they try to make sense of the world around them. He called this process **equilibration**, but recognised that learning involves being off-balance (**disequilibrium**) because new problems or tasks mean that changes in thinking are necessary. Piaget suggested that knowledge is stored in mental files or folders (**schemas** or *schemata*), which allow it to be stored with other similar information (see Figure 4.1).

Piaget's stages of development are related to maturation and occur in a fixed order, making it impossible to leave out or skip a stage. Each stage has particular characteristics which identify it, so for example the *sensori-motor* stage (0–2 years approximately) sees the child's thinking as involving the senses and motor activity. During this stage **object permanence** (the understanding that objects have a separate, permanent existence) develops and the child begins to be capable of *goal-directed actions*. The *preoperational stage* (2–7 years approximately) sees the development of logical mental operations (thinking through actions logically before carrying them out), while the *concrete operational stage* (7–11 years approximately) involves the recognition of the logical stability of the physical world. The *formal operational* stage (11 years onwards) sees the ability of abstract thought developing which can be used to formulate and test hypotheses. Piaget did not develop his theory beyond this stage, and thus assumed that there were no significant changes once formal operational thinking was acquired.

Within the learning situation

Piaget's theory has implications for teachers because it highlights the importance of presenting tasks which are neither too difficult nor too easy in order that learning takes place (so disequilibrium becomes equilibrium). This involves active learning, as individuals construct their own understanding at each level of their cognitive development and must be able to incorporate information into their own schemas. To do this they must act upon the information in some way which should include both physical manipulation of objects (such as using building blocks or shapes when working out mathematical problems) and mental manipulation of ideas (for example, a lesson about different jobs might include pictures of people and learners asked to guess their jobs, leading to issues around double classification such as woman, sister, mother, manager, chemist etc.).

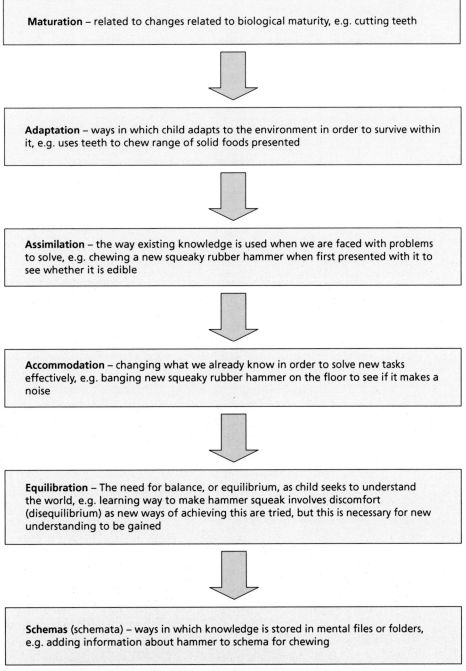

Figure 4.1 Piaget's theory of cognitive development

Source: Vivienne Walkup, after Piaget.

? Stop and reflect

A teacher wishes to encourage formal operational thinking in a class of 11-year-olds. She/he decides to take the following actions, based on Piaget's ideas:

- *Continue to develop concrete operational thinking (i.e. that which reinforces the logical stability of the physical world) by using established teaching methods and materials (e.g. simple visual aids such as pictures).*

- *At the same time, she/he begins to introduce more sophisticated methods (such as graphs and complex diagrams) in order to support the development of formal operational thinking (i.e. involving abstract thought and hypotheses).*

- *Give learners opportunities to explore hypothetical questions and solve problems using scientific reasoning (e.g. presenting both sides of an argument, or designing experiments to answer questions).*

- *Provide materials and ideas relevant to the young people's lives (e.g. addressing relevant current topics such as social messaging sites, youth cultures or compulsory education).*

On reflection, were these ideas incorporated into your own learning experiences? If so, did they result in 'deeper' (lasting) learning for you?

Piaget's theory has been criticised because it overlooks cultural differences and assumes that all children develop in the same way, whereas children and adults often think in ways which are inconsistent with his ideas. Piaget's methods have also been seen as lacking in validity (whether they are actually measuring what they set out to, i.e. children's cognitive development, or other things such as how they might be distracted by misleading information) and reliability (whether the same results would be obtained when the experiments were repeated with different participants). Many of Piaget's experiments were not confirmed when replicated, which led to children's abilities being underestimated. Vygotsky's sociocultural perspective, however, does take these factors into account.

Vygotsky's sociocultural approach

Lev Vygotsky (1978, 1986 and 1987) believed that human activities must be understood within the context of their cultural setting, and suggested that mental structures and thinking processes are related to our interactions with others. Thus our culture, and the way this is communicated (through **cultural tools**) are key factors in our cognitive development. Vygotsky thought that unlearned abilities such as attention, perception and memory, are built upon by the context which the child is part of. Cultural tools are structures within that context, such as language and number systems, which shape the thinking of those using them, as well as enable them to develop. They are passed from generation to generation, they are complex, and they influence the thinking of that culture. In particular, Vygotsky stressed the importance of **language** in cognitive development, suggesting that it allows external speech to become **verbal thought**, which allows individuals to reflect, think, plan and control behaviour. As language is invented by a particular culture, it also forms part of that culture's thinking.

Vygotsky also believed that people learn best when the task to be learnt is within their grasp but just beyond what they already know. He identified the importance of the distance between a person's *actual* developmental level and their *potential* developmental level at any one point, and called this the ***zone of proximal development*** (ZPD). Full development of potential relies upon the guidance or *scaffolding* of more competent peers.

Within the learning situation

Vygotsky's ideas suggest that a child's learning development is affected by the culture which they are part of, including family environment. The curriculum within schools should take account of this and involve building language development through active problem-solving to encourage cognitive abilities (see Chapter 2 for a full discussion of the National Curriculum). Sensitive scaffolding by educators (such as giving information, reminders, clues and encouragement) should be timely and gradually allow learners to do more independently as they become competent. Tasks should be within the learner's zone of proximal development, so that they are adapted to the learner's current levels, but include challenges to move them to their potential level.

Connect and explore

The following article (available online at **http://condor.admin.ccny.cuny.edu/~group4/ Van%20Der%20Stuyf/Van%20Der%20Stuyf%20Paper.doc**) includes a helpful summary of using scaffolding within the learning situation: Van Der Stuyf, R. (2002) Scaffolding as a Teaching Strategy, *Adolescent Learning and Development*, Section 0500A, November 2002.

Vygotsky's theory has been criticised for its generality and lack of research basis, as well as failing to take biological factors into account. Vygotsky died young, and perhaps would have developed some of his ideas further: instead these were to be developed by others (Gredler, 2005; Kozulin, 2003). Information processing approaches to learning present a different way of understanding cognitive processes which have clear significance within the learning situation.

Information processing approaches

In this approach, the computer is seen as an analogy for the human mind. It is not rooted in the work of a single theorist but draws upon the work of many. Information processing theorists suggest that it is useful to consider similarities between the mind and a computer in order to gain insights into complex abilities such as human problem-solving and cognitive development. The computer's 'hardware' can be compared with the physical structure of the brain, including nerves and tissue, and the 'software' might be the programmes or strategies used to deal with the world. Age-related changes might stem from changes or growth in the basic system and its capacity (this is similar to Piaget's ideas about maturation), or from the learning needed to use the programmes available (adaptation).

Memory is a key part of the information processing approach and is based on the ideas of several key theorists (Atkinson and Shiffrin, 1968; Gagne, 1985; Neisser, 1976). The typical information processing model of memory proposes that information is encoded in **sensory memory** where **attention** and **perception** determine what is retained for future use. In **working memory** new information connects with knowledge from **long-term memory**. If thoroughly processed and connected, the new information becomes part of long-term memory (see Figure 4.2).

Sensory memory represents information from the environment that is experienced through the senses (sight, hearing, touch, taste and smell) and transmitted very quickly to the brain as electrical impulses. Attention is critical here if the information is to be passed to the next stage, while perception determines the way that the information is understood.

Working memory, originally called short-term memory, is whatever is currently being thought about. It is brief and limited in capacity, but it allows new information to be 'worked' upon using what is already known and then either lost (forgotten) or passed for storage in the long-term memory.

Long-term memory (LTM) forms the knowledge base of the human brain and allows large amounts of information to be stored indefinitely. Retrieval of information

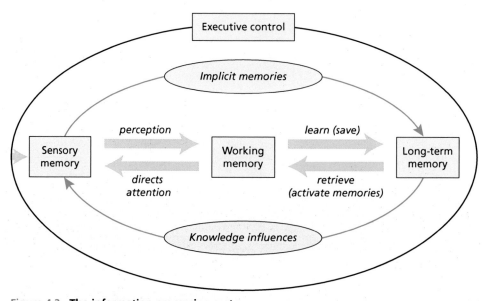

Figure 4.2 The information processing system

Source: Woolfolk, Hughes and Walkup (2008) *Psychology in Education*, Figure 7.1, p. 297.

from the LTM, however, is not always straightforward, and cues may be needed to assist recall. So, for example, verbal or written clues or hints can trigger memory. The use of multiple choice questions provides this as learners find it much easier to identify the correct answer when they see or hear it but might struggle to recall the answer otherwise.

Within the learning situation

Information processing approaches suggest that gaining the *attention* (sensory memory) of learners is critical if they are to process information and learning is to take place. Information processing approaches also stress the importance of relating new learning (working memory) to what is already known (long-term memory), so that new information is likely to be processed and stored. The use of repetition helps to keep information in working memory long enough that it can be stored in LTM. **Mnemonics** also help to encourage new learning by association, because this involves linking old and new information and helps with transfer to long-term memory.

? Stop and reflect

- *Information processing approaches are useful because they allow cognition to be broken down into separate elements which can be examined. This is particularly useful when addressing SEN conditions such as dyslexia. However, information processing views are often criticised because they take little account of physical, social and emotional aspects of individuals. These are clearly integrated in the real world where factors such as being hungry, frightened or angry can affect someone's ability to attend to learning tasks.*

- *Reflect upon your own learning experiences: have your own mental processes ever been affected by factors other than cognitive ones? For example, as you read this, are you aware of any physical, social or emotional factors affecting your concentration, such as being thirsty, hungry or angry?*

The model of memory, which is a critical part of the information processing approach, is a theoretical one not rooted in biological structures. Those who take a more biological view of cognitive development argue that it is the actual physical structure of the brain and the way that it develops which is significant in cognitive development.

The brain and cognitive development

At birth, the human brain is primed and ready for engaging with life yet it requires a further three years to establish connections between neurons (the nerve cells which transmit and receive information). These connections are formed when impulses are passed between **neurons**, using **axons** (long nerve fibres) to

111

| At birth | 6 years old | 14 years old |

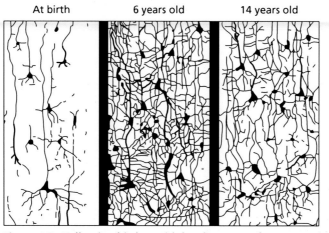

Figure 4.3   **Following birth, rapid development of synapses during early years and these are 'pruned' by the age of 14 years**

send these messages and **dendrites** (short branches from nerve cells) to receive them. Synapses (connections) are then formed which become increasingly complex as the child develops. It may help if you think of brain development as rather like a tree growing more branches and twigs as it matures (see Figure 4.3). During your first three years of life, the brain produces far more synapses than it needs even as an adult, and a 'pruning' process occurs, meaning that only those neurons which are actually used will survive and become a permanent part of the brain (Bransford, Brown and Cocking, 2000).

It seems, then, that both biological factors (which are the result of nature) and experiential ones (the result of nurture) are involved in the development of the human brain. The brain cells form the framework, but the connections made in childhood influence what happens to that framework. This is relevant for the cognitive development of children as it suggests that stimulation is important for healthy development.

Research from animal and human studies shows that both experiences and direct teaching cause changes in the organisation and structure of the brain. For example, deaf individuals who use sign language have different patterns of electrical activity in their brains compared with deaf people who do not use sign language (Campbell, MacSweeney and Waters, 2007). This is an example of a change in the brain caused by experience (i.e. the learning and use of sign language).

Shaywitz and his colleagues (2004) reported a dramatic demonstration of brain changes in children following instruction. The researchers studied 28 children aged 6 to 9 who were 'good' readers, and 49 children who were 'poor' readers. A process known as functional **magnetic-resonance imaging (MRI)** showed differences in the brain activity of the two groups. The poor readers underused parts of their brains' left hemisphere and sometimes overused their right hemispheres. After over 100 hours of intensive instruction in letter–sound combinations, the brains of the poor readers started to function more like those of the good readers and continued this functioning a year later. Poor readers who received the standard support and were used as a control/comparison group did not show the brain function changes, which suggests that the improvements in those receiving intensive instruction were not simply due to natural developmental processes but were the result of the extra stimulation.

One clear connection between the brain and classroom learning is in the area of emotions and stress. Anxiety interferes with learning, whereas challenge, interest and curiosity can support learning. If learners feel unsafe and anxious, they are not likely to be able to focus their attention on learning (Sylvester, 2003). However, learning also suffers if learners are not challenged or interested. Keeping the level of challenge and support 'just right' is often difficult for teachers, and helping learners to regulate their own emotions and motivation is an important goal for education. Research suggests that it takes until the age of 20 for the biological processes of brain development to produce a fully functional prefrontal cortex which regulates impulsive behaviour (Weinberger, 2001). Thus, learners within statutory education still lack the brain development to balance impulse with reason and planning. Weinberger suggests that parents have to 'loan' their children a prefrontal cortex, by helping them to set rules and limits and make plans, until the child's own prefrontal cortex can take over.

Within the learning situation

It is clear that the brain and learning are intimately related, which has implications for those working with learners. As the brain is relatively plastic, enriched active learning environments and flexible instructional strategies are likely to support cognitive development in young children and learning in adults. It is also apparent that many cognitive functions are *differentiated* – they are associated with different parts of the brain. Thus, learners are likely to have preferred modes of processing (visual or verbal, for example) as well as different capabilities in these different modes (Driscoll, 2005). Using different modes of instruction, and activities that draw on different senses, may support learning – for example, using shapes and solid objects to teach mathematical concepts. Schools and teachers can also play major roles in cognitive and emotional development by providing appropriate environments for these developing, but sometimes impulsive, brains (Meece, 2002).

Since the mid 1990s much has been written about brain-based education. Many publications for parents and teachers have useful ideas, but some may oversimplify the complexities of the brain by suggesting we should be teaching to different sides of the brain. Nearly all tasks, and particularly the complex skills and abilities that are taught in educational contexts, require the participation of many different areas of the brain in constant communication with each other. For example, the right side of the brain is better at working out the meaning of a story, but the left side is where grammar and syntax are understood, so both sides of the brain have to work together in reading. These functional differences between the brain's hemispheres, however, are more relative than absolute; one hemisphere is simply more efficient than the other in performing certain tasks (Bruer, 1999).

Connect and explore

Go to the Centre for Brain and Cognitive Development website at **http://www. cbcd.bbk.ac.uk** to find out about the different types of cognitive research which are happening.

Intelligence

The concept of intelligence is an important and controversial area in education. Even definitions of what intelligence is and how it can be measured vary among experts, but it is usually assumed that intelligence involves *the ability to acquire and use knowledge for solving problems and adapting to the world*. Gardner's model of multiple intelligences, which suggests that intelligence is both a biological and psychological potential to solve problems, is popular within education. The eight types of intelligence included within this framework are:

- linguistic (verbal)
- musical
- spatial
- logical-mathematical
- bodily-kinesthetic (movement)
- interpersonal (understanding others)
- intrapersonal (understanding self) and
- naturalist (observing and understanding natural and human-made patterns and systems) (Gardner, 1998).

Some critics suggest that several intelligences are really talents (including bodily-kinesthetic skill and musical ability – see Chapter 9 for more on the concept of talent) or personality traits (interpersonal ability). The idea that there are several 'intelligences' is not new at all. Many researchers have identified verbal and spatial abilities as being distinct elements of intelligence. In addition, the eight intelligences are not as independent of one another as Gardner's model might suggest; there are correlations among the abilities. For instance, logical-mathematical and spatial intelligences are highly correlated (Sattler, 2001), implying that these 'separate abilities' may not be so separate after all. Recent evidence linking musical and spatial abilities has prompted Gardner to consider that there may be connections among the intelligences (Gardner, 1998), so the theory is still developing.

However, Gardner (1998, 2003) has responded to critics by identifying a number of myths and misconceptions about multiple intelligences theory and schooling. One is that intelligences are the same as learning styles. Gardner doesn't believe that people actually have consistent learning styles. Another misconception is that multiple intelligences theory disproves the idea of a general ability (known as g). This is not the case, but multiple intelligences theory does question how useful g is as an explanation for human achievements.

An advantage of Gardner's perspective is that it expands teachers' thinking about learner abilities and ways of teaching. Critics argue that the theory has sometimes been reduced to oversimplified models such as visual, auditory, kinesthetic (VAK) approaches. Similarly there may be a tendency for teachers to include every 'intelligence' or ability in every lesson, no matter how inappropriate. More positively, multiple intelligences theory might lead to helpful outcomes within the classroom by providing more varied learning opportunities (White, 2004).

History of education

Testing intelligence

The use of intelligence tests became popular as a means of testing children for selective education within British schools in the first half of the twentieth century. Children took an examination called the 11+ which calculated their **IQ (intelligence quotient)** by comparing their **mental age** score (determined by their performance on these tests) with their actual or **chronological age**:

$$\text{Intelligence Quotient} = \text{Mental Age/Chronological Age} \times 100$$

So a child who had a mental age of 6 years and a chronological age of 8 years would have an IQ of 75, as seen below:

$$6/8 \times 100 = 600/8 = 75 \text{ (100 is the average IQ)}$$

The outcome of the 11+ determined which type of secondary education children progressed to. Testing therefore assumed intelligence to be a fairly fixed trait which predicted future performance. A child was sent either to grammar school (for high achievers likely to pursue academic or professional careers), technical school, although these were less common (for moderate achievers likely to become skilled white collar or practical workers) or secondary modern school (for lower achievers likely to become unskilled workers).

Concerns grew about the ability of IQ tests as predictors of future performance as well as increasing awareness of social inequalities which were reinforced by this type of differentiation at secondary level. The Education Act of 1964 began the process of introducing a single type of 'comprehensive' school, and by the end of the 1970s most schools in England were based on comprehensive principles.

Currently IQ tests are only used within a small number of UK Local Education Authorities that still retain grammar schools and in some independent schools (see Chapter 1 for more on this).

Howard Gardner's theory of multiple intelligences includes intrapersonal and interpersonal intelligences, or intelligence about self and others. This relates to the notion of **emotional intelligence** (or EI as it is sometimes known), an idea which is based on the work of Mayer and Salovey (1997), and which is increasingly recognised as being an important part of healthy development and education. In the UK, emotional development is promoted within the Foundation Stage (for 3 to 5-year-olds) of the National Curriculum, and forms part of personal, social and health education (PSHE) for older children and young adults (Bradley, 2003). At the centre of emotional intelligence are four broad abilities: perceiving, integrating, understanding, and managing emotions (Mayer and Cobb, 2000).

Within the learning situation

Activities which help to build these abilities may encourage cooperative behaviours and reduce antisocial activities such as the use of insults and bullying. Some research, such as that by Graham in the USA (1996), has found that the use of techniques (including role plays) to help aggressive boys read the intentions of others encouraged empathy. More recently, UK-based research has concluded that emotional intelligence is relevant to academic achievement and deviant behaviour at school, particularly for vulnerable and disadvantaged adolescents (Petrides et al., 2004).

Controversies

'The notion of emotional intelligence is useful within educational settings and learning situations'

Agree:

- The inclusion of emotional intelligence (EI) measures in assessments of children and intervention programmes, such as programmes for aggressive boys learning to read the intentions and emotions of others (Graham, 1996), seem to be useful in informing future research and social provision.

- The key point is that success in life requires more than cognitive or intellectual skills, and teachers are important influences in helping learners develop all of their capabilities.

Disagree:

- Some researchers have criticised the notion of emotional intelligence, saying that it is not a cluster of capabilities, but rather a set of personality traits, or the application of general intelligence to social situations (Izard, 2001; Nestor-Baker, 1999).

- One of the problems with innovations in educational psychology is that they are often presented inaccurately within the media and therefore become vague and misunderstood. The concept of emotional intelligence is an example of this, as many journalists use the term loosely or inaccurately which results in misunderstanding.

What do you think? Which side of the argument do you favour?

↖ *Connect and explore*

Find out more about the relationship between emotional intelligence, academic ability and deviant behaviour by reading the following research article:

Petrides, K.V. (2004) The role of trait emotional intelligence in academic performances and deviant behavior at school, *Personality and Individual Differences,* 36, pp. 277–93, available at: **http://www.psychometriclab.com/admins/files/PAID%20(2004)%20-%20T_EI.pdf.**

Learning preferences

The way a person approaches learning and studying is known as his or her **learning style**. Although many different learning styles have been described, one theme that unites most of the styles is the difference between deep and surface approaches to processing information in learning situations (Snow, Corno and Jackson, 1996). Individuals who have a *deep processing approach* see the learning activities as a means for understanding some underlying concepts or meanings, perhaps by relating to their own experience. Learners who take a *surface processing approach*, on the other hand, focus on memorising the learning materials, rather than understanding them. So surface processors may be trying to remember information in order to be ready for a test. Surface processing learners tend to be motivated by rewards, grades, external standards, and the desire to be evaluated positively by others (although obviously the situation influences these tendencies). By contrast, deep processing learners are motivated by a need to understand and see learning as worthwhile for its own sake.

Since the late 1970s, a great deal has been written about differences in individuals' **learning preferences** (Dunn, Dunn and Price, 2000; Dunn and Griggs, 2003; Gregorc, 1982; Keefe, 1982). Learning preferences are often called *learning styles* in these writings, but preferences is a more accurate label because the 'styles' are determined by your preferences for particular learning environments so may vary – for example, where, when, with whom, or with what lighting, food or music you like to study. There are a number of instruments for assessing people's learning preferences: the learning style inventory (Dunn, Dunn and Price, 1984), learning styles inventory (revised) (Kolb, 1985), and the learning style profile (Keefe and Monk, 1986). However, tests of learning style have been strongly criticised for lacking evidence of reliability and validity (Snider, 1990; Wintergerst, DeCapua and Itzen, 2001). In fact, in an extensive examination of learning styles instruments, researchers at the Learning Skills Research Centre in England concluded, 'with regard to Dunn and Dunn (Section 3.2), Gregorc (Section 3.1) and Riding (Section 4.1), our examination of the reliability and validity of their learning style instruments strongly suggests that they should not be used in education or business' (Coffield, et al., 2004:127). However, they are included here as they are currently commonly referred to within discussions about education and learning.

Within the learning situation

Some proponents of learning styles believe that individuals learn more when they study in their preferred setting and manner (Dunn, Beaudry and Klavas, 1989; Lovelace, 2005). There is evidence that very bright learners need less structure and prefer quiet, solitary learning (Torrance, 1986). However, most educational psychologists are sceptical about the value of learning preferences (Stahl, 2002), so why are these ideas so popular? Part of the answer is that many commercial enterprises have profited from selling advice to teachers by making claims about the importance of learning styles (Coffield et al., 2004). Some of the teaching ideas may be useful, but not necessarily because they are based on learning styles.

It is worth remembering that learners, especially younger ones, may not be the best judges of how they should learn. Sometimes learners, particularly those who have experienced genuine difficulty, prefer whatever is easy and comfortable, whereas 'real' learning can be hard and uncomfortable. Sometimes, individuals prefer to learn in a certain way because they have no alternatives (for example, they may prefer pictures because they are unable to read, or do not have access to very much written material) and it is the only way they know how to approach the task. These learners may benefit from developing new – and perhaps more effective – ways of learning. One final consideration: many advocates of the learning styles imply that the differences in the learner are what matter, but recent research favours viewing the person in context with the entire teaching–learning system as a better way to understand people's learning (Coffield et al., 2004).

Activity

Make a list of which parts of this chapter you have found easiest to learn. Are there similarities between these? If so, what are they? Perhaps it is in terms of whether it is in written text or in diagrammatic or tabular form? Think back to when and where you were studying these. Was it in a particular place or at a particular time? Perhaps you prefer to listen to music or have a snack as you study in order to help you focus best? Do these things apply in most learning situations or do they vary?

If you have identified some fairly consistent factors above, this links in with the learning styles or preferences discussed earlier. However, if you have found that it is more to do with the topics which are most interesting to you rather than the format or context, the section on motivation which follows may be more relevant.

Motivation

Most educators agree that motivating learners is one of the critical tasks of teaching, regardless of the context. In order to learn, individuals must be cognitively, emotionally and behaviourally engaged in the subject matter.

Motivation is usually defined as *an internal state that arouses, directs and maintains behaviour.* Psychologists studying motivation have focused on five basic questions:

1 *What choices do people make about their behaviour?* Why do some learners, for example, focus on their homework while others watch television?

2 *How long does it take to get started?* Why do some learners start their homework straight away, while others procrastinate?

3 *What is the intensity or level of involvement in the chosen activity?* Once the learner has begun a task, is she/he absorbed and focused, or just going through the motions?

4 *What causes a person to persist or to give up?* Will a learner read the entire assignment or just a few pages?

5 *What is the individual thinking and feeling while engaged in the activity?* Is the learner enjoying Shakespeare, feeling competent, or worrying about a forthcoming test (Graham and Weiner, 1996; Pintrich, Marx and Boyle, 1993)?

Answering these questions about real learners is a challenge, as many factors both internal and external influence motivation.

A classic distinction in motivation is between *intrinsic* and *extrinsic*. **Intrinsic motivation** is the natural tendency to seek out and conquer challenges in the pursuit of personal interests and using capabilities (Deci and Ryan, 1985; Reeve, 1996). When people are intrinsically motivated, they do not need incentives or punishments, because *the activity itself is rewarding.* In contrast, when something is done in order to earn a good grade, avoid punishment, please the teacher, or for some other reason that has very little to do with the task itself, then **extrinsic motivation** is involved. Here individuals are not really interested in the activity for its own sake; but only about what is gained by doing it.

According to psychologists who adopt the intrinsic/extrinsic concept of motivation, it is impossible to tell just by looking at the person and their behaviour whether behaviour is intrinsically or extrinsically motivated. The essential difference between the two types of motivation is the person's reason for acting, that is, whether the **locus of causality** for the action (the location of the cause) is internal or external – inside or outside the person. Learners who read or practise their backstroke or paint may be reading, swimming or painting because they freely chose the activity based on personal interests (*internal locus* of causality/intrinsic motivation), or because someone or something else outside is influencing them (*external locus* of causality/extrinsic motivation) (Reeve, 1996).

Recently, the notion of intrinsic and extrinsic motivation as two ends of a continuum has been challenged, and plausible suggestions about both being involved are made (Covington and Mueller, 2001). Educators must encourage and nurture intrinsic motivation, while making sure that extrinsic motivation supports learning (Brophy, 1988, 2003). To do this, they need to know about the factors that influence motivation.

Behavioural approaches to motivation

According to the behavioural view, pioneered by theorists such as J.B. Watson, Skinner and Pavlov, an understanding of learner motivation begins with a careful analysis of the **rewards** and **incentives** present in the learning environment. A *reward* is an attractive object or event supplied as a consequence of a particular behaviour, and an *incentive* is an object or event that encourages or discourages behaviour. So, for example, the promise of an A+ may be an incentive, but actually receiving the grade is a reward. If individuals are consistently reinforced for certain behaviours, they may develop habits or tendencies to act in certain ways.

Providing grades, stars, stickers and other reinforcers for learning – or demerits/black marks/unhappy faces for misbehaviour – is an attempt to motivate learners by extrinsic means. Of course, in any individual case, other factors may affect how a learner behaves, because all individuals are complex human beings. An alternative way of explaining motivation, which takes more account of internal factors, is a humanistic approach.

Humanistic approaches to motivation

From the humanistic perspective, to motivate means to encourage someone's inner resources – their sense of competence, self-esteem, autonomy and self-actualisation (successful personal development). Maslow's theory (1970), which suggested that humans have a **hierarchy of needs** ranging from basic lower-level needs (such as food, warmth, shelter, survival and safety) to the top-level of self-actualisation (or the fulfilment of one's potential), has been an influential humanistic explanation of motivation (see Figure 4.4).

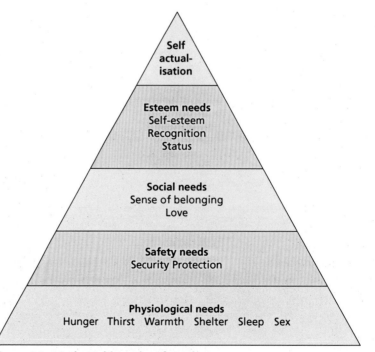

Figure 4.4 Maslow's hierarchy of needs

Source: Woolfolk, Hughes and Walkup (2008) *Psychology in Education*, Figure 10.1, p. 442.

Maslow (1968) called the four lower-level needs – for survival, then safety, followed by belonging, and then self-esteem – **deficiency needs**. This means that when these needs are satisfied, the motivation for fulfilling them decreases. He termed the top-level 'growth needs' or **being needs**. When these are met, a person's motivation does not cease; instead, it increases to seek further fulfilment. Unlike deficiency needs, these 'being needs' can never be completely filled. For example, the more successful you are in your efforts to develop as an educator, the harder you are likely to strive for even greater improvement.

Maslow's theory has been criticised because people do not always appear to behave as the theory would predict. Most of us move back and forth between different types of needs, and may even be motivated by many different needs at the same time. Some people, such as those dedicated to saving lives or discovering new things, may deny themselves safety or friendship in order to achieve knowledge, understanding or greater self-esteem.

However, criticisms aside, Maslow's theory does give us a way of looking at the whole person, whose physical, emotional and intellectual needs are all interrelated. Think about Maslow's hierarchy in reference to the following examples:

- A child whose feelings of safety and sense of belonging are threatened by divorce may have little interest in learning how to divide fractions.
- If school is a fearful, unpredictable place where neither teachers nor pupils know where they stand, they are likely to be more concerned with security and less with learning or teaching.
- Belonging to a social group and maintaining self-esteem within that group are important to learners. If doing what the teacher says conflicts with group rules, learners may choose to ignore the teacher's wishes or even defy the teacher.

Cognitive and social cognitive approaches to motivation

In cognitive theories, people are viewed as active and curious, searching for information to solve personally relevant problems. Thus, cognitive theorists emphasise intrinsic motivation. In many ways, cognitive theories of motivation developed as a reaction to the behavioural views. Cognitive theorists believe that behaviour is determined by our thinking, not simply by whether we have been rewarded or punished for the behaviour in the past (Stipek, 2002). Behaviour is initiated and regulated by plans (Miller, Galanter and Pribram, 1960), goals (Locke and Latham, 2002), schemas (Ortony, Clore and Collins, 1988), expectations (Vroom, 1964), and attributions (Weiner, 2000).

Theories that take into account *both* the behaviourists' concern with the effects or outcomes of behaviour *and* the cognitivists' interest in the impact of individual thinking are sometimes called **expectancy value theories** (Eccles, 1983). This means that motivation is seen as the product of two main forces: the individual's expectation of reaching a goal, and the value of that goal to him/her. In other words, the important questions are, 'If I try hard, can I succeed?' and 'If I succeed, will the outcome be valuable or rewarding to me?' Motivation is a product of these two forces, because if the answer to either question is 'no' there is no motivation to work towards the goal. For example, if I believe I have a good chance of selection for the badminton team (high expectation), and if making the team is very important to me (high value), then my motivation should be strong. However, if either factor is zero (if I believe I haven't a chance of making the team, or I couldn't care less about playing badminton), then my motivation will be zero too (Tollefson, 2000). The element of *cost* may also be added to the expectancy value model, as values have to be considered in relation to the cost of pursuing them. So, for example, this might be the amount of time or effort required, what the alternatives are, and what the risks of failure are (Wigfield and Eccles, 2002). The next approach focuses on the importance of the social context within motivation.

Sociocultural conceptions of motivation

Sociocultural views of motivation emphasise participation in 'communities of practice'. This means that people engage in activities to maintain their identities and their interpersonal relations within a community, which can be defined at many levels, such as a school, a family, a neighbourhood, and so on. Thus, learners are motivated to learn if they are members of a classroom or school community that values learning. Just as we learn through socialisation to speak or dress or order food in restaurants – by watching and learning from more capable members of the same culture – we also learn to be learners by watching and imitating members of our educational community. In other words, we learn by the company we keep (Hickey, 2003; Rogoff, Turkanis and Bartlett, 2001).

The concept of identity is central in sociocultural views of motivation. When we see ourselves as tennis players or sculptors or engineers or teachers or psychologists, we have an identity within a group. Part of our socialisation involves moving from legitimate peripheral participation to central participation in that group. **Legitimate peripheral participation** means that beginners are genuinely involved in the work of the group, even if their abilities are undeveloped and their contributions are comparatively small. The novice weaver learns to dye wool before spinning and weaving, and the novice teacher learns to tutor one child before working with the whole group. Each task is a piece of the work of the expert. The identities of both the novice and the expert are bound up in their participation in the community. They are both motivated to learn the values and practices of the community to maintain their identity as community members (Lave and Wenger, 1991).

The challenge in these approaches is to be sure that all learners are fully participating members of the community, because motivation comes from both identity and legitimate participation. Thus, engagement is 'meaningful participation in a context where to-be-learned knowledge is valued and used' (Hickey, 2003:411).

The behavioural, humanistic, cognitive and sociocultural approaches to motivation are summarised in Table 4.1. These theories differ in the ways in which they explain motivation, but each contributes in its own way towards a comprehensive understanding.

As we shall now see, most contemporary explanations of motivation include a discussion of personal factors such as learners' self-beliefs, as these are clearly important when considering their motivation to learn (Murphy and Alexander, 2000).

Table 4.1 **Four views of motivation**

	Behavioural	*Humanistic*	*Cognitive*	*Sociocultural*
Source of motivation	Extrinsic	Intrinsic	Intrinsic	Intrinsic
Important influences	Reinforcers, rewards, incentives and punishers	Need for self-esteem, self-fulfilment and self-determination	Beliefs, attributions for success and failure, expectations	Engaged participation in learning communities; maintaining identity through participation in activities of group
Key theorists	Skinner	Maslow Deci	Weiner Graham	Lave Wenger

Source: Woolfolk, Hughes and Walkup (2008) *Psychology in Education*, Table 10.1, p. 444.

Personal factors in motivation

Beliefs, goals, attributions and self-schemas

When ability is seen as fixed (this is known as entity theory) then learners are likely to see this as a stable, uncontrollable characteristic which is unchangeable ('I'm no good at spelling and there's nothing I can do about it'). Therefore, they are likely to set **performance goals** rather than **mastery goals** when engaging with learning tasks ('I must learn these words so that I don't look stupid in class'). Performance goals are concerned with being seen to perform well for an audience and avoid looking incompetent or unintelligent. However, if learners see ability as something which can be changed or is improvable (incremental theory) they may set mastery goals which involve getting to grips with the task and learning how to improve for their own sake rather than from concern about their audience ('I'm no good at spelling but I'll work hard to learn as I really need to get better'). They might not be too concerned about initial failure or being seen as incompetent as long as they are improving.

These ideas relate to learners' beliefs about the causes of success or failure and the control they have over learning. **Weiner's attribution theory** extends this and suggests that the way learners explain events (i.e. to what factors they *attribute* their successes and failures) influences their motivation and behaviour (Weiner, 1986, 1994, 2000). Most attributed causes of success or failure involve the source or *locus* of success or failure, the *stability* of it (whether it is long term or likely to change) and whether or not it is *controllable*. Most motivational problems occur when learners see failures as external (down to luck or the way of the world) uncontrollable events, in which case they are likely to become resigned and feel helpless. The concept of *learned helplessness* (Seligman, 1975), which is the expectation based on previous experiences that all one's efforts will fail, is relevant here as this links with beliefs about one's ability to succeed, and therefore motivation to attempt to learn.

Activity

Think back to the last assessment result you received (whether for a formal piece of written coursework or perhaps for some 'real-world' demand such as an interview or driving test).

Make a note of how you explained this outcome to yourself. To what factors did you *attribute* this outcome? Link these with some of the ideas from Weiner's theory and think about your *locus of control*. Does this apply to most test/assessment situations? Is it helpful for your continued engagement with achieving the outcome? Or are you feeling there is little to be done about this because it is always the case (learned helplessness)?

You may have identified some of the factors discussed such as *locus of control*, *stability* and *controllability*.

Both attributions and self-efficacy interact in the learning situation. **Self-efficacy** is a term used to describe how competent individuals view themselves in particular situations, so this may apply to learning different subjects or tackling different types of problem. For example, a learner may say, 'I'm pretty good at science generally, so I know I failed this time because I didn't check my answers' (which would signify *high* self-efficacy). Alternatively, they may think, 'I just can't do science and I'll never be able to learn' (suggesting they have *low* self-efficacy).

Beliefs about self-worth are connected with and underpin attributions and self-efficacy. Covington (1992) suggests there are three types of learner motivational sets:

- **mastery-oriented learners** who value achievement, see ability as improvable and have a low fear of failure;
- **failure-avoiding learners** who have a high fear of failure, set performance goals and stick to what they know;
- **failure-accepting learners** who believe that they fail because of low ability and that there is little they can do to change this.

Within the learning situation

There are a range of challenges which teachers face as they try to identify the different types of leaner, and encourage self-efficacy and self-worth. For example, within statutory education (up to the age of 16 in the UK) attendance is compulsory, classes may be large, classrooms are public places where students are assessed and there are strict routines to keep to. Within post-compulsory situations a different set of 'rules' and conditions apply: mature learners may lack self-esteem, have difficulties in managing financially and domestically, or lack adequate time to commit to their studies. However, if teachers are to encourage motivation to learn they need to involve learners productively in tasks, so that they develop internal motivation to learn as a trait (intrinsic), and think deeply (cognitively) about them. The **academic tasks** which are set for learners have different values, depending upon their expectations of success and the value they place upon this success. Eccles and Wigfield (2001) suggest that tasks have four elements which are relevant to motivation: *importance* (does doing well on this matter?); *interest* (is it enjoyable or have intrinsic value?); *utility* (will it help to achieve a goal?) and *cost* (will it make me look stupid or leave less time for a desired activity?). These illustrate the complex way in which personal and environmental influences constantly interact.

Currently within education there is interest in the use of **authentic tasks** to encourage motivation. These tasks have connections with 'real-world' or everyday situations, and are likely to be more meaningful and interesting to some learners than academic tasks, which they may perceive as irrelevant. Authentic tasks involve problem-solving, which means that learners are required to think deeply about what they are doing, and become more autonomous by making decisions about what should be done and finding solutions in given situations.

As we saw at the start of the chapter in Case study 4.1, supporting **autonomy** is a key aspect of the teacher's role. However, choice is not the norm within educational settings, where most of the time teachers rather than students are the ones 'in charge' even though this is at odds with numerous theories and research which argue that a sense of internal locus of control and self-determination are critical for developing learners' intrinsic motivation. However, providing unbounded choices may be frightening to some learners (Dyson, 1997), so clearly there do need to be some boundaries. A compromise may be to present a range of options, and offer within that some potential for personal choice (as in the case study, where learners were given a specific problem to solve, but were allowed to determine their own way of solving it). Of course, there are differences between learners, and some students are likely to want and need more support and guidance than others. It is important, then, for the teacher to be sensitive to their needs, providing reassurance and support where necessary for those who may be scared of working on their own initiative but allowing those who are ready for more autonomy to take charge.

Recognising achievement is also important for improvement, persistence and creativity, both in terms of personal achievement and for making comparisons with other learners. Feedback given should be specific and realistic to achieve a positive effect (Smith, 2005), but praise for its own sake, which lacks credibility, is too frequent or mistimed, may not be effective (see Chapter 5 for more on this).

Strategies to encourage motivation and learning

Theories and research into motivation and learning can be drawn together in order to inform practice. Four basic conditions emerge which provide the foundation for strategies to be put into place:

1 Organised teaching space with minimal interruptions.
2 Patient and supportive teacher who avoids humiliating learners for making mistakes. Mistakes should be seen as a normal and necessary part of learning (Clifford, 1990, 1991).
3 The work must be challenging but reasonable – if it is too difficult or easy, learners will be less motivated to learn and will be more likely to complete work quickly rather than engage with it fully.
4 Learning tasks should be authentic and have meaning for learners (Stipek, 1993).

Until these basic conditions have been met it is unlikely that any motivational strategies will succeed and even then the effects which teachers might have upon learners' motivation are influenced by the following questions learners might be asking themselves, consciously or unconsciously:

- Can I succeed at this task?
- Do I want to succeed?
- What do I need to do to succeed?
- What will be the cost of my engaging with this task?

Teachers wish to encourage confidence in learners so that they approach their work with enthusiasm and energy. They will want them to see the value of the task and make an effort to learn for its own sake rather than to earn a reward or finish it quickly. Teachers want to encourage learners to have self-belief and recognise that they will succeed if they use appropriate strategies rather than use self-defeating strategies which confirm their inability to learn.

Conclusion

This chapter has considered a range of psychological theories and models which are used to apply to education and the learning situation. Beginning with an outline of some of the connections and tensions between learning and education the chapter then moved on to provide discussion of behavioural approaches to learning which stress the role of the environment. Theories such as classical and operant conditioning were considered in terms of informing teachers' understanding of learners' responses to learning. Cognitive views such as those by Piaget and Vygotsky were seen as important to teachers' understanding of the way that human thinking develops and these were followed by more current views which compare human thinking with computers in order to examine the way that information is processed by individuals. The role of memory is particularly important here for teachers as it provides insights into capacity, storage and retrieval of information and suggests ways of facilitating learning. The chapter then moved on to discuss the close interaction between the brain and learning, drawing upon research which reports changes in the brain following learning and considering ways in which teachers can support this. The controversial notion of intelligence and testing is presented with models of multiple intelligences leading to a critical discussion of learning preferences. Theoretical accounts of motivation (behavioural, humanistic, cognitive, social cognitive and sociocultural) were discussed in terms of their usefulness for educators before moving on to the importance of personal factors in motivation such as beliefs, goals, attributions and views of the self. The chapter concluded by drawing together the conditions necessary for educators to encourage motivation. There is a more detailed discussion of applying psychology to behaviour within the learning situation in the chapters which follow in this part: 'Understanding and managing the behaviour of learners' and 'Communication and change'.

Case study 4.2
Putting learning theory to the test

Marilena is a fairly quiet person who has joined an evening class at a college of further education in order to improve her basic skills. She lacks confidence in her oral abilities and is in a state of high anxiety about her first assessment task which involves students preparing a five-minute presentation about an item of current news. Marilena is sure that she will fail in this task because she always finds herself stammering and blushing when she has to speak in a group situation. She remembers only too clearly the first time that she had to speak in front of a class when she was at primary school. On this occasion the teacher had become impatient with Marilena because she was so timid that no one could hear her voice. She had told her that if she did not 'speak up' she would have to stay in at playtime and despite the fact that Marilena had tried to speak louder the rest of the class had started giggling and she could not be heard. This had resulted in not only her but the whole class being kept in and many of the children had been angry and unkind after that and teased her to the point of bullying. From that time onwards she had always avoided similar situations and she now thinks to herself, 'I hate public speaking. I'm not sure I can do this. Why can't this be a written report? Perhaps I just won't come next week.'

Question for discussion

1 *Review this chapter and consider which theories/concepts might be helpful in understanding and supporting Marilena's learning and development.*

Summary

Behavioural views of learning

Behavioural learning theories assume that the outcome of learning is a change in behaviour, and stress the effects of external events upon individuals. The role of *conditioning* is seen as critical within behavioural approaches, which are based on the work of key theorists such as Ivan Pavlov (1927) and B.F. Skinner (1953). *Classical conditioning* involves learning by association and helps to explain involuntary responses to various situations. Operant conditioning focuses on ways in which behaviour is strengthened or weakened by the events that go before it or the consequences which follow it.

Cognitive views of learning

Cognitive theorists view learners as being at the centre of their own learning rather than responding to the rewards and punishments around them. Piaget's theory of cognitive development suggests that children and young people develop their cognitive abilities in stages. Vygotsky's sociocultural approach suggests that our activities must be understood within the context of our cultural setting and our interactions with others. In particular, Vygotsky stressed the importance of language in cognitive development, and defined the distance between a

▶

person's *actual* developmental level and their *potential* developmental level as the zone of proximal development (ZPD). Information processing approaches suggest that it is useful to consider similarities between the mind and a computer, and emphasise the role of memory in learning.

The brain and cognitive development

Both biological factors (which are the result of nature) and experiential ones (the result of nurture) are involved in the development of the human brain. Research from animal and human studies shows that both experiences and direct teaching cause changes in the organisation and structure of the brain.

Intelligence

Gardner's model of multiple intelligences suggests that intelligence is both a biological and a psychological potential to solve problems. This relates to the notion of emotional intelligence (EI).

Learning preferences

Individuals who have a *deep processing approach* see the learning activities as a means for understanding some underlying concepts or meanings, perhaps by relating to their own experience. Learners who take a *surface processing* approach focus on memorising the learning materials, rather than understanding them.

Motivation

Motivation is usually defined as *an internal state that arouses, directs and maintains behaviour.* A classic distinction in motivation is between intrinsic and extrinsic, the difference being whether the locus of causality for the action (the location of the cause) is inside or outside the person. Behavioural approaches to motivation focus on rewards and incentives. Humanistic approaches, such as Maslow's hierarchy of needs, focus on the individual and the fulfilment of one's potential as motivation. Sociocultural views of motivation emphasise participation in 'communities of practice'.

Personal factors in motivation

Beliefs, goals, attributions and self-schemas relate to learners' beliefs about the causes of success or failure and the control they have over learning. Theories and research into motivation and learning can be drawn together in order to inform practice.

References

Atkinson, R.C. and Shiffrin, R.M. (1968) Human memory: A proposed system and its control processes, in K. Spence and J. Spence (eds) *The psychology of learning and motivation*, 2, pp. 89–195, New York: Academic Press.

Bacchus, J.R., Baldwin, M.W. and Packer, D.J. (2004) Increasing implicit self-esteem through classical conditioning, *Psychological Science*, 15(7), pp. 498–502.

Bradley, P. (2003) *Emotional Intelligence,* Report to Executive Member for Education and Lifelong Learning, available at www.portsmouth.gov.uk/media/ecll20040106r_item04.pdf.

Bransford, J., Brown, A. and Cocking, R. (2000) How People Learn: Brain, mind, experience and school, Washington: National Academy Press.

Brophy, J.E. (1988) On motivating students, in D. Berliner and B. Rosenshine (eds) *Talks to teachers,* pp. 201–45, New York: Random House.

Brophy, J.E. (2003) An interview with Jere Brophy by B. Gaedke and M. Shaughnessy.

Bruer, John T. (1999) In search of . . . brain-based education, *Phi Delta Kappan,* 80, pp. 648–57.

Campbell, R., MacSweeney, C. and Waters, D. (2007) Sign language and the brain: A review, *The Journal of Deaf Studies and Deaf Education,* 13(1), pp. 3–20.

Clifford, M.M. (1990) Students need challenge, not easy success, *Educational Leadership,* 48(1), pp. 22–26.

Clifford, M.M. (1991) Risk taking: Empirical and educational considerations, *Educational Psychologist,* 26, pp. 263–98.

Coffield, F.J., Moseley, D.V., Hall, E. and Ecclestone, K. (2004) *Learning styles and pedagogy in post-16 learning: A systematic and critical review,* London: Learning and Skills Research Centre/University of Newcastle upon Tyne.

Covington, M.V. (1992) *Making the grade: A self-worth perspective on motivation and school reform,* New York: Holt, Rinehart & Winston.

Covington, M.V. and Mueller, K.J. (2001) Intrinsic versus extrinsic motivation: An approach/avoidance reformulation, *Education Psychology Review,* 13, pp. 157–76.

Cowley, S. (2003a) *Sue Cowley's teaching clinic,* London: Continuum.

Cowley, S. (2003b) *How to survive your first year in teaching,* 2nd edn, London: Continuum.

Cowley, S. (2006) *Getting the buggers to behave,* 3rd edn, London: Continuum.

Deci, E.L. and Ryan, R.M. (1985) *Intrinsic motivation and self-determination in human behavior,* New York: Plenum.

Driscoll, M.P. (2005) *Psychology of learning for instruction,* 3rd edn, Boston: Allyn & Bacon.

Dunn, R., Beaudry, J.S. and Klavas, A. (1989) Survey of research on learning styles, *Educational Leadership,* 47(7), pp. 50–58.

Dunn, R., Dunn, K. and Price, G.E. (1984) *Learning Style Inventory,* Lawrence, KS: Price Systems.

Dunn, R., Dunn, K. and Price, G.E. (2000) *Learning Style Inventory,* Lawrence, KS: Price Systems.

Dunn, R. and Griggs, S. (2003) *Synthesis of the Dunn and Dunn Learning-Style Model Research: Who, what, when, where, and so what?* New York: St. John's University.

Eccles, J. (1983) Expectancies, values and academic behaviours, in J.T. Spence (ed.) *Achievement and achievement motives,* pp. 75–146, San Francisco: Freeman.

Dyson, A.H. (1997) *Writing superheroes: Contemporary childhood, popular culture, and classroom literacy,* New York: Teachers College Press.

Eccles, J.S. and Wigfield, A. (2001) Academic Achievement Motivation, Development of, in N.J. Smelser and P.B. Baltes (eds) *International encyclopedia of the social & behavioral sciences,* pp. 14–20, Oxford, UK: Pergamon.

Gagne, E.D. (1985) *The cognitive psychology of school learning,* Boston: Little, Brown.

Gardner, H. (1998) A multiplicity of intelligences, *Scientific American Presents,* 9(4), pp. 18–23.

Gardner, H. (2003, 21 April). *Multiple intelligence after twenty years,* Paper presented at the American Educational Research Association, Chicago, Illinois.

Graham, S. (1996) How causal beliefs influence the academic and social motivation of African-American children, in G.G. Brannigan (ed.) *The enlightened educator: Research adventures in the schools,* pp. 111–26, New York: McGraw-Hill.

Graham, S. (1998) Self-blame and peer victimization in middle school: An attributional analysis, *Developmental Psychology,* 34, pp. 587–99.

Graham, S. and Weiner, B. (1996) Theories and principles of motivation, in D. Berliner and R.C. Calfee (eds) *Handbook of educational psychology,* pp. 63–84, New York: Macmillan.

Gredler, M.E. (2005) *Learning and instruction: Theory into practice,* 5th edn, Boston: Allyn & Bacon.

Gregorc, A.F. (1982) *Gregorc Style Delineator: Development, technical, and administrative manual,* Maynard, MA: Gabriel Systems.

Hickey, D.T. (2003) Engaged participation vs. marginal non-participation: A stridently sociocultural model of achievement motivation, *Elementary School Journal,* 103(4), pp. 401–29.

Hill, W.F. (2002) *Learning: A survey of psychological interpretations,* 7th edn, Boston: Allyn & Bacon.

Izard, C.E. (2001) Emotional intelligence or adaptive emotions? *Emotion,* 1, pp. 249–57.

Keefe, J.W. (1982) Assessing student learning styles: An overview, in *Student learning styles and brain behavior.* Reston, VA: National Association of Secondary School Principals.

Keefe, J.W. and Monk, J.S. (1986) *Learning style profile examiner's manual,* Reston, VA: National Association of Secondary School Principals.

Kolb, D. (1985) *Learning style inventory*, Boston: McBer & Company.

Kozulin, A. (ed.) (2003) *Vygotsky's educational theory in cultural context*, Cambridge, UK: Cambridge University Press.

Lave, J. and Wenger, E. (1991) *Situated learning: Legitimate peripheral participation,* Cambridge, MA: Cambridge University Press.

Locke, E.A. and Latham, G.P. (2002) Building a practically useful theory of goal setting and task motivation: A 35-year odyssey, *American Psychologist,* 57, pp. 705–17.

Lovelace, M.K. (2005) Meta-analysis of experimental research based on the Dunn and Dunn Model, *The Journal of Educational Research,* 98, pp. 176–83.

Maslow, A.H. (1968) *Toward a psychology of being,* 2nd edn, New York: Van Nostrand.

Maslow, A.H. (1970) *Motivation and personality,* 2nd edn, New York: Harper & Row.

Mayer, J.D. and Cobb, C.D. (2000) Educational policy on emotional intelligence: Does it make sense? *Educational Psychology Review,* 12, pp. 163–83.

Mayer, J. and Salovey, P. (1997) *Emotional Development and Emotional Intelligence: Educational Implications,* New York: Basic Books. (Available at http://eqi.org/4bmodel.htm)

Meece, J.L. (2002) *Child and adolescent development for educators*, 2nd edn, New York: McGraw-Hill.

Menzies, R. (1937) Conditioned vasomotor responses in human subjects, *Journal of Psychology,* 4, pp. 75–120.

Miller, G.A., Galanter, E. and Pribram, K.H. (1960) *Plans and the structure of behavior,* New York: Holt, Rinehart & Winston.

Murphy, P.K. and Alexander, P.A. (2000) A motivated exploration of motivation terminology, *Contemporary Educational Psychology,* 25, pp. 3–53.

Neisser, U. (1976) *Cognition and reality,* San Francisco: Freeman.

Nestor-Baker, N.S. (1999) *Tacit knowledge in the superintendency: An exploratory analysis,* unpublished doctoral dissertation, the Ohio State University, Columbus, OH.

Ortony, A., Clore, G.L. and Collins, A. (1988) *The cognitive structure of emotions,* Cambridge: Cambridge University Press.

Pavlov, I.P. (1927) *Conditioned reflexes: An investigation of the physiological activity of the cerebral cortex*, translated and edited by G.V. Anrep, London: Oxford University Press. Available at http://psychclassics.yorku.ca/ Pavlov/lecture10.htm.

Petrides, K., Frederickson, N. and Furnham, A. (2004) The role of trait emotional intelligence in academic performance and deviant behaviour at school, *Personality and Individual Differences,* 36, pp. 277–93.

Piaget, J. (1954) *The construction of reality in the child* (M. Cook, Trans.), New York: Basic Books.

Piaget, J. (1963) *Origins of intelligence in children,* New York: Norton.

Reeve, J. (1996) *Motivating others: Nurturing inner motivational resources,* Boston: Allyn & Bacon.

Pintrich, P.R., Marx, R.W. and Boyle, R.A. (1993) Beyond cold conceptual change: The role of motivational beliefs and classroom contextual factors in the process of conceptual change, *Review of Educational Research,* 63, pp. 167–99.

Reeve, J. (1996) *Motivating others: Nurturing inner motivational resources,* Boston: Allyn & Bacon.

Rogers, B. (2000) *Behaviour management: A whole school approach,* London: Chapman.

Rogers, B. (2002) (ed.) *Teacher leadership and behaviour management,* London: Paul Chapman.

Rogers, B. (2004) (ed.) *How to manage children's challenging behaviour,* London: Paul Chapman.

Rogers, B. (2006) *Classroom behaviour,* 2nd edn, London: Paul Chapman.

Rogers, C.R. (1969) *Freedom to learn: A view of what education might become,* Columbus, OH: Charles Merrill.

Rogoff, B., Turkanis, C.G. and Bartlett, L. (2001) *Learning together: Children and adults in a school community,* New York: Oxford.

Sattler, J.M. (2001) *Assessment of children: Cognitive applications,* 4th edn, San Diego, CA: Jerome M. Sattler, Inc.

Seligman, M. (1975) *Helplessness: On depression, development, and death,* San Francisco: Freeman.

Shaywitz, B.A., Shaywitz, S.E., Pugh, K.R., Mencl, W.E., Fulbright, R.K. and Skudlarksi, P. (2004) Development of left occipitotemporal systems for skilled reading in children after a phonologically-based intervention, *Biological Psychiatry,* 55, pp. 926–33.

Skinner, B.F. (1953) *Science and human behavior,* New York: Macmillan.

Smith, C. (2005) *Pupil motivation inquiry: Response from members of the eppi review of motivation group,* available at http://www.scottish.parliament.uk/business/committees/education/inquiries/pmi/University%20of%20Glasgow.pdf.

Snider, V.E. (1990) What we know about learning styles from research in special education, *Educational Leadership,* 48(2), p. 53.

Snow, R.E., Corno, L. and Jackson, D. (1996) Individual differences in affective and cognitive functions, in D. Berliner and R. Calfee (eds) *Handbook of educational psychology,* pp. 243–310, New York: Macmillan.

Stahl, S.A. (2002) Different strokes for different folks? In L. Abbeduto (ed.) *Taking sides: Clashing on controversial issues in educational psychology,* pp. 98–107, Guilford: McGraw-Hill.

Stipek, D.J. (1993) *Motivation to learn,* 2nd edn, Boston: Allyn & Bacon.

Stipek, D.J. (2002) *Motivation to learn: Integrating theory and practice,* 4th edn, Boston: Allyn & Bacon.

Sylvester, R. (2003) *A biological brain in a cultural classroom,* 2nd edn, Thousand Oaks, CA: Sage.

Tollefson, N. (2000) Classroom applications of cognitive theories of motivation, *Education Psychology Review,* 12, pp. 63–83.

Torrance, E.P. (1986) Teaching creative and gifted learners, in M. Wittrock (ed.) *Handbook of research on teaching,* 3rd edn, pp. 630–47, New York: Macmillan.

Van Der Stuyf, R. (2002) Scaffolding as a teaching strategy, *Adolescent Learning and Development,* Section 0500A, November 2002.

Vroom, V. (1964) *Work and motivation,* New York: Wiley.

Vygotsky, L.S. (1978) *Mind in society: The development of higher mental process,* Cambridge, MA: Harvard University Press.

Vygotsky, L.S. (1986) *Thought and language,* Cambridge, MA: MIT Press.

Vygotsky, L.S. (1987) The genetic roots of thinking and speech, in R.W. Rieber and A.S. Carton (eds) *Problems of general psychology, Vol. 1, Collected works,* pp. 101–20, New York: Plenum. (Work originally published in 1934.)

Weinberger, D. (2001) A brain too young for good judgment *The New York Times,* 10 March, p. A13.

Weiner, B. (1986) *An attributional theory of motivation and emotion,* New York: Springer.

Weiner, B. (1994) Ability versus effort revisited: The moral determinants of achievement evaluation an achievement as a moral system, *Educational Psychologist,* 29, pp. 163–72.

Weiner, B. (2000) Interpersonal and intrapersonal theories of motivation from an attributional perspective, *Educational Psychology Review,* 12, pp. 1–14.

White, J. (2004) Howard Gardner: The myth of multiple intelligences. Lecture at Institute of Education, University of London, 17 November 2004. Available at http://k1.ioe.ac.uk/schools/mst/LTU/phil/HowardGardner_171104.pdf.

Wigfield, A. and Eccles, J. (2002) The development of competence beliefs, expectancies of success, and achievement values from childhood through adolescence, in A. Wigfield and J. Eccles (eds) *Development of achievement motivation,* pp. 91–120, San Diego: Academic Press.

Wintergerst, A.C., DeCapua, A. and Itzen, R.C. (2001) The construct validity of one learning styles instrument, *System,* 29(3) pp. 385–403.

Woolfolk, A., Hughes, M. and Walkup, V. (2008), *Psychology in Education,* Harlow: Pearson Education.

5

Understanding and managing the behaviour of learners

Ann Kenny

Contents

Introduction

What is the relationship between learning and behaviour? Why do some pupils apparently seek to sabotage their own learning? Why are some teachers better than others at managing pupil behaviour? Is it to do with experience, personality, the ability to form relationships, or are they just more interesting as people? Does this make them 'better' teachers than those who struggle to manage learner behaviour?

In a moment, you will read a case study which embodies some of these complexities, for example, the nature of the curriculum, the effectiveness of the teacher, learners' willingness to engage, and teachers' feelings about pupils. But such questions have no simple answers: classrooms are complex social environments, where wider social and political influences interact with the organisational structure of the school and informal group processes to influence behavioural outcomes.

This chapter introduces you to some of the current issues around the management of behaviour. Although the chapter refers to behaviour in schools, the ideas have a much wider application which also includes **post-compulsory education, further education** colleges, universities and beyond. The chapter considers the contribution of psychology to some of the strategies suggested to improve behaviour. We begin by looking at some of the psychological approaches to behaviour management: behavioural, cognitive and humanistic. The chapter then looks at behaviour management policies, and examines the role played by government. It then focuses on practical behaviour management approaches, and attempts to grapple with the question of why some learners misbehave. We do not set out to offer you easy answers, but we do attempt to introduce you to some interesting debates in the area.

This chapter aims to:

- Introduce some of the main psychological theories and approaches to behaviour management.

- Identify some of the key policies which influence behaviour management in schools and other learning environments today.

- Explore behaviour management in practice, with particular reference to the whole school approach.

- Describe and evaluate the whole school approach.

Case study 5.1
Managing behaviour in and out of class

Sixteen pupils are present for the Year 9 maths class. The session has been running for twenty-five minutes of a one-hour lesson. Each pupil has been given their own workbook and worksheets with clear instructions for the lesson. The teacher is talking with three boys, explaining the task again, and working through an example with them. The room appears calm, with small groups of young people sitting and talking quietly. However, about half of the group are off task.

Peter is sitting at the back of the classroom on his own; he is leaning forward on his table and appears to be writing. He is sitting quietly, listening to his iPod on earphones.

Two girls sitting near the window, shout across to the teacher: 'Sir, sir, the sun is my eyes and I can't see!'

Without waiting for a reply, one of the girls, Alison, stands on the desk and starts to pull the blinds down. Rachel shouts out: 'It's too dark, sir!'

Alison shouts, 'Shut your gob, you bitch!'

The teacher calmly asks Alison to sit down and get on with her work.

'But she called me a bitch, sir!'

The teacher calmly asks Rachel to get on with her work.

'She's a bitch, sir!'

The teacher responds by saying, 'OK, OK that's enough.'

The teacher returns to working with the three boys.

Two girls at the back shout: 'Sir, we've been waiting for ages!'

The teacher asks Peter to take his earphones out and put his iPod away, so that he can get on with the work that has been set. Peter does as he is told and waits for an opportunity to put his earphones back in. The lesson continues like this until five minutes before the end, when pupils start to pack up their things to go to their next lesson before being asked to do so by the teacher.

Rachel looks at her mobile phone; she has a message which reads: BITCH.

'Sir, she called me a bitch!'

'No I didn't!' shouts Alison.

As the children file out of the classroom into the corridor, they join other children who are going downstairs for the next lesson. There is some pushing and jostling as the children change classrooms to go to their English class. Children recognise each other, shout out greetings and stop and chat. Mrs Jones, the English teacher, is standing at her door waiting for her class of twenty-eight children to arrive. As they arrive at their desks the noise levels are high. The teacher begins to settle the class by greeting children as they come in. She greets Peter, enquiring jokingly whether his iPod is in his bag. She asks him to hand out some worksheets which he appears happy to do. Rachel comes in and sits at the opposite side of the room to Alison. Rachel gets out her mobile phone. Mrs Jones asks her to put it away. Rachel shouts out, 'I just wanted to show you this, Miss – Alison called me a bitch.' This causes the other children to laugh and shout out, increasing the level of noise.

'No I didn't, Miss!' shouts Alison from the other side of the room.

'Rachel, turn your phone off now and put it on my desk.'

'But that's not fair, Miss!'

'I said *now*, Rachel.'

Rachel walks resentfully to the teacher and hands her the phone.

Mrs Jones starts to explain the task she wants the children to complete; the class settles quickly and the pupils get on with their work.

Questions for discussion

1 *Make a list of the behaviours that you think are unacceptable in both classes.*

2 *Why do some pupils actively disengage from particular subjects?*

3 *Is quiet disengagement (like Peter's) a behavioural problem?*

4 *How can teachers deal with persistent attention-seeking behaviour?*

5 *Who is responsible for behaviour in the corridors, toilets, outside/off-limit space and the playground?*

6 *Why does the behaviour from the maths class continue between lessons and into the next session?*

Psychological approaches to behaviour management

The behavioural approach to managing behaviour

The **behavioural approach** assumes that behaviour can be controlled; it is simply a matter of finding the right formula. The origin of these ideas comes from B.F. Skinner (1904–1990) and his work on operant conditioning (see Chapter 4). Behaviourists point out that behaviour has consequences: individuals are more likely to repeat behaviour if it is rewarded in some way. **Reinforcement** is used to shape behaviour, placing the emphasis on positive praise. Individuals will also tend to want to avoid negative consequences, like being removed from their social group. Behavioural approaches attempt to make clear and explicit what behaviours are unacceptable, and to communicate that certain behaviours have consequences.

Landrum and Kauffman (2006) hold that the application of behavioural strategies to school and classroom management involve five basic operations:

1 Positive reinforcement.
2 Negative reinforcement.
3 Extinction.
4 Response cost.
5 Punishment.

Let us now look at each of these operations in turn.

Positive reinforcement

Positive reinforcement occurs when something that follows behaviour increases the chances of the behaviour occurring again. This is generally referred to as a reward, and can take the form of an object (a sticker with a smiley face), an activity (extra playtime), or a gesture (a smile or praise):

> The premise of the technique is straightforward: teachers attend positively to students when they are engaged in desired, appropriate task related activity or social behaviour.
>
> Landrum and Kauffman, 2006:48

Madsen et al. (1968) conducted research in an American primary school from November to the end of the school year, and wanted to determine the effects of classroom behaviour by looking at three conditions.

1 Classroom rules.
2 Rules, plus ignoring inappropriate behaviour.
3 Rules, plus ignoring inappropriate behaviour, plus praising appropriate behaviour.

The research concluded that rules alone exerted little effect on classroom behaviour. Ignoring inappropriate behaviour and showing approval for appropriate behaviour were very effective in achieving better classroom behaviour. Showing approval for appropriate behaviour was seen as the most effective approach in changing classroom behaviour. Madsen argues that the implications for the study are that:

> teachers can be taught systematic procedures and can use them to gain more effective behaviours from students.
>
> Madsen et al., 1968:150

Madsen's research highlights some of the problems of using behavioural techniques: they are time consuming and require a high degree of expertise. Ignoring the behaviour of a difficult child can cause problems for other children in understanding what is expected of them.

Sometimes a whole class or group can be rewarded. Canter and Canter (2001) point out that the goal of a **whole class approach** is to get the group to work towards a reward that will be given to the entire class. This can help the teacher to find a solution to a problem the class is experiencing:

> A classwide recognition system is particularly effective when working on specific classwide problem behaviour. Such a problem might be students noisily entering the classroom after lunch, or students having trouble concentrating on the assigned work during small-group activities.
>
> Canter and Canter, 2001:54

One way of devising a simple tracking system for younger learners is to put a 'marble in the jar' every time the desirable behaviour is observed. When the jar is full, the whole class get a reward. Teachers need to be skilled observers to make this work well; otherwise some children can end up feeling aggrieved that their good behaviour has not been recognised. However, positive reinforcement is not always effective: children can become praise dependent, focusing on the reward itself rather than understanding why they are receiving it. Hanko (1994) describes how children with low self-esteem may refuse praise to ensure that they avoid the risk of failing again. Teachers can find it difficult to give positive praise; Shores et al. (1993) point out that teachers tend to display higher rates of disapproval compared with approval.

Negative reinforcement

Individuals are more likely to avoid behaviour if it has negative consequences. Negative reinforcement involves the removal or avoidance of a stimulus that students find unpleasant. For example, telling a group of students they will fail their GCSEs if they do not complete their homework is a negative reinforcement. The teacher wants the group to work harder, but rather than stressing the potential rewards of hard work, she highlights the negative consequences. Failure is the negative consequence which students will want to avoid by completing their homework. Landrum and Kaufman (2006) stress that negative reinforcement is a 'powerful behavioural operation' but it is not, and perhaps should not, be built into behaviour management plans. Instead, educational professionals should be aware of the potential of negatively reinforcing events and try to avoid them. Teachers may inadvertently reinforce behaviours by giving attention to unwanted behaviour because it is sometimes difficult to ignore some behaviours; for example,

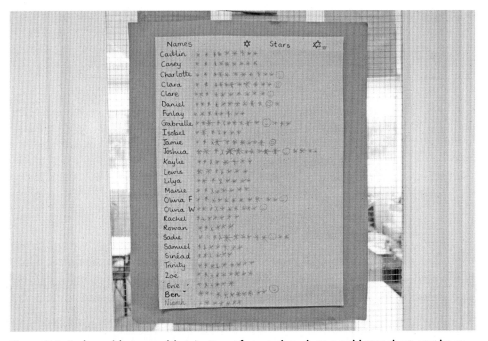

Figure 5.1 A classwide recognition system of reward, such as a gold star chart, can be a powerful positive reinforcer

Source: Pearson Education Ltd./Jules Selmes.

if a child is disruptive in maths because he/she does not like it or finds it too difficult, and is sent out of the class, then the behaviour is rewarded because the child has managed to avoid something he/she does not like or finds unpleasant. In this case the behaviour is likely to occur again because it has been negatively reinforced. Although Landrum and Kaufman (2006) stress that negative reinforcement should not be used as part of a discipline policy, it is often used informally by teachers. Students can feel unfairly treated if they are subjected to negative reinforcement such as threats or expressions of disapproval. Miller et al. (2002) in their research found that there was agreement among pupils, who felt that the main cause of pupil misbehaviour was the unfairness of teachers' actions.

Extinction

Extinction occurs when a conditioned response is either reduced or disappears. Behaviour will decrease when the reinforcement that has been maintaining it is removed. Extinction is often used in the classroom to reduce the attention a teacher gives to a pupil who misbehaves. **Planned ignoring** is a strategy that is used to reduce or change behaviour. Extinction is useful in reducing negative behaviours like shouting out answers rather than the student raising their hand and waiting to be asked. This behaviour may inadvertently have been reinforced through teachers responding to it, or asking the student not to shout out. **Tactical ignoring** when the student is shouting out while responding positively when the appropriate behaviour is displayed should, according to Madsen et al. (1968), reduce the behaviour. The problem is that some types of behaviour that are dangerous or unacceptable cannot simply be ignored. Disruptive behaviour ignored by the teacher can be reinforced by the rest of the class, which means that ignoring will have no effect. Alberto and Troutman (2009) point out that, as well as extinction taking a long time to change behaviour, it is also difficult to implement. It may also have the effect of encouraging even more of the behaviour the teacher wishes to extinguish.

Response cost punishment

This occurs when a penalty is applied every time behaviour is repeated. In **response cost punishment** a previously earned reinforcer can be removed. A child who has earned several stars for producing good work may have one removed for talking when they have been asked to stop. This enables the teacher to address problems immediately. Alberto and Troutman (2009) liken response cost programming to a system of fines. However, students who do not get many positive reinforcements 'like marbles in the jar' may become frustrated and feel they have nothing left to lose. Ellis and Tod (2009) express scepticism about removing rewards, and suggest that rewards, once given, should not be taken away:

> Our argument is that any reward given is for the piece of positive behaviour that has occurred and any subsequent misbehaviour does not change that fact. To remove the reward effectively sends the message that the earlier positive behaviour counted for nothing.
>
> Ellis and Tod, 2009:155

Punishment

A punishment occurs when something aversive happens after behaviour. This lowers the probability of the behaviour being repeated. Punishments are often regarded as a last resort in dealing with behaviour problems. Punishments in schools can range from mild aversives like reprimanding the student, which is likely to cause emotional discomfort, to harsher approaches which involve the removal of the student from the social group, for example isolation and **exclusion** from school. For a punishment to be effective it should be given as soon after the offence as possible, be appropriate and be unpleasant. However, some pupils see getting a detention or being sent out of the room as a badge of honour which contributes to their status.

Kyriacou (2009) stresses the point that the use of punishments does not deal with the causes of misbehaviour and offers extremely poor models of human relationships to children. Punishments carry risks that students may retaliate and increase negative behaviours. Children can simply learn not to repeat the behaviour when the person who applied the punishment is present. Therefore, the behaviour can be repeated in a different context, confirming that the child has not changed the behaviour (Alberto and Troutman, 2009).

Later in the chapter, we will return to some specific behavioural approaches to examine them in more depth. First though, it is important to recognise that behavioural theory is just one way of looking at managing behaviour. Critics of behavioural theory would argue that to portray people as simply responding to stimuli on the basis of sanctions and rewards reduces the rich complexity of human creativity to simple responses based on environmental conditions. As we shall see, other approaches emphasise internal influences on behaviour, like thinking (cognition) and emotion.

Controversies

'The behavioural approach should be put to practical use to manage the behaviour of learners'

Agree:

- Schools need clear guidelines about rules, rewards and sanctions to ensure that everybody is clear about what is expected of them. All children have the potential to misbehave and they need be controlled. Their behaviour should be conditioned by their environment so that they learn to behave in ways that are acceptable. It is the role of the school and the teacher to create the correct environmental conditions, by using both positive and negative reinforcement.

- Research in behavioural psychology using animals like rats and pigeons can provide insight into human behaviour because they have similar physiological imperatives like the need to eat and drink. Like humans, they have to adapt to their environment: this means they inevitably have to learn new behaviours.

- You can learn a lot about behaviour by simply observing what children actually do – how they think or feel is not central. Observation helps us to avoid prejudice and stereotyping because it involves objectively measuring what people actually do and therefore approaches problems in a much more scientific way. This approach empowers teachers by letting them assert their authority, enabling them to seek solutions to behavioural problems.

Disagree:

- Teachers undergo training to enable them to make professional judgements; they should not be straitjacketed into organisational structures that can undermine their autonomy.

- Children are inherently good. They develop the social skills they need through interaction with others. Children have the potential to think for themselves and to exercise judgement, which enables them to develop self-discipline; it is the role of the school and the teacher to foster this.

- You cannot fully understand human behaviour through observation; it is important to understand how children think and feel.

- Humans are very different from animals; it is not possible to understand complex social behaviour, like free will, by looking at rats and pigeons.

- These traditional approaches to learning, which are based on crude methods of authority and control, are outmoded and simply encourage conformity. In a society that increasingly demands flexible and creative workers with sophisticated social skills, these behavioural approaches have no place. In fact they are repressive, authoritarian and damaging to children's development. Children must be allowed to make mistakes without feeling the constant threat of sanctions.

- Teachers now spend too much time stamping planners, ticking the board or getting children to put marbles in a jar, rather than forming good relationships which are the foundation for good teaching and learning. To manage behaviour effectively teachers need to work in a 'no blame' environment, where they can discuss poor pupil behaviour with colleagues, in order to pursue a range of solutions based on their professional judgement and expertise.

What do you think? Which side of the argument do you favour?

Cognitive approaches to managing behaviour

Cognitive psychologists are interested in thinking processes: they argue that humans have a unique capacity to think, since the human brain is 'hard wired' to perform a wide range of cognitive functions. Therefore, cognitive functions like thinking and reasoning play an important part in the way people behave. This perspective, like behaviourism, recognises the importance of how behaviour, feelings and thinking interact, but the **cognitive approach** argues that problem behaviour arises as a result of how situations are perceived or interpreted. Like behaviourism, determining the cause of a particular behaviour is not required to facilitate change. According to this approach, 'faulty or maladaptive thinking' is often the cause of disruptive behaviour. Visser (2000) points out that, if teachers want to change the behaviour of a student, they must change the thinking processes that go with it. Feelings like anger and anxiety have an important influence on thinking because negative emotions can result in maladaptive behaviours:

> Emotions often intervene with carefully rehearsed plans to stand up for yourself. The student who does not trust teachers, because of previous experiences, expects future encounters to be similarly unpleasant. This can influence his or her thinking, motivation, emotions and behaviour, and result in defensive behaviour and putting up a barrier.
>
> Chaplain, 2003:179

Ellis (1962) stresses that there are two ways of thinking about any situation: people can behave 'rationally' or 'irrationally'. For example, when undergraduates get their marked assignments returned to them, they can look at the grade, read the comments made by their tutor and make a rational decision about the grade they were given. They might conclude that if they had read more widely, and applied theories more effectively, they would have improved their grade. Alternatively they can behave irrationally. For example, if a high-achieving student gets a much lower assignment grade than they expected, rather than reading the comments made by the tutor, the assignment grade might trigger strong negative emotions. This can result in what Ellis describes as **'awfulising'** or **'catastrophising'**. The student thinks they should have received a higher mark because they worked so hard. There will also be a tendency for the student to generalise these feelings to other events. The student may feel that the essay grade, despite previous evidence to the contrary, indicates that they are generally no good at essay writing, or they may have recriminations about their tutor. It is possible to dispute these irrational beliefs. The tutor's role is to help the student to restructure their thinking. The ultimate aim for the teacher is to help students to manage themselves and become independent.

Wearmouth et al. (2005) emphasise how this approach places importance on emotional **self-regulation** and **self-management** to enable children 'to cope with feelings such as violence, bullying, disaffection and isolation'. Research by Dwivedi and Gupta (2000) looked at a group of boys who exhibited episodes of anger-driven behaviour at school; they had all received fixed-term exclusions or were at risk of permanent exclusion. During school time the boys were taken through a ten-week programme, meeting for forty minutes per week to help them manage their feelings of anger. At the end of the training the boys appeared to cope with their feelings of anger more effectively. Post-training responses revealed that the boys expressed higher levels of self-efficacy and control over their anger:

> The students told us that they had gained from listening to other students' comments, that they found it easier to talk in a group, were more aware of their triggers and felt that they were not reacting as aggressively as before.
>
> Dwivedi and Gupta, 2000:79

However, the study does not say whether the changes to the boys' cognition were long term or just a result of their getting more attention during the study (this is known as the Hawthorn effect).

This process of self-regulation involves cognitive restructuring and is a method that teachers can use to help pupils change their thinking around issues which promote behavioural problems. For example, setting targets around a child who has strong emotional outbursts can help them to become more aware of what triggers the feeling and help them to respond in a different way. According to Kyriacou (2009), students should be 'encouraged to think about their own thinking'; this helps them to be more independent and self-reliant and to become much more consciously aware of how they approach behavioural situations, so that they have a wider range of strategies at their disposal. Ayers, Clarke and Murray (2000) point to a range of strategies that teachers can use to help pupils to improve their behaviour. For example, they suggest interviewing students to assess their level of awareness about their problem behaviour. Students could also be asked to complete rating scales about their behaviour to see if their view of an incident is consistent with that of the teacher. Pupils may not be fully aware of the impact of some types of disruptive behaviour on others, and this process of reflection can help pupils to become consciously aware of how they affect others. Wearmouth et al. (2005) stress that enhancing emotional management skills can help children to deal with feelings of jealousy and anxiety.

Teachers can also benefit from developing greater emotional regulation and self-management. Chaplain (2003) provides an interesting example of irrational thinking from the teacher's perspective. For example, when the teacher is in the classroom, irrational thinking would be,

> 'I must be able to control any class at any time; if I cannot it is awful and means I am a worthless teacher.' This demand causes anxiety, depression, lack of assertiveness and feelings of incompetence.
>
> Chaplain, 2003:180

This is irrational because it is not possible to be in total control of a class at all times. Students will be disruptive and teachers have 'bad' days. A rational thinker would make a judgement based on the evidence and might conclude that the class were disruptive because the lesson could have been planned better. However, what Ellis and others might describe as irrational thinking might appear perfectly rational to pupils and teachers. Therefore, pupil misbehaviour might be a result of boredom, or occur as a direct result of feeling unfairly treated by the teacher.

Teachers are constantly working to develop the cognitive skills of learners by helping them to process information and engage in the curriculum. However, as a therapeutic approach, getting people to change deep-rooted emotional responses can be challenging. At what point should the teacher or school intervene? In more extreme cases involving anxiety, depression, eating disorders or persistent violent conduct it is likely that external agencies like the psychiatric service or the police will be involved. When Ellis formulated these ideas he had a therapeutic situation in mind between a counsellor and client. The skills required to deal with complex emotional issues using cognitive approaches involve a degree of expertise that teachers may find difficult to acquire, and they may have no aspirations to be involved in the emotional regulation of pupils with serious mental heath problems (see Chapter 6 for more on this).

The Steer Report (2009) warns against complacency about behaviour management and highlights the importance of the contribution of social, emotional and behavioural development to learning (SEAL). It also highlights that pupils may need to be taught about how to behave appropriately and helped to foster the social skills required to manage difficult emotions and interact more positively with others. (We will look at the Steer Report in more detail later in the chapter.) Emotional intelligence includes a number of characteristics including the ability for self-awareness, managing our feelings, self-motivation, empathy and being able to develop positive relationships. These policy shifts suggests that some pupils need to be taught behaviours and helped to develop skills to manage difficult and strong emotions like anger or impulses which may be disruptive in the classroom. In addition, learners should be helped to develop empathy and warm relationships. It is thought that the development of these skills contributes to increased levels of motivation and improved attendance, all of which contribute to improved learning. Porter (2006) points out that the cognitive approach is implicit in teaching any skill. For example, it can be used to help children to deal with issues like anger and aggression, and can also be used to develop parenting skills.

Humanistic approaches to managing behaviour

Humanistic theory places emphasis on democracy in the classroom and the importance of fostering mutual respect between teachers and learners. It says that children deserve the same consideration as adults; children are simply people who have not yet accumulated as many skills as adults. The importance of human relationships based on empathy, genuineness (also known as congruence) and unconditional positive regard (non-judgemental warmth) are basic conditions on which respect and mutual understanding are built. This approach, unlike behaviourism, assumes that all children are basically good and have an innate capacity for psychological growth if they are exposed to the right conditions. It also assumes that children have the capacity to reflect on their own thoughts and feelings in response to experiences. This quality of reflection helps them to make choices about their actions. Gatongi (2007) considers how the **humanistic approach** could be applied to the classroom to help teachers manage behaviour by placing greater emphasis on the relationship between teachers and pupils above all else:

> A teacher can approach the management of student behaviour in a more proactive manner through building a positive and trusting relationship. The teacher establishes himself/herself as a teacher who cares about the pupil's well being in and out of school. This can help create an atmosphere in which the student's self-esteem can flourish.
>
> Gatongi, 2007:210

Glasser (1969) applied humanistic principles to education, arguing that despite past histories people have the potential to be autonomous and choose both present and future behaviours. Glasser called this 'reality theory', because it deals with behaviour in the present without reference to the past. Schools should be somewhere children want to be, where there is shared responsibility between the pupil and teacher; it should be a place where children get their needs met. Disruptive behaviour is caused by unmet needs, for example poor teaching, or a sense of powerlessness, especially where students feel a lack of recognition:

> Students in a situation where they are unable to say 'I'm at least a little bit important' will not work very hard to preserve or improve that situation.
>
> Brant, 1988

Humanists like Glasser might therefore view the National Curriculum as counterproductive to learning, it is simply a straitjacket which limits the autonomy of the student and teacher, and is likely to lead to unmet needs (see Chapter 2 for more on this).

From the humanistic perspective, schools should have rules that are fair, and these rules should reflect what Tauber (2007) refers to as a cause-and-effect relationship. If a school rule is 'no running in the corridors', this makes sense if it is explained that running in a confined space might cause an accident. This rule will make sense to pupils because it exists for their benefit and protection. Wherever possible, students should be involved in forming classroom rules, to foster a sense of ownership and responsibility. When rules are broken, as is inevitable because people make mistakes, the student should be given the opportunity to explain their behaviour, evaluate it, and come up with a plan to change it.

Tauber (2007) suggests that if students are not willing to comply or come up with a plan they should be given restorative time away from the group in a quiet safe environment, where they stay until the plan is formed. Students who find this type of activity difficult could be presented with two plans to choose from. When the student comes up with an acceptable plan to change their own behavior they can rejoin the group.

Although the sentiments embodied in the humanistic approach are consistent with those that many teachers aspire to, the weight of rules, sanctions and rewards makes it difficult to imagine how it could be implemented. An educational system driven by targets, such as the National Curriculum and continued testing of children through Standard Assessment Tests (SATs), appears to be the antithesis of this approach. That is not to say that educational professionals do not take a humanistic approach to children in their care, rather that the present emphasis on rules, sanctions and rewards militates against the adoption of whole school approaches using a humanistic perspective.

? Stop and reflect

These ideas may also seem a little woolly and vague compared with the other approaches: what do you do, for example, if the pupil plays truant from restorative time out? Should the student just be allowed back to school? If so, what message does this send out to other children?

An interesting approach to managing behaviour based on humanistic principles has been piloted since 2004 by the Scottish Executive Education Department. The scheme has introduced restorative approaches based on a 'humanistic and person-centered' understanding of the individual, group and community. The definition of restorative practice used in the pilot was:

- where staff and pupils act towards each other in a helpful and non-judgmental way;
- where they work to understand the impact of their actions on others;
- where there are fair processes that allow everyone to learn from any harm that may have been done;
- where responses to difficult behaviour have positive outcomes for everyone. (McCluskey et al., 2007:211)

McCluskey et al. (2007) explain that the restorative practices used in the pilot were concerned with prevention, response and intervention and reparation. As well as developing important skills, restorative practices provide a means through which disagreements, differences of opinion and tensions can be expressed and managed to reduce harm. The aspirations of the pilot scheme foster individual and community responsibility, while encouraging children with behavioural difficulties to reflect on the impact their behaviour has on other pupils. Hendry (2009) explains how the origin of restorative practice has it roots in the criminal justice system, where offenders are given the opportunity to meet with victims of their crime and listen to how their actions have affected them. These ideas have been developed in the Scottish pilot into a more humanistic approach.

Another method used to resolve conflict between students is **circle time** (Mosley, 1996), which has strict rules, as follows:

- No one can put anyone down.
- No one may use any name negatively.
- When they speak, everyone must listen.
- Everyone has a turn and chance to speak.
- All views are taken seriously.
- Members of the class team suggest ways of solving problems.
- Individuals can accept the help or politely refuse it. (Wearmouth et al., 2005:184)

Students need very good verbal and negotiation skills to participate fully in this type of group. Very young children will not be able to engage in restorative practices because they have not got the verbal skill to resolve serious conflicts. Steer (2009) stressed how important it is to deal with the disruptive behaviour as early as possible. **Nurture groups** have been increasingly used to help young children who display disruptive behaviour. Nurture groups were devised by Marjorie Boxall who set up the first groups in the 1970s in London. Cooper and Whitehead (2007) point out that they were set up because of the emotional problems and disruptive behaviour evident among children entering infant and primary school. Nurture groups are generally run by a teacher and teaching assistant, who provide a nurturing environment where the focus of attention is on communicating on a one-to-one basis, helping children to resolve emotional issues and building their interpersonal and social skills. Children are integrated back into the mainstream when they are deemed ready by the teacher. Bennathan and Boxhall (2000) suggest that some children have attachment problems, which make it difficult for them to form the relationships with teachers and other children that are essential for full participation in school so the group helps with these issues.

> The nurture group attempts to create the features of adequate parenting within school. Opportunities are provided to develop trust, security, positive mood and identity through attachment to a reliable, attentive and caring adult and to develop autonomy through the provision of secure, controlled and graduated experiences in a familiar environment.
>
> Wearmouth et al., 2005:107

Research by Cooper and Whitehead (2007) found that children in nurture groups improved their social, emotional and behavioural functioning, especially those with social, emotional and behavioural difficulties. In the same study, qualitative data also illustrated how mainstream staff within the school had become more nurturing to pupils.

Activity

Psychologist Sue Reynolds presented her research (summarised here), which looked at whether children benefited from being placed in nurture groups, to the Educational and Child Psychology Annual Conference (2007):

- In all, 179 children (aged five to seven) took part in the study. They were vulnerable, withdrawn, exhibited behavioural difficulties, had problems communicating or displayed some form of developmental delay.

- The children were first assessed and rated on self-image, self-esteem and emotional maturity before being allocated either to a nurture group (made up of six to eight children with lower scores) or the control group which attended schools with similar levels of deprivation but no nurture group.

- Children in the nurture group made improvements in all of the categories, sometimes overtaking the control group.

  1 Could the improvement be related to other factors than the nature of the nurture group itself?

  2 Make a list which includes strengths and weaknesses of the project. Would it be possible to resolve any of these? If so, how might this be done?

Although it is important to exercise caution with these findings, as the improvement could simply be related to being in a smaller class and getting more attention, children in the nurture group were reported as being much more socially involved with their friends and able to respond to requests from adults.

> Some features to be found in nurture groups include easy physical contact between adult and child; warmth and intimacy and family atmosphere; good humoured acceptance of the children and their behaviour; familiar and reassuring routines, a focus on tidying up and putting away; the provision of food in structured contexts; the opportunity to play and the appropriate participation by adults; adults talking about and encouraging reflection by children on trouble-provoking situations and their own feelings and opportunities for children to develop increasing autonomy.
>
> Wearmouth et al., 2005:107

We have now seen a range of approaches – behavioural, cognitive and humanistic – which can inform behaviour management. In reality, however, learner behaviour is not the sole concern of the educator: it is also an important social and political issue, and one in which governments can, and do, intervene.

Policy approaches to behaviour management

Government reports and guidelines on pupil behaviour can provide some insight into the dominant concerns about the behaviour of learners, and offer some guidance about how behavioural issues can be managed on a day-to-day basis. But how far can any policy hope to direct what goes on in schools and colleges on a day-to-day basis? The modern classroom is a dynamic environment, characterised by rapidly changing group processes. Within this context, teachers are required to make instant, subjective judgements about what constitutes misbehaviour; inevitably, these judgements are not always consistent (as we saw in the case study at the beginning of the chapter). Kyriacou (2009) points out that, while there may be agreement among teachers about the seriousness of some forms of misbehaviour (such as refusal to work or aggressive behaviour), there are also many behaviours that are open to the interpretation of the teacher (for example, the amount of noise, or how much talking is allowed). This creates inconsistency between teachers:

> The teacher must judge what degree of such misbehaviour can be tolerated, and what degree requires action. There are thus two grey areas here: first, the point at which such misbehaviour is deemed to have occurred, and second the point at which such misbehaviour requires action.
>
> Kyriacou, 2009:121

Teachers may respond differently to the same behaviours within a class, and likewise pupils may respond to the same actions from two teachers in different ways. Pupils are likely to have favourite particular subjects and teachers, while teachers might simply prefer pupils who are more compliant or motivated, or easier to manage. Although this may appear to be down to the individual teacher and students involved, it is important to realise that both teachers and pupils operate within wider structural influences, for example school and classroom policies, the support received from senior management and government guidelines.

The Elton Report

The Elton Report (1989) is an important starting point in contextualising some of the concerns raised about behavioural issues in schools. Miller (2003) points out that the report represents the beginning of legislative intervention into behaviour management. It was the result of concerns raised in the media about a perceived worsening of pupil behaviour and a concern that teachers were not up to the job. Ellis and Tod (2009) stress that this resulted in a moral panic at the time, fuelled by a perceived increase in violent behaviour in schools. This, they argue, was seen particularly by the media as contributing to moral decline and a collapse of the social fabric of society.

Although some data on school exclusions was available at the time of the report, the Elton Report really highlighted that information about misbehaviour in schools was limited. It was therefore not possible to confirm or refute the media's claims, so further research was commissioned to support the report. Sheffield University was asked to examine teachers' perceptions and concerns about discipline: 3,500 teachers were surveyed in 220 primary schools and 250 secondary schools, with a response rate of 89 per cent in primary and 79 per cent in secondary. Research evidence from the report indicated that some schools were more effective at managing behaviour:

> When we visited schools we were struck by the differences in their 'feel' or atmosphere. Our conversations with teachers left us convinced that some schools have a more positive atmosphere than others. It was in these positive schools that we tended to see the work and behaviour which impressed us most. We found that we could not explain these different school atmospheres by saying that the pupils came from different home backgrounds. Almost all of the schools we visited were in what many teachers would describe as difficult urban areas. We had to conclude that these differences had something to do with what went on in the schools themselves.
>
> DES, 1989:88

The Elton Report also pointed to the variation between teachers and their ability to manage groups as central to behaviour management. While the report emphasised the importance of building good relationships between teacher and pupils, it commented that group management skills were 'the single most important factor' in achieving good standards of classroom behaviour:

> Teachers with good group management skills are able to establish positive relationships with their classes based on mutual respect. They can create a classroom climate in which pupils lose rather than gain popularity with their classmates by causing trouble. They can also spot a disruptive incident in the making, choose an appropriate tactic to deal with it and nip it in the bud.
>
> DES, 1989:67-68

However, according to the report, teachers who lack group management skills struggle in the classroom, often finding it difficult to assert their authority:

> Our evidence suggests however that there are teachers who lack confidence in their own ability to deal with disruption and who see their classes as potentially hostile. They create a negative classroom atmosphere by frequent criticism and rare praise. They make use of loud public reprimands and threats. They are sometimes sarcastic. They tend to react aggressively to minor incidents. Their methods increase the danger of a major confrontation not only with individual pupils but with the whole class.
>
> DES, 1989:68

The Elton Report claimed that the skills required to be an effective teacher can be taught and learned. However, the report's findings did suggest that there were failures both in the way teachers were trained, and in senior management teams' ability to manage schools effectively. If all teachers in a school are experiencing similar problems with the same group of pupils, this is often an indication of a failure at senior management level. This concern about the inconsistency in approach between teachers within the same school and in different schools led to one of the central recommendations in the Elton Report, that schools should adopt a '**whole school approach**' to behaviour management. We will examine what this means, and look at examples of a 'whole school approach', in the next section.

After Elton – policy developments

The introduction of the National Curriculum in 1988 overshadowed the advisory recommendations of the Elton Report. Policies around inclusive education resulted in conflicting agendas in education. In addition, the Elton Report arguably failed to contextualise how low levels of achievement and poor behaviour are the result of wider social and economic factors rooted in class and poverty. Nevertheless, in the two decades since, further legislation and guidance have taken forward some of the key recommendations in the Elton Report. For example, the DfE Circular 8/94, Pupil Behaviour and Discipline, stressed the importance of a whole school approach. Ellis and Tod (2009) point to the specific aims of the circular, which were to:

- Help schools to manage behaviour effectively.
- Help schools to promote respect for others among young people.
- Promote firm action against all forms of bullying.
- Reduce levels of truancy from school.
- Reduce the poor behaviour that leads to pupils being excluded, either temporarily or permanently. (Ellis and Tod, 2009:33)

A further DfE circular (9/94) made recommendations about children with emotional and behavioural difficulties. This group was referred to in the Elton Report but without any real clarity. The report suggested that some children are subjected to a greater number of risk factors that make them more likely to engage in seriously disruptive behaviour:

> In the case of attendance, the picture of the pupil most at risk seems fairly clear – a low achiever from a severely disadvantaged home background. In the case of seriously disruptive behaviour, the picture of the pupil most likely to be involved seems less clear in terms of his or her material circumstances, such as quality of housing and family income. Some other characteristics can, however, be identified. Our survey and other evidence, such as LEA exclusion statistics, indicate that boys are about four times more likely to be involved than girls. They are likely to be rated as of below average ability by their teachers and to have a history of low achievement at school. They are also likely to come from highly stressed family backgrounds.
>
> DES, 1989:147

Miller (2003) (referring to circular 9/94) identifies three distinct groups of children that may present behavioural issues:

1 The first group are children who are 'naughty and disruptive' but are responsive to behaviour management techniques. This group of children are more likely to engage in low level disruption but will be responsive to teacher demands.

2 The second, very small group, are those children described as having severe mental illness, who require specialist care outside the scope of the school.

3 The third group are categorised as having emotional and behavioural difficulties. According to Daniels and Garner (1999), many of these children exhibit behaviours such as being withdrawn, displaying frustration, anger, disruptive and antisocial behaviour, as well as more serious problems like substance abuse, depressive or suicidal attitudes, and violence.

Ellis and Tod (2009) stress that the problem of trying to categorise children with emotional and behaviour difficulties is the strong contextual influence in which these children are judged, and this might lead to undesirable results such as labelling and stereotyping. Wearmouth et al. (2004) are highly critical of the term 'education and behavioural difficulties' (EBD) and argue that it is:

> a category which substitutes quasi-clinical assessment about putative need for more straightforward judgements about right and wrong. It enables and legitimates clinically orientated judgements about the causes of behaviour – emotional difficulties – which allow schools to evade serious scrutiny of its own routines and procedures. Moreover, the judgements made about children occur in the absence of the panoply of protections which exist for adults who behave oddly or unacceptably.
>
> Wearmouth et al., 2004:48

The problem, then, with the term EBD is a lack of any real definition (perhaps inevitable given the nature of human complexity) about what constitutes such behaviour, and a fear that, once imposed, such labels are difficult for pupils in a relatively powerless position to change.

The Elton Report had expressed concern about the negative attitudes some teachers harboured about parents, and revealed that many teachers thought that parents were responsible for the misbehaviour of their children at school. The report recommended that Local Education Authorities, the government, school governors and headteachers shared a responsibility to foster a closer relationship between parents and schools. Subsequent guidance from the government required all schools to produce home school agreements which should be signed by both a representative of the school and parents to indicate their understanding of their responsibility for children's school behaviour and attendance (Miller, 2003). Research by Harris and Goodall (2008) suggests that parental engagement can have a positive effect on student behaviour:

> Students were clear that if there was no home based consequence to bad behaviour at school, such behaviour would continue.
>
> Harris and Goodall, 2008:283

However, the research also highlights the considerable barriers faced by parents in participating in school, for example the lack of time, full-time employment, childcare facilities, and difficulties in communication with teachers and schools. Tomlinson (2005) further suggests that these barriers have a disproportionate impact on families with low incomes, single parents and ethnic minorities.

The Steer Report

The Steer Report (2009) reiterated many of the issues raised by the Elton Report and pointed out that:

> There is strong evidence from a range of sources that the overall standard of behaviour achieved by schools is good and has improved in recent years.
>
> Steer, 2009:2

Although some of the definitions of words like 'satisfactory' or 'good' used by Ofsted in their reports are vague (and are sometimes redefined), a 2005 report, *Challenging Behaviour*, found that most pupil behaviour in schools was satisfactory or better. It identified low level disruptive behaviour as the main problem for teachers. Ellis and Tod (2009), commenting on the Steer Report, argued that 'there is little new to discover about the management of pupil behaviour as the key principles have been known for a long time' (Ellis and Tod, 2009:42). However, it is clear that the key recommendations in the report which have been accepted by the government have shifted the emphasis on school behaviour in a range of different directions. For example, 'satisfactory' behaviour is no longer acceptable; schools are expected to raise the standard of behaviour further. The Steer Report emphasised the following:

- children with behavioural problems and SEN (see Chapter 9) should be identified early and intervention should take place;
- Parent Support Advisors should be employed to enable school–home relationships to grow;
- parenting classes should be offered by the LEA to ensure that support to parents is available;

- nurture groups should be used with pupils who exhibit poor behaviour, and improved access to child and mental health services;
- disruptive children should be withdrawn if necessary, and isolation rooms should be used where appropriate;
- schools should work more closely with external agencies (for example social services, the police), and educational provision should be made for children who are excluded;
- schools should be involved in behaviour and attendance partnerships;
- teachers needed to be more aware of their legal duties, especially to exercise discipline beyond the school gates.

Like the Elton Report, Steer (2009) placed emphasis on a range of strategies to improve pupil behaviour:

- excellent classroom practice and an appropriate curriculum;
- a whole school approach, based on consistency and clearly communicated sanctions and rewards used by all staff;
- strong leadership and in-service training in behaviour management approaches;
- school–parent partnerships and pupil support;
- improved teacher training.

New initiatives by the government have tended to focus on social and emotional aspects of learning (SEAL, 2007). This development has been influenced by policies like *Every Child Matters* (2003), which place emphasis on children being healthy and safe, able to enjoy and achieve, make a positive contribution to social groups/communities and achieve economic well-being. In this particular context, it is not surprising that the Steer Report recommends that children with disruptive behaviour should be identified earlier and nurture groups used to improve their behaviour. In addition, parenting classes are suggested to provide help and support to those parents who are struggling or have poor parenting skills. Social factors outside the school have also been given greater consideration, for example working more closely with external agencies, dealing with problems of pupil attendance and a consideration of discipline beyond the school gates. However, some of the recommendations in the report do raise serious concerns about the role of schools in society, which, already engulfed by demands on their time, must now address the emotional issues of the child and the deficits of parents.

Activity

DfES (2005) *Learning Behaviour: The Report of the Practitioners on School Behaviour and Discipline* (The Steer Report): http://www.teachernet.gov.uk/wholeschool/behaviour/steer/.

Read Chapter 5: Exclusions
One of the most controversial recommendations in this report is the use of withdrawal rooms (sometimes called isolation rooms). Do you think these punitive measures work

▶

with children who display disruptive behaviour, or is being sent to the isolation unit simply a badge of honour?

Read Chapter 8: Support and guidance for pupils and parents
What is your view of nurture groups in primary schools? What is your reaction to young children (aged between 5 and 7) displaying disruptive behaviour? How do you explain their behaviour and what do you think the causes are?

Steer suggests that Pupil–Parent Support Workers (now referred to as Pupil Support Advisors, or PSAs) should be employed to support families with children who are disruptive; in addition, they should be able to provide an important link to other agencies. What is your reaction to this new role; in what way can you see PSAs making a contribution to the improvement of children with behavioural difficulties?

⬉ Connect and explore

Ecclestone, K. and Hayes, D. (2008) *The Dangerous Rise of Therapeutic Education*, London: Routledge

Read some or all of this to provide you with some really interesting debate about initiatives such as nurture groups and SEAL (DfES, 2007). Ecclestone and Hayes (2008) have been critical of what they call 'therapeutic education' in schools and they argue that the preoccupation with emotional needs has undermined independent thought and created overprotected students who now require a whole range of support services to function within education.

Behaviour management in practice

In this chapter, we have so far looked at some of the psychological theory behind behaviour management approaches and seen some of the ways in which government policy has attempted to guide and regulate what happens in classrooms. We now turn to look at behaviour management practice in more detail, as the area where theory and policy are put to the test. To this end, we return now to a particular behaviour management approach – the whole school approach – examining some of its applications and variations. The two approaches described both use a behavioural approach to behaviour management.

The whole school approach: behavioural theory in action

Ellis and Tod (2009) refer to **'tariff systems'** as a way of explaining some whole school approaches which have developed rigid systems of behaviour management and are underpinned by the behavioural approach. The term 'tariff' refers to the cost of something: under these systems the school explicitly states the cost for unacceptable behaviour and rewards for acceptable behaviour. These systems are usually brought into schools by Local Education Authorities that buy the whole behaviour package, including staff training. We will look now at two examples of tariff systems, **Assertive Discipline** and **BfL** (**Behaviour for Learning** – not to be confused with the TDA website behaviour4learning, or Ellis and Tod's textbook *Behaviour for Learning* [2009] which take a different approach to behaviour management).

Assertive Discipline and BfL are based on the observation that very bright children and those who exhibit unacceptable behaviour often get the most attention in schools. In comparison, the children who come to school every day on time, with the right equipment and willing to work, get less attention simply because they are doing what is expected of them. Both BfL and Assertive Discipline set about changing this balance by ensuring that the children in the middle, who may lack attention, are positively rewarded for their efforts.

A whole school approach: BfL (Behaviour for Learning)

BfL is a system rooted in the behavioural approach, built on rules, rewards and sanctions. It is not concerned with the causes of behaviour, only the behaviour itself. In 1988, Dexter Hutt became the head teacher of a failing school in Birmingham called Ninestiles. At that time only 6 per cent of children at the school achieved five GCSEs grade A–C:

> Students were underachieving and teachers were streaming heavily focusing on higher streams with lots of people in lower streams not attending. Children were left with bad feelings about their time at school.
>
> www.TeacherNet.gov.uk

By 2006, the proportion of children at the school gaining five GCSEs grade A–C was 83 per cent. Although the changes at the school were complex, there was a clear emphasis on behaviour management. The BfL approach was developed and refined within the school over a ten-year period. Ninestiles is now designated as a Leading Edge School by the government, with approval from the Teacher Development Agency to train its own teachers. Ninestiles Plus, the company set up by the now Sir Dexter, has contributed to the improvement of schools in other regions.

BfL depends on the support of governors, the senior management team, teachers and support staff. It is built on the expectation that behaviour management will be implemented by all staff within the school. In some schools this approach is supported by BfL lessons, which are delivered by personal tutors. It is based on a system of incremental rewards and sanctions, with the emphasis on rewarding positive behaviour. Although this approach can be implemented in different ways, the common theme is that pupils are encouraged to accumulate rewards (for example reward stamps will carry a particular value). Rewards are given for effort, attainment, contributions in class and producing homework to a good standard. Like behaviourism, the focus is on positive reinforcement to ensure recognition of those children who come to school every day with the correct equipment, uniform and attitude. School rules are on display in the corridors, classrooms and communicated to the whole school through assemblies, tutor groups and by teachers in the classroom.

As well as rewards, there are sanctions and expectations placed upon pupils who are expected, for example, to have the correct uniform and equipment, to attend classes regularly and punctually, and to submit any homework set. Pupils are made aware of the consequences of breaking the rules. If the rules are broken, sanctions escalate, moving from an initial verbal warning to written comments to detention and eventually isolation, fixed-term exclusions and finally permanent exclusions. Verbal warnings give pupils the opportunity to think about the consequences of their behaviour before the teacher moves on to the next level of sanctions. The first verbal warning has to be explicitly stated; for example, the teacher might say, 'I have asked you to get on with your work twice, I am now giving you a verbal warning'. Serious misbehaviour is dealt with by handing out the severest sanctions; for example, verbal abuse to staff, deliberate acts of aggression and bullying result immediately in the severest punishments.

One of the more controversial aspects of this approach is to place students in isolation. Isolation rooms are cubicles where students cannot see or speak to anyone else. Breaks are also spent in isolation and lunch is brought to the cubicle. Students are allowed out for a specified number of toilet breaks. Student materials are provided by teachers, usually in the form of worksheets, to ensure that pupils in isolation have no contact with their friends. This form of punishment is used to separate pupils from social contact with their friends; for some students interaction with a social group might be the most important aspect of school.

Stop and reflect

Recall the humanistic idea of 'restorative time away' outlined by Tauber (2007). In what way do you think restorative time away is different from the isolation rooms used in the BfL model of behaviour management?

BfL programmes start from the assumption that however good teachers are, and however exciting the curriculum is, it cannot be delivered if learners are badly behaved. Although individual schools will manage strategies for behaviour differently, they will have zero tolerance to unacceptable behaviour. Students are expected to do as they are asked by teachers the first time and every time. They are expected to show respect, listen to the teacher and to other students and work to the best of their ability.

Within the learning situation

A whole school policy based on BfL might use a system of sanctions and rewards. Imagine a pupil who cannot settle in class: the teacher might respond initially by asking the pupil whether he understands the task, and whether he needs some help. If the disruptive behaviour continues, the teacher might proceed by giving the pupil a verbal warning, with the additional threat that the next one will be a written warning. In a BfL system, warnings can have a cumulative effect: for example, perhaps three written warnings in a week results in a detention. Rewards are equally important as sanctions, however: if the pupil gets to the end of the lesson without a written warning, the teacher might give him two reward stamps. Like warnings, rewards can be put to cumulative effect: for example, if a learner collects enough stamps throughout the year, he might be allowed to go to Alton Towers with all the other students who have collected enough rewards.

A whole school approach: Assertive Discipline

Like BfL, Assertive Discipline is a whole school approach based on behavioural principles (Skinner, 1953; Whedall and Merrett, 1984), which uses rules, sanctions and rewards to manage the behaviour of learners. Assertive Discipline, according to Wearmouth and colleagues (2005), is a highly structured approach to classroom management. Whereas BfL tends to place emphasis on the overall system of behaviour management and how it is implemented within the school, what is required for this approach to work is an 'assertive teacher'. It is a whole school approach because where this behaviour management model is used all teachers are expected to be assertive in the same way. This approach is critical of 'timid teachers' who are unable to communicate clearly what they require from their pupils and do not follow through sanctions with action. Canter and Canter (1976) also describe 'aggressive' or 'hostile' teachers as problematic, because they lower the self-esteem of pupils by constantly using intimidating tactics like using negative reinforcements such as threats and overly harsh sanctions. Canter and Canter (2001) define an assertive teacher as someone who is able to communicate behavioural expectations clearly and where the words and actions of the teacher should send the following message:

> I am committed to being the leader in this classroom, a leader who will establish an environment in which I can teach and my students can learn. To reach this goal, I am committed to teaching my students the behaviour they need to learn to allow them to succeed in school. In turn, I will guide them to make the choices that lead to success in life. I care too much about my students to allow them to behave in a manner that is not in their best interests and in the best interests of the class.
>
> Canter and Canter, 2001:8

Although this assertion by Canter and Canter begs the question 'isn't this what all teachers want?' they advocate a distinct behaviourist approach for achieving this goal. According to Jones (1987), the 'assertive teacher' uses assertive body language, to establish authority and self-assurance. Consequently the use of eye contact, tone of voice, facial expressions and gestures help to establish the teacher's authority. For example, sometimes a frown or moving closer to a student may be enough to discourage disruptiveness.

Like BfL, teachers draw up a discipline plan which makes the rules of behaviour and sanctions for breaches of behaviour explicit. Canter and Canter (2001) claim that the plan should consist of rules, supportive feedback and corrective actions. Examples of such rules are:

- Be in your seat when the bell rings.
- Do not leave the classroom without permission.
- No swearing, or teasing.

Supportive feedback should reinforce acceptable behaviour and reward students who are doing what they have been asked to do. By highlighting positive behaviour, children have a role model and can see what good behaviour looks like and copy it. A class-wide recognition system can be used to motivate students to learn a new behaviour by being given a reward for displaying the desired

Figure 5.2 **Assertive Discipline relies on body language as well as behaviour. How can you tell that this teacher is in control?**
Source: Pearson Education Ltd./Sophie Bluy.

behaviour, for example more outdoor time, or free reading time. Assertive Discipline takes both a paternalistic and authoritarian approach to what it describes as corrective action. Canter and Canter (2001) claim that teachers need to apply sanctions consistently and appropriately, moving from a verbal warning to being moved away from friends. Whereas the BfL approach has clear procedures for persistent or difficult behaviour, the processes are less clear for Assertive Discipline. In the first instance teachers are expected to deal with the problem and involve parents and the head teacher if the behaviour continues. This places a disproportionate responsibility on the teacher who may feel that they are to blame for pupil misbehaviour because they are not assertive enough.

Within the learning situation

Imagine you are a teacher finding it difficult to settle your class after lunch. They display a range of behaviours which by themselves are not problematic, but which taken together are extremely disruptive. They chat, leave their seats more often than usual, squabble, tell tales and insist that they need the toilet. You decide to use supportive feedback and explain to the children that if they settle and listen carefully to what you would like them to do, they will be allowed to put a marble in the jar. This means following the rules. When the jar is full, all the children will be allowed to work on their favourite activity. Having explained this, you ask the students to get the book out of their desk. You comment to the whole class that one girl already has her book out, earning a marble (reward) for the class.

? *Stop and reflect*

Star charts, ticks on the board, verbal praise or marbles in the jar are often used to control and manipulate the behaviour of very young children; what do you think are the pros and cons of this approach as an appropriate way to change behaviour?

Assessing BfL and Assertive Discipline

BfL and Assertive Discipline provide an overarching system to manage behaviour. However, Ellis and Tod (2009) point to how these approaches can become mechanistic and formulaic if they do not encourage discussion or problem-solving. Although both theories appear to offer pupils a choice, there is usually only one option if they want to avoid sanctions, which means they really have no choice. Porter (2000) raises ethical concerns about the degree of control these types of approaches impose on children, pointing out that it is neither desirable nor possible to exercise this degree of control over 'someone else's behaviour':

> To attempt to do so is counter productive as it teaches the opposite skills to those we are trying to instil, helps to create disciplinary problems that teachers struggle with, and reduces students' motivation to learn and a willingness to accept responsibility for the effects of their actions on others.
>
> Porter, 2000:204

Both approaches detach behaviour from learning and the curriculum. Ellis and Tod (2009) argue that the curriculum is central to behaviour. BfL and Assertive Discipline use the principles of behaviourism to create the preconditions for learning, but do not explain how learning itself takes place. These approaches tend to ignore both the ideological position of the teacher and their professional training and skill. Teachers make judgements about pupils based on previous knowledge and experience. BfL and Assertive Discipline ignore the sophisticated and complex understanding teachers employ to manage behaviour, which are often based on an understanding of the deeper cognitive and emotional motivations of students in their care. Watkins and Wagner (2000) suggest that teachers are 'invited to be more automata rather than professionals or even humans'.

> This can lead to some pupils being escalated rapidly through to exclusion as class teachers rigidly adhere to the predefined sequence of consequences without recognising when an alternative approach might be more appropriate.
>
> Ellis and Tod, 2009:161

It may also be seen as contradictory that, while Elton (1989), Ofsted (2005) and Steer (2009) all point to generally good behaviour in schools, BfL and Assertive Discipline insist that pupils need to be managed prescriptively. Students are confined to a compulsory education system in which their lives are controlled and constrained by others. In this situation is low level disruption normal and to be expected? Would adults' behaviour be any different were they similarly confined?

Commentators like Ball (2007) point to how the partnership between the state and private consultancies can be a source of big business for the private sector.

Assertive Discipline and BfL involve schools buying in training and support materials for whole school training. The impact of such expensive strategies are not researched independently.

Although all state schools are required to have a whole school approach to behaviour, there are significant barriers to achieving this. Miller (2003) conceptualises the debate around barriers to whole school behaviour management policies by considering how teachers and pupils are able to thwart their implementation.

Barriers to a whole school approach: Teachers

Schools, like all organisations, are socially complex and heterogeneous; they are made up of people with different ideologies, personal values and political orientations. Schools that choose to promote values embodied in approaches like Assertive Discipline and BfL will place a high premium on obeying the rules to ensure academic success. However, within the same school, teachers can fundamentally disagree about the best approach to managing behaviour. Some teachers will be much more liberal in their relationships with students, emphasising the importance of cooperation, negotiation and compromise. Others will foster a more humanistic approach, encouraging self-awareness and self-discipline. Teachers are not a homogeneous group; they develop strategies to protect their own values about teaching, learning and managing behaviour. For example, teachers can appear to support the school policy about behaviour management in staff meetings, but ignore it in their own classrooms. In this way they learn to mediate complex organisational structures to protect their professional integrity.

Teacher responses to behaviour are not always consistent and can vary depending on how the behaviour is perceived: this is because teachers are often concerned with the *cause* of a particular behaviour. According to Woolfolk-Hoy and Weinstein (2006), when the reason for unacceptable behaviour can be attributed to the student, like lack of effort or laziness, the teacher is more likely to react in a negative way. If behaviour is attributed to a cause outside the student's control, teachers are more likely to respond in a supportive way and avoid giving punishments.

Miller (2003) discusses the role of **counter-cultures** in staff rooms where teachers depend on each other for information about pupils. Counter-cultures, in this case, are smaller groups within organisations that form their own sense of identity, expressing values that may oppose those of the organisation. Hammersley (1984) described how conversation in staffrooms played a role in the construction of labels and stereotypes. Maclure and Jones (2009) illustrate this process in their research in primary school, by looking at how teachers develop discourses around the concept of the 'proper child'. To be defined as 'good', children are judged against the model of the proper child. Some who do not meet the requirements of this 'idealised model' are likely to develop reputations which stay with them:

> Once a child's reputation has begun to circulate in the staffroom, dining room and amongst other parents, it may be very difficult for his/her behaviour not to be interpreted as a 'sign' of such imputed character traits. Children who have acquired a strong reputation may therefore find it harder to be good – or rather, to be recognised as good.
>
> Maclure and Jones, 2009:4

This process of stereotyping and scapegoating (singling out and blaming) some pupils can result in some children not getting a fair chance to develop new behaviours, and counters the aspirations of BfL and Assertive Discipline that children should be given the opportunity to start each day afresh.

Miller (2003) also highlights the lack of technical language around issues of behaviour; for example, what do terms like 'low level disruption' and 'lack of focus' actually mean, and do all teachers have a common understanding of these terms? At what point does 'lack of focus' become translated into being 'bored', or 'having an off day'? There is also a lack of commonly agreed standards about what constitutes good behaviour management. Therefore, the focus of poor pupil behaviour is skewed towards blaming teachers, who are accused of being either too timid or too aggressive, poorly prepared or not willing to use their powers fully. Without a 'no blame culture', teachers may not feel they can openly admit to finding some students difficult to manage without appearing inadequate or unable to cope.

Barriers to a whole school approach: Pupils

It is now more than three decades since Paul Willis (1977) wrote about how some working-class boys experienced a deep sense of alienation within the school system, which they counter by developing anti-school behaviour and rejecting the values of the school. Willis described students flouting school rules about dress codes, and concentrating more on getting a laugh from the class than on academic success. Willis found that pupils do not experience schools in the same way: class, gender and ethnicity can have an important influence, not only on the school children go to, but on the quality of their educational experience. This behaviour of resistance, according to Willis, is deep rooted and determined by the social structure. Social class and cultural capital still have a determinate effect on educational achievement: for many working-class children, rejecting the system before it rejects you is a way of accommodating school failure. The DES (2003) Youth Cohort Studies provide evidence of poor achievement at GCSE among the working class, while blacks, Pakistanis and Bangladeshis still lag behind white pupils in their levels of achievement. What is the relationship between behaviour and achievement?

Research by Ofsted (2005, 2006) points out that older boys, especially those aged 13 and upwards, are more likely to show disruptive behaviour. However, research by Lucey and Walkerdine (1999) demonstrated that both middle-class and working-class boys displayed the same stereotypical male behaviour, but that middle-class boys were more likely than working-class boys to achieve academically. They argue that this contradiction can be understood by looking at the social constraints placed on black and working-class boys, who do not have the option of being working class and studious. Whole school policies cannot always change the individual's sense of being outside the school system, and rigid school rules are likely to give some children something to rebel against.

The debate about the whole school approach is complicated by Ofsted's (2005) finding that primary schools tend to have fewer behavioural problems. In primary schools pupils tend to have one teacher, and this makes it easier for children to understand the rules of the classroom: because the teacher is constant, there is less change during each day. These children are also younger and may be easier to exert authority over. However, in large comprehensive schools with pupils aged 11–16, learners will encounter a number of teachers throughout the course of the day. A whole school approach may be much more difficult to manage in these circumstances, where sub-cultural factors among both pupils and teachers can have a greater impact. Johnson (1999) points out that primary schools are less likely to take radical action like excluding pupils; they tend to contain them, sometimes by using internal segregation (for example by asking teaching assistants to work with children on a one-to-one basis) so that the immediate behavioural problem is controlled. This is supported by Steer (2009) who expressed concern that earlier intervention with some children in primary school was the only way help them in the long term.

Conclusion

Psychological approaches have helped to inform the debate about behaviour management, but the presentation of competing theoretical approaches does not always help in the application to practice. Psychology explains the causes of misbehaviour by considering thinking, feelings and behaviour. Behaviourists contribute to the debate by looking at how the environment shapes behaviour through positive and negative reinforcement. Managing behaviour depends on finding the optimum balance of rules, rewards and sanctions. Cognitive psychologists argue that disruptive behaviour is related to faulty thinking, and behaviour management is all about getting pupils to think rationally. Humanistic psychology places much more emphasis on affective concerns. These theories present a dichotomous relationship, which does not always appear to be reconcilable in practice. When teachers are dealing with a problem pupil, they do not always have time to consider whether the issue is best dealt with by considering feelings, thinking or behaviour. Psychology does contribute to what Ecclestone and Hayes (2009) describe as therapeutic education by redefining behaviour in schools; for example, emotional outbursts become 'irrational thinking', and disruptive tendencies become 'unmet needs'. Imbuing young children with a range of psychological dysfunctions can result in long-term labels that are difficult to change. Teachers require training in skills to use psychological approaches effectively, and yet again this raises boundary tensions about the role of the teacher. Many of the interventions referred to in this chapter were undertaken and monitored by trained psychologists whose role is to advise and observe. In a busy classroom, this sort of attention to detail is not always possible or desirable. More importantly, psychological approaches do not consider how behaviour and the curriculum are linked.

Many of the recommendations of the Elton Report (1989) are now embodied in the way educationalists think about behaviour, for example the emphasis on a whole school approach and the importance of explicit rules, rewards and sanctions. Although Steer (2009) supports many of Elton's recommendations, there is a notable shift towards the influence of social and emotional factors on behaviour. That is not say that the importance of rules, rewards and sanctions has been superseded, only that new concerns have been raised about the causes of disruptive behaviour. Steer points to the importance of identifying pupils with disruptive behaviour earlier, particularly in primary schools, and taking responsibility for teaching children how to behave. There also appear to be new expectations from teachers about their role, which suggests a much broader pastoral function.

A new direction for behaviour management is evident in the ideas behind 'Behaviour for Learning' put forward by Garner (2005) and Ellis and Tod (2009) who reassert the central role of the curriculum in behaviour management (for more information, see http://www.behaviour4learning.ac.uk). Therefore the emphasis shifts from a small minority of disruptive pupils to creating a positive learning environment for all students. As well as the priority given to the relationship between pupils and the teacher, effective lesson planning is seen as central to engaging pupils and reducing low level disruption. This approach recognises the need for rules and sanctions, but not at the expense of good relationships. Although the curriculum is central, it requires teachers to make it interesting enough to engage learners. Johnson (1999) does stress that behavioural problems and low achievement tend to be concentrated in some schools; it is therefore not possible to have a complete discussion about pupil behaviour without reference to issues of class and ethnicity.

Case study 5.2
Alternative approaches to managing behaviour

Alison attends her local sixth form college. She is in the first year of her A levels and achieved one A, two Bs and three Cs in her GCSEs. The college have higher entry requirements but offered her a place because she comes from one of the most deprived areas of the city and her previous school were convinced that she had the potential to do well academically and go on to university. Alison is always pleasant and polite; she makes insightful contributions to classroom discussion, and clearly does some reading beyond her taught sessions. It is the first week in November after half-term and Alison's personal tutor asks to see the Head of Department. It appears that Alison is constantly late, especially for the first sessions in the morning, often missing up to half an hour of the lesson. She has failed to do any homework and now claims to have lost several of her textbooks. Her mobile phone goes off constantly and there always seems to be some family crisis for her to deal with. She spends most of her break and lunchtime returning calls. Her teachers have tried all methods at their disposal, offering sanctions and rewards, but are now at a complete loss about how to proceed. Her tutor does not think it worthwhile for Alison to continue on the course if something does not change. Her tutor has also noticed that Alison seems to have formed a close relationship with her sociology lecturer, Miss Baxter.

The Head of Department sets up a meeting with Alison at the end of the day. Alison's story was very poignant. She had complex family arrangements where she stayed with her mum for three nights a week, her dad for two and her stepdad for two. If she left any of her files, papers or books at one of the houses they tended to either disappear or be defaced. She suspects that her brother sold her books for psychology and sociology. It is difficult for her to study because she has a lot of responsibility for younger children and often has to make them dinner, collect and take them to school and babysit. She appeared to be doing her best under overwhelming odds. She did not complain about the demands made on her by her family but accepted them as reasonable.

Miss Baxter thought it would be a good idea if she took over the role of her personal tutor. She negotiated with the team to allow some morning lateness if Alison had to

▶

take her brothers and sisters to school. This would be explained to the other students in the group, stressing that Alison had family commitments which made it difficult for her to get to her class on time. It was also arranged for Alison to have a staff locker where she could leave her books and files. She was allowed to stay behind at the end of the day and given a space to work in. She agreed to turn off her phone while she was in class, explaining to her family that it would be confiscated if it was left on. Alison managed to finish her A levels, although it was never easy for her; she got grades high enough to go to university but decided that she wanted to earn some money.

This case study illustrates how sanctions and rewards can only go so far in managing the behaviour of learners. Alison was encouraged by her previous school to keep studying, even though it was difficult for her. At college her lecturers, with the support of the senior management team, were able to offer Alison a range of solutions to allow her to continue to study, treating her with mutual respect and positive self-regard.

Questions for discussion

1 *Would the sorts of solutions offered by the humanistic approach be possible in a large secondary school?*

2 *Behavioural approaches are seen as authoritarian, imposing rules, rewards and sanctions from the outside to encourage acceptable student behaviour, while the humanistic approach encourages internal reflection and self-discipline. Does this thinking, which sees these processes as dichotomous, reflect human behaviour in practice?*

Summary

Psychological approaches to behaviour management

Psychological approaches try to make sense of behaviour by looking at a range of psychological processes. The field of psychology is divided into diverse perspectives/approaches which place emphasis on different underlying factors that influence behaviour. This chapter has examined a range of different psychological approaches and applied them to managing the behaviour of learners. The following approaches have been explored:

- the behavioural approach;
- the cognitive approach;
- the humanistic approach.

The behavioural approach to managing behaviour assumes that behaviour is largely determined by the environment and that new behaviours can be taught and learned. The methods used to change behaviour are positive reinforcement, negative reinforcement, and punishment.

The cognitive approach to managing behaviour assumes that problem behaviour arises as a direct result of how situations are perceived or interpreted by the learner or the teacher. According to this approach, 'faulty or maladaptive thinking' is often the cause of disruptive or badly managed behaviour.

▶

The humanistic approach to managing behaviour places emphasis on democracy in the classroom and the importance of fostering mutual respect between teachers and learners. This approach assumes that all children are basically good and have an innate capacity for psychological growth if they are exposed to the right conditions. Disruptive or badly managed behaviour is simply the result of unmet needs.

Policy approaches to behaviour management

There are a number of **influential reports** about managing the behaviour of learners, which are reflected in government policy; some of these have been heavily influenced by psychological approaches, particularly the behavioural approach.

The Elton Report (1989) was the result of concerns raised in the media about a perceived worsening of pupil behaviour and a concern that teachers were not up to the job. It pointed to the variation between teachers and their ability to manage groups as central to behaviour management.

Policy in the years after the Elton Report tried to identify groups of learners who presented particular behavioural issues. Government policies to address these issues included the introduction of home–school agreements.

The Steer Report (2009) identified low level disruptive behaviour as the main problem for teachers, and placed more emphasis on schools using strategies like a whole school approach and nurture groups to raise the standards of behaviour in the classroom.

Behaviour management in practice

A range of different approaches to whole school behaviour have emerged in different schools; some whole school approaches have developed rigid systems of behaviour management and are underpinned by the behavioural approach. Two such examples of these approaches are Assertive Discipline and Behaviour for Learning (BfL).

Assertive Discipline is a whole school approach based on behavioural principles, which places emphasis on the role of the 'assertive teacher'. All teachers are expected to be assertive in the same way, and 'timid teachers' are criticised for not having enough control over their pupils. According to this approach, 'timid' teachers are largely to blame for disruptive behaviour in the classroom.

Behaviour for Learning (BfL) is built on the expectation that behaviour management will be implemented by all staff within the school. It is based on a system of incremental rewards and sanctions, with the emphasis on rewarding positive behaviour.

Assertive Discipline and BfL provide an overarching system to manage behaviour, but it is argued that they can become mechanistic and formulaic because they do not encourage discussion or problem-solving.

Evaluation of the whole school approach: There are **barriers to a whole school approach,** which make it difficult for a single approach to managing behaviour to work.

Teachers are not a homogeneous group. Even within the same school, teachers can disagree about the best approach to managing behaviour. Some teachers will

▶

163

be much more liberal in their relationships with students, while others will foster a more humanistic approach, encouraging self-awareness and self-discipline.

Pupils are not a homogeneous group and can be an obstacle to the implementation of whole school policies. Teachers cannot always change how pupils feel about themselves, especially if they have problems outside school or have no sense of belonging to the 'system'. Rigid school rules are likely to give some children something to rebel against. Psychological approaches to managing the behaviour of learners have contributed to a greater understanding of the causes of pupil behaviour and the difficulties teachers face on a daily basis. It has also raised important questions about the curriculum, social factors and issues of motivation which are all contributory factors to how pupils see themselves as learners.

References

Alberto, P.A. and Troutman, A.C. (2009) *Applied Behavior Analysis of Teachers*, London: Pearson.

Ayers, H., Clarke, D. and Murray, A. (2000) *Perspectives on Behaviour: A Practical Guide to Effective Interventions for Teachers*, Oxon: David Fulton.

Ball, S.J. (2007) *Education plc: Private sector participation in public sector education*, London: Routledge.

Bennathan, M. and Boxhall, M. (2000) *Effective intervention in primary schools: Nurture groups*, 2nd edn, London: Fulton, cited in Cooper and Whitebread (2007).

Brandt, R. (1988) On students' needs and team learning: A conversation with William Glasser, *Educational Leadership*, 45(6), pp. 38–45, cited in Tauber (2007).

Canter, L. and Canter, M. (1976) *Assertive discipline: A take charge approach for today's educators*, Santa Monica, CA: Canter and Associates.

Canter, L. and Canter, M. (2001) *Assertive discipline: Positive behavior management for today's classroom*, Santa Monica, CA: Canter and Associates.

Chaplain, R. (2003) *Teaching without disruption in the secondary school: A model for managing pupil behaviour*, London: RouledgeFalmer.

Cooper, P. and Whitebread, D. (2007) The effectiveness of nurture groups on student progress: evidence from a national research study, *Emotional and Behavioural Difficulties*, 12(3), pp. 171–90.

Daniels, H. and Garner P. (1999) *World year book of Education 1999*, Inclusive Education, Routledge.

Department of Education and Science (1989) *Discipline in Schools* (The Elton Report), London: HMSO.

Department of Education and Science (1994) *Pupil Behaviour and Discipline*, Circular 8/94, London: DfE, cited in Miller (2003:15).

Department of Education and Science (1994) *The Education of Children with Emotional and Behavioural Difficulties*, Circular 9/94, London: DfE, cited in Ellis and Tod (2009:35).

Department for Education and Skills (2003) *Youth Cohort Studies: The Activities and Experiences of 18-year-olds: England and Wales (2002)*, London: DfES.

Department for Education and Skills (2003) *Every Child Matters*, London: DfES.

Department for Education and Skills (2005) *Learning Behaviour: The Report of the Practitioners on School Behaviour and Discipline* (The Steer Report), London, Nottingham: DfES.

Department for Education and Skills (2007) *Social and Emotional Aspects of Learning* (SEAL), Nottingham: DfES.

Department for Education and Skills (2009) *Learning Behaviour: Lessons Learned* (The Steer Report), Nottingham: DfES.

Dwivedi, K. and Gupta, A. (2000) 'Keeping it cool': Anger management through group work, *Support for Learning*, 15(2), pp. 76–81.

Ecclestone, K. and Hayes, D. (2008) *The Dangerous Rise of Therapeutic Education*, London: Routledge.

Ellis, A. (1962) *Reason and emotion in psychotherapy*, Secaucus, NJ: Lyle Stuart.

Ellis, S. and Tod, J. (2009) *Behaviour for Learning: Proactive approaches to behaviour management*, Oxon: Routledge.

Elton (1989) See Department of Educational Science (1989).

Garner, P. (2005) Behaviour for Learning, in Capel, S., Leask, M. and Turner, T. (eds) *Learning to Teach in the Secondary School: A Companion to School Experience*, Oxon: Routledge.

Gatongi, F. (2007) Person-centred approach in schools: Is it the answer to disruptive behaviour in our classrooms? *Counselling Psychology Quarterly*, 20(2), pp. 205–11.

Glasser, W. (1969) *Schools without failure*, New York: Harper & Row.

Hammersley, M. (1984) Staffroom news, in Hargreaves, A. and Wood P. (eds) *Classrooms and Staffrooms: Sociology of Teachers and Teaching*, The Open University.

Hanko, G. (1994) Discouraged children: When praise does not help, *British Journal of Special Education*, 12(4), pp. 166–68.

Harris, A. and Goodall, J. (2008) Do parents know they matter? Engaging all parents in learning, *Educational Research*, 50(3), pp. 277–89.

Hendry, R. (2009) *Building and Restoring Respectful Relationships in Schools: A guide to using restorative practice*, Oxon: Routledge.

Johnson, M. (1999) *Failing School, Failing City*, Jon Carpenter Publishing.

Jones, F.H. (1987) *Positive Classroom Discipline*, New York: McGraw-Hill.

Kyriacou, C. (2009) *Effective Teaching Schools: Theory and Practice*, Cheltenham: Nelson Thornes.

Landrum, T.J. and Kauffman, J.M. (2006) Behavioural Approaches to Classroom Management, in Evertson, C.M. and Weinstein, C.S. (eds) *Handbook of Classroom Management*, USA: Taylor & Francis Group.

Lucey, H. and Walkerdine, V. (1999) Boys' underachievement, social class and changing masculinities, in T. Cox (ed.) *Combating Educational disadvantage*, London: Falmer.

MacLure, M. and Jones, L. (2008) *Becoming a problem: How and why children acquire a reputation as 'naughty' in the earliest years at school*, Economic and Social Research Council.

Madsen, C.H., Becker, W.C. and Thomas, D.R. (1968) Rules, praise, and ignoring: Elements of elementary classroom control, *Journal of Applied Behavioural Analysis*, 1(2), pp. 139–50.

McCluskey, G., Lloyd, G., Stead, J., Kane, J. and Weedon, E. (2007) 'I was dead restorative toady': From restorative justice to restorative approaches in school, *Cambridge Journal of Education*, 38(2), pp. 199–216.

Miller, A. (2003) *Teachers, parents and classroom behaviour: A psychosocial approach*, Buckingham: Open University Press.

Miller, A., Ferguson, E. and Moore, E. (2002) Parents' and pupils' causal attributions for difficult classroom behaviour, *British Journal of Educational Psychology*, 72; pp. 27–40.

Mosley, J. (1996) *Quality Circle Time in the primary classroom: Your essential guide to enhancing self esteem, self discipline and positive relationships*, Cambridge: LDA.

Office for Standards in Education (2005) *Managing challenging Behaviour*, London: HMSO.

Office for Standards in Education (2006) *Improving behaviour*, London: Her Majesty's Stationery Office.

Porter, L. (2000) *Behaviour in schools: Theory and practice for teachers*, Buckingham, PA: Open University Press.

Porter, L. (2006) *Behaviour in schools: Theory and practice for teachers*, Buckingham, PA: Open University Press.

Reynolds, S. (2007) Educational and Child Psychology Annual Conference. Online conference report: http://www.bps.org.uk/media-centre/press-releases/releases$/division-of-educational-and-child-psychology/nurture.cfm, last viewed 4 April 2010.

Shores, R.E., Jack, S.L., Gunter, P.L., Ellis, D.N., DeBriere, T.J., and Wehby, J.H. (1993) Classroom interactions of children with behaviour disorders, *Journal of Emotional and Behavioural Disorders*, 1, pp. 27–39.

Steer (2005) See Department for Education and Skills (2005).

Steer (2009) See Department for Education and Skills (2009).

Tauber, R.T. (2007) *Classroom Management: Sound theory and effective practice*, Westport: Praeger.

Tomlinson, S. (2005) *Education in a post-welfare society*, Open University Press.

Visser, J. (2000) *Managing behaviour in classrooms*, London: David Fulton.

Watkins and Wagner (2000, cited in Ellis and Tod:161).

Wearmouth, J., Glynn, T., Robin, C., Berryman, R. and Berryman, M. (2004) *Behaviour Management in Schools: Issues and challenges*, London: David Fulton.

Wearmouth, J., Glynn, T. and Berryman, M. (2005) *Perspectives on Student Behaviour in Schools: Exploring theory and developing practice*, Oxon: Routledge.

Willis, P. (1977) *Learning to Labour: How working class kids get working class jobs*, Farnborough: Saxon House.

Woolfolk-Hoy, A. and Weinstein, C.S. (2006) Student and Teacher Perspectives on Classroom Management, in Evertson, C.M. and Weinstein, C.S. (eds) *Handbook of Classroom Management*, USA: Taylor & Francis Group.

6

Communication and change: transactional analysis and cognitive behavioural theory

Vivienne Walkup

Contents

Introduction

Within education, debates about problematic behaviour continue to be at the centre of many national initiatives and media reports. Social inclusion policies mean that schools and colleges often struggle to meet targets such as reducing truancy and increasing achievement as they deal with issues of challenging behaviour. The details and underpinnings of these policies are explored elsewhere in this text (see Chapters 5 and 9), but here the focus is on the importance of interpersonal communications and clear thinking as a critical part of understanding problematic behaviour and non-productive learning experiences. This chapter aims to contribute to the issue of understanding behaviour and explores effective ways of reacting to learners in order to improve successful learning. Working with others effectively within any kind of learning situation involves forming relationships and clear communications. The process of forming relationships between teachers and learners may be difficult and many teachers feel unprepared for the challenges involved in making these connections although increasingly they are pressured by societal concerns about student behaviour (Rogers, 2000). Currently behavioural management models within the UK education system draw heavily upon learning theory and behavioural concepts such as establishing rules, using rewards and consequences and monitoring behaviour (as we saw in Chapter 5). This chapter looks at two alternative or additional models which are useful within the learning situation to facilitate working relationships, enhance communications and encourage clear thinking. These are **transactional analysis (TA)** and **cognitive behavioural theory (CBT)**.

This chapter aims to:

- Provide an outline of transactional analysis and consider ways in which it is useful within the learning situation.

- Consider ways in which transactional analysis and cognitive behavioural theory are similar and different.

- Explore cognitive behavioural theory and its value within education.

- Critically evaluate these models in terms of their theoretical underpinnings and their applications within educational contexts.

Case study 6.1
Communications failure?

Kyle is twenty years old and is taking an Access course (available to adults without the necessary higher education entry qualifications) as he wishes to enter university and gain a degree. He left school at sixteen to study music at college but dropped out after a few months saying it was not what he had expected and he felt it was leading him nowhere. Since then he has been working in retail but recognises that he will always be on low pay unless he acquires further qualifications. On the Access course Kyle engages well in class discussions but has handed in no written work. His tutor asks him about this.

Tutor: 'Kyle, still no work from you, I see.'

Kyle: 'No, sorry, I had trouble with the PC at home. I'll get it done by Monday and hand it in.'

The work is not handed in on Monday, however, and Kyle himself fails to appear in the lesson. A week further on the tutor rings Kyle on his mobile as his home number was not answered and asks about his work.

Tutor: 'What's happening Kyle? Am I to assume you've left the course?'

Kyle: 'No, I've been ill. I'll get it done for you and bring it in next week.'

The situation continues in this way with Kyle repeatedly making promises but failing to submit any written work. Therefore Kyle fails the course.

Questions for discussion

1 *How would you respond to this situation if you were the tutor?*
2 *In what ways might you be able to deal with Kyle differently so that a more positive outcome is achieved?*

What is transactional analysis?

Communication is the most fundamental and important aspect of human relationships. Generally, communication runs fairly smoothly and we are hardly aware of it but when we encounter problems such as misunderstandings or inappropriate responses to our communications it is important to address these if learning is to take place. Transactional analysis (TA) is a theory about human personality and interactions which draws upon a range of psychological approaches including psychodynamic, humanistic, cognitive and behavioural (see definitions and discussion of these perspectives throughout this chapter). TA is rooted in the work of Eric Berne (a clinical psychologist in the USA) in the 1960s (Berne, 1961, 1964, 1972) and was originally applied to psychotherapy but has developed to include applications in education and organisational development. The underlying principles or philosophy of TA are outlined here.

Philosophy of TA

TA is based on the following philosophical assumptions about the essence of people:

- People are OK (everyone has value and is worthy of respect).
- Everyone has the capacity to think (apart from those with serious brain damage).
- People decide their own destiny and can make changes to this (we are responsible for our own thinking and behaviour so can change this). (Stewart and Joines, 1987)

It is useful to understand these principles within the context of the learning situation as they underpin the whole framework of TA, so let us think about the first assumption ('People are OK') in those terms. Berne liked to keep terminology simple and jargon free and used everyday language such as 'OK' where possible to make things easily understandable and accessible to all (you will notice this throughout our exploration of TA). Notions of human beings as valuable and worthy of respect are central to *humanistic* approaches to understanding people's minds and behaviour. Humanistic approaches to psychology (founded by Abraham

Maslow and Carl Rogers, among others) assume that human beings are intrinsically good, worthy of respect and striving towards developing their potential (see Chapter 4 for discussion of humanistic approaches to motivation).

It may seem difficult to envisage a frustrated teacher or student being able to see that the behaviour of the other is OK when they are filled with anger, dislike or fear. However, what Berne meant by saying that everyone is OK was that each individual is essentially a worthwhile human being in their own right. Therefore, we might be annoyed by the *behaviour* of the person and not 'OK' with this, but that does not mean that the person himself is not 'OK'. So it might be that, for example, a certain individual is bullying another, behaving maliciously, distracting others, taking no part in the group activities or constantly in a state of stress about the work they are being asked to do. Clearly this person is exhibiting behaviour which is not OK but the person could still be thought of, on balance, as being OK. It indicates rather that she/he is not functioning in an OK way within this learning context. This is an important distinction: it means that the person can change his/her 'not-OK' behaviour as it is only one aspect of them, whereas it would be impossible to change their 'essence' or fundamental self. From the person's perspective this is therefore not a rejection of them but of their behaviour, so is likely to elicit a less negative response.

Let us think now about the second assumption (Everyone has the capacity to think) as, again, this is an essential ingredient in the learning process, regardless of the type of learning or the age of the learner. Berne recognised that individuals (apart from those with organic brain damage) were responsible for their own thoughts and behaviour. So, in the learning situation it may be that the person in the teaching role invites and encourages learning to take place but is not responsible for the way that the person in the student role thinks about their own learning. It might be, for example, that in a group of twenty learners one person is bored and complains that the lesson is dull. The teacher might be invited to think that he/she is responsible for this because he/she has produced a boring lesson which is not stimulating or exciting enough. However, TA would place the responsibility for this with the learner as he/she has the capacity to think in an active way about what he/she is learning but is choosing not to. Therefore 'boredom' is in the mind of the beholder!

The third assumption (People decide their own destiny and can make changes to this) links directly with this because thinking about our actions and recognising that we have choices means that we have opportunities for change. So the learner who is complaining about boredom could reflect and recognise that he/she is bored because he is not bothering to listen or prepare for this lesson: this means that he/she is not following what is happening properly. Or it could be that they have not had enough sleep or that they have other problems on their minds. This gives him/her options about whether to change this behaviour to avoid being bored next time, or to continue being bored which will result in their learning less completely, or not learning at all. Whichever option is taken, it becomes a conscious choice wherein the learner assumes responsibility for his/her own thoughts and actions. Both of these assumptions (the capacity to think, and to decide one's own destiny) draw upon **cognitive behavioural approaches** to understanding human behaviour because they focus on the way that individuals process and respond to information. These are explored more fully later in this chapter.

? Stop and reflect

- *Look again at the philosophy of TA. Do you find any of these principles surprising? If so, in what ways?*
- *Do any of them challenge your own way of thinking about yourself and/or others?*

The key principles upon which TA is built are also fundamental to education itself, as within education assumptions are made about including and providing opportunities for all (people are OK), engaging learners in thinking (everyone can think) and encouraging development (everyone can change). Let us look now at the central structure of TA. The basic framework includes a number of concepts which are particularly relevant within education. These concepts will be outlined and discussed here with reference to a range of educational contexts. We begin then with the 'ego state' model before moving on to 'transactions', 'strokes' and 'time structuring'.

The ego-state model

The 'ego state' model describes the way personality is *structured*, suggesting that people have three parts to their personality: 'parent', 'adult' and 'child'. (This is similar in some ways to Freud's notions of '**id**', '**ego**' and '**superego**' and is the foundation of TA (Stewart & Joines, 1987) and in this way draws upon **psychodynamic approaches** to psychology.)

Psychodynamic approaches to psychology are based on the work of Sigmund Freud and stress the importance of early childhood experiences and the unconscious mind. Personality is described as a dynamic mechanism consisting of the *id* (basic instincts and desires), the *ego* (finds realistic ways of meeting needs of the *id*) and the *superego* (morality and ideals).

Psychodynamic theory assumes that we move between these different aspects of our personality as we interact with the world. In TA terms this equates with when we are involved in conversations or 'transactions' either with others or with ourselves. Each ego state has its own consistent ways of thinking, feeling and behaving (Berne, 1966), as listed below.

- *Parent*: aspects of ourselves which we have copied from our own parents or caregivers.
- *Adult*: direct response to the present (here-and-now) situation using all the resources and knowledge we have at our disposal.
- *Child*: reversion to childhood feelings, thoughts and behaviour which we learned as strategies for survival.

Controversies

Has Eric Berne oversimplified?

Let us look here at two of the debates about TA so that we can consider these as we read the rest of the chapter.

Berne has been criticised by some writers who argue that he has reduced Freud's work to a simplistic model which does not accurately represent psychodynamic theory.

Agree: Shertzer and Stone (1980) suggested that TA is 'little more than a warmed-over simplified psychoanalytical theory' (p. 210).

Disagree: Berne deliberately shifted the focus of psychodynamics and used simple language in order to provide an accessible theoretical model. He focused on internal processes to the analysis of interpersonal interactions in order to address change rather than simply gain insight into the person's problems. John McLeod (1993:85) acknowledges this:

> The use of everyday language . . . serves to demystify psychodynamic ideas and make them more accessible and relevant to ordinary people. The concept of ego states also implies a great deal more conscious awareness of these structures and how they operate than is assumed in traditional psychoanalysis.

TA is also accused of being a 'Pop' psychology which lacks depth.

Agree: Clinebell (1981) comments on '. . . the oversimplified way in which the PAC ego states are often described' (p. 7).

Disagree: In his original work Berne stressed the importance of a time dimension in the ego state model. He defined parent and child as both echoing the past whereas adult was a response to the present 'here-and-now' using fully the person's developed resources and abilities. All three ego states include thinking, feeling and behaviours, which is different from the later, oversimplified model which assumes that 'Adult is thinking, Child is feeling and Parent is oughts and shoulds'. (Stewart and Joines, 1987:xiii).

What do you think? Which side of the argument do you favour?

The **structural ego state model** is usually represented diagrammatically, as shown in Figure 6.1.

When we think about any kind of learning situation it becomes clear that these ego states have a particular significance. Let us consider this for a moment.

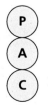

Figure 6.1 **The structural ego state model**
Source: http://www.ta-tutor.com/ztatutor.html

Activity

Visualise yourself as a student entering a classroom or learning space. As you enter, you see the teacher/lecturer look at her watch. Are you:

(a) Afraid of being told off for being late?

(b) Annoyed by the teacher's petty clock-watching?

(c) Certain that you are on time for the lesson?

Which ego-state are you in?
  You may recognise your reactions as similar to one of those listed below:

● If you are feeling frightened that you were going to be 'told off' and you have a sinking feeling in your stomach, you are in your child ego state.

● If you feel that the tutor is out of date and should not be using such obvious ways of managing the classroom, you are in your parent ego state.

● If you wait to see what happens next as you are sure that you were within time, you are in your adult ego state.

The ego state you are in at any given moment is relevant when you interact with others, who will also be in one of their three ego states. If you recognised that you were in the child ego state in the 'teacher looking at her watch' situation, you would be communicating this by your behaviour. You might, for example, be looking up at the teacher and raising your shoulders, lowering your head, fiddling nervously with your hands or smiling apologetically depending upon the types of behaviour you learned to use when in situations you saw as threatening as a child. If you were in the parent ego state, you might be shaking your head, raising your eyebrows, looking towards the ceiling or pursing your lips as one of your own parent figures did to show disapproval. If you recognised that you were in the adult ego state, you would be behaving and thinking in a 'grown-up' way, appropriate to the situation. So you might, for instance, appear fairly relaxed and be waiting for eye-to-eye contact with the teacher in order to find out why she is looking at her watch. Now let us think about the way this is likely to impact upon us as we *function* in the world.

The **functional ego state model** is shown in Figure 6.2 and includes additional categories within the parent and child ego states. These are:

● **Parent** is divided into *controlling or critical parent* (attempting to control or 'put down' other people) and *nurturing* parent (caring, protecting and looking after other people).

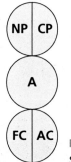

Figure 6.2 **The functional ego state model**
Source: http://www.ta-tutor.com/ztatutor.html

- **Child** is divided into *adapted child* (responding to rules and expectations learned in childhood) and *free child* (spontaneous response taking no account of rules or expectations).

[It is assumed that **adult** includes all of our 'grown-up' ways of managing and responding to the current situation or the 'here-and-now' so this is not sub-divided.]

When we think about the ways we operate in the learning situation (whether as a pupil/student or a teacher/lecturer/facilitator) this model becomes very useful in terms of understanding and improving our working relationships. Let us think about our own experiences for a moment, with the help of the following activity.

Activity

Reflect for a moment upon a teacher or lecturer that you remember well. Was he/she communicating from a particular ego state that you are now able to identify? Have a look at these examples and see if you recognise the ego states involved:

1 You must pay attention to this or you will fail the exam. (Controlling/critical parent)

2 I know it is difficult to concentrate while there is noise outside. I will go and have a word with the people concerned. (Nurturing parent)

3 Let's read this poem through together and then talk about what we think it means. (Adult)

4 Come on, let's go outside – it's too warm to work on a day like this. (Free child)

5 I do hope you like the lesson today and that you will all be quiet for me. (Adapted child)

When we think about these examples of ego states it is clear that there are a number of possible ego states for those in the teaching/lecturing role. It is also apparent that the use of a particular ego state is likely to invite a particular response, so for example:

- *Teacher 1* (controlling parent) is likely to evoke feelings of fear, apprehension or rebelliousness which are rooted in the learner's adapted child ego state. This is hardly a healthy position for someone in the learning situation who is aiming to take in information and gain understanding because it means that they are responding to the demands of the teacher's parent ego state rather than engaging in the here-and-now learning from their own adult ego state.

- *Teacher 2* is communicating from the nurturing parent ego state, which again is likely to evoke an adapted child response, perhaps invite the learner to feel cared for but rather helpless, as someone is fighting on their behalf. Again, this is not likely to elicit the kind of adult thinking required to grasp knowledge.

- *Teacher 3* does invite an adult response as he/she directs and encourages a here-and-now response to the stimulus (poem). There is no attempt to force or protect the pupil/student here, but an acknowledgement of sharing the learning experience.

- *Teacher 4* in free child shares her/his spontaneous responses with the group of learners, allowing these to direct them away from the required task and

Figure 6.3 **Communication between learners and educators is affected by their ego states. What kind of exchange do you think is happening in this picture?**
Source: Getty Images: Echo.

inviting them to respond from their own free child ego states. However, this might evoke the critical parent ego state from some students who could see this as irresponsible and unfair.

- *Teacher 5*, coming from adapted child, is appealing to the nurturing parent ego states of her/his learners thus signalling that he/she is not adequate and putting her/him at the mercy of the group.

Ego states and the ways in which they affect communications are of central importance whenever two people communicate. Berne called these communications *transactions* (hence transactional analysis), a term which we will now explore.

Transactions

A **transaction** is the basic unit of social interaction in TA. Eric Berne defined a transaction as follows:

> A transaction consisting of a single stimulus and a single response, verbal or non-verbal, is the unit of social action. It is called a transaction because each party gains something from it, and that is why he engages in it.
>
> Berne, 1972:20

When two people meet and one person presents some form of communication (*stimulus*) and the other person responds (*response*) a simple transaction has taken place. So, for example, a person joining a group of adult learners for an evening class might look at the teacher and say, 'Hello' to which the teacher might reply,

'Hello there.' It is possible for either of the two people to use any of their three ego states so potentially there are six ego states involved in any meeting between two people. Transactions are identified as being *complementary*, *crossed* or *ulterior*:

Complementary transactions

Complementary transactions refer to those which are smooth and have an ordinary 'feel' to them. They are called complementary because they involve the ego state which is addressed being the one which responds and **when shown on a drawing the lines of communication (or vectors) are parallel.** So, in the example above, the adult learner is sending a stimulus from her adult ego state to the teacher's adult ego state when she says, 'Hello' and the teacher responds from adult, directing her response to the adult learner's adult, replying, 'Hello there.' This is represented diagrammatically in Figure 6.4a.

It is also possible to have complementary (parallel) transactions between the following ego states:

- *Parent to child/child to parent.* For example the teacher might say, 'Make sure that you take notes' (controlling parent to adapted child) and the student replies, 'Yes, I'm writing everything down' (adapted child to controlling parent).

- *Parent to parent/parent to parent.* For example, the learner could comment, 'I do think the younger students are lazy – they never do any work' (controlling parent to controlling parent) and the teacher might reply, 'Yes, they certainly don't realise the opportunity they have to improve themselves' (controlling parent back to controlling parent).

- *Child to child/child to child.* For example, an adult learner might say, 'Let's finish early tonight so we can go down the pub' (free child to free child) and the tutor replies, 'Go on then – we could catch Happy Hour if we're quick!' (free child to free child).

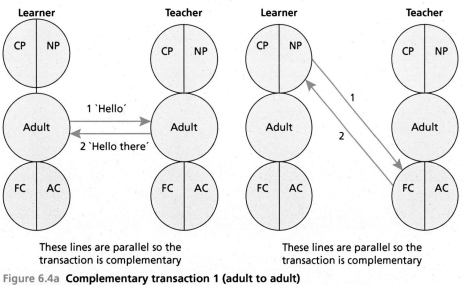

These lines are parallel so the transaction is complementary

These lines are parallel so the transaction is complementary

Figure 6.4a **Complementary transaction 1 (adult to adult)**
Source: Vivienne Walkup.

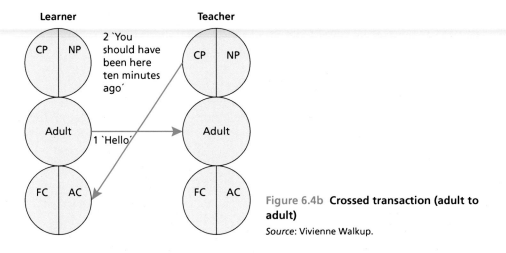

Figure 6.4b **Crossed transaction (adult to adult)**

Source: Vivienne Walkup.

Complementary transactions have a predictable, almost comfortable 'feel' to them and can continue indefinitely depending upon the topic. However, crossed transactions have an unexpected and uncomfortable 'feel' to them: let us look at these now.

Crossed transactions

Crossed transactions are the ones which cause us trouble in our communications with others. They involve transactions which are directed towards a particular ego state in the receiver but the response comes from another ego state and the communication lines are crossed. So, if we return to the earlier example of the adult leaner entering the room and saying, 'Hello' to the tutor (A–A) but make this into a crossed transaction, it would mean that the tutor might reply, 'You should have been here ten minutes ago' (critical parent–adapted child). See Figure 6.4b for a diagram of this.

The four most commonly occurring types of crossed transactions are:

- adult adult–parent child AA–PC.

- adult adult–child parent AA–CP (stimulus 'Hello' AA/ Response 'Oh, I'm sorry I haven't brought you a handbook' CP).

- child parent–adult adult CP–AA ('Where on earth have you been hiding?' PC/ Response 'Hello there, welcome to the psychology class' AA). Crossed transactions often involve negative feelings and tend to either end quickly or escalate into 'rows'.

Activity

See if you can identify the ego states and types of transactions involved in the following:

1 (a) 'I will not tolerate any lateness in my class. You must always be here on time.'
   (b) 'Oh dear, I'm really sorry.'

2 (a) 'I'm really tired so I'm staying in bed today.'
   (b) 'Good idea, I'll join you.'

3 (a) 'I'm sorry to hear you've got problems at home. Would you like some extra support?'
   (b) 'I really don't think it's any of your business. You shouldn't stick your nose in.'

> ↖ *Connect and explore*
>
> Berne's notions of non-verbal communication were confirmed by work by Albert Mehrabian, a well-known American educational psychologist. Mehrabian's research on body language (1971) suggested that only 7 per cent of human communications are through spoken words. Although Mehrabian's findings have been challenged (what about written communication or understanding someone speaking in a foreign language?) they provide important insights into the role of non-verbal communication.
>
> For more on this read: **Mehrabian, A.** (2007) *Non-verbal Communication*. Edison: Transaction Publishers (preview available through Google Book Search).

Let us move now to the third type: ulterior transactions.

Ulterior transactions

Ulterior transactions convey two messages simultaneously, and often result in the receiver feeling confused. In ulterior transactions, there is a difference between the actual words spoken or overt social-level message and the psychological-level message which is conveyed covertly through non-verbal communication. For example, the 'Hello' spoken by the student entering the classroom might seem to be an AA communication, but if accompanied by non-verbal signals such as a rising tone of voice, raised eyebrows and hands on hips then the transaction is actually PC. Berne stressed that it was the covert message which determined the outcome of the transaction because human beings learn to read signals before they learn language (Berne, 1964).

Ulterior transactions invite us into the targeted ego states but are often difficult to pinpoint. We may, for example, feel that we are being rebuked (parent–child) but the actual words seem inoffensive and invite a response from the ego state addressed at the psychological level. See Figure 6.4c for a diagram of this type of transaction.

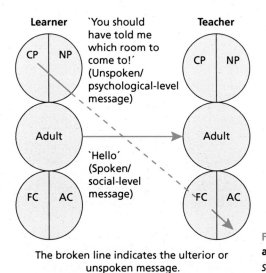

The broken line indicates the ulterior or unspoken message.

Figure 6.4c Ulterior transaction: adult to adult (parent to child)
Source: Vivienne Walkup.

Why are transactions so important?

If learning is to take place then individuals need to be in adult mode so that they may respond to the information or stimulus in the here and now using all of their developed resources. This is not a conscious choice on the part of the learner but knowledge of TA can assist those in the teaching role particularly when communications (and therefore learning) are not progressing smoothly. Now that we have looked at different types of transactions and thought about some ways they can be spotted and changed within the learning situation, let us now explore two further TA concepts: Berne's notion of 'strokes' and how they are involved in 'games'.

Strokes

Berne suggested that human beings have a fundamental need for recognition which he called '**strokes**'. This name is derived from an infant's need for tactile stimulation or literal strokes which are essential for its healthy development and growth.

Connect and explore

Berne's ideas of the importance of human stimulation for healthy growth were based on the work of Renee Spitz (1945, 1946) which found that over a third of infants in an institution for abandoned babies did not survive despite adequate standards of cleanliness, food and medical care. This was compared with children reared by mothers in prison where conditions were much poorer in these respects but all the children survived. The critical difference was in the level of physical contact as those in the foundling institution (orphanage) were often in incubators whereas in the poorer prison they were held by the mothers. This suggested that people need physical contact (strokes) to survive.

More current research (Ackerman, 1990; Walsh, 1991; Field, 1995, 1998; and Jinon, 1996) involving premature infants has also indicated the need for tactile stimulation in order for both physical and psychological development to proceed normally (Patterson and Hidore, 1997). This has been taken on board by maternity units in hospitals which now ensure that even tiny premature babies are physically 'stroked' by those caring for them.

The following articles provide more details of research in this area:

Caulfield, R. (2000) Beneficial effects of tactile stimulation on early development. *Early Childhood Education Journal*, 27(4), pp. 255–57.

Patterson, C. (1997) The primary prevention of psychosocial disorders: a person-centred perspective, *The Person-Centred Journal*, 4(1).

As we mature, this need for physical strokes is largely replaced by other kinds of strokes or recognition such as verbal interactions (conversations) or non-verbal communication (such as smiles, frowns, waves and gestures). As the human need for strokes is critical, much of our time is spent in gathering strokes in order for them to feel that we are alive. However, there are a number of different kinds of strokes and not all of them are pleasant. The list below demonstrates the different sorts of strokes, both positive and negative:

- Positive unconditional – e.g. 'you are wonderful'.
- Positive conditional – e.g. 'you have done a really good assignment'.
- Negative conditional – e.g. 'this is a really poor piece of work'.
- Negative unconditional – e.g. 'you are worthless'.

Berne suggested that any strokes are better than no strokes at all (Stewart and Joines, 1997), so while it might seem strange that people may seek negative strokes, they may do so because they have learnt that it is easier to gain these and, although painful, they are nevertheless powerful forms of strokes.

These ideas provide us with powerful insights into interactions within the learning situation. Think about these with reference to your own experience.

? Stop and reflect

What type of stroke did you most often receive in school, college or other learning situations? Did these differ depending upon the context/teacher? Were some teachers always telling students off, while others gave more praise?

It might be that you received praise or recognition for producing good pieces of work (positive conditional) or found it easier to gain strokes by behaving as the class clown (negative conditional from the teacher plus positive conditional from some peers). These stroke-seeking behaviours might vary depending upon the way in which they are responded to. Some teachers/facilitators deliver praise effectively, but others are much more likely to reprimand or punish, so the behaviour of the learners is linked with this. It is important, therefore, for those in the position of delivering strokes to be aware of the impact they are likely to have upon behaviour (for more on rewards and behaviour management, see Chapter 5).

When we think about strokes in terms of the ego states and transactions taking place, it helps us to understand the process better, because we can see that there is much to be gained through our interactions with others, namely recognition. Let us now move on to consider 'games', another important aspect of TA which connects with ego states, transactions and strokes.

Games

'**Games**' within TA are different from our usual understanding of such activities. In TA they are anything but fun and involve ulterior transactions, negative strokes and repetition. If, for example, you have had a 'row' with someone and walk away saying to yourself, 'Why do I always do this? We never seem to get anywhere' or something similar, you have been playing a game in TA terms. Berne offered a number of definitions which are summed up succinctly by Van Joines:

> A game is the process of doing something with an ulterior motive that:
> 1 is outside adult awareness;
> 2 does not become explicit until the participants switch the way they are behaving;
> 3 results in everyone feeling confused, misunderstood and wanting to blame the other person.
>
> Stewart and Joines, 1987

This clearly explains that we do not always know when we are playing games, that they involve a kind of 'switch' or role change and they result in confusion and misery. Games can occur in any situation and are common within classrooms, staff rooms and other educational situations. Because they are played without conscious awareness neither of the two 'players' is in the here-and-now adult ego state position. Berne suggested that games are played by all of us in order to gain (negative) strokes and that there are different levels or degrees of games (Berne, 1964). These range from those which are uncomfortable but socially acceptable and relatively harmless (first degree), to second degree games involving things (such as minor law breaking, e.g. damaging property, drinking and driving, taking illegal drugs) you would not easily share with others and third degree games (e.g. physical violence or abuse to self or others including suicide) which result in serious, often permanent consequences (death, divorce, prosecution, hospital, etc.).

Within the learning situation

It is likely that first degree games are the ones most commonly encountered although more serious versions may sometimes occur. Awareness of game-playing and ways of dealing with games is extremely useful if effective (adult) learning is to occur.

Berne (1964) identified a sequence that games go through, which he presented in the following formula:

Con + Gimmick + Response → Switch → Cross-up → Pay-off

The '**Con**' is the non-verbal, ulterior transaction which invites the other person into the game.

The '**Gimmick**' is the response from the other person which signals that he/she has been 'hooked' and is willing to play.

The '**Response**' may consist of a number of transactions (could last for moments or years) which continue the game, until:

The '**Switch**' happens. This is when there is a sudden change in the transactions signalling the end.

The '**Cross-up**' occurs immediately following the switch when the second player feels confused or surprised by the sudden change in the transactions.

The '**Pay-off**' is the negative feelings (strokes) experienced by both players following the end of the game.

Before we look at an example of a game and identify the different parts of the formula within it, let us examine a model called the 'drama triangle', devised by Stephen Karpman (1968) which is helpful in terms of analysing games (see Figure 6.5).

As you can see in Figure 6.5, three positions are identified which players take up and move between when taking part in a game: 'Victim', 'Rescuer' and 'Persecutor'. Once the invitation to play a game has been offered and accepted (moving out of

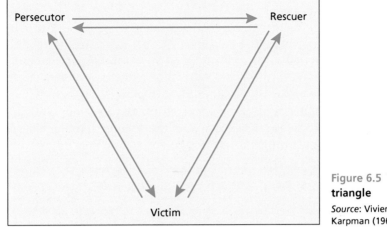

Figure 6.5 **The drama triangle**

Source: Vivienne Walkup, after Karpman (1968).

adult awareness) each player will be on one of the points of the triangle. Let us look at the example below in order to illustrate both the drama triangle and the game formula:

> *Anna:* I can't do my assignment because I can't find any information on the project you set us.
>
> *Tutor:* Have you looked at the reading list? I've included plenty of relevant material there.
>
> *Anna:* Yes, but all of the books you suggested were on loan and I can't afford to buy any.
>
> *Tutor:* OK, but there are plenty of online resources as well. Have you seen those?
>
> *Anna:* Yes, but I cannot access them from home so they're useless.
>
> *Tutor:* Oh dear, that is difficult for you. Why don't you go to the help desk in the resource centre to see if they can advise you on this?
>
> *Anna:* I have, but they say I need a new computer and I haven't got the money to buy one.
>
> *Tutor:* Well, shall I contact the financial advisers and ask about ways in which you can apply for funding to support you?
>
> *Anna:* No, I won't be eligible for any support because I have a part-time job. You see it's useless, I just can't do my work. Thanks for trying to help anyway. *(She sighs and leaves)*

This example illustrates a pair of games which Berne referred to as *Why don't you?* and *Yes but* (Berne, 1964) and these may be familiar to many of you reading this chapter. To begin with Anna issues the **Con** in the **Victim** position (adapted child/I am helpless and cannot think/solve problems myself) and invites the tutor to move into the **Rescuer** position (nurturing parent/I will make this OK for you as you cannot do it yourself). Although the tutor appears to be in adult mode at the beginning and makes appropriate helpful suggestions to her student, she becomes drawn into the game (the **Gimmick**) as the original problem becomes increasingly complicated. Several transactions form the **Response** element until the **Switch** occurs when Anna moves from her *Victim* position to *Persecutor* (critical parent/ rejecting the help and options offered as ineffective) and the tutor feels that she has been taken by surprise (**Cross-up**) and moves to the *Victim* position. The **Pay-off** is the feeling of frustration and inadequacy experienced by the tutor and Anna's feeling of indignation and disappointment at the tutor which confirms her belief that others are to blame for her failure. Thus, negative strokes are experienced by both players. This game is often encountered between teachers and learners and, although the details will differ, the end result is that both parties feel 'bad' and the learner fails to take responsibility for his/her own learning.

Within the learning situation

A number of other games were named by Berne, some of which are listed below with examples of how they might be played within the learning situation:

- **Now I've got you, you son of a bitch (NIGYSOB)** is often paired with **Kick me** and might involve a pupil/student repeatedly behaving in an unacceptable way (in *Persecutor* position but inviting 'kicks' or rejection) and the teacher/tutor tolerating this passively (*Victim*) until she suddenly moves to *Persecutor,* losing control, shouting loudly and sending the pupil from her class (**NIGYSOB** – offloading her anger and feeling blameless).

- **Blemish** is often played by teachers who give only negative feedback to a student (*Persecutor*), inviting the learner into a *Victim* position where they might play **Stupid** or **You can't make me.**

This list is by no means exhaustive and you may have your own versions or different ones altogether. It is more important to know how to recognise and deal with games than to name them so let us move on to that here.

Connect and explore

For a more detailed explanation and exploration about games see **Berne's** (1964) publication *Games people play*. For a brief summary of this book and the games listed within it, go to **http://www.ericberne.com** and click on 'Games people play'.

Stop and reflect

Now that you have some understanding of games, think of one which you have played recently – either as Player 1 (the instigator) or Player 2 (the person drawn into the game) and write answers to the following questions:

- *How did the game begin (what were the 'con' and 'gimmick')?*
- *Which position did you take up in the game? Where did you move to?*
- *What was the 'Pay-off'? Have you played this game before?*

Dealing with games

Games are prolific within the learning situation for a variety of reasons including underlying stereotypical assumptions about power, parent figures and childlike passive behaviour so that learners may unconsciously assume that they are there to be given all the answers by the teacher who is the expert. This places them in a passive, powerless child position with the teacher being assumed to be the active, powerful parent. Therefore we need to be aware of games and the **options** available to deal with them.

Options are the choices we have about the transactions which are occurring (Karpman, 1971) and may be used at any point in the game to interrupt it. Recognising that we are playing a game is the first step: once this has happened we are able to choose a positive ego state and move out of the game. This involves a *crossed* transaction (ego state addressed is not the one which responds) to interrupt the flow of the *complementary* transactions within the game. We do not, of course, have the power to change the other person's response but we can take ourselves out of the game. If you think about the example you used in the last 'Stop and reflect' activity again, consider how you would opt out of the game in future. An effective option is to move into the adult ego state because this means that we are in the here-and-now with all of our developed reasoning powers at our disposal.

Activity

Turn back to the example with Anna and her tutor: how might the tutor have stopped the game? The tutor could have crossed the transactions by staying in or moving back to adult from nurturing parent and perhaps asking Anna whether she has thought of any ways round her problems. This is then addressing Anna's adult rather than adapted child and inviting her to take appropriate responsibility for her own learning and, although there are no guarantees that Anna would respond from adult, it means that the game is diffused because the tutor is not playing and receiving a negative Pay-off.

It is helpful to note that games always involve *discounts* which occur in the opening con and throughout the various stages. A *discount* means that a person is ignoring possible solutions to the problem, but is not aware of this. So Anna is *discounting* her own ability to find ways round the difficulties she has. This means that she is out of adult and not operating in the here-and-now but reverting to earlier child behaviours where she looked to parental figures to do her thinking for her. The longer this continues, the less likely she is to develop her own adult problem-solving skills so those in the teaching situation are not facilitating learning by attempting to rescue their learners.

It is also important to remember that games provide strong negative strokes, which indicates that the person instigating the game is looking to top up their required amount of strokes or 'stroke bank'. Therefore, if those in the teacher role provide effective strokes freely, this should help to discourage the use of games. These are not simply positive strokes given for no reason (named 'plastic fuzzies' by Claude Steiner, 1974) but a combination of positive and negative conditional strokes to guide the learner and provide recognition of her/his individuality. For example, a teacher might comment on the excellent improvement made in a piece of work and

Figure 6.6 A learning contract drawn up by a teacher and student can formalise and clarify the communication process
Source: Getty Images: DK images.

then give feedback on how the errors made could be corrected and enhanced. He/she might also employ ***contract-making*** with learners in order to encourage adult thinking and ownership of responsibility. Let us look briefly at how this might work.

Contracts

Berne used the term '**contracts**' to describe ways in which those using TA in professional contexts (such as therapists, teachers and managers) can encourage change by setting out specifically what changes are possible and necessary, and how these are to be carried out. The use of contracts within educational situations helps to promote clear, open agreements about desired goals and ways of achieving these. SMART targets are currently used within statutory education in the UK (Ofsted, 2006) and the elements involved in these are similar to TA contracts in that they include Specific, Measurable, Appropriate, Recorded and Time-framed goals for learners to work towards.

Drawing up a contract in TA involves adult thinking on the part of both parties (learner and educator) which informs the agreement reached after discussion. So if, for example, a learner was disappointed with his grades and wanted to improve them in future and the tutor wanted to ensure that this was not the beginning of a game (Yes but, NIGYSOB, Stupid, or another game), a contract might be drawn up between them. In this contract the teacher would record what he was prepared to do in order to support the learner and the learner would commit to actions he would carry out (such as regular study, reading or attendance) in order to improve his chances of gaining higher grades. Details of the process and recording of the changing behaviour would be noted, such as the timings of the planned activities and a list of his current grades to provide a baseline.

Within the learning situation

Rhianna is a Year 11 (15/16-year-old) pupil who will be taking GCSEs at the end of the year. She is currently underperforming in terms of coursework (predicted overall B but work at E standard) for a number of subjects and this will affect the outcome of her exam results. During a discussion with her year tutor Rhianna revealed that she was leaving her work to the last minute and so rushing it. This resulted in poor-quality work which was brief and littered with errors. A contract was drawn up which clearly laid out the responsibilities of both Rhianna and her year tutor.

Rhianna

- Agreed that she would work productively on each of the three pieces of coursework for two hours per week and bring her work to her year tutor on a weekly basis (Fridays at 2 p.m.) until the end of the autumn term when the final coursework is submitted.
- She also contracted to listen carefully to the comments made by her year tutor and seek help from relevant subject teachers if she needed support. Attend to any areas for amendment suggested.
- She also agreed to meet with the year tutor in January to discuss her results and measure progress towards B grades from E grades.

Year tutor

- Agreed to meet Rhianna on Fridays at 2 p.m. on a weekly basis in order to read and feedback on the progress she has made on each of the pieces of coursework she is working on.
- The year tutor also contracted to support her requests for access to relevant subject teachers.
- The year tutor contracted to meet with Rhianna in January to discuss her results and measure progress towards Bs from Es.

Let us now turn to a key underlying assumption in TA known as **life-script** to help gain further insight into ourselves and others.

Life-scripts

The kinds of games we play, the ego states we favour, the strokes we like to receive and the types of transactions we have are all linked to our '**life-script**' according to TA theory. A life-script is defined by Berne as 'a life-plan made in childhood, reinforced by the parents, justified by subsequent events and culminating in a chosen alternative' (Berne, 1972). In effect this means that we make early decisions about ourselves when we are very young (from birth to seven years of age) which are then amended slightly as we pass through adolescence. These early decisions are based on our perceptions of the world around us and those in it and are focused on survival for us as infants and young children. Although the decisions made sense then, they are not appropriate for our later life as we mature and develop our abilities and skills, but they will nevertheless influence our views of ourselves and the world. One of the basic assumptions we might make is concerned with whether we saw the world as safe (OK) or hostile (not OK) and ourselves as welcome and secure within it (OK) or unwelcome or at risk (not OK). Berne called these **life positions** (Berne, 1966) and saw them as underpinning the rest of the story or script we create about ourselves as *'winners'* (defined as achieving the enhancing goals set for ourselves) or *'losers'* (not achieving our aims and feeling unhappy with this). Let us examine these here in more detail:

Life positions are represented as four different combinations of ways in which we view the world:

1 I'm OK, you're OK.

2 I'm not OK, you're OK.

3 I'm OK, you're not OK.

4 I'm not OK, you're not OK.

Once we have adopted one of these positions we are likely to construct our script around this and see ourselves in these terms. Although, as adults, we are likely to move between a number of these positions as we encounter the challenges of daily life, we will tend to favour the original position in times of stress. So, if we originally adopt the first position we have a generally positive view of ourselves and others which will inform the 'winning' script we write. Moving to the second option means that we put ourselves into a 'losing' script position because we consider others as more successful, able and valuable than ourselves and thus invite criticism and victimisation. If we take the third option we see others as less valuable and so seek to maintain superiority in order to feel OK ('losing' script). The fourth option is the most negative of all as it involves a view of self and others as worthless, leading to depression and futility (losing script).

When we apply these positions to those involved in any form of education it allows us to understand some of the basic difficulties which might be encountered by both those wishing to learn and those wishing to teach. Here are some examples of how this might occur:

I'm OK, you're OK

Chris: I don't get this bit, Sir. I understand down to Macbeth's speech but then I get lost. Would you go over it again, please?

Teacher: Yes, of course. How are the rest of you with this? ('Not sure' noises from class). OK, I'm going to tackle it another way to make sure it's clear.

I'm not OK, you're OK

Chris: I don't get this, Sir. You explain it well and everything but I'm just thick.

Teacher: Where abouts did you get lost, Chris?

Chris: I don't understand any of it, I never do.

I'm OK, you're not OK

Chris: It's impossible to understand this.

Teacher: OK – let's go over it again.

Chris: No, don't bother, you don't explain clearly. I'll ask my dad when I get home.

I'm not OK, you're not OK

Chris: I just don't get this!

Teacher: Where did you get lost, Chris?

Chris: It's pointless trying to help – I don't understand anything you say. I'm just stupid and there's nothing you can do about it.

Being able to recognise these positions and link them with the other TA concepts (ego states, transactions, strokes, games, life positions and scripts) we have discussed here can be a valuable tool for us in our relationships with others. Within educational contexts where the aim is to develop the ability to think clearly and solve problems, it becomes particularly helpful. Some institutions, such as the school featured in the video clip below, include TA within their framework and teach the basic framework to learners in order to enhance communications and facilitate effective learning. This allows teachers and pupils to use concepts such as critical parent, adapted child and adult when addressing problematic issues and behaviour.

↖ *Connect and explore*

Go to the Teachers TV website at **www.teachers.tv** to view an actual example of TA being used within a middle school: 'Primary management – transactional analysis' and an example of TA training for head teachers: 'Stress relief for heads-transactional analysis and communications'. Both of these were posted in 2006 and they present real world, contemporary insights into TA in practice within education.

Evaluation of TA

Before we move on to look at cognitive behavioural theory (CBT), another model which is useful to improve thinking and learning within education, let us consider some of the strengths of TA and criticisms which are levelled at TA:

Strengths

- Provides a comprehensive, theoretical framework for counselling and analysing communications in a range of contexts including education, counselling, healthcare and other organisations.
- The underlying principles are empowering to individuals as they assume people are equal and worthy of respect.
- Encourages open communication and self-awareness.
- Offers an accessible and practical working model which aims to effect positive change.

Criticisms

Oversimplification of a complex theoretical framework:

- Berne's deliberate use of everyday terms was seen by some as an oversimplification of some heavily theoretical concepts, e.g. Freud's notions of *id*, *ego* and *superego*.

- 'Pop' psychology – in the 1960s TA became something of a 'cult' psychology in the USA particularly, enjoying wide popularity following the publication of *Games people play* in 1964. This resulted in some of the basic ideas becoming trivialised and distorted (Stewart and Joines, 1987), e.g. misunderstanding the notions of parent, adult and child to mean that the adult only involves thinking and reasoning whereas Berne defined it as the fully integrated response to the here-and-now (thoughts, feelings and experience). (See Controversies, p. 171.)

Now that you have acquired some grasp of TA and before we move on to cognitive behavioural theory let us think back to the case study of Kyle at the beginning of the chapter and about the transactions taking place there. The tutor's first question seems to be A–A (Kyle, still no work from you, I see) but Kyle responds from AC–CP (No, sorry, I had trouble with the PC at home. I'll get it done by Monday and hand it in), which suggests that the tutor's words were actually CP–AC. The next transaction is similar as the tutor seems to be asking for here-and-now information (A–A) (What is happening, Kyle? Am I to assume you've left the course?) but receives an AC–CP response (No, I've been ill. I'll get it dome for you and bring it in next week). It seems that the tutor is sending an *ulterior* message to the student which is evoking the adapted child response. In order to engage Kyle's adult he needs to check carefully that he is communicating in a straight, unambiguous way. For example:

Tutor: The deadline for handing coursework in has now passed. Anyone who has not handed work in needs to speak to their tutor.

Kyle: Would it be possible for me to have an extension? The PC at home is not working?

Tutor: There are plenty of PCs here. Do you think you could arrange work here?

Kyle: Yeah. I suppose I could. I'd have to arrange things.

Tutor: We need to agree a realistic extension date, then.

Kyle: I think I'd need two weeks.

Tutor: OK, that is the maximum time limit. The regulations state that longer than that will incur a fail.

Here we see the tutor in straight adult with no judgemental overtones, simply stating the facts and negotiating within the rules and regulations. This invites Kyle to think in the here-and-now about the situation and he responds appropriately. Of course there are no guarantees that Kyle will engage with the coursework or complete the course itself, but this will be his decision.

Can you see alternative ways of analysing the transactions between Kyle and his tutor? It is quite possible that you might as we cannot be sure about the non-verbal communications taking place (such as facial expressions, posture and tone of voice). The important thing is that you recognise the possibility of ending or avoiding games by using adult communication.

Let us now look at cognitive behavioural theory and see how this helps us to understand and address some problems with thinking and learning.

Cognitive behavioural theory

There are similarities between cognitive behavioural theory (CBT) and TA in that both seek to encourage clear thinking and problem solving and that both have wide applications. CBT is used widely and is currently extremely popular within clinical settings as a therapy as well as to address problem behaviours among young people such as school failure (McLaughlin and Vacha, 1992; Quinn et al., 1998), criminal and violent behaviour (Lipsey et al., 2001), substance abuse (Waldron and Kaminer, 2004), and teenage pregnancy. However, TA and CBT differ in the ways in which they analyse and address problems We will first look briefly at some of the background to CBT before moving on to look at the basic principles and how these are relevant within education.

History of education

CBT

- *Behavioural approaches* originated in the work of J.B. Watson in the first half of the twentieth century (Watson, 1913). Watson wanted to create an objective, scientific theory of human psychology which challenged the 'introspective' view current at this time. He and others, such as Pavlov (1927) and Skinner (1953), believed that only observable actions mattered because only they could be recorded and measured. Thus experiments (many of them on animals) formed much of the research supporting this approach. This was understandable at a time when science emerged as a dominant model within western culture.

- *Cognitive approaches* take the opposite view in some ways, believing that it is thought and internal processes that drive behaviour, and that it is therefore important to make a distinction between what happens (events) and the ways in which theses are interpreted by individuals (cognitions). Within psychology, cognitive approaches focus on processes such as memory, attention, perception and information processing in order to understand humans. There is no single starting point for this wide-ranging and diverse approach but it began to emerge as a central discipline in the 1950s with the work of psychologists such as Chomsky (1957), Bruner (1956), Miller (1956) and Newell and Simon (1958).

Background to CBT

It can seem confusing when reading about CBT to find that there are different versions of it, that these are still developing, and that it might be described as a 'movement' rather than a single model (Westbrook et al., 2007). However, CBT mainly stems from the work of Albert Ellis (1962) and Aaron Beck (1976), and draws upon two main influences – behavioural theory and cognitive theory. Let us look at each of these in order to understand where CBT has developed from.

CBT has emerged from these as a combined theoretical framework which draws upon elements of both approaches. We will now look at some of these and explore their usefulness within educational contexts.

Behavioural beliefs, such as the important role of behaviour in determining psychological states, are included within CBT. So if certain behaviours have in the past produced positive results we are likely to feel happy about them and to repeat them: for example, if we have found that smiling at people when we see them produces a smile back, this makes us feel happy, so we are more likely to smile in future, and so on. If, however, we do not receive a smile in return but a sneer or a blank response, then we may wonder why this person does not like us and begin to feel depressed or unlovable. Then we might smile less and look miserable, which is unlikely to evoke a positive response in others and therefore confirm to us that we are not liked by others.

When **applying behavioural principles** to problems the following are likely to be included:

- specifying goals;
- making decisions about how to reach those goals; and
- measuring progress to provide feedback.

These link with **cognitive beliefs** (how we think about ourselves) which precede our feelings and subsequent behaviour. It follows, then, that if our cognitions are changed or modified both feelings and behaviour will change, so changing a learner's appraisal of a situation will lead to an improved response to it.

When applying cognitive principles to problems linked with learning there are a number of approaches which can be used including cognitive therapies (Beck, 1963, 1964; Ellis, 1962) and self-instruction strategies (Meichenbaum, 1977). The main focus here will be on using some of the principles from cognitive therapies as these are seen as most appropriate when addressing negative thinking and encouraging more optimistic attitudes in learners (Barnes, 2000) and this will be followed by a shorter discussion of useful self-instruction strategies.

CBT assumes that individuals hold different beliefs about the world and process the information they receive from the world differently. So the same situation might result in different reactions from different people – the following Activity box describes an example of this.

Activity

Imagine that you are summoned unexpectedly to see the head teacher/principal of the institution where you are studying. Answer the following questions:

- How do you explain this event?
- How do you feel?
- What do you do?

Reflection
You may have *explained* this in a number of ways, such as:

(a) 'Oh no, my results must have been worse than I thought – I'm going to be thrown out', or:

(b) 'That woman/man probably wants to check my enrolment yet again', or

(c) 'I expect she/he wants to talk to me about my options for next year.'

▶

How you *explain* it will influence the way you *feel* about the event, for example:

(a) you might feel scared or perhaps a little angry depending upon how important this course is to you;

(b) then you might feel irritated or angry at what seems to be a waste of time or incompetence on the part of the institution;

(c) you might be pleased that someone is taking an interest in your future.

As you may have noticed, there are already a number of options for how you might feel depending upon your view of your world, but let's now think about the possible consequences of this or what you do:

(a) you approach the Head's office with dread, your heart pounding and become very defensive;

(b) you scowl with impatience as you enter and appear surly;

(c) you enter the office feeling happy and cared for.

Thinking irrationally

As we can see, it is the way the event is perceived that determines the feelings and actions which follow rather than the event itself. Thus when addressing problems and issues the following are likely to be included:

- identifying cognitive 'distortions';
- using logic and searching for evidence to challenge distortions;
- substituting more rational thoughts; and
- planning new thought patterns.

Drawing upon the work of Ellis (1962) and Beck (1976), let us look at some of the ways in which they identify 'irrational thoughts' or 'cognitive **distortions**' and apply these to the learning situation:

- *Overgeneralisation* – where wide-ranging conclusions are drawn from small instances, for example 'I failed my maths test so that means I'm useless at maths and it's not worth me making an effort because I'll obviously fail again.'
- *Distortions* – sometimes referred to as 'all or nothing' or 'black and white' thinking, for example 'I did not get all As in my coursework so that means I'll never be a good student.'
- *Catastrophising* – where faults or errors are magnified but positive achievements are played down, for example 'I only got an A through luck – I am usually the worst in the group.'
- *Absolutes* – using absolute terms such as 'never', 'must', 'have to', 'ought' or 'always', for example 'I must always get the highest mark.'
- *Fortune-telling* – predicting the (negative) outcome of an event, for example 'I know I'm going to hate this course.'

Being able to spot some of these (which you may already have recognised in yourself or others as you read through the examples) provides insights for both

Table 6.1 **The ABCDE theory of psychological functioning**

A *Activator*	B *Beliefs*	C *Consequence*	D *Disputing*	E *Effective response*
Event Situation	Personal meanings	– emotions – behaviour – biology	Ways to break up rigid thinking	New ways of responding

Source: Albert Ellis (1962).

teachers and learners in whatever learning context they might be in. Having become aware of irrational thinking the next step is to challenge it: is there evidence to support what you are thinking? Is this a reasonable conclusion? Even if it were true that you will never be a straight 'A' student, do you feel better or worse for thinking you won't be? The aim here is to encourage realistic thinking which is more likely to help the person reach sensible, well-informed decisions.

ABC theory

Albert Ellis devised an ABC (Activator, Beliefs, Consequences) theory of psychological functioning (part of the REBT approach) which shows how problems develop, and added DE (Disputing arguments and Effective response) to include ways of dealing with these problems (see Table 6.1).

As you can see, this is based on the assumption that thought is dominated by emotional needs which precede logical thinking. In other words, we may not think clearly because our emotional response comes first and gets in the way of our ability to think rationally. These emotional needs may be based on basic irrational assumptions such as:

- 'I must do well at all times.'
- 'People must treat me fairly and give me what I need.'
- 'I am a bad unlovable person if I get rejected.'
- 'I can't stand it when life is really unfair.'
- 'I need to be loved by someone who matters to me a lot.'

? Stop and reflect

Do you recognise any of the above assumptions as being part of the way that you respond to certain situations? Check that you understand why they are irrational assumptions by challenging them, e.g. is it possible for anyone to do well at all times?

One of the key processes involved in the cognitive approach is the concept of *metacognition*. This means thinking about or reflecting upon the way that we think and it is a fairly sophisticated process which is increasingly encouraged within educational settings. Using metacognition allows us to recognise how we think and explore ways in which we might want to change this. Within the ABCDE framework metacognition occurs at the D stage as the person thinks about the ways they respond to certain activators, challenges these and chooses new ways of thinking. In TA this is activated in the adult ego state where 'here-and-now' thinking occurs; irrational assumptions, on the other hand, would be located in the adapted child ego state.

The aim of applying cognitive and behavioural principles in this way is to allow the individual to have insight into their own problems and provide them with the tools and support to change things. Let us now move on to another useful aspect of CBT which involves self-management by learners.

Self-management and self-instruction

Self-management generally means getting learners involved in the basic steps of a behaviour change programme. There is a stage in cognitive development when young children seem to guide themselves through a task using private speech (Vygotsky, 1978, 1986). They talk to themselves, often repeating the words of a parent or teacher. In cognitive behaviour modification, learners are taught directly how to use **self-instruction**. Meichenbaum (1977) outlined the steps:

1 An adult model performs a task while talking to him- or herself out loud (cognitive modelling).
2 The child performs the same task under the direction of the model's instructions (overt, external guidance).
3 The child performs the task while instructing him- or herself aloud (overt, self-guidance).
4 The child whispers the instructions to him- or herself as he/she goes through the task (faded, overt self-guidance).
5 The child performs the task while guiding his/her performance via private speech (covert self-instruction) (p. 32).

Brenda Manning and Beverly Payne (1996) list four skills that can increase student learning: *listening, planning, working* and *checking*. How might cognitive self-instruction help learners develop these skills? One possibility is to use personal booklets or class posters that prompt learners to 'talk to themselves' about these skills. For example, one class of 10 to 11-year-olds in the USA designed a set of prompts for each of the four skills and displayed these around the classroom. The prompts for listening included: 'Does this make sense?' 'Do I understand this?' 'I need to ask a question now before I forget,' 'Pay attention!' 'Can I do what he's telling us to do?' Planning prompts were: 'Do I have everything together that I need?' 'Am I paying attention to this and not my friends?' 'Let me get organised first.' 'What order will I do this in?' 'I know this already'.

Actually, cognitive behaviour modification as it is practised by Meichenbaum and others has many more components than just teaching learners to use self-instruction. Meichenbaum's methods also include dialogue and interaction between teacher and learner, modelling, guided discovery, motivational strategies, feedback, careful matching of the task with the learner's developmental level, and other principles of good teaching. The learner is even involved in designing the programme (Harris, 1990; Harris and Pressley, 1991). Given all this, it is no surprise that learners seem to be able to generalise the skills developed with cognitive behaviour modification to new learning situations (Harris, Graham and Pressley, 1991).

As we did earlier in the chapter with TA, let us now consider some of the strengths of CBT and some of the criticisms which are directed at it before concluding the chapter:

Evaluation of CBT

Strengths

- Provides a straightforward, practical framework which emphasises action (McLeod, 2003).
- Effectiveness confirmed by plenty of research support in many areas including school refusal (King et al., 2000) and anger management for children at risk of exclusion (Humphrey and Brooks, 2006).

Criticisms

- Although cognitive behavioural approaches claim to be scientific there is little evidence of the validity of the assumptions made such as the link between distorted cognitions and behaviour/feelings; for example, just because I know that flying is the safest form of transport doesn't mean that I lose my fear of flying.

Connect and explore

Read **Rob Barnes'** account of a small-scale project which used REBT (Rational Emotive Behaviour Therapy) in the form of a therapeutic board game with 10-year-old pupils to dispute irrational thinking and encourage discussion:

Barnes, R. (2000) Mrs Miggins in the classroom, *British Journal of Special Education*, 27(1), pp. 22–28.

Conclusion

Both CBT and TA are focused on finding workable solutions to problems and helping people become more aware of their own thoughts and emotions. Thus they are linked with the 'emotional intelligence' principle which is currently being recognised as having increasing importance within schools and is included within subjects such as PSHE (personal, social and health education) and voluntary programmes such as SEAL (social and emotional aspects of learning) – see Chapter 5, 'Understanding and managing behaviour'.

Currently there is growing awareness of TA within educational contexts and it is becoming increasingly popular as a means of providing understanding the teacher/pupil relationship. Thus, it provides an alternative or addition to the traditional behaviour management approaches which have dominated the UK educational scene for a number of decades and includes philosophical assumptions which emphasise mutual respect and individual responsibility. It is not applied as a therapeutic tool within educational settings but rather as an alternative way of facilitating learning and teaching. Writers such as Giles Barrow and Trudi Newton have published work which outlines ways in which TA may be used to improve behaviour and raise self-esteem (2001, 2004) and Sandra Newell and David Jeffery apply TA to behaviour management in the classroom (2002).

Similarly, a range of CBT strategies are increasingly included within educational contexts as suggested perspectives for understanding and improving behaviour (Ayers et al., 2000; Squires, 2001).

Case study 6.2
Using the ABCDE framework

Jolie did very badly in science in her recent SATs tests. (*A: Activator*).

She tells herself that this is because she is stupid. This makes her feel ashamed and inferior to her classmates and she thinks that they will make fun of her. (*B: Beliefs*)

Jolie has begun to waste time in lessons by talking and kicking the backs of other pupils' chairs when they are writing. (*C: Consequences*)

Using the **ABCDE** framework to improve this situation would involve *D: Disputing* Jolie's beliefs (B) by applying arguments to attack the irrational beliefs. This might be along the lines of:

- Are there any other possible reasons why you might have failed the tests?
- Do you think that you worked hard during the year to make sure you understood the work you were doing?
- Are you the only person who has failed these tests?
- Have your classmates made fun of you in the past?
- Do you have friends at school?

In the course of questioning her belief that she failed the maths test because she is stupid, Jolie is encouraged to provide more rational responses to the arguments, such as:

- I failed my science tests because I didn't do any revision.
- I did not understand some of the topics we did during the year but I did not ask the teacher for help with them.
- Three other people in my class also failed and one of them is in the top set.
- No, my classmates haven't made fun of me before.
- I've got two really good friends and some people I'm sort of friendly with.

In this way Jolie is disputing her irrational beliefs *(B)* and replacing these with more realistic and effective ones *(E)*. This means that she has the option of addressing the actual problems with science (such as seeking help with understanding and spending time working on this) rather than remaining rooted in her negative thinking which will keep her where she is (believing that she is stupid and incapable of changing that).

Behavioural aspects would also be included alongside the cognitive ones detailed here and these might be in terms of setting specific goals – such as passing the next science test; arranging help and support and keeping to revision timetables; measuring change, perhaps involving reviews of progress with her teacher and so on.

Questions for discussion

Do you think the ABCDE framework is 'just a theory', or do you think it has practical value in learning and teaching situations?

Summary

What is transactional analysis?

- TA is a theory about human personality and interactions based on the principles that people are equally valuable, able to think and capable of changing.

- The *ego state model* is at the centre of the theory and suggests three parts of personality (parent, adult and child) each of which has consistent ways of thinking, feeling and behaving.

- *Transactions* are the basic units of human interactions between two people involving potentially six ego states. They may be complementary, crossed or ulterior.

- For learning to take place effectively individuals need to be in adult so that they are able to respond to the here-and-now.

- *Strokes* are the human being's fundamental need for recognition which develop from tactile stimulation in infancy to a range of different types (such as verbal and non-verbal communication). They may be conditional, unconditional, positive or negative.

- Playing *games* is the process of doing something with an ulterior motive which results in a negative outcome. Games involve a specific formula (Con, Gimmick, Response, Switch, Cross-up and Pay-off) and within this players move around the drama triangle (Victim, Persecutor and Rescuer).

- *Options* allow individuals to make choices about the transactions they take part in and avoid playing games.

- The use of *contracts* can encourage change by setting out clear routes to change (similar to SMART targets in education).

- The term *life-script* is used to describe early decisions people make about their lives which informs the way they view the world (I'm OK, you're OK; I'm not OK, you're OK; I'm OK, you're not OK; I'm not OK, you're not OK).

Evaluation of TA: TA provides a clear, useful framework which empowers individuals and allows change to be effected. However, it may be that its status as a 'pop' psychology in the 1960s resulted in an oversimplification of some of it.

Cognitive behavioural theory

- *Both TA and CBT* encourage clear thinking and problem solving and have wide applications but they differ in the ways they analyse and address problems. CBT draws upon behavioural and cognitive beliefs.

- *Behavioural theory* assumes that psychological responses have been learned so when applying behavioural principles to problems it is likely that this will involve specifying goals, making decisions about how these might be reached and then measuring progress to provide feedback.

- *Cognitive beliefs* assume that how we think about ourselves precedes our feelings and subsequent behaviours so if cognitions are changed then feelings

▶

and behaviour will also change. There are a number of therapeutic approaches linked with CBT but within the learning situation addressing negative thinking and encouraging more optimistic issues are important.

- *Thinking irrationally* by overgeneralising, distorting, catastrophising, dealing in absolutes and fortune-telling (Ellis, 1962; Beck, 1976) often leads to negative attitudes. Being able to spot these and challenge them allows changes to be made.

- *The ABC theory* devised by Albert Ellis is a framework which shows how problems develop (Activator, Beliefs, Consequences) and how they can be changed (D: Disputing and E: replacing with Effective ways of thinking).

- *Self-management and self-instruction* involves changing behaviour by modelling and encouraging the use of 'self-talk' or instruction to guide learners through performance on a task. However, *cognitive behaviour modification* has more components including dialogue, interaction, guided discovery, motivational strategies and matching tasks with developmental level and seems generalisable to other learning situations.

Evaluation of CBT: Strengths of CBT include its effectiveness (plenty of research support for this) and the straightforward, practical framework it provides.

References

Ayers, H., Clarke, D. and Murray, A. (2000) *Perspectives on behaviour: A practical guide to interventions for teachers*, 2nd edn, Oxon: David Fulton.

Barnes, R. (2000) Mrs Miggins in the classroom, *British Journal of Special Education*, 11(1), pp. 22–28.

Barrow, G. and Newton, T. (2001) *Improving behaviour and raising self-esteem in the classroom*, UK: Taylor Francis.

Barrow, G. and Newton, T. (2004) *Walking the talk*, London: David Fulton.

Beck, A. (1963) Thinking and depression, 1: Idiosyncratic content and cognitive distortions, *Archives of General Psychiatry*, Vol. 9, pp. 324–33.

Beck, A. (1964) Thinking and depression, 2: Theory and therapy, *Archives of General Psychiatry*, Vol. 10, pp. 561–71.

Beck, A. (1976) *Cognitive therapy and the emotional disorders*, Harmondsworth: Penguin.

Berne, E. (1961) *Transactional analysis in psychotherapy: A systematic individual and social psychiatry*, New York: Grove Press.

Berne, E. (1964) *Games people play*, New York: Grove Press.

Berne, E. (1966) *Principles of group treatment*, New York: Oxford University Press.

Berne, E. (1972) *What do you say after you say hello?* New York: Grove Press.

Bruner, J., Goodnow, J. and Austin, G. (1956) *A study of thinking*, New York: John Wiley.

Chomsky, N. (1957) *Syntactic structures*, The Hague: Mouton.

Clinebell, H. (1981) *Contemporary growth therapies*, California: Abingdon Press.

D'Zurilla, T. (1986) *Problem-solving therapy: A social competence approach to clinical intervention*, New York: Springer.

Ellis, A. (1962) *Reason and emotion in psychotherapy*, New York: Lyle Stuart.

Field, T. (1995) Massage therapy for infants and children, *Journal of Developmental and Behavioural Paediatrics*, Vol. 16, pp. 105–11.

Field, T. (1998) Touch therapy effects on development, *International Journal of Behavioural Development*, Vol. 22, pp. 779–97.

Harris, K.R. (1990) Developing self-regulated learners: The role of private speech and self-instruction, *Educational Psychologist*, 25, pp. 35–50.

Harris, K.R., Graham, S. and Pressley, M. (1991) Cognitive-behavioral approaches in reading and written language: Developing self-regulated learners, in N.N. Singh and I.L. Beale (eds) *Learning disabilities: Nature, theory, and treatment*, pp. 415–51, New York: Springer-Verlag.

Harris, K.R. and Pressley, M. (1991) The nature of cognitive strategy instruction: Interactive strategy construction, *Exceptional Children*, 57, 392–404.

Humphrey, N. and Brooks, G. (2006) An evaluation of a short cognitive-behavioural anger management intervention for pupils at risk of exclusion, *Emotional and Behavioural Difficulties*, 11(1), pp. 5–23.

Jinon, S. (1996) The effect of infant massage on growth of preterm infants, in Yabes-Almirante, C. and de Luna, M. (eds) *Increasingly safe and successful pregnancies*, pp. 265–69, Amsterdam: Elsevier.

Karpman, S. (1968) Fairy tales and script drama analysis, *Transactional Analysis Bulletin*, 7(26), pp. 39–43.

Karpman, S. (1971) Options, *Transactional Analysis Journal*, 1(1), pp. 79–87.

King, N., Tonge, B., Heyne, D. and Ollendick, T. (2000) Research on the cognitive-behavioral treatment of school refusal: A review and recommendations, *Clinical Psychology Review*, Vol. 20, pp. 495–507.

Lipsey, M., Chapman, G. and Landenberger, N. (2001) *Research findings from prevention and intervention studies: Cognitive-behavioral programs for offenders*, The American Academy of Political and Social Science.

Manning, B.H. and Payne, B.D. (1996) *Self-talk for teachers and students: Metacognitive strategies for personal and classroom use*, Boston: Allyn & Bacon.

McLaughlin, T.F. and Vacha, E. (1992) School programs for at-risk children and youth: A review, *Education and Treatment of Children*, Vol. 15, pp. 255–67.

Mcleod, J. (1993) *An introduction to counselling*, Buckingham: Open University Press.

McLeod, J. (2003) *An introduction to counselling*, 3rd edn, Buckingham: Open University Press.

Mehrabian, A. (1971) *Silent messages*, Belmont: Wadsworth.

Meichenbaum, D.H. and Goodman, J. (1971) Training impulsive children to talk to themselves: A means of developing self-control, *Journal of Abnormal Psychology*, 77(2), pp. 115–26.

Miller, G. (1956) The magic number seven, plus or minus two: Some limits on our capacity for processing information, *Psychology Review*, Vol. 63, pp. 81–93.

Newell, S. and Jeffery, D. (2002) *Behaviour management in the classroom: A transactional analysis approach*, London: David Fulton.

Newell, A., Shaw, J. and Simon, H. (1958) Elements of a theory of human problem solving, *Psychological Review*, Vol. 65, pp. 151–66.

Ofsted (2006) *Evaluation of the manageability of the joint area review and corporate assessment process*, available at www.ofsted.gov.uk/publications.

Pavlov, I. (1927) *Conditioned reflexes* (trans. G. Antrep), London: Oxford University Press.

Quinn, M., Osher, D., Hoffman, C. and Hanley, T. (1998) *Safe, drug-free, and effective schools for ALL students: What works!* Washington, DC: Center for Effective Collaboration and Practice, American Institutes for Research.

Rogers, B. (2000) *Behaviour management: A whole school approach*, London: Paul Chapman.

Shertzer, B. and Stone, S. (1980) *Fundamentals of counselling*, Boston: Houghton Mifflin.

Skinner, B.F. (1953) *Science and human behaviour*, New York: MacMillan.

Spitz, R. (1945) Hospitalism, in Eissler, R. (ed.) *The psychoanalytic study of the child* (Vol. 1), New York: International Universities Press.

Spitz, R. (1946) Hospitalism: A follow-up report, in Eissler, R. (ed.) *The psychoanalytic study of the child* (Vol. 11), New York: International Universities Press.

Squires, G. Using cognitive behavioural psychology with groups of pupils to improve self-control of behaviour, *Educational Psychology in Practice*, 17(4), pp. 317–35.

Steiner, C. (1974) *Scripts people live: Transactional analysis of life scripts*, New York: Grove Weidenfeld.

Stewart, I. and Joines, V. (1987) *TA today: A new introduction to transactional analysis*, Nottingham: Lifespace Publishing.

Vygotsky, L.S. (1978) *Mind in society: The development of higher mental process*, Cambridge, MA: Harvard University Press.

Vygotsky, L.S. (1986) *Thought and language*, Cambridge, MA: MIT Press.

Waldron, H. and Kaminer, Y. (2004) On the learning curve: Cognitive-behavioral therapies for adolescent substance abuse, *Addiction*, Vol. 99, pp. 93–105.

Watson, J.B. (1913) Psychology as the behaviourist views it, *Psychology Review*, Vol. 20, pp. 158–77.

Westbrook, D., Kennerley, H. and Kirk, J. (2007) *An introduction to cognitive behaviour therapy*, London: Sage.

Part 3

CONTEMPORARY POLICIES AND DEBATES IN EDUCATION

7

Contemporary education policies and issues

Deborah Outhwaite

Contents

Introduction

We often hear about education being described as a political 'football'. This chapter explains how and why this has been the case since 1997. There were three main strands of the Labour government's education policy: equality, accountability and choice. This chapter explains these three strands in the light of the social policy changes that took place under the Labour government 1997–2010, and explains how the Liberal–Conservative coalition government elected in May 2010 aims to put its own stamp on education policies. Many of the contemporary issues raised here come from a wider sociological debate within education policy. This debate closely links to **social exclusion** and education, and what measures have been put in place to tackle such exclusion. Social exclusion occurs when individuals are excluded from taking part in society fully, whether it is being left out of schooling or housing, or a particular group such as 'hoodies' being excluded from shopping centres because of their dress code.

Some of the ideas and policies covered in this chapter are:

- Social justice and the alleviation of child poverty.
- Social policies such as Sure Start.
- Excellence in Cities, Excellence in Schools and the National Challenge schemes.
- Every Child Matters and extended services provision.
- City Academies Programme.
- Widening participation.

You are likely to have heard about some or all of these policies before, although you may not know exactly what they all mean. In this chapter, some are covered in depth, others are mentioned in passing, but there are many educational issues (see the Activity box on p. 204), so it should not be assumed that this is an exhaustive list. When you have read about them, follow the web-links to look into the policies in more detail. Once you have an understanding of what they are, you will be able to refer to them, where appropriate, in your written work.

When the Labour government came to power in 1997, it was to implement a fairly radical agenda, wanting to change lots of areas from devolution (such as who controls education policy in Wales and Northern Ireland) through to further EU involvement, leading to changes in legislation that had a knock-on effect on education, as will be discussed below. Some of these policies were targeted through the use of **'joined-up' government**. The term joined-up government refers to increasing collaboration and cooperation between the many distinct departments that make up an administration. There was a push by New Labour in 1998 to get government departments working together in Whitehall (this is a shorthand term for the offices of the UK government), in order to achieve many of the wide-ranging policies that were specifically developed by the government to target social exclusion. Such policies often combined staff from the areas of health, housing, social services and the Treasury with education, in order to work convincingly with sections or groups of the population that had long been ignored by government policies; examples of these groups include lone-parent mothers and unskilled workers.

This chapter aims to:

- Highlight some of these policies.
- Demonstrate that education policy has played a pivotal role in the development of policies to create social justice in the UK (aimed at achieving a fair and equitable society for all).

Case study 7.1
The history of Sure Start Children's Centres

Sure Start Children's Centres were developed from earlier Sure Start-funded settings, including Sure Start local programmes, Neighbourhood Nurseries and Early Excellence centres. Other existing providers, such as (state) maintained nursery schools, primary schools and other local Early Years provision, including voluntary and private settings, have also provided the basis for Sure Start Children's Centres.

Sure Start grew out of the recognition that deprivation was blighting the lives of too many children and families in disadvantaged areas. It was established in 1997, and within two years the first Sure Start local programmes were set up. Their remit was to bring together early education, childcare, health and family support for the benefit of young children (under the age of four) living in disadvantaged areas and their parents. Local programmes were area-based initiatives which had the aim of improving the health and well-being of families and children from before birth to age four. The original target was to establish 250 Sure Start local programmes by March 2002, starting with 'trailblazer' programmes set up during 1999 and 2000. In 2000, this was expanded so that more families could benefit.

By the end of 2003, there were 524 Sure Start local programmes serving the most deprived communities. Furthermore, in 2001 the Neighbourhood Nurseries programme aimed to create 45,000 new high-quality, accessible and affordable, full-day care places for children under five in the poorest areas of England. From 2004, these programmes have formed the basis of Sure Start Children's Centres with over 2,500 centres now serving young children and their families. By 2010, 3,500 Children's Centres had been established, one for every community, with the Liberal–Conservative coalition stating that it intended to continue the funding of them.

Sure Start Centres are educational, as this case study shows, aiming to give children a good start in their lives and in their learning. However, Sure Start has not been without criticism: research conducted on staff revealed them to believe in, and act uniformly in, early interventions in family settings which are perceived as dysfunctional (Ball, 2008).

Research by Belsky et al. (2006) and Astle (2007), cited in Reay (2008), 'has shown that Sure Start overwhelmed and alienated working-class mothers leaving middle-class families to reap the benefits of extra provision and funding' (Reay, 2008:645).

Source: http://www.dcsf.gov.uk/everychildmatters/earlyyears/surestart/surestartchildrenscentres/history/ history/, viewed 09/07/09.

Questions for discussion

1 *In what ways do you think that working-class parents may have felt 'alienated' by Sure Start?*

2 *What do you think is meant by Reay's comments that middle-class families have reaped the benefits of Sure Start? Is it possible to address these issues? If so, how might that be done?*

Activity

Defining contemporary education issues

Look down the list of contemporary education issues on the left. What do you think each one means?

Then, for each issue, look at the list on the right for potential reasons for importance. Did your understanding of the issue match the reason given here?

Issue	Potential reasons for importance?
Looked-after children	Poverty and child protection (CP) issues
Refugee/asylum children	Use of immigration detention centres
Traveller children	Poverty and human rights issues
Home schooling	Increasing trend, different schools utilise in varying ways
Allocation of school places	Increasing parental fraud on applications and changes in use of CCTV footage by LEAs
Assessments	SATs, changing school assessment methods
2009 new Ofsted framework	Limiting factors, value for money, evidence trails
School choice	Increasingly diversified education system
Academies Programme	Flagship Labour policy (now adopted by the Liberal–Conservative coalition)
Access to HE	Widening participation
Increase in school leaving age to 18 in 2013	Labour government skills policy, every student educated to L3
Multiculturalism	Issues with urban versus rural schools
Increase in faith schools	Schools diversity policy
Preoccupation with boys' underachievement	Biased direction of education policies
Increase in numbers of teaching assistants and higher level TAs	Accelerated feminisation of the teaching profession
Teen pregnancy	Underachievement of white working-class girls

The role of government in education

There is a large degree of overlap between what we regard as contemporary issues in education policy, and government policy initiatives. Policies start as ideas from individuals, or groups of people (sometimes who come together collectively, and are known as 'think-tanks') or political parties and work their way through a process (see History box) in order to become an Act of Parliament. Although voter apathy (people not voting in elections – only 65.1 per cent of the electorate voted in 2010) has been on the rise in recent years, elections of governments make a huge difference to what policies actually end up being implemented.

History of education

How does an idea become an Act of Parliament?

First, ideas tend to be published in a **Green Paper**, to consult public and specialist opinions to see what need there is for changes to the legislation in an area. Once soundings have been taken from think-tanks and pressure groups in an area, the legislation is drafted by civil servants to become a **White Paper**. This formal document then calls for responses, which can be written into the proposed **Bill**, which is what the legislation is called as it goes through three 'readings' in both Houses of Parliament (the Commons and the Lords). When a Bill has been passed it becomes an **Act**, which has to be obeyed. Usually ideas come from the governing party as they are the ones elected to office to change how the country is run, but occasionally a Private Member's Bill or an Opposition Party Bill can also become law if enough of the governing party agree with it and the government of the day have given it enough time to have 'safe passage' through both Houses to be enacted.

The policies that governments end up adopting as new Acts of Parliament are therefore fundamentally significant to the direction that they take the country in. These will be analysed along with Labour's approach to education that was implemented up to 2010.

Government policies, such as those introduced by the Labour governments of 1997–2010, can impact on education even if they do not originate from the circles of education policy. These government policies hoped to help socially excluded groups learn the skills to integrate fully in society and aimed to target spending on certain groups in the population in order to alleviate poverty. The main groups chosen were the under-25s, the long-term unemployed, lone parents, those with disabilities, and the over-50s. Smaller schemes were subsequently set up for aspiring unemployed musicians, and those who did not speak English as a first language. Here there is a strong overlap between education and other government policies. The cost of these policies was indirectly spent through the education system, either on retraining or reskilling individuals (when their original training has become outdated or is no longer required in the economy), or providing courses that people had missed out on such as '**basic skills**': reading, writing, numeracy and ICT. In addition, there was funded childcare for some of the parents involved in the scheme. These policies, known as the 'New Deal', were largely designed by Professor Layard from the Centre for Economic Performance at the London School of Economics. More than a decade later, a more flexible version of the scheme was introduced for young people (i.e. the under-25s) in October 2009, with a focus on retraining and work experience placements.

Table 7.1 **The New Deal: a summary**

Social group	Policies
Under-25s	Work placements
Over-50s	Reskilling
Disabled	Basic skills
Lone parents	Subsidised childcare
Long-term unemployed	Retraining

Source: Layard, 2001.

The impact of the European Union, devolution, and the Third Way

Following the landslide election of New Labour in 1997, it was apparent that the new government had a different ideological base from previous Labour governments. Giddens (1998) argued that their reformed ideology had brought them into power, and justified the policies that they were busy implementing; he subsequently published *The Third Way*, which had been written after conversations with Tony Blair that connected the issues of social exclusion and social justice, and how the Labour government wanted to set about creating a fairer society for all (see Connect and explore, opposite). This was labelled as the **Third Way** because the two previous 'big ideas' – **capitalism** (the First Way) and **socialism** (the Second Way) – were considered to be inadequate on their own, and had therefore failed in policy terms. Capitalism was considered to have failed by the Labour government of 1945 because it relied on market interventions, only with the government not stepping in when it needed to. The 1945 Labour government changed that with the creation of services such as the NHS and welfare payments. Socialism, though, was also considered by New Labour to have failed as it led to some of the discontent experienced in the 1970s, and also failed to acknowledge the role that the markets can have in social policy, such as private schools, private nursing homes and all the charitable sector.

Policies that are often included in the discussion on the Third Way include the minimum wage, the maximum working week, extended maternity and paternity leave, as well as the Flexible Working Time Directive which enabled employees to have time off to look after elderly parents or children up to the age of 16. However, New Labour were more pro-European than other previously elected governments, and many of these policies that were put forward under the Third Way banner were being put forward by the EU. For example, the very first act of the New Labour government was to send Robin Cook, the Foreign Secretary in 1997, to the EU institutions in order to sign the 'Social Chapter'. This was a very important decision, as the previous Conservative government had decided to negotiate 'an opt-out' from this legislation in 1992, arguing that the British people and businesses didn't want it. New Labour argued that it was essential for the UK to take advantage of these Social Chapter policies, and that meant instituting policies such as the minimum wage. This had a huge knock-on impact, not only in the areas of pay and entitlements, but also more directly in education, in the area of harmonisation of education policies. Although this is something that the EU have never directly tried to do, as more people work across EU member states there is a need to understand the qualifications that people have.

↖ Connect and explore

'CORA': New Labour ideology and the Third Way

Community: building links from the grassroots upwards.

Opportunity: making sure that opportunities are available to all.

Responsibility: ensuring that everyone understands that they have a role to play in society.

Accountability: making sure that people understand that they are accountable for their actions.

Source: Giddens, A. (1998) *The Third Way*, Cambridge: Polity Press.

As was mentioned briefly above, devolution was one of the radical ideas that were put forward in 1997, and implemented in London, Northern Ireland, Wales and Scotland over the next few years, following successful referendums on the issues of whether the people living in these areas wanted their own **Assemblies** or, in the case of Scotland, a Parliament. It is important to remember here that Scotland has always maintained control of its own education system, and has different types of qualification for further education (called Highers) in comparison with the rest of the UK, with a longer, usually four-year, undergraduate course. Giving control of education policy to these Assemblies (except for London's Greater London Assembly) has had a significant impact on their education systems, with Wales, for example, establishing far more Welsh-speaking schools and being able to divert funding into areas that they consider culturally significant. Scotland used its Parliament's tax-raising powers in order to scrap university tuition fees for Scottish students at Scottish universities, a move agreed with by the Liberal Democrat party nationally.

Social mobility, education and social policy

To enable us to understand Labour's education policies, it is necessary to demonstrate how the quest for social justice has played such a central role in the creation of these policies. To do this, we first need to look at how wealth is distributed in the UK today, and to understand how wealth transfers from generation to generation, in order to see how this impacts on our education system in the twenty-first century. As we shall see in Chapter 9, the term '**inclusion**' implies that all individuals have the right, and should be afforded the opportunity, to participate fully in all that society has to offer; but some **socio-economic groups** can access different parts of the system to their benefit. One of the major criticisms of the Labour Party's time in government has been the increase in middle-class **hegemony**, or political knowledge, power and control (Reay, 2008). Despite putting forward policies aimed at those who are excluded, the gap between those who are successful and the rest in society has increased – not decreased – leading to speculation that not enough has been done to hold back the inequalities in society (Toynbee and Walker, 2008).

Failing schools (sometimes known as 'sink schools') often result in a loss of middle-class students, leaving schools in deprived areas with far less additional parental and economic resources than schools in more affluent areas. Schools fail because they lose students and, as students leave, the schools receive less funding (as funding follows the individual student), and so with smaller budgets it becomes increasingly difficult to improve a challenging school. Arguably, such a reduction of direct funding for schools and the resources that parents bring to schools (often located in deprived areas) is one of their biggest issues (Tomlinson, 2008). The UK has one of the most highly stratified societies in the world, where large divisions exist between high and low earners, and this position enables top earners to send their children to independent schools, or move to the areas with the best state schools. Such purchase of privilege, with 'topped-up' education including tutoring, foreign trips, books and internet access, means that as a society little social mobility, or movement between the socio-economic groups, takes place. Blanden and Machin (2007) have argued that the chances of children improving on their parents' position in society are now at their lowest point in the last twenty years. Similarly, if parents come from a professional family, their children are therefore much more likely to become professionals themselves.

In January 2009, as part of the government's *New Opportunities* White Paper, Prime Minister Gordon Brown set up the Panel on Fair Access to the Professions in the UK under the guidance of Alan Milburn (a former Labour Minister). The Labour government had decided that not enough progress was being made on social mobility, and the panel's remit was to 'advise on how we can make a professional career genuinely open to as wide a pool of talent as possible' (Milburn, A.,

Figure 7.1 **Gordon Brown**
Source: Getty Images: Hulton Archive.

2009:5). The Milburn Report (2009) argued that the rise of factors such as internships (often unpaid work experience) helped the social networks of already well-connected children, and made them seven times more likely to end up as middle-class professionals than children from less privileged backgrounds. Recommendations from the report to change this position included advertising potential work placements in order to overcome class disadvantages.

➤ Connect and explore

Unleashing Aspiration: A brief summary of the findings of the Panel on Fair Access to the Professions, July 2009

There were 88 recommendations from this Panel on how the government should address the increasing inequality of access to the professions, including:

- Ensuring that social mobility explicitly be the top overarching social policy priority for this and future governments.
- Establishing an expert social mobility commission.
- Reforming and rebranding the Gifted and Talented programme.
- Establishing a national scheme for career mentoring into the professions.
- Establishing a 'Yes, you can' scheme to encourage young people to choose professional careers.
- Establishing a database of people who would be prepared to talk to their former schools about their professional career.
- Overhauling work experience placements to align them better with students' career aspirations.
- Looking at professional regulators and encouraging them to address fair access.
- Encouraging corporate social responsibility.
- Establishing a Fair Access Charter Mark to reward organisations that make fair access a priority.

Source: Milburn, A. (2009) *Unleashing Aspiration: The Final Report of the Panel on Fair Access to the Professions*, available at: http://www.cabinetoffice.gov.uk/media/227102/fair-access.pdf (viewed 06/06/10).

Britain has long been portrayed as a **meritocracy** (a system based on ability rather than wealth) by Conservative politicians such as John Major (Prime Minister 1990–1997), where everyone is born with equal opportunities (Saunders, 2001). However, despite policies such as Sure Start (see Case study 7.1) targeted at disadvantaged communities, many opportunities are influenced by social background. When ability is rewarded, social advantage is often also effectively being documented: results in IQ tests and exams can reflect social advantages, and the income and wealth of these advantaged groups ensure class reproduction, as analysed by Blanden and Machin (2007). For example, in 2008, from approximately 3,500 A grades awarded at A level, fewer than 200 went to children from disadvantaged backgrounds who qualified for free school meals.

Social justice and the alleviation of child poverty

Policies to reduce social exclusion included a flagship New Labour policy on ending child poverty. When Labour came to office in 1997, think-tanks, such as the Joseph Rowntree Foundation and the Child Poverty Action Group, claimed that one in three children under the age of 16 in the UK were living in poverty. Much pressure had been exerted on the Labour Party while in Opposition (prior to 1997) to do something about this once elected, and a raft of measures that linked into the education system were pushed through the Treasury. The policies included the Baby Bond, where £500 was given to the poorest families in the UK to save for their child's future (and £250 to all other families); if families had then saved this money successfully it was to be topped up at 18 years of age. Child Tax Credit (CTC), and the Working Families Tax Credit (WFTC) were also designed to boost the income of low-paid groups in society, and reduce some of the material inequalities that families with children face. Many families find themselves very poorly off when they have children, as one partner (usually the woman) often has to give up work in order to look after the children until at least school age, as their earnings very often do not cover the childcare costs. The Labour government therefore set out to massively increase the number of places of childcare available, and subsidise the costs. A major part of this childcare push was to reduce the number of children living in poverty and to enable parents to work or retrain. This is because the educational research in this area shows us that children from working parents (as opposed to benefit-dependent parents) are better off, both financially and in terms of educational achievements (Raffo et al., 2007). The government's answer to this perceived lack of appropriate childcare was the creation of the Sure Start scheme in 1997. The Liberal–Conservative government elected in May 2010 have said that they will continue to fund the Sure Start scheme, but other policies such as the Baby Bond were phased out from July 2010, providing us with an example of how the change of a government can make a real difference to the changes in government policies.

➤ Connect and explore

2009 Child Poverty Bill

Eradicating **child poverty** is an important issue which needs a new approach if it is to work and improve children's life chances for the longer term. Read about the Child Poverty Bill, which aims to lift a further 500,000 children out of poverty, at: http://www.commonsleader.gov.uk/output/page2654.asp. After 12 years of trying to implement anti-poverty strategies, the Labour government decided to resort to using legal measures.

Generally, Labour and Liberal Democrat politicians agree more with the notion of **relative poverty** (having less than 60 per cent of the median income in society) and many of the policies introduced since 1997 try to prevent or remove poverty of this type. These policies are motivated by the idea that if you can help lift families with young children out of poverty then their chances of gaining a better education will be substantially improved. It is estimated that 2.8 million children (20 per cent) were still living in poverty in the UK in 2009. Labour pledged to end child poverty from 1999 onwards and, ten years on, 600,000 children are being lifted out of poverty helped by Tax Credits and Back to Work schemes, according to the government's own figures from 2009. Since 1997, overall wealth has increased unevenly in society, particularly at the top end, and so those who are relatively poor find themselves even worse off. A good example is how the pay gap between staff has changed: in 1997, a doorman of a City bank earned seventeen times less than a director; ten years later it was seventy times less (Toynbee and Walker, 2008).

Every Child Matters and extended services provision

In its second term in office, the Labour government was forced to address the proposition that every child matters, after an eight-year-old girl, Victoria Climbié, was murdered by her aunt in London. The lack of communication between agencies dealing with Victoria – namely health, education and social services – meant that a complete re-evaluation of the system took place. This resulted in the government redesigning how services work from birth to age nineteen.

The aim of Every Child Matters is to give all children the support they need to:

- be healthy
- stay safe
- enjoy and achieve
- make a positive contribution
- achieve economic well-being.

The Labour government was, yet again, forced to re-address these issues in its third term in office, following the 'Baby P' murder in London, when a mother and her boyfriend were subsequently sentenced for the murder and neglect of a toddler, who had been known to the range of local authorities but who had not been sufficiently protected. It is this sort of high-profile failure of provision that made politicians look as though they were not dealing with the communities that the Labour government set out to help, despite the policies that had been put in place. One of the outcomes of the 'Baby P' tragedy was a speeding up of the implementation of the extended services provision in order to further protect vulnerable children.

Case study 7.2
Extended services provision

It is essential that schools work with the local authority and local providers, and all with each other, in order to provide access to a core offer of extended services, including the following:

- a varied menu of activities (including study support, play/recreation, sport, music, arts and crafts and other special interest clubs, volunteering and business and enterprise activities), in a safe place, for primary and secondary schools;

▶

- childcare: 8:00 a.m. to 6:00 p.m., 48 weeks a year for primary schools;
- parenting support – including family learning;
- swift and easy access to targeted and specialist services such as speech and language therapy;
- community access to facilities including adult learning, ICT and sports facilities.

These will often be provided beyond the school day but not necessarily by teachers or on the school site.

What are the benefits?

There is evidence that extended services can help to:

- improve pupil attainment, self-confidence, motivation and attendance;
- reduce exclusion rates;
- better enable teachers to focus on teaching and learning;
- enhance children's and families' access to services.

Ofsted will report during school inspections on how extended services are contributing to improved outcomes for children and young people.

Questions for discussion

1 *Consider the changes suggested by the extended services provision above. Can you see ways in which these measures will help to avoid cases such as that of 'Baby P'?*

2 *How might there still be problems for some children?*

Excellence in Cities, Excellence in Schools and the National Challenge schemes

In March 1999, the government launched the Excellence in Cities (EiC) programme in England to try to resolve the educational problems of inner-city areas. It was intended to raise standards and transform the culture of low expectations and achievement: £200 million was spent in 2001–2002, and £300 million in 2002–2003. In November 2001, the Education Action Zones (EAZs) first introduced in 1998 were phased out and incorporated into the Excellence in Schools scheme, where community liaison partnerships became the central focus. Schools were encouraged to share expertise across Key Stages as opposed to paying for outside expertise or being able to 'top-up' their budgets from the EAZ scheme. Many LEAs established 'Learning Communities' from 2003 onwards, where expertise was shared across a range of local schools, sometimes through the facilitation of Advanced Skills Teachers (ASTs). Many of these Learning Communities are still in existence today, and have been used to help with the introduction of the new 14–19 diploma.

The EiC programme's main strands were:

- In-school learning mentors.
- Learning support units for difficult pupils.
- Programmes to stretch the most able 5–10 per cent of pupils.

- City learning centres to promote school and community learning through state-of-the-art technology.
- Encouraging schools to become beacons and specialists (beacon status was a term used at the end of the 1990s to highlight an area of expertise in a particular subject, with additional funding being awarded if beacon status had been achieved).

Many of the above points are now well integrated into state schools, and the EiC programme has been gradually phased out and replaced with the National Challenge.

The **National Challenge** was launched in 2008. It is a programme of support that is intended to secure higher standards in all secondary schools so that, by 2011, at least 30 per cent of pupils in every school will gain five or more GCSEs at A* to C, including both English and mathematics. The National Challenge is, again, about tackling the link between deprivation and low educational attainment – again highlighting the link between social policy and education policy. This is a programme that had aimed under the Labour government to build sustainable improvement in secondary schools. This was a policy that also acknowledged that they had been in power for ten years, and still had yet to get every school to a benchmark of 30 per cent – despite record spending on education post-1999. The Labour government put in place support for schools below the 30 per cent threshold, including 'a National Challenge adviser' for each one. These advisers will work closely with the head teacher, supporting the school directly and organising additional support for the school's needs to be met effectively.

Although the Liberal–Conservative coalition is unlikely to continue to call this scheme by its Labour name, some sort of policy to help the schools that achieve the least is likely to continue under every government, as they always have to be seen to be having an influence on these underperforming schools. The answer for the Liberal–Conservative government, though, is probably through the City Academies Programme.

City Academies Programme

The City Academies Programme built on the legacy of City Technology Colleges (CTCs) from the previous Conservative governments of the 1980s and 1990s. The Labour government argued that the City Academies Programme provided **academies** that were all-ability, state-funded schools established and managed by sponsors from a wide range of backgrounds including high-performing schools and colleges, universities, individual philanthropists, businesses, the voluntary sector and the faith communities. Some of these academies were established by educational providers with long histories, and others brought with them a record of success in other enterprises which they were then able to apply to their academies in partnership with experienced school managers, albeit of their own choosing. The sponsors of an academy have a huge say in the running of the school, including the recruitment of the school's leadership team.

The Labour government argued that sponsors challenge traditional thinking on how schools are run and what they should be like for students. Such sponsors therefore seek to make a complete break with cultures of low aspiration which afflict too many communities and their schools. The government was therefore happy to entrust the governance of academies to these new bodies. The system that the government set up was that, on establishing an academy, the sponsor had to set up an endowment fund, the proceeds of which are then spent by the academy trust on measures to counteract the impact of deprivation on education in their local community; this is then left to their own discretion, as they are accountable to themselves, not the governing body.

The governing body and the head teacher have responsibility for managing the academy. In order to determine the ethos and leadership of the academy, and ensure clear responsibility and accountability, the private sector or charitable sponsor always appoints the majority of the governors. This is the case even when a local authority is acting as a co-sponsor for wider purposes. The number of governors on an academy governing body is not prescribed, but the government's expectation was for the body to be relatively small.

All academies are bound by the same School Admissions Code, **SEN Code of Practice**, and exclusions guidance as all other state-funded schools. All new academies are also required to follow the National Curriculum programmes of study in English, maths, science and ICT. All academies – like the large majority of secondary schools – have specialist school status, and have a specialism in one or more subjects. Each academy is unique because of the programme's focus on fitting each academy to its community and circumstances. This is a scheme that is currently under expansion (see page 223).

Case study 7.3
A student in a City Academy school, summer 2009

Profile

Name: Stephen

Age: 16

Educational status: Functionally illiterate

Reading age: 6 years old

Programme of study: BTEC Physical Education (four GCSE C grade equivalents)

Background

Stephen managed to leave school with four C grade equivalents, using a vocational course, whereas he would have failed had he been entered for GCSEs. Stephen wants to stay on at the school's sixth form, but the school refuses as it is aware that he is functionally illiterate; the school passes him on to a college, which accepts him with his certificate, unaware of his reading age.

Is he unique?

Stephen is not alone; the government's new diploma route for 14–19s pushes them into vocational routes early and closes down other options for them: from the school's viewpoint, the only way it is ever going to gain a 'value added' score for Stephen is to place him on a vocational route, not a GCSE programme.

Stephen's name has been changed and the name of the school has been withheld from publication. 44,000 children leave school illiterate every year (Hansard, 2006).

Questions for discussion

1 *How do you see Stephen's future at college and beyond progressing?*

2 *Do you consider that he has been disadvantaged by his educational experiences?*

3 *How does Stephen's experience fit into the issues raised in this chapter?*

Widening participation

Until 1979, university students were provided with grants and a free place in higher education (HE), but a rise in student numbers during the 1980s increased pressure on state funding. The Conservative government introduced the student loans system in 1992 – which was the first use of market forces in higher education (Bloor, 2008). This is significant because prior to this date the HE sector had been largely protected from marketisation (where market forces, such as private companies, are actively involved in state education, as opposed to the government running state education), when other areas of education, such as secondary schools, had been forced to adapt to the market through the publication of league tables since the 1988 Education Reform Act. **Tuition fees**, where HE students were expected to contribute towards the cost of their undergraduate courses, were established through legislation that went through Parliament in 2004, with two amendments. The first amendment imposed a duty on the Education Secretary to impose a £3,000 cap on any university that tried to charge higher fees. Second, any move to raise the £3,000 limit on fees after 2010 will require a vote in both Houses of Parliament.

The argument that the Labour government had put forward to justify undergraduate course fees is that the socio-economic take-up of university places was biased towards higher social classes. Therefore, an amount for fees was charged, so that the money raised could be spent on expanding the **lifelong learning** sector, and widening student participation would encourage universities to compete against each other for state funding. The National Union of Students (NUS) has long campaigned that fees are unfair and act as a deterrent to students from poorer backgrounds going to university. As we saw earlier, the Liberal Democrats believe that it deters poorer students, and the Scottish Parliament voted to scrap such a policy for Scottish students in Scottish universities, under the powers accorded to them through **devolution**.

The Labour government's target was to get 50 per cent of young people into higher education by 2010. However, this figure remains unachieved to date with a combined total of 43 per cent of 17 to 30-year-old English domiciled first-time participants in an HEI (higher education institution) in 2007–2008. The Liberal–Conservative coalition is not aiming to maintain such an ambitious target in this decade, as HE cuts were among the first casualties of cutting the government deficit when the coalition came to power.

Connect and explore

Social Mobility: Universities Changing Lives

This report for the million+ think-tank, published March 2009, argued that post-92 universities have had a significant impact on social mobility in the UK, summarised as follows:

- There is a significant amount of occupational mobility generated by the universities that subscribe to million+. Many graduates get the opportunity to move from manual backgrounds into professional and managerial careers.

- Eight per cent of graduates from million+ member universities come from professional families – but 17 per cent have similar professional or managerial careers three and a half years after graduating.

- The diverse population that attends million+ member universities includes a much higher proportion of black and Asian students compared with the average for all UK universities.

- These 28 universities have significantly more women graduates and graduates who have studied later in life – providing opportunities for social mobility which add value in terms of other equality indicators.

- Graduates from these universities earn an average of around £22,000 three and a half years after graduation.

- Three and a half years after graduating, wages of million+ member universities are likely to be nearly 15 per cent higher than wages of people who have lower qualifications, many of whom could have progressed to university but did not do so.

- The wages of these graduates are likely to be 60 per cent higher than those of people with no qualifications.

Source: Rodda, M., Tilbury, L. and Tough, S. (2009) *Social Mobility: Universities Changing Lives*, million+, London: Institute of Education.

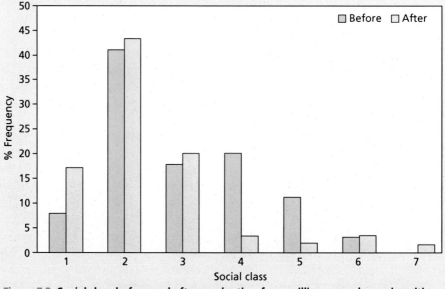

Figure 7.2 Social class before and after graduation from million+ member universities
Source: Table 1, p. 6, million+ Report: http://www.millionplus.ac.uk/documents/MOBILITY_190309.pdf

Criticisms of Labour in office 1997–2010

Blair 1997–2007

At the start of this chapter we mentioned three strands that characterise education policy under Labour: equality, choice and accountability. We will now look at each of these strands in more detail.

Equality

This suggests a belief in an egalitarian system where everyone has the right to start their lives from a level playing field. Clearly such a level playing field does not exist, and therefore many of Labour's policies have been targeted at helping those who are disadvantaged in society. Many Labour policies attempted to address the position of inequality at birth – such as the Baby Bond, tax credits for lower earners and the Sure Start scheme discussed above. However, criticisms of a lot of these policies were that they were 'gimmicky' or of insufficient funding to really make a difference to the lives of poorer families. Many of the tax credits in particular were overcomplicated, with individuals sometimes having to pay back thousands of pounds. Another criticism was that, when a government continues to address educational inequalities by repeatedly talking about failing schools and low standards, invariably it increases concerns about the education system. It can act to lower morale on the staff working in the system, and it can put people off wanting to work in the education system.

Choice

Historically, the comprehensive system was meant to bring about such equality, its aim being to educate all classes of children together. Dismantling the comprehensive

Figure 7.3 Tony Blair, visiting a school in south London during the 1997 General Election campaign

Source: Getty Images: Hulton Archive.

system and replacing it with a choice of diverse schools and academies that do not try individually to cater for all needs, but instead encouraging particular schools to concentrate on particular needs, was a major part of Labour policy. This has led to a major criticism of Tony Blair's time in office: that decisions taken by the Labour government to increase so-called choice in the education system, and enable families to 'choose' their preferred type of education since 1997, have in fact led to further class entrenchment, or a lack of choice for people from lower social class groups. Despite rhetoric from the government (Ball, 2003) that argued for further choice and social mobility, many of Labour's education policies have inadvertently resulted in confirming class positioning (Ball, 2003; Tomlinson, 2008; Whitty, 2001). For example, students from working-class backgrounds often find themselves attending post-92 universities (Ball et al., 2002). As we have seen, these universities improve the life chances for people that attend them, but don't often offer the opportunities to study subjects such as medicine, so students from lower social class groups can still be denied opportunities to improve their class position.

Accountability

In terms of accountability, we have seen that many policies have been about tackling social exclusion, but the accountability for these policies has not been passed on (as the Third Way proposed) to the people and various communities. Instead – using policies such as the City Academies Programme – it has bypassed elected government officers and been given to private companies or charitable organisations such as independent schools. These new academies are an extension of the government's drive to introduce marketisation and the accountability is not left with the local community but with the business partners who often fail to understand the complex community issues at stake. For example, Gorard (2009) argues that there is evidence that the academies have not applied all the criteria that apply to state schools, and because the governors are from business sectors and want the schools to be successful, higher rates of exclusion have applied to students.

❓ Stop and reflect

What do you see as the main barriers for students from working-class families who wish to apply to older, traditional universities?

Brown 2007–2010

Gordon Brown was Chancellor of the Exchequer for the ten years that Tony Blair was Prime Minister. The policies introduced during Blair's years in office were funded by Brown's Treasury. Many of the policies such as tax credits and Sure Start were therefore considered 'Brownite' not 'Blairite' policies in the first place. The difference is that Blair was ideologically happier with the introduction of market forces into education, whereas Brown saw this as the only way to gain the effective funding needed to improve the system. However, in relation to education policy there was a continued dichotomy under Brown's leadership that existed under Blair's premiership. Middle-class families strive to achieve what Ball describes as 'narrative coherence' (Ball, 2003:173) in order for their children's families to have the same chances and opportunities and, although Labour governments don't have a problem with people working hard, they do want people from socially excluded groups to achieve more. Brownite policies can be reviewed as very much taking place through the workplace, encouraging (or penalising) those who don't want to take part in education or training.

Controversies

Did Labour go far enough?

Agree: Tony Blair came to power in 1997 and formed the first Labour government for eighteen years. The previous Conservative governments presided over an educational system that was underfunded and divisive. New Labour invested more money into education and were ambitious in their desire to see new school buildings and infrastructure. Their aim was to tackle the conditions of poverty which held back so many working-class children on run down, neglected housing estates. It was thought that Sure Start could intervene in family life and counter some of the long-term deprivation which devastates so many young lives. More children than any other time in history now take exams and pass them as a result of Labour government policies. Higher education also expanded, creating opportunities for increased numbers of the population to be the first generation in their own families to have access to degree-level education, leading to widening participation and greater access to education. Failing schools and poor teaching were tackled head on with exacting targets set throughout children's school lives, which were monitored by Ofsted to force standards up. The Labour governments of 1997–2010 have undoubtedly implemented a great many policies which have improved education, and led to a silent revolution in social change.

Disagree: The Labour government presided over a period of spin and ideology, claiming to be the agents of change while reinforcing social inequality and unequal access to valuable life chances such as education. The greatest obstacle to inequality is private education. Children from private schools still have the best opportunities and are more likely to end up in the most privileged positions in society. Britain can never be described as a meritocracy; it is simply a society based on inequality, class and privilege. Labour's educational policies have overwhelmingly benefited middle-class children whose parents use their economic advantage to buy housing which gives them access to the best schools. Economic advantage enables the middle classes to segregate themselves from ethic minorities, the poor and the working class. The expansion of the higher education sector has simply meant that more middle-class children benefit from higher education and the employment opportunities that go with it. Despite spending on projects like Sure Start, the number of children in poverty has remained the same. The Labour governments were ultimately not able to change the deep-rooted nature of inequality that afflicts British society; they were not radical enough and missed a real opportunity to use educational policy to bring about fundamental social change.

What do you think? Which side of the argument do you favour?

Activity

Write an introduction outlining the main points you would raise in response to the following question:

How well do you think the Labour governments have addressed educational inequalities during their time in office?

The Conservatives in Opposition 1997–2010

Historically, Conservative politicians believe in the concept of absolute poverty. Absolute poverty is defined as being without water, food, shelter and clothing. Aside from homelessness this exists far less in the developed world, where welfare systems are common, than in less developed nations where they still have to rely on charitable and religious organisations to provide relief. On the basis of this definition, the Conservatives have argued that poverty in the UK today does not stop children from achieving in education in the way it does in underdeveloped countries, and often consider that those who are marginalised are often at fault. The welfare state (government-provided education, housing and social services) is often blamed in New Right theory. New Right theory is the idea that responsibility for services should rest as much as possible with the individual, and not with the state. The Conservatives, up to 1997, argued that the welfare state was responsible for the creation of a benefit-dependent 'underclass' who choose to be welfare reliant (Murray, 1999). As was discussed earlier in this chapter, research in this area tells us that the children of these benefit-dependent families are far less likely to achieve in education than if these individuals can find work (Raffo et al., 2007).

Yet the election of the 1997 Labour government that seemed to believe in this notion of 'big government', where many of the solutions to these problems lay in the state finding help for families, led the Conservatives in Opposition to have a rethink about their belief in New Right theory. After the further loss of both the 2001 and 2005 General Elections, and three Conservative Party leaders, David Cameron was elected as leader of a Conservative Party that he aimed to restyle as a compassionate and green party. Heavily influenced through the recent work of Iain Duncan Smith (the former Conservative Party leader), the notion of New Right theory has been challenged inside the contemporary Conservative Party, with David Cameron's 'Compassionate Conservatism' (2007) becoming successful.

The Conservative Party under Cameron continued to be vocal in its opposition to many Labour government decisions on education, largely because, as was discussed earlier, many of the solutions that a Labour government put forward come from the state. Iain Duncan Smith, who led the Conservative Party between 2001 and 2003, went on to establish the Centre for Social Justice (CSJ). This proved to be very influential on the policies of Cameron's Conservative Party. In 2006, Duncan Smith published a report called 'Breakdown Britain' (clearly the Conservatives had a vested interest in making the UK seem as though it was 'broken' under a Labour government), which has a section on educational failure that has been regularly updated (see below). As of May 2009, the Conservative Party had adopted 65 policies from the CSJ, while the Labour government had also adopted 18 CSJ policies (see http://www.centreforsocialjustice.org.uk/default.asp, viewed 22/07/09).

In the 2010 General Election, Cameron put forward some of these ideas as part of a 'Big Society' that he wanted to see created under a Conservative government. This idea held that the power of the state would start to be reclaimed by individuals and social groups rather than being held on to by government organisations. In effect, Cameron was re-asserting the accountability factor of the Labour governments, asking voters to choose something different from what they had already been given.

Connect and explore

'Breakdown Britain': educational failure?

Educational inequality matters, and government needs to place far more emphasis on the most underachieving pupils in our education system to improve social justice and social mobility. Children spend just 15 per cent of their time in school; it is family background, cultural factors and material needs which have the most significant impact on educational outcomes.

Five key paths to poverty:

- Family breakdown
- Educational failure
- Economic dependence
- Addictions
- Indebtedness.

Issues which contribute to the failure of the education system to address the needs of the disadvantaged include:

- Government policy and funding
- Lack of parental involvement
- Unmet material needs
- Social and cultural influences
- The curriculum and structure of schooling
- Poor pupil behaviour
- Lack of school leadership.

Source: http://www.centreforsocialjustice.org.uk/client/downloads/BB_educational_failure.pdf, CSJ, December 2006 (viewed 21/07/09).

Conservative policy towards higher education has also seen some changes, and might appear to have been in a state of flux in recent years. At the 2005 General Election, the Conservative Party pledged to scrap both the 50 per cent target for higher education and top-up (or variable) fees. This policy has since been dropped by David Cameron. The Conservative Party underwent a lengthy policy review, and published a Green Paper on Skills in 2007; this argued that much of the expansion in HE was unnecessary, and the party was not prepared to accept the new 14–19 diploma that the Labour government had proposed.

Liberal Democrat education policies

In stark contrast to the Conservative position, the Liberal Democrats have been consistent in their policy to scrap all student fees in higher education, and would instead raise funds via progressive taxation: charging higher tax payers more. Education always plays a significant role in Liberal Democrat policies, largely because, despite having far fewer MPs than the other two main parties, they often have success at local levels, and are in power in local authorities throughout the UK, therefore often having considerable control over education policy and its implementation. Notable ideas that are similar to the Conservative Party include that of the 'Pupil Premium' (Liberal Democrat Manifesto, 2010:36) where schools that accept pupils who come from disadvantaged backgrounds will receive a higher amount of funding, to spend as they choose.

Among a range of other policies, the Liberal Democrats would also like to scrap the Qualifications and Curriculum Development Agency (QCDA), Ofsted and Ofqual (the qualifications and examinations regulator), and replace them with an independent Education Standards Authority (ESA). In addition to scrapping the 50 per cent target of young people attending university, the party also believes in 'designing a trial scheme whereby the best students from the lowest achieving schools are guaranteed a place in Higher Education' (Liberal Democrat Manifesto, 2010:39).

2010 onwards: the Liberal–Conservative Coalition

Although the Conservative party under Cameron has become more successful, they were not able to win the number of seats needed for an outright victory in the 2010 General Election. This meant that, after talks with both Labour and the Conservatives, the Liberal Democrats chose to enter into a formal five-year coalition agreement with the Conservatives. Clearly both parties put different ideas to the electorate, on what education policy should be if either of them won the election, and so a consensus had to be determined between them on the direction of this new education policy.

This consensus has comprised a range of statements that form the basis of government policy for the five years through to 2015. Interestingly one of the first acts of this government in May 2010 was to scrap the Department for Children, Schools and Families (DCSF), which had integrated many education policies with the social policies discussed earlier in the chapter, and create the Department for Education (DfE). This alone shows the difference in emphasis between the two administrations with the coalition putting schools as a central part of their policy, while still acknowledging some of the inequalities that were discussed earlier. For example, the statement on schools issued by the coalition states:

> The Government believes that we need to reform our school system to tackle educational inequality, which has widened in recent years, and to give greater powers to parents and pupils to choose a good school. We want to ensure high standards of discipline in the

classroom, robust standards and the highest quality teaching. We also believe that the state should help parents, community groups and others come together to improve the education system by starting new schools.

The Coalition Programme for Government, 2010:28

The Conservative Party in Opposition were good at listening to potential voters, and as a consequence radically altered the ways in which they portray policy decisions. The Conservatives were aware that there have been many popular education policies under Blair and Brown that have tackled educational inequalities. Indeed, many of these policies were based on the notions of parental choice that the last Conservative governments introduced in the 1980s and 1990s, so in fact the current Conservative hierarchy agree with many of the previous Labour government's policies if not the tactics used. However, as the CSJ research shows, the Conservatives often disagreed with the last Labour government on how future change should be carried out: one of the the the most notable sections of the coalition's programme refers to giving:

> . . . parents, teachers, charities and local communities the chance to set up new schools, as part of our plans to allow new providers to enter the state school system in response to parental demand; that all schools have greater freedom over the curriculum; and that all schools are held properly to account.

The Coalition Programme for Government, 2010:29

This is going to be achieved in part through an extension to the Academies Programme. Indeed, Michael Gove, the Secretary of State, wrote to all the schools that the government's inspection body, Ofsted, had rated as 'Outstanding', inviting them to apply for academy status in May 2010. Case study 7.4, on page 226, gives an example of both the type of charity that might want to take part in the setting up of a new school and the successes that can be achieved as an academy.

The coalition have identified the lack of social mobility in the UK, and have identified the idea of diverting more resources to pupils from disadvantaged backgrounds as part of a long-term supply-side revolution that will address the current gaps that they have identified in education:

> We will fund a significant premium for disadvantaged pupils from outside the schools budget by reductions in spending elsewhere.

The Coalition Programme for Government, 2010:29

This is a policy that was in the programmes for government (known as manifestos) of both the Conservatives and Liberal Democrats, so consensus on the inclusion of it in the coalition's programme was straightforward, but there are other areas between the parties that are not as easily solved. For example, the coalition has also committed to a full review of the higher education sector; this may leave the government under pressure from the Russell Group (the UK's top 20 research universities), which wants to see an increase in funding, irrespective of where additional resourcing comes from. An increase in university fees is one option but this has two problems. First, as we discussed early on in this chapter, it would require a supportive vote in both Houses of Parliament, something unlikely to be achieved under the Coalition government. Second, although the Liberal Democrats were firmly against the issue of tuition fees, and wanted to see them scrapped, not increased, they were nevertheless sanctioned by the Government and subsequently introduced to begin in 2012.

↖ Connect and explore

Useful think-tank websites

Adam Smith Institute: http://www.adamsmith.org/ Founded in 1977 to impart the ideas of the free market, this has been very influential on the Conservative Party, in particular see: **http://www.adamsmith.org/education/**.

Centre for Social Justice: http://www.centreforsocialjustice.org.uk/ Founded by Conservative politicians, this is very influential inside Cameron's Conservative party.

Centre for Policy Studies: http://www.cps.org.uk/ An independent think-tank that was founded by prominent Conservative politicians in the 1970s; its aim is to promote economic liberalism.

Child Poverty Action Group: http://www.cpag.org.uk/ CPAG is a leading charity campaigning for the abolition of child poverty in the UK and for a better deal for low-income families and children.

Compass: http://www.compassonline.org.uk/ Aims to give direction to the democratic left in the UK, through influencing Labour Party policies.

Demos: http://www.demos.co.uk/ A London-based think-tank that deals with welfare issues; influenced New Labour in its early days.

IPPR: http://www.ippr.org.uk/ The Institute for Public Policy Research is an important think-tank that has influenced Labour, but is unafraid of being critical of government policies.

Joseph Rowntree Foundation: http://www.jrf.org.uk/ An important poverty research group, for the specialist education section see: http://www.jrf.org.uk/work/workarea/education-and-poverty.

Million+: http://www.millionplus.ac.uk/ A university think-tank of a group of 28 leading post-1992 universities; see in particular the *Social Mobility: Universities Changing Lives* report: http://www.millionplus.ac.uk/documents/MOBILITY_190309.pdf.

The Russell Group: http://www.russellgroup.ac.uk/about.html The leading 20 research-focused universities in the UK; they are highly selective.

The Sutton Trust: http://www.suttontrust.com/ A very important educational charity that concentrates on research on the disadvantaged in education; for the specialist reports section see: **http://www.suttontrust.com/annualreports.asp**.

Political Parties websites:
The Conservative Party: http://www.conservatives.com/
The Green Party: http://www.greenparty.org.uk/
The Labour Party: http://www.labour.org.uk/
The Liberal Democrats: http://www.libdems.org.uk/
The UK Independence Party: http://www.ukip.org/

Conclusion

This chapter has shown that there is a large number of ever-changing contemporary educational issues in the UK. To return to our theme of equality, choice and accountability, we have seen that in the early years of New Labour a variety of substantial policy changes were made in education, heavily influenced by the idea of social justice and creating a fairer society. The Labour governments 1997–2010 targeted education as a major area of social change, raising expectations on many levels. There has been much criticism that Labour has failed to live up to the high expectations that it created (Tomlinson, 2008). A major criticism of the Labour administrations has been that Labour did not listen when policies were not working in the particular way the government wished them to. For example, in relation to the City Academies Programme, Gorard (2009) has identified how the intake of schools changed and the needs of students locally were often not met, despite the improvements in the schools themselves. Indeed, the new policy issued by the Coalition government relating to academies stated that it would 'ensure that all new Academies have an inclusive admissions policy' (Coalition Programme for Government, 2010:29). This suggests that the parties are sensitive, perhaps, to some of the controversies that have already occurred in this arena.

We have witnessed how external indicators such as social mobility were highlighted by the Brown government in 2009, in an attempt to recapture the initiative on education policy. The Labour government's notion of equality was always going to be a challenge to adhere to, given that the policy of school diversity was high on Blair's list of priorities. When specialist school status and City Academies were introduced, schools were trying to attract different groups of children, and this inevitably makes it harder for those who were already marginalised. As Lynch and Moran (2006) have argued, parents of some children are actively discouraged by the use of some systems, such as exclusive types of school uniform. The extent of social exclusion makes the notion of equality difficult for many people, particularly in urban areas where schools tend to be rather polarised: outstanding or failing. The provision provided by the state is far from equal across small areas of inner cities, and it is this aggravated difference that means that parents often feel that no real choice exists within the system: there are over-subscribed schools that parents are unlikely to get their children into, or under-subscribed schools that parents would not want their children to attend (Ball, 2003). However, we have also seen that the issue of inequality has been raised by the Coalition government and therefore is unlikely to disappear from the educational policy agenda, with future policies being characterised by how it is dealt with.

In terms of accountability, it could be argued that Labour policies have been dichotomous, arguing that they wanted to increase parental accountability within the system, such as increasing use of home–school contracts, where parents and schools enter into agreements regarding the education of their children on an annual basis. However, Reay (2008) has argued that ultimately using such policies makes schools less accountable to parents through the diverse models that they now use. In addition, critics of the City Academies Programme, such as Gorard

(2009), argue that Academy schools are not accountable to the parental body, but ultimately to their private finance investors, thus reducing the overall accountability to parents. As the Academies Programme is to be significantly widened through 2011 and 2012, it seems reasonable to assume that some of the issues of accountability will remain with this contemporary education policy for some time to come.

Choice, as has been demonstrated in this chapter, is often something that parents have when their financial positioning (or what sociologists call their economic capital) is significant enough to enable them to move into 'good' school catchments or pay for additional support such as tutoring, or pay for independent education. Choice becomes something far less significant if you have children in an urban area that you cannot afford to leave or access other forms of services; as Reay comments, 'few working-class parents can afford the cost of hiring private tutors and sending children to Kumon maths classes even if they have the inclination' (Reay, 2008:643). Social justice, as we have seen, was a major theme that Blair took into office in 1997. Equality also appears to be a theme that has followed the Coalition government into power, as it remains one of our most important contemporary education issues of the twenty-first century.

Case study 7.4
Springboard for Children

This is a charity based in Peckham which works with local volunteers to improve literacy in disadvantaged primary schools through intensive one-on-one teaching. Each child has a 30–40 minute session per week for as long as is needed, sometimes for several weeks or months. Children graduate from Springboard literacy programmes with similar literacy levels to their peers and increased confidence, raised expectations and enthusiasm for learning. The project is hugely successful, with 96 per cent of pupils returning to mainstream lessons with a reading age appropriate for their year group. According to 'Hub Manager' Janet Bristow: 'We always make the programme fit the child rather than the child fit the programme.'

Phoenix High School

This school was once called a 'Hell School' by the media. Attendance was poor, behaviour appalling and staff morale extremely low.

Over the past 12 years, the head teacher William Atkinson and his team have raised the self-esteem of the whole school community. The atmosphere is calm and focused and pupils are smartly dressed and polite. The walls are covered with photos of pupils with their GCSE results, forming a 'Hall of Fame' aimed at raising the aspirations and creating a sense of shared mission. One of the school leadership team's key areas of focus has been getting parents and the community on board; as William Atkinson himself says, 'parental involvement is the most important thing you can do outside teaching and learning.'

Since William Atkinson took over the school, the percentage of pupils achieving five GCSEs A*–C has risen from 4 per cent to 77 per cent.

Source: http://www.centreforsocialjustice.org.uk/default.asp?pageRef=311 (viewed 06/06/10).

Summary

The role of government in education

Labour government policies hoped to help socially excluded groups learn the skills to integrate fully in society and aimed to target spending on certain groups in the population in order to alleviate poverty. The main groups chosen were the under-25s, the long-term unemployed, lone parents, those with disabilities, and the over-50s. Here there is a strong overlap between education and other government policies.

The impact of the European Union, devolution, and the Third Way

The Labour government wanted to set about creating a fairer society for all. This was labelled the Third Way, the two previous 'big ideas' being capitalism (the First Way) and socialism (the Second Way). New Labour were more pro-European than other previously elected governments, and many of these policies that were put forward under the Third Way banner were being put forward by the EU. Devolution involved giving control of education policy to separate Assemblies for Wales, Scotland and Northern Ireland, with significant impact on their education systems.

Social mobility, education and social policy

The UK has one of the most highly stratified societies in the world, where large divisions exist between high and low earners, and this position enables top earners to send their children to independent schools, or move to the areas with the best state schools. Such purchase of privilege, with 'topped-up' education including tutoring, foreign trips, books and internet access, means that as a society little social mobility, or movement between the socio-economic groups, takes place.

Social justice and the alleviation of child poverty

Policies to reduce social exclusion have included the Baby Bond, Child Tax Credits (CTC), Working Families Tax Credit (WFTC), and Sure Start.

Every Child Matters and extended services provision

The aim of Every Child Matters is to give all children the support they need to:

- be healthy
- stay safe
- enjoy and achieve
- make a positive contribution
- achieve economic well-being.

▶

Extended services provision includes:

- a varied menu of activities, in a safe place, for primary and secondary schools
- childcare: 8:00am to 6:00pm, 48 weeks a year for primary schools
- parenting support, including family learning
- swift and easy access to targeted and specialist services such as speech and language therapy
- community access to facilities including adult learning, ICT and sports facilities.

Excellence in Cities, Excellence in Schools and the National Challenge schemes

The National Challenge was launched in 2008. It is a programme of support that is intended to secure higher standards in all secondary schools so that, by 2011, at least 30 per cent of pupils in every school will gain five or more GCSEs at A* to C, including both English and mathematics. The National Challenge is, again, about tackling the link between deprivation and low educational attainment – again highlighting the link between social policy and education policy. Forerunners to the National Challenge were the Excellence in Cities (EiC) and Excellence in Schools initiatives.

City Academies Programme

The City Academies Programme aimed to provide Academies that were all-ability, state-funded schools established and managed by sponsors from a wide range of backgrounds, including high performing schools and colleges, universities, individual philanthropists, businesses, the voluntary sector and the faith communities.

Widening participation

The Labour government's target was to get 50 per cent of young people into higher education by 2010. However, this figure remains unachieved to date with a combined total of 43 per cent of 17 to 30-year-old English domiciled first-time participants in an HEI (higher education institution) in 2007–2008. The Liberal–Conservative coalition is not aiming to maintain such an ambitious target in this decade, as HE cuts were among the first casualties of cutting the government deficit when it came to power.

Criticisms of Labour in office 1997–2010

The policies introduced during Tony Blair's years in office were funded by Gordon Brown's Treasury. Many of the policies, such as tax credits and Sure Start, were therefore considered 'Brownite' not 'Blairite' policies in the first place. The difference is that Blair was ideologically happier with the introduction of market forces into education, whereas Brown saw this as the only way to gain the effective funding needed to improve the system.

The Conservatives in Opposition 1997–2010

The Conservative Party under Cameron continued to be vocal in its opposition to many Labour government decisions on education, largely because, as was discussed earlier, many of the solutions that a Labour government put forward come from the state. Iain Duncan Smith, who led the Conservative Party between 2001

▶

and 2003, went on to establish the Centre for Social Justice (CSJ). This proved to be very influential on the policies of Cameron's Conservative Party. In the 2010 General Election, Cameron put forward some of these ideas as part of a 'Big Society' that he wanted to see created under a Conservative government. This idea held that the power of the state would start to be reclaimed by individuals and social groups rather than being held on to by government organisations.

Liberal Democrat education policies

The Liberal Democrats have been consistent in their policy to scrap all student fees in higher education, and would instead raise funds via progressive taxation: charging higher tax payers more. Among a range of other policies, the Liberal Democrats would also like to scrap the Qualifications and Curriculum Development Agency (QCDA), Ofsted and Ofqual (the qualifications and examinations regulator), and replace them with an independent Education Standards Authority (ESA).

2010 onwards: the Liberal–Conservative Coalition

The Liberal–Conservative Coalition has issued a range of statements that form the basis of government policy for the five years through to 2015. Interestingly one of the first acts of this government in May 2010 was to scrap the Department for Children, Schools and Families (DCSF), which had integrated many education policies with the social policies discussed earlier in the chapter, and create the Department for Education (DfE). This alone shows the difference in emphasis between the two administrations, with the Coalition putting schools as a central part of its policy, while still acknowledging some of the inequalities that were discussed in this chapter.

References

Ball, S., Davies, J., David, M. and Reay, D. (2002) 'Classification' and 'Judgement': social class and the 'cognitive structures' of choice of Higher Education, *British Journal of Sociology of Education*, 23(1), pp. 51–72.

Ball, S.J. (2003) The Risks of Social Reproduction: the middle classes and education markets, *London Review of Education*, 1(3), pp. 163–75.

Ball, S.J. (2008) *The education debate*, Bristol: The Policy Press.

Blanden, J. and Machin, S. (2007) *Recent changes in intergenerational mobility in Britain*, Report for the Sutton Trust (Economics Department, University of Surrey, and Centre for Economic Performance, London School of Economics).

Bloor, K. (2008) *A Level Politics*, 2nd edn, London: The Book Guild.

City Academies Programme, DfES: http://www.standards.dfes.gov.uk/academies/what_are_academies/?version=1, accessed 21 July 2009.

Conservative Party: http://www.conservatives.com/Policy/Where_we_stand/Universities_and_Skills.aspx, viewed 16 July 2009.

Crompton, R. (2008) *Class and Stratification*, 3rd edn, Cambridge: Polity Press.

DCSF, Every Child Matters: http://www.dcsf.gov.uk/everychildmatters/about/aboutecm/, viewed 16 July 2009.

DCSF, National Challenge Scheme: http://www.dcsf.gov.uk/nationalchallenge/, viewed 16 July 2009.

Giddens, A. (1998) *The Third Way: The Renewal of Social Democracy*, Cambridge: Polity Press.

Gorard, S. (2009) What are Academies the answer to? *Journal of Education Policy*, 24(1), pp. 101–13.

Hansard (2006) Written answer to question from John Hayes, 22 May 2006.

Layard, R. (2001) *Welfare-to-Work and the New Deal*, Centre for Economic Performance, London: London School of Economics.

Lynch, M. and Moran, M. (2006) Markets, schools and the convertibility of economic capital: The complex dynamics of class choice, *British Journal of Sociology of Education*, 27(2), pp. 221–35.

Milburn, A. (2009) *Unleashing Aspiration: The Final Report of The Panel on Fair Access to the Professions:* http://www.cabinetoffice.gov.uk/media/227102/fair-access.pdf, viewed 6 June 2010.

Murray, C. (1999) The Underclass Revisited, available at: http://www.aei.org/docLib/20040311_book268text.pdf, viewed 22 July 2009.

Raffo, C., Dyson, A., Gunter, H., Hall, D., Jones, L. and Kalambouka, A. (2007) *Education and poverty: A critical review of theory, policy, and practice*, York: Joseph Rowntree Foundation.

Reay, D. (2008) Tony Blair, the promotion of the 'active' educational citizen, and middle-class hegemony, *Oxford Review of Education*, 34(6), pp. 639–50.

Rodda, M., Tilbury, L. and Tough, S. (2009) *Social Mobility: Universities Changing Lives*, million+ think-tank, London: Institute of Education, available at: http://www.millionplus.ac.uk/documents/MOBILITY_190309.pdf, viewed 21 July 2009.

The history of Sure Start Children's Centres: http://www.dcsf.gov.uk/everychildmatters/earlyyears/surestart/surestartchildrenscentres/history/history/, viewed 9 July 2009.

Teachernet, Extended Schools Provision: http://www.teachernet.gov.uk/wholeschool/extendedschools/, viewed 16 July 2009.

Saunders, P. (2004) 'Fair Go': Do we want to live in a meritocracy? *Policy*, 20(1), pp. 3–10.

Tomlinson, S. (2008) *Education in a post-welfare society*, 2nd edn, Maidenhead: Open University Press.

Toynbee, P. and Walker, D. (2008) *Unjust Rewards: Exposing Greed and Inequality in Britain Today*, London: Granta Books.

Whitty, G. (2001) Education, social class and social exclusion, *Journal of Education Policy*, 16(4), pp. 287–95.

8

Lifelong learning

Vanessa Cottle

Contents

Introduction

There is something very self-explanatory in the term lifelong learning – that is, learning throughout one's life; however, this chapter examines some of the implications of lifelong learning for those diverse groups of people who engage with it and who are often motivated by factors outside their own control. We begin by taking a broad look at the concept of lifelong learning by offering some definitions; then consider some key government documents that have shaped the current concept and purpose of lifelong learning. These documents include reports commissioned by governments to inform decisions that will be made about forthcoming policy; Green Papers which are put together to provide opportunity for consultation and further discussion and White Papers, or policy documents, which come about as a result of the finalised Green Paper. Ultimately, White Papers inform legislation. Finally, this chapter considers how educational and training institutions, in all their guises, can provide the steps on a ladder towards increased employability prospects for adults. Adults engaged in lifelong learning include those who bring with them all manner of barriers to learning, including psychological, learning and physical difficulties, as well as those who are aspirational and find learning fulfilling.

Much of this chapter offers a practical perspective of lifelong learning as a means by which individuals improve their employment and career prospects and achieve increased personal fulfilment through formal education and training. Therefore, this chapter will be of interest to all education studies students, particularly those of you who may become motivated to practise in the lifelong learning sector.

This chapter aims to:

- Explore the concept of lifelong learning.
- Consider key government drivers for the implementation of lifelong learning.
- Investigate the ways in which lifelong learning is put into practice.

Case study 8.1
The Alleygates Project: opening the door to lifelong learning

Alternatives (Lighthouse Project) is a voluntary sector training provider in Knowsley, Liverpool, that specialises in work with ex-offenders and people recovering from alcohol and substance misuse. It provides learning activities, which lead to qualifications, in skills for life (i.e. literacy and numeracy), hospitality and catering, furniture making, information technology, hair and beauty, and metalwork. The aim of the organisation is to enable recovering substance users to fulfil their potential and to live socially integrated lives.

One particularly successful aspect of its work was the Alleygates Project, which taught welding and fabrication skills in the production of security gates for the ends of alleys. In addition to the skills learned there was also a 'windfall' contribution to improving the lives of the community members because the use of these gates significantly reduced the incidence of break-ins to the buildings accessed via these alleys. The participants grew in self-esteem not only as a result of the employability skills in welding and fabrication, but also as a result of providing something of value to the community. Instances where this occurred included hospitality, where economical, balanced meals using fresh ingredients were cooked, then shared, and in hair and beauty personal presentation classes developed a pride in their own appearance. They even made furniture of a very good standard that could be used to furnish their homes as their lives became more settled.

Participants involved in this kind of project have previously led chaotic lifestyles caused by life experiences often shaped by prison and lack of interest in their own physical and mental well-being. These lifestyles are often characterised by lack of structure and routine in daily life such as going to work, eating regularly, having the same place to sleep each night and inappropriate or no friendship groups. The project provided structure and support in the form of requiring commitment to attend classes with expert staff available to teach new skills and to refer those in need of advice to, for example, housing or benefit counsellors. The project also encouraged them to keep clean, value each other's differences and commit to attend; consequently they developed qualities such as self-discipline and respect for themselves and others.

One participant had been a heavy drug user for many years. The high level of commitment and concentrated activity required to attend the project and complete qualifications had helped him to give up the habit. The project had promoted a change in an old, dysfunctional lifestyle to one with a positive future which in turn helped the participant restore good relationships in family life. Increased confidence was particularly important in raising aspirations to apply for paid work.

Source: Alternatives (Lighthouse Project), adapted from The Annual Report of Her Majesty's Chief Inspector of Education, Children's Services and Skills 2007/08.

Questions for discussion

1 *What is it about each of the learning activities described above that will contribute to learners' self-esteem?*

2 *Why is it important to replace a chaotic life with structure?*

3 *How might investment in this type of provision have a positive impact on social cohesion within a community and the economy of the country?*

The concept of lifelong learning

What do we mean by lifelong learning?

We begin with a straightforward definition of lifelong learning as a process of learning that goes on through the duration of an individual's life. As Field (2006:1) puts it, lifelong learning '. . . can be almost as unconscious as breathing'. As a student engaged in learning you may already have identified that, in order to achieve the career you aspire to, you will need to undertake postgraduate study. You may have been required to draw up personal and professional development action plans as part of a study skills or career development module to help you improve your personal learning skills and professional employability qualities. These plans oblige you to anticipate what future training you need to achieve your intended career goals and they apply whether you are a full-time student with no current employment, a student with part-time employment or a part-time student. Employees in most occupations are required to attend, some would say endure, events which range from health and safety training lasting for only one hour to long-term, in-service postgraduate courses. Whatever form they take, these examples reflect several rationales for engaging in lifelong learning. These range from personal desires to make a difference to the lives of others, preparing for career progression or responding to the demands of organisations and government legislation which begin with a requirement that we are all literate and numerate and employable. All of these, however, do depend on the preparedness of 'someone' to provide funding; this 'someone' could be the Government, the employer or the individual.

You should now be starting to develop a concept of lifelong learning. In fact, as a student in higher education you are already part of the process because, as Blanda et al. (2009:4) explain, lifelong learning is 'a period of formal education or training which occurs after a break from continuous, full-time education', though many would argue it should include all learning from birth, whether formal or informal. The difference in these two approaches underpins some of the tensions to be uncovered when considering lifelong learning. If we consider Blanda et al.'s 2009 suggestion we get the sense that lifelong learning is for adults who are already educated and whose new learning is formal and planned with a focus on developing vocational skills, much as described in the examples considered above. If we accept the 'cradle to grave' proposition we have to accept the validity of informal, incidental (or even accidental), more personal contexts for learning. These could include a baby's cognitive and psychomotor development as she/he learns to, for example, talk and walk; a child learning to tie a shoelace or play a few chords on a recorder; a teenager learning to enjoy new fashions and an adult learning about the wonder of architecture through international travel.

As a student you will recognise learning experiences other than the formal learning offered by your lecturers. You may have had to learn how to budget for the first time, or how to use a new washing machine; you may have had to learn how to find your way around a new city, how to organise your study time around family commitments and how to enhance your communication skills in order to make new friends. You are unlikely to go many weeks without watching some illuminating documentary on TV from which you learn something new. These incidental or **informal learning** experiences are essential to your being able to cope with the kinds of new situations you will face throughout your life. Certainly, John Denham, the then Secretary of State for Innovation, Universities and Skills, in The Learning Revolution White Paper (policy document) (2009) seemed to believe that the outcomes of learning for its own sake contribute to a society we can be proud of.

We now have some simple views of lifelong learning; from these ideas we can begin to see that the term may have different meanings to different people and, therefore, formulating one specific definition is difficult. The following ideas and challenges proposed by Foskett (2002) go some way to capturing the ideas behind lifelong learning:

Lifelong Learning is the process of engaging individuals, communities and organisations in recognising the importance of learning to personal, cultural, social and economic development at all stages of people's lives. It is essentially a cultural reformation, and widening participation is one of the key processes of reconstruction that it requires. The ultimate objective of both widening participation and Lifelong Learning is a transition to a learning society in which education and training, both formal and informal, are a high profile and high status activity for all, with a community commitment to the value of learning.

Foskett, 2002:80

Here, Foskett is drawing on the concept of **cultural capital**, as discussed by Bourdieu and Passeron (1977), which explains how individuals are locked into cycles of, for example, unemployment and poor education that are inherent within the socio-economic class to which they were born. Foskett (2002) claims that lifelong learning is a process that can reform and reconstruct these cultural ties, and that policy which succeeds in opening up educational opportunities to those who would not traditionally take advantage of them (i.e. widening participation which you will read more about later in this chapter) is required to achieve this end.

History of education

Lifelong learning

The idea of learning throughout life is not a new one. The National Institute of Adult Continuing Education NIACE (2009), in the Annexe (additional document) to The Learning Revolution White Paper (DIUS, 2009:49) gives a flavour of the historical origins of lifelong learning in the UK. This refers to the debates of the seventeenth century generated by groups known as Levellers, who challenged how parliament operated; also, how in the eighteenth century the new idea of coffee houses allowed socially and educationally diverse individuals to engage in everyday as well as more intellectual and philosophical discussion; and how the temperance movement of the nineteenth century stimulated debate about the squalor and degradation arising from the extreme use of alcohol by the poor. These examples demonstrate how informal situations can generate insights, or learning, that can lead to social change.

Later, in 1903, the Workers Education Association (WEA) was established 'to support the educational needs of working men and women' (Workers Education Association, n.d.). Today the WEA continues to offer formal adult education classes as a voluntary movement committed to widening participation. NIACE itself was founded in 1921 with the purpose of supporting adult learners and learning providers and today continues to promote lifelong learning opportunities for adults with a particular interest in increasing participation for those who experience barriers to learning. However, it was not until the 1970s, according to Morgan-Klein and Osborn (2007), that lifelong learning first became a subject for debate with the publication for UNESCO of the 1972 Faure Report, Learning to Be. Then, as the 1990s drew to a close the focus of lifelong learning policy outcomes encompassed learning for self-fulfilment, social stability and economic growth, with the emphasis being on the latter. The early 2000s saw the beginnings of a return to recognising the value of informal learning in achieving lifelong learning, particularly for a population with a growing number of healthy, retired individuals.

What is the purpose of lifelong learning?

You should now begin to see how lifelong learning can contribute to a **cycle of improvement**; for example, achieving qualifications can lead to better job prospects with better pay.

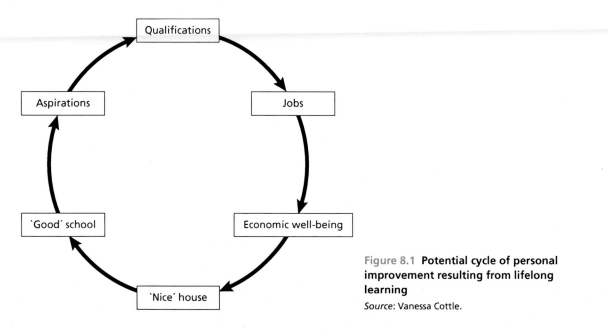

Figure 8.1 Potential cycle of personal improvement resulting from lifelong learning
Source: Vanessa Cottle.

As a consequence of successful learning, the lifelong learner's levels of self-esteem, or at least concept of themselves as a learner (Marsh and O'Mara, 2008), and confidence are improved. This probably leads to better chances in achieving higher qualifications which, in turn, lead to better job prospects. This upward spiral of success does not need to rest with the individual lifelong learner. In addition, your partner and family may experience the material effects of success such as new clothes or even a new car or new house; perhaps your new house is in a locality with a better school for your children (see Figure 8.1). The potential impact of these improvements in economic capital begins to be far reaching. You may be able to develop cultural and **social capital** for example; culturally you may develop an interest in buying new books, visiting the theatre and travelling abroad, and socially your new neighbour, or new colleague at work, might know just the right make of computer at the right price for you to purchase to help with your children's homework. In this way, both you and your children will develop a use of language known as 'elaborated code' which fits a teacher's expectations of those who are bright and able (Bernstein, 1971, cited by Atherton, 2010). Being 'labelled' as bright, a child is treated as such; the resulting positive effects on personal self-esteem may mean that they become more likely to achieve higher levels of qualifications and better job prospects. With improved self-esteem and confidence, together with possibly fewer financial worries, people are likely to become generally happier – therefore, health is likely to be maintained for longer. As a healthy person you are in a position to take more advantage of learning opportunities and use the outcomes of these positively.

Another consequence of a healthy, well-paid population is that the government will benefit from the higher income taxes paid and probably fewer demands on the health services and benefits they provide. This is very timely as the age for receiving state pension gradually rises (from age 60 for women and 65 for men to 68 by 2046 for everyone), coupled with the uncertainty surrounding many private pensions, leaves no alternative for many but to try to remain in employment for longer than they intended. An ability to earn more and spend more should stimulate the economy to grow faster, thereby creating more and better paid employment.

If you are well qualified and up to date in your occupational knowledge and skills you can contribute to increased productivity. For example, an electrician has to be prepared to work to professional standards and with new techniques; a teacher has to be abreast of developing subject knowledge and innovative methods of teaching. New technologies, which need an innovative workforce to develop, influence many of these kinds of changes which in turn generate a need for **continuous professional development (CPD)**. All this assumes that employment opportunities are available and, indeed, development economists such as Easterly (2002) do debate the contribution of education to economic growth.

Taking all this into account, you should begin to understand how lifelong learning can potentially serve the purposes of: ensuring you have the right skills and knowledge for employment; providing job security; keeping you ready to respond to changes in the employment arena, for example the impact of technology; contributing to economic growth; raising your quality of life and, not least, raising your own personal self-esteem and confidence. In short, effective lifelong learning should benefit individuals, society and the country as it plays its part in a global economy where technology has increased the possibilities to compete internationally (Curtis and Pettigrew, 2010). David Blunkett (1998), the then Secretary of State for Education, forecast the flavour of policy and strategy to come in this way:

> Learning is the key to prosperity – for each of us as individuals, as well as for the nation as a whole. Investment in human capital will be the foundation of success in the knowledge-based global economy of the twenty-first century . . . learning throughout life will build human capital by encouraging the acquisition of knowledge and skills and emphasising creativity and imagination. The fostering of an enquiring mind and the love of learning are essential to our future success . . .

↖ Connect and explore

Read the introduction to the report 'The Learning Age', a paper which sets out the aims, purpose and strategies for lifelong learning during the life of the Labour government. Find out why the learning age and the information and knowledge economy were felt to be so important.

Introduction to the Green Paper Consultation on Adult Learning, available from: http://www.lifelonglearning.co.uk/greenpaper/index.htm.

It can be seen that New Labour government (1997–2010) policy gave a clear purpose to the notion of lifelong learning. Later in this chapter you will read about the commitments made to provide a range of opportunities for everyone to participate in lifelong learning. In particular, those considered to be disengaged from learning (for example those who have had poor learning experiences caused by failure, learning difficulties or ill-health) have been targeted, but why is this so important? To begin to answer this question, consider the following points:

- Statistics show that UK productivity is trailing other countries, including Italy, France and the United States (Office for National Statistics, 2010), in the global market which puts our international competitors in a position to take business opportunities away from the UK.

- Worldwide technology could become a major threat to employment; for example, building a website for a company based in London can easily be done anywhere in the world by someone with the right skills and software – and wages are much lower in many growing economies such as India. Lifelong learning can help develop the innovative work practices needed to improve the competitiveness of the UK companies.

- Those who are disadvantaged tend to do less well during initial, compulsory periods of education, which results in poor employment rates (use this website for some statistics which demonstrate this: http://www.dwp.gov.uk/publications/policy-publications/opportunity-for-all/indicators/table-of-indicators/people-of-working-age/indicator-19/). A second chance at learning can make a difference to their employment opportunities.

- Adults with poor basic skills are more likely to be unemployed or be employed in low-paid unskilled jobs, which are increasingly rare (Sabates, 2008)

- Twelve per cent of working age in the UK have no qualifications and, of those, only 47 per cent are employed compared with between 71 per cent and 88 per cent (depending on the nature of qualification) of those with qualifications (Morgan and Hubble, 2008).

- There is still inequality between the highest and lowest income rates which in turn reflects social class divisions. The 2003–2004 Family Expenditure Survey demonstrates that:

> The poorest 20 per cent of households received just under half the average final income, while the richest 20 per cent received nearly twice the national average.
>
> Haralambos and Holborn, 2008:36

- High rates of child poverty make the above problems worse by increasing a future negative downward spiral of failure, poor health and unemployment. According to Her Majesty's Revenue and Customs website, child poverty refers to children who live with families that receive benefits and whose income 'is less than 60% median income' for that type of household.

- In spite of the emphasis on employer targets, the national and the international economy, the Foresight report on Mental Capital and Well being confirms that to 'Keep Learning' is one way to maintain good mental health and well-being (Foresight, cited by DIUS, 2009:11).

The overall vision for lifelong learning is, therefore, to build a new culture of learning where everyone is prepared to be, and values being, engaged in learning at recurrent times throughout life. This culture of learning, according to government aims, would equip the country not only with a workforce which has the creativity and innovation to increase personal prosperity and be rewarded by resulting personal fulfilment, but it will also help build a cohesive society which, according to Curtis and Pettigrew (2010:134), increases 'tolerance for gender and racial equality' thereby providing a sense of belonging and responsibility. Within this vision, as defined by DfEE 1998, there is a social challenge to change individuals' attitudes to ongoing learning and to their aspirations for employment as well as an economic challenge to meet the workforce skills gap so that the UK can remain economically competitive globally (DfEE, 1998). The challenge of widening participation continues to be key to achieving this vision.

Widening participation

In 1997 two reports on widening participation were published; these were *Learning Works: Widening Participation in Further Education* and *Higher Education in the Learning Society* (they became known as the Kennedy Report and the Dearing Report respectively). Helena Kennedy chaired the committee responsible for the *Learning Works* report and continues to support widening participation through the Helena Kennedy Foundation which champions social action, social mobility and social justice. She proposed that lifelong learning should bridge the gulf, which widens over time, between the two extremes of those who succeed and those who do not. Table 8.1 provides a simple illustration of these two groups. While it should not be read as a precise description of specific groups in society, it does illustrate how cultural and social capital can lead to success and where lack of it can lead to early underachievement due to missed opportunities in education, which in turn compromises progression into paid employment and associated advantages. The aim of widening participation is specifically to attract non-traditional learners into further and higher education. These non-traditional learners are those without the social and cultural capital referred to earlier; they tend to be those who do not succeed due to non-participation in learning and, therefore, are less likely to have the opportunity to improve their socio-economic status (i.e. achieve social mobility, a concept you can read more about in Chapter 5). The Fryer Report (1997) describes these

Table 8.1 **Those who succeed and those who do not**

Those who succeed	*Those who do not succeed*
• Parents in employment	• One parent family out of employment
• Well prepared for learning by experiences outside school environment	• Not prepared for learning due to lack of adult time and attention
• Access to environment conducive to study (e.g. personal study area without distraction, personal computer)	• Inadequate facilities for study (e.g. house cold and damp with only shared spaces and no resources)
• Attendance at 'good' school with a culture and practices focused on high achievement of children who are already learning in the home environment	• Lack of encouragement to attend school • School resources focused on supporting children to reach a level of 'readiness' for learning, rather than on actual learning
• Motivational family and peer role models enhance aspirations to succeed	• Role models disengaged from formal learning and education
• Family culture of progressing to next stage of education and/or professional career	• Family culture develops insufficient self-esteem to aspire to employment

learners by using the emotive term 'casualties', which seems to suggest they are suffering or at risk. The report identifies a number of categories of casualties including:

> . . . unskilled manual workers; part-time and temporary workers; people without qualifications, unemployed people; . . . lone parents; low-income earners; some ethnic and linguistic minority groups, older adults, people with learning difficulties and/or disabilities; people with literacy and/or numeracy difficulties, ex-offenders, disaffected youth and those living in isolated locations.
>
> Elliott, 1999:105

? Stop and reflect

Re-read the above section and list the different types of 'capital' discussed. Then try to analyse the effect of these on your education to date and in the future.

Lifelong learning: policy and practice

For more than a decade much New Labour government thinking, policy and funding was invested into developing lifelong learning and the Coalition government of 2010 continues in this vein. This section provides a summary of the key policy themes which have impacted on practice. Although the earliest of these policies are now over a decade old, they continue to be significant and to resonate in more recent policy.

In 1997 two reports were published (Kennedy and Dearing) which together encompassed all post-compulsory education and training, being focused on further education and higher education respectively. As previously mentioned, a particularly powerful message that came from these two reports was that of widening participation; they galvanised the notion that it was not enough for learning to be delivered to those who had easy access to it. To make a difference, those who did not have a culture of learning should be given opportunities to do so – it was, after all, these groups that would benefit most from learning. The Fryer Report (1997) focused on adult learning in the community and workplace, including libraries.

Later, in 1999, the Moser Report had far-reaching implications when adult inability to read and write at functional levels was revealed. This document set targets which would shake up the approach taken to teach illiterate adults. This included writing a new literacy and numeracy curriculum document and new qualifications for basic skills teachers.

Learning to Succeed (DfEE) 1999 put forward the programme of change to achieve previous targets, though there were concerns about the focus on personal prosperity rather than community capacity. The importance of this White Paper is clear as it led the way for the Learning and Skills Act 2000 which put the policy into legislation.

In 2003 and 2005 the government published two White Papers to facilitate their Skills Strategy. It became clear that lifelong learning must provide adults with employment skills as a first priority, which would in turn provide for personal fulfilment. In 2006 the Leitch Review published by HM Treasury strongly reinforced the need for the skills gap to be closed.

More recently *Building Britain's Future* (Her Majesty's Government, 2009) and *Ambition 2020* (United Kingdom Commission for Employment and Skills, 2009) continue the same theme of how post-16 learning must contribute to the economic success of the country.

The above documents contain a number of common themes which continue to have a strong influence on the shape of how providers of lifelong learning work; these are summarised below:

Barriers to, and the widening of, participation

In order to promote widening participation for those who would not traditionally engage with learning, providers are expected to remove barriers that contribute to the non-participation in learning. These barriers were identified in the Fryer Report (1997) and included:

> . . . shortage of money for course fees and related expenses, lack of confidence, lack of outreach provision, lack of tutorial support when studying, lack of personal support, courses organised at inappropriate times and inaccessible places designed to be economic for the provider rather than the learner.
>
> Elliott, 1999:105

Information advice and guidance (IAG)

The barrier of not knowing what opportunities exist for career options and related learning opportunities provokes the need to promote lifelong learning through focused information, advice and guidance (IAG). Organisations, such as Job Centres and Connexions services which are in contact with the unemployed, work with providers to provide IAG.

All adults to become functionally literate and numerate

The need to ensure that all adults are able to use literacy and numeracy skills at least at level 2 (which is equivalent to a GCSE grade between A* and C) becomes increasingly important as high-skill jobs replace low-skill jobs. More recently these skills have been referred to as functional skills and now include information and communication technology skills.

Give responsibility to a wider range of providers

Encouraging private training organisations, voluntary sector organisations and community projects as well as the traditional FECs to deliver courses is seen as a strategy to overcome many barriers to access which are mentioned elsewhere in this chapter.

Measurement of achievement

The development of qualifications to measure achievement and progression at all levels places the emphasis on formal learning. To acknowledge that many adults do develop skills through life experience informally, systems which accredit prior experiences and learning (APEL), for example National Vocational Qualifications, are encouraged. APEL is a process of accrediting part of a qualification by recognising experiences that adults accrue during their lives often as a result of informal learning. This can eliminate the need to re-experience the negative feelings and past failures of formal education while reducing the time period required to achieve a recognised qualification. Certification of learning is important as a means of both auditing whether or not providers have achieved government targets and measuring individual suitability for employment.

Improve quality of provision

An infrastructure of quality checks (e.g. inspections, audits and professionalisation of the lifelong learning sector) to ensure that learning opportunities are effective (that is, lecturers are competent and qualifications achieved truly reflect learners' capability) has increasingly been embedded into management systems.

The skills gap

In order to help develop the skills deemed necessary to fill the skills gap and make individuals employable, funding mechanisms are designed so that providers of learning offer approved subjects and courses rather than leisure-type courses.

Activity

Devise a short questionnaire aimed at finding out the extent to which the above themes have benefited fellow students – or family and friends – as lifelong learners. Analyse your findings to find out which barriers to learning have and have not been addressed.

Lifelong learning in practice

Taking into account the reports, White Papers and reviews referred to above, there can be no doubt that there has been a government determination that we all become involved with lifelong learning of some sort or another. This section considers how the lifelong learning sector seeks to achieve this.

Lifelong learning providers deliver the types of learning programmes to meet the needs of the following:

- Academic and vocational learning for all those *normally* over the age of compulsory education.
- Vocational education and training for adults seeking employment.
- Workforce development on behalf of employers for those already in employment.
- Basic literacy and numeracy skills (functional skills) improvement to achieve government targets in qualifications at level 2.
- Second chance general education for adults who have previously failed or want/need to change.
- Learning for leisure, personal and community development.

↖ Connect and explore

To help you put into context the range of learning available within the above visit **http://www.direct.gov.uk/en/EducationAndLearning/QualificationsExplained/ DG_10039017** and browse the table which defines the qualifications and credit framework and levels of learning.

The lifelong learning sector tends to place learning providers into the following categories;

- Further education colleges (FECs) – the 14–19 Reforms of 2007 extend the lower age range studying within FECs to 14.
- Higher education – comprises learning and qualifications from level 4, first-year degree (A level qualifications equate to level 3), upwards and is commonly found in universities, but also occurs in the workplace and FECs.
- **Work-based learning** – practical learning in the workplace often backed up with theory lessons at an FEC, private training provider or university.
- **Offender learning** – mostly associated with prison education and the development of functional skills. It also applies to offenders who attend learning opportunities in the community.
- **Adult and community learning (ACL)** – often based in outreach centres managed by the local FEC and aims to provide functional skills and other basic learning opportunities which are often delivered through short, focused projects.
- Museums and libraries and archives – similar to ACL but located in the museums and libraries to take advantage of facilities and informal learning opportunities.

Each of these categories is considered below, but it is worth mentioning that the boundaries of these categories tend to overlap and often change.

Further education colleges

Nearly ten years before Bill Rammell (2005:i), the then Minister of State at the Department of Education and Skills and later at the Department of Innovation, Universities and Skills with responsibility for Lifelong Learning, Further and Higher Education, claimed: 'Further education is the engine room for skills and social justice in this country,' the Fryer Report (1997) also emphasised the importance of further education in ensuring the efficacy of lifelong learning. FECs have been traditionally viewed as providing a wide range of study choices for the post-compulsory age group of learners. However, for many years a small percentage of schoolchildren from Key Stage 4 (GCSE level) have studied at their local college. These programmes, sometimes known as Link Courses, were aimed at children who were likely to benefit from the more 'grown-up' feel of a vocational context as they studied courses not available in school. Being released from school for one or two half days a week was often perceived as a particularly motivating privilege for otherwise disengaged learners. With the 14–19 Reforms (14–19 Education and Skills White Paper, 2005), 14 has become an accepted starting age for attending FECs; there is no upper limit.

The strength of the FEC is its ability to be flexible and responsive to economic and political changes which impact on educational and training preferences. One example is that, after the Moser Report (1999) was published, FECs were able to offer the expertise necessary to provide basic skills courses for the increasing numbers of illiterate and innumerate adults seeking courses. Another example of flexibility is that, as a result of the Further Education and Training Bill 2006, FECs may be granted powers to award and manage their own **foundation degrees**. Foundation degrees include vocational and associated academic learning at level 4 and 5 and were developed in response to government drives to widen participation by engaging 50 per cent of 18 to 30-year-olds in higher education by 2010. Foundation degrees provide opportunities for those from a vocational background to relate real-life practice to theory by engaging in a period of academic study alongside voluntary or paid work experience. They can then progress, if they wish, to the final stage of an honours degree.

Unlike schools, FECs do not follow the National Curriculum, but rather respond to local needs. For example, in areas where farming is prevalent you will find agricultural and horticultural colleges. Most offer A level and other academic courses at level 3 and, where departments are large enough, they may become known as sixth form colleges. You or someone you know may have attended sixth form college which gave you an opportunity to continue studying your school subjects, but without the constraints that a school might impose on you. Technically, sixth form colleges provide further education; they focus on level 3 qualifications and offer very little level 1 or 2 work. But FECs encompass very much more than sixth form colleges. They offer vocational subjects including construction trades, IT, hairdressing, beauty, engineering, business studies and functional skills. Academic courses are also offered, including undergraduate work in some colleges' higher education centres, for example foundation degrees. However, it is the vocational programmes starting at pre-entry levels that make FECs significant for the kinds of lifelong learning aspirations mentioned in the reports discussed earlier.

Partnerships and further education

The notion of partnerships is a key element in the way FECs work. It is by providing partnerships within the community that many of the barriers identified by Fryer (1997) are removed and disengaged learners in particular are reached. Partnerships with higher education enable colleges to develop and deliver a range of level 4, 5 and 6 programmes. The advantage of this for learners is that they are able to remain in familiar, local environments to progress their study and, for colleges, it is the extra funding brought in by these courses. Partnership between a college and a university usually provides progression routes for learners, with a guaranteed interview to named degrees when a named qualification, for example Access to HE, has been achieved.

Table 8.2 demonstrates two routes through lifelong learning that might apply to learners currently at school. The non-traditional route takes longer because the learner is out of full-time education sooner, but ultimately the same goals as those reached by the traditional route are possible. For the disengaged learner who has left school lacking qualifications and possessing poor functional skills the route is only possible once this lack is addressed. The time taken to develop functional skills depends on how quickly the barriers to learning can be overcome.

Table 8.2 **Traditional and non-traditional routes to success or how a further education college can widen participation: towards a career in teaching**

Traditional route	Non-traditional route
• Attends primary school	• Attends primary school
• Attends secondary school, gains 5 GCSE grades A*–C including maths, English and science	• Attends secondary school – Diploma L1 in society, health and development
• Attends sixth form, gains 3 A levels	• Achieves modern apprenticeship while working in local nursery
• Achieves university degree	• Leaves employment to become full-time parent of two children
• Achieves Post-Graduate Certificate in Education	• Enrols and passes part-time Access to HE course
• Gains job as teacher	• Gains job as teaching assistant (TA) during term time when children start school
• Becomes parent to two children who go to nursery and continues full-time employment	• Achieves foundation degree with a merit – FD studied as part of employment requirements of being a TA
• Attends in-service short courses to keep up to date with teaching, learning and assessment policy (e.g. behaviour management)	• Studies part time at FEC, while still in full-time work as TA, to achieve the final year of a BA (Hons) Education Studies Degree
• Studies in-service Masters in Education Degree in anticipation of promotion	• Accepted on to a Graduate Teaching Programme which means being employed as an unqualified teacher while studying and building a portfolio of evidence which, once accredited, leads to Qualified Teacher Status
	• In-service short courses to keep up to date with teaching, learning and assessment policy (e.g. behaviour management)
	• In-service Masters in Education Degree in anticipation of promotion

Activity

Think about the two routes above. What are the benefits and limitations of each for (a) the individual's personal fulfilment and (b) the economy? Is there anything here that might address problems of social cohesion?

Connect and explore

To get a real feel for the structure of further education, read **Adrian Perry's** report entitled: *If I were you, I wouldn't start from here: Comments on the Structure and Organisation of Further Education for the Foster Review of Further Education*, available at **www.dius.gov.uk** – search for Adrian Perry, 2009.

To learn more about further education's role in promoting community cohesion, read the consultation document *The Role of FE Providers in Promoting Community Cohesion, Fostering Shared Values and Preventing Violent Extremism* (2008), available at **www.dius.gov.uk/publications.html**.

Adult and community learning

The purpose of adult and community learning (ACL) is to provide courses which meet the needs and interests of particular groups of people. These courses should provide the kinds of learning opportunities that are taught in an enjoyable and achievable manner; they should be available in familiar, safe environments where people work and live. ACL can take place just about anywhere in outreach centres such as schools, village halls, specific local adult centres, health centres and, increasingly as with all learning opportunities, online virtual classrooms. This diverse range of locations is essential in helping prospective learners take their first steps into study. Once the barrier of geographical access is removed, trained staff can provide support to overcome other barriers, such as poor attitude, motivation, ability, finance and previous negative experiences, more easily. Categories of learners involved might include any of these complex groups: refugees; asylum seekers; women-only groups; those with learning difficulties, mental health problems and addictions; offenders in the community and those with poor literacy and numeracy skills – many of these are the 'casualties' mentioned previously in this chapter. These 'casualties' tend to be vulnerable and sensitive to possible failure and their development as lifelong learners needs to be handled with care.

The provision is funded, managed and delivered through a range of bodies including: local authorities, which often offer adult education evening classes in local school buildings; FEC outreach centres; one-off Lottery projects particularly targeted at specific community schemes; Sure Start centres (read more about Sure Start in Chapter 5) and the WEA. This approach allows learning opportunities to expand and contract as necessary to provide for the diverse needs within the community. This range of agencies raises questions of quality, consistency, continuity and accountability; however, partnerships that successfully address these challenges can deliver appropriate and enabling courses. Many projects, such as New Deal, provide access to short work experience opportunities with training and progression into the next stage of learning in mainstream further education when individuals are successful in their learning. (For more information about New Deal use this link: http://www.direct.gov.uk/en/Employment/Jobseekers/programmesandservices/DG_173717.)

Unfortunately, short-term projects tend to capture the willing minority, while the really disengaged and disadvantaged often do not recognise their own needs and continue to be difficult to reach. Research by Appleby and Bathmaker (2006) reveals that, although the first overall target for literacy, language and numeracy achievements had been achieved, less than 50 per cent of the qualifications were achieved by the intended priority groups. On the other hand, for those who do engage, success is measured in many ways, not just through qualifications. You may wish to re-read Case study 8.1 to see examples of how, as a result of the opportunities provided, individuals grow in confidence and self-esteem, and they develop life skills and job skills in readiness for employment, perhaps in community projects similar to the ones in which they undertook their own learning.

Within the learning situation

The range of community initiatives is as diverse as those whose needs it intends to address. Here is a case study of how one school made successful links with the community and claims to have improved individual lives.

Mitchell High School Business and Enterprise College is located in an area characterised by all of the common indicators of deprivation, in particular high unemployment rates.

Many of the students at the comprehensive school are from families where unemployment is now in the third generation and little value is given to education. High teenage pregnancies, coupled with low aspirations and poor life chances, all featured in the overall picture.

In setting up the community learning centre (CLC), the head teacher knew the school had a role to play in supporting community members to re-engage in education and to take up employment opportunities. She also knew that to engage learners the centre needed to be responsive to their needs, so residents were consulted about what they were looking for and what would entice them into the centre. The centre accomplished 60 per cent for A*–C at GCSE (a rise of 31 per cent since opening in 2003); has been re-accredited with the Matrix standard for work in the communitry. The CLC now has a culture, both in school and out, that values education and promotes achievement.

Source: http://www.teachingexpertise.com/articles/successful-community-learning-centre-case-study-5462

Connect and explore

For more case studies of adult and community learning, see the Ofsted report entitled *The Role of Adult Learning in Community Renewal: Neighbourhood Learning in Deprived Communities Programme*, available at **www.ofsted.gov.uk**; click on Publications, then on Research, then thematic reports for September 2008.

For an in-depth, but readable, research report about adult attitudes, barriers related to learning and socio-economic effects, see *Segmentation of Adults by Attitudes Towards Learning and Barriers to Learning*, David Chilvers (2008), published by DIUS and available at **www.dcsf.gov.uk/research**.

Work-based learning

In this section of the chapter we will visit some examples of work-based learning, sometimes known as continuing professional development (CPD). We examine why workplaces encourage employees to engage in ongoing learning and the impact it may have for employees.

To begin with, the government has a number of policies which encourage work-based learning, including:

- **The National Apprenticeships Service** ensures that apprenticeship places are identified appropriately in areas of need, for example construction.

- **The Skills Pledge** is a public commitment that employers are encouraged to make by the government. They pledge to offer their workforce opportunities to retrain to level 2 achievement.

- **Train to Gain** is a national skills service which encourages organisations to train employees by matching the needs of the employer to appropriate local provision from level 2 through to management levels.

- **Time to Train** allows employees to request time away from work for the purpose of training and is covered by the Apprenticeships, Skills, Children and Learning Act 2009.

- **Extra funding** for small and medium-sized enterprises (SMEs) so that they will be able to offer the same kind of opportunities as larger companies.

Connect and explore

Find out much more about the Skills Strategy, the history of apprenticeships and where current legislation is taking us by reading Research Paper 09/14, dated 18 February 2009, by accessing **http://www.parliament.uk**.

Apprenticeships are seen as particularly important within the work-based learning context, with large amounts of government funding being invested in them. They have been promoted by the Labour government as being a high quality route into a skilled job and the plan to increase the 150,000 places by another 35,000 (BIS, 2009) by 2011 was extended by the Coalition government to 50,000 (Hayes, 2010). The Apprenticeship route provides young people with secure employment for approximately two years while studying for a nationally recognised qualification. Qualifications are National Vocational Qualifications (NVQs), achievement of which depends on demonstrating competence in the workplace, as well as proficiency in literacy, numeracy and information technology. NVQs enable many to achieve some APEL, but practical skills are usually developed within the workplace and the underpinning theory and functional skills within the classroom at a local FEC or similar provider. Although strongly associated with apprenticeships, NVQs are not confined to 'first jobbers', for example they can be offered as part of redundancy packages to help equip individuals for new careers. There is also evidence (Conlon and Vignoles, 2005) that, for those between the ages of 26 and 34, achievement of NVQs can lead to higher wages and encourage learners to continue studying for further qualifications. NVQs can also be embedded within diplomas, which now encourage work-based learning from the age of 14 while learners are still within compulsory education.

Apprenticeship places are not always taken up, which could reflect rejection by those who do not value vocational qualifications; reluctance by employers to undertake the bureaucratic demands of apprenticeship schemes or, as highlighted earlier in the chapter, a need for improved information, advice and guidance mechanisms. However, Data Service 2010, an independently managed organisation, established and funded by the Department for Business, Innovation and Skills and supported by the Skills Funding Agency to act as a single, central point of information for further education, reveals some encouraging statistics. They claim that in 2008/09 there was the highest ever recorded level of people starting apprenticeships and gaining higher success rates; respective increases of 6.8 per cent and 27.4 per cent compared with 2007/08. Their statistics also confirm that Train to Gain recruitment and achievements for 2008/09 also increased, though direct comparisons with previous years cannot be made due to funding changes.

These statistics do seem to indicate that many employers take their responsibility to provide education and training very seriously. Indeed, many become their own awarding bodies so that learning and qualifications exactly meet the specific needs of the organisation. For example: the Royal Mail has worked with City & Guilds to develop an NVQ Level 2 in Mail Operations to meet their specific training needs; B&Q, owned by the Kingfisher Group, identified in their 2010/11 milestones that they hope to extend NVQ or City and Guild's qualifications to a further 9,500 staff; and McDonald's, which has been an awarding body in the UK since 2008, offers an online learning platform which has been specifically designed for its employees. (You can view McDonald's approach to education and training by using this link: http://www.mcdonalds.co.uk/about-us/schools-and-students/schools-and-students.shtml.) While this does show a commitment to training and skills development, when companies do develop their own training this can reduce or replace apprenticeship schemes that would otherwise be offered. In-house training can also be so specific to one employer that it could limit an individual's opportunity to progress with an alternative employer. Other work-based learning routes can lead to more advanced academic qualifications achieved externally through a university.

All this learning activity generates a cost to the employing organisation in the following ways: training implies that unqualified staff are employed, other staff time is deployed to deliver training, payment of course fees and the possible loss of a newly qualified employee to a competing organisation which did not have to pay for the training. It follows, therefore, that employers will be keen to ensure that the CPD training in which they have invested accrues benefits for the organisation. It is for this reason that training opportunities are often linked to the organisation's mission statement. When this kind of system is in place we begin to see a **learning organisation (LO)**. As the mission statement and related objectives change to keep pace with external demands on the organisation, so must the training and education planned for the employees. This benefits both the employee, who is learning to continue earning, and the organisation, which evolves in line with its chosen strategic direction. This cost/benefit calculation has to work in favour of the organisation so that it maintains its economic viability.

However, as we have seen earlier in the chapter, the lifelong learning concept includes personal fulfilment and wider social changes in the lives of individuals. The types of skills required for this type of outcome are generic, **transferable skills** rather than job-specific skills. They are important whatever the nature of your job; for example, a teacher with an excellent command of their particular subject will still need excellent communication and organisational skills in order to be excellent at their job. These generic, transferable skills improve employment chances and can make personal life more fulfilling; they include resilience, empathy and goal setting. However, where government targets and economic goals are the driving force of lifelong learning it is easy to see that the following ideal definition of a learning organisation may be difficult to achieve:

> Where people continually expand their capacity to create the results they truly desire, where new and expansive patterns of thinking are nurtured, where collective aspiration is set free and where people are continually learning together.
>
> Senge, 1990, cited in Keep, 2000:3

This picture defines the LO as one where the employees are liberated to change that organisation rather than the organisation changing the employee.

In order to gauge the benefits accrued from the costs of CPD a process of evaluation takes place. When evaluating the success of the training provided for employees, the LO may begin by asking some basic questions of the trainees such as 'Did you enjoy the training?' and 'Did you learn from the training?' This process encourages trainee employees to feel valued; to feel that the training was for them personally and to feel that they have, in some way, ownership of their training; it also provides some immediate feedback about the quality of the training. However, of much greater interest to the LO will be questions such as 'Are you able to apply this training within your job?' and 'Did the application of your training generate improvements in the organisation's profits?' Of course, this is the bottom line: lifelong learning within work-based learning has a tension between benefits for the individual and benefits for the organisation. Other questions that are pertinent to work-based learning include: 'Do employees really need more skills?' and if they do, 'Is the workplace equipped to deliver them?' Also, does training create a false promise for employees? After all, there are only so many 'top jobs' and not everyone is capable of doing, or indeed seeks, such a job if it is available.

Within the learning situation

All organisations should include an induction to the company; this might be an informal chat for an hour or so with a line manager, or it may be a more protracted procedure where new entrants spend a week experiencing work in different departments. Many professional jobs carry with them a requirement for CPD in order to maintain professional status. Recent requirements for further education lecturers require that they undertake at least 30 hours a year of recorded CPD in order to maintain their professional licence with their professional body, the Institute for Learning. As the professional body for practitioners in the lifelong learning sector, the Institute for Learning (IFL) recommends the following kind of CPD:

- gaining Skills for Life qualifications, supporting and embedding literacy, numeracy and English for speakers of other languages;
- organising trips, residentials and work placements;
- reading the latest journal articles in your subject;
- attending conferences; and
- shadowing experts at work.

You can find out more about IFL at http://www.ifl.ac.uk/.

So, even where employers may not want to invest in training their employees, professional bodies require individuals to demonstrate specified standards of skills and knowledge to demonstrate their competence and to earn continued recognition within a career route. Legislation ensures that only those individuals who meet IFL standards and requirements are employed as practitioners in the lifelong learning sector.

Activity

The 14–19 Reforms bring into focus the debate surrounding the different value society places on academic and vocational learning.

Write down notes to explain why you believe an A level in an academic subject (e.g. history) should, or should not, carry the same value as a level 3 vocational subject (e.g. IT). (A level passes are equivalent to level 3 as identified in the qualifications and credit framework.) Where do you see non-certificated learning that takes place in the workplace fitting in to this debate?

Offender learning

Offenders are one of the most difficult categories of lifelong learner to reach, whether the offenders are confined to prison or serving their sentence within the community. This section considers the particular challenges that make this aspect of the lifelong learning sector different. According to the National Audit Office (2008:9), in 2008 there were '35,000 offenders in prison whose literacy and numeracy levels were below level 1'; this represented almost one-half of all prisoners. Ofsted (2008:7) claims that offenders' skills are 'below level 1 for over 60% of those assessed' and that 'nearly all . . . young people entering secure settings have skills below the national average.' Uden (2004:1) explains:

> [The] whole offending cohort is disproportionately composed of the poor and the poorly educated. It is disproportionately black. Very large numbers suffer from mental and physical illness and from drug or alcohol dependency. It is clear that taken together they form a significant element within that wider group of non-participants in learning who have always been a central concern for NIACE [National Institute of Adult Continuing Education] and who are increasingly targeted by the Government's Basic Skills, Widening Participation and Skills strategies.

The purpose of offender learning is to equip offenders to lead a productive life in their community by developing their personal and social skills, including parenting and employability skills. It is perhaps this area of lifelong learning that can contribute to improved social cohesion, where individuals value each other's difference, more than any other. However, as the number of unskilled job vacancies falls, the chances of offender rehabilitation through meaningful employment decreases due to their very poor level of qualifications in both basic skills and vocational subjects. Successful offender learning would benefit both the economy and the community, but the challenges to success are more significant than the barriers faced by other lifelong learners. Those offenders who have not previously engaged with learning face the same barriers as any other adult, including lack of motivation, lack of self-esteem and lack of learning skills. However, these barriers are compounded for offenders, particularly during a prison sentence which is a clear label of failure and of being a 'bad person' and during which an individual may perceive themselves as having little control over their own life. This depressing state can lead individuals to avoid being proactive even when positive opportunities present themselves. In addition, provision for education and training for offenders is often in conflict with the need to meet their physical and mental health needs. Consider the learning situation case study below.

Within the learning situation

Between 8 and 13 female prisoners attend their morning basic literacy class. The number of learners in attendance fluctuates according to release dates, court appearances or privileges being removed. Education is classed as a 'job' and prisoners are paid for attendance, just enough to buy some toiletries or cigarettes. Within the group most have no qualifications, though one or two have studied to undergraduate level. Most have some form of mental health and/or learning problem including a range of addictions and dyslexia. Some have health problems such as diabetes and epilepsy; some have a combination of these difficulties.

In order to prepare for the session the day's attendance list has to be checked as well as individual learning plans (ILPs) to identify what level of learning the students have reached and which worksheets they have each completed. Appropriate work – enough to maintain attention without being overwhelmed – then has to be selected for each student on the list. The panic button in each classroom is tested, a noisy necessity though rarely needed in practice. The staff room door is locked and handbags, wallets and purses are carefully put away; mobile phones were checked in at the main gate that morning when keys were allocated and attached around waists on long chains within leather pouches.

The session cannot begin on time as there is a short lock-down while the roll is called again. Finally, the learners arrive, some chatting and bumptious, others subdued. Not everyone on the original list has arrived, one or two have meetings with prison officers to discuss early release, one has been released, one is back on suicide watch and another kept in their cell. Two new learners have joined the group and there are no prepared materials for them as the initial assessment which informs their ILP has not yet been processed. Instead they have to be satisfied with sharing a worksheet that may be too difficult or too easy. After five minutes of clambering to sort out miscellaneous stationery, the more long-term and settled learner is engaged with study, others just want to chat, bicker or rest their head on the table. Calls around the room include: 'Miss, can I carry on with my book I'm writing?' (this learner can only concentrate on a personal journal detailing a young life of extraordinary abuse which probably offers some explanation of the self-harm covering forearms in deep, leathery scars); 'Come on everyone start your worksheets' – 'Can't Miss, am waiting for meds'; 'Can't Miss, I've been refused early release'; 'Can't Miss, my letter from home didn't arrive.' Ten minutes into the already late start of the session and the call comes to allow them out for medication (meds) – often methadone. About 5 of the 8 remaining students wander off – when they return their demeanour has changed from almost asleep to agitated and over-eager, but certainly no more in readiness to learn than they were before going to the pharmacy. Ten minutes later the whole group is released for a weekly library visit. By the time they return it is time to clear up and lock everything away. The learners return to their cells and the update of the ILPs confirms that the total amount of learning is minimal, even for the few keen ones, due to the constant, everyday disruptions which exacerbate the already many barriers experienced in this setting.

Source: Based on a range of experiences of the author.

Figure 8.2 **Offenders face challenges to success which are more significant than the barriers faced by other lifelong learners.**
Source: Getty Images: Thinkstock.

This learning situation highlights some of the emotional, medical and other barriers that offenders face when they try to access learning. Prison education is contracted out to providers such as FECs, with the contract going to whichever submits the best bid. It is the provider's responsibility to ensure that arrangements are in place, including staffing, to provide the same quality learning experiences as available for all other lifelong learners. However, resources and skilled staff are not always available. It is clear that when dealing with a cohort, no matter how small, who by the nature of their situation all have special needs and many of whom have possibly volatile dispositions, specially trained and highly experienced staff are essential. Many people find prisons uncomfortable places to work in and they are often located in remote areas, so it is understandable that such staff may be at a premium. One significant issue that can be identified in the learning situation above, and which is highlighted by both Uden (2004) and Ofsted (2008), is to do with problems of continuity. Lack of continuity constitutes a significant demotivator for learners. As Uden (2004) notes, this can occur within one session of learning, the beginning of a prison sentence, during transfers between prisons and when they are released to become ex-offenders in the community; initial assessments often have to be retaken when their ILPs are incomplete or do not follow them. This lack of continuity increases the problems of improving offenders' skills as encouraged by Public Service Agreement targets for education DIUS (2007). However, while the importance of basic skills, especially literacy, cannot be underestimated (Dugdale and Clark, 2008), basic skills alone do not gain employment. Offenders need to develop their self-esteem and confidence, as well as in some cases having to overcome a range of health and mental health problems associated with drug and alcohol addiction. Then, to become really employable, vocational skills such as construction, catering, business studies, basic IT and dressmaking are offered in prisons, though the emphasis remains on basic skills. With so many barriers blocking the way to success it seems to be the lucky few who come through with meaningful job skills, while for many the process will seem disappointing and even demotivating. However, for those offenders in the minority who do engage in education and are ready for higher levels of learning, access to paper-based distance learning courses such as Open University is available.

Out of prison as lifelong learners, offenders often experience as many difficulties as they did in prison. Their lives tend to be chaotic: they can experience homelessness, benefit issues and health and drug problems as well as unemployment. For these reasons offenders are probably the most likely of all lifelong learners to be dependent on individual support from a range of agencies to keep them motivated, engaged and ultimately successful. As Uden (2004:11) recommends:

> A successful strategy for the education and training of offenders and ex-offenders will need agencies in both the Criminal Justice and Education and Training sectors to work together in national and local partnerships to secure coherence and improvement in the delivery of services to offenders and ex-offenders in the community.

This is a promising strategy, and will include the funding agencies such as the Learning and Skills Council; providers which offer quality education and training; heads of Learning and Skills based in prisons to liaise effectively with the prison authorities; a probation service to ensure ex-offenders and offenders in the community continue their education without having to undergo further, apparently meaningless initial assessment; Job Centre Plus facilities to match learners with likely employment; case officers and even general practitioners to provide medical and mental health care. Once again the notion of partnership is a key to success in lifelong learning, but will take great efforts on all sides to achieve.

? Stop and reflect

Think about your own experiences of learning; have any of these changed your approach to life? Think about your personal attitudes and qualities; do you have what it takes to work with offenders in a learning context to help them change their approach to life? Do you believe this would be a positive way to invest your time?

Museums and libraries

The Learning Revolution White Paper (2009) invites organisations to sign the informal adult learning pledge as ambassadors for informal learning and this is at the heart of the role of museums, libraries and archives within lifelong learning. This White Paper, unlike the earlier ones in this chapter, emphasises the importance of learning for learning's sake and acknowledges that, while this may not lead to a formal qualification, the benefits are worth investing in. This section will discuss how museums and libraries specifically facilitate this, and present the controversy surrounding informal learning.

This chapter has already acknowledged that widening participation of lifelong learning is about re-engaging those who are most difficult to reach or who are unwilling to seek out learning for themselves. Many such learners rejected a school curriculum that did not suit them; therefore, it is reasonable to suppose that an alternative curriculum, i.e. a way of learning and being taught, could be beneficial. The learning opportunities that are available in museums and libraries tend to require the learner to be self-directed; their curricula do not control and encourage dependency as can the school curriculum. Museums and libraries must meet the needs of a range of learners from individual children and adults of every age to school and community groups who come with diverse purposes and contexts. Learners in these situations have to take responsibility for themselves; they will self-differenti- ate to choose materials and topics appealing and accessible to them personally rather than others; they will make sense of things in their own ways and in their own time. As discussed by Gorard and Rees (2002), learners who have already found their own identity as failures in a formal setting may well respond much better in an informal environment. Davis and Gardner (1999) suggest that the potential success of learning in museums may also have something to do with the way multiple intel- ligences are catered for. There is also much more reflection time than would be available in formal settings, which are constrained by funding methodologies and which set time limits for achievement, as in two years to achieve a GCSE for exam- ple. Concrete experiences are also very much a part of museum and library learning. Museums encourage visitors to interact with displays and engage in discussions on their own terms and at their own levels with expert curators. It is no surprise that books and increasingly computers are the tools of learning in libraries – often the first port of call for those who cannot afford their own computer.

Within the learning situation

There are many examples of good practice cited by NIACE (2008:65–67): here are some examples relating to museums and libraries:

- Relay Project, developed by Leeds libraries, will create opportunities for different communities to share experiences and perspectives of conflicts past and present through creative writing and technology. The project is aimed at refugees and will incorporate the use of ICT.
- Prisoners attended creative writing workshops in the prison library and produced CDs of themselves reading stories for their children.
- Bournemouth libraries used peer support volunteers to run Silver Surfer ICT sessions.
- Salford Museum worked with young people aged 16 to 25 to re-engage them with learning. Audio diaries and photographic records were created and several young people went on to take NVQs.
- Middlesbrough College library offers 13-week placements in the library to people who have been unemployed, with health problems, for some time.
- English for speakers of other languages (ESOL) is an important part of the British Museum's social inclusion and audience development work. Museum collections are used to promote the skills of listening, speaking, reading and writing English. Learn- ers study world cultures, often their own, and are able to learn through objects in a dedicated and stimulating environment.

The examples above represent the diverse range of learning activities available within libraries and museums. However, while learning can be 'casual or even accidental as far as the learner is concerned' (NIACE, 2008:3) there must still be a careful approach to the planning of quality learning experiences. This implies an element of 'measurement' in order to determine whether or not the learning has been a quality experience. The type of outcome required in this context is subjective, which goes some way to explain why informal learning, unlike formal qualifications, is not easily communicated to prospective employers. However, with a little imagination such outcomes could be instrumental in a renewed interest in the use of APEL towards gaining a full, formal qualification, as argued for by Burke and Jackson (2007).

The Learning Revolution White Paper (2009) has developed overarching principles as a possible way of validating the worth of informal learning, but the partnerships required to support museums and libraries in the development of their pedagogical approaches, including APEL, and funding structures could shift the balance back from informal to formal learning.

Connect and explore

This chapter provides a picture of the current situation of what lifelong learning means in a very practical sense. For a view of the future of lifelong learning, read *Learning Through Life* (2009) published by NIACE and available online at: **www.niace.org.uk/ lifelonglearningenquiry**.

Controversies

'Informal learning should be encouraged and acknowledged as an effective, relevant and appropriate means of lifelong learning'

Agree

- Informal learning overcomes many barriers that present themselves to disengaged learners in a variety of ways:
  - It is a response to individual needs so subjects and topics chosen are directly relevant to the learner at the time of engagement with learning.
  - The process begins when the learner is ready to learn and can develop a freedom to learn (Rogers and Freiberg, 1994).
  - The learner is able to access learning in places and at times that are convenient.

- Learners have to be self-directed and take responsibility for themselves; they are able to differentiate for themselves; they tend to be highly self-motivated to learn what they see as important to themselves, resulting in a tendency to be deep learners. They can develop a range of employability skills and qualities which could include literacy, IT and commitment/enthusiasm. These represent 3 of the top 6 of 12 employability skills identified by Martin et al. (2008) in their research into what employers expect from possible employees.

- The pedagogy within the informal learning situation is one which allows the learner to make meaning or grasp and synthesise concepts in their own way. This is largely because a range of multiple intelligences can be catered for (Davis and Gardner, 1999). For example, within a museum a learner can meet the needs of their visual, auditory and kinaesthetic senses as they walk around, connect with art images and musical experiences or experience touching the objects available for concrete exploration. They can do this in their own time and at their own pace, re-visiting ideas and focusing on whatever pleases them at a particular moment without an externally imposed structure as in a school or other formal learning environments.

- The self-esteem and confidence developed through informal learning can prepare and motivate the individual to take their first steps into more formal, structured learning situations within the community or at a local FE college.

- Informal learning through relationships and situations encountered within the workplace is, perhaps, the only way to really learn the complexities of any job role for which formal learning can only provide a generic framework.

- Informal learning can be used for credits towards formal qualifications through the process of APEL.

Disagree

- Those who are disengaged or out of touch with learning need a more formal approach with focused support to get them started.

- While some employability skills may be developed, many others such as communication, team-working, numeracy and personal presentation are much less likely to develop through informal learning. In the Martin et al. (2008) research report it was found that, along with literacy skills, timekeeping was the skill most highly prized by employers – a skill unlikely to be developed in informal learning where the individual is accountable only to him/herself and where there are no deadlines or business routines to adhere to.

- The ad hoc nature of informal learning makes it difficult to plan specific goals so learning is less productive and effective than formal learning.

- Learning achieved will be difficult, if not impossible, to measure for prospective employers who depend on nationally recognised qualifications to determine the suitability of job applicants.

- Because informal learning cannot be measured easily, quality aspects cannot be attributed to the process, making it difficult to allocate funding appropriately to providers.

- Informal learning is often perceived as learning for leisure; it does not focus on the development of vocational skills demanded by employers and as such cannot contribute to economic growth. It would, therefore, be inappropriate were public funding to be directed towards it.

- Without well-defined qualification progression routes the learner has nowhere to go with their learning.

What do you think? Which side of the argument do you favour?

? *Stop and reflect*

Think about all the learning you have encountered in your life to date. Can you separate the formal, structured learning from the informal, incidental learning? Which learning has led to most personal fulfilment, which will lead to better employment prospects for you, and has any stimulated your social conscience and helped you value diversity in your fellow man?

Activity

Consider this controversy to help you decide whether you will support learning for self-fulfilment or learning for employability.

Conclusion

Lifelong learning in the context of post-compulsory learning is probably so embedded in most of our lives that it may be easy to miss how it impacts upon us. It would be very easy, for example, to miss the amount of government determination for us to engage in lifelong learning in a very particular way. The key documents that have been discussed in this chapter represent over a decade of government dedication to lifelong learning. But many more documents with their associated aims and targets continue to be published and implemented.

For almost the last 15 years lifelong learning policies have consistently maintained that the purposes of lifelong learning are to:

- create economic renewal so that the country can remain competitive in a global market;
- ensure social cohesion where communities and individuals within communities are confident and competent enough to have purposeful and productive employment rather than divert their energies into disruptive behaviours, such as addictions, that can lead to crime; and
- personal fulfilment – learning should lead to achievement, growth in self-esteem, heightened self-confidence and motivation.

These recurring themes would seem to suggest that lifelong learning aims are never achieved. However, the case studies provided do give many examples of success; they also give insights into the practical problems experienced by practitioners and providers.

It follows that skills development and the acquisition of qualifications can lead to increased employment opportunities, but compare the following two quotes of over ten years apart:

> Younger employees and those who already have good educational qualifications receive more training. People with degrees are six times more likely to be trained than people with no qualifications.

> The Learning Age Report, 1998

. . . the data suggest that participation among individuals with strong initial qualifications is significantly higher than among the least qualified, such that these opportunities often do not reach those who need them most.

OECD, 2009:5

These quotes imply that, with regard to accessing learning, it is still those who already have a culture of learning that continue to access learning, certainly with regard to achieving qualifications. In ten years of lifelong learning little has changed to widen participation to non-traditional learners. Without overcoming the barriers experienced by these non-traditional learners, the aim of filling the skills gap to grow the economy is unlikely to be achieved; it is also non-traditional learners who need the personal fulfilment to improve their self-esteem and confidence. So, while there are many successes and positive statistics, there is still some way to go to eradicate the disengaged and reach non-traditional learners.

Case study 8.2
Work-based learning

The context for this case study is a large general hospital, providing healthcare services to nearly half a million people. It employs approximately 3,500 staff, more than 400 volunteers and has a total daily population of 8,000 people; the site is the size of a small town.

This is a complex organisation which employs people working in a great variety of disciplines – in the clinical field, in engineering, administration, warehousing, medical support, care assistance, management and more. Staff are employed at various stages of their careers including, among others, those on work experience, school leavers, university graduates and ex-offenders. Some are very well qualified, others are not, and some have physical disabilities and mental health issues.

The hospital's vision statement clearly spells out the importance of all staff to the overall clinical effectiveness of the organisation and excellent care of the patients. A vital part in achieving this is that all staff, whether doctor or cleaner, are trained to and work to professional standards. A training provider experienced in work-based learning trains a range of hospital staff – customer service people, team leaders, managers and administrative staff – as well as providing curriculum-based NVQ courses in health management, warehousing, business management and IT. The hospital employs a Work-based Learning Advisor for Widening Participation who is responsible for working with candidates on a one-to-one basis, running advice and guidance sessions for them, identifying their precise training needs and tailoring courses accordingly – as well as monitoring the results.

The Trust is happy with the way the training is progressing and one NVQ trainee, Melanie, explains about her experience: 'The tutor sat down with me and went through how the course would be delivered. We chose the most suitable units for my job as a secretary and I had to complete maths and English tests. It's a long time since I was at school and I was very nervous about all this. But I needn't have been – I was put at my ease and by the time she left I was really very excited about the whole thing.' Melanie's tutor visited her regularly while she was studying, helping her manage her time, supporting her studies, encouraging her and dealing with any specific problems she was having. Melanie is highly motivated and she believes that her qualification will give her security, prospects and an income that will provide her children with the opportunity she never had to stay on at school. Her tutor is also highly motivated and works hard to ensure that Melanie achieves her goals within the time scale prescribed by the provider that employs her. These time scales are important as the provider's achievement targets are bound by them which in turn, when met, releases the funding that secures the tutor's job.

The Trust believes that bringing NVQ training to the workplace allows the staff to improve the specific skills they use in their jobs, improves their career development and has a positive effect on morale. This kind of reward gives staff an extra reason to make a long-term contribution to the success of the hospital, and it should reduce staff turnover and benefit the trust by enabling it to improve competitiveness and stay ahead.

Source: Adapted from Train to Gain: Case Study on the Ipswich Hospital NHS Trust: www.traintogain.gov.uk/casestudiesitems/East_of_England, viewed August 2009.

Questions for discussion

1 *Identify all the categories of staff mentioned in the case study and create two lists, one list being those least likely to resist training offered and one list being those most likely to resist training offered. Justify your two lists.*

2 *Think about the purposes of lifelong learning: improved economy, improved social cohesion and personal fulfilment. To what extent will the training provided address these issues?*

3 *Could informal learning address any of the training needs that this hospital has? Explain your answers.*

4 *What role might a further education college have in providing learning opportunities for this hospital?*

5 *Can you see any place for adult and community learning within this case study?*

6 *What disadvantages might engaging with work-based learning bring for an employee?*

Summary

The concept of lifelong learning

A straightforward definition of lifelong learning is a process of learning that goes on through the duration of an individual's life! As Field (2006:1) puts it, lifelong learning 'can be almost as unconscious as breathing'. Lifelong learning has been with us in one form or another for hundreds of years and as early as the seventeenth and eighteenth centuries adult learning was recognised as contributing to the quality of people's lives. Today there is a drive to develop a culture of learning for all, but not just to enhance life quality. Today, imperatives of national competitiveness in the global market are at the forefront of government thinking and targets.

▶

Lifelong learning: policy and practice

A number of key government documents have influenced lifelong learning, and those drawn on in this chapter are:

- *Learning Works: Widening Participation in Further Education*, 1997 – The Kennedy Report
- *Higher Education in the Learning Society*, 1997 – The Dearing Report
- *Learning for the 21st Century*, 1997 – The Fryer Report
- *A Fresh Start – Improving Literacy and Numeracy*, 1999 – The Moser Report
- *Learning to Succeed – A New Framework for Post-16 Learning*, 1999 – DfEE
- The Skills Strategy White Papers: *21st Century Skills*, 2003, and *Skills: Getting on in Business, Getting on at Work*, 2005
- *Prosperity for all in the Global Economy – World Class Skills*, Leitch, 2006
- *Building Britain's Future*, 2009

A number of common themes apparent within these documents have influenced how lifelong learning policy is translated into practice; in particular these are:

- Removing barriers to learning.
- Widening participation.
- Improved information, advice and guidance.
- Measurement of achievement.
- Bridging the skills gap, with an emphasis on functional skills, i.e. literacy, numeracy and IT.
- Increasing the range of providers of learning opportunities and partnerships between providers.
- Emphasis on quality provision.
- Funding mechanisms which drive curricula.

Lifelong learning in practice

Further education colleges, work-based learning, offender learning, adult and community learning, and museums and libraries all have their place in the jigsaw of lifelong learning. The edges between them are blurred, which reflects the need for partnerships. They all have targets to meet and funding entitlements which drive them to offer the provision that is deemed appropriate by government.

FECs do not follow the National Curriculum; they respond to local needs. They deliver both vocational and academic subjects; many have specialist departments such as agriculture, art or even HE and offer courses across the range of levels from pre-level 1 to level 6.

Adult and community learning is about providing learning where people live and work and is usually more concerned with basic skills and motivating learners to feel comfortable about learning in the hope that their self-esteem will improve sufficiently for progression into more mainstream learning contexts.

Work-based learning includes training apprentices up to level 4; employees who need to access level 2 qualifications, which is often through Train to Gain schemes; and employees who need to update their job knowledge and job skills, as work practices change, to maintain and move careers forward. Many large organisations provide their own training, though much will be delivered by external providers and funded by the organisation. In all cases the aim of the organisation will be that education and training enables employees to meet the goals of that organisation.

Offender learning is specifically about people in prison or on community sentences. Mostly, but not exclusively, it is again about disengaged learners achieving basic skills qualifications up to level 2. There are great challenges with offenders who, by their nature, have disproportionate barriers to their engaging with learning. These barriers include mental health problems, addiction problems, learning difficulties, and lack of practical support from family and friends as well as other practical problems such as poor or no housing.

Museums and libraries are valuable places for engaging in informal learning. *The Learning Revolution* (2009) report on informal learning has added weight to this aspect of lifelong learning and brings libraries and museums into the fore. Libraries are also in a position to bring basic IT to many who would never have access to this and most offer short courses to local people.

References

14–19 Education and Skills White Paper (2005), London: HMSO.

Appleby, Y. and Bathmaker, A. (2006) The New Skills Agenda: increased lifelong learning or new sites of inequality? In *British Educational Research Journal*, 32(5), pp. 703–17, available at http://ejournals.ebsco.com/direct.asp?ArticleID=4626B30652A5ECF32B98, viewed August 2010.

Apprentices, Skills, Children and Learning Act (2009), London: HMSO.

Atherton, J.S. (2010) *Doceo: Language Codes*, available at http://www.doceo.co.uk/background/=language_codes.htm, viewed August 2010.

BIS (2009) *Skills for Growth: The National Skills Strategy Executive Summary*, Department for Business Innovation and Skills, available at http://www.bis.gov.uk/assets/biscore/corporate/docs/s/skills-strategy-summary.pdf, viewed August 2010.

Blanda, J., Stugis, P., Buscha, F. and Unwin, P. (2009) *The Effect of Lifelong Learning on Intra-generational Social Mobility*, DIUS (copyright University of Surrey), available at www.webarchive.nationalarchives.gov.uk, viewed January 2010.

Blunkett, D. (1998) Introduction, the Green Paper Consultation on Adult Learning, available at http://www.lifelonglearning.co.uk/greenpaper/index.htm, viewed January 2010.

Bourdieu, P. and Passeron, J. (1977) *Reproduction in Education, Society and Culture*, London, California, New Delhi: Sage Publications Ltd.

Burke, P. J. and Jackson, S. (2007) *Reconceputalising Lifelong Learning: Feminist Interventions*, Abingdon: Routledge.

Conlon, A. and Vignoles, A. (2005) *An Analysis of the Benefit of NVQ 2 Qualifications Acquired at Age 26–34*, London: Centre for Economics of Education.

Curtis, W. and Pettigrew, A. (2010) *Education Studies Reflective Reader*, Exeter: Learning Matters Ltd.

Data Service (2010) *Post-16 Education and Skills: Learner Participation Outcomes and Level of Highest Qualification Held*, Coventry: Data Service, available at *www.thedataservice.org.uk/statistics*, viewed January 2010.

Davis, J. and Gardner, H. (1999) Open Windows, Open Doors, in Hooper-Greenhill, E. (ed.) *The Educational Role of the Museum*, London: Routledge.

Dearing, R. (1997) *National Committee of Inquiry into Higher Education* (Dearing Report) available at https://bei.leeds.ac.uk/Partners/NCIHE/, viewed January 2010.

Denham, J. (2009) Ministerial Foreword in Secretary of State for Innovation, Universities and Skills, *The Learning Revolution*, DIUS, available at http://www.dius.gov.uk/skills/engaging_learners/informal_adult_learning/white_paper, viewed January 2010.

DfEE (1998) *The Learning Age: A Renaissance for a New Britain*, Department for Education and Employment, available at http://www.lifelonglearning.co.uk/green-paper/index.htm, viewed July 2010.

DfEE (1999) *Learning to Succeed – a New Framework for Post-16 Learning: A Summary*, Nottingham: Department for Education and Employment.

DfES (2006) *Further Education and Training Bill*, available at http://www.publications.parliament.uk/pa/pabills/200607/further_education_and_training.htm, viewed January 2010.

DIUS (n.d.) *About the Skills Strategy*, available at http://www.dcsf.gov.uk/skillsstrategy.

DIUS (2007) *The Offenders' Learning and Skills Service (OLASS) in England: A brief guide*, Department for Innovation, Universities and Skills, available at www.dius.gov.uk/offenderlearning, viewed January 2010.

DIUS (2009) *The Learning Revolution*, available at http://www.dius.gov.uk/skills/engaging_learners/informal_adult_learning/white_paper, viewed January 2010.

Dugdale, G. and Clark, C. (2008) *Literacy Changes Lives: An advocacy resource*, London: National Literacy Trust, available at http://www.literacytrust.org.uk/research/nlt_research, viewed August 2010.

Easterly, W. (2002) *The Elusive Quest for Growth: Economists' Adventures and Misadventures in the Tropics*, London: MIT Press.

Elliott, G. (1999) *Lifelong Learning: The Politics of the New Learning Environment*, London: Jessica Kingsley Publishers.

Field, J. (2006) *Lifelong Learning and the New Educational Order*, 2nd edn, Stoke on Trent: Trentham Books.

Foskett, N. (2002) Marketing Imperative or Cultural Challenge? Embedding Widening Participation in the Further Education Sector, *Research in Post-Compulsory Education*, 7(1).

Fryer, R. (1997) *Learning for the 21st Century: First report of the Naitonal Advisory Group for Continuing Education and Lifelong Learning*, London: Department for Education and Employment, available at http://www.lifelonglearning.co.uk/nagcell/prov04.htm, viewed March 2009.

Gorard and Rees (2002) *Creating a Learning Society? Learning Careers and Policies for a Lifelong Learning Society*, Bristol: The Policy Press.

Haralambos, M. and Holborn, M. (2008) *Sociology Themes and Perspectives*, 2nd edn, London: Collins.

Hayes, J. (2010) *Association of Learning Providers: Summer Conference*, speech presented at Riverbank Plaza Hotel, London, available at http://www.bis.gov.uk/news/speeches/john-hayes-assoc-learning-providers, viewed August 2010.

Her Majesty's Government (2009) *Building Britain's Future*, Norwich: Stationery Office.

Her Majesty's Revenue and Customs (n.d.) *Child Poverty*, available at www.hmrc.gov.uk/stats/personal-tax-credits/child_poverty.htm, viewed July 2010.

Institute for Learning (2010) *Example Activities for your CPD*, IFL, available at http://www.ifl.ac.uk/cpd/effective-cpd-activities-2010, viewed August 2010.

Keep, E. (2000) *Learning Organisations, Lifelong Learning and the Mystery of the Vanishing Employers*, available at http://www.skope.ox.ac.uk/publications/learning-organisations-lifelong-learning-and-mystery-vanishing-employer, viewed January 2010.

Kennedy, H. (1997) *Learning Works: Widening Participation in Further Education*, Department for Employment and Education.

Leitch, S. (2006) *Prosperity for All in the Global Economy – World Class Skills*, London: Stationery Office.

Learning and Skills Act 2000, London: HMSO.

Learning and Skills Council (2006) *Learning for Living and Work: Improving education and training opportunities for people with learning difficulties and/or disabilities*, Learning and Skills Council.

Marsh, H.W. and O'Mara, A. (2008) Reciprocal effects between academic self-concept, self-esteem, achievement, and attainment over seven adolescent years: Unidimensional and multidimensional perspectives of self-concept, *Personality and Social Psychology Bulletin*, 34(4), pp. 542–52, available at http://ejournals.ebsco.com/direct.asp?ArticleID=4A9DA3F499B5965E1422, viewed August 2010.

Martin, R., Villeneuve-Smith, F., Marshall, L. and McKenzie, E. (2008) *Employability Skills Explored*, London: Learning and Skills Network.

Morgan, B. and Hubble, S. (2008) *Skills: Statistics and Recent Developments*, House of Commons Library.

Morgan-Klein, B. and Osborne, M. (2007) *The Concepts and Practices of Lifelong Learning*, London: Routledge.

Moser, C. (1999) *A Fresh Start – Improving Literacy and Numeracy: Summary and Recommendations*, DfEE, available at http://www.lifelonglearning.co.uk/mosergroup/freshsum.pdf, viewed August 2009.

National Audit Office (2008) *Skills for Life: Progress in Improving Adult Literacy and Numeracy*, London: Stationery Office, available at www.nao.org.uk, viewed August 2010.

NIACE (2008) *Adult and Family Learning in Museums, Libraries and Archives*, Leicester: NIACE.

OECD (2009) *Education at a Glance 2009: Summary of key findings*, available at http://www.oecd.org/infobycountry/0,3380,en_2649_39263238_1_70432_119829_1_1,00.html, viewed August 2010.

Office for National Statistics (2010) *Comparisons of Productivity*, available at http://www.statistics.gov.uk/cci/nugget.asp?id=160, viewed August 2010.

Ofsted (2008) *The Annual Report of Her Majesty's Chief Inspector of Education, Children's Services and Skills*, House of Commons, available at www.ofsted.gov.uk, viewed January 2010.

Rammell, B. (2005) *Learning and Skills: The agenda for change*, Learning and Skills Council.

Rogers, C.R. and Freiberg, H.J. (1994) *Freedom to Learn*, 3rd edn, Columbus: Merrill/Macmillan.

Sabates, R. (2008) *The Impact of Lifelong Learning on Poverty Reduction: Inquiry into the Future of Lifelong Learning, Public Value Paper 1*, Leicester: NIACE.

Uden, T. (2004) *Learning's not a Crime: Education and training for offenders and ex-offenders in the Community*, Leicester: NIACE.

United Kingdom Commission for Employment and Skills (2009) *Ambition 2020: World Class Skills and Jobs for the UK*, UKCES, available at www.ukces.org.uk, viewed January 2010.

Workers Education Association (nd) *About WEA*, available at http://www.wea.org.uk/aboutus/index.htm, viewed August 2010.

9

The inclusion debate and special educational needs (SEN)

Jenny Thompson

Contents

Introduction

In 2004, the UK government unveiled a new strategy document which demonstrated their commitment to the development of an inclusive education system. The **special educational needs (SEN)** strategy document *Removing Barriers to Achievement* (DfES, 2004) provides a clear argument for supporting a move towards inclusion. In order to try to understand the complexities of SEN and inclusion, it is important to be aware that the distinction may not always be made between pupils who are recognised as having SEN and those who have not (Postlethwaite and Hackney, 1989, cited in Hodkinson and Vickerman, 2009). Although there are divergent views on what SEN is, perhaps the most controversial aspect of the debate over SEN and inclusion is whether children identified as having SEN may be educated in a mainstream or 'special' school.

This chapter looks at inclusion, and focuses on how learners with special educational needs may be included in the mainstream education environment. In addition to SEN, the chapter also looks at another term used to identify particular learner needs – **'gifted and talented'** – and, again, examines the ways in which these learners are included (or not included) in mainstream environments.

This chapter aims to:

- Provide a definition of inclusion.
- Explore theories of inclusive education.
- Consider special educational needs in the context of historical perspectives.
- Explain what the term 'special educational needs' (SEN) means today.
- Consider the impact of the National Curriculum on the education of pupils with SEN.
- Discuss whether it is possible to include a pupil with Autistic Spectrum Disorder in a mainstream school environment.
- Explore the challenges of including a gifted and talented pupil in a mainstream school environment.

Case study 9.1
Sharp rise in number of special needs pupils

Sarah Teather, the new Children's Minister, last week ordered a Green Paper on youngsters with special educational needs (SEN), amid concerns that the diagnosis may be being overused to explain simple bad behaviour – or even in order to get more money for schools.

It has now emerged that the number of children aged between two and four who were assessed as having special needs by nurseries has risen by 19 per cent in two years to 31,350. Another 8,280 were diagnosed as needing a legal 'statement' setting out the support they are entitled to, a rise of eight per cent since 2008.

The Green Paper ordered by Miss Teather into special educational needs and the lives of disabled children will be published in the autumn.

She is concerned that parents are being given insufficient advice and support following a diagnosis of SEN, with some beginning to question whether their child may have been inaccurately labelled as having special needs when in fact they may just be badly behaved.

Figures released by the Department for Education also show that twice as many male as female pupils are registered as having special needs, suggesting that naughtiness by over-exuberant little boys may be being misinterpreted as a syndrome such as Attention Deficit Hyperactivity Disorder.

There is no medical test for SEN, and diagnosis is performed by experts observing the child's behaviour.

As well as the possibility of overzealous use of the term SEN by experts, there have been suggestions that diagnoses may be occurring for more cynical reasons, as schools and even parents seek to take advantage of the extra help given to children with special needs.

Schools have a 'perverse incentive' to enlist as many children with SEN as possible, in order to improve their standing in league tables, while parents with an SEN child have more chance of getting them into the school of their choice.

Earlier this year, Philippa Stobbs, a senior government adviser and expert on special needs, said children were being 'over-labelled' when they might simply be falling behind in school. She went on: 'I don't think it's very helpful to infer that children behind in their learning have SEN. . . . They are only working below the standards they should be achieving. . . . Teachers need to sidestep the label and look at children's progress in a more responsible way, using their age and prior attainment.'

Dr Gwynedd Lloyd, an education researcher at the University of Edinburgh, added: 'You can't do a blood test to check whether you've got ADHD – it's diagnosed through a behavioural checklist. . . . Getting out of your seat and running about is an example – half the kids in a school could qualify under that criterion.'

Ministers are said to believe that children who are genuinely in need of support, and their parents, should have more targeted help. Announcing the Green Paper, Miss Teather said: 'We want to make sure that the most vulnerable children get the best quality of support and care. . . . Children with special educational needs and disabilities should have the same opportunities as their peers. . . . The system needs to be more family friendly so that parents don't feel they have to battle to get the support their child needs.'

Source: Rosa Prince, *Daily Telegraph*, 22 July 2010, available at: http://www.telegraph.co.uk/education/educationnews/7904999/Sharp-rise-in-number-of-special-needs-pupils.html

Questions for discussion

1 *Where would you draw the line between 'bad behaviour' and 'special needs'?*

2 *From reading this article, do you think it presents special educational needs in a positive or a negative light?*

3 *As this article says, 'there is no medical test for SEN.' Would teachers' and teaching assistants' jobs be any easier if there was?*

Defining inclusion

Society has become much more aware of the term 'inclusion' over the past decade. Within the English educational system, an inclusive approach to education became evident from 1997 with the election of New Labour. As Hodkinson (2009) suggests, Labour's Green Paper *Excellence for All Children* was an attempt to reform education and place inclusion firmly on the political agenda.

The 'Excellence for All Children' initiative was greeted with a good deal of criticism including that by Clough and Corbett (2000:9), who argued that the Green Paper:

> implies that inclusion at schools will promote inclusion in society as adults. However, this is clearly a naïve view since many other factors are involved such as appropriate curriculum, adequate transition planning and available support services.

Following the implementation of the Green Paper in 1997, the Labour government introduced a revised curriculum in 2000, with a view to addressing any deficiencies with the previous SEN policy. Curriculum 2000 focused on three core inclusive principles:

- Setting suitable learning challenges.
- Responding to pupils' diverse learning needs.
- Overcoming potential barriers to learning and assessment for individuals and groups of pupils.

There are two key perspectives to consider when focusing on special educational needs and inclusion. First, there is the perspective of the government departments and educational policy-makers who offer guidance in relation to SEN systems and inclusive education. We may broadly refer to this as being the 'policy perspective'. Second, there is the perspective of the education professionals, practitioners, families and administrators, who battle every day to meet the individual needs of SEN children (Farrell, 2004, cited in Hodkinson and Vickerman, 2009). This second, 'practical perspective' is perhaps less well documented than the policy perspective, but may be more reflective of what actually goes on at the 'ground level' of the inclusion debate.

History of education

The origins of SEN, 1870–1944

Compulsory schooling in the UK began in 1870 with the introduction of the Elementary Education Act and school boards. School boards had a duty to promote good relationships between the school, its parents and the community and also form a channel for the flow of information between these groups. They consisted of a group of individuals who were involved in determining the overall policies, objectives and ethos at the school. As a result of the Act and pressure applied by these boards, children with disabilities were seen as unfit to be taught in a large class situation. The solution was to provide segregated education for these children in the form of a special school. As a result of this segregation disabled children were often denied access to activities in the local school as the emphasis was on the medical condition rather than their educational opportunities.

There was not a shift in the situation until later years, when the 1944 Education Act was passed towards the end of the Second World War. This Act radically changed the structure of education; every child including those with disabilities would now be entitled to statutory education at primary and secondary school. The 1944 Act made it the responsibility of the Local Education Authorities to decide whether a child needed special educational treatment.

Inclusion has been defined in many different ways, which, not surprisingly, causes confusion for those involved in education, including academics and students. Inclusion, as defined by Michael Farrell (2003:27) in relation to mainstream schools, 'encourages the school to review its structures, approaches to teaching, pupil grouping and use of support to enable the school to meet the diverse learning needs of all its pupils.' Farrell, an expert in the field of special educational needs (2003:29), points out that inclusion may be understood in three ways:

- The social inclusion and education of children presently excluded from education.
- The inclusion of pupils currently in mainstream schools.
- The balance of pupils in mainstream and special schools.

In contrast, The UK Centre for Studies in Inclusive Education (2008) provides a broader definition of inclusion, involving staff and the community as well as students:

Inclusion in education involves:

- Valuing all students and staff equally.
- Increasing the participation of students in, and reducing their exclusion from, the cultures, curricula and communities of local schools.
- Restructuring the cultures, policies and practices in schools so that they respond to the diversity of students in the locality.
- Reducing barriers to learning and participation for all students, not only those with impairments or those who are categorised as 'having special educational needs'.
- Learning from attempts to overcome barriers to the access and participation of particular students to make changes for the benefit of students more widely.
- Viewing the difference between students as resources to support learning, rather than as problems to be overcome.
- Acknowledging the right of students to an education in their locality.
- Improving schools for staff as well as for students.
- Emphasising the role of schools in building community and developing values, as well as in increasing achievement.
- Fostering mutually sustaining relationships between schools and communities.
- Recognising that inclusion in education is one aspect of inclusion in society.

CSIE, 2008

For the purposes of this chapter, the term 'inclusion' will be defined according to the Every Disabled Child Matters Inclusion Charter (2007): 'All children have the right to be included in every aspect of society.' This clearly encompasses not only education but all areas of society and therefore takes a **holistic approach** to the child ('holistic' in this case meaning that the whole child is considered). This definition also supports the Disability Discrimination Act 1995, which specifically states that disabled children should not have to ask or fight to be included in the things that other children do.

Labour policies often emphasised that in order to move towards inclusion it was important to value diversity and show respect for all individuals – but how do we demonstrate this? How can we let individuals know that we respect them?

To answer these questions, we need to look not only at the notions of diversity and respect, but also at the related ideas of equity and entitlement. We saw in Chapter 5 how a whole school approach may be used to effectively monitor and evaluate the progress of all pupils. In the context of inclusion and SEN, this approach highlights the need for careful planning of lessons by teachers in order that any barriers to learning are removed, and any pupil who is at risk of underperformance should be identified in order that personalised learning needs may be met (Cheminais, 2006: 44). Inclusive schools should also be willing to offer opportunities to pupils who have previously been excluded from other schools due to past difficulties. But in reality this presents several practical problems – for example, why would any school want to take on difficult and challenging learners who have been excluded from other schools?

? Stop and reflect

- *Consider the various definitions of inclusion and decide for yourself what is important when considering this notion. Justify your answer.*
- *Identify and list any obstacles which would need to be overcome in order to implement a programme of inclusion in a mainstream learning environment.*

Models of disability

When looking at the challenges of inclusion within education it is worth reflecting upon the underlying models or assumptions about 'disability' as these have an impact on the nature of provision. The two major models are known as the 'medical' and the 'social' model of disability.

The medical model of disability

The **'medical' model of disability** paints a picture of the person being defined in relation to a medical condition and promotes the view of a person not only being 'disabled', but also as being dependent on the medical profession to be cured or cared for. The focus is on sickness rather than health. The model was based on assessments of impairments, specifically in relation to what the individual was *unable* to do, rather than what the individual was *able* to do. Historically, the employment of medical ideas has formed a significant part of the identification and placement of children with the school system (Corbett and Norwich, 2005, cited in Hodkinson and Vickerman, 2009:19). In the early part of the twentieth century children were given medically diagnosed categories based on clinical assessments (such as intelligence and personality tests) and those identified as having special educational needs were sent to separate, special schools. The medical model continued to prevail through the educational reforms of 1944 when eleven categories of 'handicap' were identified and children were given 'treatment' according to these, still within special schools. It was not until the 1960s and 1970s that behavioural psychologists rejected the medical model and suggested that teachers could help modify some of the children's learning difficulties by using techniques such as operant conditioning (discussed in Chapter 4). This was important because it suggested that it was possible to help learners with particular difficulties and placed the responsibility on the teacher (Lewis, 1995). It also helped pave the way for later legislation (such as the Warnock Report in 1978 and the Education Act of 1993) which promoted the inclusion of children with special educational needs within mainstream schools.

Today, the medical model is viewed critically as dehumanising children and the disabled by treating them as objects (Lewis, 1995), and for its emphasis on the disabled individual as 'deficient' (Clough and Corbett, 2000:12). The assumption of dependency within the model on others to change their situation and the resulting 'cycle of dependency' is also very difficult to break (Reiser, 2008) and may lead to *learned helplessness* or the expectation of failure (see Chapter 4 for a more detailed discussion of the idea of learned helplessness).

The social model of disability

In contrast, the **social model of disability** focuses on the experience of the individual, environmental factors and preventative measures, rather than cure by the medical profession (Bailey, 1998, cited in Clough and Corbett, 2000:11). It views the position of disabled people as being socially created, and suggests that discriminatory practices, whereby individuals are socially excluded, are reinforced by images in the media, which magnify attitudes that are already present in society. Through fear, ignorance and prejudice, barriers and discrimination develop (Reiser, 2008). Individuals who do not have special educational needs are not born with these attitudes; they learn them through contact with others. Therefore, to tackle discrimination and ensure effective inclusion, it is imperative that educating individuals about special educational needs starts at school. In order to do this there are many issues to consider:

- Schools should have a positive attitude towards the notion of an inclusive school. This is only possible if there is a willingness on the part of the teacher to accept the challenge of adapting the classroom and environment and resources to suit the needs of the individual with special educational needs.

- Schools should involve both teachers and support staff in the development and implementation of a policy statement highlighting the school's inclusive practices. This process should be proactive rather than reactive, so that strategies are put into place for dealing with problems before they arise, rather than coming across as emergency responses (Westwood, 1997:191).

- Improved training for teachers, to increase their knowledge of special educational needs and equip them for dealing with adapting curriculum content and resource materials. Without this training, it is doubtful that an inclusive environment will exist.

- Encouraging group work and peer assistance in order to tackle any discrimination. By focusing on cooperative learning, teachers and teaching assistants can try to ensure that individuals with special educational needs are included (Westwood, 1997:192).

Activity

Imagine you are a primary teacher with a class of 32 children, one of whom, Peter, never seems to be able to keep quiet in lessons. Peter has physical disabilities and as a result he is unable to walk unaided. Peter demonstrates symptoms of **Attention Deficit Hyperactivity Disorder (ADHD);** he shouts out inappropriate answers and often makes noises to gain the attention of the rest of the class, especially when he is unable to understand a task. He finds it very hard to concentrate and becomes very frustrated as he is unable to move around without his wheelchair. When he is given a literacy task he starts misbehaving. Peter is very low ability and struggles to complete any task relating to literacy skills.

- Consider the medical model notion that it is the individual child's condition which means that they are unable to learn.

- Do you think that the medical model is sufficient to explain Peter's behaviour? Can you identify other factors which may affect the individual pupil's ability to learn in a mainstream environment?

Special educational needs: policy perspectives

In 1978, a government commission chaired by Baroness Mary Warnock produced a report highlighting the need to identify children with 'special educational needs' and provide for them accordingly. The term *special educational needs* (SEN) was thus introduced into UK legislation. This was a significant departure from the view of disabled children as being medically unfit for educational involvement. The Warnock Report (1978) highlighted two groups of children with SEN: those who experience difficulty at school, but who would normally have their needs met within the existing framework of their schools; and those whose needs were the focus of additional, specialised provision, as a result of more complex learning difficulties.

The Warnock Report heralded a further significant piece of legislation for special education, in the form of the 1981 Education Act. This resulted in a marked shift of emphasis from the segregation of children with special educational needs to the inclusion of these children. The 1981 Act had a major influence on teachers who were now obliged to take responsibility for pupils with SEN, and follow standardised procedures implemented following the Act for identifying and assessing children.

In 1988, the Education Reform Act also legislated for pupils with special educational needs. This Act articulated the requirement for all children to have a right to a 'balanced and broadly based curriculum which is relevant to their individual needs' (OPSI, 2008). The Education Reform Act introduced **local management of schools (LMS)**, a scheme which provided schools with differing levels of resources depending on the number of SEN pupils on the school roll. By placing the responsibility on local management in schools, the government ensured specific funding was provided for each individual with special educational needs.

Subsequently, the 1993 Education Act (Part 3) introduced new elements, including the setting up of the SEN tribunal (an independent body who considered parents' appeals against the decisions of local authorities with regard to an individual's special educational needs) and the *Code of Practice on the Identification and Assessment of Special Educational Needs* (DfE, 1994a). This Code of Practice stipulates that schools and LEAs are required to make provision for pupils with SEN. Following the 1993 Act and the Code of Practice (1994), more emphasis was placed on schools and parents as decision-makers with regard to the issuing of a statement of special educational needs and the provision offered, although final decisions were still made by the LEAs (Cowne, 2003).

The SEN Code of Practice (2001) was introduced in order to provide practical advice to LEAs, maintained schools (which are schools maintained by the local authority, i.e. funded by the government) and independent schools (which are schools that receive little or no funding from government sources and are sometimes called private schools, or more confusingly in the UK, 'public schools') with regard to carrying out their statutory duties to identify, assess and make provision for children's special educational needs. The SEN Code of Practice has made a significant contribution to the inclusion debate: the introduction of the Code means that, when parents choose to send their child to a mainstream school, the education service is obliged to do everything possible to support this choice (GovernorNet, 2008).

↖ *Connect and explore*

This website is a useful site to inform the reader of current educational policies in relation to SEN and responsibilities of local authorities in ensuring an inclusive approach to education: **http://www.governornet.co.uk/cropArticle.cfm?topicAreaId= 1&contentId=275&mode=bg.**

The move towards inclusion in school was further identified by the Salamanca Statement in 1994 (UNESCO, 2004), which advocated that schools should assist children with special educational needs and disabilities to become economically active and to provide these children with the skills needed in everyday life (UNESCO, 1994, cited in Hodkinson and Vickerman, 2009). Every Child Matters: Change for Children in Schools was a policy introduced in 2003 to 'create a shared programme of change to improve outcomes for all children and young people' (DCSF, 2009). Every Child Matters identifies that five outcomes are key to well-being in childhood and later life:

- Being healthy
- Staying safe
- Enjoying and achieving
- Making a positive contribution
- Achieving economic well-being (Every Child Matters, 2004).

The Every Child Matters (ECM) agenda has had a significant impact on pupils with special educational needs. It places emphasis on schools adopting more of a multi-agency approach, whereby organisations which are involved in providing services for children (including social workers, voluntary groups, and general practitioners) will be 'joined up' in their sharing of ideas in order to ensure that the needs of individual children with SEN are met. This will be achieved through the use of the common assessment framework which aims to promote more effective early identification of additional needs. This is a standardised approach to conducting assessments on the individual's additional needs with a view to deciding how these should be met (DCSF, 2009). Teachers play a significant role as facilitators and supporters of children's learning and well-being. This is a much more holistic approach to the child (meaning that all aspects of the child's life are considered, not just their school life), ensuring that both the child's well-being and learning are taken into consideration.

In summary, if an inclusive approach is to be adopted it is crucial that the focus should be on the individual child. The teaching and learning of children with special educational needs has been much improved since 1987, and the introduction of policies, Acts and initiatives demonstrate that improvements are taking place on a continuous basis. However, in order to ensure that we do not become complacent, it is essential that the government provide funding to meet the demands of society, specifically in relation to training and development for teachers in order to meet the individual needs of a child with SEN.

? Stop and reflect

- *How have policies influenced the education of children with special educational needs since 1870?*
- *What are the implications of meeting the needs of a child with SEN within the existing framework of their school?*

Defining SEN in the twenty-first century

Today, the term special educational needs (SEN) is used to describe a diverse range of difficulties whereby a child or young person is prevented from learning at a rate and level similar to children of the same age. According to a key document, the Special Educational Needs Code of Practice (DfES, 2001), children have SEN if they have a learning difficulty which calls for special educational provision to be made for them.

Below is a summary of key points from the SEN Code of Practice (2001). Four principal areas of special educational need are identified:

1 Communication and interaction (for example, a child with Autistic Spectrum Disorder may demonstrate difficulties with speech and language).
2 Cognition and learning (for example, a child with dyslexia may demonstrate difficulties with processing language and in acquiring literacy skills).

3 Behaviour, emotional and social development (for example, a child with symptoms of ADHD may demonstrate challenging or attention-seeking behaviour).

4 Sensory and/or physical needs (for example, a child who has hearing impairments, or a child with cerebral palsy).

Within these areas children are considered to have a learning difficulty if they:

(a) have a significantly greater difficulty in learning than the majority of children of the same age; or

(b) have a disability which prevents or hinders them from making use of educational facilities of a kind generally provided for children of the same age in schools within the area of the Local Education Authority; or

(c) are under compulsory school age and fall within the definition at (a) or (b) above or would so do if special educational provision was not made for them. Children must not be regarded as having a learning difficulty solely because the language or form of language of their home is different from the language in which they will be taught.

Special educational provision means:

(a) for children of two or over, educational provision which is additional to, or otherwise different from, the educational provision made generally for children of their age in schools maintained by the LEA, other than special schools, in the area;

(b) for children under two, educational provision of any kind.

Connect and explore

Go online to view the full SEN Code of Practice guidance document: **http://www.teachernet.gov.uk/_doc/3724/SENCodeOfPractice.pdf**.

While there is a clear definition of SEN presented in the Code of Practice, it is also apparent that it applies to a range of learning difficulties which are very diverse in nature. With this in mind, the role of special educational needs coordinator (SENCO) was created in order to provide advice for mainstream teachers, and to support pupils with special educational needs. As we shall see in the next section, the SENCO is one of a growing number of 'stakeholders' (interested parties) in the continuing debates around SEN and inclusion.

Stakeholders in SEN and inclusion

In response to the Green Paper *Excellence for All Children: Meeting Special Educational Needs* (DfEE, 1997), special educational needs regional partnerships (SEN RPs) were established, with a broad remit to improve regional coordination of SEN provision and services by developing more inclusive policies and practices. Their aim was to improve the efficiency of special education processes and services and to improve inter-agency working locally and regionally (Teachernet, 2009). These partnerships were developed with a view to engaging **stakeholders** who were concerned with SEN and inclusion issues.

Stakeholders have a very important part to play in relation to the UK agenda regarding provision for pupils with special educational needs, as they are involved in making crucial decisions in relation to the education of SEN children. So who are these 'stakeholders'? First, the British government is considered a key stakeholder – as the policy-maker for the SEN and inclusion agenda, they are the driving force of inclusive practice in education in the UK. In an ideal world, the government's stakeholder role would involve nurturing positive partnerships at the local and regional level, between professionals who are able to work together to find solutions to problems of inclusion.

Our second stakeholder group is parents and guardians. Parents of children with SEN are able to offer first-hand experience in relation to the individual needs of their children. Parents are very important stakeholders in education, and express this not only through their natural interest in their children's education and welfare, but also through advisory roles such as parent governorship, or membership of a PTA (Parent–Teacher Association). Some parents also work in a voluntary capacity, assisting in the classroom, reinforcing classroom programmes and collaborating with teachers to develop the curriculum for both mainstream and SEN learners. Without this collaborative partnership, there may be a lack of understanding in terms of meeting the individual needs of a pupil with SEN.

A third set of stakeholders, SENCOs, are involved with whole school SEN policies in order to address a wide range of issues relating to SEN, including:

- Admission arrangements for children with SEN.
- Coordination of provision to assist with the identification, assessment and monitoring of progress for children with SEN.
- The organisation of a curriculum that allows for children with SEN to participate as fully as possible in all school activities.
- Ensuring staff development.
- Developing partnerships with parents.
- Linking with outside agencies to offer a multi-agency approach.

Outside agencies such as Connexions, social services, health professionals and educational psychologists also have a key part to play in ensuring the inclusion of SEN pupils in the mainstream educational environment. By offering their expertise, the individual needs of the pupil may be addressed more effectively.

Ultimately, teachers are also stakeholders, with a key role in ensuring that government policies are implemented at a local level, specifically within practice. They are responsible for ensuring that the provision of opportunities for all children is available, so that all children are able to participate in all activities wherever possible. Teaching staff work closely with teaching assistants in order to ensure the successful inclusion of pupils with SEN, and the role of the teaching assistant is very important, especially in terms of their professional relationship with the teacher and class.

SEN pupils and the National Curriculum: an inclusive approach?

In order to gain a broader picture of the issues of an inclusive education for pupils with SEN, we need to take into account other factors involved with inclusive education. We will now consider the National Curriculum and its impact on the SEN pupil. Since the National Curriculum was introduced in 1988, it has been subject to much debate in relation to meeting the needs of the pupil with SEN. The Qualifications and Curriculum Authority (2009) Statutory Inclusion Statement outlines three principles for inclusion:

- Setting suitable learning challenges.
- Responding to pupils' diverse learning needs.
- Overcoming potential barriers to learning and assessment for individuals and groups of pupils. (Department for Education and Employment Qualifications and Curriculum Authority, 1999, cited in Farrell, 2003:32)

The National Curriculum was designed to offer every child the entitlement to a 'broad, balanced and differentiated' curriculum across a range of programmes of study. As we saw in Chapter 7, the two principal aims of the National Curriculum are:

- To provide opportunities for all pupils to learn and achieve.
- To promote pupils' spiritual, moral, social and cultural development and prepare all pupils for the opportunities, responsibilities and experiences of life.

It can, however, be argued that the National Curriculum was planned with little reference to pupils with special needs, as it:

- Lays emphasis on attainment targets which may not be considered the most effective system when aiming to provide for SEN pupils.
- Is organised around subjects including literacy and numeracy.
- Is a very rigid approach in that literacy and numeracy hours are given priority over other subjects such as art and drama. Some SEN learners are more suited to kinaesthetic learning and with this in mind the literacy and numeracy hours may not best suit their needs.

? Stop and reflect

- *How does the National Curriculum meet the needs of SEN pupils?*
- *Does failure to offer the National Curriculum to SEN pupils result in unequal access to education?*

In 2004, the Office for Standards in Education (Ofsted) conducted research in 114 schools in the UK, based on the impact of the inclusion framework, with a specific focus on educational inclusion and raising attainment among pupils with SEN. During this research special attention was given to progress made in literacy by pupils with SEN. The main findings indicate that the inclusion framework

'Removing Barriers to Achievement' (2004) has contributed to growing awareness of the benefits of inclusion, and demonstrate some improvement in practice since the SENDA (2001). However, the research highlighted a lack of benchmarks against which SEN achievement can be measured, and an inconsistent approach by some schools in comparison with other schools, regarding expectations of achievement in SEN pupils.

Furthermore, of the schools visited, few considered the progress of SEN pupils towards meeting targets in the core subjects. There was evidence that they seldom linked the progress of SEN pupils to the provision the school had made, and many staff were actually aware that their pupils were not making sufficient progress; however, they tended not to analyse why this was the case (Ofsted, 2004). Without this analysis, schools were left in a situation whereby they were unable to evaluate whether they were actually doing the best they could for SEN pupils and this raises the question, can pupils with special educational needs be included in a mainstream school successfully? Farrell (2006:1) suggests:

> To communicate and to interact is of such central importance, not only in education but in everyday life, that it will be apparent that, where a child or young person experiences significant difficulties in these areas, it is essential that suitable educational provision is put in place to help ensure that the pupil makes the best progress possible.

Without suitable educational provision, it is likely that the individual will fall short of the education system and as a result may fail to meet his/her maximum learning potential; however, if an inclusive approach is taken, bearing in mind the individual needs of the pupil with SEN, a positive outcome may be achieved.

Can a pupil with SEN be included in a mainstream school environment?

For the purpose of this chapter, the emphasis will be placed on **autism** or **Autistic Spectrum Disorder (ASD)**, which is one of many special educational needs. However, we begin with a brief discussion of two other special educational needs: **dyslexia** and Attention Deficit Hyperactivity Disorder (ADHD).

Including a pupil with dyslexia: a challenge?

Dyslexia is a specific learning difficulty which may affect areas of spelling, reading, writing and mathematics; a pupil may display the following symptoms:

- Lack of concentration
- Reversing of words and letters in written work
- Difficulty in reading, writing and/or spelling
- Difficulty with speech development
- Difficulty with organisation
- Difficulty with the concept of right/left
- Difficulty with structuring ideas.

Although dyslexia is a complex SEN, it may be possible to include a pupil with the symptoms in a mainstream educational environment with the right amount of support. Stakes and Hornby (2000) suggest that the vast majority of children with specific learning difficulties such as dyslexia may be educated in a mainstream classroom.

It is imperative that strategies are implemented to ensure inclusive and effective classroom management in relation to a pupil with SEN. The individual needs of the pupil must be taken into account at all times and it is important to remember that each pupil who has dyslexia may display different symptoms. When working with a pupil who is dyslexic it is very important to offer clear instruction, in sizeable chunks, rather than overloading the pupil with information. This will allow the pupil time to process the information sufficiently. A pupil with dyslexia may need extra time when completing written tasks as he/she may have difficulty with fine motor skills. If a pupil is not given this time, he/she may become very frustrated and be left with a feeling of failure and this may result in negative behaviour.

It is important to concentrate on a pupil's strengths and encourage these rather than focus on what he/she cannot do due to difficulties in relation to dyslexia. An effective strategy when teaching a pupil with dyslexia is to emphasise the use of oral/practical approaches rather than placing emphasis on written work which will be very difficult to master, although when working with a pupil on written tasks it is important to highlight the important spelling errors to assist the child with progression. A child who has dyslexia may respond positively to visual aids as these will reinforce understanding and, by using a range of teaching strategies (such as audio, visual and kinaesthetic), effective inclusion is more likely.

Including a pupil with ADHD: a challenge?

Attention Deficit Hyperactivity Disorder (ADHD) is a term used currently to describe disruptive behavioural disorders marked by overactivity, excessive difficulty sustaining attention and impulsivity. The American Psychiatric Association (APA, 1994) includes diagnostic criteria which relate to three types of ADHD seen in children:

- Hyperactive/impulsive type – Impulsive behaviour in children with ADHD may be displayed in the form of shouting out answers in class when they have been asked to 'put your hand up and wait to be asked to answer a question'. They may also find it difficult when playing games where they have to turn take.

- Inattentive type – Children with ADHD may exhibit difficulties when working on educational tasks and other tasks, as they may find it very difficult to sustain attention. If they are disinterested in a task these difficulties may appear to be exacerbated as they will find the task dull and boring.

- Combined hyperactive-impulsive/inattentive type – Hyperactivity can include behaviours including hand/foot tapping, fidgeting, talking, and walking around at a very fast pace when the child should be seated and working on educational tasks.

ADHD is a complex special educational need, and as such a mainstream school may have a limited capacity to include a child with ADHD effectively. The school's effectiveness is dependent on the staff being aware of ADHD and taking measures to enable a child to achieve. A child with ADHD may behave impulsively in situations which cause him/her stress, and display inappropriate behaviour, possibly resulting in aggressive behaviour towards staff and pupils. Confronting a child with ADHD can further exacerbate aggressive behaviour. It is important that the behavioural needs of a child with ADHD are met prior to the point where a child becomes very stressed or aggressive. By observing the trigger behaviours and intervening at an early stage, these outbursts of negative behaviour may be avoided.

There are many things that a teacher may do to support a child with ADHD in a mainstream classroom. However, it is essential that a child with ADHD is placed in an educational setting which will maximise opportunities for him/her, and this may not be a mainstream school. It may be that a child with ADHD is educated in a mainstream school in a learning support unit, and wherever appropriate integrated into the curriculum. Additional support might take a number of forms. Marjorie Boxall (cited in Hughes and Cooper, 2007) advocates that 'nurture groups' are a positive way of ensuring educational engagement. By questioning the setting in which the student is to be 'included', we are able to ascertain if a child with ADHD is actively supported and if the circumstances do not do this and promote a child's social, emotional and cognitive engagement, we are not providing an inclusive experience and a nurture group setting may better suit the needs of the child.

In summary, by taking a proactive approach to dealing with behavioural issues demonstrated by a child with ADHD, teachers may be able to avoid any changes to a child's routine in order to reduce stressful situations and the onset of inappropriate behaviours. By providing the child with the necessary support and involving them in the process throughout, effective inclusion in the mainstream environment may be possible.

Can a pupil with ASD be included in a mainstream school environment?

Communication can be very difficult for an individual with Autistic Spectrum Disorder, or autism. In order to explore the issues faced by pupils with autism, and the possibility of educating the autistic pupil in a mainstream school environment, we must first highlight the various difficulties which might be involved.

In the mid-1940s Leo Kanner, a child psychiatrist, formally identified autism as a set of characteristics. More recently, Wing (1996) identified the condition as a 'triad of impairments' (Wing, 1996, cited in Plimley and Bowen, 2006). The three main areas of developmental differences are:

- difficulty with social communication;
- difficulty with social interaction;
- difficulty with social imagination.

↖ *Connect and explore*

This website is useful as a starting point to learn more about Autistic Spectrum Disorder: **www.nas.org.uk**.

Common characteristics of children with Autistic Spectrum Disorder

Individuals with Autistic Spectrum Disorder, sometimes referred to as Autistic Spectrum Condition, are all unique, and as such different behaviours and characteristics will be displayed across individuals. We will now look at the most commonly noted areas of difference.

Communication: The general symptoms may include difficulty with social relationships, and a child with ASD may appear very remote to others. They may demonstrate the following symptoms:

- lack of speech;
- limited conversation;
- speech likely to develop more slowly than is the norm for children of the same age;
- unable to respond spontaneously;
- unable to share social situations;
- lack of desire to communicate.

Social interaction: A child with ASD may have difficulty with verbal and non-verbal communication, have an inability to understand sarcasm and may take meaning literally. They may demonstrate the following symptoms:

- unable to form social bonds;
- avoid eye contact;
- limited play skills;
- inability to understand others' thinking;
- inability to understand others' feelings;
- difficulty with tolerating peers.

Social imagination: A child with ASD may find it difficult to play with others and use imagination and/or creativity. They may demonstrate the following symptoms:

- unable to use own imagination to create pictures;
- unable to understand jokes;
- have difficulty in initiating play with other children;
- may prefer to be left alone;
- lack of imitation of other individuals' actions. (Plimley and Bowen, 2006:4–5)

Autism is a lifelong developmental disability: however, although many of the characteristics appear in each autistic individual, the condition will affect each individual in very different ways and degrees (hence the notion of a spectrum). Some individuals with autism are able to live relatively normal lives, while others will require a lifetime of specialist support (the National Autistic Society, UK, 2008). While physical disabilities are often visible and apparent, the difficulties of the autistic individual are often hidden until they try to communicate or interact with others. This special educational need is very hard to detect in comparison with an individual who is physically disabled and uses a wheelchair; however, by observing the behaviour of a child with ASD, the symptoms become apparent.

One of the principles of the SEN Code of Practice is that the individual with special educational needs should be educated in a mainstream school wherever possible. As a result of this, a child with special educational needs must now have a clear case that his or her needs may not be met in a mainstream school in order to be educated in a special school. A variety of special schools exist including schools for the hearing impaired, schools for the blind, specialist schools for children with epilepsy, schools for children with severe learning difficulties and moderate learning difficulties (including schools for autistic children).

? Stop and reflect

If each individual case of ASD is different, how can the ideas presented in the 'spectrum' model proposed by Wing help our practical understanding of this SEN?

Including a pupil with autism: a challenge?

The concept of inclusion in a mainstream environment when focusing on the autistic pupil is very difficult. Buckton (2000, cited in Clough and Corbett, 2000) argues that mainstream education is not always suitable for autistic pupils, as the difficulties which are faced by these pupils in relation to social understanding may impact on their ability to function in the mainstream environment. Buckton, an educationalist, uses the experience of a colleague who is a high functioning autistic individual to reinforce his argument. This colleague reflects that her feelings are very mixed in relation to mainstream education, as she had a very bad experience as a pupil prior to the Warnock Report of 1978: she was completely isolated and her teachers failed to understand her autistic traits, because she did not understand the tasks she was asked to do and so failed to complete them. The teachers misread this behaviour for stubbornness, referring to her as a 'rude child' (Buckton, 2000, cited in Clough and Corbett, 2000:148). This highlights the particular difficulties which may be faced by the autistic pupil being educated in a mainstream school environment prior to the shift in attitudes to SEN following the Warnock Report in 1978.

Controversies

'SEN learners can never be fully included in mainstream learning environments'

Agree: Bill Tuckey's article 'The boy in the corner: Why do children with special needs still get such a raw educational deal?' in *The Independent*: Education (April, 2010) argued that the government's long-standing policy of inclusion within mainstream schools did not work. The parent of a son with a diagnosis of autism, Tuckey challenged politicians Ed Balls and Michael Gove to respond to the frustrations encountered by both parents and children suggesting that 'a more united parental voice in the whole special-needs debate might help change things.' His view is representative of many parents who experience the ongoing problems of supporting their child's learning in an environment which seems inappropriate for them.

Disagree: Tara Flood, director of the Alliance for Inclusive Education, is worried that the Conservatives could 'turn the clock back 40 years' for children with SEN and fears the return of 'segregation', which is more concerned with providing care than education. Flood argues that educational inclusion needs to go further and that politicians should 'encourage the aspirations of disabled or SEN children and young people in their manifestos' (Higgs, 2010: Children and Young People Now, 4 May).

In order to be properly inclusive it is important that all children are given access to mainstream education. As long as schools plan their provision carefully and there is adequate support from specially trained teachers and teaching assistants there is every chance that this will be a positive experience leading to improved social inclusion.

What do you think? Which side of the argument do you favour?

Autistic individuals can find it very difficult to adapt to any change in their routines, and find the educational environment very challenging. While they are able to act on their environment, learn skills and in some cases develop language, learners with autism are often unable to make sense of many of the activities they take part in (Mesibov et al., 2006:21). Tony Attwood (Attwood, 1998, cited in Hesmondhalgh and Breakey, 2001:17) uses the analogy of building a brick wall to stress that every single part of life for the autistic individual has to be in place in order if progression is to occur. Just as one missing brick can impact on the whole structure of the wall, so can the structure of an autistic individual's life depend on any given aspect.

Autistic individuals are also often unable to generalise appropriately, and as such may learn one set of rules in one situation (for example, undressing in a bedroom), but may try to generalise this to another situation (for example by undressing in the middle of a shop, not realising this is an inappropriate context). This poses many problems in a school environment, specifically in relation to the changes which are frequently taking place; for example, there may be a change of staff or a change of routine which cannot be avoided due to staff illness. Something as apparently trivial as a session finishing five minutes late may cause heightened anxiety for the autistic pupil, who is unable to cope with the concept of change. As a result of the change in setting, the individual may start behaving erratically or even become violent.

Professor Gary Mesibov (2008), who has studied autistic individuals extensively, advocates that the autistic pupil is unable to share experiences with others, and as such will find group activities confusing, as they have to pay attention to too many different things at one time. Autistic pupils are unable to conceive that other individuals think differently from themselves, and are unable to engage and disengage easily as they are more narrowly engaged and focus intently on fewer things. Classrooms are often noisy, very active and full of clutter. Autistic individuals have problems with over-stimulation and this may lead to a marked effect on the behaviour of the autistic pupil in the classroom. Many autistic individuals are very sensitive to touch, noise, smell, movement, lights, food and sunlight; for example, if an autistic person is touched unexpectedly, the effect can almost be like receiving an electric shock. Bearing these traits in mind, it may seem an almost impossible task to include the autistic pupil in a mainstream school environment, but we will now consider how this may be possible.

If a school is to provide an inclusive mainstream environment for the autistic individual, three groups of people are crucial: the staff who provide support for the autistic pupils; the teachers; and the mainstream pupils. In the majority of special schools which cater for autistic pupils, the staff-to-student ratio is very high, as some pupils require one-to-one support. Staff have to be both a support mechanism for the autistic pupil, and develop mainstream pupils' understanding of their SEN peers. Hesmondhalgh and Breakey (2001:52) support the notion that the success of any inclusive education is largely dependent on the mainstream pupils. From the outset, mainstream pupils need to be aware of communication disorders such as Autistic Spectrum Disorder in order that they are able to understand autistic pupils and the difficulties they face. It is also useful for mainstream pupils to understand that a disability may not always be visible, and that individuals with special educational needs can achieve and make progress in the same way as mainstream pupils. This is very hard to achieve as children will need to be specifically educated in order to accept this concept.

The level of independence of autistic individuals varies: with this in mind it is desirable that the autistic pupil, who is unable to function independently in a school environment, has a 'safe haven' at school, where he/she feels secure and safe. Many mainstream schools have specific areas allocated for teaching pupils with special educational needs, and depending on how severe the autistic traits of the individual are, it may be that the pupil on first arriving at the school may spend the majority of his/her time in the special educational needs unit, with high levels of support. Over time, he/she may be integrated into the mainstream environment wherever possible, with support as and when required. Again, this can be an important stage when moving towards inclusion.

The TEACCH programme: towards inclusion

We can try to structure the mainstream environment to suit the individual needs of the autistic pupil in order that inclusion can be successful. Mesibov et al. (2006) advocate that the concept of structure is fundamental to ensuring the successful education of autistic individuals. With this in mind, Eric Schopler, an American psychologist who conducted research into autism in the early 1970s, founded the Treatment and Education of Autistic and related Communication handicapped CHildren (TEACCH) programme. The focus of the TEACCH programme is to develop highly structured settings for learning, around a person's skills, interests and needs. This approach shifts the priority from inclusion on to the individual. The structured TEACCH approach includes physical organisation, daily schedules and work systems, as described in Table 9.1.

Table 9.1 **The TEACCH approach**

Physical organisation

Physical organisation clarifies boundaries for the autistic pupil and minimises distractions and unwanted stimulation in order to keep the autistic pupil focused on the task in hand. It also adds contextual cues for the autistic pupil to make meaning of their world, for example placing books in one specific area, and computers in another, in order to avoid confusion. Failure to provide these contextual clues might make it practically impossible for the autistic pupil to make sense of his/her world. In the context of the classroom, some autistic pupils may find it extremely disturbing if chairs are not placed in a structured way.

Source: www.educationphotos.co.uk/walmsley. Copyright © John Walmsley 2011. All rights reserved.

Daily schedules

It is important to provide clear beginnings and endings for the autistic pupil in a practical way. This may be in the form of a written and/or pictorial schedule, and may require a system whereby, when a task is finished, the pupil removes the word/picture from the schedule to reinforce the achievement of the task. Daily schedules can also provide visual stimuli which link to concrete experience; for example, a picture of a bus at the end of the schedule may indicate it is home time.

Source: Alamy Images: Blend Images.

Work systems

The individual work system gives the autistic pupil a systematic strategy to approach the work that needs to be completed (Mesibov et al., 2006). For example, written work systems may include written instructions to reinforce what actually needs to be done. Matching work systems ask the pupil to match a picture to a completed task to reinforce achievement.

Source: Pearson Education Ltd./Photodisc/Geoff Manasse.

The TEACCH approach has been used very widely internationally since 1978. Since 1984, programmes for adults, including social skill groups and supported employment, have been the focus of the programme. By replacing the existing gap between parents and professionals with a professional model, individuals are able to make valuable contributions to the larger society (Mesibov, Shea, Schopler, 2006:11). This programme aims to provide a structured approach for autistic learners, as without this structured approach the autistic individual may be held back by an inability to work independently in a variety of situations (Mesibov, 2008). Mesibov suggests that, if these techniques are adopted and implemented in mainstream schools consistently, autistic pupils may be included in these environments successfully. He argues that 'adults brought up using these practices are now the most productive and successful in the world with lives that are full, rich and meaningful' (2008).

Activity

Connect to **http://www.nas.org.uk/nas/jsp/polopoly.jsp?d=297&a=3630** and read the information about the TEACCH programme. Answer these questions to reinforce your learning about the TEACCH programme.

- What is the key focus of the TEACCH approach?
- How can the TEACCH approach support effective learning?
- By adopting the TEACCH approach, would the autistic pupil be able to function effectively in a mainstream educational environment?

What does gifted and talented mean?

In the past, giftedness related to academic skills and talented related to non-academic ability, for example drama. More recently, gifted and talented learners have been defined as 'Children and young people with one or more abilities developed to a level significantly ahead of their year group (or with the potential to develop those abilities)' (Department for Children, Schools and Families, 2008).

The DCSF define gifted learners as those who have the ability to excel academically in one or more subjects such as mathematics, English or science. Talented learners are defined as those who have the ability to excel in practical skills such as artistic performance, sport or a vocational subject area (DCSF, 2008).

While the terms 'gifted' and 'talented' appear to reinforce high achievers in school, low academic attainers can also be identified as gifted and talented, where there is clear evidence to support this identification (DCSF, 2009). The DCSF (2008) encourage schools in identifying gifted and talented learners to focus on the following:

- Learners aged 11–19 who meet the eligibility criteria.
- Learners aged 4–19 who are gifted and talented relative to their peers in their own year group and school/college.
- Learners who demonstrate a range of abilities including talent in the arts and sport and ability rather than achievement so that underachievers may also be identified.

The Labour government's expectation was that special schools will also identify gifted and talented learners and as such enrol these individuals as members of the 'Young Gifted and Talented Learner Academy', which was set up in 2007 to provide support and opportunities for gifted and talented children aged 4 to 19. The Academy offers children the opportunity to take part in activities which will challenge them and will enable them to meet other gifted and talented pupils with similar interests.

The Learner Academy is funded and supported by the Department for Children, Schools and Families and its aim is to provide opportunities within and beyond the classroom for gifted and talented young people.

The work of Renzulli has been very influential as a framework for the creation of opportunities for gifted and talented children. Renzulli (1977, cited in Hymer and Michel, 2002:12) argues that 'above average ability is necessary but not sufficient for giftedness to emerge.' Renzulli believes that enrichment activities (activities to promote learning and enrich the regular curriculum taught in schools) can create opportunities for individuals to discover their interests, gifts and talents. Renzulli also believes that the family, the peer group and the school are very important influences on whether an individual is gifted or not (Monks, 1992, cited in Hymer and Michel, 2002:13). Renzulli's model is evident in a variety of settings, including the DfES's *Excellence in Cities* initiative (Warwick, 2001, cited in Hymer and Michel, 2002).

Within the learning situation

Renzulli considers that gifted children are those who are able to develop the three traits demonstrated in Figure 9.1 by applying these traits to any valuable area of human performance. In practice, if only one set of these traits were presented, for example a pupil was a very divergent thinker, this child would not, under Renzulli's model, be considered gifted. Through their interaction the three traits can be seen as equal partners in contributing to giftedness. Central to Renzulli's model is the notion of school enrichment activities, in order that all pupils are offered the opportunity to discover their gifts and talents.

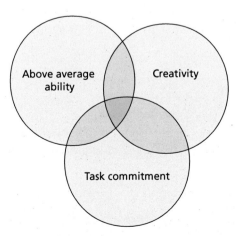

Figure 9.1 **Renzulli's three-ring model of giftedness**

Table 9.2 **Gardner's multiple intelligences**

Intelligence	Example
Bodily kinaesthetic (used for touch and reflex)	Bodily-kinaesthetic intelligence focuses on the ability to use mental ability to coordinate bodily movements
Interpersonal (used for communicating with others)	Interpersonal intelligence focuses on the ability to understand the intentions and desires of other people. Educators are an example of individuals who have interpersonal intelligence as they are able to work effectively with others because they can understand intentions, motivations and desires of others
Intrapersonal (used for self-discovery and analysis)	Intrapersonal intelligence is involved with the ability to understand the self and appreciate feelings and fears. This enables a person to control their own life as they have a good understanding of how they feel and what motivates them in order to take control of their life
Linguistic (used for reading, writing and speech)	This is involved with the ability to learn languages and to use language effectively to express oneself. A poet is an example of an individual with linguistic intelligence
Logical (mathematical; used for maths, logic and systems)	This intelligence focuses on the ability to problem solve, specifically in mathematics. A physicist is an example of an individual with logical intelligence
Musical (used for rhythm, music and lyrics)	Musical intelligence involves the ability to perform and compose music specifically in relation to musical rhythms, tones and pitches. Musicians are examples of individuals with musical intelligence
Visual spatial (used for visualisation and art)	Spatial intelligence involves the ability to visualise patterns of wide space and more confined areas. An actor is an example of an individual who would display spatial intelligence
Naturalist	Naturalist intelligence enables human beings to recognise, categorise and draw upon certain features of the environment

Source: www.Teachingexpertise.com, 2008.

Over the past 20 years, psychologist Howard Gardner's **theory of multiple intelligences** has been very influential in the field of education. Gardner suggests that individuals should be given the opportunity to excel using non-academic forms, and highlights several different types of intelligence, as shown in Table 9.2.

? Stop and reflect

- *What are the key characteristics of a gifted learner?*
- *What are the key characteristics of a talented learner?*
- *Who should schools include in their gifted and talented populations?*

Gifted and talented learners are not always recognised: frustration may be demonstrated when work is considered too easy and fails to challenge the individual. Learning difficulties such as difficulties with literacy may mask the potential of one who has a talent, for example, in woodwork. The Qualifications Curriculum Authority suggests that gifted and talented pupils are likely to:

- think quickly and accurately;
- work systematically;
- generate creative working solutions;
- work flexibly, processing unfamiliar information and applying knowledge, experience and insight to unfamiliar situations;
- communicate their thoughts and ideas well;
- be determined, diligent and interested in uncovering patterns;
- achieve, or show potential, in a wide range of contexts;
- be particularly creative;
- show great sensitivity or empathy;
- demonstrate particular physical dexterity or skill;
- make sound judgements;
- be outstanding leaders or team members;
- be fascinated by, or passionate about, a particular subject or aspect of the curriculum;
- demonstrate high levels of attainment across a range of subjects within a particular subject, or aspects of work. (QCA, 2008)

It is important to be careful that, when identifying gifted and talented learners, they may not demonstrate all of these characteristics. Gifted and talented learners may be identified by teachers or parents who notice that the individual has either a 'gift' or 'talent'; this will be considered in the next section of this chapter.

Connect and explore

This website provides excellent, clear guidance for identifying gifted and talented children: **http://ygt.dcsf.gov.uk/FileLinks/312_Identifying%20Gifted%20and %20Talented%20Learners%20final%20version.doc.**

The expectation is that all schools and colleges will identify some learners who are gifted in comparison with the majority of their peers (year group), some learners who are talented in arts and sport, and some underachievers who are identified by way of their ability in arts and sport rather than achievement in academic subjects (DCSF, 2008). It is not necessary for each institution to identify a fixed percentage of gifted and talented learners: there is no 'quota system' for identifying gifted and talented individuals. Gifted and talented learners may be identified at any stage in their development and it is very important that, once identified, provision is appropriately challenging, caters for the needs of the individual, and allows them to further excel in their specific area. Although this is the aim, in reality does this occur? Today's system of identification aims to ensure that the individual's needs are taken into consideration and met accordingly; however, due to limited funding and resources this may not always be possible.

> ↖ *Connect and explore*
>
> Excellence in Cities is a programme which sets out to improve the education of city children, and builds on existing policies to raise standards by focusing on the individual needs of the pupils.
>
> To review the full report, go to: **http://www.standards.dfes.gov.uk/search/?mode= basic_search&pagenumber=1&x=54&y=11&d=all&search_string=excellence+in+cities.**
>
> View the summary to find out what an effective school should be aiming for in order to ensure an inclusive approach towards gifted and talented learners.

Let us now look at ways in which gifted and talented learners may be identified, and the strategies which can be implemented to ensure that an inclusive approach is adopted towards these learners.

Methods of identifying gifted and talented pupils

It is important to provide numerous opportunities for learners to discover gifts and talents. Regular assessments need to be conducted, especially in the case of new pupils joining mainstream schools, as previous achievements often fail to be forwarded by previous schools. There may also be a need to place greater emphasis on the use of non-verbal assessments if the pupil's language skills are underdeveloped.

Gardner emphasises that a crucial stage in the identification of a gifted or talented pupil is the creation of an environment which enriches and stimulates learning, giving all students the opportunity to reveal their unique strengths (Hymer and Michel, 2002). With this in mind, it is imperative that an effective learning environment is created, in order to stretch the individual while ensuring that students who are less able are not excluded. It is important that the practitioner takes a holistic approach, offering lots of different opportunities for learning in different contexts, especially in the case of pupils who demonstrate a lack of interest.

Taking a holistic view of the child includes considering their home life – gifted and talented traits may emerge at home as well as at school. This means that parents can also identify an individual child's abilities, and point them out: this may occur in a formal context, such as at parents' evenings, or less formally if parents meet teachers when dropping off or collecting their child from school. Effective communication between parent and school, specifically the teacher or SENCO, is important in order to identify the child as gifted and talented.

Identification may not always be straightforward. For some pupils, the school environment will not encourage them to demonstrate their excellence in a particular area, and so they may benefit from opportunities provided away from school. Examples of these may be summer schools or residential trips. By taking the individual away from their normal home or school environment, they may participate in activities which they would not be involved in at school or at home: in this way, specific talents may be identified which may otherwise be overlooked. By making the pupil's attendance voluntary, he/she may demonstrate a gift or talent which is not overtly related to school work, but which can subsequently be utilised in other educational environments.

Including a gifted and talented learner: a challenge?

Freeman (1988, cited in Hymer and Michel, 2002) advocates that, in order to create an inclusive approach to gifted and talented learners, an enriched environment is crucial whereby high-quality teaching focusing on gifted and talented students is based on the following:

Task demand

New knowledge is presented within the context of a conceptual framework, not as facts in isolation. For example, when teaching children about the world, this needs to be defined specifically in relation to whether it is being referred to as the whole world, as in the Earth, or whether it is being referred to in relation to the world of knowledge a specific person has.

- The teacher stimulates thinking by taking a problem-posing as well as a problem-solving approach to issues and material. This involves using unstructured problems in learning, placing the emphasis on open-ended tasks to stimulate the gifted and talented learner.
- Abstract as well as basic concepts are emphasised. An example of this is demonstrated in the use of the concept 'tree'. This has an abstract concept, 'plant'.
- High-quality materials are used, and reading levels demand complex, novel responses. As gifted and talented learners may have well-developed word knowledge and language skills compared with other children of the same age, the use of language used may need to be adapted to match the understanding of the learner, which may involve creative use of language, ensuring that the needs of the learner are met.

Use of language

- The intellectual demands of a lesson are recognised by the level, speed and quality of the verbal interactions that go on within it.
- The appropriate technical language is used, rather than a simplified version.
- Word-play is encouraged, whereby words are used to reinforce learning.
- Questioning is considered part of everyday learning, to stimulate thinking and creative problem-solving.

Communication

- Students explain out loud, comparing old and new learning and ideas with their peers.
- Research skills are taught, whereby pupils will research ideas independently, using the internet and other resources, so that pupils can expand on ideas for themselves.

Encouragement to excellence

- Students get own-time rewards on demonstration of high achievement. This takes the form of individual projects in accordance with an agreed teacher–student contract, whereby the student and teacher reach an agreement with regard to expectations in relation to the project to be undertaken.
- Goals are set to a high standard.
- Mentors are appointed; these may include other gifted and talented pupils who are at a higher level than the mentee.
- Creative abilities are nurtured by allowing the gifted and talented learner to explore ideas and develop these.
- Projects are completed and work is monitored. (Joan Freeman, 1998, cited in Hymer and Michel, 2002:60)

It is important to ensure that these opportunities are available for all students, enabling an enriched environment and an inclusive approach to gifted and talented education. We also need to consider the possibility of **acceleration** in order to meet the academic and social needs of gifted and talented students. The purpose of acceleration is to advance pupils who excel (those who demonstrate that they are achieving at a faster rate than peers of the same age) through the curriculum more quickly. Southern and Jones (2004, cited in Balchin et al., 2009:195) identified five dimensions of acceleration: pacing, salience, peers, access and timing. Rogers (2004, cited in Balchin et al., 2009:196) categorises acceleration into **'subject-based acceleration'** and **'grade-based acceleration'**. Rogers advocates that grade-based acceleration will reduce the number of years the pupil is in education, whereas subject-based acceleration offers opportunities for the pupil to increase subject knowledge at an earlier age than peers.

Kulik (2004, cited in Balchin et al., 2009:198) suggests that 'acceleration is positively related to educational ambition.' However, while the academic effects of acceleration are positive, the social effects should also be considered. Issues such as interpersonal skills, emotional maturity and the motivation to accelerate need to be addressed so that the gifted pupil is able to excel. Balchin et al. (2009:199) further suggest that 'effective social skills and social maturity are needed to complement exceptional academic skills.'

? Stop and reflect

- *What impact might acceleration have on the social aspects of the gifted pupil?*
- *Make a list of strategies which may be put into place to ensure that the gifted pupil remains motivated while on an accelerated programme.*
- *Consider the label of 'gifted' or 'talented': what effect might this label have on the pupil?*

The role of schools is very important in meeting the needs of gifted and talented pupils. By ensuring that high-quality admission and induction procedures are in place, including initial assessments, pupils who are gifted and talented are more likely to be identified at an early stage. This will help them to settle in to the new environment and they are more likely to learn effectively as a result. To carry out these initial assessments, a gifted and talented coordinator should be identified as the main person. The coordinator will have overall responsibility for ensuring that the needs of gifted and talented pupils are met in order that they are able to excel in their area of excellence. It is also imperative that, when identified, the gifted and talented learner is set challenges which enable them to achieve, and that progress is monitored on a regular basis to ensure that they are able to reach their maximum learning potential.

Appropriate programmes of professional development for all staff involved in the education of gifted and talented pupils should be put in place by management. Failure to do this may result in the gifted and talented learner becoming demotivated and as a result the individual may not reach their maximum potential in relation to their giftedness or talent. This may involve working in partnership with outside agencies and parents to support and extend pupil learning.

Author Rita Cheminais (2006:47), who has been involved in writing many texts in relation to the Every Child Matters agenda, identifies the following strategies for removing barriers to learning, which are crucial if the needs of the gifted and talented learner are to be met:

- Use plenty of open questions and set open-ended tasks.
- Provide opportunities to use and apply multiple intelligences.
- Develop pupils' higher-order thinking skills, e.g. exploration, reflection, evaluation, prediction, observation.
- Put extra challenges on learning, e.g. time limit, word limit.
- Develop analytical skills, e.g. investigative reporting.
- Set a quiz question, puzzle, problem or unusual word for the week activity.
- Provide opportunities for collaborative group work, role plays, hot-seating activities.
- Give options on how to present their work and findings, e.g. diary account, newspaper report, interview, audio/visual presentations.
- Seek opportunities for cross-Key Stage working whereby gifted and talented learners work at a level appropriate to them and at times at a Key Stage higher than their expected achievement rate in relation to their age.
- Provide emotional support.

Conclusion

In conclusion, the term inclusion is only useful if it is used in the correct context. If a child with SEN who has complex learning difficulties and behavioural problems is placed in a mainstream school it may be that this child is excluded rather than included. It is imperative that the individual is offered a choice with regard to attending either a mainstream or special school, as, without this choice, it is unlikely that the child will feel 'included'. If an SEN child is placed in a mainstream educational environment and the strategies suggested in this chapter are developed and implemented consistently, pupils with special educational needs are more likely to be successfully included in a mainstream school environment. Effective schools, with staff who are willing to take on the challenge of developing and implementing an inclusive policy for SEN learners, will be successful in offering an inclusive environment for each and every learner regardless of any disability of gift/talent. By taking a more holistic approach to meeting the varying needs of pupils, the five key outcomes of the Every Child Matters agenda, which include being healthy, staying safe, enjoying and achieving, making a positive contribution and achieving economic well-being, will be met, and the shift toward an inclusive society will become more apparent.

Case study 9.2
The rise and fall of NAGTY

The last Labour government (1997–2010) made considerable progress in the provision for students identified as gifted and talented, making it a statutory responsibility for schools to provide for the differing abilities of all pupils. Guidance about the 'education of the able, gifted and talented child' was included in governmental guidance as a topic of teacher training (Monks and Pfluger, in CCEA, 2005).

In England a number of initiatives were launched:

- Excellence in Cities (launched in 1999) was targeted to support schools in deprived areas and included aims for gifted and talented pupils such as identification, provision and support both in and out of schools. Each school had a coordinator who worked with other schools and learning mentors to 'champion' these students.

- Physical education school sports and clubs links (PESSCL) strategy for gifted and talented students (part of the DfES) was created to establish pathways for young people with potential to achieve in sport.

- The Student Academy provides opportunities for peer activities to allow stimulation and debate (e.g. summer schools, online forums and internet-based learning).

- Study groups set up with specialist areas and topics such as Classics (art and artefacts in Greek and Roman cultures) and ethics and philosophy (What is betrayal?).

- NAGTY summer schools provide residential courses, at universities, usually led by lecturers with a range of topics such as legal studies, robotics, advanced maths and creative writing, as well as activities such as drama and sports to encourage social interactions. Outreach provision is also provided in a range of locations across England and Wales.

- NAGTY's higher education gateway is part of the national DfES project called AimHigher to provide advice and information about HE entry particularly among non-traditional groups.

- A range of other initiatives including the Student Council for gifted and talented students, Gifted Entrepreneurs programme (training to run a business), the Professional Academy (working with school to help with provision for gifted and talented learners), Ambassador schools (to support other schools and exemplify best practice), think-tanks and so on.

Now that there is a new coalition government in place (Conservative and Liberal Democrat) it seems that NAGTY will cease to exist. There is therefore considerable reshuffling in progress with the NAGTY website announcing: 'A new UK Government took office on 11 May. As a result the content on this site may not reflect current Government policy. All statutory guidance and legislation published on this site continues to reflect the current legal position unless indicated otherwise' (viewed 26 August 2010).

Reaction to this change varies with a range of opinions reported in *The Guardian*: *Education* under the question:

> The National Academy for Gifted and Talented Youth, which offers extra support for gifted children in state schools, is to be scrapped and funds redirected to help children from disadvantaged backgrounds to get to university. Was the national G&T scheme a field day for pushy parents, or a valuable support system for children in danger of not realising their full potential?

> Murray, 2 February 2010

Question for discussion

While reported views and viewpoints were mixed, the general feeling was that this might be a loss which is difficult to recoup. What do you think?

Summary

A definition of inclusion

There are many differing definitions for the term 'inclusion'; however, the Every Disabled Matters Inclusion Charter suggests that all children should have the right to be included in every aspect of society, taking a holistic approach to inclusion.

Theories of inclusive education: models of disability

Theorists have proposed two models of inclusive education: the medical model, which relies on the disabled individual as being totally dependent on the medical profession, and the social model, which in contrast focuses on the experience of the individual, environmental factors and preventative measures rather than cure by the medical profession.

Special educational needs: policy perspectives

When schooling began in 1870 with the introduction of the Elementary Education Act, children with disabilities were seen as unfit to be taught in a large class situation and, as a result, were segregated from mainstream children. As the emphasis shifted when the 1944 Education Act was passed at the end of the Second World War, every child, including those with disabilities, had the right to statutory education at primary and secondary school. Following this, in 1978, as a result of the Warnock Report, the term SEN was introduced into UK legislation, thus ending the discrimination of children with SEN. The 1981 Education Act emerged and this had a major influence on teachers, who were now obliged to take responsibility

▶

for pupils with SEN and follow standardised procedures for identifying and assessing these pupils. The Education Reform Act 1988 was also very influential as this identified that all pupils had the right to a 'balanced and broadly based curriculum relevant to their individual needs'. The SEN Code of Practice was introduced in 2001 with a view to offering guidance for parents and educators in relation to the education of individuals with SEN.

Defining SEN in the twenty-first century

Special educational needs (SEN) is a term used to describe a diverse range of difficulties whereby a child or young person is prevented from learning at a rate and level similar to those children at the same age.

There are four principle areas of special educational needs: communication and interaction; cognition and learning; behaviour, emotional and social development; and sensory and/or physical needs.

Stakeholders in SEN and inclusion

Stakeholders have a very important part to play in relation to the UK agenda for inclusion and key stakeholders include the government, which drives the inclusion agenda forward by nurturing positive partnerships at a regional and local level to provide solutions to any issues faced in relation to education.

Parents as stakeholders offer expertise in many ways in their roles as parent governors. They are very influential when schools are developing policies specifically in relation to children with SEN and are able to provide first-hand experience to teachers who are tasked with developing the curriculum to meet the needs of each individual child with SEN.

As stakeholders, SENCOs are involved with whole school SEN policies in order to address a wide range of issues relating to the coordination of provision for children with SEN and teachers have a crucial role as stakeholders in ensuring that national policies are implemented at a local level, in practice by providing opportunities for all children in order that an effective inclusive educational experience is offered.

Outside agencies such as Connexions, social services, health professionals and educational psychologists also have a key part to play in ensuring the inclusion of SEN pupils in the mainstream educational environment. By offering their expertise, the individual needs of the pupil may be addressed more effectively.

What is the impact of the National Curriculum on the SEN pupil?

The National Curriculum was designed to offer every child the entitlement to a 'broad, balanced and differentiated' curriculum across a range of programmes of study; however, it is suggested that the National Curriculum was planned with little reference to pupils with SEN as it lays emphasis on attainment targets, is organised around subjects including literacy and numeracy and is a very rigid approach. This fails to take into account the individual needs of pupils with SEN.

Can a pupil with ASD be included in a mainstream school environment?

Autism is a condition which was formally identified as a set of characteristics in the mid-1940s by Leo Kanner, a child psychiatrist. The three main areas of developmental differences are: difficulty with social communication, social inter-action and social imagination. This condition will affect each individual in very different ways; while some individuals with autism are able to live relatively every-day lives, others require support throughout their lifetime.

When looking at the concept of inclusion and the autistic pupil, it is quite clear that, predominantly, the autistic pupil would find it very difficult to function in the mainstream environment, due to the difficulties faced in relation to social un-derstanding; however, this is not always the case and some pupils with autism may cope in a mainstream environment, given the right amount of support from staff and pupils at the school.

A structured routine is of paramount importance to the autistic individual, and the TEACCH approach founded by Gary Mesibov is a technique adapted in main-stream schools consistently to include autistic individuals in this environment.

What are gifted and talented learners?

Gifted and talented young people are learners identified with one or more ability developed to a level significantly ahead of their year group. There are many theorists who suggest differing views of gifted and talented. Renzulli proposes that the notion of gifted and talented is determined by enrichment activities to promote learning and enrich the regular curriculum taught in schools as a means of influencing whether the individual is gifted or not. In contrast, Howard Gardner suggests that individuals have multiple intelligences and that there is a relationship between the individual and his/her talents, the domain (which is the discipline whereby individuals are able to express their talents) and the field (which includes the people who actually judge the indi-vidual's work).

Methods of identifying gifted and talented pupils

It is imperative that there are numerous opportunities for learners to discover gifts and talents, and regular assessments should be conducted in order to ensure that these gifts/talents are recognised. Teachers, staff and parents may identify an individual child's abilities, and it is paramount that effective communication be-tween parent and school ensues in order that the child may be identified as gifted and talented.

Including a gifted and talented learner: a challenge?

When considering inclusion and the gifted and talented learner, an enriched environment is crucial to this process. The role of schools is very important in meeting the needs of gifted and talented learners. By offering high-quality admission and induction processes, individuals who are gifted and talented are more likely to be recognised. Individual pupils need to be given the opportunity to accelerate in order to meet their academic and social needs, and a gifted and talented coordinator should be identified in order to ensure that the needs of the pupils are met.

References

American Psychiatric Association (1994) *Diagnostic and Statistical Manual of Mental Disorders*, 4th edn, Washington, DC: APA.

American Psychiatric Association (2000) *Diagnostic and Statistic Manual of Mental Disorders*, 4th edn, Text Revision, Washington DC: APA.

Balchin, T., Hymer, B. and Matthews, D.J. (2009) *The Routledge International Companion to Gifted Education*, Oxon: Routledge.

Because Films Inspire (2008) *Medical Model vs Social Model*: http://www.bfi.org.uk/education/teaching/disability/thinking/medical.html.

CCEA (2006) *Gifted and talented children in (and out) of the classroom*, A Report for the Council of Curriculum, Examinations and Assessment, 28 February: http://www.nicurriculum.org.uk/docs/inclusion_and_sen/gifted/gifted_children_060306.pdf.

Centre for Studies on Inclusive Education (2008) *What is Inclusion?* http://www.csie.org.uk/inclusion/what.shtml, November 2008.

Cheminais, R. (2006) Every Child Matters: A Practical Guide for Teachers, Oxon: Routledge.

Clough, P. and Corbett, J. (2000) *Theories of Inclusive Education: A student's guide*, London: Sage.

Cole, B.A. (2005) Mission Impossible? Special educational needs, inclusion and the re-conceptualization of the role of the SENCO in England and Wales, in *European Journal of Special Needs Education*, 20(3), pp. 287–307.

Cowne, E. (2003) *The SENCO Handbook: Working within a whole-school approach*, 4th edn, London: Fulton.

Department for Children Schools and Families (2009) Every Child Matters: http://www.dcsf.gov.uk/everychildmatters/, November 2009.

Department for Children, Schools and Families (2009) Common Assessment Framework: http://www.dcsf.gov.uk/everychildmatters/strategy/deliveringservices1/caf/cafframework/, November 2009.

Department for Children, Schools and Families (2008) Identifying Gifted and Talented Learners – getting started: http://ygt.dcsf.gov.uk/FileLinks/312_new_guidance.pdf.

DES (1944) *Education Act*, London: HMSO.

DES (1981) *Education Act*, London: HMSO.

DfE (1994a) *The Code of Practice on the Identification and Assessment of Special Educational Needs*, London: HMSO.

DfES (2001) *The Special Educational Needs Code of Practice*: http://www.teachernet.gov.uk/_doc/3724/SENCodeOfPractice.pdf.

DfES (2002) *Removing Barriers to Achievement*: http://www.standards.dfes.gov.uk/eyfs/resources/downloads/removing-barriers.pdf.

DFES (2004) *Removing Barriers to Achievement*: http://www.standards.dfes.gov.uk/eyfs/resources/downloads/removing-barriers.pdf.

DFES (2008) Identifying Gifted and Talented Learners: http://ygt.dcsf.gov.uk/FileLinks/312_Identifying%20Gifted%20and%20Talented%20Learners%20final%20version.doc.

Every Child Matters (2004) *Change for Children*: http://www.everychildmatters.gov.uk/aims.

Every Disabled Child Matters (2007) *The Inclusion Charter* http://www.edcm.org.uk/pdfs/the_inclusion_charter.pdf.

Farrell, M. (2003) *Understanding Special Educational Needs: A guide for student teachers*, London: RoutledgeFalmer.

GovernorNet (2008) *Children with Special Educational Needs – Overview*: http://www.governornet.co.uk/cropArticle.cfm?topicAreaId=1&contentId=275&mode=bg.

Hesmondalgh, M. and Breakey, C. (2001) *Access and Inclusion for Children with Autistic Spectrum Disorders: 'Let Me In'*, London: Jessica Kingsley.

Hymer, B. and Michel, D. (2002) *Gifted and Talented Learners: Creating a Policy for Inclusion*, Oxon: David Fulton.

Lewis, A. (1995) *Children's Understanding of Disability*, London: Routledge.

Lorenz, S. (2002) *First Steps in Inclusion: A handbook for parents, teachers, governors and LEAs*, London: David Fulton.

Mesibov, G.B., Shea, V. and Schopler, E. (2006) *The TEACCH Approach to Autism Spectrum Disorders*, New York: Springer.

Murray, J. (2010) Farewell to the gifted and talented scheme: the National Academy for Gifted and Talented Youth, which offered extra support for gifted children in state schools, is to be scrapped. Does it matter? *The Guardian: Education*, 2 February 2010.

National Autistic Society (2008) *Our experience of inclusion in mainstream school*: http://www.nas.org.uk/nas/jsp/polopoly.jsp?d=123&a=14609&view=print.

Ofsted (2004) Special Educational Needs and Disability: Towards Inclusive Schools: http://www.ofsted.gov.uk/Ofsted-home/Publications-and-research/Browse-all-by/Documents-by-type/Thematic-reports/Special-educational-needs-and-disability-towards-inclusive-schools.

OPSI (2008) *Education Reform Act 1988*: http://www.opsi.gov.uk/acts/acts1988/ukpga_19880040_en_1.

Plimley, L. and Bowen, M. (2006) *Supporting Pupils with Autistic Spectrum Disorders*, London: Sage.

QCA (2008) *Identifying gifted and talented learners: Characteristics to look for*: http://www.qca.org.uk/qca_1960.aspx.

Reiser (2008) *The Social Model of Disability*: http://inclusion.uwe.ac.uk/inclusionweek/articles/socmod.htm.

Shuttleworth, V. (2000) *The Special Educational Needs Coordinator*, London: Pearson Education.

Somerset County Council (2006) *Meeting the needs of gifted and talented pupils in Somerset schools and colleges*: http://www.six.somerset.gov.uk/equalities/do_download.asp?did=23460.

Teachernet (2008) National Curriculum: http://www.teachernet.gov.uk/management/atoz/n/nationalcurriculum/.

Teachernet (2009) Evaluation of the Special Educational Needs Regional Partnerships: http://www.teachernet.gov.uk/_doc/10513/NfER%20final%20eval%20report.pdf, December 2009.

Teaching Expertise (2008) *Howard Gardner – more than multiple intelligences*: http://www.teachingexpertise.com/articles/howard-gardner-more-than-multiple-intelligences-1678.

Tuckey, B. (2010) The boy in the corner: Why do children with special needs still get such a raw deal? *The Independent: Education*, 11 April 2010.

United Nations Educational, Scientific and Cultural Organization (2004) The Salamanca Statement: http://www.unesco.org/education/pdf/SALAMA_E.PDF.

Westwood, P. (1997) *Commonsense Methods for Children with Special Needs*, London: Routledge.

Part 4

NEW PERSPECTIVES IN EDUCATION

10

Literacy learning
in a postmodern world

Laura-Lee Duval

Contents

Introduction

The limits of my language means the limits of my world.

Wittgenstein (1889–1951)

Contemporary discourse surrounding **literacy** rests upon the premise that it is an essential prerequisite of economic inclusion, i.e. participation in the world of work. In fact, it is so much more. Being literate means being able to make sense of our personal and social worlds; it means being able to communicate, to learn, to inform, to share, to explore, to create, to act and react confidently in a world of words and images. Readers and writers can explore the past, negotiate the present, and shape the future. This is the essence of inclusion: the literate person is equipped to play a full part in society's activities and take advantage of its opportunities. Conversely, low levels of literacy, defined as poor reading, writing, speaking and listening skills (Rose, 2006) limits life chances. For Wittgenstein (an Austrian-born British philosopher), restraints on the ability to use language to encode and decode messages (spoken and written) hinder communications which are those means by which people make and share meaning. Literacy constrains individual and collective thinking and thus understanding (Richter, 2004). Just what constitutes a 'literacy fit for purpose' in a digital age is the subject of much debate.

A **paradigm shift**, meaning a change from one way of thinking to another, in pedagogy, those strategies and methods we use to teach children, is emerging concerning **technoliteracy** (Marsh, 2003). Literacy is no longer limited to the printed page; individuals create and access symbolic and visual texts through computers, mobile phones and a host of audio/visual media (Goodwin, 2005). Such **multimodal** texts use a combination of media to transmit messages to communicate meaning, for example film and computer games (McLean, 2007) (Figure 10.1).

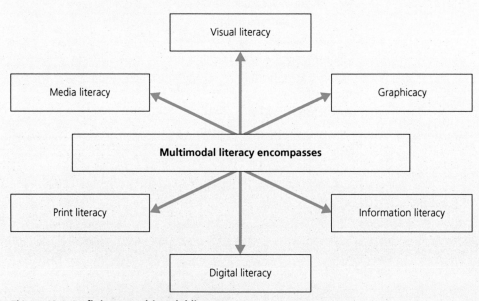

Figure 10.1 Defining a multimodal literacy
Source: Adapted from McLean, 2007.

This chapter explores how the natural enthusiasm for multimodal literacy among the young might be harnessed. The internet has, at one and the same time, expanded and shrunk our world. It has redefined time and distance and unbounded our transactions and interactions. Online we can access goods and services and people and communities anywhere in the world. A technological curriculum is needed, one that engages, empowers and equips individuals for participation in this global marketplace and citizenship in the global village. Literacy is the key to not just surviving but thriving in this postmodern world of diverse and multiple meanings predicated upon increasingly sophisticated and accessible technologies. In an arena where *creativity*, the active involvement of learners in the discourse, design, production and distribution of knowledge is feasible, we need not a re-think but a *new-think* about literacy strategy.

This chapter aims to:

- Help you develop an understanding of the context in which postmodern multimodal literacies are emerging.
- Explore the functional and the creative approaches to literacy learning and teaching.
- Consider how such approaches might be affected by new technologies.
- Reflect upon potential opportunities and threats of embracing new modes of literacy LTA (learning, teaching and assessment) practices for educators.

Read the following case study to help you begin to think about the implications (positive and negative) of using electronic media as pedagogical tools for learners, teachers and institutions.

Case study 10.1
Unprecedented opportunities in online learning

Philip is an education studies lecturer in a modern university. His philosophical stance is aligned with social constructivism, a theory of learning that holds that 'what the learner has to *do* to create knowledge is the important thing' (Biggs, 2003:12). He leads a final year module: 'Competing literacies', and has designed the curriculum to include theoretical, experiential and reflective learning elements. This module focuses on how learners extract meaning from a range of textual forms: books, film, lyrics and computer games. Students also explore the potential opportunities and possible threats of using interactive and connected technologies in literacy teaching. It offers an ideal opportunity to mediate learning activities and assessment using Web 2.0 tools, for example wikis and blogs (Mayes and de Freitas, 2007) to facilitate online collaborative and individual work respectively.

The assessment comprises two parts. First, a collaborative project results in a critical evaluation of textual forms and is presented for peer/tutor view through the VLE (virtual learning environment). Students also act as 'critical friends' to three other groups through the electronic discussion board. Philip considered that using a wiki to e-collaborate would encourage experiential learning and extend students' transferable skills. Second is an individual reflective journal, comprising students' reflections on their theoretical and experiential learning through a series of directed tasks. Presenting an electronic blog would afford the opportunity to stream video and audio files to augment (enhance) and cement their learning.

As Philip redesigned the assessments, he conducted a SWOT analysis (Cottrell, 2003) by listing all the potential strengths, weaknesses, opportunities and threats he could think of. That the modes of activity were now electronic texts was a potential strength; in using a range of textual forms to learn about a range of textual forms students would be *doing* what they were studying. A potential weakness might be the computing competence and confidence of individual students. Addressing this afforded the opportunity for peer expert teaching based on Vygotsky's (1978) social learning theory: IT literate students (the 'experts') would guide the less-skilled in a supportive social environment. Philip then considered the nature and degree of impact of potential threats; risk analysis is about ensuring students' personal safety in any learning environment, including the virtual (Shea, 1994). Just as educational researchers must consider ethics (British Education Research Association, 2004) so are there always ethical issues attendant to what teachers ask learners to do.

Philip knew that social networking sites, as with mobile phone technology, had generated so-called *cyber-bullying* (Woolcock, 2009). He knew of cases of student-to-student bullying online, with messages/images disseminated to 'friends,' and friends of friends compounding the impact. Equally worrying was reported abuse of teaching staff by students reacting to dissatisfaction about their courses and tutors (Nikkhah and Henry, 2009). Philip thus restricted the wiki and blog privacy settings to himself and his two tutor colleagues. Satisfied the students would be safe, he looked forward to the next semester and his 'e-group'.

Questions for discussion

1 *Look again at Philip's SWOT analysis – do you think he has considered all the possible strengths, weaknesses, opportunities and threats? Can you think of any others?*

2 *Do you think that restricting privacy settings in wikis and blogs is 'enough' when working with students in online settings?*

A paradigm shift in literacy pedagogy: meaning over mechanics

Literacy persists as a contemporary issue in education, with a particular focus on teacher strategies for learner achievement. It continues to excite heated debate between and within principal stakeholder groups (government, employers, educational policy-makers, teachers, parents and students). It prompts banner headlines in the media especially when SATs (Standard Assessment Tests), GCSE (General Certificate of Secondary Education) and A (Advanced) level results are released into the public domain. Why should this be? Quite simply, too many children and young people appear to be struggling, first within the education system (compulsory, further and higher) and later in the world of work (DCFS 2009:1). This discussion focuses especially on technoliteracy but it is worth noting another aspect of the multiple nature of literacy, **'vernacular literacy'**. Researchers at the Teaching and Learning Research Programme (TLRP) consider that it is important to appreciate that people develop different sets of literacies depending on the context and goal (personal/educational) and therefore:

> In order to distinguish between those literacies in which people engage for purposes of their own and reading and writing in educational contexts, the term 'vernacular literacy practices' has been used.
>
> TLRP, 2008:2

Table 10.1 **The mismatch that students experience as literacy practitioners in their personal and educational lives**

Student literacy practices	College literacy practices
Tend to be communicative, and:	Tend to be more limited, for example:
• Purposeful to the student	• Reading handouts, PowerPoint presentations and textbooks
• Oriented to a clear audience	
• Generative, involving meaning-making, creativity and getting things done	• The ubiquitous 'doing research on the internet'
• Shared, i.e. interactive, participatory and collaborative	• The writing of essays or reports
• In tune with students' values and identities	• The completion of worksheets
• Non-linear with varied reading paths	• Furthermore, students received mixed messages about the genres and tasks expected of them, for example, the notions of an essay or a report were used in a wide variety of ways as were terms such as to discuss, to research, to analyse
• Multimodal, combining symbols, pictures, colours and music	
• Multimedia, combining paper and electronic media	
• Under the students' control and self-determined in terms of activity, time and place	
• Varied rather than repetitive	
• Learned through participation	

Source: Adapted from TLRP, 2008.

Working with FE teachers and learners, the research identifies a number of common characteristics of vernacular literacy practices which are generally at odds with what they are asked to demonstrate at assessment in a formal educational curriculum. Furthermore, vernacular literacy practices are not viewed as valuable in an educational context.

The findings of this report, *Literacies for Learning in Further Education*, suggested that college educators needed to address aspects of curricular and qualification design, how literacy development could best be supported, CPD (continuing professional development) for staff and practitioner research, and that these findings:

> Have implications for other parts of the education system . . . that can be drawn upon in any pedagogical context.
>
> TLRP, 2008:3

A decade earlier, although not using the term 'vernacular literacy practices' directly, Lankshear and Knobel (1997:1) identified that the general perception is that conventional classroom literacy practices are insufficient to meet the demands of a fast-developing and rapidly changing world. This is a world embedded in technologies that spawn unique forms of literacy. Each makes related demands on users, i.e. the different but related skills needed to read (interpret), for example, film and computer games. The implications of these inadequacies are wide and deep and impact upon national economic performance, community cohesion and personal progression.

Evans (2004) is one of a growing band of literacy educationalists that claims that the disaffection and consequent disengagement of young people with literacy is the result of a mismatch between their experiences of technology in their personal and school lives. While children naturally appropriate technoliteracies in their interactions, for example, with computer games, CDs, DVDs, videos, and their communications through the internet and mobile phones (Kellner and Share, 2005), schools are regularly failing to integrate these new technologies within and across curricula. Where practice is ostensibly innovative, i.e. appears at first glance to be new and exciting, Lankshear and Knobel (1997:2) argue it tends to assimilate technology into existing educational structures rather than accept the challenge that new media might offer. They suggest that generally educators offer precisely the same texts as before but in a different format: an online chapter, a podcast activity, a DVD clip or an SMS (Short Message Service) text. Matthewman et al. (2004:156) agree, describing this as a 'typical "add ICT" to an existing practice approach'. There is a reluctance among educators to explore the pedagogical potential of interactive learning; consequently we continue to teach using traditional methods to a contemporary generation that has come to be termed the connected generation (Johnson, 2005). Indeed, George Siemens, author of *Knowing Knowledge* (2006:42), posits that 'connectivism is a learning theory for the digital age'. By this he means, as he explains on his blog (Siemens, 2009), that:

> Learning has changed over the last several decades. The theories of behaviourism, cognitivism, and constructivism provide an effect view of learning in many environments. They fall short, however, when learning moves into informal, networked, technology-enabled arena.

Sims (2008) concurs with this notion that current literacy LTA practice remains teacher-centred. Primacy, i.e. the greatest importance, is conferred on the notion of a transfer of knowledge, clearly measurable through assessment: the 'effect view of learning' that Siemens describes. Sims (2008:153) argues that:

> These emergent technologies and interactions have opened doorways to new ways of learning and that these deserve new models of thinking about the teaching and learning dynamic.

The result, then, is discord between the knowledge and skills young people expect to learn and develop to function in their world of immersion in multiple textual forms, and the content-heavy, received knowledge focus of the compulsory education system constrained by state mechanisms of social control (for a full discussion of these, see Chapter 7: 'Contemporary policies and issues'). Figure 10.2 outlines the developing context of multimodal literacies with respect to learner experiences and expectations. It is adapted from a presentation delivered at the annual strategic conference of the National Association of Advisers in Computer Education by Niel McLean, Executive Director, Institutional Development, of the British Educational Communications and Technology Agency. It demonstrates a clear paradigm shift in the way the learner and learning are viewed.

According to Matthewman et al. (2004:153), 'Working with multimodal texts creates tensions for English teachers', hence the notion of *competing* rather than

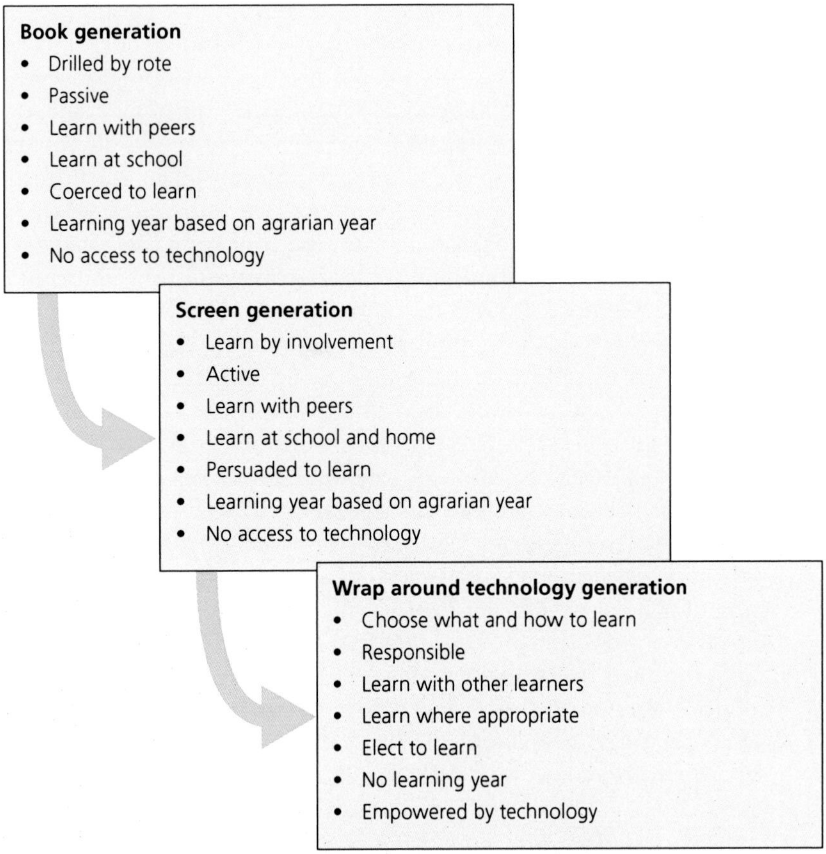

Book generation
- Drilled by rote
- Passive
- Learn with peers
- Learn at school
- Coerced to learn
- Learning year based on agrarian year
- No access to technology

Screen generation
- Learn by involvement
- Active
- Learn with peers
- Learn at school and home
- Persuaded to learn
- Learning year based on agrarian year
- No access to technology

Wrap around technology generation
- Choose what and how to learn
- Responsible
- Learn with other learners
- Learn where appropriate
- Elect to learn
- No learning year
- Empowered by technology

Figure 10.2 **The developing context of multimodal literacies**
Source: Adapted from McLean, 2007.

complementary literacies (Martin, 2005). The view that literacies compete suggests that the conventional way of accessing text is superior, and sufficient to the task of addressing young people's learning needs. Enthusiasts of technoliteracy argue the opposite; they view literacy pedagogy as an approach to literacy teaching in which literacies work together, that is, complement one another. Such an approach demands a change from one way of thinking to another (a paradigm shift) about literacy teaching away from a transferential to a more 'transformatory mindset' (Matthewman, 2004:156), as discussed below.

Transformational learning: the prerequisite of agency and actualisation

Transformational learning is learner-centred; it goes beyond the notion that it is sufficient for teachers to simply transfer knowledge to their learners. Transformational learning is a **meta-cognitive** process; it refers to what individuals *do* with incoming information, how they make meaning from and with it; 'thus education is about conceptual change, not just the acquisition of information' (Biggs, 2003:13). This deficiency or failure to understand the need for transformational learning in a postmodern world was flagged up over a decade ago by Lankshear (1997) in his book *Changing Literacies*. He argued that as the postmodern technological era, characterised by unprecedented change in economic and social spheres, began to take hold in the early 1990s, somehow education, the producer of economic workers and social citizens, was failing to grasp the significance of transformational learning. Technology, primarily the internet, was redefining how we work and how we play; we needed a new way of thinking, of making meaning concerning our transactions and interactions. This is the key point; the ability to make meaning facilitates the development of personal **agency**. In understanding our world and the multiple messages it sends us we are able to respond appropriately and in our own best interests.

Agency is integral to our personal identity; it refers to how we settle upon our self image, how we think about ourselves in the context of the messages we receive about ourselves. These messages can be explicit and direct, for example the attitudes of others towards us, or implicit and indirect, those interpretations we put upon how we are treated, whether or not we seem to fit, whether we are valued. This is what Sartre (1946) called the 'existential self'. Another way in which we work out who we are or might be is by comparing ourselves with the attributes and deficits of others: our 'categorical self'. As children and young people negotiate the world to make sense of it and of themselves in order to make judgements about how to think and act, they are seeking to understand degrees of power and control, their own and that of others. Zimmerman and Cleary (2006:45) consider that 'personal agency refers to one's capability to originate and direct actions for given purposes' and that it is inextricably linked with and 'influenced by the belief in one's effectiveness in performing specific tasks . . . self-efficacy'. In learning settings, children and young people are subordinate to the more powerful and controlling discourses of teachers. Kornfeld and Prothro (2005:218) urge teachers to use 'literature in the classroom [for learners] to explore conceptions of curriculum and teaching'. They use Harry Potter as an exemplar of a text that offers the opportunity for open debate about notions of schooling (form and purpose) and power relations, where:

> teachers and students together examine their lived experience and envision ways to enhance their lives and sense of efficacy in the world around them.
>
> Kornfeld and Prothro, 2005:219

In this way, they argue, the components of self-determination – 'autonomy, relatedness and competence' (Sheldon and Kasser, 2001:35) – are fostered within the individual. In other words, the individual develops personal agency in the context of their socio-cultural world and has the skills, the ability to function, not just economically as a worker, but is psychologically equipped to self-actualise (Maslow, 1954) (Figure 10.3). To self-actualise is to fulfil the potential each of us has as a unique entity, in order to be a critical actor in the story of our own lives.

According to Herrington (2008), agency and actualisation are key characteristics of effective knowledge workers, those who work with information to identify problems and create solutions and who comprise the human capital of competitive business. In a developed society **empowerment** and employability are inextricably linked.

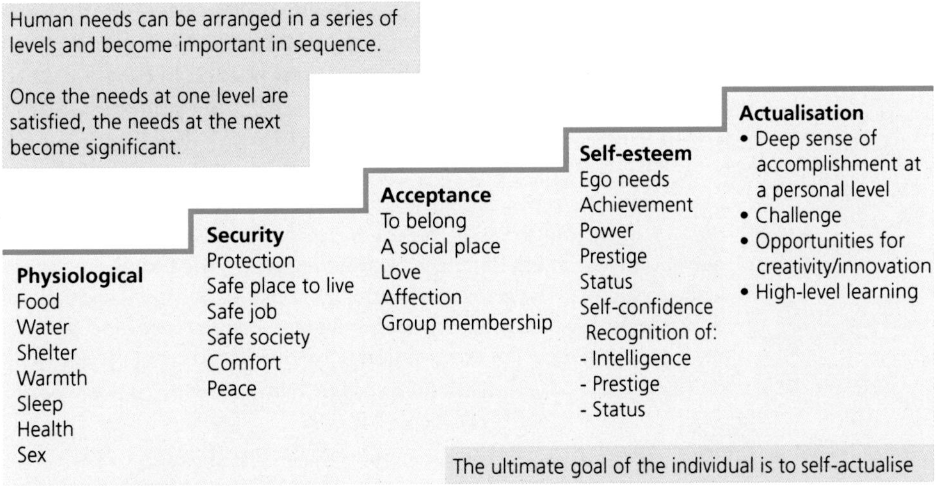

Human needs can be arranged in a series of
levels and become important in sequence.

Once the needs at one level are
satisfied, the needs at the next
become significant.

Actualisation
- Deep sense of
  accomplishment at
  a personal level
- Challenge
- Opportunities for
  creativity/innovation
- High-level learning

Self-esteem
Ego needs
Achievement
Power
Prestige
Status
Self-confidence
  Recognition of:
- Intelligence
- Prestige
- Status

Acceptance
To belong
A social place
Love
Affection
Group membership

Security
Protection
Safe place to live
Safe job
Safe society
Comfort
Peace

Physiological
Food
Water
Shelter
Warmth
Sleep
Health
Sex

The ultimate goal of the individual is to self-actualise

Figure 10.3 **Maslow's hierarchy of needs**
Source: Maslow, 1954.

Connect and explore

Theoretical enquiry outside academia

Undergraduates are regularly encouraged to explore a range of resources to initiate enquiry into particular educational issues but then are often exhorted to return to the body of educational research literature that exists for supporting evidence. In fact, business commits substantial funds and energy into research in order to make the most of its workforce (human capital) through effective management strategies. Understanding how people learn and perform (act and react) is fundamental to educational and employment success. These resources can be very useful as an alternative lens for looking at familiar theories and new works from the business rather than the academic world. In fact, the notion of theoretical research as the preserve of the academic may have had its day. The more graduates that enter the workplace, the greater the bank of research skills employers have at their disposal.

A useful start point is Herrington's (2008) article 6: *Maslow's hierarchy, societal change and the knowledge worker revolution*, available from **http://www.pateo.com/article6.html** (note mention of the characteristics of the postmodern era, effective practice is underpinned by theory and culturally contextualised). To navigate the site for other articles use the left-hand lists.

Radical educational thinkers: using education to oppress

Supporters of a transformational literacy, that which embeds multiple (connected) media in the curriculum, are the radical educators of the day. In parallel with earlier radical thinkers, for example Paulo Freire (1921–1997) and Ivan Illich (1926–2002), they view the 'banking' notion of education, where the teacher deposits knowledge in his or her students, as simply inadequate to meet the challenges of our age. Paulo Freire viewed education as a dialogue between learner and teacher; he was interested in the power of education, particularly how, through literacy, an individual might be personally empowered and so liberated from the constraints of ignorance (Smith, 2002). Ivan Illich believed that the state, through its control of what was learned, when and how and by whom, sought to limit learning to a formal education; he called for the **deschooling** of society:

> Many students, especially those who are poor, intuitively know what the schools do for them. They school them to confuse process and substance. Once these become blurred, a new logic is assumed: the more treatment there is, the better are the results; or, escalation leads to success. The pupil is thereby 'schooled' to confuse teaching with learning, grade advancement with education, a diploma with competence, and fluency with the ability to say something new. His imagination is 'schooled' to accept service in place of value.
>
> Illich, 1973, cited in Smith, 2008: http://www.infed.org/thinkers/et-illic.htm

Freire's (1972) theory, that literacy education (content and modes of delivery) is used to oppress, and Illich and Verne's (1976) assertion that a prescriptive pedagogy serves the oppressors, the rulers of the state, are still pertinent in developing countries. By exposing learners only to sufficient literacy to serve the economic needs of a nation, they argue, is to subjugate the individual, to repress their rights to fulfil their potential, their capacity to self-actualise.

The paucity of definitions of literacy offered by repressive governments clearly demonstrates the positive correlation between the complexity of a society's economic needs and the availability of state-funded mass education. This is particularly evident in developing countries. It thus might be argued that literacy is a **social construct**. A social construct is a set of meanings that a society applies to a particular issue; what a society considers something to mean arises from that society's history (what has gone before) and culture (their world view or ideological perspective). For example, in the Islamic republic of Pakistan, a country where 65 per cent of the population (167 million) is rural, literacy is defined as the ability to 'read a newspaper and write a simple letter in any language' (Latif, 2009:427). In terms of employability, where literacy is not needed to perform work, the state does not provide. In terms of empowerment, as Latif (2009) reports, in a patriarchal, primarily feudal society, literacy can be withheld or limited; only 20 per cent of rural girls have access to the most basic schooling. China also discerns between the literacy needs of rural and urban workers, and this is clearly delineated in their definition of literacy, cited from the online Asia Pacific Literacy Database:

> One who can recognize more than 1500 Chinese characters (for a farmer) and 2000 characters (for an office worker or urban resident).
>
> UNESCO, 2002

Connect and explore

For a wider picture of international definitions of literacy as indicators of economic development, visit the Canadian Education Association (2009) web page: 'Focus on Literacy: framing the debate': **http://www.cea-ace.ca/foo.cfm?subsection=lit&page=fra&subpage=wha&subsubpage=som**.

In more complex societies in the developed world, definitions of literacy are correspondingly more complex, encompassing new concepts; for example the notions of employability, of meaning-making, of agency, of citizenship and of lifelong learning. Yet even this 2001 definition drawn up by the Scottish Executive in their review of adult literacy teaching makes no mention of technology:

> The ability to read, write and use numeracy, to handle information, to express ideas and opinions, to make decisions and solve problems, as family members, workers, citizens and lifelong learners.

> Scottish Executive, 2001, cited in Macdonald, 2005:
> http://www.literacytrust.org.uk/Pubs/macdonald2.html

According to Macdonald (2005) this definition acknowledges that literacy is constructed upon the 'social, cultural, economic and political context of the learner'. This implies an appreciation of the learner as a participant in a dynamic environment, one where literacy is currency. Yet how can this be wholly true if the *technological context* is not given equal weight? This deficit suggests an implicit rather than explicit example of educational oppression. The overt or surface message focuses upon a literacy that empowers the individual, with the ability to read, write and use numeracy etc. but the covert or deeper message focuses on literacy for employability. When Leitch (2006:7) suggests ' "economically valuable skills" is our mantra', is he not arguing for just enough 'literacy to do', rather than sufficient 'literacy to be' or the perpetuation of the status quo (Freire, 1972)? This is a position where literacy creates a functional worker rather than an 'actualised' learner. In this way society continues, with all its inequalities unchallenged.

Functional illiteracy: a national and personal tragedy

The Leitch (2006) *Review of Skills* was commissioned by the government with a remit to research the skills the country has (in its existing and potential workforce) and the skills we need to compete globally. Its vision is aspirational. The aim is that the UK becomes a world-class leader in skills by 2020. This is also the target year for the ending of child poverty associated with a low-skilled workforce (Hirsh, 2008). Lifelong learning is viewed as the corrective response to the estimated 5 (of 35) million working adults lacking **functional literacy**, that is, they are not sufficiently literate to participate in society (Leitch, 2006). Across the whole adult population the figure is higher: one in five, according to Machin and McNally (2005), are ill-equipped to function in a workplace that demands literacy skills. Each year this ill-equipped and therefore disempowered group is joined by poorly qualified school leavers. Half of school leavers leave without 5 GCSEs including English and mathematics at grade C or above (HM Chief Inspector of Education, Children's Services and Skills, 2007/08). Once out of the compulsory schooling system, 20 per cent of teenagers are subsequently designated as NEET (Not in Education, Employment or Training) (DCSF, 2009:1) and are thus vulnerable to a range of social problems such as substance abuse, mental health problems and homelessness (Youth Access, 2009). According to Cassen and Kingdon (2007) these statistics demonstrate that social disadvantage, identified as low levels of economic, social and cultural capital continues or perpetuates for a significant proportion of society. Clearly the 'literacy problem' has not been resolved for marginalised groups in society. Such groups are separated from the rest of society, for example gypsy travellers, refugees, and the impoverished of any ethnic group (all people have an ethnicity). For them, social disadvantage and attendant low expectations are passed from one generation to the next (Tomlinson, 2008).

The case for literacy initiatives that work and consequently begin the process of improving social justice and upgrading outcomes for such groups (see Chapter 7: 'Contemporary policies and issues') is clearly compelling. Less evident, because it is more difficult to isolate and quantify, is the impact of disengagement (boredom) that results in achievements being of a lower academic level than might have been the case had a learning event been more stimulating. According to Mann and Robinson (2009:243):

> boredom stems from a situation where none of the possible things that a person can realistically do appeal to the person in question. This renders the person inactive, and generally unhappy.

Inactive, unhappy learners do not learn; they suffer the learning environment until they can escape it for activities that are meaningful to them. This is the argument of advocates of multimodal literacies, that before we can teach, we must reach.

Moving towards a postmodern definition of literacy

The mantra of the Blair government on election in 1997 was 'Education, Education, Education', meaning that education was the key to a more prosperous future for the nation and the individual. A decade later, investment in education had risen significantly and accounted for 5.6 per cent GDP (Gross Domestic Product), with more teachers and teacher-support workers employed in more schools than ever before (Coughlan, 2007). Yet, despite funding a wholesale overhaul of every aspect of educational provision and implementing a raft of literacy initiatives (e.g. Book Start Crawl to encourage early reading; Reading is Fundamental, UK, to encourage parental involvement; and Reading Connects, which encourages whole school reading communities), low levels of achievement persist among disadvantaged groups and levels of truancy (which may be an indicator of boredom) are rising across the whole state school student population (Tobin, 2009). Real world literacy has moved beyond the currently state-accepted definition of: reading and writing, speaking and listening. In fact, speaking and listening were added only recently as a direct result of the Rose Report: an independent review of the teaching of early reading (2006) (Palmer, 2006). Literacy, like numeracy, continues to attract particular government scrutiny. The main points of Labour's literacy strategy are outlined in the history box opposite.

History of education

A brief review of literacy strategies

1996   David Blunkett (Labour Shadow Education Minister) tasked to review literacy teaching in primary schools and piloted the 'Literacy Hour' as part of the National Literacy Project (NLP) for Key Stages 1 and 2.

1998   The NLP gave rise to a national roll-out of the National Literacy Strategy (NLS) in the context of the National Curriculum and SATs (Standard Assessment Tests) at Key Stages 1, 2 and 3.

2001   The secondary stage of the strategy rolled out for Key Stage 3.

2003   Report 'Excellence and Enjoyment: A Strategy for Primary Schools' attempted to address an overemphasis on the teaching of mechanical skills to the detriment of reading for pleasure and writing creatively.

2005   Strategy for Key Stage 4 completed, strategies renamed as Primary National Strategy and Secondary National Strategy to incorporate the approaches of the existing literacy and numeracy strategies.

2006   Following the Rose Report (2006), the primary framework for literacy and mathematics added 'speaking and listening' to 'reading and writing' to expand the existing definition of literacy.

2008   Key Stage 3 SATs abolished following complaints that they encourage teaching to the test, create anxiety, are unreliable and costly and are not a reliable indicator of progression and potential at age fourteen.

2009   Publication of the Rose Report (2009): 'An independent review of the primary curriculum' (further discussion in text).

Source: Adapted from the website of the Literacy Trust: http://www.literacytrust.org.uk/Policy/strat.html#Background.

You are strongly recommended to consult the website of the National Literacy Trust, a wealth of all things 'literary' including a wide range of pertinent research and practical resources. As you read through, consider the locus of power in educational policy-making and implementation; are teachers agents of the state or are they agents of change, and are these notions mutually exclusive? The next section explores the parameters of teacher power. This is important in moving into a new postmodern era of literacy teaching; stakeholders in education need to be clear about what postmodern literacy might be, and what it might demand in terms of support and resources. According to Matthewman et al. (2004:154), literacy strategy in schools uses a mainly:

> psychological and operational approach which focuses on the individual's acquisition of basic skills of language competence.

Yet there are alternative approaches that, taken together, might reasonably extend this simplistic model of literacy to a more complex set of aims and objectives more suited to the diverse nature of contemporary multimodal literacies. Matthewman et al. (2004) argue for a model that draws from the socio-cultural context, the 'reading the word and the world' approach put forward by Freire and

Macedo (1987, cited in Matthewman et al., 2004:154). Critical literacy emerges from this socio-cultural premise; it:

> stresses the active critiquing of power relations within texts in the interests of inclusion and social justice... Its aim is to empower . . . in terms of rewriting, transforming and creating texts (and by implication challenging the social and cultural status quo.
>
> Matthewman et al., 2004:155

In so doing it involves active engagement with a text to the extent that it can be challenged and changed by technoliterate readers, a far cry from the passive acceptance of received knowledge spawned by a dominant ideology.

Literacy: whose responsibility, whose ideology?

Free provision and compulsory duration of the study of literacy (reading and writing) and indeed numeracy for the masses as determined by the state is linked with techno-logical advances. As the creation of wealth, through production and commerce, becomes increasingly sophisticated, so the need for an increasingly literate and numerate workforce becomes evident. Nineteenth-century industrialisation enabled mass production and demanded mass free education; this interrelationship between the economy and the education system was cast in the form of the 1870 Elementary Education Act, also known as the Forster Act (Gillard, 2007). At this time the state con-trolled who learned, when and for how long; however, the locus of control of teach-ing itself, that is, who decided curriculum content and modes of delivery, rested with teachers. This teacher autonomy was ensconced in law by the Balfour Act (1902) which introduced secondary education and teacher training. This Act defined the role of the teacher and the position of the state (as the national Board of Education):

> The high function of the teacher was to prepare the child for the life of a good citizen, to create or foster the aptitude for work and the intelligent use of leisure. The only uni-formity of practice the Board wishes to see is that all teachers should think for them-selves and adapt the curriculum to the needs of the children in their charge.
>
> Board of Education, 1905, cited in Gillard, 2007: http://dialspace.dial.pipex.com/ prod/dialspace/town/plaza/kbr30/history/text03.shtml

However, disquiet about mass educational achievement rumbled through the corridors of power. As agents of the state but not especially accountable to it, the teaching profession was viewed as a law unto itself. The state school system existed to provide suitably skilled candidates for the workplace in the context of a marketplace that was to remain produc-tion based and labour intensive for generations. As the need for literate workers increased over time, employers began to complain to government that school leavers were unequal to the demands of a modern industrial society. This turned the spotlight on the educa-tors; there was a sense of mystery surrounding what teachers actually taught, an enigma which became known as the 'Secret Garden of the Curriculum'.

This was the pivotal theme of Callaghan's (Labour Prime Minister) 1976 Ruskin speech where education, and thus literacy, was seen as too important to leave to chance or to teachers. This prompted the 'Great Debate' (Adams and Calvert, 2005:2) which effectively terminated a teacher-driven curriculum and served as the precursor of a National Curriculum. In 1979 the political ideology of the debate changed, swinging to the right with the election of Margaret Thatcher. By 1988, for the first time, the Secretary of State was to be responsible for all the dimensions of the curriculum; centralisation of the what, who, where, when and how of education was under total government control.

The National Curriculum was drawn up by a **quango** (quasi-autonomous non-government organisation); no teachers were involved. It was implemented in 1988. The election of New Labour (1997) did not see its overturn despite the change in political perspectives. National politics, i.e. between left and right, are traditionally polarised and new governments notorious for undoing what a previous administration has done in the name of ideology; not this time. The National Curriculum remained, and Education Minister David Blunkett was determined to focus the spotlight on the processes and products, the quantity and quality of literacy teaching. State control of the curriculum allowed the prescription of every minute of the daily literacy hour:

> . . . every teacher in the land received a personal copy of its Framework for Teaching, setting out term-by-term coverage, down to the last spelling rule.
>
> Palmer, 2006:1

In reviewing the literacy hour, Palmer (2006) concludes that literacy teaching has improved in terms of bringing back **phonics**, and ensuring that teachers are fully versed in the mechanics of reading and writing. Phonics, now referred to as synthetic phonics, is a teaching methodology that uses the sounds made by small groups of letters (phonemes) as building blocks which children blend to make words. The system had been replaced in the 1960s by whole-word recognition techniques such as 'look and say' as this avoided rote learning of the alphabet. This method was criticised, however, for allowing children to guess words based on other clues on the page, or to memorise stories, thus masking their true reading abilities (Blair, 2005). Palmer (2006) worries that even the return of phonics will not be sufficient to foster a notion of reading for pleasure and writing creatively given what she regards as the prevailing testing culture in both primary and secondary strategies.

 Connect and explore

For a pertinent analysis of the strictures or constraints of the testing criteria and their emphasis on technical skills to the detriment of the meaning of the story, read **D'Arcy** (2002) 'A comparison of two types of response, interpretive and skills-based, to a Yr 6 story: "Three Wishes"'. In this paper D'Arcy emphasises the need for early development of critical thinking skills, namely evidence of engagement (how did the text make me feel?) and appreciation (how did the author do that?). These skills are transferable when different media are deemed to be 'textual'. Faced with a text message, a film, a song or a computer game, discerning 'readers' will be skilled in engagement and appreciation and thus able to critically evaluate how they felt (about what they learned/experienced) and how the author/creator of the message achieved that. Engagement and appreciation are essential to augment and cement learning throughout life. The role of the teacher must therefore be to get them reading, and to *keep* them reading.

Where did all the fun go and why does it matter?

The themes of engagement and appreciation of a text are apparent in the government's report 'Excellence and Enjoyment: A Strategy for Primary Schools' (DfES, 2003). In the introduction, Charles Clarke (the then Secretary of State for Education and Skills) states that 'excellent teaching gives children the life chances they deserve' and 'enjoyment is the birthright of every child'. In the context of rigorous testing, these statements may appear rather incongruous (Palmer, 2006) but there is a subtle shift in who is responsible for excellence and enjoyment:

> I want every primary school to be able to build on their own strengths to serve the needs of their own children. To do this, they will work with parents and the whole community; they will think creatively about how they use the skills of everyone in the school. And they themselves will take responsibility for making what they do better all the time. I want every school to drive its own improvement, to set its own challenging targets, and to work tirelessly to build on success.
>
> Clarke, 2003, quoted in DfES, 2003:2

This implies the need for a less prescriptive primary curriculum, an implication that had not filtered through when the Rose Review (2006) was announced.

In the Controversies box which follows, we will consider the different goals of reading, and whether literacy is 'about' meaning – i.e. the content of what is written (e.g. a story) – or **mechanics** – i.e. the process of reading and understanding language.

Controversies

'It is possible to read for meaning and mechanics'

Agree:

- The literacy hour can and does include popular books as a source for encouraging the understanding of language and its mechanics.
- It may be helpful to children if the passage they are given for comprehension or as part of a vocabulary exercise is one that they recognise.

Disagree:

- The idea of 'reading for pleasure' and writing creatively is not easily combined with the testing strategy culture at both primary and secondary levels (Palmer, 2006).
- A number of popular children's authors including Philip Pullman, Michael Rosen and Jacqueline Wilson argue that: 'Books – proper books – in all their richness, completeness and variety – lie at the heart of real achievement in both reading and writing' (Powling, 2006:26). Therefore, to treat them as anything other than complete entities to be enjoyed is to deny their purpose.
- Rosen challenges the use of reading mechanically when asking young people to 'count the adjectives in the first page of Harry Potter' (Rosen, 2005, quoted in

Katbamma, 2005), and in the same *Guardian* interview adds: 'The literacy hour doesn't encourage the idea that books are for you, that they are yours. It says that they are texts which can be quizzed.'

- When presenting pupils with short passages from books to illustrate grammatical structures and vocabulary there is an underlying flawed assumption that children's language development is dependent upon first recognising and labelling it. In fact, from approximately four years old children have been using such structures in their speech (Powling, 2006).

What do you think? Where do you stand in this debate?

Can you enjoy a text first and then 'dissect it' for syntax or similar? Does that spoil the memory of it? Does it put readers off reading, knowing that a post-mortem of a favourite character or story must inevitably follow? D'Arcy (2002) argued for interpretive skills (engagement and appreciation) to be natural products of the reading process but are they the only ones? Is there a problem if books are categorised as either learning tools or pleasurable activities (the first may well become associated with school and the second with home)? What of children whose home is a bookless zone?

This is an interesting debate to reflect upon when considering the need to engage children and young people in the reading process, and to counter their reluctance in the face of multiple distractions.

Challenging reluctancy: an international imperative

In his book *Promoting Reading for Pleasure in the Primary School* Lockwood, a lecturer in English and Education (2008), draws attention to the findings of international research carried out on behalf of the OECD (Organisation for Economic Co-operation and Development) into the reading habits of 15-year-olds. The report concluded:

- Being more enthusiastic about reading and being a frequent reader was more of an advantage on its own than having well-educated parents in good jobs.
- Finding ways to engage students in reading may be one of the most effective ways to leverage social change. (OECD, 2003, cited in Lockwood, 2008:4)

These remarkable claims have substantive implications for initiatives to redress social injustice as well as for reading and writing, that is, decoding and encoding texts, in the context of the connected generation. They provide **empirical evidence** that reading for pleasure changes lives. Yet, so far, there has been little, if any, tangible return on literacy efforts despite all the initiatives, directives, strands and standards. Teachers have tried to make students do it, and do more of it more often with more assessments to little or no avail. What needs redefining, advocates of multimodal literacy argue, is what 'it' is. They argue that technology can (and must) be used in the pursuit of excellence and enjoyment to develop the skills of engagement and appreciation in postmodern readers and writers. As we shall see in the next section, they appear, in Sir Jim Rose, to have found a champion.

↖ *Connect and explore*

Read the full report:

Kirsch, I. et al. (2000) *Reading for Change: Performance and Engagement. Results from PISA 2000*, available from: **www.oecd.org/dataoecd/43/54/33690904.pdf**.

Of particular interest and relevance are Chapters 5: 'The reading engagement of 15-year-olds', and 16: 'The relationship between background characteristics and reading literacy'.

Cometh the hour; cometh the report?

Rose's (2009) latest independent review appears to address this deficit in literary achievement. Reviewing the whole primary curriculum in 2009, the report firmly establishes ICT (information and communications technology) as one of the four cornerstones (alongside literacy, numeracy and personal development) of a curriculum fit for purpose. Rose captures precisely what proponents of a digital literacy have been calling for:

> To argue against the importance of ICT in the primary curriculum is to ignore the increasing digitization of information worldwide. This will require digital literacy of all children for their full participation in society. Information required for leisure, work, finance, communication and citizenship will be mediated electronically. In all branches of knowledge, all professions and all vocations, the effective use of new technologies will be vital. Children not only need to learn to use specific devices and applications, they also need to understand the fundamental concepts of safe and critical use. The review therefore calls for an understanding of technology to be taught and ingrained in curriculum design and delivery.
>
> Rose, 2009:70

There is here a recognition that a digital literacy is not about fads and fashions but a genuine acknowledgement of the link between human activity and technology in every sphere of life. George Cole, a journalist who regularly reports on ICT and education in the Guardian Online (2009) interviewed key players in this field about the report. Generally the reception of Rose's recommendation has been positive. NAACE (the National Association of Advisors for Computers in Education) welcomed the move to embed ICT in the curriculum and the provision of teacher training and support. BECTA (British Education Communications and Technology Agency) submitted five key skills areas to the review: finding and selecting information, creating, manipulating and processing information, collaborating, communicating and sharing information, and refining and improving work. These key skills all rest upon D'Arcy's (2002) notions of engagement and appreciation as being pivotal to critical reading and writing. The key, according to BECTA's executive director (quoted in Cole, 2009) is:

> that children are prepared and really equipped to make intelligent and discriminatory use of the technology.

Making intelligent and discriminatory use of technology is what the Rose Report (2006:70) describes as the 'fundamental concepts of safe and critical use' that must be taught. This presupposes, of course, that teachers have an understanding of those fundamental concepts, especially in the context of an apparently less restrictive literacy curriculum. The DCSF (2009:2) report *Your child, your school, our future: Building a twenty-first century school system* suggests that the daily literacy hour is to remain in place but will no longer be prescriptive in content, nor centrally supported (resourced). While the former might be cause for celebration, the latter has created some concern. The idea is that 'good' schools will connect with lower-performing schools to share best practice and resources. It will be interesting to see whether this good (and cheap) intention manifests. The intention to reduce investment in education (Wintour and Curtis, 2009), of which literacy is the lynchpin (Goodwin, 2005), is a clear indicator that educationalists need to do more with less, and more so since the credit crunch of 2008/09. Rose's (2009) recommendations have been accepted by the government and an implementation date of 2011 has been set (DCSF, 2009). In 2010, however, there has been a General Election which has resulted in a change in government and thus a change in political perspectives (although, as we saw earlier, a long-awaited change of government in 1997 did not result in the anticipated demise of the National Curriculum).

The possible implications of political change

Untangling party political rhetoric concerning educational debates is not straightforward; most issues are reduced to sound-bites and snappy slogans. A search of the Conservative's school reform plan 'Raising the bar: Closing the gap' (2007) has no entries for ICT or computer, and four for technology. Rather the focus is upon behaviour management strategies including parental contracts. The section ends with this statement:

> Poor behaviour and truancy from school overwhelmingly stem from a fundamental disengagement from education. And this disengagement begins at an early age: it starts when a child first begins to read.
>
> Conservatives, 2007:27

This is an astonishing statement especially as the only remedy (in a report that is already over two years old: 'Learning to read: Reading to learn') is a single proposal to improve training in synthetic phonics for teachers. While this might well be appropriate, what of the wider world, the digital world in which even very young children are not just engaged but immersed? There is a hint of back to basics here, a return to a traditional transferential system of teaching where the teacher banks knowledge in his or her passive and compliant learners. The reality is that we have nowhere to go back to; today's connected generation need a connected education from the outset. This is the fundamental concept underpinning the teaching of literacy by another independent review, the Cambridge Primary Review: 'Children, their world, their education' (Alexander, 2009). This sets out the rationale for and recommendations of the analysis of a significant body of research into all aspects of primary education undertaken by over 100 academics and educationalists over a six-year period. According to Mortimer (2009), none of the mainstream political parties has yet accepted its findings. According to an analysis of its implications for literacy by the National Literacy Trust (NLT) it:

> recommends that ICT should remain part of the language, oracy and literacy domain of learning. This is a significant diversion from the Jim Rose review, which recommends that ICT be its own cross curricula discipline.
>
> NLT, 2009

The NLT welcome this, believing that an integration of ICT into the literacy domain would:

> deconstruct the unhelpful false divide between literacy and digital or media literacy . . . [it would] help bridge the gap between online and offline literacy.
>
> NLT, 2009, online

This is an interesting diversification from Rose's (2009:70) call for 'technology to be . . . ingrained in curriculum design and delivery'. This implies that technology would be embedded in any literacy domain *as well as* all the other curricula domains. Rose (2006) had already introduced oracy, that is, listening and speaking, to the primary literacy curriculum in 2006 and emphasised the importance of comprehension and communication through the reintroduction of synthetic phonics. Linebarger (2004) has conducted significant research demonstrating the potential language benefits of television for infants and toddlers; might there not therefore be a role for *any* media offering an audio and visual component in early reading? According to Mioduser et al. (2000), the evidence for the use of computer-based instruction for young children (5–6 years), especially those at high risk of developing learning disabilities, is compelling:

> Results clearly indicated that children at high risk who received the reading intervention program with computer materials significantly improved their phonological awareness, word recognition, and letter naming skills relative to their peers who received a reading intervention program with only printed materials and those who received no formal reading intervention program.
>
> Mioduser, et al., 2000:54

Literacy is too important to be embroiled in power politics at any level. Policy-makers are tasked to create cohesive and effective strategies that promote literacy learning using all the means at their disposal.

Activity

Notions of power sharing to navigate a digital world

Use the search facility in YouTube: (**http://youtube.com**) to locate the video *Technology Fear Factor in Education*. (When you use YouTube to augment your learning, look to the right to see and select related videos.) This short but highly pertinent video message was ▶

created by Vikki Davis ('Cool Cat'). A keen teacher/technocrat, she charges parents in particular to go with their children on this incredible journey into the virtual world. Her website (http://coolcatteacher.blogspot.com) is a model of good practice when it comes to the radical notion of teachers and learners working together to formulate just what new (or postmodern) knowledge might be. She is able to relinquish her (traditional) power as a teacher to the extent that she is an active learner alongside her pupils in what Illich and Verne (1976) would have called a learning community.

Embracing technoliteracies: face the fear and do it anyway

Contemporary radical thinkers might argue that there are no rational or reasonable arguments for spurning technoliteracies simply because it is not a matter of choice; **telematics** (the blending of technologies) is entrenched in the 3D sensate, interactive, interconnected world of contemporary learners from a very young age (Peltoniemi, 2003). In response to Rose's (2009) review, BECTA (cited in Cole, 2009) raises the concern that around 70 per cent of primary schools do not use technology well with respect to system support, staff training and student innovation. The first conflict for young learners is that their 3D world is not generally replicated, let alone extended, in their school experiences. Instead, many leave their multimodal world at the school gate and enter a 2D, primarily passive learning environment. It is perhaps not surprising that they feel increasingly disconnected and at an increasingly young age. In recognition of this disparity and to counter it, the Rose Review (2009) suggests that some of the technological skills which are currently introduced in Key Stage 3 should be brought in much earlier. Current and future educators should therefore set aside their own ideological beliefs (and any reluctance) in order to 'approach the whole area from an appropriately skeptical and socially critical perspective' (Lankshear and Knobel:2, 1997:138).

Ideological beliefs are by their nature entrenched, not easy to uproot. Reluctancies can take many forms: fear of the unknown (what does this mean to me?); fear of change (what will happen if?); fear of loss of status (in this situation my learner knows more than me, what if my ignorance is detected?); fear of the new (how does this technology work?); fear of failure (supposing it all goes wrong?) and fear of exposure (I just want to keep my head down and do my job) (Kimber, 2002). Some or all of these fears manifest when considering competing literacies. There are the innovators (those that are first to journey into a new virtual world) and there are the tokenists (those that take a day trip in order to tick a box). For some, our language and our stories are so culturally important to us that the very notion of using text-speak to translate Shakespeare, or of teaching history through computer games, may very well be anathema, representing not education but 'edutainment'. The purist argument has no place in the diversity of postmodern literacy. To teach, one must first reach; failure is not an option: the personal costs are too high and the economic benefits too great.

The means of delivering learning is being revolutionised. In a bid to cut costs the city of San Francisco intends to replace *all* textbooks with digital versions and has started the process (California Learning Resource Network, 2009). In other US states schools are piloting smart phones (PDAs, personal digital assistants) as learning tools in the classroom and in the home (Long, 2009). As the pilot leader explains:

> Cell phones aren't going to go away. Mobile technology isn't going away . . . Right now what we're telling kids is 'You go home and use whatever technology you want but when you get to school we're going to ask you to step back in time.' It doesn't make any sense.
>
> Menchofer, Ohio Technology Coordinator, quoted in Long, 2009

Advocates of a multimodal literacy recognise the reality of a world immersed in technology and are beginning to explore what the shape of new-thinking might be.

 **Stop and reflect**

Before you read on, think about your relationships with technology in your own life. Is it a relationship based on convenience or necessity? What devices do you have access to and how would you feel if that access were denied you? Some students have difficulty in avoiding potential distractions when studying, for example msn messenger, Facebook and texting; but really, do we need to be available 24/7? Think back, how did you connect with people before these connective technologies arrived? Who did you ask before you asked Google?

Embracing technoliteracies: seeing through a glass darkly

We will explore the pedagogical opportunities and threats of these and other technologies in the next chapter. For now we need to have a rationale for investing time, energy and effort in new-thinking, because the notion that learning should be fun, that it should be creative, that it should be conducted in what might be termed 'free space' through the offerings of multimodal media, challenges our existing order. This is a journey with an unspecified destination but one that is essential if we are to fully explore what literacy is and why it matters if we (collectively and individually) are not just to survive but thrive in a globalised world constructed upon the efficacy of technologically mediated communication. Postmodernism deconstructs barriers to individual progression; it is a move away from the old, comfortable order of things through the accessibility of mass communications (including text and images) to the individual. It is a world of opportunities, and equally a world of threats. There are divides (digital and generational). What there is not is the option to stay where we are. An interesting reflection is that, actually, the journey may not be particularly long, simply because the future is coming to us; we are the prosumers (producer/consumer) of the now. If you do no other activity in this chapter, do this next one!

Activity

Meet the new you

Use the search facility in YouTube to locate the video *Prosumers*.

How did you engage with this text? How did it make you feel? What did you appreciate about this text? Can you identify the devices the creator used to make you feel like this? What age group of learners would you share this with? Does the message empower or enslave?

Packing the essentials for a new journey: appreciating contextual concepts

All new learning demands that we arm ourselves with an appropriate set of tools; the means we have to critically evaluate the topic at hand. We need to know what **postmodernism** is, and what *ideology* is, in order to contextualise how readers and writers are meaning-makers. Messages are underpinned and overlaid by our conscious and unconscious beliefs be they narrative or informative (loosely defined as fictional/non-fictional) and independent of the medium used to transmit/receive them. In the literate classroom:

> [Readers] bring to a text their social and cultural histories. At the same time the texts they read and the talk that occurs around that reading are constantly reshaping these social and cultural identities.
>
> Deblase, 2003:624

The learning potential of different media can only be fully exploited if we understand the learning process. Bloom's (1956) *Taxonomy of Learning Domains* models *how learners learn* and their likely aspirations. It thus provides a means of mapping developmental needs with mediated activities designed to foster engagement to achieve multiple goals. An example of this might be an early years computer game that makes learning spelling fun, and at the same time develops hand–eye coordination.

The next step is to consider *what a text is*, or might be, to take our understanding from the general to the specific. It is important in any discourse to ensure that all participants agree a contextualised definition for the subject under investigation. Language is a social construct, expressed through signs and signifiers (actual words and their imposed meanings). A brief review of the work of Saussere (1857–1913) provides a framework within which to debate the perceived opportunities and threats of text-speak – the language of much mobile and virtual communication. From here we move to the notion of **multiple literacies** which hinges upon the fact that the word 'text' no longer signifies purely the concept of the written (usually printed) word. Rather it has come to encompass any mediated message. The final tool we need is an understanding of potential barriers to participation in digital literacy. This is the notion of **digital divides** concerning an individual's access to and attitude towards technology.

Postmodernism

This section rests upon the premise that technoliteracy must emerge; this is because, quite simply, traditional literacy practice associated with the modern era is insufficient for the demands of a (postmodern) society powered by technology (Evans, 2004). An age is defined by historic changes in the way members of a society see things (what we may broadly think of as art/architecture), think about things (theory) and produce things (economics). Therefore, an age is characterised by commonly held values and beliefs and their manifestations in every facet of cultural life through societal structures and operations.

> ↖ *Connect and explore*
>
> For a very accessible discussion of historic ages and theories of progress, read **Curtis and Pettigrew** (2009) *Learning in Contemporary Culture*.

In postmodernism, the prefix 'post' (meaning 'after') has been added to the term used to describe the period 1900–1990 (approximately) according to Haralambos and Holborn (2008). This was known as the modern age (Latin 'modo' meaning 'just now'). So postmodernism challenges the tenets of the modern age, i.e. that time immediately before this time. Haralambos and Holborn (2008) identify the guiding principles of western culture during the greater part of the twentieth century as a belief in:

- The possibility of human progress.
- The superiority of rational thought over emotion.
- Technology and science to resolve human problems.
- Ability and rights of humans to shape their own lives.
- Manufacturing to improve living standards.

Postmodernism is not straightforward to define because it is the story of where we are living at present. It must come about because:

> In effect we have gone beyond the world view of modernism, it is an inadequate term to describe *the diversity and pace of change we are experiencing* . . . but we use this term knowing that it does not specify where we are going . . .
>
> Jenks, 1995, cited in Appignanesi and Garratt, 1999:3

Bleakley (2006) discusses the links between education and the postmodern condition made by Lyotard (1984) in his book *The Postmodern Condition: A Report on Knowledge*. Lyotard argued that education was becoming commodified (it was turning into something that could be bought and sold). Commodification prized performativity (doing) and information over **scholarship** (knowing) because the computer had become the major shaping force upon educational practices.

The concept of scholarship – the notion of pursuing knowledge for its own sake – is one of the arguments against accepting technology put forward by those wishing to conserve what they view as ideologically appropriate. This is an example of hegemonic practice. A hegemony is the dominant elite in any society and it is in their interests to control what is known and by whom. McLaren (1993:7) explores this notion through the lens of a Freirian perspective:

> My central argument is that pedagogies always produce specific forms of practical competency – literacies – that for the most part have been pressed into the service of the dominant culture. This situation occurs because of the ways in which knowledge is inscribed in the social: certain linguistic competencies, forms of narrative address, and signs of ideological solidarity are privileged over others.

This argument is perhaps the most telling we have met so far. British society is in transition, as the earlier quote suggests, and is almost schizophrenic about its identity. Genuine debate about diversity is stifled; the laws that rightly protect various groups from tangible expressions of hostility may well have driven them underground where they fester in the darkness of ignorance. Change creates fear; fear induces prejudice; prejudice can quickly become extremism. For those who have thrived on the notion of a single knowledge being always right and unquestionable, a diverse postmodern education is potentially subversive. It may even be dangerous because if knowledge is socially constructed (invented by the people for the people) then the dominant groups are under threat. The education system is an agent of social control through the transmission of cultural invariables (Lawton, 1986). When those variables are challenged then the (hegemonic) status quo is at risk. Furthermore, postmodern constructivism is the *equal* valuing of each concept of socially constructed knowledge(s). Knowledge is constructed by information, the conduit of which is technology, ergo (therefore) technology itself is dangerous and its use must be controlled if not censored. According to Said (1999:1),

> There can be no civilized society in which the life of the mind is ruled dogmatically by laws of what is forbidden and what cannot be read.

What Said is referring to is that the internet makes information freely available to ordinary people. What they read is not restricted to the materials their rulers or government would wish them to read. Ordinary people have access to extraordinary banks of information. They can come together online and collaborate to challenge the status quo (how things are) of their country and culture. As well as receiving messages, they can also transmit. It is this access, to mass broadcasting, that makes rulers uncomfortable. Similarly individuals can exchange messages and intimacies without first meeting. It is this notion, of inappropriate and illusory relationships, that makes those responsible for the well-being of children and young people uncomfortable. It is the role of parents and educators to help them stay safe and sensible, the 'fundamental concepts' Rose (2006:70) refers to.

Whether children and young people read from a page or a screen, the task of the educator is to instil critical reading strategies. According to Kurland (2002), critical readers are empowered to engage in dialogue with a text to ask what it says (on the lines), what it means (between the lines) and whether it matters (beyond the lines). In this way they develop sophisticated strategies capable of identifying, contextualising and evaluating ideologies.

↖ *Connect and explore*

Dan Kurland's excellent website offers resources about:

- Learning to read and write
- Critical reading and critical thinking
- Reading ideas as well as words
- The ingredients of texts
- What a text says, does and means
- A grammar for reading and writing.

Kurland, D. (2002) How the Language Really Works: The Fundamentals of Critical Reading and Effective Writing: **http://www.criticalreading.com/index.html**

Can any text be free of ideology? According to Hollindale, a lecturer in English and critic of children's fiction (1992), the answer is no, because there is always evidence of the writer's aim in writing (sending or publishing the message) in the first place. Ideology is deemed a conceptual category (Wallace, 2009), that is, it is a way of thinking about sets (categories) of ideas and beliefs or concepts. These are ways of connecting ideas that are similar at a general level but when defined more specifically the definition reflects the context. For example, an educationalist will define ideology in one way, an economist slightly (but significantly) differently:

> At its most basic level, it can be used to refer to a set of beliefs and ideas which inform all the practices of a profession such as teaching . . . they inform . . . training . . . reflect . . . values [and] represent what appear to be 'common-sense' ideas – ideas which are taken for granted and rarely questioned or analysed analytically.
>
> Wallace, 2009:133

Wallace (2009) goes on to suggest that the work of Saussure (which we discuss below under the heading 'What is a text?') underpins the theories of Althusser (1918–90), a Marxist academic who postulated that ideology is so critical to the structure of society that individuals actually derive personal identity from the dominant cultural structures or 'ideological state apparatuses, one of which was education' (p. 133). It is not just what we read as part of the curriculum that contributes to our own ideologies but what we read as we operate within the societal systems we inhabit. Wallace (2009) discusses these readings as tangible signs: how informational posters are designed and displayed, and intangible signs, how the teacher talks to pupils, how the classroom is (hierarchically) designed – all these elements send messages. In this theory the written word, the visual image, the spoken word, even the physical staging of the learning environment are all messages. For the child who belongs to the dominant culture (in terms of colour, class and creed), which is the originator and perpetrator of these signs, there is little to fear; the process of absorption or interpellation, as Althusser termed it (Felluga, 2003), into that culture is not unsettling. For the child who lacks the appropriate **habitus** (Bourdieu, 1998), that is, the ability to receive and absorb this dominant cultural capital, there is no adaptive mechanism supplied by the system (Dumais, 2002): this child will simply sink or swim. In a postmodern society with its attendant diversities, with respect to colour, class and creed, and in a post-welfare society predicated on a contracting welfare state (Ainley, 1999), this position is neither attractive nor tenable from any ideological stance. A **post-welfare society** is one in which the adult individual is expected to meet their own needs, to be economically self-sufficient rather than dependent upon the state as provider.

Critical reading strategies are not just tools to discern the provenance of messages. They are the tools through which we might interpret the messages that we receive about who we are, the world we live in, and what it (this life) is all about (Sartre, 1946). This is important because, according to Sartre (1905–1980), an influential French existentialist philosopher, each of us has two essential selves. The first is our existential self: who am I? The second is our categorical self (because it references one individual against another): who am I compared with you? When a child takes the first question into school and does not recognise themselves, and then asks this second question but finds no satisfactory (meaningful) answer, the result must surely be disengagement. Critical reading strategies enable an individual child or young person to navigate their world and negotiate their place within it because they are able to recognise messages that confirm who they are and challenge how things are. This is the development of student agency (Kornfeld and Prothro, 2005) referred to earlier.

How learners learn

Bloom's (1956) **taxonomy** (classification) of learning processes comprises three developmental domains: cognitive, affective and psychomotor. These relate to growth in mental skills (knowledge), emotional areas (affective) and physicality (skills) respectively. All are active to some degree as learning occurs; one may be prioritised over another depending on the learning event and the intended outcome. This framework provides a useful tool when thinking about the use of multimodal texts to offer different learning opportunities. In this way we can create a reading scheme that, in the round, provides scaffolded learning (see Chapter 4: 'The psychology of learning and education'). We can facilitate progression from the simple to the complex in order to develop not just mechanical processing abilities but also to develop higher-order skills, for example the ability to interpret and evaluate, to make meaning. When readers read, whatever they read, they are experiencing the text from all three domains. They are thinking (cognitive), feeling (affective) and doing (physical) to a greater or lesser extent. Thus a reading scheme, even for very young learners, may be constructed using an appropriate combination of books, film clips, audio (vocal/musical) and computer games.

This notion, of multiple competences, maps neatly on to the 3D nature of postmodern literacy delivered through a technological curriculum because it meets the demands of all three domains simultaneously. Multiple competences are the lynchpin of a holistic teaching methodology (Figure 10.4).

There is a tendency in modernist teaching to separate the three domains: now we are thinking, in a moment we'll be feeling and then we'll be doing. In fact, the

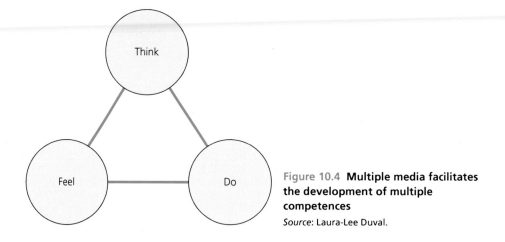

Figure 10.4 Multiple media facilitates the development of multiple competences

Source: Laura-Lee Duval.

three are so inextricably interlinked that to ask learners to effectively turn off two-thirds of their inner lives at the point of learning could be considered a potential precursor of later disaffection. Bloom (1956) did not subdivide the third category (psychomotor) but later researchers have enabled a greater understanding of the influence of physical maturation on the learning process.

So what did Bloom (1956) have to say that informs what we do over half a century later? His major contribution was to suggest that the cognitive domain comprises six categories; each revolves around the development of an ability to use information in a certain way (see Table 10.2).

The affective domain refers to emotional intelligence, or how we deal with our feelings. Learning is heavily based on motivation, enthusiasm, how we have dealt with past experiences, how we view our current situation, and our expectations of the future. We make emotional decisions about phenomena (see Table 10.3).

Simpson (1972, cited in Clarke, 2009) developed Bloom's categories to offer subdivisions of psychomotor development which relate to our speed, precision, distance and execution of an action. We first take in sensory clues (*perception*) and this triggers the process of getting '*set*' to act based on our readiness and mindsets. These help to produce a *guided response* to the stimulus, a response based on how

Table 10.2 **The thinking domain**

Domain: Cognitive	How learners use information
Knowledge	To recall it
Comprehension	To understand it and communicate it to another
Application	To use it in a new situation
Analysis	To deconstruct it in order to examine components/relationships
Synthesis	To reconstruct it in order to create new meaning
Evaluation	To reliably assess the value of that information

Source: Adapted from Clarke, 2009.

Table 10.3 **The feeling domain**

Domain: Affective	How learners use phenomena
Receiving it	What do we absorb and what do we reject?
Responding to it	What do we react to and how?
Valuing it	Does this matter to us? Why? How do we show this?
Organising it	What matters to us? Why? How do we show this?
Internalising it	How open are we to change, to the unfamiliar?

Source: Adapted from Clarke, 2009.

we learn, for example through observation, imitation, trial and error. The next subdivision Simpson calls *mechanism* meaning how we move forward into taking on new learning. Achieving proficiency is referred to as acquiring (developing) a *complex overt response*. In this way we are able to adapt, to use what is known here to work there, the notion of transferable skills. Success here guides us to move learning forward to solve new problems, a process Simpson describes as *origination*.

So what does all this mean in terms of literacy teaching? Once we know how learners learn, that there are three domains of learning (cognitive, affective and psychomotor) and that each of these domains comprises graduating skills sets as the learner moves from novice to expert, we are in a position to design a curriculum that develops thinking, feeling and doing simultaneously. Multimodal literacies offer an opportunity to use technologies to achieve this holistic model of learning. For example, young learners involved in a video project are thinking (about their textual and visual messages), feeling (experiencing the moment) and using physical skills to handle equipment and explore body language. Similarly, a computer game can simultaneously engage the cognitive (problem-solving), affective (pleasure at winning) and psychomotor (moving the mouse/using the keypad) domains.

Activity

Thinking, feeling and doing

To experience how even very simple computer games can satisfy all three of a learner's learning domains, try these links:

- Word Sailing (spelling game): **http://miniclip.com/games/word-sailing/en/**. Make words and win the race!
- Bunch (problem-solving game): **http://miniclip.games.com/bunch/en/**. Create bunches of coloured balls using only valid moves, collect points and move up through five levels of increasing difficulty.

As you play, be aware of how you are thinking, feeling and doing.

▶

Thinking: How hard are you working to understand the game's units (what you have, resources and options) and rules (how you can use these) to score points? Are you aware of increasing concentration and focus?

Feeling: Are you enjoying learning the game? Or frustrated? Is there a help screen or is the game intuitive? When you score well are you excited? Does a low score disappoint you? How does the game motivate you to try again?

Doing: Be aware of the visual clues you are using about where you are in the game; are you keeping an eye on the timer? What are your hands doing? Can you detect increasingly proficient hand–eye coordination as the game becomes more familiar? How does the sound affect you? Does the backing track add to the experience? Does the speeding up of the timer urge you to think and move more quickly as time runs out?

Reflection: How did these games appeal (or not) to you? Could they be used as learning activities in the process of becoming multimodally literate (revisit Figure 10.1 if you are unsure of the components of multimodal literacy)? Can you map sub-domains of activity from Bloom's cognitive and affective, and Simpson's psychomotor master domains?

There is much more for you to read and explore about this/these frameworks. The point is that texts are the medium through which we explore our thoughts and feelings, and multimodal texts extend our experience into the sensate (the physical world). What is labelled a virtual world can often be more real to us than any traditional reading activity might offer. We can and do engage strategically with words and pictures on a printed page but the level of engagement in all three domains is significantly intensified when a technology allows us to immerse ourselves in a 'text'; we are no longer observing 'the moment' but experiencing it. When we think, feel and do, at one and the same time, then we are learning indeed.

Connect and explore

- Much of the above has been adapted from 'Big Dog and Little Dog's Performance Juxtaposition' (Clarke, 2009), a commercial training company that refers to Bloom's (1956) taxonomy as the KSA (knowledge, skills and attitude) methodology. This resource is really readable:

  Clarke, D. (2009) *Bloom's taxonomy of learning domains, the three types of learning*, available from **http://www.nwlink.com/~Donclark/hrd/bloom.html**.

- Highly recommended: use the spectacular mind map to access jargon-free learning theories. This link is about Bloom's taxonomy but do review the links on the left of the screen – a substantial bank of resources:

  Atherton, J.S. (2009) *Learning and Teaching; Bloom's taxonomy*, available from **http://www.learningandteaching.info/learning/bloomtax.htm**.

- Nice and simple offering from North Carolina State University: **http://faculty.chass.ncsu.edu/slatta/hi216/learning/bloom.htm**.

How might a text be constructed?

Ferdinand de Saussure (1857–1913) was philosophically a **structuralist**, meaning that he explored phenomena in terms of units and rules. This view defines units as being parts of something, and rules as controlling how units can be put together (i.e. how they are structured) in order to make something else. Saussure's perspective is, therefore, a very useful way of understanding language and thus literary texts, those deliberately constructed to communicate meaning from writer to reader. If we think of the units as words and the rules as syntax (grammar) then we can grasp that words plus syntax equals a sentence having meaning (the 'something else made'). Units and rules, then, determine how we structure language to communicate and interpret, and for each culture both are socially constructed; we have language conventions.

This explanation gives you a way of thinking about how text is constructed by writers and deconstructed by readers as part of the processes of decoding and encoding text. In practical terms, young readers start with phonemes as units, and words are the 'something else' they make when they are structured to make meaning.

Connect and explore

For an excellent resource on teaching children to read, visit Murray (2009) University of Auburn: Reading Genie: **http://www.auburn.edu/academic/education/reading_genie/**

Klages (2001) describes how Saussure viewed structure as a conceptual system having three essential properties. First is 'wholeness' and this refers to the need for both units and rules to exist in order for the system to function. Second, 'transformation' identifies the system as dynamic, not static, because new units can be added (subject to existing rules) to create new meaning. For example, when the word 'text' is used as a noun it traditionally referred to 'a piece of writing' but more recently it has also come to be interpreted as the name for 'a transmitted message' (by any media). Third, the system was also deemed 'self-regulating', meaning it could be added to but the basic structure could not be changed; the effect is a serious distortion of intended meaning. Lynne Truss (2003) captured the comical absurdity of some grammatical infringements in her book *Eats, Shoots and Leaves* (a definition of giant panda behaviour). Although very funny, her underlying message was serious. When we disrupt conventional language structure, we run the risk of being misunderstood. Misunderstanding can have consequences that lie anywhere on the continuum of harmless to harmful (think of misreadings of medical instructions).

Thus language is seen as a structured signifying system. This is where the notion of text-speak being anathema to language and literacy purists comes in. But is this actually a true representation? Before we look at text-speak in detail, there is one more area where Saussure can illuminate understanding. This is in the notion of how words make meaning. The basic linguistic unit has two parts, the signifier and the signified, which combine to make a sign (the study of which is called **semiotics**). When we ask ourselves what a particular sign means (in our cultural context) we are practising semiotic thinking. The simplest way to understand this is to work through the next activity.

Activity

Applying semiotics

Think of the word tree; you can probably see one in your mind's eye. When you thought the word, you 'heard' it. This is the signifier, the 'sound image' of a word. When you hear a sound image it prompts the connection with the concept associated with the sound and you bring the concept to mind. The important thing about signs is that meanings are imposed on them: these impositions are agreed within the language conventions of a society and are apparently arbitrary: a tree is called a tree, it is not called a sheep.

Why does all this matter? If the relationship between the signifier (the sound image) and the signified (the idea associated with the sound) is changed then the result is ambiguity (lack of clarity) or multiplicity of meaning. Text comprises signs that imply meaning, so critical reading skills are vital if readers are to be able not only to decode (access) but to decipher (discern) the meaning which the author intended. Of course, there is often also space for individual interpretation by the reader but to be in a position to interpret we must first be able to decode messages – this involves the use of a socially constructed yet highly structured mechanism, that of language. This is the case even where the definition of a text goes beyond the written word towards multiple literacies.

Activity

Signs and signifiers are culturally located

Language, we have said, is socially constructed. When we approach texts (in whatever form) we do so within the context of our own societal/cultural heritage; we understand what 'our' signs signify. How does that change when we move outside our native language? Perhaps you enjoy the spectacle of Bollywood films but cannot read all but the simplest signs (visual/musical/speech). Perhaps you admire the exquisite beauty of Chinese silk art, the drawings and characters but cannot read them. We may glean a surface understanding from commonalities we may recognise but we are unlikely to be able to appreciate the subtleties of the message.

Watch this short clip: *Culture differences Personal space*, created by a global bank to appreciate how different signs signify different meanings in different cultures: **http://www.youtube.com/watch?v=mUCODUvKbzE.**

What are technoliteracies?

Any form of communication can be said to have an associated literacy in a postmodern context where being literate infers an ability to understand, to critique, and to create messages; for example, people may claim to be 'IT literate'. Meaning is conveyed through the use of symbols (letters, numbers and characters), graphical (static) images, visual (moving) images, and sounds (voices, instruments). These are described as 'abstract' cultural tools by Erstad et al. (2007:184) and, when combined with 'concrete' cultural tools (such as the mobile phone or the computer), give rise to multimodal or technoliteracies, each of which has an associated syntactic structure, that is, units and rules that govern how they are constructed. The components of multimodal literacy (see Figure 10.1) are:

- Media literacy
- Visual literacy
- Graphicacy
- Print literacy
- Information literacy
- Digital literacy.

These are all underpinned by technologies, hence 'technoliteracy' is an umbrella term used to describe them collectively. We saw earlier that signs have meanings imposed upon them; what signs signify is socially constructed, that is, agreed within the language conventions of a society. This is where the transferable skills of engagement (how did the 'text' make me feel?) and appreciation (how did the author do that?), which D'Arcy (2002) argued were critical components of early reading and writing curricula, come in. Once embedded within the child's reading approach, these skills are then ready to be honed as the child matures (emotionally and cognitively). It is therefore the role of educators (and parents) to facilitate the development of these skills through presenting the child with appropriate materials. The developing child is thus able to bring an appropriately sophisticated methodology to negotiate increasingly complex mediated literacies and make meaning from and with them. Schema/genre theory is a model of learning that matches how children learn to the textual materials that can facilitate learning.

Figure 10.5 illustrates how Piaget's schema theory of child development (see Chapter 4: 'The psychology of learning and education') can be mapped on to the genre categorisation of literature. The genre approach uses the mechanism of schematic development to appreciate that, as a child matures, their ability to process information becomes increasingly sophisticated and wide ranging. The goal is the schematic development of metacognitive abilities, for example insight,

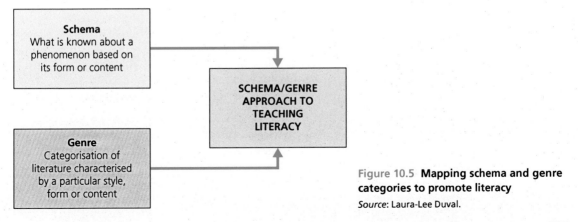

Figure 10.5 **Mapping schema and genre categories to promote literacy**
Source: Laura-Lee Duval.

critical thinking skills and self-expression. In practice, teachers and parents can use this theory to encourage cognitive and affective maturation:

> Each type of literature presented to a young reader serves two important functions, to develop a schema for the literary genre and to encourage the application of thinking skills in a variety of literary engagements.
>
> Smith, 1991, cited in Smith, 1994:2

When Smith was writing he was focusing on literary genres relating to the written (printed) word; he was talking about three basic categories of writings: prose, poetry and drama-script. It is not too far a leap to see how his theory can be extended to capture the multiple literacies that characterise today's literary landscape. In essence, when presenting literary texts in any form to the developing child we start with the simple and move towards the increasingly complex in step with the child's increasingly sophisticated ability to process information regardless of the underlying technologies used to produce those texts.

Technology affords individuals the concrete means to participate in mass communication. Young people in particular are able to blend abstract tools (text-speak, photographs, video, audio, music recordings) and upload these representations of their textual interpretations to social networking sites, blogs and personal websites. They read and respond to postings on discussion boards and in forums. For **synchronous** (real time) rather than **asynchronous communication** there are chat sites and web cams. Children and young people are sharing writings, songs, images, and their interests with 'virtual' friends who are strangers, i.e. they have not met them in the real world. To situate popular culture outside traditional curricula, to view it (and its media) as subcultural or not mainstream, and thus subversive, meaning that it undermines traditional (dominant) culture, is to deny:

> the critical educator . . . a logical connection between lived experiences and the school culture.
>
> Morrell, 2002:2

Far from being subversive, Morrell (2002) argues, popular culture is an exchange between dominant and subordinate cultures; ideologically it occupies a 'compromise equilibrium' (Gramsci, 1971, cited in Morrell, 2002:2). This is called a 'transactional learning space' by Erstad et al. (2007:185) and is a two-way street for sending and receiving messages that negate time and space constraints. A (student) reader in one time and place can access and hear (and re-hear) a lecture from a world-renowned lecturer no matter when it was made or where. Another reader (a lecturer) might be accessing amateur hip hop music videos created and disseminated through YouTube or My Space. Which is education, which is entertainment? The lecturer-reader could be researching popular culture, or enjoying it; the student-reader could be cramming before a deadline or immersed in an area of his/her own interest. The point is this space exists and in it things happen. It is transactional – an exchange between one person and another or more – in a virtual rather than a real world context; nevertheless it is as real and as valid to those who participate in it.

There are some commentators who spurn this notion of compromise, of exchange, choosing to see any foray into youth culture by adults as an insidious infantilisation process. Somehow, the virtual world has become associated with play (because it is unreal?), which is naturally the province of the young, rather than with the serious, the province of maturity. When adults embrace the virtual world, Calcutt (2001) argues they are 'de-maturing' themselves. He also believes that the allure of technology blinds them from realising they are joining with such practices, for example text-messaging. He abhors the political veneration of youth, the idea that, because young people can use these technologies with ease, somehow what they produce has more value than traditional communications. Young people must, by the natural order of things (maturation), lack wisdom. Gluck et al. (2005:198) studied the notion of wisdom, defining it as something 'more than cognition . . . context-dependent [and] . . . gained through life experience'. The implication for detractors is that, while youngsters may know which keys to press, that is, how to send a message, adults should retain their position as the guardians of which message to send.

The debate has thus become about the role, if any, of popular culture (and its associated technologies) in contemporary literacy teaching and learning. On the one hand, advocates such as Morrell (2002) believe that before we can teach we must reach, and that the way to do this is to meet children and young people where they are. Conversely, traditionalists such as Calcutt (2001) see no rationale for change; it is the role of the adult to instil wisdom in the maturing child and they cannot do this if they themselves 'play' at life.

Digital divides

This section is called 'Digital divides'. The plural is intentional. The original concept related to the divide between those who had access to technology and those who did not (Suoranta, 2003). This is a critical component of the move towards social justice; exclusion from social activities disadvantages individuals and communities according to the Champion for Digital Inclusion, Martha Lane Fox, appointed by the government to spearhead the campaign to encourage nationwide participation with internet activities given her background as a successful e-entrepreneur (she was co-founder of the lucrative web-based travel service Lastminute.com). The current 'Get Connected' campaign (http://www.scie.org.uk/workforce/getconnected/index.asp) targets this group, described as 'digitally disadvantaged' by Lane Fox in her interview with Hard Talk (BBC News, 2009). At the very least these groups lack access to information about government services and cheaper commercial services; many government departments are only available though the internet, and many commercial organisations offer discounts to internet consumers. But this divide is not only practical but political. Commercial stakeholders are infusing funds into education. According to the website of Business in the Community (2009), a business–community outreach charity and a Prince's Charity Trust, the supermarket Tesco has delivered more than £100 million pounds worth of ICT equipment since the inception of its voucher redemption scheme 'Computers for Schools' in 1992. While some might balk ideologically at the private funding of public sector services, an integral element of globalisation is outreach, the facilitation of global villages on a local scale. Such school/community/business partnerships are an example of how the local can be connected to the global through digital technology. Digitalisation

Figure 10.6 Why might the generational 'digital divide' favour younger users?
Source: Pearson Education Ltd./Rob Judges.

costs, however, and new ways of footing the bill have to be found; governments alone cannot meet all the costs of a nation 'getting connected'.

The second digital divide might be termed 'generational' (Calcutt, 2001:1). This divide is attitudinal; it is rooted in mainstream ideology, i.e. it concerns the mind-sets and beliefs of the dominant culture. The divergence between the technological aptitudes of the young and the old is, in this context, not only mismatched but ad-versarial. Not only do they not understand each other, but each is suspicious of the other. Why such a controversial divergence? The key is in the transition from the World Wide Web (generally read only) to Web 2.0 technologies (instant interactiv-ity). Web 2.0 has led to an explosion in the number of available media devices and an increasing connectivity between them. Connectivity refers to how information (textual/graphic/visual) can be moved from one technology to another, for exam-ple photographs taken on a mobile phone can be uploaded to the PC (personal computer) and disseminated (broadcast) via the internet. This, in turn, has led to an unprecedented capacity for individuals to receive and transmit mass communi-cations, to immerse themselves in a sea of technology. As we have seen, Calcutt (2001:2) dismisses emerging subcultures as the transcendence of 'the banality of teenage interactions', if not a genuine fear that the acceptance, let alone integra-tion, of 'yoof culture' might dilute traditions and standards. ('Yoof culture' as a phrase is credited to the television producer/presenter Janet Street Porter, who made programmes for young people in the 1980s and famously had difficulty pro-nouncing the word 'youth'.) For others (Davis, 2009), teaching young users to nav-igate and participate safely in a virtual world, and reaching them through their lived experience of multiple media (Morrell, 2002), is an essential prerequisite of a holistic postmodern education, one fit for purpose. It is the task of educators, they argue, to equip contemporary learners with the tools to self-actualise, reach their potential, in today's digitalised world. These aspirations are set out in the 'Every Child Matters' (DfES, 2004) agenda. This identifies five outcomes for children and young people: to be healthy, to stay safe, to enjoy and achieve, to make a positive contribution, and to achieve economic well-being. If adults are to make these aspirations a reality, they must understand the world that children are growing up into, and that includes understanding the reliance of that world upon technologies to communicate, to learn, work and play.

Taking control: technology as the slave of pedagogy, not its master

Much of the information we have about technoliteracies is necessarily axiomatic, that is, we have absorbed facts and figures and experiences (our own and that of others) about it but there is little if any 'hard science' associated with it, or any rigorous empirical evidence. There simply has not been the time to evaluate efficacy of practice on any kind of grand scale. However, small pockets of evaluative research offer interesting and often encouraging views on what might be achieved, but we have no established bank of literature to refer to. This is cutting-edge postmodernism; technology appears to dictate the pace of change. It is important, therefore, that we maintain a sense of perspective, that technology is always the slave of pedagogy and never its master.

Activity

Digital divides or digital democracy?

Andy Carvin is the host of the PBS Teachers (US) web initiative, Learning.now: a *weblog that explores how new technology and Internet culture affect how educators teach and children learn.*

The focus of this posting is access to personal political capital through technology. Carvin (2008) acknowledges that those who are immersed in Web 2.0 connectivity need to be mindful of the needs (and rights) of those who are not. At the outset of President Obama's election campaign, event tickets were only available online. This effectively excluded much of his targeted constituency of disadvantaged, disenfranchised and impoverished citizens, the very groups he was promising to include. In any context, when technology is the master of operations rather than its slave, human rights are rendered invisible.

Carvin, A. (2008) Random Acts of Journalism, available from **http://www.pbs.org/teachers/learning.now/2008/06/random_acts_of_journalism.html**.

Now consider the three strands of the citizenship curriculum: social and moral responsibility, community involvement, and political literacy. How would you ensure that young people are fully able to participate in a technological world?

Now bookmark the home page of PBS so that you can access a whole range of research and resources relating to technoliteracies.

Conclusion

In this chapter you have encountered the notion of multiple literacies with an especial focus on technoliteracy in the context of the vernacular literary practices of young learners. The facets of multimodal literacy (print literacy, visual literacy, graphicacy, media literacy, information literacy, digital literacy) have been cast as essential skills for active participation in a postmodern world of diverse and multiple meanings. They are the key to employability and personal empowerment (agency and self-actualisation) for the connected 'wrap around technology' generation. There has been a paradigm shift in literacy teaching, one prioritising meaning over mechanics, and this has led to a call for transformational learning embedded in a technological curriculum. You have encountered radical educators, past and present, and discovered how limiting the definition of literacy can be used to oppress and disadvantage certain social groupings because literacy is a social construct. The national imperative for a literate workforce was outlined through discussion of government reports, for example Leitch's (2006) 'Review of Skills', and in the light of these considered the achievements and underachievements of children and young people in state schools and colleges. Government initiatives to raise standards were mapped, culminating in a consideration of the recommendations of the most recent, Rose's (2009) 'Review of the Primary Curriculum' which strongly advocated the need for a digital literacy for all children.

Having contextualised the debate, the discussion moved on to why educators may be reluctant to embrace notions of a postmodern digital literacy. This raised questions about what postmodern is, and the influences of ideology in meaning-making. We then focused on how learners learn, using a recognised taxonomy of learning domains to understand the notion of deep learning, comprising action on the part of the learner in terms of thinking, feeling and doing at one and the same time. How texts are constructed and deconstructed was explored in the light of structuralism, the theory of units being combined under the control of rules to make something else, a hypothesis that is transferable from print to graphic and visual and auditory texts and any combination of them. The next topic was the importance of critical reading skills, the ability to discern valid and invalid messages. Finally we extended our understanding of digital divides, appreciating that many are excluded from participation in a digital society through a lack of equipment and education but also that some people choose to self-exclude on the basis of their personal beliefs and feelings about the validity of mediated messages. As these people are generally adults, this is termed the generational divide. In this way we have armed ourselves with the tools to move forward to learning about engaging with innovative practice, the subject of the next chapter.

Unanticipated threats in online learning

Recall from Case study 10.1 the story of Philip, a lecturer who designed online assessments using wikis and blogs. The assessments involved students using VLEs, blogs and wikis to comment on and criticise each other's work. Philip did a SWOT analysis (strengths, weaknesses, opportunities, threats), and restricted wiki/blog privacy settings to himself and his two tutor colleagues in the interests of ethics and student safety.

Five weeks in, Philip was challenged to rethink his strategy on a day which rapidly went from bad to worse. An email from a distressed female student reported abuse of personal information. She claimed receipt of texts of a sexual nature from multiple unidentified numbers. She strongly suspected that her number, available on the wiki for other group members, had been passed on by a male member who had posted some 'odd comments and, last night, an offensive image' on their wiki. Philip immediately accessed the wiki.

What he read concerned him greatly. The group was exploring textual representations of women in computer games aimed at men, the Lara Croft effect (Dovey and Kennedy, 2006), to critically evaluate the objectification of women by male game designers and players (primarily male). The male student's posts came perilously close to sexual harassment. Comparisons were made between her and Lara Croft in terms of bodily prowess. Facially the student looked nothing like her. To redress this, he had superimposed her head (having snapped her unawares presumably via mobile phone) to the body of Lara Croft and uploaded it. The access logs showed other members had not yet seen it, so Philip took a screenshot as evidence and deleted the image from the wiki. Despite his suspicions, no electronic log could prove that the same person who had posted the image had distributed her phone number.

Next Philip checked the offender's reflective blog. His concern elevated to alarm, not about its scholarship; it was coherent; it comprised well constructed supported and evidenced arguments, drawn from the literature and personal experience respectively, as per the assignment brief. The problem was that the student had not only critically evaluated textual forms but also his tutors' performance and competence. Although anonymous both were easily identifiable through the description of their sessions and Philip worried that they would be called to account when management investigated the whole incident. Suddenly the notion that e-writing could be used to harm became very real. He could not control access by management to this blog but at least the privacy settings would prevent its becoming common knowledge among students.

His relief didn't last very long. In his inbox he noticed an all-user message from the student in question. It revealed a threat he had not remotely considered. All users are listed and accessible through the VLE; exploiting this, the student had disseminated his blog link for wider comment. Philip realised that each recipient had the potential for further dissemination. The flood gates had opened, a tide of malicious data was surging from the virtual to the real world and Philip had no means of stemming the flow.

Questions for discussion

1 *What are the advantages and disadvantages of using wikis to facilitate communications between diverse student groups working together?*

2 *What safeguards might be put in place to guide these communications and how might these be enforced?*

3 *Should tutors have access to the process of collaboration rather than only the product? Think about the impact of observation (and tracking) on the learning process, about personal privacy, about informal communications, e.g. use of text speak/emoticons (between students) being potentially viewed by a marking tutor schooled in academic discourse.*

Summary

A paradigm shift in literacy pedagogy

A paradigm shift in the teaching of literacy is emerging as we embrace technoliteracy through computers, mobile phones and other audio/visual media. Being literate means being able to make sense of our personal and social worlds, to communicate, to learn, to inform, to share, to explore, to create, to act and react confidently in a world of words and images.

Literacy in its limited sense (reading and writing) continues to excite heated debate within education because many children and young people appear to be struggling, first within the education system and later in the world of work. However, literacy is increasingly multimodal in nature and includes visual, graphical, media, informational, technological, digital and print forms.

Transformational learning: the prerequisite of agency and actualisation

Transformational, learner-centred learning embeds multiple media and seeks to democratise the teaching and learning process as it encourages meaning-making and personal agency.

Moving towards a postmodern definition of literacy

A postmodern definition of literacy challenges the simplistic notion of receiving knowledge and learning how to read and write. It stresses the importance of active interpretation in order to empower the learner.

The possible implications of political change

The National Curriculum meant that the literacy hour was highly prescriptive and related to tests rather than allowing children to appreciate texts. The Rose Report (2009) recommended the increased use of technology but the recent change of government may affect the implementation of this.

Embracing technoliteracies

Embracing technoliteracies means moving away from a comfortable 'familiar' position for many educators and developing new ways of thinking and doing. Postmodernism is a complex term which assumes that individuals interpret the world through the lens of their own experiences and values. Thus a postmodern literacy must assume the engagement of the person in the process for it to be meaningful.

Within texts of any kind there will be ideological assumptions because of the creator's aims which are part of his/her way of thinking about ideas or beliefs (ideology).

Children and young people have a natural enthusiasm for multimodal literacy which could be usefully harnessed within education but there is a gap between their personal, social experiences of technology and their educational encounters with technology which may account for disengagement.

How learners learn

Bloom's taxonomy (1956) classifies the learning process into cognitive, affective and psychomotor (thinking, feeling and doing) areas which link with the use of technologies within multimodal learning.

How might a text be constructed?

Structural views see texts as being constructed and deconstructed in terms of units (such as words and rules of grammar) which are deliberately arranged to communicate meaning to another.

Critical reading skills are an essential part of the communication process as they involve the ability to detect messages which are valid and invalid.

Digital divides

Many people are excluded in a digital society as they lack equipment, education and/or motivation. Adults who choose not to take part in technological advances become part of a generational divide.

References

Adams, P. and Calvert, M. (2005) A square peg in a round hole: citizenship and problems with 'curriculum' – the English secondary school problem, Paper presented at 'Learning Beyond Cognition' Biennial Conference of the European Affective Education Network.

Ainley, P. (1999) Learning Policy, Towards the Certified Society, Paper presented at the British Educational Research Association Annual Conference September 2–5 1999, available from http://www.leeds.ac.uk/educol/documents/000001186.doc.

Alexander, R. (2009) *Children, their World, their Education: Final Report and Recommendations of the Cambridge Primary Review*, London: Routledge.

Appignanesi, R. and Garratt, C. (1999) *Introducing Postmodernism*, Cambridge: Icon Books.

BBC News (2009) Hard Talk: 'Brutal numbers' point to digital disadvantage, available from http://news.bbc.co.uk/1/hi/programmes/hardtalk/8303522.stm.

Biggs, J. (2003) *Teaching for Quality Learning at University*, 2nd edn, Berkshire: Open University Press.

Blair, A. (2005) Q&A: What are phonics? In Times Online, available from http://www.timesonline.co.uk/tol/news/uk/article598574.ece.

Bleakley, A. (2006) *Education Research in the Post Modern*, available from http://www.edu.plymouth.ac.uk/resined/postmodernism/pmhome.htm.

Bloom, B.S. (1956) *Taxonomy of Educational Objectives, Handbook I: The Cognitive Domain*, New York: David McKay.

Bourdieu, P. (1998) *Practical Reason*, Cambridge: Polity Press.

British Educational Researchers Association (2004) Revised Ethical Guidelines for Educational Research, available from http://www.bera.ac.uk/files/guidelines/ethica1.pdf.

Business in the Community (2009) Tesco Computers for Schools, available from http://www.bitc.org.uk/resources/case_studies/afe903crbtescocomp.html.

Calcutt, A. (2001) Generation Txt: mixed messages, available from http://spiked-online.com/Articles/0000000054DF.htm.

California Learning Resource Network (2009) Free Digital Textbook Initiative Review Results, available from http://www.clrn.org/fdti/.

Canadian Education Association (2009) Focus on Literacy: Framing the debate, available from http://www.cea-ace.ca/foo.cfm?subsection=lit&page=fra&subpage=wha&subsubpage=som.

Cassen, G. and Kingdon, R. (2007) Understanding Low Achievement in English Schools, for Centre for Analysis of Social Exclusion, London School of Economics and Political Science, available from http://en.scientificcommons.org/35764142.

Clarke, D. (2009) *Bloom's taxonomy of learning domains: The three types of learning*, available from http://www.nwlink.com/~Donclark/hrd/bloom.html.

Cole, G. (2009) Rose Report places technology centre stage in primary curriculum, in Guardian Online, available from http://www.guardian.co.uk/resource/rose-report-technology-primary-curriculum.

Conservative Party (2007) Raising the bar: closing the gap, available from http://www.conservatives.com/Policy/Where_we_stand/Schools.aspx.

Cottrell, S. (2003) *Skills for Success: The Personal Development Planning Handbook*, Hampshire: Palgrave-Macmillan.

Coughlan, S. (2007) 'Education, education, education', in BBC News, available from http://news.bbc.co.uk/1/hi/education/6564933.stm.

Curtis and Pettigrew (2009) *Learning in Contemporary Culture*, Exeter: Learning Matters.

D'Arcy, P. (2002) A comparison between two kinds of response, Interpretive and Skill-based, to a Y6 story: 'Three Wishes', *English in Education*, 36(2), pp. 40–49.

Davis, V. (2009) The Cool Cat Blog, available from http://coolcatteacher.blogspot.com/.

DCSF (2009:1) 14–19 Reform: 16–18-year-olds NEET, available from http://www.dcsf.gov.uk/14-19/index.cfm?go=site.home&sid=42&pid=343&ctype=None&ptype=Contents.

DCFS (2009:2) *Your child, your schools, our future: Building a 21st-century schools system.*

DfES (2003) Excellence and Enjoyment: A strategy for primary schools, available from http://nationalstrategies.standards.dcsf.gov.uk/node/88755.

DfES (2004) Every Child Matters, available from http://www.dcsf.gov.uk/everychildmatters/publications/.

Deblase, G. (2003) Acknowledging Agency While Accommodating Romance: Girls Negotiating Meaning, 'Literacy Transactions', *Journal of Adolescent & Adult Literacy*, 46, pp. 24–35.

Dovey, J. and Kennedy, H.W. (2006) *Game Cultures: Computer Games as New Media*, Berkshire: Open University Press.

Dumais, S.A. (2002) Cultural Capital, Gender and School Success: The Role of Habitus, *Sociology of Education*, 75(1), pp. 44–68.

Erstad, O. et al. (2007) Re-mixing multimodal resources: Multiliteracies and digital production in Norwegian media education, *Learning, Media and Technology*, 32(2), pp. 183–98.

Evans, J. (2004) *Literacy Moves on*, London: David Fulton.

Felluga, D. (2003) Introductory Guide to Critical Theory: Modules on Althusser: On Ideology, available from http://www.cla.purdue.edu/academic/engl/theory/marxism/modules/althusserideologymainframe.html.

Freire, P. (1972) *Pedagogy of the Oppressed*, London: Penguin Books.

Gillard D. (2007) Education in England: A brief history, available from www.dg.dial.pipex.com/history/.

Gluck, J. et al. (2005) The wisdom of experience: autobiographical narratives across adulthood, *International Journal of Behavioural Development*, 29(3), pp. 197–208.

Goodwin, P. (2005) *The Literate Classroom*, 2nd edn, London: David Fulton.

Haralambos, M. and Holborn, M. (2008) *Sociology Themes and Perspectives*, London: Collins.

HM Chief Inspector of Education (07/08) Children's Services and Skills, available from http://www.ofsted.gov.uk/.

Herrington, A. (2008) article 6: Maslow's hierarchy, societal change and the knowledge worker revolution, available from http://www.pateo.com/article6.html.

Hirsch, D. (2008) What is Needed to End Child Poverty in 2020? available from http://www.jrf.org.uk/sites/files/jrf/2275_0.pdf.

Hollindale, P. (1992) (ed.) *Literature for Children*, London: Routledge.

Illich, I. and Verne, E. (1976) *Imprisoned in the Global Classroom*, London: Writers and Readers Publishing Cooperative.

Johnson, S. (2005) *Everything bad is good for you*, London: Penguin.

Katbamma, M. (2005) True Crime: SATS are killing our stories, in Guardian Online, available from http://www.guardian.co.uk/education/2005/nov/08/schools.news2.

Kellner, D. and Share, J. (2005) Toward Critical Media Literacy: Core concepts, debates, organizations, and policy, *Discourse: studies in the cultural politics of education*, 26(3), pp. 369–86.

Kimber, K, et al. (2002) Reclaiming Teacher Agency in a Student-Centred Digital World, *Asia-Pacific Journal of Teacher Education*, 30(2), pp. 155–67.

Kirsch, I. et al. (2000) *Reading for Change: Performance and Engagement*, Results from PISA 2000, available from http://www.oecd.org/dataoecd/43/54/33690904.pdf.

Klages, M. (2001) Structuralism and Saussure, available from http://www.colorado.edu/English/courses/ENGL2012Klages/saussure.html.

Kornfeld, J. and Prothro, L. (2005) Envisioning Possibility: Schooling and Student Agency in Children's and Young Adult Literature, *Children's Literature in Education*, 36(3), pp. 217–39.

Kurland, D. (2002) How the Language Really Works: The Fundamentals of Critical Reading and Effective Writing, available from http://www.criticalreading.com/index.html.

Johnson, S. (2005) *Everything Bad is Good for You: Why Popular Culture is Making Us Smarter*, London: Penguin.

Lankshear, C. and Knobel, M. (1997:1) Literacy, new technologies and old patterns, in Lankshear, C. (1997) *Changing Literacies*, Buckingham: Open University Press.

Lankshear, C. and Knobel, M. (1997:2) Different Worlds? Technology-mediated classroom learning and students' social practices with new technologies in home and community settings, in Lankshear, C. (1997) *Changing Literacies*, Buckingham: Open University Press.

Lankshear, C. et al. (1997) *Changing Literacies*, Buckingham: Open University Press.

Latif, A. (2009) A Critical Analysis of Enrollment and Literacy Rates of Girls and Women in Pakistan, *Educational Studies*, 45(5), pp. 424–39.

Lawton, D. (1986) *Education, Culture and the National Curriculum*, London: Hodder & Stoughton.

Leitch, S. (2006) Leitch Review of Skills, available from http://www.dcsf.gov.uk/furthereducation/index.cfm?fuseaction=content.view&CategoryID=21&ContentID=37.

Linebarger, D. (2004) Young children, language and television, *Literacy Today*, 40, available from http://www.literacytrust.org.uk/pubs/linebarger.html.

Lockwood, M. (2008) *Promoting Reading for Pleasure in the Primary School*, London: Sage.

Long, C. (2009) Schools slowly add phones, PDAs to curriculum, available from http://www.msnbc.msn.com/id/32112813/ns/tech_and_science-tech_and_gadgets.

MacDonald, F. (2005) *Adult Literacies in Scotland, Literacy Today*, available from http://www.literacytrust.org.uk/Pubs/macdonald2.html.

McLean, N. (2007) Multimodal Literacies, presented at the NAACE annual strategic conference, available from http://events.becta.org.uk/content_files/corporate/resources/events/2007/feb/niel_mclean_naace.ppt.

McLaren, P. (1993) Critical Literacy and Postcolonial Praxis: A Freirian Perspective, *College Literature*, 20(1), pp. 7–28.

Machin, S. and McNally, S. (2005) *The Literacy Hour*, London: London School of Economics, Centre for the Economics of Education.

Mann, S. and Robinson, A. (2009) Boredom in the lecture theatre: An investigation into the contributors, moderators and outcomes of boredom amongst university students, *British Educational Research Journal*, 35(2), pp. 243–58.

Marsh, J. (2003) The Techno-literacy Practices of Young Children, *Journal of Early Childhood Research*, 2(1), pp. 51–66.

Martin, A. (2005) DigEuLit – a European Framework for Digital Literacy: A Progress Report, *Journal of E-Literacy*, Vol. 2, available from http://www.elearningeuropa.info.

Maslow, A. (1954) *Motivation and Personality*, New York: Harper & Row.

Matthewman, S. with Blight, A. and Davies, C. (2004) What does Multimodality Mean for English? Creative Tensions in Teaching New Texts and New Literacies, *Education, Communication & Information*, 4(1), pp. 153–76.

Mayes, T. and de Freitas, S. (2007) Learning and e-learning: The role of theory, in Beetham, H. and Sharpe, R. (2007) *Rethinking Pedagogy for a Digital Age: Designing and delivering e-learning*, Oxon: Routledge.

Mioduser, D., Tur-Kaspa, H. and Leitner, I. (2000) The learning value of computer-based instruction of early reading skills, *Journal of Computer Assisted Learning*, Vol. 16, pp. 54–63.

Morrell, E. (2002) Toward a critical pedagogy of popular culture: Literacy development among urban youth, *Journal of Adolescent & Adult Literacy*, 46(1), available from http://www.readingonline.org/newliteracies/lit_index.asp?HREF=/newliteracies/jaal/9-02_column/index.html.

Mortimer, P. (2009) Cambridge review team, take heart – your ideas may yet triumph, in Guardian Online, available from http://www.guardian.co.uk/education/2009/nov/03/cambridge-primary-review-peter-mortimore.

National Literacy Trust (2009) *The Cambridge Primary Review: Children, their world, their education: Final report and recommendations of the Cambridge Primary Review*, available from http://www.literacytrust.org.uk/Policy/strat.html.

Nikkhah, R. and Henry, J. (2009) Facebook bullying students 'should be expelled', *The Telegraph* (10 January 2009).

Palmer, S. (2006) National Literacy Strategy – good or bad? Available from http://www.literacytrust.org.uk/Policy/strat.html.

Peltoniemi, T. (2003) Young People and the New technologies – Perspectives on Internet and Mobile Services in Drug and Alcohol Prevention, available from http://www.kolumbus.fi/teuvo.peltoniemi/Peltoniemi_publications.htm.

Richter, D.J. (2004) Ludwig Wittgenstein (1889–1951), available from http://www.iep.utm.edu/wittgens/#H1.

Rose, J. (2006) Independent review of the teaching of early reading, available from http://www.jceps.com/index.php?pageID=article&articleID=16.

Rose, J. (2009) Independent review of the primary curriculum: Final Report, available from http://www.dcsf.gov.uk/primarycurriculumreview/.

Said, E. (1999) Literature and literalism, in *Al-Ahram Weekly*, Issue 414, available from http://weekly.ahram.org.eg/1999/414/cu1.htm.

Satre, J.P. (1946) Existentialism is a Humanism, available from http://www.marxists.org/reference/archive/sartre/works/exist/sartre.htm.

Shea, V. (1994) *Netiquette*, San Francisco: Albion, also available online from http://www.albion.com/netiquette/book/index.html.

Sheldon, K.M. and Kasser, T. (2001) Goals, Congruence and Positive Well-being: New Empirical Support for Humanistic Theories, *Journal of Humanistic Psychology*, 41(1), pp. 30–40.

Sims, R. (2008) Rethinking (e)learning: A manifesto for connected generations, *Distance Education*, 29(2), pp. 153–64.

Siemens, G. (2006) Knowing Knowledge, available from http://www.knowingknowledge.com.

Siemens, G. (2009) Connectivism, available from http://www.connectivism.ca/?page_id=2.

Smith, C.B. (1994) Helping Children Understand Literary Genres, available from http://www.vtaide.com/png/ERIC/Literary-Genres.htm.

Smith, K. (2008) Ivan Illich: Deschooling, conviviality and the possibilities for informal education and lifelong learning, available from http://www.infed.org/thinkers/et-illic.htm.

Suoranta, J. (2003) The world divided in two: Digital divide, information and communication technologies, and the 'youth question', in *Journal for Critical Education Policy Studies*, 1(2), available from http://www.jceps.com/index.php?pageID=article&articleID=16.

Teaching & Learning Research Programme (2008) Literacies for Learning in Further Education, available from http://www.tlrp.org/dspace/retrieve/3692/IvanicRB50final.pdf.

Tobin, L. (2009) How to solve the problem of truancy? In Guardian Online, available from http://www.guardian.co.uk/education/2009/nov/03/bunking-off-school-pupils-truancy.

Tomlinson, S. (2008) *Education in a post-welfare society*, 2nd edn, Buckingham: Open University Press.

Truss, L. (2003) *Eats, Shoots and Leaves*, London: Profile Books Ltd.

UNESCO (2002) National Literacy Policies: China, available http://www.accu.or.jp/litdbase/policy/chn/index.htm, viewed October 2009.

Vygotsky, L. (1978) Interaction between Learning and Development, *Mind in Society*, (Trans. M. Cole), Cambridge, MA: Harvard University Press.

Wallace, S. (2009) (ed.) *Oxford Dictionary of Education*, Oxford: Oxford University Press.

Wintour, P. and Curtis, P. (2009) Ed Balls sets out schools savings to strike blow in battle of the cuts, in Guardian Online, available from http://www.guardian.co.uk/politics/2009/sep/20/ed-balls-chools-savings-cuts.

Woolcock, N. (2009) Soaring number of teachers say they are 'cyberbully victims', in Times Online, available from http://www.timesonline.co.uk/tol/life_and_style/education/article3213130.ece.

Youth Access (2009) Submission to the Children: Schools and Families Select Committee inquiry into young people not in education, employment or training, available from http://www.youthaccess.org.uk.

Zimmerman, B.J. and Cleary, T.J. (2006) Adolescents' development of personal agency, in Pajares, F. and Urdan, T. (2006) (eds) *Self-efficacy Beliefs of Adolescents*, Greenwich: Information Age Publishing.

11

Engaging with innovative practice

Laura-Lee Duval

Contents

Introduction

The previous chapter, 'Literacy learning in a postmodern world', introduced a range of theoretical perspectives to contextualise how educators might harness the power of the multiple technologies that have captured the imagination and enthusiasm of young learners so as to encourage the development of multiple literacy competences in formal educational settings. We explored the potential of connected technologies in terms of the strengths, weaknesses, opportunities and threats. The chapter argued that there has been a paradigm shift in what we understand contemporary literacy to be, that today it is much more than simply reading and writing the printed word. The term multimodal literacies, we saw, embraces media literacy, visual literacy, graphicacy, print literacy, information literacy and digital literacy.

This is an important shift because illiteracy negatively impacts upon an individual's life chances. Marginalised groups, those without access to technology, and/or lacking the multiple competences needed to function in a technological word are significantly disadvantaged politically, economically, socially and personally. We discussed how a postmodern world is one characterised by diversity and change and that the pace of change is speeding up, driven by technological advances. Such change in the order of things demands a positive response from educators charged with equipping young learners with the tools they need to thrive, not just survive in this new landscape. The chapter made reference to recent government reports, and the findings of organisations and commentators working to make change happen. Change challenges existing ideologies. We explored why some people are reluctant to embrace the notion of new thinking about literacy teaching and learning. Finally, we explored theories of how learners learn and how texts are constructed in order to develop an understanding of how we might match one with the other so as to counter endemic disaffection with learning among many young people.

This chapter, 'Engaging with innovative practice', explores some of the innovative practice that educators are using in a range of educational settings. We look first at the language of a significant mode of digital transmissions, text-speak. Moving from the symbolism of the written word we consider the symbolism integral to visual media. Media literacy has long been associated with 'reading' visual broadcasts: there is an accepted syntagm (a combination of conventions and codes) of film and television programme-making techniques that demand a viewing grammar (Harris, 2002). The use of sound, the human voice, a musical instrument, an audible effect is part of that **syntagm**. It offers cues and clues to the audience, for example the frighteningly evocative backing track signalling the impending appearance of a monstrous white shark in the 1975 blockbuster *Jaws*. Music is integral to culture and subcultures; therefore, we consider the notion of literacy in lyrics and how this might foster engagement. The final section explores computer games and their educational potential.

Our route is necessarily linear; we need to break down the notion of media to explore its constituent parts but the reality is that all these parts connect. Not only do they connect but they have changed beyond recognition. We were never passive receivers of information; as homo significans (Chandler, 2009), we are creatures that attach significance to the signs we meet (see the previous chapter for a discussion of the work of Saussure). What this means is that we are inherently meaning-makers. The change is that connectivity redefines us not simply as active audiences – we are interactive users.

This is particularly evident in the context of computer game playing; however, it is just as relevant in every literary sphere as we are able to develop a readership (online), record images, events and sounds, make music and create virtual environments.

This chapter aims to:

- Consider the challenges various techno-phenomena present, for example text-speak, Web 2.0 interactivities and computer gaming.
- Help you become familiar with a range of technologies that can be used for learning.
- Explore examples of innovative practice.

Read the following case study to help you begin to think of the implications (positive and negative) of using electronic media as pedagogical tools for learners, teachers and institutions.

Case study 11.1
Using the virtual world to navigate the real one

The City College of Southampton serves an ethnically diverse population and as such is one of the largest providers of English for speakers for other languages (ESOL). The challenge for the college is to integrate a significantly diverse cohort of learners, having multiple mother-tongues, and educational experiences and achievements between them, into the college and wider community. In 2005 they reported on their innovative programme called 'Any time, any place learning: multimedia learning with mobile phones', designed to achieve this.

Tutors had to, at one and the same time, cope with the limited ICT experience of many students and motivate them to learn the linguistic skills they needed, quickly. To achieve this they created a techno-curriculum underpinned by mobile phone technology connected with internet publishing software (mediaBoard). This software hosts text messages and image/audio files. First, the tutor uploaded an image, in this case a map of the college campus and created zoned areas within it. Working in pairs students visited the zones and sent back messages in the form of text messages, photographs and audio files. In this way, a composite picture could be built up of the college campus at the start of the course for newly enrolled learners. As they advanced in terms of technological competence and linguistic confidence they moved out into the wider community.

The outcomes are positive. Students are orienting themselves using technology and peer support in the context of tutor guidance, and simultaneously learning language skills (grammar, idiom, pronunciation). The report concludes that learners benefited from multi-sensory learning experiences with respect to motivation and self-esteem (see student agency in the previous chapter). The technological underpinning also facilitated inclusion for less mobile students; they could ask questions of their peers in the field. The students' work was published on the web, creating a resource that could be revisited by the participants and serve as an inspirational prompt for future cohorts.

Read the report at http://www.elearning.ac.uk/innoprac/learner/southampton.html. Bookmark the JISC homepage URL so that you can return to this excellent resource from the Joint Information Systems Committee which supports post-16 and higher education and research in the UK in providing leadership in the use of ICT (information and communications technology).

Questions for discussion

1 *What issues might such a programme raise in terms of*
- *funding*
- *supporting the technologies*
- *the student learning experience*
- *tutor capabilities?*

2 *Language competence is the precursor of literacy skill development; is there a place for text messaging in language learning in our schools?*

Multiple technologies: identifying possibilities

In this opening section we consider a variety of technologies and contexts which offer new possibilities and perspectives of what 'literacy' means: **'text-speak'**; visual texts; sound texts; literacy in lyrics; and the importance of the personal computer.

Text-speak

According to Milian (2009), the texting revolution was sparked in the mid-1990s by the emergence of a new mode of personal communication on to the market, the text message. Mobile phone users were no longer restricted to voicemail; a textual option now existed. The dominance of the SMS (Short Message Service) by young people as a social tool took the mobile communications industry completely by storm (Milian, 2009). Very rapidly 'text-speak' emerged (and is continuing to evolve) as an expedient response to the main constraint of SMS, the 160 characters per message limit. Text-speak is considered a representational 'language' given its reliance upon abbreviated phonetics and substitutive letters, numbers and characters (Urban Dictionary, 2009). Unexpectedly, Generation Txt was born (Calcutt, 2001:1).

Texting was viewed initially (by adults) as a teenage activity and dismissed as having no place in a formal literacy curriculum. The controversial, even radical, idea that it might has resulted in an essentially polarised debate. For detractors, according any credence to a subcultural language that breaks the syntactic rules inherent to Standard English is anathema. There is profound concern that the informality of text-speak will pervade, and subsequently subvert, formal written communications. Conversely, to the advocates of experimentation, this is a golden opportunity to negate youth disaffection, i.e. disaffection towards 'old' texts. They seek to harness young learners' enthusiasm for this form of textual expression and use it as an entry point into conventional literacy learning:

> The emergence of SMS is noteworthy for literacy educators and researchers for at least two of its characteristics: first, the rapid evolution of a new form of text and the accompanying skills; and second, the ways in which this new textual form reflects contemporary social relationships.
>
> Carrington, 2004:216

It is not that young learners can't and won't read: the successful and rapid integration indicates that they are reading (and writing) profusely; what they are looking to access is a textual form that reflects their lived experience outside school, inside.

The purpose of text-speak is for 'text' to verbalise or 'speak' a message to a recipient. There is no oral component to this language. Why has it arisen? Is it a pragmatic response to the cost of phone calls and transport? Is it evidence of the inherent laziness often associated with adolescence? Calcutt (2001) argues that it is socially constructed in the sense that it has arisen almost spontaneously to address a deep-rooted social need, the need to connect. He reasoned that its meteoric success was about timing; the technology arrived just as young people were becoming increasingly physically isolated in a climate of parental fear and anxiety. Texting filled the gap. It was private and generally safe and young people had control over access to their mobile numbers. It also exercised their creativity and ingenuity in learning how to compress longer missives into a format that the recipient could decode and understand, could read.

How does text-speak work? Text-speak functions primarily through the use of phonetic abbreviations and/or the use of substitutive letters (graphemes), characters and numbers (Urban Dictionary, 2009); for example, 'great' shortens to GR8, upper or lower case, although capitals can be considered as the verbal equivalent of shouting. One of the difficulties associated with compressing a rich language into a semi-abbreviated, coded and symbolic configuration is the loss of nuance or tone. The very shortness of the message can make it appear abrupt. This has been partially resolved by the use of 'emoticons', either actual pictograms or combinations of punctuation characters to denote different expressions, for example, happy [☺], sad [☻], or confused [☺]. Combinations of graphic and grapheme can 'extend the range of meanings available' (Carrington, 2004:218). Similarly, 'initialisms' are used to represent short fixed phrases (LOL: laughing out loud). According to the text-speak website Netlingo (2009) they are called 'initialisms' rather than 'acronyms' because acronyms are intended to form a new word that can be spoken. In user communities they start out as a novelty and, if the consensus is that they work, they become the norm. To the outsider the dynamics of texting requires more than manual dexterity, it requires that those who wish to participate learn the conventions of texting just as they were required to learn the conventions of the language from which it derives. This is part of the excitement for young people, its perceived exclusivity; this is a form of text that can often perplex the uninitiated reader.

The web, however, offers a variety of deciphering facilities, for example Netlingo.com and urbandictionary.com. There are also glossaries in book form such as Jansen's (2003) *Net Lingo: The Internet Dictionary,* although whether these are up to date given that this is an evolving language is questionable. There is evidence that coding rather than abbreviation is now being used, for example '143' signifies 'I love you', while 'I hate you' is denoted by '182' (Netlingo, 2009). Here there is no possible correlation between the original words and the resulting code string. It is this type of exclusivity that worries some adults; young people's transactions and interactions can be impossible to monitor, making young people themselves difficult to protect.

These concerns extend to connected media, for example instant messaging and social networking sites. Here it becomes 'net-speak' for which there is a 'neti-quette' which refers to the social conventions of online interaction. Text-speak is thus a dynamic language created by young people to do the job they want it to do, to maintain contact with their community (Carrington, 2004). In so doing they have usurped the traditional roles of parents and educators as monitors of their interactions and transmissions. The practical convenience of texting, however, is no longer the preserve of the teenager; adults are using it as a cheap and quick means of information exchange.

↖ *Connect and explore*

How 'stranger danger' changed the way children play

Steve Humphries, producer of 'Hop, Skip and Jump: the story of children's play' broadcast on the BBC in 2009, charts the changes in parental attitudes to children's freedom in this article available from **http://news.bbc.co.uk/1/hi/magazine/8399749.stm**.

Is the threat of 'stranger danger' the only reason for limiting external unsupervised activity? What about the rise in car ownership, notions of freely available drugs, rising teenage pregnancy statistics and reports of racially motivated attacks? Can you think of other social issues that impinge upon young people's freedom to physically connect with the outside world?

From subcultural to mainstream

Texting is now the most common form of mobile communication; in 2008 American users alone sent over 1 trillion texts (Park, 2009). The texting phenomenon has permeated social relations across the board. Adults are joining in in droves, primarily because of the relative instancy of response from younger family members (they are more likely to reply to a text message than respond to a phone message or 'snail mail' or conventional post). This intimates that the young are shaping the behaviours of their seniors. Whether older users are simply adopting the convenience of SMS or wholly embracing the culture (in terms of moving out of their comfort zone and using text-speak rather than Standard English) is yet to be researched in any depth.

Users are also getting younger. More than half of all British children aged five to nine years own a mobile phone (Times online, 2009). They are set to be joined by an even younger generation with the imminent release in the UK of a modified handset designed to be used by toddlers. The Firefly supersedes the 'TeddyPhone' which is essentially a mobile tracking device (BBC, 2005). More than 7,000 Firefly mobiles have already been sold in Ireland, suggesting a rise in parental approval. These are functional cell phones having just five keys: on, off, mum, dad (represented pictorially) and a twenty-number phonebook. Khan (2009), digital and media correspondent for the *Telegraph*, reports concerns that such a device negates parental responsibility. While still restricted in functionality, it is far more sophisticated than the TeddyPhone; for example, it can receive (but not send) texts. The target market is parents and the sales pitch revolves around child safety. What this indicates is the creeping normalisation of mobile technology as integral to every aspect of personal life in contemporary society. Very young children are not able to use text-speak from the outset but familiarity with the medium from an early age creates an expectation that they will develop increasingly sophisticated schemas for more complex functions as they mature. This has significant implications for early learning curricula; we need to new-think not just for older children and teenagers but for the very young who are being socialised into connectivity.

Knowing how to achieve this is problematic. Certainly society is in a transitional state, a period of adjustment, with respect to what all this might mean. Just what do the norms and mores of this new technology and attendant language imply for our cultural (communal) and thus personal (individual) notions of identity? Because language and culture are inextricably linked, any change in either has significant consequences for the other:

> Our particular cultural heritage, via language, has shaped the way we think about the world in almost imperceptible ways.
>
> Adams, 2003:231

The key phrase here is 'via language'. For young people this is their language; yet some educators appear to refuse to consider this with any sincerity. There is a perceived discomfort about the whole process of texting; it has evident expediency, but value? There is, for some, the deep concern that an acceptance of a casualness in language will lead to a casualness in cognitive and behavioural practices among young people. Yet Carrington (2004:217) disputes this approach:

> It is inappropriate to dismiss this phenomenon as a fad or as simply a shorthand and inferior form of 'real' text.

The most recent messaging phenomenon is Twitter, which restricts messages (or 'tweets') to 140 characters. It has found surprising acceptance among adults; the chief executive of Twitter believes this is because of its usefulness in broadcasting ideas, questions and answers and marketing information; it is a 'one-to-many' network (Cain Miller, 2009). The GuardianEdu website uses Twitter to alert signed-up members to educational journalism. Classroom 2.0, a social network for educators interested in technoliteracies, has a tagged discussion thread that reports Twitter is being used to send out messages from schools to parents and pupils. More radically, Texas students are using Twitter to contribute to group discussions in lectures; individuals can text their comment which is sent to a central website where it is displayed instantly. Professor Rankin (History Professor) views Twitter as a way of encouraging shy students to participate, and believes that the character limit challenges randomness; students have to pare their messages which requires critical thought and discernment (Kirkpatrick, 2009).

Activity

The Twitter Experiment – UT Dallas

Input the above term into the YouTube search engine and find out how the students respond to this technology. One advantage is that there is a record of session activities and discussions which can be revisited at the student's leisure. Another is that students are encouraged to leave their comfort zone in the safety of anonymity.

There is an array of information about using Twitter for educational purposes; a particularly useful web page offering one hundred tips, applications and resources for teachers is part of the Online College Degree website. One idea is to create a Twittory, which, like the game Consequences, encourages collaborative story writing: each person in the learning group adds a tweet to move a story forward.

? *Stop and reflect*

Identifying the opportunities and threats concerning Twitter

*Information about how Twitter works and what you need to make it work can be found on the Frequently Asked Questions page at Twitter Support: **http://help.twitter.com/forums/10711/entries/13920**. How might this technology be used to create a global classroom that is information rich, inclusive and inviting?*

Some educators are using text-speak to teach Shakespeare. Learners often find the original language archaic and problematic. While the themes are universal, Shakespearian text is often inaccessible to them, in the same way text-speak is for the uninitiated. Using text-speak adds a third language to the mix; it can serve as a translational tool, one that is contemporary and fun to play with. Using translations back and forth requires analytical thinking; it also encourages learners to develop summarising skills when used in SMS format. Modern translations are available online from the SparkNotes website; these can be put into an online translator using lingo2word.com (Education Week, 2009). For example, this is the opening dialogue of *Macbeth*: wen wl 3 mEt agn, n thunder, lytnin or n rain? wen d hurlyburly's done, wen d battle's 404 n 1, that'll B ere d set of sun. Note the use of code here: '404' means 'lost'. SMS demands a close focus on the words and how they might be represented faithfully in abbreviated form. It is this focus that drives the learner to search for the *meaning* of Shakespeare's language.

Not all education is classroom based of course. Peltoniemi (2003:2) works in the field of drug and alcohol guidance and argues that:

> Mobile phones, as well as telematics in general, are instruments of personal power, especially for the young. It gives them a feeling of control and command.

Telematics, as we saw in the previous chapter, is a term describing the blending of technologies. Far from depersonalising the counselling experience (an adult perspective), Web 2.0 technologies allow greater interaction, and, for educators, the means to reach far more people than would ever be possible in a face-to-face environment. Peltoniemi (2003) cites the Textari-Helppi programme in Finland where young people could text for help with any problem that was troubling them and receive immediate (and anonymous) advice.

There is little doubt that the evils versus efficacy of text-speak will continue to attract vigorous debate, just as visual media has excited controversy:

> Thirty years ago we would perhaps not have recognised the notion that we 'read' media texts such as television and film.
>
> Bell, 2005, quoted in Ofsted, 2009

The fact that educators, as the above Ofsted report illustrates, are accepting of the notion of a visual literacy is indicative of a growing willingness to expand upon traditional definitions of literacy and explore new notions of multimodality.

Visual texts

According to Christian Metz (cited in Jensen, 2002), film is so difficult to explain because it is so easy to understand. Metz (1931–1993) was a French structuralist critic who used Saussure's structural semiotics to understand the language of film. Suassure's work was covered in the previous chapter but, briefly, structuralism explores phenomena in terms of units and rules. Units are parts of something and rules control how those units can be put together (structured) to make something else, for example language. Metz said that visual language is created through camera. This language is based on conventions and uses basic tools, for example frame, shot, cut, sequence, scene and sound techniques, and, as such, film is the result of choices and constraints.

↖ Connect and explore

Do we learn to 'read' television and film?

Jensen's excellent article explores the semiotics of cinema through a discussion of the work of structuralist critics including Metz. It helps us understand how with film we are presented not with visual suggestions, as happens with the printed sentence (or paragraph), but rather with a visual statement, the image. In the film *The Lord of the Rings*, for example, we no longer have to imagine Frodo as we do with the book; here, we are presented with him.

Jensen, R.B. (2002) Do we learn to 'read' television and film and do televisual and filmic codes constitute a 'language'? Available from **http://www.aber.ac.uk/media/students/rbj0001.html**.

The key points to remember are that: images are not neutral; they transmit a message that represents the ideology of the image-maker. Images can be denotative (represent something) and connotative (connect with something) and so involve the use of symbolism and stereotypes. Audio and music are similarly message-bearing; they are usually emotive, triggering affective responses. When all these units have been brought together to make 'something else', the final

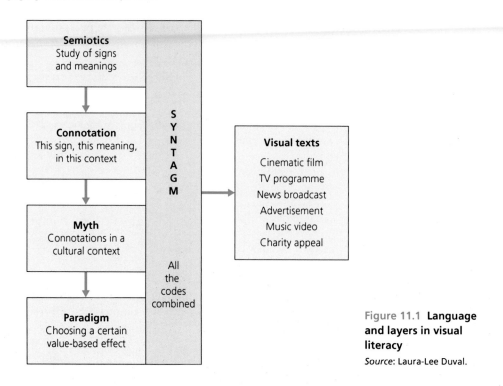

Figure 11.1 Language and layers in visual literacy
Source: Laura-Lee Duval.

product is cut and shaped through the editing process. It is for this reason that media literacy is taught at Key Stage 3 (and is likely to be brought forward to Key Stage 2 if the recommendations of the Rose (2009) Independent Review of the Primary Curriculum are adopted). Figure 11.1 illustrates the links between filmic and televisual semiotics, connotations, myths and paradigms as codes combined in a syntagm, the basic 'ingredients' of visual texts.

According to Bazalgette (2003:1):

> The job of fostering media literacy has been enshrined in the Communications Act of 2003 as a responsibility of Ofcom, the (then) new regulatory body for electronic media.

Prior to this Act, interested parties were invited to report to early consultations. One such group was the Department for Culture, Media and Sport: Broadcasting Policy Division (2001) which, in its media literacy statement, suggested that Key Stage 3 media literacy should aim to produce learners who can:

- Distinguish fact from fiction
- Appreciate different levels of realism
- Understand mechanisms of reproduction
- Differentiate reportage from advocacy
- Assess commercial messages within programmes
- Critically assess advertising

- Understand economic and presentational imperatives that underlie news management
- Explain and justify media preferences.

These learning outcomes now form the base criteria for media literacy at this level.

Connect and explore

These three papers usefully cast light on why and how media literacy came to the fore of the literacy debate at the outset of the twenty-first century.

Thoughts from a freelance writer, researcher and consultant in media education. Bazalgette, C. (2003) Literacy and the media (QCA Futures: meeting the challenge), available from **http://www.qcda.gov.uk/libraryAssets/media/11466_bazalgette_literary_and_media.pdf**.

Department for Culture, Media and Sport. Broadcasting Policy Division (2001) media literacy statement available from **http://culture.gov.uk/PDF/media_lit_2001.pdf**.

Contextualisation of the founding theorists of media literacy through developments at the end of the twentieth century. Wilcox, D. (2002) Media Literacy Paper, available from **http://www.ofcom.org.uk/consult/condocs/strategymedialit/responses/ah/hhs.pdf**.

This approach is necessary to equip young learners with the skills to discern truth and reality, and to make appropriate choices in a postmodern world. Postmodernism was discussed in the previous chapter but, briefly, it is, according to Bleakley (2004), a world in which any truth or reality is fragmented and subjective, where texts are heavily intertextualised (layered with meanings) and socially constructed, that is culturally and historically determined. Contemporary media literacy studies is a reflection of a paradigm change in attitudes towards the media. The protectionist stance of early curricula (1980s), one which 'reflected a long-standing suspicion of the media and popular culture' (Wilcox, 2002:5), has been superseded by a recognition that learning to read visual texts prepares students for the world as it is, one which is heavily mediated:

> Media education is now no longer so automatically opposed to students' experiences of the media. It does not begin from the view that the media are necessarily and inevitably harmful, or that young people are simply passive victims of media influence. It does not aim to shield them from the influence of the media but to enable them to make informed decisions on their own behalf.
>
> Buckingham, 1998, cited in Wilcox, 2002:6

Thus, acquiring media literacy is another route to acquiring student agency (Kornfeld and Prothro, 2005), the ability to make meaning from multiple messages and to respond appropriately in the best interests of oneself and one's community.

Activity

Visual texts, then and now

Then (YouTube and use the keywords Ed Murrow speech)
Ed Murrow was a radical American journalist turned broadcaster with the advent of early television. His 1958 speech to the RTNDA (Radio-Television News Directors Association), challenging the media moguls of the day, was made famous in the 2005 film *Good Night and Good Luck* (starring George Clooney as Ed Murrow). Murrow warned that television should not be just an entertaining distraction, a place to sell products:

> This instrument (television) can teach, it can illuminate; yes, and it can even inspire. But it can do so only to the extent that humans are determined to use it to those ends. Otherwise it is merely wires and lights in a box. There is a great and perhaps decisive battle to be fought against ignorance, intolerance and indifference. This weapon of television could be useful.

To read the transcript: http://www.turnoffyouryv.com/commentary/hiddenagenda/murrow.html

Now (YouTube: Peter Packer and the Digital Media Literacy Summit)
Peter Packer is a strategy adviser to the UK Film Council and also advises the Digital Media Literacy Task Force which sets out some of the priorities for media literacy teaching:

> It's about being creative with media, yes, but also about having a critical understanding of media, and furthermore knowing a bit about the context, the cultural context . . . different countries, different forms; different ways of presenting messages through media.

Watch the clip to find out more about how the task force works in practice and who is influential in media literacy today.

There is a plethora of research and information concerning the use of visual media to augment learning, and as a learning process in its own right through critical study of what is being presented and how. Morrell (2002:4) used 'popular films as academic texts worthy of critical interrogation' to include marginalised groups of learners, and to use these as routes into canonical texts (film and book). The module that connected *Native Son* and *A Time to Kill* (film versions of the novels) led students to explore their perceptions of injustices as learners in an impoverished environment, and to reproduce and disseminate their findings through a magazine they created:

> They were able to translate their analyses into quality oral debates and expository pieces . . . classroom activities laid the groundwork for more traditional academic work while fostering student activism.
>
> Morrell, 2002:5

Here activism can be linked with agency, with constructing a personal identity through negotiating conflicting presentations of who we might be, and how things are and, critically, how they might be (Kornfeld and Prothro, 2005).

↖ *Connect and explore*

For a very accessible argument concerning the whole debate about incorporating popular culture into the traditional curriculum, read Gair's (1998) comprehensive review of Giroux's (1997) book *Pedagogy and the Politics of Hope: Theory, Culture, and Schooling*. Although written before the digital explosion, Giroux's call for a critical pedagogy embodies notions of diversity and inclusion in a postmodern context.

Today, the visual reader can also be a visual writer, a creator of visual texts, through the advent of Web 2.0 tools (which allow individuals to create and broadcast video and audio files). Dovey and Kennedy (2006) argue that, when consumers of visual texts become producers of them, a new definition of media studies is required.

The Ofsted (2009) report 'English at the Crossroads' highlights case studies where television is used not just to inform or demonstrate to learners as viewers but as the basis for further literacy work. For example, Key Stage 3 learners (11–14 years) critiqued television news items and then created their own news reports. In the past these would have been written (scripted) and then acted out, a one-time event. Now young people have access to technologies that enable them to actually create a news report, one that can be filmed, edited, sound-checked, have titles and music added and broadcast via the internet. This multimodal approach to producing and disseminating text demands an ability to engage with and appreciate a range of literacies that complement each other. The same is true of longer pieces of film; mobile video cameras, automatic upload and editing software have placed the power of mass media in the hands of the young (Potter, 2005) and promote opportunities for experiential learning. Experiential learning meets the needs of the three learning domains identified by Bloom (1958) and discussed fully in the previous chapter. These are the cognitive, the affective and the psychomotor. New media studies facilitates simultaneous and focused thinking, feeling and doing.

Table 11.1 **Dovey and Kennedy present a useful comparative analysis of the differences between media studies and new media studies**

Media studies	New media studies
The effects of technology are socially determined	The nature of society is technologically determined
Active audiences	Interactive users
Interpretation	Experience
Spectatorship	Immersion
Representation	Simulation
Centralised media	Ubiquitous media
Consumer	Participant/co-creator
Work	Play

Source: adapted from Game Cultures: Computer Games as New Media (Dovey, J. and Kennedy, H.W., 2006).

> ⬉ *Connect and explore*
>
> ## Children's self-representation in digital video format
>
> **Potter, J.** (2005) 'This Brings Back a Lot of Memories' – a case study in the analysis of digital video production by young learners, *Education, Communication & Information*, 5(1), pp. 5–23.
>
> This excellent case study tracks the literary practices of two eleven-year-old boys who wanted to 'celebrate their time at primary school, just before they left and went their separate ways to their respective secondary schools.' The resulting video evidences the 'sophistication of these manipulators of moving image literacy as they merge sound, image, cultural reference and performance into a representation and celebration of their identity at a particular place and time' (p. 6).

Sound texts

Podcasts are audio files which listeners can download from the internet and access through MP3 players (MP3 is the technical jargon for the digital compression of large files into smaller ones). Video can also be transmitted. The educational innovation they offer is that a teacher can record information which students can then access on demand. In the educational context of diverse learning styles and approaches, these might seem particularly useful for auditory learners. Experiments for podcasting lectures suggest that the facility to listen again (and again and again if necessary) gives students an opportunity to cement their learning at their own pace which gives them advantages over the one time/one delivery approach that teaching is predicated upon (Brittain and Johnson, 2008). Any notion that the podcast could ever replace the traditional lecture is disputed by Hearnshaw (2006) who points out that lectures are not just orally transmitted facts but concepts and ideas that are demonstrated through diagrams, elucidated through anecdote, and made real through teacher–learner and learner–learner interaction. What is more useful is the exchange of intellectual information through free or subscription podcast feeds. A web feed is the server on which the podcasts are stored; subscribers buy software called a podcatcher which automatically 'catches' new casts as they are made and uploaded to the feed; this means the user no longer has to search for updates, as they arrive automatically.

Podcasts can also be created by students. Learners at Salford City Academy are using podcasts to broadcast to the local community as part of the three-stranded citizenship curriculum designed to foster 'social and moral responsibility, community involvement and political literacy' (QCA, 1998, cited in Adams and Calvert, 2005:11). The podcasts are broadcast through the internet radio station the students have set up. According to a case study on the National Curriculum website (2009:1), the aim is for learners 'to act as effective advocates for their community'; to achieve this they use a 'focused-conversation approach'. This encourages critical thinking through 'four levels of structured questioning: objective, reflective, interpretive and decisional'. The resulting questions are then posed during a live broadcast which is recorded, to be played when the listener wants to listen.

Literacy in lyrics

Continuing his theme of bringing popular culture into the classroom, Morrell (2002:3) uses hip-hop to reach students:

> Many rappers consider themselves educators and see at least a portion of their mission as raising the consciousness of their communities.

The teaching context was the poetry curriculum, viewing the artist as a poet; his poetry could be subject to the same critical methods of analysis as mainstream poets. In this way, the notion that poetry is representational and contextual, links were made between rap and canonical (classic) texts. Again, learners moved from consuming to producing, empowered to represent themselves and their communities through a new genre – poetry – that was, in fact, there all the time, posing as rap music. The appropriation of rap by white youth is also a unifying phenomenon, or can be, in the classroom. This is described as 'Goin' Gangsta . . . white youth who dress and act like non-white inner city "gangstas"' (Bernstein, 1995, cited in Solomon and Maasik, 1999:348). Song, musical poetry, unites; it excites debate and facilitates dialogue; it can be used as a medium through which we might better understand each other.

Activity

Can Eminem's 'Stan' be a teaching tool?

Read the following article to contextualise rap as a literacy: Kun, J. (1994) *Reading, Writing and Rap: Literacy as Rap Sound System*, available from **http://bad.eserver.org/issues/1994/12/kun.html**.

Search YouTube for the video of Eminem's 'Stan' and locate the lyrics using a lyric finder via Google. How might you use the poem to spark debate about the implications of a culture of celebrity worship? Can you help learners identify the ideological messages within and behind the lines, first on the printed page (or computer screen), then as an audio file and ultimately as a video clip? Are different literacy skills required to 'read' the same text through multiple media?

I am PC (or Mac)

So far we have considered a range of connected media and their associated literacies in a linear manner. Where they all merge is in the domain of the personal computer. This is perhaps the most problematic area of media literacy for educators, given its complexity. Nevertheless, computer literacy is a prerequisite of participation in a postmodern world. The embedding of digital technologies in every facet of contemporary life generates urgent and significant challenges for twenty-first-century schools (DCSF, 2009:2). With respect to preparation for employability it is generally accepted that:

> Skills that were once seen as high level are increasingly seen as basic skills . . . Even in those occupations traditionally thought of as low skilled there has been a dramatic growth in the use of IT.
>
> Leitch, 2006:33

What constitutes this skill set continues to evolve. With the advent of Web 2.0 technologies, the personal computer, whether sited in the workplace, school or home, has become much more than a mere text/number processing tool. The interactivity facilitated by these new applications (for example software to create, capture and share audio/video/image/text files and web pages) is revolutionising not just how we work but also how we play. Technology permeates not just our economic lives but also our social interactions and personal efficacy, dimensions of reality that have critical implications for educators because:

> Digital technologies themselves are understood to exert powerful agency in so far as our whole relationship with the external world is now heavily mediated.
>
> Dovey and Kennedy, 2006:4

'Heavily mediated' means a significant proportion of our everyday interactions take place through some form of media, for example communicating with friends through Facebook, paying a bill using an online bank account, reading an online newspaper, catching up with missed television programmes through iPlayer. It is no longer sufficient to teach purely functional skills (applications) to produce static documents. Today's users have direct access to cyberspace, a virtual world that offers unprecedented opportunities for creativity, socialisation and self-actualisation but which also has the potential to threaten. Just as we teach young learners how to navigate the real world, so we must equip them to operate safely and successfully in a virtual one. In the previous chapter, we discussed the rise of the prosumer. Anyone with the skills to create a **blog**, for example, has an instant and limitless (global) audience. Anyone with the skills to create a **wiki** can share information with collaborative partners. Anyone with the skills to play computer games can enter a virtual world, create an **avatar** (a virtual identity) and interact with countless numbers of like-minded people. Videos and images (captured by a mobile phone) can be uploaded to a global platform in minutes. The offer of the PC has extended from the observable to the experiential; today it permeates the sensorium (all our senses). This is the 3D world of contemporary learners; actors characterised by an unprecedented kinship with machines (Dovey and Kennedy, 2006).

Our deepening relationship with the internet and connected technologies

So far our journey into competing literacies has been comparatively smooth. We have travelled with relative ease from the established literacy of the written word as presented to us through the book (and its derivatives) into the more complex decoding of visual images (film), and explored the reaching and teaching of auditory learners for whom the language (literacy) of musical forms, not least the efficacy of the human voice, is key. We have considered our understandings of the era in which we operate and contextualised our discoveries with notions of postmodernism, ideology, agency and habitus (discussed in the previous chapter). We have updated our definition of literacy to one where the focus is on making meaning from multiple messages in the context of the affordances of the medium of transmission. In essence we have moved through increasingly complex reading processes to interpret visual cues of symbols, words and images (static and moving, silent and musical).

Hopefully we have adopted a critical distance as we explore each new find, careful not to assume, willing to set aside our own preconceptions; looking to learn, to think and to wonder. This is not quite as easy as it might seem at first glance; personal histories, ideologies and mindsets are often deeply entrenched – we need to see with new eyes.

We can already identify (to some extent) with the opportunities and threats associated with relatively benign technologies. We understand traditional literary genres: the story, the poem, the play. We enjoy the book, the song, the film, how what we can relate to is presented to us by others for our perpetual consumption. We have learned about a new language, text-speak, one we may be fully immersed in but through social rather than educational processes, and the jury may still be out on the appropriateness of connecting the linguistics of outside and inside school.

? Stop and reflect

- *What is multimodal literacy?*
- *How does it reflect a postmodern world?*
- *Why are mediated human interactions relevant to notions of social justice?*

Web 2.0: the portal from the real to the virtual world

We are about to enter the hinterland of computer/human relations. It will require us to open up, not just our eyes but our hearts and minds. Really grasping the essentiality of computer literacy demands that we challenge (and not automatically accept) some big ideas that have to do with how we teach the literacy of the virtual world, and how we imbue learners with the tools to move beyond functionality to self-actualisation, from employability to empowerment.

As educators, we need to break down barriers. We need to talk to one another; we need to be able to challenge what the social constructs of our roles are (teacher, facilitator, counsellor, social worker), to admit that sometimes we don't get it (new areas of practice) and, most importantly, to acknowledge the opportunities and threats afforded us through connected communication. Before we look at the theory, examine your own stance on debate surrounding multimodal literacy. What are your preconceptions? Perhaps you are a reluctant second lifer, or perhaps gaming is second nature. Is there a place for games, simulations and virtual worlds in formal learning?

> ### Connect and explore
>
> ## Computer games as learning tools?
>
> EDUCAUSE (a nonprofit organisation whose mission is to advance higher education by promoting the intelligent use of information technology) are firm advocates of computer games as pedagogical tools. They posit that:
>
>> Games, simulations, and virtual worlds provide educators with an opportunity to engage learners in an immersive and interactive environment that requires knowledge, decision making, and information management skills . . . Research suggests that these environments can play a significant role in facilitating learning through engagement, group participation, immediate feedback, and providing real-world contexts.
>
> For a rich source of research and resources, visit their site at: **http://www.educause. edu/ELI/LearningTechnologies/GamesSimulationsandVirtualWorl/11263**.
>
> A particularly interesting overview (on that page) is provided by Foreman, J. (2004) Game-Based Learning: How to Delight and Instruct in the 21st Century, *EDUCAUSE Review*, 39(5), pp. 51–66. Available from **http://www.educause.edu/EDUCAUSE+Review/ EDUCAUSEReviewMagazineVolume39/GameBasedLearningHowtoDelighta/157927**, viewed October 2009.

The rise of the cyborg

According to Dovey and Kennedy (2006), a radically new aspect of human psychology has emerged. This notion began to take hold in the mid-1980s when Donna Haraway, now Professor of Feminist Theory and Technoscience (at the European Graduate School, Switzerland), described this new entity as a '**cyborg**'. What it might mean to be a cyborg has been developed by other theorists. Certainly cyborgs occupy cyberspace and operate in cybercultures:

> What began as Cold War effort to speed up communications has become cyberspace, an electronic geography that reterritorializes pre-existing geographies, opening up new and social cultural worlds that are only beginning to be explored but that quite probably are already redefining what it means to be human.
>
> Poster, 2002, cited in Dovey and Kennedy, 2006:5

Cybernetics describes the positive feedback loop between humans and technologies: for example, technology drives the activities a human can perform; in turn, the experiential nature and results of this activity drives the human to further push at technological barriers. One feeds the other and the appetite appears endless, hence the designation of the loop as positive; there is, as yet, no brake on the system.

The literate cyborg

If all this sounds a little fantastic, the stuff of modern (rather than postmodern) Hollywood blockbusters, something quite alluring (as entertainment) but alien (as a lived reality), think again. In the developed world, we are so entrenched in consumption, in novelty and acquisition, we rarely exercise critical distance in considering what we do, how and why. A constant stream of new, faster, racier technologies is offered, it seems, almost daily. Our society is connected in ways we barely notice; the doctor logs direct into the hospital appointments database, the academic feeds grades into the student profile database, the TV salesperson alerts the TV Licensing Authorities of a sale, the local garage uploads MOT results directly to the DVLA, you transfer monies from one place to another online and so on. You may not consider yourself a cyborg but could you bear to be denied access to your mobile phone, your email account, your social networking space, the internet itself?

> With modernity, mechanical models of physical and social life gave way to models centered on production and maximization of life itself, including the coupling of the body and machines in new ways, in factories, schools, hospitals and family homes.
>
> Escobar, 2000, cited in Dovey and Kennedy, 2006:15

We live in a connected world and this has profound implications for what it means to be human, and what it means to be to be included.

The Digital Inclusion Task Force

As discussed in the previous chapter, Martha Lane Fox (founder of Lastminute.com and internet millionaire) has become the champion of the Digital Inclusion Task Force (Wakefield, 2009). In an interview with BBC news she explained how the British government is anxious to save money by offering more services online (the majority of its transactions, 80 per cent, are already internet-based). The decision to do this further disadvantages those who lack access and/or computer skills (25 per cent of the population). This group is the hardest to reach in terms of digital inclusion. There are 6,000 UK online centres; places where people can access computers in their community, for example local libraries. They are, however, in the main not well or regularly attended by most of the local populace. Some 17 million Britons have never been online, and 43 per cent would choose to remain offline even with the offer of subsidised, or free, hardware and software and household broadband connections. This has significant implications for the educational outcomes of some of the poorest and most excluded children growing up in a digital world. Parental involvement in education is a critical component in achievement (Tomlinson, 2008). When a parent cannot provide support in terms of equipment or skills it is incumbent upon the school to do more, in terms of the provision of a digital education. For some adults the preconception that the internet user is somehow a solitary, if not sad, soul still persists.

The Controversies box overleaf illustrates some of the differences of opinion around whether the internet is a positive or negative force in terms of social inclusion or isolation.

Controversies

'The internet can make you lonely and isolated'

Agree:

- The notion that the internet not only exacerbates but causes loneliness was set in motion by the findings of the 'HomeNet Study' (Kraut et al., 1998, cited in Whitty and McLaughlin, 2005:1436).

- It was quickly captured and disseminated by the media and, a decade later, has some resonance with the public consciousness of those not yet connected (including parents who see their children engrossed in multimedia communication).

- Some survey research indicates that online social relationships are weaker than offline ones (Parks et al., 1998) and other findings suggested that people who use the internet heavily spend less time with family and friends (Cole, 2000; Nie and Erbring, 2000).

- Whitty and McLaughlin (2005) conducted a research project with undergraduates to explore the relationship between loneliness and internet self-efficacy. Their aim was to challenge some of the myths concerning the image of the cyborg, paying particular attention to:

  > Whether the Internet is detrimental to one's psychological health or whether, instead, it might enhance one's well-being.
  >
  > Whitty and McLaughlin, 2005:1436

Disagree:

- It is, perhaps, this pervasive belief that the computer fractures rather than enhances inter- and intrapersonal interactions among those who are self-excluded from internet interactivity that underlies the polarisation of this debate. Much work has been done in the intervening decade to dispel Kraut et al.'s (1998) assertions; their original methodology has been dismissed as invalid. Not only was the sample size limited but the participants were novice users; none had accessed the internet before Kraut supplied them with free equipment and connections.

- According to LaRose et al. (2001, cited in Whitty and McLaughlin, 2005), drawing conclusions about the effects of long-term internet use by psychologically profiling short-term users was fundamentally flawed. The length of time this group spent online and the stress they experienced was far more likely to be correlated with trying to work out how to use the internet. Indeed, a follow-up study found that the same participants had developed considerable self-efficacy:

  > Could it be that the participants in the HomeNet study became more Internet savvy over time?
  >
  > Whitty and McLaughlin, 2005:1436

What do you think? Which side of the argument do you favour?

The key point here is not whether Kraut et al. (1998) were wrong or misguided, but that it is a classic example of the power of the (established) media to disseminate a message that can reshape the core of a generation. Popular news culture, of which newspapers and television magazine programmes are an integral part, is not about fact. It's about persuasion of readers and viewers (income generators); people elect (and pay) to read/view journalistic styles that reflect their own beliefs and values. Broadcasting media (newspapers and news channels) are corporations; they exist primarily for profit (the BBC is exempt from this). Corporations have agendas; their first obligation is to their shareholders, not the truth (Bakan, 2004); they do not have to check the validity of their sources for stories. Why is this important? If we are to successfully (and fruitfully) navigate the virtual world, we must understand what is going on in our own, real world.

Today, newspapers themselves are under threat; the internet (via connected devices) has made news accessible 24/7. But who are we reading and why should we believe them? Understanding notions of agenda and profit are tools we need in order to understand how language is used to persuade. Persuasion is a technique of argumentation. Politicians do it; they use rhetoric as a language to persuade. Teachers do it; they appeal to authority (established teaching methods). Advertisers do it; they appeal to novelty. The power of fallacious arguments is their capacity to persuade, and their commonplace usage.

Activity

Understanding how we are persuaded by forms of words

Don Lindsay is a computer scientist and engineer who worked in higher education and who has a passion for helping students understand fallacious arguments and how they are used to persuade and misdirect. Fallacious arguments are the antithesis of objective critical thinking and discourse. Use this link to explore examples of commonly used fallacious arguments: **http://www.don-lindsay-archive.org/skeptic/arguments.html**.

Why does this matter? Here we return to ideology, and acknowledging that every message arises from an agenda. The confusion it imbues in us shows postmodernism at its best and worst. At best we are free (once we are armed) to make informed choices; at worst we are ill-equipped to self-actualise or even self-preserve. This has implications for inclusion and something called critical distance, the ability to stand back from a message and interpret it objectively on multiple levels rather than simply accept it wholesale.

The implications of cyberculture

According to Dovey and Kennedy (2006:16), Haraway credited the cyborg with:

> the radical potential to undermine binary hierarchies of 'race', class and gender through new forms of representation and new metaphors for being.

In other words, this was the *opportunity* for a radical rethink (new think?) of the very structures of society and thus the inequities inherent to it. The old order could be challenged through new media which 'unsettles pre-existing identity formations: national, gendered, ethnic, racialist' (Poster, 2002, cited in Dovey and Kennedy, 2006:16). This theme, of the potential of cybernetic feedback to radicalise the very fabric of human society, to facilitate the wholesale deconstruction of inequitable relations and replace them with new equitable social constructs, appears, to the uninitiated, somewhat grand to say the least. Simply put, Poster was arguing that the arrival of this new form of hybrid and neutral human offers the human race the opportunity to rebuild society, this time without the social injustices we know today where people are discriminated against or disadvantaged because of their nationality, gender, ethnicity or race. This conundrum regarding power relations is captured in the theory of technicity:

> The significant aspect of the new term 'technicity' is to encapsulate, in conceptual terms, the connections between an identity based on certain types of attitude, practices, preferences and so on and the importance of technology as a construction of that identity.
>
> Dovey and Kennedy, 2006:17

Poster argued that in front of the computer we are all invisible and thus all equal. We are different in terms of our likes and dislikes, but fundamentally we share an equal status.

? Stop and reflect

Who are you interacting with?

When you play a game over the internet, you have no idea of the nationality, gender, ethnicity, race or religion of the person/people you are interacting with; you deal only with the persona, the identity that person or group opts to present you with. Similarly, you can create your own identity, use a name or build an avatar that may or may not represent you as you are in the real world. When it comes to making purchases or accessing services online, you will not be discriminated against because the key issue is what you want (and whether you can pay for it, or are entitled to it), nor who you are as a member of a specific social grouping. The internet allows us to reinvent and re-present ourselves and to join with others who have the same attitudes, practices and preferences as we do. The next time you interact online, take time to see how much you can really identify about the person/people you are interacting with.

This anonymous equality can, in itself, be threatening:

> An invisible computer is most likely a monopolist's best friend . . . Molecular society emerges in a paradoxical moment, as great transformations always do. The irruption of popular empowerment coincides with the climax phase in the evolution of oligopolies, a final division of very great spoils.
>
> Moulthrop, 2004, cited in Dovey and Kennedy, 2006:9

Moulthrop is building on Poster's argument that in front of the computer we are all invisible and all equal, and that the rise (irruption) of this new social group comprising these new components or molecules (cyborgs) has happened at the same time that oligopolies, sometimes called oligarchies, have emerged. An **oligopoly** is a small group of people within whose hands the seat of power lies. Let's think about this for a moment. We have already said that, when the power or at least the opportunity for instant access to mass communications through technology is available to the individual, there are inevitable consequences. These can be opportunities: a CV, a dance/song video, a recipe, an invention sent across the world that brings (due to its 'hit' rate) instant success, personally and perhaps commercially gratifying. Or they can be a threat: cyber bullying, the release of a picture that discredits someone, the foolishness of the employee who (having invited his boss to be his Facebook friend) later posted how he was chucking a sickie . . . needless to say he was somewhat unceremoniously chucked himself (Aulia, 2008).

Moulthrop draws our attention to the idea that any belief we have of being in control of our transactions is an illusion. He argues that, instead, we are being fed just enough to satisfy our emotional, social and cognitive (and, should we join the Nintendo Wii generation, physical) appetites to make us believe that we are in control. To all intents and purposes this seems a manageable transaction: we feed into the computer; it feeds back to us; we are done and we turn it off. The pay-off is a relaxing (entertaining), or industrious (ordering groceries, booking a holiday online) evening. Yet, while we sleep, thousands of bytes of data are being processed about us. The sites we visit are being digitally noted; someone you have never met knows what you like to eat, to purchase, how much you drink/date/smoke and with what/whom and where you like to play. You are feeding a machine you may not know existed, and it is turning you into a new form of human.

The rise of the prosumer

In the previous chapter you were asked to watch the prosumer clip on YouTube. Before we think about the implications of the notion of a prosumer society run by an oligarchy, one in which we are passively subsumed (the reality) rather than actively consuming (the rhetoric), let's weigh up what is or what might be going on here and what it might mean for us. This is the society Moulthrop identifies, one in which media literate individuals buy into the illusion of the computer as an emancipatory tool, one which frees and extends their choices, when, in fact, this sense of personal control is an illusion sold to them by media moguls, those who truly hold the power.

It should be clearly understood that access to this world is inherently defined by access to literacy as a basic participatory tool; to join it, you must be able to use a computer. If it is to become an emancipatory one, one that really does free and extend our choices then our education system must commit to a 180-degree turn. Rose (2006) offers some hope but, at the time of writing, his placement of ICT at the heart of the curriculum is a suggestion. It is insufficient to our day to simply pay lip service to the notion of the computer as a means to an (informed) end. If we do not teach children and young people the skills to adopt a critical distance to the potential opportunities and threats this world presents then effectively we are sending our children out there alone. Michael Carr-Gregg, a leading Australian psychologist and author of *Real Wired Child* (2007), likens this to a re-run of *Lord of the Flies*, except this time it is not accidental abandonment but wilful neglect. He considers that we are putting our children in a boat with no adults to guide them as they arrive in this new and undiscovered land. We are almost asking for 'there be dragons' to be their epitaph, if not physically, then cognitively, emotionally and socially. This concern underpins the creation of the 'Click Clever, Click Safe Code', a campaign created by UKCCIS (the UK Council for Child Internet Safety). Their website offers internet safety advice for young people and their parents using the code:

> *Zip it:* Keep your personal stuff private and think about what you do and say online.
>
> *Block it:* Block people who send nasty messages, and don't open unknown links and attachments.
>
> *Flag it:* Flag up with someone you trust if anything upsets you or if someone asks to meet you offline.

(http://clickcleverclicksafe.direct.gov.uk/index.html, 2010)

UKCCIS is an amalgam of representatives from government, children's charities and industry (including Microsoft, BT, Yahoo, CEOP and the NSPCC). It was inaugurated following a review led by Dr Tanya Byron, a government-appointed psychologist and popular presenter of television series such as *Little Angels* and *The House of Tiny Tearaways*, which helped dysfunctional families develop coping and resolution strategies. The campaign is being rolled out to children and young people in the state school sector (including Early Years settings) and to parents through the media; Byron refers to it as the 'Green Cross Code' for coping with online traffic (Fildes, 2009).

Activity

Zip it, Block it, Flag it: the online Green Cross Code

Primary and secondary schools are being introduced to the code. This link: **http://news. bbc.co.uk/1/hi/technology/8398763.stm** accesses Fildes' (2009) online article and contains three video clips.

1 A primary school teacher talks about the need to teach internet safety – note the class are competing with children around the world, using the mass platform Mathletics, a computer 'game' designed to help make learning maths fun: **http:// www.mathletics.co.uk/**.

2 Secondary school pupils give their views of school web blocks and the assistant headteacher explains the thinking behind the Local Authority (LA) filtering system where the LA block all sites not considered educational in order to take responsibility away from individual schools.

3 Dr Tanya Byron discusses the rationale for the campaign.

How would you introduce the notion of internet safety to children and young people who might perceive the review's recommendations that parents use filters and locate computers in family spaces as challenging their trustworthiness?

Let's review what we have learned so far in this section:

- The internet has changed, from a bank of information from which we might safely draw information.

- We hold, even if we do not know it, deeply held beliefs about what is right and what is wrong, what is safe and what is not.
- That advocates of this new world have powerful and persuasive arguments.
- That detractors – provided their timing is right with respect to exposure in populist media – can influence a generation.
- That technology can be hijacked – just as the young snatched the potential for text-speak and made it their own, so can huge corporations manipulate this new world.
- That technology can be blamed for the human condition. In a world where happiness is predicated on the work ethic (leading to the pleasure principle, i.e. that time off is infinitely more enjoyable than time on), then over-involvement with a machine simply results in isolation.
- That language (and thus literature in all its multimodal forms) can be used to persuade and that simply because 'it is written' does not make it true.
- That we are not in control but that through education we can identify not just opportunities but also threats, personal, national and global.

These premises underpin the UNESCO (2004) report 'New Ignorances, New Literacies: Learning to Live Together in a Globalizing World'. International contributors such as Swee-Hin, Laureate of the UNESCO Peace Education Prize 2000, acknowledge that connectedness is inextricably linked to notions of social justice, social responsibility and ultimately social cohesion:

> Today, an increasing number of children and adults worldwide, especially when personal and social resources permit, are travelers in cyberspace. While the Internet has undoubtedly facilitated ease and speed of communications, unparalleled access to information and provide creative tools for education, nevertheless its significant role in promoting stereotypes and increasingly hate, racism and ideologies of violence needs urgent attention.
>
> Swee-Hin, 2004, cited in UNESCO, 2004:153

A computer literacy that is fit for purpose is thus regarded as key to navigating this world safely and successfully; we need not only to be able to find information, but also the discernment to handle it appropriately.

Getting started: educating young people in multiple connected literacies

Today the internet has multiple applications; we need a new taxonomy to begin to think about its effectiveness in education. A simple framework might be to categorise **cyber-interactions** (the activities we do that are mediated through computers) as informative, instructive or immersive (or a combination of these at its most complex). Here the subdivisions are about receiving information, interacting for instruction and ultimately fully experiential learning through immersion, what is referred to as a 'digital education' by organisations such as TEEM (Teachers Evaluating Educational Multimedia).

McFarlane et al. (2002) Report on the Educational Use of Games, available from http://www.teem.org.uk/publications/teem_gamesined_full.pdf.

This report canvassed teachers' evaluation of games in a classroom context, parents' views on software usage and primary and secondary pupils' experiences of game playing to consider the implications for successful computer game design for classroom use. The main recommendations concerned design and navigation issues: accuracy of content, save and restart facilities, teacher information and volume control. Successful elements were pupil collaboration, no timed-out function, and the inclusion of useful knowledge. The main issues for the curriculum, the review concluded, were that, although the majority of participants in the study (teachers, parents and pupils) commented on the value of games in making them think and collaborate, it was debatable whether these two attributes alone could justify their inclusion in the school curriculum as it was then framed and resourced; games need to add more value to warrant a place.

A later report by UNESCO (2006) Unlimited learning, computer and video games in the learning landscape: http://www.elspa.com/assets/files/u/unlimitedlearningth-eroleofcomputerandvideogamesint_344.pdf suggests significant progress in the potential of games to provide educational value: 'This report is an important step in beginning the challenging and exciting process of developing potentially powerful new partnerships between the games industry and education' (Lord Puttnam of Queensgate, CBE, President of UNICEF UK, 2006:1).

The informative internet

The opportunity for learners to access a vast range of information has given rise to concerns about a 'copy-and-paste generation' (Powell, 2008, http://efoundations. typepad.com/efoundations/2008/01/the-copy-and-pa.html). The implication (if not the evidence) is that learners of all ages are roaming the internet like digital hunter-gatherers. They know how to find information and they know how to store it. According to a recent survey conducted by ATL (the Association of Teachers and Lecturers, 2008), over half of teachers have been presented with plagiarised work for assessment. **Plagiarism** is a concept that needs to be taught and taught early. Think back to the prosumer clip; this appears to suggest that in the future the notion of intellectual property might be incongruous in an information society. The rationale for this is that, now that there are so many digital voices, how can we be certain who can claim ownership of an idea? References are useful guides to further reading, the argument goes, but rarely add to the income of internet authors who choose to upload their thinking (university access to journal articles *does* produce revenue through subscription). This is a purely economic argument, one that ignores the ethics of intellectual property ownership. A computer literacy fit for purpose must be rooted in ethical practice.

Much of the debate around plagiarism is associated with the notion of cheating but it is deeper than that. It is also about shallow learning. One threat is that cutting and pasting masquerades as progress. Learners appear to achieve until they reach a level where application (of ideas, theories or models) is required. The move from descriptive to interpretive and ultimately critically evaluative thinking is impeded when learners cannot perceive the value in putting things into their own words. Until the turn of the century, this skill was essential when education was delivered through a limited range of textbooks; copying out in longhand was laborious and would quickly be identified. The sheer speed of the computer processor in locating and capturing information is an affordance of the medium that affects the thinking processes of the user:

> It seems that today's youth simply do not have the time and patience to learn about the world in the same way we did. They have different means at their disposal. For young people, the screen has become such an attractive and irresistible power as the Sirens who bedazzled Odysseus.
>
> Livaneli, 2004, cited in UNESCO, 2004:89

While this may seem rather a quaint way of describing our relationship with the PC, it does draw attention to the fact that it is easy to get distracted when learning in this way. It is not just the potential lure of entertainment, for example social networking sites, instant messaging and games. Even when we stay on task there are so many links to further (and possibly) better information we might use in our studies, it is easy to find ourselves with heaps of information but consequently less time to read it to any depth.

Another threat concerns the **validity** of information. Learners need the skills to identify the authority of a text, the agenda of the writer (producer), in order to be able to test its **reliability**. Unless learners can make meaning out of what they encounter then the medium becomes the message. This was what McLuhan (1911–1980) predicted, i.e. the message is an end unto itself so what appears to be active engagement is actually passive acceptance, the antithesis of agency and actualisation. In other words, we are absorbed by the quantity of what we have found, rather than the quality. We think we are working hard but in fact we are taking a surface rather than a deep approach to learning, we are meeting a short-term objective (getting the assignment done), rather than the long-term (how has doing this assignment moved me forward in my thinking, feeling and doing?).

The instructional internet

Web 2.0 applications offer a plethora of opportunities for instruction by facilitating an action and response relationship (I do, the computer does) between the user and the machine. It is this relationship that underpins the whole debate about games and gaming. The essence of a computer game is that it is built upon a reward system, i.e. you can win. This, according to Johnson (2005:34) is what accounts for its success; it is able to 'tap into the brain's natural reward circuitry'. Achievement brings pleasure; as we have seen, humans are sensate beings; what we enjoy (cognitively, emotionally and physically) we seek more of. Games encourage this seeking behaviour; the neuroscience or study of the nervous system that supports this assertion comes from work into neural activity in the case of drug addiction (Johnson, 2005). It is this subtle connotation with addictive potential that disturbs some detractors. Similarly, pleasure invokes excitement, and excitement is not easy to control in the learning environment. According to McFarlane et al. (2002), who wrote the TEEM report referred to earlier, a further concern is that some games are notionally educational; in fact the actual content and links with the curriculum can appear incidental to learners as well as teachers. This was a significant conclusion of the report although individual games were not singled out and identified.

There are still some dissenters who demand evidence that learning through games must be empirically shown to be more effective than learning from books before they can be countenanced. This is an interesting notion because it ignores the fact that, in order to teach, one must first reach. A pilot scheme using games consoles to teach maths by Learning and Teaching Scotland (LTS) has been criticised by an Edinburgh University Professor. The argument is economic:

> This study shows there is no advantage – why should we spend money on finding out more rather than spending money on good teaching and good learning?
>
> Professor Della Sala, quoted in a BBC2 interview, November 2009

Surely there is no greater imperative than 'finding out more' to appreciate what does constitute 'good teaching and good learning' in a multimodal world? This appears to be an example of a generational divide; maths is indeed a serious subject but does that imply that how it is learned cannot be fun? (Revisit the Mathletics website referred to earlier.)

Enjoyment of computer activities was noted by many of the teachers who contributed to the TEEM research. Their difficulties centred on a mismatch between game content and the curriculum and time. Many commented that there was not sufficient time to become competent in playing the game and to develop an awareness of its strengths and limitations. It also takes time to actually play a game; if it is to have any educational value then learners need to be instructed beforehand and de-briefed afterwards. One area that might have been seen as a problem, the supply of equipment, had an unanticipated benefit as it forced collaboration which was perceived to be more successful in transferable skills development than lone working. The integration of computer games into schools can thus be problematic; these problems are 'present in primary schools, but significantly more acute in secondary' (McFarlane et al., 2002:16) because numbers of learners are higher, and their learning needs significantly more complex.

The immersive internet

So far we have looked at degrees of computer use, to access information and to receive instruction. The relationship between user and machine is perceived to be relatively benign in both cases. It is where stimulation becomes simulation that the greatest fears manifest among educators. When experiential learning goes beyond a kind of active but distinctly separate responder, to a deep sensory immersion in a game, one where the user leaves one world for another; for example, in Second Life there can be a sense of discomfort (if not outright fear) among spectators. There is little general or common knowledge about the nature of games and, as we have discussed, ignorance can perpetuate fear.

So what is simulation? According to Aarseth (2004, cited in Dovey and Kennedy, 2006:10):

> Simulation is the hermeneutic Other of narratives; the alternative mode of discourse, bottom up and emergent where stories are top-down and preplanned. In simulations, knowledge and experience is created by the player's actions and strategies, rather than recreated by a writer or moviemaker.

Hermeneutics refers to ways of interpreting, understanding texts. Here the implication is that we need new ways to understand how readers read a story that they themselves are creating in a virtual place but in real time. An immersive computer scenario is not like a dramatic play that the player plays to a script written by someone else; here they are writing the script themselves and as they go. This means that rules are not externally imposed in terms of the unfolding of events to the player; there are, however, as Johnson (2005) points out, physical and philosophical conditions and consequences – actions evoke reactions. Games are effectively models, models which simulate or mimic three-dimensional environments. Immersed players thus negotiate with the text using 'model-based thinking' (Gee, 2009:4) premised on the principles of Newtonian mechanics or modelling physics (Hestenes, 1992, cited in Gee, 2009). In other words, just as what goes up must come down in the real world, so it must in the virtual one, although it is possible for humans (or at least their avatars) to fly in Second Life. Gee (2009) juxtaposes this claim with a quote from the designer of Sim City and Spore taken from Mastrapa's (2008:2) blog:

> If you look at any kid playing a game, what they do is they go up and they grab the controller and they start pushing buttons randomly. They observe the results. They start building a model in their head for how the buttons are mapped. Then they start trying to set high-level goals. They start building a more and more elaborate model in their head of the underlying simulation in our game. And they're doing it purely through the scientific method. They observe data. They craft and experiment and do interactions to test their experiment. They observe their results then they increase the resolution of their model. And that's pretty much exactly what the scientific method is. So I think any kid, almost inherently, knows that and recognizes it as such.

This captures perfectly the learning experience games offer. The games experience is so intense and so all encompassing that we have to move out of the familiar hermeneutics associated with reading text to adopt new models (from other disciplines) to understand human behaviour when that human is totally immersed in possibility. To the uninitiated, all this may seem a step too far, an attempt to legitimise the informal (and thus capture the lucrative education market). But Johnson (2005) disputes the notion that games are chaotic. Rather, game playing is about 'finding order and meaning in the world, and making decisions that help create that order' (p. 62).

The game play experience is about *thinking, feeling* and *doing* simultaneously. Thus game play accommodates all three of Bloom's (1956) learning domains in the context of a pleasurable experience. Humans are sensate beings; we return to what we find pleasurable to re-experience that pleasure. We are also able to defer gratification if the wait generates a higher intensity of pleasure. Computer games, as has been said, are about reward. They persuade gamers that it is worth taking the time, making the effort, and spending the energy to learn how objects work, how your avatar can move on the ground or in the air. It is worth strategising what you want and how you're going to get it, the seeking behaviour that we are wired to crave (Yoffe, 2009). As games software has become increasingly sophisticated, so educators have started to look at virtual worlds as potential pedagogical tools, a means of harnessing seeking behaviours for formal learning and skills development.

Second Life, described in Case study 11.2 opposite, is an example of how learning can be accessed using computer games (as a product). Other educators are using the creation of computer games (as a process) by learners to develop multiple skills and literacies (Kirkpatrick, 2008). Game creation involves many stages and solutions, from inception to the marketplace, and these demand that learners develop what Gee (2009:4) refers to as:

> Twenty-first century skills . . . an embodied empathy for complex systems; 'grit' (passion + persistence); playfulness that leads to innovation: design thinking; collaborations in which groups are smarter than the smartest person in the group and; real understanding that leads to problem solving and not just test passing.

Learners new to the internet, whether they are using it for information, for instruction or ultimately for immersion, are motivated to persevere with steep learning curves for the reward of achievement. The technology is new; the pedagogical concept is not. Dewey (1910/1991:224) was writing about the notion of deep learning a century ago:

> Let the facts be presented so as to stimulate imagination and culture ensues naturally enough.

Conclusion

One of the central messages of this chapter, and of Chapter 10, is that boundaries are critical in our personal and social lives. We have explored how those boundaries are being pushed against, if not completely relocated, by forces beyond any group's control. Navigating the connected world demands action rather than assumption. In an educational setting, cyborgs must learn to agree conduct, and they must do so with the informed guidance of educators.

There is hope: in the Ofsted (2009) report 'English at the Crossroads', a previous chief inspector, David Bell, is quoted as saying:

> What is immediately clear . . . is how much more is expected of readers than 30 years ago. The skills needed to read a novel at home are vastly different from those required to search on the internet, read and compose a text message or review a number of different reports on a handheld device such as a BlackBerry . . .Thirty years ago we would

perhaps not have recognised the notion that we 'read' media texts such as television and film . . . Increasingly, texts that were exclusively verbal such as newspapers are extending the notion of visual literacy. Many texts, including those enjoyed by children, now express meaning through both verbal and nonverbal or visual means. As technological changes multiply, therefore, each generation needs to rethink the concepts of literacy and reading.

The message of advocates of technoliteracy is that the natural enthusiasm for multimodal literacy among the young can and must be harnessed through a technological curriculum. This is new-think.

Case study 11.2
Second Life: I log on, therefore I am

Second Life (SL), perhaps one of the best known online simulation games, is referred to by Kamel Boulos et al. (2007:233) as a kind of 'collaborative 3-D wiki space' (see Figure 11.2). What makes SL so popular, they suggest, is the advanced technologies embedded within it, for example a 'unique in-world weather system, with realistic day-night cycle support' and that members can create a 'fully textured high-resolution avatar that can be finely customised'. The particular interest of these researchers was the use of SL in medical and health education. One of the positive features of simulation is that it provides users with an opportunity to practise activities that have an associated risk with their decision-making process, for example in the development of clinical skills.

Much of what this game carries in terms of information is available through the 'real' internet; simulation allows groups comprising very large populations to come together and organise their 'second lives' in a way that suits their discipline best. For example ISTE (the International Society for Technology in Education) has an island (area) in Second Life. According to their introductory notecard (this is an SL object or device that players can click on to find out more about where they are), ISTE represents 85,000 professional members. ISTE Island is where they can meet (as customised avatar forms), exchange ideas through lectures and seminars (audio) or, in informal groups, talk (through a microphone or via text chat using instant messaging) to each other, and locate resources such as lesson activities, podcasting software, ideas for best practice.

Many universities have a presence in SL. Shephard (2007) reports that many are offering courses that include an element of Second Life activity. There is as yet little, if any, rigorous (peer-reviewed) research into this phenomenon but online tutor evaluations of pockets of experience indicate some common issues for tutors. There is regular reference to the need for high-specification computers and the time required for new gamers to adapt to the navigational and 'netiquette' demands of SL. One especially pertinent point is that replication of real-life facilities for transmissive rather than active learning is not neutral but negative. Students resent layers of complexity to access what they can already access simply (Parker and Webber, 2008). For example, simply replicating the student experience on campus online by putting materials up that they can already access via the VLE is frustrating. Students need to consider that it is worth learning a new application because it brings different (and greater) rewards.

Customising an Avatar

Members can:

- Fully customise a sophisticated avatar
- Fly within a location
- Teleport to different places
- Purchase land
- Build content
- Visit cultural sites
- Visit new places
- Take snapshots and keep/send them
- Socialise with other cultures
- Navigate multi-media content video
- Browse virtual libraries/document collections
- Play multi-player games from a range of genres
- Develop social skills through realistic voice chat and instant messaging
- Develop professional practice skills using simulated scenarios
- Attend and participate in live events (concerts, meetings)
- Build communities (learning, support, special interest)
- Buy, sell and advertise virtual and real-life goods and services, trading in Linden dollars which are exchangeable with US Dollars

Flying

Figure 11.2 **The lure of virtual worlds such as Second Life**

Source: Adapted from Kamel Boulos et al. (2007); screen shots: Laura-Lee Duval.

Acklam Grange school in Middlesbrough has become one of the first in the UK to hold lessons in the world of Second Life (BBC, 2009). The school used a 'locked down area', according to the headmaster, John Bate, so that the group could use 3D immersive learning to develop multiple literacies while accessing 'facts' about how the heart works. Go online to watch the video at: http://news.bbc.co.uk/newsbeat/hi/technology/newsid_7869000/7869303.stm.

Questions for discussion

1 *Do you think that VLEs like Second Life can offer any learning opportunities that real life cannot?*

2 *From your own experience of using technology in your education to date, what were the best 'interactive' experiences? Why were they successful? How did they help you learn?*

Summary

In this and the previous chapter we have explored a paradigmatic change in thinking about contemporary literacy. We contextualised the need to rethink in the light of the prevailing debate about literacy, learner achievement and under-achievement, and the demands of a global world driven by unprecedented technological advances. We recognised how learning has changed, how far apart the inside and outside of the classroom experiences have become, and how teaching and learning are subsequently being reframed with consequences for both teachers and learners. We have come across notions of student and teacher agency. The familiar power hierarchy of our educational system is subtly shifting in places. When learners are more in-the-know than teachers it can engender fears of redundancy (as in not being useful rather than unemployed, although that may come to be the case as younger technoliterate graduates move into the system). Redundancy is a precursor of reluctancy; reluctancy is an emotional response that can lead to rejection of new ways of literacy teaching, hence the notion that advocates of multimodal literacies are radical educators.

Radical educators (Friere, Illich) have always been involved with notions of social injustice, of disadvantage and oppression. We explored definitions of literacy that were far from postmodern; rather, they represented the economic needs of the time and the place, literacy as a social construct. This brought us to think about the consequences of illiteracy and to move away from the psychological model of a learner who is disengaged (it's their fault) to a consideration of what we are asking them to engage with (could it be our fault?).

We know that levels of learning, at least when they are provided free at the point of need by the state, in state-controlled primary, secondary and tertiary education, correlate to the needs of the state. A brief journey through just over a decade of literacy teaching shows almost a desperate approach to teaching children to read. We then explored the politics that contextualises all this, to consider who is responsible for literacy teaching in terms of content and delivery. We were exploring the ideology that underpinned this teaching. Again this indicates a shift in power, from teachers to the state, and recently, from the state to teachers – but, we asked, is that the transfer of power, or accountability?

Research and reflection then suggested some hope in Rose's (2009) review of curriculum content where ICT was established as one of the cornerstones (alongside

▶

literacy, numeracy and personal development) of a curriculum fit for purpose. The General Election in 2010 will determine whether there is the political will for these recommendations to become embedded in a holistic approach to literacy teaching.

We then moved on from historical and contemporary issues to think about the future. To be equipped for this journey we armed ourselves with a pertinent selection of evaluative tools, notably an understanding of what postmodernism means, what a text might be, the ideologies that underpin messages, how learners learn (in a 3D way, that is, exploring and experiencing multiple competences). We learned that actually we should not be taken aback by these new ways of thinking and feeling as part of the learning process. Human beings like rules, and need structure. Saussure (1857–1913) wrote over a century ago but he gave us a map to navigate text-speak, something he could never have imagined. The point is that he captured our need for certainty (the rules) but also our love of novelty (the units).

Our next step took us to the frequent disconnection of adults from the connected generation. Educators and parents as well as other interested parties are being asked to 'up our game' exponentially. We are asked to step outside our comfort zone over and over again, to embrace popular culture, which, as we have seen, has been called a 'compromise equilibrium' and a 'transactional learning' space. Digital divides must be bridged, practically and culturally.

To this end we explored innovative practice. We looked at the revamping of characteristics of new media studies. Much of this was predicated on an understanding of text-speak, the language of connectedness. We met with innovation (people who do choose to innovate, because they see the wider picture) and reluctance (people who do not innovate because to do so would take them out of their comfort zone). We looked at a range of connected textual devices and schemes, all building up to three distinct categories of using the internet: for information, for instruction, for immersion. Contemporary young learners are digital natives (Prensky, 2001) well-versed in experiential learning, thinking, feeling and doing, outside the classroom; contemporary literacy practices must embrace these attributes within.

References

Adams, M. (2003) The reflexive self and culture: a critique, *British Journal of Sociology*, 54(2), pp. 221–38.

Adams, P. and Calvert, M. (2005) A square peg in a round hole: citizenship and problems with 'curriculum' – the English secondary school problem, Paper presented at 'Learning Beyond Cognition' Biennial Conference of the European Affective Education Network.

Association of Teachers and Lecturers (2008) *School work plagued by plagiarism*, available from http://www.atl.org.uk/media-office/media-archive/School-work-plagued-by-plagiarism-ATL-survey.asp.

Aulia, M. (2008) Sick leave facer caught on facebook, available from http://www.cravingtech.com/sick-leave-faker-caught-on-facebook.html.

Bakan, J. (2004) *The Corporation: The Pathological Pursuit of Profit and Power*, London: Constable & Robinson Ltd.

Bazalgette, C. (2003) Literacy and the media, available from http://www.qcda.gov.uk/libraryAssets/media/11466_bazalgette_literacy~_and_media.pdf.

BBC News (2005) TeddyPhone Launched for Kids, available from http://news.bbc.co.uk/cbbcnews/hi/newsid_4480000/newsid_4482700/4482732.stm.

BBC News (2009) Computer consoles 'no better' than books for learning, available from http://news.bbc.co.uk/1/hi/scotland/8368940.stm.

Bleakley, A. (2006) *Education Research in the Post Modern*, available from http://www.edu.plymouth.ac.uk/resined/postmodernism/pmhome.htm.

Bloom, B.S. (1956) *Taxonomy of Educational Objectives, Handbook I: The Cognitive Domain*, New York: David McKay.

Brittain, S. and Johnson, L. (2008) Podcasting Lectures: Lessons Learned from Formative and Summative Evaluations, *Academic Interceptions*, No. 2, available from http://edcommunity.apple.com/ali/story.php?itemID=15224&version=3552&pageID=8795.

Cain Miller, C. (2009) Who's driving Twitter's popularity? Not teens, *New York Times*, available from http://www.nytimes.com/2009/08/26/technology/internet/26twitter.html.

Calcutt, A. (2001) *Generation Txt: mixed messages*, available from http://spiked-online.com/Articles/0000000054DF.htm.

Carr-Gregg, M. (2007) *Real Wired Child*, Australia: Penguin Books.

Carrington, V. (2004) Text and Literacies of the Shi Jinrui, *British Journal of Sociology of Education*, 25(2), pp. 215–28.

Chandler, D. (2001) Lecture: Visual participation 1, available from http://www.aber.ac.uk/mediamodules/MC10220/visper01.html.

Chandler, D. (2009) Semiotics for beginners, available from http://www.over.ac.uk/media/Documents/S4B/Sem02.html.

Cole, J. (2000) Surveying the digital future: The UCLA Internet Report. Downloaded from http://WWW.CCP.UCLA.EDU/pages/internet-report.asp, 17 November 2000.

DCSF (2009:1) Case Studies: Community Broadcasting, available from http://curriculum.qcda.gov.uk/key-stages-3-and-4/case_studies/.

DCFS (2009:2) *Your child, your schools, our future: Building a 21st century schools system*.

Department for Culture, Media and Sport Broadcasting Policy Division (2001), Media Literacy Statement, available from http://www.culture.gov.uk/PDF/media_lit_2001.pdf.

Dewey, J. (1910/1991) *How we think*, New York: Prometheus Books.

Dovey, J. and Kennedy, H.W. (2006) *Game Cultures: Computer Games as New Media*, Berkshire: Open University Press.

Education Week (2009) Are Shakespeare and Texting Compatible? *Associated Press*, available from http://www.newstin.com/tag/us/137119134.

Fildes, J. (2009) *Internet Safety for Children Target*, available from http://news.bbc.co.uk/1/hi/technology/8398763.stm.

Gair, M. (1998) *Review: Giroux, Henry A. (1997). Pedagogy and the Politics of Hope: Theory, Culture, and Schooling*, Boulder, CO: Westview Press, available from http://edrev.asu.edu/reviews/rev39.htm.

Gee, J.P. (2009) Pedagogy, Innovation and Education in 3-D Virtual Worlds, *Journal of Virtual Worlds Research*, available from http://journals.tdl.org/jvwr/article/view/624/453.

Harris, K. (2002) *Is Television Like a Language Which we Read?* Available from http://www.aber.ac.uk/media/Students/kjh0001.html, viewed November 2009.

Hearnshaw, R. (2006) Will podcasting finally kill the lecture? Guardian Online, available from http://www.guardian.co.uk/education/2006/sep/19/elearning.highereducation.

Jensen, R.B. (2002) Do we learn to 'read' television and film and do televisual and filmic codes constitute a 'language'? Available from http://www.aber.ac.uk/media/Students/rbj0001.html.

Johnson, S. (2005) *Everything bad is good for you*, London: Penguin.

Kamel Boulos, et al. (2007) Second Life: an overview of the potential of 3-D virtual worlds in medical and health education, *Health Information and Libraries Journal*, Vol. 24, pp. 233–45.

Khan, U. (2009) Firefly mobile phone designed for four year olds, Telegraph Online, available from http://www.telegraph.co.uk/technology/mobile-phones/5611280/Firefly-mobile-phone-designed-for-four-year-olds.html.

Kirkpatrick, D. (2008) Computer Games as Liberal Arts? *Fortune Magazine*, available from http://money.cnn.com/2008/06/06/technology/games_change.fortune/index.htm.

Kirkpatrick, M. (2009) How one teacher uses Twitter in the classroom, *Read Write Web*, available from http://www.readwriteweb.com/archives/how_one_teacher_uses_twitter_in_the_classroom.php.

Kornfeld, J. and Prothro, L. (2005) Envisioning Possibility: Schooling and Student Agency in Children's and Young Adult Literature, *Children's Literature in Education*, 36(3), pp. 217–39.

Kun, J. (1994) *Reading, Writing and Rap: Literacy as Rap Sound System*, available from http://bad.eserver.org/issues/1994/12/kun.html.

Leitch, S. (2006) *Leitch Review of Skills,* available from http://www.dcsf.gov.uk/furthereducation/index.cfm?fuseaction=content.view&CategoryID=21&ContentID=37.

McFarlane et al. (2002) Report on the Educational Use of Games, available from http://www.teem.org.uk/publications/teem_gamesined_full.pdf.

Milian, M. (2009) Why text messages are limited to 160 characters, *Los Angeles Times*, available from http://latimesblogs.latimes.com/technology/2009/05/invented-text-messaging.html.

Morrell, E. (2002) Toward a critical pedagogy of popular culture: Literacy development among urban youth, *Journal of Adolescent & Adult Literacy*, 46(1), available from http://www.readingonline.org/newliteracies/lit_index.asp?HREF=/newliteracies/jaal/9-02_column/index.html.

Netlingo (2009) Guide to Text and Chat, available from http://www.netlingo.com/index.php.

Nie, N. and Erbring, L. (2000) Internet and society: SIQSS Internet study, available from http://www.stanford.edu/group/siqss/Press_Release/internetStudy.html.

Ofsted (2009) English at the Crossroads, available from http://www.ofsted.gov.uk/Ofsted-home/News/Press-and-media/2009/June/English-at-the-crossroads.

Park (2009) *Americans sent 1 trillion SMS text messages in 2008*, available from http://www.intomobile.com/2009/04/06/americans-sent-1-trillion-sms-text-messages-in-2008.html.

Parks, M. and Roberts, L. (1998) Making MOOsic: The development of personal relationships on-line and a comparison to their off-line counterparts, *Journal of Social and Personal Relationships*, Vol. 15, p. 517.

Parker, L. and Webber, S. (2008) *Introduction to Second Life for Inquiry-Based Learning*, available from http://www.slideshare.net/cilass.slideshare/introduction-to-second-life-for-inquirybased-learning.

Peltoniemi, T. (2003) *Young People and the New technologies – Perspectives on Internet and Mobile Services in Drug and Alcohol Prevention*, available from http://www.kolumbus.fi/teuvo.peltoniemi/Peltoniemi_publications.htm.

Potter, J. (2005) 'This Brings Back a Lot of Memories' – a case study in the analysis of digital video production by young learners, *Education, Communication & Information*, 5(1), pp. 5–23.

Powell, A. (2008) The Copy and Paste Generation, available from http://efoundations.typepad.com/efoundations/2008/01/the-copy-and-pa.html.

Prensky, M. (2001) Digital Natives, Digital Immigrants, in *On The Horizon*: MCB University Press, 9(5), available from http://www.marcprensky.com/writing/.

Rose, J. (2006) Independent review of the teaching of early reading, available from http://www.jceps.com/index.php?pageID=article&articleID=16.

Rose, J. (2009) Independent Review of the Primary Curriculum: Final Report, available from http://www.dcsf.gov.uk/primarycurriculumreview.

Shepherd, J. (2009) It's a world of possibilities, Guardian Online, available from http://www.guardian.co.uk/education/2007/may/08/students.elearning.

Solomon J. and Maasik, S. (1999) *Signs of Life*, Bedford: St Martins.

Times online (2009) Mobile phones for children: a boon or a peril? Available from http://women.timesonline.co.uk/tol/life_and_style/women/families/article6556283.ece.

Tomlinson, S. (2008) *Education in a post-welfare society*, 2nd edn, Buckingham: Open University Press.

UK Council for Child Internet Safety (2010) Click Clever Click Safe Campaign, available from http://www.clickcleverclicksafe.direct.gov.uk.

UNESCO (2004) New Ignorances, New Literacies: Learning to Live Together in a Globalizing World, available from http://unesdoc.unesco.org/images/0013/001395/139524e.pdf.

Urban Dictionary (2009) Urban dictionary is the dictionary you wrote. Define your world, available from http://www.urbandictionary.com/define.php?term=Text%20Speak.

Wakefield, J. (2009) Your country needs you connected, available from http://news.bbc.co.uk/1/hi/technology/8152221.stm.

Whitty, M.T. and McLaughlin, D. (2005) Online recreation: the relationship between loneliness, Internet self-efficacy and the use of the Internet for entertainment purposes, *Computers in Human Behaviour*, 3(3), pp. 1435–46.

Wilcox, D. (2002) Media Literacy Paper, available from http://www.ofcom.org/consult/condocs/strategy-medialit/responses/ah/hhs.pdf.

Yoffe, E. (2009) Seeking: How the brain hard-wires us to love Google, Twitter and texting. And why that's dangerous, *Slate*, available from http://www.slate.com/id/2224932/pagenum/all/#p2.

12

International education

John Dolan

Contents

Introduction

Your School

Your school knows your name –
Sharin, Abdul, Aysha, Rayhan, Lauren, Jack –
And who you are.
Your school knows the most important thing to know
You are a star, a star

Carol Ann Duffy

What ideas are prompted when you read the phrases '**Third World**' and 'developing country'? We obviously can't be sure, but guess that such things as 'poverty . . . underdeveloped . . . dependency . . . aid . . . disease . . . Africa . . . disasters . . .

383

Asia' might have featured in your thinking. That's understandable; we're very used to seeing images and reports about 'Third World problems' in the western media. And many are affected enough by such stories to provide financial or other support to help.

However, at the start of this chapter, we want to challenge you to think in rather different ways about the 'Third World', and about issues of **development** and **underdevelopment**.

Those who live in these **developing countries** make up around 80 per cent of the world's population. All of these areas of the world have cultural histories stretching back thousands of years. They sustain successful social systems, despite poverty, diseases and the exploitation of their economic natural resources by multinational corporations based in the developed 'west'. Many have accepted a disproportionate number of refugees to live in them. Some, such as India and Brazil, are beginning to emerge as major economic forces in their own right, and several others will probably do so within the next 20 years. India, additionally, has already produced 13 Nobel Prize laureates. In other words, far from being a 'third world' these countries are the **Majority World**. This term was first used over twenty years ago by the internationally renowned Bangladeshi photographer and educationalist Shahidul Alam. He insists on defining this community of nations in terms of what it is, rather than what it lacks. Alam's definition is disputed by others, as you might expect, but is increasingly used by those with an interest in international development.

Alfred Sauvy first coined the expression 'Third World' ('tiers monde' in French) in 1952, as a deficit concept for nations characterised by poverty and dependence on economically more privileged (and usually former colonising) countries. The term is considered to be derogatory by most of those working in the fields of international understanding and development. '**Colonisation**' refers to the historical process by which the nationals of one state (or nation) extend political and economic control over another area. This is usually achieved as a result of organisational, economic or technological superiority possessed by the colonising state, leading to the military and civil subjugation of the indigenous (native) population of the area now dominated and, invariably, economically exploited. The legacy of past colonisations remains evidenced in many countries of present-day Africa, Asia and South America: local languages and knowledge traditions are often marginalised with systems of schooling mirroring closely those found in the former colonising state; much of their economic activities are controlled and directed by companies and interests located in European or North American countries; political structures are often fragmented and weakened by corruption (Said, 1978).

The study of international education is about greater understanding of issues of **globalisation** and of the development of awareness of **global citizenship**. These are two terms found increasingly in the study of education, and so let us offer brief explanations of them. 'Globalisation' is a concept that refers to the system of interaction among the countries of the world and involves technological, economic, political and cultural exchanges made possible largely by advances in communication (especially electronic communications, ICT) and transportation. Too often in contemporary usage it reduces to efforts to develop a global economy, but at best the notion can describe the growing and mutually shared understandings and interconnectivities between nations and the individuals who make them up. 'Global citizenship' is about under-standing the need to tackle injustice and inequality, and having the desire to work actively to do so. It is also about valuing the knowledge and experience of others around the world, and about being willing to learn from them, their culture and their histories.

If these aims are to be achieved, though, then each of us (education professionals and students, and school pupils) has to be prepared to cross some borders in our own knowledge: we need to know something about the way education is structured and organised, and to think about the way learning and teaching takes place in schools in other countries.

This chapter aims to:

- Provide an outline of the historical development and current state of debates about 'international education'.

- Consider ways in which equity in educational opportunities, especially for young women, are changing in the Majority World.

- Explore the supply and accountability of teachers in selected countries of the Majority World.

- Investigate how changes in educational ICT (information and communication tech-nologies, including computers and mobile or cell phones) might impact on these matters in the future.

- Critically evaluate these topics in terms of relevant theoretical underpinnings and their wider educational significance.

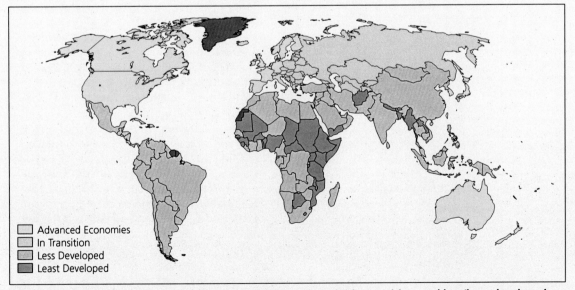

Figure 12.1 World map showing advanced economies, economies in transition, and less/least developed countries

Source: WHITIA World Health Imaging, Telemedicine & Informatics Alliance, 2009.

Evelyn, Accra, Ghana

We will focus on the school day of just one student attending a High School in the city of Accra, Ghana, in West Africa. We will call her Evelyn, which is quite a common first name for girls in parts of Ghana. Accra is the modern capital of Ghana, a West African country with a well developed school system established since its Education Act of 1960. Almost all major secondary schools today, especially exclusively boys and girls' schools, are mission- or church-related institutions.

Ghana is just one of the 50 or so nations that make up the present day continent of Africa. Prior to 1957, when it became an independent nation, the country was known as 'The Gold Coast', a name indicating something of its historical economic status as a colonial territory. Present day Africa is a continent with a fascinating diversity of peoples, who make up about 10% of the world population. No one country (much less, one person) can be 'typical' of present-day Africa. However, a focus on one person living in one country provides us with a lens through which something of this richly diverse, fast changing part of the world can be glimpsed and better understood.

Ghana has a total of 5,450 junior secondary schools, and 503 senior secondary schools. Evelyn is in the 9th Grade, her final year in a girl's junior high school. She hopes to shortly commence a further three years of study at senior high school. Her home is two kilometres from the school. Accra is just one of the modern cities of Africa where one third of the continent's population lives and where life goes on at a pace far removed from the quiet rural lives of the majority of the African peoples.

Like many young people living in the south of Ghana close to the Atlantic coast, Evelyn comes from a Christian family. She lives with her mother and father, two younger sisters and one older brother in a modest home, which is built from brick, packed earth and with a straw roof. In the north, the majority of people are Sunni Muslims, and amongst Muslim Ghanaians family size tends to be greater.

She walks to school every day and says that it is safe to do so since wild animals are found more commonly in the north of the country. There are city buses in big towns like Accra, though most people can only afford to travel by matatus, a minibus, or other public transportation nowadays found in many African countries. Evelyn, like most of the students at her school, cannot afford to use them on a daily basis. So they walk to school. The school day is usually eight hours but can go up to 11 hours. Success in education is often the necessary precursor of an individual being able to find a well-paid job in adult life and for a society to improve its national economy, and so children and teachers are willing to devote time and energy to it. Parents have to pay for their children's school text books and uniforms, even though many families still struggle to make ends meet financially.

At her junior high school, Evelyn follows a required curriculum of three core subjects – English, Mathematics, and Science, and a mix of technical and vocational training. At senior high school, she hopes to continue with her core subjects but also to study Geography, Economics and Literature. Some students, though, can choose to follow 'electives' in more scientific subjects such as Additional Mathematics, Chemistry, Biology and Physics.

Generally, classes are held in classrooms, and occasionally outside for Physical Education and sporting activities, Natural Science laboratories, and Technology. Her classes are taught by lecture, and are the only source of information since students are financially unable to purchase books.

After school and on non-school days, Marguerite works with the family on domestic and field tasks, but she, along with her classmates, has homework to do, usually in the school's library. Her least favourite job at home is helping with the family's laundry. This is done by filling a large bucket with water and some soap, letting it sit for awhile, and then rinsing, before hanging it out to dry – quite a task.

Evelyn enjoys school, because the students organise field trips and other after-school activities. These activities are usually supervised by her teachers. Evelyn shares the common African attitude of having great respect for her teachers, viewing them as both sources of knowledge and role models for herself.

Ghana is an economically developing nation. The discovery of major offshore oil reserves was announced in June 2007, encouraging expectations of a major economic boost. However, oil is not expected to flow for some years. In recent years, young people here have been watching helplessly as the level of unemployment, particularly among educated young people, has continued to grow. Most Ghanaians do not have the financial means or experience to set up their own businesses. However, Evelyn lives in one of the most established democracies in Africa, enjoying a stable, lasting peace, which places Ghana well in terms of its future economic growth.

Because of the influence of the radio and television, many young Africans are in contact with other cultures. The US Population Reference Bureau suggests that as many as 40% of Africa's population are under 15 years of age. Evelyn prefers western styles of clothing, of hairstyles, etc. Like most young people, she identifies with famous singers, actors and football players. From documentaries on TV, she has some access to current technical progress and scientific discoveries.

Evelyn dreams of a time when she will be able to travel, either for the purpose of education, or for tourism or to start a professional life. Her view of her own future, and that of other young Ghanaians, is optimistic: "If you believe there are opportunities you will look out for them. If you don't believe they are there you won't look for them. With God's help, everything is possible."

You can read what they say for themselves, and see photographs of young Ghanian school students' lives, in a resource produced by the International Education and Resource Network (iEARN). This is available at http://pbskids.org/africa/myworld/westafrica.html.

Questions for discussion

1. *What are the similarities between Evelyn's experiences of education and of life more generally, and those of a typical young girl living in the UK?*

2. *What are the main differences between them, and how do these affect your own thinking about the organisation and purposes of schooling?*

3. *What do you think might be the lasting legacy of colonial influence in the curriculum and system of schooling still found in many countries of the Majority World? Think, in particular, about what the case study information tells you about the curriculum of school and about the influence of religion in Evelyn's life today.*

Four trends in international education

The term 'international education' means different things to different people. This is not entirely surprising, since fine slicing of terms and information is at the very heart of any academic field. It is important to keep in mind, though, that in an age of rapid political and social change such as ours, new features will emerge in intellectual debates, such as those now characterising the field of international (and the nearly synonymous notion of 'comparative') education. In part, these features result from new technologies, while others reflect political transitions, such as the rise to dominance of **neo-conservative** ideology in the USA and Europe in the past 15 years or so.

In brief, this ideology (or school of thought) maintains that the optimal economic system is achieved by giving free rein to market participants, privatisation, minimal restrictions on international trade, and the shrinking of government intervention in the economy. Alongside these economic concerns, neo-conservatives also argue for an emphasis on individual endeavour and 'freedom of action'. How much freedom one might have when facing the economic deprivation and political crisis that is so often found in the Majority World might be debatable, however. The force of neo-conservative thinking is often summed up in the term 'globalisation'. This notion encapsulates a variety of developments, such as the growing interdependence of systems of economic exchange and production as more and more established companies outsource manufacturing processes and jobs to countries in the Majority World, in order to cut their own costs through reducing wage and associated costs.

Comparative education is best understood, therefore, as not only something which embraces and 'widens the form and extent of cross border transactions between people's assets, goods and services' (Lubbers, 1998), but also as something which involves the transfer of a range of politico-social ideas.

Don't worry, though, it's not going to be a very lengthy review of ideas and debates: instead, four main trends (or 'trajectories') are going to be identified and explained. Remember, too, that it isn't the case that any one or more of these four directions of debate has been abandoned, nor that any is 'better' than the others. For different times and for differing purposes, everyone interested in 'international education' is likely to make use of any one (or more) of them. Familiarity with all four is going to equip you to reach decisions on how you reach your own understanding of these notions – which, after all, is the real purpose of your reading this chapter.

Let's begin by outlining our four trends.

Describing national systems of education

Describing national systems of education and their constituent elements has been the traditional focus of *comparative education* since its earliest days in the first

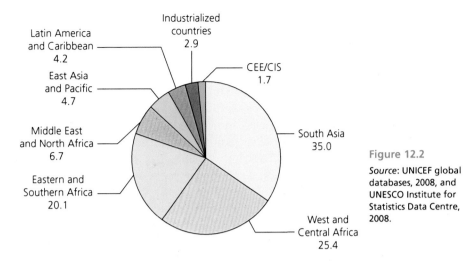

Figure 12.2

Source: UNICEF global databases, 2008, and UNESCO Institute for Statistics Data Centre, 2008.

half of the twentieth century. To begin with, early workers in the field were content to provide narrative, descriptive accounts of the particular features of one or more specific, differing system. There was, for example, intense interest among western educationalists in describing the Soviet education system following the success of the Sputnik space exploration programme of the late 1950s and early 1960s (Trace, 1961). You probably noted something of this tradition for yourself as you read and reflected on Case study 12.1. You probably found as much interest in the details of Marguerite's reported experience of her home and schoolday life as you did in pondering its wider significance as an example of post-colonial education provision in a Majority World country. We've already suggested that none of the four trajectories in the development of international education has been abandoned or surpassed, and so it isn't surprising that interest in, and accounts of, various nations' systems of education can still be found in the literature of international education.

 Connect and explore

UNESCO's International Bureau of Education/WDE World Data on Education, the foremost publication on a global scale of comparative education provision, covers a wide range of topics, including the official rationale for education, outcome measures of student achievements, finances, equipment, educational research and current issues. Its website is a useful 'starting point' resource, the most ready and reliable source for comparative education enquiries of this sort: http://www.ibe.unesco.org/en.html.

The process of economic and political development

Our first trend, with its focus on the 'different' (the 'other'), is all well and good. However, the academic interest in comparative education after the end of the Second World War assumed a more critical edge. The late 1940s and early 1950s was a period of reconstruction in Europe and elsewhere following war damage and the shift from a wartime to a peacetime economy, and of decolonisation when former colonial powers recognised and conceded to the desire for independence of previously subjugated territories (colonies) and their populations. In this period, 'comparative educators' sought to explore the place and contribution of societal institutions such as education in the process of economic and political development in these changing circumstances. By the late 1950s, a body of research and theory had been mainly produced by academics working in the economically prosperous nations and which tended to emphasise the role of education as a driver of economic *modernisation*.

McClelland (1961), for example, focused on the relationship between individuals' values within a society and the implications of these for economic and technological growth and change. And since most former colonial countries adopted (or, perhaps more accurately, had imposed on them) an educational system modelled on that of the dominant colonial power, comparison was made on the basis of the extent to which such systems were successful in replicating processes and outcomes familiar to the colonial power. Such 'dependency' is central to theorised notions of post-colonial inequality, which argue that imposed measures of effectiveness reflect more the concerns of the developed and previously colonising states rather than the local circumstances, values and needs of the now independent, former colony. This theory is also in opposition to notions of 'modernisation', which saw the less developed countries being able to catch up with the economically dominant nations (Frank, 1969).

This body of research and debate endures into the present day. In 2003, for instance, the Canadian academic David Wilson defined *comparative education* as:

> an intersection of the social sciences, education and cross-national study which attempts to use cross-national data to test propositions about the relationship between education and society and between teaching practices and learning outcomes.

Another academic, Rogers (1993), could well have been writing about classrooms in almost any reasonably affluent region when he suggested that if one were to walk into 'almost any school in America today you walk in to a time warp where the basic tools of learning have not changed in decades.' Think back to Case study 12.1 with its emphasis on students' dependency on what the teacher says and on the textbook. Might you now agree when we suggest that the same may well be true of schools in regions only aspiring to prosperity, where the lingering influence of former colonial values and culture can be seen?

Transfer of models of education

Rogers' tone was, perhaps, symptomatic of a widespread impatience in the last two decades or so of the twentieth century with the slow pace of change in education policy and provision more generally. Wilson (2003) had gone on to suggest that a more appropriate approach might be that of an *international education*, concerned with 'the application of descriptions, analyses and insights learned in one or more nations to the problems of developing educational systems and institutions in other countries.' In other words, trying to see how far solutions and answers to education challenges generated in one (or more) developed states might be appropriate for the meeting of apparently similar challenges in Majority World contexts. A twin term now often encountered in the literature of comparative education for such an approach is **development education**. Somewhat inevitably, given what has been suggested about the transfer of models of education policy and provision, such transfer has tended to be in only one direction from developed to dependent (former colonial) regions.

There are problems with this particular form of comparative education, however. Research undertaken for both the World Bank and UNICEF as early as the 1990s drew attention to the fact that, although governments throughout the world invest heavily in education, they spend remarkably little on monitoring and evaluating their investment. Management of most of the world's education systems occurs without adequate information and analysis. Continuing attempts at creating an international education database are often unreliable, leaving out crucial measures of quality, process and output, but ignoring at least equally important differences between local contexts, cultures and social aspirations. In other words, we would suggest that such attempts are often about as useful to the concerns of global citizenship and international education as might be a comparison between chalk and cheese.

These shortcomings are due in part to the limited professional capacity most countries have to gather education statistics and carry out education research. There is also strong resistance from educators and policy-makers to being evaluated. As recently as 2006, for example, the Commonwealth Consortium for Education confessed that 'Comparative data on the quality of schooling across [23 countries of] the Commonwealth is thin.' Little surprise, then, that some have drawn attention to the fact that globally education research does not receive the same priority from governments as does research on agriculture, health or the economy. There is also a danger that problems in education may only receive 'quick-fix' solutions and that gathered statistics and data are culturally and socially decontextualised, leading to the sort of inappropriate conclusions, comparisons and transfer of generalised practice that we have already mentioned (Watson, 2001). Perhaps growing levels of activism in many parts of the world (such as the 'Make Poverty History' campaign against poverty and indebtedness, and volunteering involvement in education development in many countries, such as those sponsored by the UK's VSO organisation) will contribute to a change in this poorly informed, superficial kind of thinking.

A post-structuralist approach

In the second of the approaches to international education already outlined in this chapter, we saw how McClelland (1961) emphasised the importance of the relationship between 'values' and the role of education as a driver of 'modernisation'. Our fourth approach has been shaped by the work of researchers such as Inkeles and Smith (1974) who sought to synthesise these ideas with those developed earlier. For example, Max Weber, seen by many to be the father of the modern academic discipline of sociology, argued from early in the twentieth century for the centrality of formal schooling also being a driver of such values formation. This trend in research and scholarship found expression in theories of **human capital**, in which people's skills and knowledge are valued for their contribution (actual or potential) to economic growth. Even as respected an education academic and researcher as Patricia Broadfoot (2000) has warned that educational systems worldwide are '. . . under intense pressure to adapt to the changing needs of the labour market.' In other words, in this approach, education becomes firmly located in the marketplace. In their turn, international educationists working in this tradition argue for the comparative appraisal of national educational systems primarily in terms of their economic efficacy (Little, 2000).

Despite the powerful effects of market forces in international education, some argue that education cannot be left to the market alone. Some current researchers (Ninnes and Burnett, 2003) take the work on antagonisms produced by Mouffe in the mid-1990s to argue that international education ought properly to focus on exploring ways in which teachers, students and processes might best acknowledge competing interests, differences and ideas. By doing so, educationalists are able to go on to explore ways of tolerating, and of even welcoming, these differing interests as creative opportunities from which to forge new structures based on democratic values.

These writers go on to argue for the need for an ethical basis to underpin study of international education. Such a basis might then promote the critical evaluation of different education policies, provision and processes in terms of the extent to which they impact on individuals in ways consistent with their developing as autonomous political agents, able to make and take decisions for themselves. Seen in this way, education is as much about effective learning and concerns as it is about cognitive and economic outcomes. (Look back at Case study 12.1 and you might be able to see hints of this approach suggested by mentions of the social experience and aspirations of Marguerite and her classmates, both individually and collectively.) In effect, educationalists and researchers such as Ninnes and Burnett reject the structuralist approach to education, initiated in the work of Weber as we mentioned earlier.

Such an essentially post-structuralist approach to educational study begins to align with a growing emphasis within international education on the extent to which schooling processes support 'the moral development of the individual by attempting to influence the formation of positive attitudes towards peace, international understandings and responsible world citizenship' (Cambridge and Thompson, 2004).

The remainder of this chapter will go on to selectively explore some of the possibilities hinted at in the work of Cambridge and Thompson. As you read these, you need to keep in mind the fact that all of them reflect our own commitment to this fourth approach within international education. We make no apologies for what is, after all, our bias. You may or may not agree with all that you go on to read in the chapter, but we aim to give you the basis from which to begin your own thinking and debates.

❓ Stop and reflect

Look again at the four approaches to the study of international education that we have outlined.

- *Do you find any of these directions of comparative study surprising? If so, in what ways?*
- *Do any of them challenge your own way of thinking about yourself? About others?*

Either way, that's OK; it shows that you're thinking things through for yourself, that you're learning. After all, finding a way of creatively responding to difference is part and parcel of what we see as the value of studying international education. Besides, as the now very well known Harvard professor of philosophy Michael Sandel has recently written: 'Sometimes an argument can change our minds' (2009). He should know. His Harvard University class, 'Justice', has been taken by more than 10,000 students in the last 20 years.

It is important, therefore, that the grounds – the criteria – for such selection are made clear. For us, the first topic, the education of girls, reflects international education's broader concern for **equity** in educational opportunities so that all have equal access to them (which then requires that all students are treated with equality when once in the educational system), and for the contribution of such opportunities to both individual aspirations and wider community development.

Our second, teacher accountability, reflects a prioritisation of the democratic basis of educational policy and provision. At its best, such accountability assures the efficacy of education processes and structures, and their compliance both with notions of equity and with individual learners' empowerment and achievement. There is always a risk, however, that 'accountability' becomes merely a managerialist and bureaucratic procedure, often at the expense of local needs and local aspirations.

Our third topic, changing education technologies, reminds us that education is a mediated process. Schools and teachers set out to teach their students a set curriculum, but their students access and make understandings of what is being taught them in terms of their own experiences and interests. Increasingly, such mediation of learning is managed through the use of fast-changing telecommunications technologies. This can be as true in the Majority World as it is in developed nations.

The education of girls

In September 2000, after nearly a decade of major conferences and summits, world leaders came together at United Nations headquarters in New York and adopted the United Nations Millennium Declaration. This committed signatory nations to a new global partnership to reduce extreme poverty and set out a series of time-bound targets – with a deadline of 2015 – now known as the Millennium Development Goals. The second of these (MDG2) requires that 'by 2015, children everywhere, boys and girls alike, will be able to complete a full course of primary schooling'.

In general terms, good progress has been made towards the achieving of this goal. Attendance data (based on household surveys – usually the most reliable method of data gathering in regions of poor infrastructure) show that the number of children of primary school age who are out of school has declined markedly in recent years, from 115 million in 2002 to 93 million in 2005–2006. Put another way, in more than 60 Majority World nations, at least 90 per cent of primary school-age children are registered in school (UNICEF global database figures up to 2006).

This progress is encouraging. Education is accepted as probably the most effective method for helping communities' transition into more functional, prosperous and independent societies (Bennett, 1993). In a world in which the poorest 40 per cent of the world's population accounts for just 5 per cent of global income and the richest 20 per cent accounts for three-quarters of world income (*2007 Human Development Report*, HDR) it is remarkable that poorer parents continue to make greater relative contribution to schooling than do more affluent parents (Shah, 1998).

And, when the engagement of girls in schooling is considered, the situation seems even better. Thirty years ago, girls represented 38 per cent of primary enrolments in low-income countries, and boys 62 per cent. But in recent years, the gender gap has narrowed, with girls representing 48 per cent and boys 52 per cent of primary enrolments (OECD/UNESCO, 2005). Gross enrolment rates for girls in some low-income countries have gone from 52 per cent to 94 per cent over that same period. Many low-income countries have registered improvements in primary school completion rates, with an average increase of 6 per cent (from 63 per cent in 1999 to 74 per cent in 2006), with the completion rate rising faster than for boys (from 57 per cent in 1999 to 70 per cent in 2006, whereas for boys the improvement was only from 63 per cent to 70 per cent) (World Bank, EdStats, 2008).

These gains really matter. For a start, MDG2 is inextricably linked to MDG3 – concerned with the promotion of gender equality and the empowerment of women. Clearly, universal primary education requires gender parity (UNICEF, 2008, *The State of the World's Children 2009*). In addition, there are several compelling benefits associated with girls' education, including the reduction of child and maternal mortality, improvement of child nutrition and health, lower fertility rates, enhancement of women's domestic role and their political participation, improvement of the economic productivity and growth, and protection of girls from HIV/AIDS, abuse and exploitation. Educating a girl dramatically reduces the chance that her child will die before the age of five, and improves her prospects of being able to support herself and have a say in her own welfare and in society.

In short, girls' education yields some of the highest returns of all development investments, yielding both private and social benefits that accrue to individuals, families and society at large (World Bank, April 2009); an educated woman has the skills, information and self-confidence that she needs to be a better parent, worker and citizen.

Yet the averages that we have quoted showing improvement in girls' access to education opportunities, and especially to primary schooling averages, hide sharp differences among regions and countries. Girls still constitute 55 per cent of all out of school children. Worldwide, for every 100 boys out of school there are 122 girls. In some countries the gender gap is much wider. For example, for every 100 boys out of school there are 426 girls in India, 316 girls in Iraq, 270 girls in Yemen, and 257 in Benin (UNESCO GMR, 2007).

Why should this be so?

There is no single explanation, of course; instead, a complicated matrix of factors influences girls' access to education. Gender differential access to school is usually caused by poverty, adverse cultural practices, schooling quality and distance to schools. However, there are some emerging challenges that reduce girls' enrolment in primary, secondary and even tertiary education. These are: HIV/AIDS, orphanhood, conflicts, emergencies and other fragile situations, gender-based violence, and the information technology gender gap.

For example, a recent report from Human Rights Watch (2001) notes that: sexual violence in schools has a negative impact on the educational and emotional needs of girls and acts as a barrier to their attaining education. 'Rape and other forms of sexual violence place girls at risk of contracting the HIV/AIDS virus . . . [which then takes] . . . its toll on the educational system and disrupted education . . . especially for girls' (Human Rights Watch, 2001). Similarly, according to a report by Action Aid (2004), girls in east and southern African countries find it particularly difficult to access education: they are expected to do household chores instead; safety is a problem; and there is no culture of valuing or prioritising the education of female children (Hillman and Jenkner, 2004).

At this point, a word of caution is needed. Keep in mind that much research on child and young people's development has been very Eurocentric and ethnocentric in character and focus. In a globalised world it is imperative to understand young people of various cultures from a position of some knowledge of the cultural achievements and values in which they live their lives. It is also necessary, we argue, to do so from a non-judgemental (**culturally relativistic**) perspective. There is always the need to respect the unique cultural assets and challenges of different parts of the world. We also need to remember that at least 80 per cent of humanity lives on less than $10 a day (Chen and Ravallion, 2008), and that for many of the world's poor families education of their children is simply beyond what is practicable from household budgets.

Let's try to illustrate some of these important points by use of a specific case. More than six years after the fall of the Taliban in Afghanistan and military intervention by the USA and the European Community, fewer than 30 per cent of eligible girls are enrolled in schools, and the infrastructure is so poor that only a tiny fraction are likely to get the education they need to enjoy the fruits of emancipation. Yet here, as everywhere else in the Majority World, all social and economic indexes show that increasing the percentage of women with a high school education will result in better overall health, a more functional democracy and increased economic performance. In Afghanistan, there is another pay-off: educated women are a strong bulwark against the extremism and conflict that still plague the country.

Yet, even within this context of violence and civil strife, progress has been made. In 2008, there were 3,446 community-based schools in Afghanistan, and

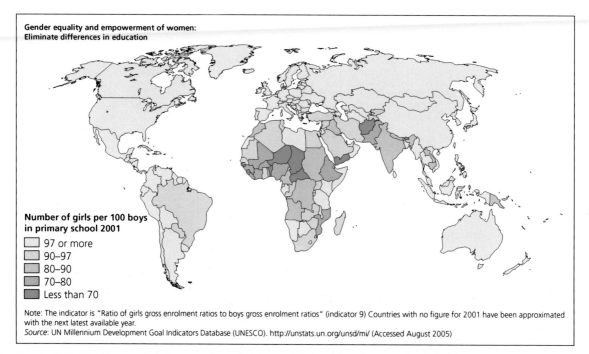

Gender equality and empowerment of women:
Eliminate differences in education

Number of girls per 100 boys
in primary school 2001

- 97 or more
- 90–97
- 80–90
- 70–80
- Less than 70

Note: The indicator is "Ratio of girls gross enrolment ratios to boys gross enrolment ratios" (indicator 9) Countries with no figure for 2001 have been approximated with the next latest available year.
Source: UN Millennium Development Goal Indicators Database (UNESCO). http://unstats.un.org/unsd/mi/ (Accessed August 2005)

Figure 12.3 **World map showing number of girls per 100 boys in primary school, 2001**

1,393 more were planned for completion in 2010. In addition, the Afghan government, supported by various development organisations such as UNICEF, is working to remove entrenched cultural barriers to girls' education and train more female teachers. This last development is an important one. In traditionalist Moslem areas such as those that make up most of the area of Afghanistan, parents are often reluctant to break from the tradition that says 'girls belong at home' and which spurns their being taught by male teachers:

> In Afghan culture, women are seen as the repository of family honour, and the education of girls – whether in terms of the design of school buildings or in the way in which classes are conducted – needs to reflect that reality.
>
> Baker, 2008

This sort of sensitive extension of education opportunities and provision, even in the difficult and tragic circumstances of Afghanistan, is proving effective. UNICEF claims that 2.2 million girls are now in school and there is expectation of a 20 per cent increase in primary school enrolment for girls by 2013 (Banbury, 2009).

Case study 12.2
A cause for hope?

Khewa refugee camp is located on the outskirts of Peshawar, in Pakistan. Official estimates published by the Pakistan government in 2009 indicate that at least 2 million registered Afghans live in such camps as Khewa. Yet the education of the young people in such camps offers hope for the future, and especially for Afghan women. As one recent young school graduate remarked when she received her twelfth-class diploma, 'I want to develop a lot of courses to teach local girls their rights and values. I want to go back to Afghanistan and make my country a learning center for all!'

Like most of the refugee camps scattered throughout Pakistan, Khewa has been slowly, but steadily, emptying. The Pakistani government's role in the reconstruction of Afghanistan has urged many refugees back into Afghanistan. The UN, too, has made concrete efforts in this regard. A devastated economy and the ongoing violence mean extreme hardship for the returnees.

For the youth, especially school-going girls, life in Afghanistan is characterised by very real physical danger. As a recently released report by Amnesty International explained, violence against females in the country is such that 'Daily Afghan women are at risk of abduction and rape by armed individuals. The government is doing little to improve their condition.' Acts of violence against women are rarely investigated or punished.

Only a few schools destroyed during the Taliban era and subsequent American invasion have been rebuilt, meaning that very few girls have educational institutions near their homes.

Rather than lose the chance of obtaining an education, many girls have decided to remain alone in the refugee camps in Pakistan while their families travel back to Afghanistan. Despite the accelerating repatriation of the Afghans, there remains a strong need for educational programmes on the Pakistani side of the border.

No one knows this better than girls like Feroza, a tenth-class student, whose parents and sister have returned to eastern Afghanistan. Her father, a physician, arranged for her to stay at Khewa and attend school. The schools in Feroza's village have been destroyed, and the area is far too volatile for her to travel to the nearest town.

'My elder sister had to stay in Afghanistan to help my mother,' explained Feroza. 'We are all sad that she cannot go to school . . . but there it is not safe. My parents are afraid she could be kidnapped if she goes out.'

Feroza has hope for her sister. 'When I go home, I will teach her everything I learned here. She is very interested in learning.'

Source: Adapted from Erica Ahmed (2005) *You! Magazine*, July.

Activity

In their recent book, *What Works in Girls' Education: Evidence and Policies from the Developing World*, Barbara Hertz and Gene Sperling identify and discuss some key features that typify successful education provision in various regions of the Majority World:

- Make girls' schooling affordable by either cutting school fees or through scholarships, or both.
- Cover both direct and indirect costs for families of sending a daughter to school – not just fees, but also the fact that the family loses the availability of the girl to earn money, to contribute to the work of the household and family, and the costs of keeping the girl safe going to and from school.
- School-based health and nutrition programmes make a real difference to attendance and retention rates in schools, along with adequate supply of clean water and sanitation to ensure privacy and maintain cultural priorities.

- Build schools local to communities and let them have flexible timetable arrangements to take account of local needs, and especially in respect of expectations of homework or other extension learning.
- Involve the community actively in the school, through such activities as parent and guardians associations, adults being involved as supplemental teachers for basic and traditional skills.
- Both curricula and pedagogies should take account of girls' interests and values, including the employment of female teachers, and the teaching of twenty-first-century knowledge and competences including numeracy, science and problem-solving.
- Maintain high-quality standards in schools – parents and communities are supportive of schooling which equips girls to improve their prospects as adults.

What is your reaction to these suggestions? Which ones do you agree or disagree with?

As Case study 12.2 indicates, in many parts of the Majority World 'It is absolutely crucial to increase the number of female teachers if you want to see more girls in school' (Oxfam, 2008).

Yet there are so few girls completing their education, so how do you grow the next generation of female teachers? The first answer would seem to be to remove all resource impediments to girls going to school. That often means constructing new buildings (including sanitary facilities) so that girls and boys might be safe and – here local values dictate – separately taught. In the meantime, unconventional inducements seem to help. In a successful programme in some rural areas of Afghanistan, for example, girls are given a free ration of oil and flour at the end of every month. This encourages their poor families to keep sending them to school. Increasing teachers' salaries would convince more parents that their daughters should take up the profession. Even qualified teachers are paid so little that their salary amounts to a tiny return on investment for families whose daughters could be spending their years in education and training in more immediately gainful ways. Increasing teachers' pay and conditions is probably the best way in which the quality of education provision can be improved in many countries around the world.

As is so often the case, the lens of equality in respect of girls' opportunities allows us to view more sharply a more generic, universal concern. It is to this topic of the supply and accountability of teachers – and, especially, of the effects of these variables on the quality of education – that we now turn.

The supply and accountability of teachers

During the past 10 to 15 years many changes have been introduced in educational systems around the world. As we have previously shown in this chapter, the adoption of the UN's Millenium Development Goals has had a significant influence on the pace and direction of these reforms. In particular, the first of these ('Target 1: Ensure that, by 2015, children everywhere, boys and girls alike, will be able to complete a full course of primary schooling') has demanded that there be structural reforms to establish longer compulsory education cycles, for all 8 to 10-year-olds in many countries in the Majority World. Fundamental shifts in the political and social systems of countries have also produced the need for the new educational structures and curriculum. Here, though, we want to concentrate on two commonly encountered concerns among those seeking to promote reform: teacher supply and teaching effectiveness. Together, these are viewed as crucial for the enhancement of the quality of education provision (UNESCO, 2005).

One of the main challenges obstructing improved education performance globally is the supply and quality of teachers. There were 27.8 million teachers in the world in 2007 – some 9.5 million more than in 1980, but still far short of the further 10.3 million needing to be recruited by 2015 (UNESCO, 2009). Most of these teachers (64 per cent) work in the poorer countries of the world, where there are still many teachers whose educational level is low and who have not taken part in formal teacher education programmes. Many of the Majority World's teachers are proportionately younger – and so less experienced – than is the case in most economically developed nations. Though not always uniform, their working conditions are often harsher, with many working up to 50 hours a week (and in two or more schools). In many countries, competing demands for cost reductions and education provision mean that teachers earn less today than they did twenty years ago, particularly in sub-Saharan Africa and Latin America (Nilsson, 2003) Additionally, many teachers work in overcrowded classrooms and in schools without water, electricity or sufficient instructional aids such as a table for the teacher or a usable chalkboard (Mehrotra, 2006).

Faced with these problems, it may not seem too surprising that Majority World teachers can become both disillusioned and difficult to retain. Such attrition is, though, a waste of both resources and expertise. However, there are indications that some comparatively simple changes can counteract these very real constraints. At the simplest of levels, there is evidence that payment incentives of about 3 per cent of annual salary paid as a bonus can result in raising the number of teachers remaining in the profession and improve the performance outcomes of the children and young people entrusted to them for their education (Muralidharan and Sundararaman, 2009).

Generally speaking, though, policies that aim to include teachers' discussions to determine change at an institutional level, together with the building of a constructive social image of the teaching profession, would seem to offer the most promise for the future of the world's children. Policies that reward those persons and institutions that are willing to improve and to learn from mistakes, and which encourage and support collaboration between them, rather than competition, would seem most effective. When these are matched to appropriate funding to modernise effectively institutions and resources and to provide opportunities to learn for those who educate teachers, then most beneficial change can be achieved. Most Majority World countries now have at least one or two policies that address these objectives. In Cuba, for instance, the last decade has seen a new emphasis on raising educational standards for all young people in every school through re-engineering of teaching and learning strategies. Secondary school teachers now spend longer with their class of students, providing more generalist teaching to them. In these ways, the initiative is intended to enlarge and deepen teachers' knowledge of students as individuals, the better to meet their particular learning needs and encourage greater learning commitment from each student. These efforts, according to UNESCO, have resulted in the teaching profession having distinctively high social status in Cuba and the recruitment of high-attaining students for programmes of teacher training and professional development (UNESCO, 2005).

 Stop and reflect

- *Do you think that the changes discussed up to now in this section would be sufficient to bring about a significant improvement in education globally?*
- *What other sorts of measures or initiatives might be introduced?*

Perhaps more common globally has been the introduction of regulatory mechanisms intended to raise education performance by the control of the day-to-day working of the teaching profession. Systems of standard setting, teacher testing, evaluation and accreditation of teacher preparation are now developing features in many countries. Such developments are not limited to countries in the Majority World, of course. The Controversies box which follows outlines some different views on accountability.

Controversies

'Accountability is the way forward if we are to improve education globally'

Agree: The United Nations Educational, Scientific and Cultural Organization (UNESCO) open their Global Monitoring Report for 2005 with the following statement:

> The quest to achieve Education For All (EFA) is fundamentally about assuring children, youth and adults gain the knowledge and skills they need to better their lives and to play a role in building more peaceful and equitable societies. This is why focusing on quality is an imperative for achieving EFA. As many societies strive to universalize basic education, they face the momentous challenge of providing conditions where genuine learning can take place for each and every learner.
>
> UNESCO, 2005:5

They stress the need for teacher supply and effectiveness which are seen as critical in the enhancement of the quality of education provision (UNESCO, 2005).

Disagree:

- Notions of 'accountability' are contested, and rightly so. What is appropriate or acceptable in economically developed nations may not take proper account of

▶

concepts of accountability found elsewhere. There are those who put forward more nuanced arguments. O'Sullivan (2005), for example, suggests that without contextualising the problems that teachers face on a daily basis, through observation of the teaching/learning process in the classroom and other settings, little can be done meaningfully to improve the situation. Producing policy documents, attainment targets, improving school leadership practices, transferring 'best practice' from one national context to another entirely different one, or simply by throwing more money at the situation are not going to lead to quality improvement. She stresses the importance of context and explores the advantages of classroom observation in helping to improve the quality of the teaching and learning that is taking place.

● A complementary set of concerns is argued by Barrett (2005), who, based on experiences in African schools, draws attention to the relationship between effective teaching and family support for schooling, and the adherence of both to traditional values which emphasise community. In particular, the value placed on the societal role of family and notions of honour (for the teacher and also for the efforts of parents to support their children emotionally and financially) need to be assured and positive. For both, traditional values also emphasise 'responsibility' – for the teacher to behave professionally and for parents to respect the contribution and worth of the teacher and the school. Though the evidence of both O'Sullivan and Barrett to support their assertions comes from work in African schools, it seems that their broad case is more widely applicable.

What do you think? Which side of the argument do you favour?

This is an interesting debate to reflect upon as we continue to look at some further issues relevant to the questions of accountability in educational provision.

In England and Wales, for example, Case, Case and Catling (2000) are not alone in identifying a dominant 'managerialist discourse in the restructuring, running and inspection of schools,' even though they – like others (Chapman, 2002) – question the beneficial impact of such systems. You may have personal experience of Ofsted school inspections, and so can begin to weigh the arguments both for and against them for yourself. Equally, you probably know already that, in the United States, incoming President Obama in 2009 chose education, along with tackling global warming and working to extend healthcare coverage, as a key issue needing immediate action (*Washington Post*, 10 March 2009). It now is generally accepted that current trends towards international accountability are strongly influenced by globalised economic forces as nations attempt to become competitive in the global market and try to shape their education systems to provide those skills most needed in the fast-changing global economy (Tatto, 2006).

A third perspective on education improvement is provided by work done on the direct professional development of teachers. Any such development aims to impact on teacher knowledge, teacher practice and, thus, to change student outcomes. Some of the most effective examples of professional development in economically developed contexts have focused on active involvement of staff in the process and have been extensive and progressive in nature. There are many examples provided in the research literature attesting to the fact that professional development undertaken in a climate of school reculturing and collaboration enhances a teacher's sense of ownership and effective involvement in processes of change and confidence about systems of professional accountability.

To cite just one example, let's look at a study at a disadvantaged primary school in Queensland, Australia, provided by Robinson and Carrington (2002). In this study, 11 teachers were supported to consider collective school beliefs, values and knowledge and the influence of these on school organisation and practice. As these teachers discussed, problem solved and developed teaching and learning strategies, they were able to focus on the needs of all their students and so raise their attainments.

Similarly, attempts to support the development of learning organisations formed through collaboration between teacher training institutions and school partners are widely reported in many countries and contexts. Work undertaken by the University of Warwick to establish 'training schools' for its PGCE programmes, for example, demonstrates how such partnerships have the ability to disseminate initiatives to large numbers of students and schools across a broad geographical area. (Harris and van Tassell, 2005)

For our purposes, though, perhaps most significant have been efforts to promote teacher collaboration and professional development within schools, and especially that which takes the form of peer coaching. Such reform appears to be a powerful catalyst of change and educational improvement. Reporting on such knowledge and skills transfer and mutual development between Cuban teachers in Jamaica and Namibia, Hickling-Hudson (2004) shows that important but often overlooked 'South-South' (Majority World) educational policy exchange is possible. Such initiatives also show that 'radically new relations' are mutually beneficial and can be essential in a decolonising twenty-first-century world for building teacher capacity and meeting local needs.

Anne Hickling-Hudson (2004), for example, has described collaboration between Cuban teachers and schools and sports programmes in Namibia. Namibia is barely twenty years old as an independent country. It is emerging from the legacy of German colonialism from 1884 to 1915, followed by the burden of South African rule from 1915 to 1990. According to Hickling-Hudson, education provision in Namibia remains highly selective, and the drop-out rates are enormous. About 389,000 children start primary school at age six to seven in Grade 1 and just over 156,000 finish it with the examination for the Certificate of Primary Education (CPE) in Grade 7.

Under current agreements with Cuba, six coaches on two-year contracts – three in athletics, one in basketball, one in wrestling and one in boxing – volunteered to work in Namibia. The policy was to rotate the coaches between Namibia's 13 regions. The coaches worked with adults, but their main emphasis was on after-school training and sports camps for schoolchildren and teens. Hickling-Hudson claims that, as a result of this programme, the expertise and experience of Cuban coaches has supported local Namibian schools to develop new education structures and enhanced opportunities for young people, and is already having a positive impact on school retention and completion rates.

It is important, too, that we remember not only that education change has to be accountable to, and understood in the context of, specific national (and even regional) contexts, but also that the Majority World nations individually and collectively are sites of resilient skills and particular valid knowledge. Initiatives such as that described by Hickling-Hudson demonstrate that Majority World countries are often well able to provide expertise and resources to each other, without remaining dependent on those of more developed economies (Dei, 2002). You will see a further instance of such mutual development in Case study 12.3.

Case study 12.3
Making the most of ICT to develop literacy in rural areas: the Kannivadi experience

In 2001, the M.S.Swaminathan Research Foundation (MSSRF) developed innovative learner-specific, community-specific literacy programmes using ICTs in the Tamil Nadu and Dindigul districts in India. Unlike conventional literacy programmes that depend on standard packages, the Kannivadi project supported individual families to develop their own learning material suitable for learners within the family and using their local vernacular language.

After carrying out preliminary and participatory appraisals to identify local literacy needs in four villages, the project negotiated with the self-help groups (SHGs) and described the potential benefits of ICT (electronic, computer-based learning materials) in spreading literacy. During these discussions, it was decided that the family would be the focal point for learning and the village community would facilitate the learning process. The villagers conducted a survey in the village and identified the illiterates and sought the cooperation of the family members in making their illiterate family member(s) literate. MSSRF entered into a contract with SHGs and channelled funds and provided PCs with touch screen, internet and digital cameras.

A critical feature of the project was that the SHGs selected animators from their own community. The animators were trained in various aspects of ICT, such as computers, the internet and digital cameras, by the Research Foundation's project team. The animators became well versed in operating PowerPoint presentations. They, in turn, requested the family members to define the important words and sentences which their illiterate members should learn, supplemented by further words and phrases supplied by the Foundation team and intended to make the material more gender sensitive.

Following training in using a digital camera, family members took suitable pictures for the words and sentences identied by them. Animators then helped them to put these materials into PowerPoint presentations. The letters, words and sentences were given sound and the family members gave their voices. Each participating member was given a CD which they could run in the computer with the touch screen. Each member could choose a fixed time convenient to her/him and they were trained to put the CD in the computer and open the PowerPoint presentation.

The words and sentences appear slowly, with the voices in the background. The learner follows the letter, numbers, words and pictures, often using their finger to do so. The learners are also trained in handling telephones and other ICT equipment. Once a week the learners meet and discuss their progress. Similarly, once a month the family members of the learners meet and discuss the progress. Each learner participated for a period of six months, at the end of which period the family members assessed the progress made by the learner.

The project inevitably encountered some problems. Minor conflicts within the community arose about unrelated issues and the project had to mobilise the community to ensure that these did not affect the progress of the projects. The other important issue was financial viability for the project overall. The Research Foundation took the view that such resources were common property resources of the villages and thus the cost if shared by every family in the village would be less than $5 per year. In addition, the project's centres were also used as communication, information and training centres for those who would like to acquire familiarity with simple computer operations. The villages paid for such facilities.

The role of ICT in helping the villagers to develop materials suitable to their culture and environment remains an important aspect in literacy programmes. The use of ICT tools that encourage and support independent learning, and to develop a sense of participation, has applicability to many regions of the Majority World. The Kannivadi project has, for example, been taken up and locally applied in several east Africa countries, such as Rwanda and Uganda (International Development Research Centre, 2004).

Source: Adapted from Dr K. Balasubramanian, COLIT project, Commonwealth of Learning.

Activity

- Make a list of what you now see as being some of the differences between the job of a teacher in the Majority World and that of a teacher in England.
- Why do you think it is important that any education changes take due account of local values and cultural traditions? Are there any circumstances in which you think that these should be ignored?
- If they were ignored, what do you think would be the implications for the education changes being proposed or introduced?

Changes in educational information and communication technologies

Case study 12.3 is taken from the extensive website of an organisation called IMFUNDO. IMFUNDO is the main team within the Department for International Development, UK (DFID), which creates partnerships to deliver ICT-based activities supporting gender equality and universal primary education in sub-Saharan Africa and other regions of the world.

Connect and explore

You might usefully spend time exploring this website for yourself to extend your knowledge and thinking about these matters. The website is rich in ideas, information and resources: **http://imfundo.digitalbrain.com/imfundo/**.

Increasingly we use computers in every area of our lives and they can provide great opportunities for business and social change. ICT-based education innovations are now embedded in the schools of developed countries that drive globalisation. In contrast, teachers in many parts of the Majority World find computers mainly only in tertiary institutions (intended for students following their completion of elementary and secondary schooling), and even then have little experience of using them for teaching purposes, rather than for personal use or research (Wycliffe and Muwanga-Zake, 2007). Unsurprisingly, therefore, children in developing countries generally do not have access to computers. Neither do they have access to clean running water or reliable electricity, so historically computers have been low down the priority list for governments and for development and aid organisations.

❓ Stop and reflect

- *How important has been the use of ICT-based technologies to your own learning (a) in school? (b) since leaving school?*
- *Is this lack of computer literacy widening the gap between our technology 'rich' youngsters and children in developing countries?*

We would suggest that the lack of computer literacy in developing countries might be creating a barrier to learning that further distances them from the modern world. Studies have shown that children who have never had access to a computer before reaching school age struggle to adapt to computer use during early years schooling. Imagine the student who has never had access to a computer trying to catch up with fellow students who have lived with and played with computers and computer games all their lives.

For these reasons, the United Nations (UN) now has an aim to supply 500,000 workstations to primary and secondary schools in developing countries by 2012. A first pilot project was completed in Burkina Faso, and further pilot projects provided 1,000 Linux desktops to schools in Rwanda, Senegal and Tanzania by the end of 2008. The project is being extended in these countries to establish further partnerships with businesses, universities and NGOs to provide budget computers, logistical support, suitable content and training (Kanter, 2009).

There is no doubt that efforts such as this by the UN are starting to have marked impact in Majority World countries. If you look at Table 12.1, you will see that the areas of greatest percentage growth in internet usage worldwide in the last decade have occurred in these nations (shown in bold). You probably weren't expecting such a marked trend, but when you remember that all of the countries that sponsor aid to developing regions have espoused ICT technologies enthusiastically, and that sponsors often dictate the direction of economic and associated development, it perhaps isn't so surprising after all.

However, you need to keep in mind some further considerations when thinking about the spread of ICT-based education (and social) changes in countries and regions so far free from the dominance of neo-liberal, market-driven ideologies that are now prevalent in economically developed ones, nations like the UK (and which we discussed earlier in this chapter). There is always potential for problems and even disappointments when ideas or innovations are transferred from one location to another, very different one (McCann, 2003).

Table 12.1 **World internet usage and population statistics**

World regions	Population (2009 est.)	Internet users 31.12.2000	Internet users (est. December 2009)	Growth 2000–09	Penetration (% population)
Africa	991,002,342	4,514,400	67,371,700	1,392.4%	6.8%
Asia	3,808,070,503	114,304,000	738,257,230	545.9%	19.4%
Europe	803,850,858	105,096,093	418,029,796	297.8%	52.0%
Middle East	202,687,005	3,284,800	57,425,046	1,648.2%	28.3%
North America	340,831,831	108,096,800	252,908,000	134.0%	74.2%
Latin America / Caribbean	586,662,468	18,068,919	179,031,479	890.8%	30.5%
Oceania / Australia	34,700,201	7,620,480	20,970,490	175.2%	60.4%
World TOTAL	6,767,805,208	360,985,492	1,733,993,741	380.3%	25.6%

Source: Adapted from http://www.internetworldstats.com/stats.htm

First, the internet remains a realm of information exchange dominated by the English language (though this is now beginning to change). Many poorly educated and uneducated people in the Majority World have no experience of using or understanding English, of course, and so there is need for use of other national languages (such as vernacular languages) to have a greater place both in cyberspace and in materials developed for teaching and learning in the countries in which these people live.

Second, purchasing computer equipment, though expensive, is not the main cost of computer-based education changes. There are continuing costs, to do with initial training and continuing professional development for teachers, mainte-nance and repair of equipment and so on, that can cost on average five times as much as the purchase costs over the first five-year period of their educational use (Cawthera, 2002).

Third, it is worth bearing in mind, too, that standard computer equipment is virtually worthless in many areas of the Majority World, where power supplies are often erratic, where people live more nomadic or socially interrupted lives and temperatures can fluctuate massively. However, even in these respects, important changes are starting to be seen. Computer designers have created solar-powered and wind-up wireless laptops that are sturdy, heat proof and child friendly. These cost less than £100 per computer and the idea is that computers and aid organisa-tions will buy them to give to children who would otherwise never experience using a computer (BBC, 2005). These computers run on open source Linux soft-ware, free of any copyright charge (which is conventional for the great majority of commercial models), and can be networked so children can talk to friends in neighbouring villages. They include simple programming tools, graphics and other applications all designed (along with a smaller keyboard and lighter keys) specifically for use by children.

So far these child-friendly laptops have taken off slowly. It is understandably hard to persuade a school that has no writing materials that they should buy computers, however cheaply. International aid organisations are more committed to feeding and clothing the population rather than bringing them technology – and perhaps rightly so: education is the responsibility of national governments, after all, and not of third parties (no matter how well intentioned). The original target for these laptops was for 150 million users worldwide by 2016 – a target that seems unlikely to be reached and for a variety of reasons, mainly to do with commercial and governmental rivalries internationally. However, there is increasing evidence that the uptake of mobile phone technology worldwide, and which gives an alternative means of accessing internet resources and applications, may well mean that a total close to this target will be achieved: 'One Mobile per Child would be a more affordable and realistic solution in networking communities in the developing world and within underserved communities in developing countries. Mobiles are small, portable, affordable and much more useable and useful than laptops' (Chhanabhai and Holt, 2009).

Finally, there are also concerns about introducing computers to people who have so far lived without the levels of connectivity that are taken for granted and expected in economically developed nations. Many parents and teachers remark nostalgically of the days before children in the UK were permanently attached to their mobile phones or linked to friends via instant messenger. Many involved in education leadership and change are starting to ask if such expectations and habits should be imported into communities that haven't had great previous involvement with these technologies. Introducing computers to children in Majority World countries may be an inspiring idea, and one that could bring these children in touch with their peers worldwide, but it's an idea that comes from the belief of those who argue for the inevitability of a globalised, homogeneous world in which computers are inevitably part of all of our future. Many communities in developing countries resist the influence of richer nations. To these communities, a good education is more about learning to farm or fish than learning how to draw simple graphics using open source software. Besides, isn't it still the case that 'the best learning happens by surprise . . . [and that] by watching young children happening to learn, it is possible to sense what learning might be', rather than relying on machines? (Carr and Lynch, 1968).

Perhaps you'll also agree that Case study 12.3 gives indication of the very real symbiotic potential that ICT-based learning has for individuals and communities in the Majority World. In our view, it provides a good example of the way in which education change that is sensitive to local values and needs, and which is properly supported, can harness and refine traditional knowledge and learning skills in ways which build confidence and competence in people and in their communities. Indeed, some argue (Cawthera, 2002) that community telecentres similar to that described in the case study is the best way to achieve effective innovation. Such centres in their operation cross generational boundaries, allowing exchange of knowledge and enthusiasm between adults (of all ages) and young people, thereby contributing to social cohesion as well as contributing to basic educational needs and changing aspirations (Perraton, 1997). In the end, innovations such those described in Case study 12.3 offer the most promising way to increase ICT usage in the Majority World, and thereby to reduce costs and make access increasingly realistic and achievable in developing regions and countries.

Despite earlier notes of scepticism, there are now grounds for believing that the relative costs of gaining access to ICT-based learning and social communication technologies will continue to fall in the future, as the use of third-generation (3G) mobile phones capable of accessing the internet grows in the economically developing regions of the world (Arnold, 2001). Already, the International Telecommunications Union (2009) suggests that mobile phone coverage in these regions has grown from 25 per cent of the population in 2000 to 58.5 per cent in 2008, and subscriber penetration is up to 31 per cent in 2008 (from 12.5 per cent in 2005). Of course, figures such as these hide marked local variations, and especially between urban and rural communities. Even so, mobile phone technologies are growing apace in all parts of the world and are likely to continue to do so. What is needed is for Majority World governments to support wireless broadband connections, and for them to then encourage individuals sharing access points to create a digital identity for each of them (by far the most likely cost-effective basis for the spread of the technology in the Majority World).

Figure 12.4 New technologies will likely be commonplace among ever-growing numbers of people worldwide

Source: Getty Images: Joseph Van Os.

? *Stop and reflect*

*To what extent do you share in the optimistic view that 3G (and 4G) mobile ICT technologies –
providing fast, mobile internet connectivity – offer hope for establishing cross-generational
global partnerships to mobilise activism in local and global initiatives to combat poverty,
environmental degradation and poor education in the Majority World and beyond?*

One such ground for this optimistic view may come from findings in southern
Africa that already suggest that these technologies are useful to break down the
globally acknowledged gender divide between girls and boys' eagerness to make
use of computer-based communications and opportunities for learning (Bovée
et. al., 2007).

Conclusion

No chapter about a topic as broad and as challenging as international comparative education can ever be exhaustive. However, this chapter has shown how the
discipline has continued and can continue to 'use cross-national data to test
propositions about the relationship between education and society and between
teaching practices and learning outcomes' (Wilson, 2003). This chapter has
demonstrated the broad scope of international (comparative) education.

Summary

Four trends in international education

The first section looked at the historical development of the academic discipline of
such education study, and charted the movement from comparative description of
systems and structures of education across the world to an insistence on examining the ethical bases of education and its effects on the lives of learners living in
particular, but diverse, cultures and economies. Notions of globalisation, of development and underdevelopment in some countries (the Majority World), and of
international competition have to be scrutinised and appraised if the purposes
and values of education are to be properly understood.

The education of girls

This section examined these notions and realities through the lens of the education opportunities afforded to girls and young women, and argued that education has the potential to provide learners with the knowledge tools and skills they
need to fashion a future for themselves. Case study 12.2 provided evidence of the
determination of young people in many parts of the world, including those experiencing profound threats and political struggles.

▶

The supply and accountability of teachers

This section of the chapter investigated the supply, accountability and effectiveness of teachers in an international context. While recognising that teachers are often limited in their efforts by their having available few classroom and learning resources, and by their students having often to interrupt their education for social, family or other reasons, nonetheless there is a growing body of evidence that suggests that teachers can make a critical difference to the future of young people, regardless of their cultural or economic location. In particular, this part of the chapter showed initiatives in which teachers in different Majority World countries are increasingly able to collaborate and support each other to develop their own effectiveness, contribute to their own professional development, and to enhance the education opportunities available to their students.

Changes in educational information and communication technologies

All of these strands were then examined in the final section of the chapter. The impact and the potentials of electronic information and communication technologies (ICT) on education increasingly suggest that they will change irrevocably how learners access and demonstrate their learning in the future. Increasingly, too, technologies commonly available across the world will be put to varied and local purposes as communities decide for themselves how best to respond to fast-changing political, economic and social circumstances.

References

Action Aid (2004) *Stop Violence Against Girls in School*, Johannesburg, South Africa: Action Aid International.

Arnold, W. (2001) *Cell Phones for the world's poor; hook up rural Asia, some say, and ease poverty*, MIT, Mass.: The Legatum Center for Development and Entrepreneurship.

Avalos, B. (2000) Policies for Teacher Education in Developing Countries, *International Journal of Educational Research*, 33(5), 457–74.

Baker, A. (2008) Afghanistan's Girl Gap, *Time Magazine*, 17 January.

Banbury, J. (2009) *Girls' Education in Afghanistan*, UNICEF, http://www.unicefusa.org/news/news-from-the-field/feeding-girls-hunger-to.html, viewed October 2009.

Barrett, A. (2005) Teacher accountability in context: Tanzanian primary school teachers' perceptions of local community and education administration, *Compare*, 35(1), 43–61.

BBC News Channel (2005) UN debut for $100 laptop, 17 November 2005, available at http://news.bbc.co.uk/1/hi/technology/4445060.stm.

Bennett, N. (1993) How can schooling help improve the lives of the Poorest? The need for radical reform, Ch. 3 in Levin, H.M. and Lockheed, M.E. (eds) *Effective schools in developing countries*, London: Falmer Press.

Bovée, C., Voogt, J. and Meelissen, M. (2007) Computer attitudes of primary and secondary students in South Africa, *Computers in Human Behavior*, 23(4), 1762–76.

Broadfoot, P. (2000) Comparative Education for the 21st Century: retrospect and prospect performance, *Comparative Ed*, 36(3).

Cambridge, J. and Thompson, J. (2004) Internationalism and Globalization as Contexts for International Education, *Compare*, 34(2).

Carr, S. and Lynch, K. (1968) Where Learning Happens, quoted in Banerjee, T. and Southworth, M. (1990) (eds) *City sense and city design: Writings and projects of Kevin Lynch*, Cambridge, Mass.: MIT Press.

Case, P., Case, S. and Catlin, S. (2000) Please Show You're Working: a critical assessment of the impact of OFSTED inspection on primary teachers, *British Journal of the Sociology of Education*, 21(4), 605–21.

Cawthera, A. (2002) *Computers in Secondary Schools in Developing Countires: Costs and other issues*, World Bank: World Links for Development.

Chapman, C. (2002) Ofsted and School Improvement: teachers' perceptions of the inspection process in schools facing challenging circumstances, *School Leadership & Management*, 22(3), 257–72.

Chen, S. and Ravallion, M. (2008) *The developing world is poorer than we thought, but no less successful in the fight against poverty*, Policy Research Working Paper 4703, Washington: World Bank, August 2008.

Chhanabhai, P. and Holt. A. (2009) One mobile per child: a tractable global health intervention, *Journal of Health Informatics in Developing Countries*, 3(2).

Commonwealth Consortium for Education (2006) Commonwealth Education Briefing Notes No. 5: *The Commonwealth and Education for All*, London: Commonwealth Consortium for Education.

Dei, G.J.S. (2002) Learning Culture, Spirituality and Local Knowledge: Implications for African Schooling, *International Review of Education*, 48(5), 335–60.

Duffy, C.A. (2009) *New and Collected Poems for Children*, London: Faber & Faber.

Frank, G.A. (1969) *Capitalism and Underdevelopment in Latin America*.

Harris, M. and van Tassell, F. (2005) The professional development school as learning organization, *European Journal of Teacher Education*, 28(2), 179–94.

Hertz, B. and Sperling, G.B. (2004) *What Works in Girls' Education: Evidence and Policies from the Developing World*, New York: Council on Foreign Relations (also available online at books.google.co.uk).

Heyneman, S.P. (1999) The Sad Story of UNESCO's Education Statistics. *International Journal of Educational Development*, 19(1), 65–7.

Hickling-Hudson, A. (2004) South-South collaboration: Cuban teachers in Jamaica and Namibia, *Comparative Education*, 40(2), 289–311.

Hillman, A.L. and Jenkner, E. (2004) Economic Issues No. 33: *Educating Children in Poor Countries*, Washington DC: International Monetary Fund.

Human Development Report (HDR) (2007) United Nations Development Program, 27 November, p. 25.

Human Rights Watch (2001) *Scared at School: Sexual Violence against Girls in South African Schools*, New York: Human Rights Watch.

Inkeles, A. and Smith, D.H. (1974) *Becoming Modern*, London: Heinemann.

International Development Research Centre (2004) Casting Curriculumnet Wider, available from http://www.idrc.ca/en/ev-64993-201-1-DO_TOPIC.html.

International Telecommunications Union (2009) Information Society Statistical Profiles, available from http://www.itu.int/ITU-D/ict/material/ISSP09-AFR_final-en.pdf.

Kanter, J. (2009) Efficient Computers in Cambodian Schools, *New York Times*.

Little, A. (2000) Development Studies and Comparative Education: context, content, comparison and contributors, *Comparative Education*, 36(3).

Lubbers, (1998) Trends in Economic and Social Globalisation: challenges and obstacles, http://www.globalize.org.

McCann, P. (2003) Global Village or Global City? The (Urban) Communications Revolution and Education, *Paedagogica Historica*, 39(1), 165–78.

McClelland, D.C. (1961) *The Achieving Society*, New York: Free Press.

Mehrotra, S. (ed.) (2006) *The Economics of Elementary Education in India: The Challenge of Public Finance, Private Provision and Household Costs*, UNICEF: Sage Publications India.

Muralidharan, K. and Sundararaman, V. (2009) *Teacher Performance Pay: Experimental Evidence from India*, National Bureau of Economic Research (NBER) Working Paper No. 15323.

Nilsson, P. (2003) *Education for All: Education Demand and Supply in Africa*, Education International Working Paper No. 12.

Ninnes, P. and Burnett, G. (2003) Comparative education research: poststructuralist possibilities, *Comparative Education*, 39(3).

O'Sullivan, M. (2005) What is Happening in the Classroom? A Common-sense Approach to Improving the Quality of Primary Education in Developing Countries, *Teacher Development*, 9(3), 301–14.

Oxfam (2008) Afghanistan: Development and Humanitarian Priorities, available at http://www.oxfam.org.uk/resources/policy/conflict_disasters/downloads/afghanistan_priorities.pdf.

Perraton, H. (1997) *International Research in Open and Distance Learning: Report of a feasibility study*, Cambridge: International Research Foundation for Open Learning.

Puryear, J.M. (1995) International education statistics and research: Status and problems, *International Journal of Educational Development*, 15(1).

Robinson, R. and Carrington, S. (2002) Professional development for inclusive schooling, *International Journal of Educational Management*, 16(5), 239–47.

Rogers, C.R. (1993) The interpersonal relationship in the facilitation of learning, in M. Thorpe, R. Edwards and

A. Hanson (eds) *Culture and processes in adult learning*, pp. 228–42, London: Routledge with Open University Press.

Said, E. (1978) *Orientalism*, London: Routledge & Kegan Paul Ltd.

Sandel, M.J. (2009) Justice: What's the Right Thing to Do? London: Allen Lane (it is also possible to see a shortened version of his Harvard classes on the web: http://justiceharvard.org).

Shah, P.J. (1998) The Full-truth in Professor Sen's Half Truth, *Business Standard*, 3 January 1998.

Tatto, M.T. (2006) Education reform and the global regulation of teachers' education, development and work: A cross-cultural analysis. *International Journal of Educational Research*, 45(4/5), 231–41.

Trace, A.S. (1961) *What Ivan Knows that Johnny Doesn't*, New York: Random.

UNESCO (2009) Projecting the Global Demand for Teachers: Meeting the Goal of Universal Primary Education by 2015, UIS Technical Paper No. 3.

UNESCO (2005) Chapter 6: The Quality Imperative, *Education For All (EFA) Global Monitoring Report*.

Watson, K. (2001) *Doing Comparative Education Research: issues and problems*, Oxford: Symposium Books.

Wilson, David N. (2003) The Future of Comparative and International Education in a Globalised World, in Mark Bray (ed.) *Comparative Education: Continuing Traditions, New Challenges, and New Paradigms*, Dordrecht, Netherlands: Kluwer.

Wycliffe, J. and Muwanga-Zake, F. (2007) Introducing educational computer programmes through evaluation: A case in South African disadvantaged schools, *International Journal of Education and Development*, 3(3), 30–48.

Conclusion

In the introduction to this book, we asked, 'What is education studies?' Even now, you may not be able to give a simple, one-sentence answer to that question, but we do hope that *Exploring Education Studies* has provided you with an informed understanding of the wide range of issues bound up in the academic study of education. Now that you have read the book, it is worth taking some time to reflect upon some of the major themes which have emerged, and which we hope you will take away with you. While these will very probably include the core disciplines of history, philosophy, psychology and sociology, within this book we have also added new dimensions which we think likely to feature in future debates about education.

We have looked back at both British and international educational history to inform current educational developments, and we have also looked ahead to highlight the importance of developing technologies and their future impact on education. Our exploration of current educational provision in schools and alternative models of schooling has drawn upon key philosophical theorists in order to critique issues such as the purpose of education and the notion of educational choices.

We have included some of the key contributions of psychology within education, some of which are currently more useful than others. Thus the well-established psychological application of behavioural approaches to managing behaviour is discussed, but moved into newer territories such as the frameworks from transactional analysis and cognitive behavioural theory to reflect changing notions of 'control' within classrooms, which acknowledge the importance of mutual respect and responsibility.

Our exploration of contemporary issues within education has been underpinned with sociological debates such as the use of social justice and social exclusion to analyse educational policies. While advances have been made in specific areas, such as lifelong learning and special educational needs, we have also seen that many disadvantages remain for economically disadvantaged learners. It remains to be seen how future governments and policy-makers will respond to these challenges.

We have also tried to give you access to some new perspectives in education. Focusing on ideas of literacy and innovative practice, we have looked at changing notions of what education means now, and where perhaps it may develop in the future. We have suggested that education must go beyond schools and books if young people are to be reached in a rapidly changing, increasingly globalised world.

Above all, it remains vital that we are able to critically examine the complexity of education as we try to ensure that it remains faithful to some of its strong, humane principles while simultaneously adapting to suit the nature of its evolving environment. Education studies provides a vital space in which this kind of academic interrogation is best carried out, and its role will continue to be more accepted and clearly defined in this respect.

Glossary

11+ (eleven plus) an examination given to learners aged 11 to determine which secondary school they will attend

academic tasks the work the learner must accomplish, including the content covered and the mental operations required

academies all-ability, state-funded schools in the UK established and managed by sponsors from a wide range of backgrounds

acceleration the process of advancing learners who excel more quickly through the curriculum, through pacing, salience, peers, access and timing

accommodation according to Piaget, the process of changing existing knowledge in order to solve new tasks

Act in the context of the UK Parliamentary system, an Act is a piece of legislation that has been passed into law by both Houses of Parliament (the Commons and the Lords)

adaptation according to Piaget, ways in which people adapt to the environment in order to survive within it

Adult and Community Learning (ACL) often based in outreach centres managed by the local further education college, and aiming to provide functional skills and other basic learning opportunities which are often delivered through short, focused projects

agency the process of how we settle upon our self-image, and how we think about ourselves

alternative schools schools which may or may not be state funded, and which offer a different teaching approach or philosophy from the majority of mainstream schools

Assemblies in the UK, devolved regional parliaments such as the Welsh Assembly and the Northern Ireland Assembly

assertive discipline a whole school behaviour management approach in which all teachers are expected to be assertive in the same way

assimilation according to Piaget, the way existing knowledge is used when we are faced with problems to solve

asynchronous communication communication between people where all the communicants are not necessarily in contact at the same time

attention focus on a stimulus

Attention Deficit Hyperactivity Disorder (ADHD) current term for disruptive behaviour disorders marked by over-activity, excessive difficulty sustaining attention or impulsiveness

authentic tasks tasks that have some connection to real-life problems the learners will face outside the classroom

autism or Autistic Spectrum Disorder (ASD) developmental disability significantly affecting verbal and non-verbal communication and social interaction, generally evident before age 3 and ranging from mild to severe

autonomous institution a school or education provider which runs itself and is not required to follow a prescribed curriculum

autonomy independence

avatar a virtual identity created for use online or in virtual/computer-simulated environments

awfulising an irrational, negative, and emotional reaction on the part of the learner in response to poor performance or failure, also known as catastrophising

axon a long, thin part of a neuron attached to the soma; divides into a few or many branches, ending in terminal buttons

basic skills in the UK, an umbrella term referring to reading, writing, numeracy and ICT

Behaviour for Learning (BfL) a whole school behaviour management approach based on a system of incremental rewards and sanctions, with the emphasis on rewarding positive behaviour

behaviour management approaches to learning which place emphasis on managing and dealing with observable behaviour

behavioural approach a behaviour management approach which assumes that behaviour can be controlled; it is simply a matter of finding the right formula

behavioural beliefs in cognitive behavioural theory (CBT), the tendency that, if certain behaviours have in the past produced positive results, we are likely to feel happy about them and repeat them

behavioural learning theories explanations of learning that focus on external events as the cause of changes in observable behaviours

being needs Maslow's top-level needs, sometimes called growth needs

Bill the name for an Act of Parliament before it is passed

blog an abbreviation of the term 'weblog', meaning an online narrative written by one person or group, usually with the capacity for other users to respond and add their own comments

capitalism an economic and political system in which property and the means of production and distribution are in private ownership, rather than in the hands of the state, and goods are produced for private profit

catastrophising where faults or errors are magnified but positive achievements are played down

child poverty the phenomenon of children living in conditions of deprivation and poverty, usually measured statistically by governments

circle time a behaviour management technique which emphasises equality and mutual respect between learners

classical conditioning association of automatic responses with new stimuli

coaching additional help and support given to learners, over and above that offered in timetabled classes

cognitive approach a behaviour management approach which argues that problem behaviour arises as a result of how situations are perceived or interpreted, and that faulty or maladaptive thinking is often the cause of disruptive behaviour

cognitive behavioural approaches approaches to understanding individuals which combine cognitive and behaviourist psychological theories

cognitive behavioural theory (CBT) a combined theoretical framework which draws upon elements of cognitive and behaviourist psychological theories

cognitive beliefs how we think about ourselves

colonisation the historical process by which the nationals of one state (or nation) extend political and economic control over another area

comparative education the use of cross-national data to test propositions about the relationship between education and society, and between teaching practices and learning outcomes

complementary transactions in transactional analysis, these transactions are smooth and have an ordinary 'feel' to them

comprehensive schools state-funded schools, attended by children with a wide range of abilities and socio-economic backgrounds, which aim to generate more social mixing and more opportunities for children to pursue diverse educational paths

compulsory education the legal requirement for children under a certain age to attend a school

conditioned response (CR) learned response to a previously neutral stimulus

conditioned stimulus (CS) stimulus that evokes an emotional or physiological response after conditioning

conditioning the process of acquiring a response to a given stimulus

conservatism a term denoting a broad political stance, sometimes called 'the Right', which traditionally supports the propertied (rich) classes and law and order, and takes a gradual approach to social reforms

continuous professional development (CPD) the drive to carry on learning and developing one's skills, even when one has achieved educational or professional goals

contracts agreements between learners and learning providers about desired goals and ways of achieving these

counselling advising students on matters not directly connected with the course being taught, e.g. personal problems

counter-cultures smaller groups within organisations that form their own sense of identity, expressing values that may oppose those of the organisation

crossed transactions in transactional analysis, these transactions are directed towards a particular ego-state in the receiver but the response comes from another ego-state, so the communication lines are crossed

cultural capital the idea that individuals exist in cycles of, for example, unemployment and education that are part of the socio-economic class into which they were born

cultural tools structures within a learning context, such as language and number systems, which shape the thinking of learners and enable them to develop

culturally relativistic taking account of differences between cultures when comparing them

cyber-interactions the activities we do that are mediated through computers

cyborg term used to describe the way in which humans interact with technologies

cycle of improvement the idea that education can lead to qualifications, which can lead to improved socio-economic prospects, which lead back to the opportunity for further education and improvement

deficiency needs Maslow's four lower-level needs, which must be satisfied first

dendrite a tree-like part of a neuron on which the terminal buttons of other neurons form synapses

deschooling in Illich's theory, the dismantling of the automatic association of learning with school

developing countries those countries or societies which are less rich, boast fewer social advances, or are more dependent upon aid from others; also known as the developing world

development the process by which countries and societies grow and improve economically, politically and socially

development education trying to see how far solutions and answers to education challenges generated in developed states might be appropriate for the meeting of similar challenges in developing world contexts

devolution the process of creating government institutions that exercise power locally rather than centrally

digital divides potential barriers to participation in digital literacy

disequilibrium according to Piaget, a state experienced by learners because new problems or tasks mean that changes in thinking are necessary

distortions 'all or nothing' or 'black and white' thinking

dyslexia a specific learning difficulty which may affect ability in the areas of spelling, reading, writing and mathematics

ego responsible for dealing with reality and meeting the needs of the id in a socially acceptable way

emotional intelligence (EI) the ability to process emotional information accurately and efficiently

empirical evidence data or findings gathered through a 'scientific' process or method

empowerment growth in confidence or ability resulting in a positive change for good

equilibration according to Piaget, the efforts of a person to maintain balance as they try to make sense of the world around them

equity fairness

exclusion process by which a learner is removed from their peer group, either temporarily or permanently

expectancy value theories expectations of motivation that emphasise individuals' expectations for success combined with their valuing of the goal

extinction in behaviour management, this occurs when a conditioned response is either reduced or disappears

extrinsic motivation motivation created by external factors such as rewards and punishments

failure-accepting learners learners who believe their failures are due to low ability and that there is little they can do to change this

failure-avoiding learners learners who avoid failure by sticking to what they know, by not taking risks or by claiming not to care about their performance

fees financial charges usually paid by the parents of learners attending private schools

foundation degrees vocational and associated academic learning at Level 4 and 5, offered by further education colleges and universities

functional ego state model a development of the structural ego state model in which the parent state is subdivided into either controlling/critical or nurturing, and the child state is subdivided into either adapted or free

functional literacy the state of being sufficiently literate to participate in society

further education in the UK, education which one pursues after compulsory schooling has ceased, but prior to higher (university-level) education

games in transactional analysis, the process of doing something with an ulterior motive that is outside adult awareness, does not become explicit until the participants switch the way they are behaving, and results in everyone feeling confused, misunderstood and wanting to blame the other person

gifted and talented gifted learners are those who have the ability to excel academically in one or more subjects such as mathematics, English or science. Talented learners are defined as those who have the ability to excel in practical skills such as artistic performance, sport or a vocational subject area

global citizenship valuing the knowledge and experience of others around the world, and about being willing to learn from them, their culture and their histories

globalisation a concept that refers to the system of interaction among the countries of the world and involves technological, economic, political, and cultural exchanges made possible largely by advances in communication (especially electronic communications, ICT) and transportation

grade-based acceleration a form of learner acceleration which reduces the number of years the pupil is in education based on their early achievement of goals

grammar school secondary schools attended by pupils who, following examination or other assessment at 11+, were labelled as being particularly academic

Green Paper the initial stage of development for a potential Act of Parliament in the UK

habitus the mindset and ability to receive and absorb cultural capital

hegemony the domination of power, control, knowledge or some other form of authority by one particular group

hermeneutics ways of interpreting and understanding texts

hierarchy of needs Maslow's model of levels of human needs, from basic physiological requirements to the need for self-actualisation

higher education learning and qualifications taking place from first year degree level upwards, commonly found in universities, but also occurring in the workplace and further education colleges

holistic approach an approach that specifies that all aspects of the learner's life are considered during assessment, not just their school life

home schooling a system which provides parents with the opportunity to keep their children away from school and educate them within the home on a full or part time basis

human capital a measure which places a value upon people's skills and knowledge and their contribution (actual or potential) to economic growth

humanistic approach a behaviour management approach which places emphasis on democracy in the classroom and the importance of fostering mutual respect between teachers and learners

id the instinctive needs and desires of a person present from birth

ideology a set of ideas and values about the world held by a group, influencing their behaviour and conversation or debate with others

incentives objects or events that encourage or discourage certain types of behaviour

inclusion the integration of all learners, including those with severe learning difficulties, into mainstream classes

informal learning learning experiences other than the formal learning offered by an institution, school, college or learning provider

information and communication technology (ICT) a taught subject dealing with how learners access knowledge through computers, the internet, and other technology-based means

information-processing approaches approaches used by cognitive psychologists to explain the workings of the brain

initial teacher training (ITT) in the UK, the process by which student teachers become qualified

inspection the process by which the UK government monitors the quality of teaching and other provision for learners in schools, colleges and other settings

intelligence quotient (IQ) score comparing mental and chronological ages

intrinsic motivation motivation associated with activities that are their own reward

joined-up government in the context of the late 1990s in Britain, this referred to increasing collaboration and cooperation between the many distinct departments that make up an administration

league tables statistical comparisons of schools, often used by government to rank schools according to how well pupils achieve in examinations

learning organisation (LO) an organisation employing people where training opportunities are often linked to the organisation's mission statement

learning preferences preferred ways of studying and learning, such as using pictures instead of text, working with other people or alone, learning in structured or unstructured situations, and so on

learning styles characteristic approaches to learning and studying

legitimate peripheral participation genuine involvement in the work of a group, even if your abilities are undeveloped and contributions are small

liberalism an ideology which prioritises the individual, rather than society as a whole, and which argues that the individual's own self-motivation underpins all action, including efforts at learning

lifelong learning education or training which occurs both within and beyond an individual's experience of compulsory education

life-script in transactional analysis, a life-plan made in childhood, reinforced by the parents, justified by subsequent events and culminating in a chosen alternative

literacy at its most basic, this refers to reading, writing, speaking and listening skills

Local Education Authorities (LEAs) in the UK, educational administrations operating through locally elected authorities (councils)

local management of schools (LMS) a scheme which provided schools with differing levels of resources depending on the number of pupils attending

locus of causality the location – internal or external – of the cause of behaviour

long-term memory the region or subset of memory where knowledge is stored permanently

magnetic-resonance imaging (MRI) neuro-imaging technique which allows observation of the structure of the brain by measuring the reverberation of hydrogen molecules in the brain as a magnetic field is passed over the head

Majority World a term which defines the developing community of nations in terms of what it is, rather than what it lacks

mastery goals a personal intention to improve abilities and learn, no matter how performance suffers

mastery-oriented learners learners who focus on learning goals because they value achievement and see ability as improvable

maturation according to Piaget, a stage of a person's development relating to changes in biological maturity

mechanics in the context of literacy, the process of reading and understanding language

medical model of disability a view of a disabled person which defines them in relation to a medical condition and promotes the view of a person not only being 'disabled', but also as being dependent on the medical profession to be cured or cared for; the focus is on sickness rather than health

mental age in intelligence testing, a score based on average abilities for that age group

mentoring a relationship where a more experienced person provides advice, guidance and resource to a less experienced one

meritocracy a system based on advancement of the individual on the basis of their ability rather than, for example, their wealth, background or class

metacognitive concerning metacognition, or knowledge about our own thinking processes

mnemonics techniques for remembering; also, the art of memory

motivation an internal state that arouses, directs and maintains behaviour

multicultural aiming to include a wide range of cultures

multimodal including many types or forms; in the case of literacies, these would include media literacy, visual literacy, graphicacy, print literacy, information literacy and digital literacy

multiple literacies the concept that 'literacy' applies to more than just the ability to read, write, speak and listen

multi-sensory approach a multi-sensory approach to learning requires children to use more than one of the senses, for example learning the shape of letters in the alphabet not only by looking at the shape of the letter, but also by drawing the shape of the letter

National Challenge a programme of support that is intended to secure higher standards in all secondary schools in the UK

National Curriculum in the UK, a legally constituted curriculum for all pupils in state education, making certain subjects mandatory for students depending on their age/level

nationalism the belief that one's country is worth supporting strongly in most situations

negative reinforcement strengthening behaviour by removing an aversive or unpleasant stimulus when the behaviour occurs

neo-conservative an ideology which maintains that the optimal economic system is achieved by giving free rein to market participants, privatisation, minimal restrictions on international trade, and the shrinking of government intervention in the economy. Alongside these economic concerns, neo-conservatives also argue for an emphasis on individual endeavour and 'freedom of action'

neo-liberalism the ideas associated with the New Right of the 1980s that market competition is the best means of guaranteeing political freedom and economic growth

neurons nerve cells that store and transfer information

nurture groups small groups of learners, often run by teachers and teaching assistants, focusing on communicating on a one-to-one basis to resolve emotional issues and build interpersonal and social skills

object permanence the understanding that objects have a separate, permanent existence

observation in Montessori schools, a key tool in assessing how a child is developing, which involves watching them interact with their surroundings

offender learning mostly associated with prison education and the development of functional skills, but also applied to offenders who attend learning opportunities in the community

oligopoly a small group of people within whose hands the seat of power lies, also known as oligarchy

operant conditioning focuses on ways in which behaviour is strengthened or weakened by the events that go before it or the consequences which follow it

options in transactional analysis, the choices we have about the transaction/s which are occurring

overgeneralisation where wide-ranging conclusions are drawn from small instances

paradigm shift a change from one way of thinking to another

pedagogy relating to teaching and the transmission of knowledge

perception the interpretation of sensory information

performance goals a personal intention to seem competent or perform well in the eyes of others

phonics a teaching methodology that uses the sounds made by small groups of letters (phonemes) as building blocks which children blend to make words

plagiarism presenting someone else's work as if it was your own, or failing to reference or correctly attribute the origin

planned ignoring a strategy that is used to change behaviour by reducing the attention a teacher gives to a pupil who misbehaves

podcasts audio files which listeners can download from the internet and access through MP3 players

positive reinforcement strengthening behaviour by presenting a desired stimulus, or reward, after the behaviour

post-compulsory education education or training pursued after a person has passed the age at which compulsory education ceases to be enforced

postmodernism postmodernism can be defined in a number of ways; in education contexts, it may be taken to refer to the process by which education has come to be seen as a commodity (something which can be bought and sold)

post-welfare society a society in which the adult individual is expected to meet their own needs and be economically self-sufficient rather than dependent upon the state as provider

prepared environment in Montessori schools, an orderly approach to both the conceptual and physical design of a classroom

psychodynamic approaches approaches to psychology based on the work of Sigmund Freud which stress the importance of early childhood experiences and the unconscious mind

punishment process that weakens or suppresses behaviour

quango an acronym, standing for 'quasi-autonomous non-government organisation'

readings in the context of the UK Parliamentary system, the process whereby a proposed new Act is scrutinised by MPs and Lords

reinforcement use of consequences to strengthen behaviour

reinforcer within operant conditioning, any consequence which strengthens the behaviour it follows

relative poverty having less than 60 per cent of the median (average) income in society

reliability the extent to which a set of findings would re-occur if a test was repeated

response cost punishment punishment by loss of reinforcers

rewards attractive objects or events supplied as a consequence of a particular behaviour

rote system a type of memorisation by repetition to facilitate automatic and accurate recall of facts

scaffolding support for learning and problem solving, which could take the form of clues, reminders, encouragement, breaking the problem down into steps, providing an example, or anything else that allows the individual to grow in independence as a learner

schema a mental storehouse or template in which a person's knowledge of the world is stored, and sense or meaning created

scholarship the notion of pursuing knowledge for its own sake

secondary modern school secondary schools attended by pupils who, following examination at 11+, were labelled as non-academic

self-actualisation fulfilling one's potential

self-efficacy a person's sense of being able to deal effectively with a particular task

self-instruction talking oneself through the steps of a task

self-management use of behavioural learning principles to change your own behaviour

self-regulation process of activating and sustaining thoughts, behaviours and emotions in order to reach goals

semiotics a branch of the study of language which says that the basic linguistic signifier has two parts, the signifier and the signified, which combine to make a sign

SEN Code of Practice in the UK, the legislation requiring that schools and LEAs make provision for pupils with SEN

sensory memory the region or subset of memory where attention and perception determine what is retained for future use, based on information from the environment experienced through the senses

social capital the idea that an individual's relationships with others create and add value and meaning to their life as part of a society

social construct a set of meanings that a society applies to a particular issue

social exclusion this occurs when individuals are excluded from taking part in society fully

social mobility the potential ability for members of a given socio-economic group to join another socio-economic group

social model of disability a view of a disabled person which focuses on the experience of the individual, environmental factors and preventative measures, rather than cure by the medical profession

socialism an economic system in which everyone benefits from the labour of others

socio-cultural views of motivation perspectives that emphasise participation, identities and interpersonal relationships within communities of practice

socio-economic group a category or group within society determined by 'status' and/or income, whether your own or your family's

special educational needs (SEN) personal conditions affecting the ability to learn or thrive in a mainstream educational environment

spiral curriculum a programme of learning in which themes are revisited again and studied in more depth as the learner develops

stakeholders groups and communities – such as central government, local government, parents, and guardians – with an interest in education

Standard Assessments Tests (SATs) tests given, usually nationwide, under uniform conditions and scored according to uniform procedures

state-funded system in the UK, a national and compulsory system of elementary education for all children, established by law

strokes refers to human beings' fundamental need for recognition, and derives from an infant's need for tactile stimulation or literal strokes which are essential for healthy development and growth

structural ego-state model model describes the way that personality is structured, suggesting that people have three parts to their personality: 'parent', 'adult' and 'child'

structuralist a kind of philosopher who uses units and rules to explore phenomena

subject-based acceleration a form of learner acceleration which offers opportunities for the pupil to increase subject knowledge at an earlier age than peers

superego holds all the moral principles and ideals acquired from parents and society

syllabus a schema or plan for what is taught to learners in a given subject and at a particular level or age range

synchronous communication communication between people where all communicants are taking part at the same time and can 'chat'; also known as real-time communication

syntagm a combination of conventions and codes attached to a given medium (e.g. film, television)

tactical ignoring a strategy that is used to change behaviour by reducing the attention a teacher gives to a pupil when they are misbehaving, while responding positively when the pupil behaves appropriately

tariff system a behaviour management technique in which the school explicitly states the cost for unacceptable behaviour and rewards for acceptable behaviour

task demand learning philosophy in which new knowledge is presented within the context of a conceptual framework, not as facts in isolation

taxonomy a system of classification

technoliteracy the ability to understand and become fluent in the use of various kinds of technology

telematics the blending of technologies

text-speak a form of abbreviated language used by mobile phone users in SMS (Short Message Service) messages

theory of multiple intelligences in Gardner's theory of intelligence, a person's eight separate abilities: logical-mathematical, linguistic, musical, spatial, bodily-kinesthetic, interpersonal, intrapersonal and naturalist

Third Way an idea which connected the issues of social exclusion and social justice, labelled as the Third Way because the two previous 'big ideas' – capitalism (the First Way) and socialism (the Second Way) – were considered to be inadequate

Third World a deficit concept for nations characterised by poverty and dependence on economically more privileged countries

transaction the basic unit of social interaction in transactional analysis, consisting of a single stimulus and a single response, verbal or non-verbal

transactional analysis (TA) a theory about human personality and interactions which focuses on people's communications (or 'transactions') with one another

transferable skills communication and organisational skills which improve employment chances and can make personal life more fulfilling, such as resilience, empathy and goal setting

transformational learning a type of learning which focuses on what individuals *do* with incoming information, and how they make meaning from it

tuition fees the payments HE students are expected to contribute towards the cost of their undergraduate courses

ulterior transactions in transactional analysis, these are transactions in which there is a difference between the actual words spoken and the psychological-level message which is conveyed covertly through non-verbal communication

unconditioned response (UR) naturally occurring emotional or physiological response

unconditioned stimulus (US) stimulus that automatically produces an emotional or physiological response

underdevelopment the relative lack or absence of socio-economic and political progress in a nation or country

validity the extent to which a concept or set of findings can reasonably be applied to a given subject

verbal thought a cognitive process which incorporates language and allows individuals to reflect, think, plan and control behaviour

vernacular literacy those literacies in which people engage for purposes of their own, generally at odds with what they are asked to demonstrate at assessment in a formal educational curriculum

virtual learning environment (VLE) a software product providing shared resources and information, with communication through email and discussion boards

White Paper a formal document, drafted by civil servants, which may go on to become a Bill and then an Act of Parliament in the UK

whole class approach a behaviour management technique which aims to get the group to work towards a reward that will be given to the entire class. Also known as a class-wide recognition system

whole school approach a system in which both learners and staff are expected to conform to a particular standard of behaviour

widening participation a policy introduced by the Labour Party to improve take-up of university places by learners from less privileged socio-economic backgrounds

wiki a web application that allows anyone visiting a website to edit content on it

work-based learning practical learning in the workplace often supported by theory lessons at a further education college, private training provider or university

working memory the region or subset of memory where new information connects with knowledge from long-term memory. Also known as short-term memory

zone of proximal development (ZPD) phase at which a child can master a task if given appropriate help and support

Index

Research Methods for Education

Peter Newby

ISBN: 9781405835749

FEATURES

- Written for people who are new to research and not confident with numbers
- A mixed methods approach, which doesn't simply prioritise quantitative or qualitative methods
- Rich supporting website with activities, multiple choice questions, data-sets, examples of good and bad research tools. This shows students how to progress their own research project and contains a remedial maths coaching tool
- Covers graphical and analytic procedures using Internet tools and spreadsheets
- Contains guidance on analytic procedures that require more advanced tools such as SPSS, Minitab
- Designed to help students produce good, valid and valuable research
- Excellent coverage of availability of secondary data sources
- Many excellent international examples and case studies specifically from education, which breaks away from a parochial focus on UK education system

Written with the novice educational researcher in mind, Research Methods in Education is designed to help students produce good quality, valid and valuable research. The text is written in an engaging style and adopts a mixed-methods approach; guidance on analytical procedures that require more advanced tools such as SPSS and Minitab are also provided.

The book is packed with exercises, examples and comparative international material from other educational contexts, all of which help to introduce this complex subject in an easy to use format for people that are new to research and are not confident with numerical information.

For more information visit our website at:
www.pearsoned.co.uk/education